Contemporary Hong Kong Government and Politics

Third Edition

Contemporary Hong Kong Government and Politics

Third Edition

Edited by
Lam Wai-man
Percy Luen-tim Lui
Wilson Wong

Hong Kong University Press
The University of Hong Kong
Pok Fu Lam Road
Hong Kong
https://hkupress.hku.hk

© 2024 Hong Kong University Press

ISBN 978-988-8842-87-2 (*Paperback*)

All rights reserved. No portion of this publication may be reproduced or transmitted in any form or by any means, electronic or mechanical, including photocopying, recording, or any information storage or retrieval system, without prior permission in writing from the publisher.

British Library Cataloguing-in-Publication Data
A catalogue record for this book is available from the British Library.

Digitally printed

Contents

Acronyms and Abbreviations	vii
About the Contributors	xi

1. Political Context 1
   LAM Wai-man

Part I: Political Institutions

2. The Executive 31
   LI Pang-kwong

3. The Legislature 52
   Percy Luen-tim LUI

4. The Judiciary 76
   LAI Yan-ho

5. The Civil Service: Institutional Conscience, Politicization, and Capacity-Building 111
   Wilson WONG

6. District Councils, Advisory Bodies, and Statutory Bodies 134
   Rami Hin-yeung CHAN

Part II: Mediating Institutions and Political Actors

7. Democratic Development in Hong Kong 161
   LAI Yan-ho and SING Ming

8. Political Parties and Elections 191
   KWONG Ying-ho and Mathew Y. H. WONG

9. Civil Society 214
   Stephan ORTMANN

10. Political Identity, Culture, and Participation 239
    LAM Wai-man

vi   Contents

11. Mass Media and Public Opinion   264
     Joseph M. CHAN and Francis L. F. LEE

Part III: Policy Environment

12. Economic Policy   293
     Wilson WONG and Raymond YUEN

13. Changes in Social Policy in Hong Kong since 1997: Old Wine in
     New Bottles?   318
     WONG Hung

14. Urban Policy: Governing Asia's World City—Ready for a Paradigm
     Shift toward People, Place, and Planet-Friendly Urban Development?   340
     NG Mee Kam

Part IV: Political Environment

15. Changing Relations between Hong Kong and the Mainland
     since 2014   371
     Peter T. Y. CHEUNG

16. Hong Kong's International Status at a Crossroads   399
     LI Hak-yin and TING Wai

17. Conclusion: Looking to the Future   428
     LAM Wai-man, Percy Luen-tim LUI, and Wilson WONG

Index   443

Acronyms and Abbreviations

ADPL	Association for Democracy and People's Livelihood
Anti-ELAB Movement	Anti-Extradition Law Amendment Bill Movement
AO	administrative officer
ASPDMC	Alliance in Support of Patriotic Democratic Movements of China
ASPO	Accountability System for Principal Officials
ATV	Asia Television Limited
AUS	Alliance of Universal Suffrage
BL	Basic Law
BORO	Bill of Rights Ordinance
BRI	Belt and Road Initiative
CCP	Chinese Communist Party
CCTV	Chinese Central Television
CE	Chief Executive
CEPA	Closer Economic Partnership Arrangement
CEPU	Chief Executive's Policy Unit
CFA	Court of Final Appeal
CFI	Court of First Instance
CLO	Liaison Office of the Central People's Government in the Hong Kong Special Administrative Region
CP	Civic Party
CPG	Central People's Government
CPI	Corruption Perceptions Index
CPPCC	Chinese People's Political Consultative Conference
CPU	Central Policy Unit

CRC	Cooperative Resource Centre
CS	Chief Secretary for Administration
CSD	Commission on Strategic Development
CSD	Council for Sustainable Development
CSNS	Committee for Safeguarding National Security in the HKSAR
CSSA	Comprehensive Social Security Assistance
CUHK	Chinese University of Hong Kong
DAB	Democratic Alliance for the Betterment and Progress of Hong Kong (formerly Democratic Alliance for the Betterment of Hong Kong)
DC	District Council
DCFC	District Council Functional Constituency
DMC	District Management Committee
DP	Democratic Party
DRC	Democratic Republic of the Congo
EC	Election Committee
EIU	Economist Intelligence Unit
EPP	Enhanced Productivity Programme
EU	European Union
ExCo	Executive Council
FC	functional constituency
FS	Financial Secretary
FYP	Five-Year Plan
G-20	Group of Twenty
GBA	Greater Bay Area
GC	geographical constituency
HA	Housing Authority
HAD	Home Affairs Department
HKAS	Hong Kong Affairs Society
HKCTU	Hong Kong Confederation of Trade Unions
HKFTU	Hong Kong Federation of Trade Unions
HKJA	Hong Kong Journalists Association
HKMA	Hong Kong Monetary Authority

HKMAO	Hong Kong and Macao Affairs Office
HKPA	Hong Kong Progressive Alliance
HKSAR	Hong Kong Special Administrative Region
HKSARG	Hong Kong Special Administrative Region government
HKUPOP	Hong Kong University Public Opinion Poll
HOS	Home Ownership Scheme
HPS	Health Protection Scheme
ICAC	Independent Commission Against Corruption
ICCPR	International Covenant on Civil and Political Rights
ICESCR	International Covenant on Economic, Social, and Cultural Rights
IGO	intergovernmental organization
ISD	Information Services Department
IT	information technology
JCPDG	Joint Committee for the Promotion of Democratic Government
KCR	Kowloon-Canton Railway
LDF	Liberal Democratic Foundation
LegCo	Legislative Council
LP	Liberal Party
LSCD	Leisure and Cultural Services Department
LSD	League of Social Democrats
MP	Meeting Point
MPF	Mandatory Provident Fund
MRIR	median rent-to-income ratio
MTR	Mass Transit Railway
NCSC	non-civil service contract
NGO	non-governmental organization
NIC	newly industrialized country
NPC	National People's Congress
NPM	new public management
NSL	National Security Law
OAA	Old Age Allowance Scheme
OCM	Occupy Central Movement
OCTS	one country, two systems

ODI	Outward Direct Investments
OSNS	Office for Safeguarding National Security in the HKSAR
PAS	Political Appointment System
PHC	private primary health car
PLC	Provisional Legislative Council
PORI	Hong Kong Public Opinion Research Institute
PR	proportional representation
PRC	People's Republic of China
PRD	Pearl River Delta
PSC	Public Service Commission
RC	Regional Council
REIT	Real Estate Investment Trust
RTHK	Radio Television Hong Kong
SAO	Senior Administrative Officer
SAR	Special Administrative Region
SARS	Severe Acute Respiratory Syndrome
SCNPC	Standing Committee of the National People's Congress
SD	sustainable development
SDU	Sustainable Development Unit
SJ	Secretary for Justice
SMW	statutory minimum wage
SSO	social service organization
TF	The Frontier
TPS	Tenants Purchase Scheme
TVB	Television Broadcasts Limited
UC	Urban Council
UDHK	United Democrats of Hong Kong
UM	Umbrella Movement
UNDP	United Nations Development Programme
WKCD	West Kowloon Cultural District
WPM	Wage Protection Movement
WTO	World Trade Organization

About the Contributors

Rami Hin-yeung CHAN is an assistant professor in the Department of Social Science and, concurrently, associate director of the Centre for Greater China Studies at the Hang Seng University of Hong Kong (HSUHK). Prior to joining HSUHK, he pursued his PhD in political science at Lingnan University, Hong Kong. His research interest is mainly on the politics of crisis management, with special focus on state-society interactions and crisis-induced policymaking. He received funding for projects related to policy capacity, migration politics, and urban development such as conducting public policy research on expatiates' and overseas returnees' migration plans under the recent social incidents in Hong Kong.

Joseph M. CHAN is emeritus professor at the School of Journalism and Communication, the Chinese University of Hong Kong, where he served as a chair professor and school director. He has published extensively in books and various international journals. The books he has coauthored or coedited pertain to media and social movements, media and political transition, comparative journalists, collective memory, and comparative communication. He was elected fellow of the International Communication Association and president of the Chinese Communication Association. He was the founding chief editor of *Communication and Society*. He received the Changjiang Chair Professorship from the Ministry of Education, China, for which he was affiliated with Fudan University.

Peter T. Y. CHEUNG is professor (practice) in the Department of Social Sciences and Policy Studies, Education University of Hong Kong. He was formerly associate professor, head, and director of the Master of Public Administration Programme, Department of Politics and Public Administration, University of Hong Kong. His research interests focus on public policy in Hong Kong, relations between Hong Kong and the Mainland, and the politics of regional development in the Greater Bay Area.

KWONG Ying-ho is an assistant professor in the Department of Social Science at the Hang Seng University of Hong Kong. His current research interests lie in contentious politics, democratization, and political economy.

LAI Yan-ho is a research fellow with the Center for Asian Law of Georgetown University Law Center (GCAL), and an associate fellow at the Hong Kong Studies Hub of the University of Surrey. He was formerly the Hong Kong Law Fellow at GCAL and a visiting researcher at King's College London Dickson Poon School of Law. He holds a PhD in law from the School of Oriental and African Studies (SOAS), University of London. His research focuses on law and society, judicial politics, legal transplantation, the legal profession, and legal mobilization in authoritarian regimes. His works can be found in *Communist and Post-communist Studies*, *Journal of Asian and African Studies*, and *Hong Kong Law Journal*.

LAM Wai-man was formerly an associate professor and head of social sciences at the School of Arts and Social Sciences, Hong Kong Metropolitan University. Her current research interests include comparative government and civil society, global governance, political culture and identity, and state-society relations. She has published widely, including book chapters and journal articles in *Citizenship Studies*, *The China Quarterly*, *Social Indicators Research*, *Journal of East Asian Studies*, and elsewhere. She is the author of *Understanding the Political Culture of Hong Kong: The Paradox of Activism and Depoliticization* (ME Sharpe 2004; Routledge 2015), and coauthor and coeditor of four other books on Hong Kong politics and public policymaking.

Francis L. F. LEE is professor at the School of Journalism and Communication, the Chinese University of Hong Kong. His most recent publications include *Memories of Tiananmen: Politics and Processes of Collective Remembering in Hong Kong, 1989–2019* (Amsterdam University Press 2021) and *Media and Protest Logics in the Digital Era* (Oxford University Press 2018). He is elected fellow of the International Communication Association and currently chief editor of the *Chinese Journal of Communication*.

LI Hak-yin is professor at the Institute for International Strategy, Tokyo International University. He was a visiting research fellow of the East Asian Institute at the National University of Singapore, and he taught at the Chinese University of Hong Kong before. His research and teaching interests mainly cover the fields of world order issues, international relations of Asia-Pacific, Chinese foreign policy, and Hong Kong's international status. His works can be found in the *Journal of Contemporary China*, *Asian Politics and Society*, *East Asian Policy* and *Place Branding and Public Diplomacy*. He is the author of *China's New World Order: Changes in the Non-Intervention Policy* (Edward Elgar 2021).

About the Contributors

LI Pang-kwong received his PhD in government from the London School of Economics and Political Science, the University of London. He is a professor of practice in the Department of Government and International Affairs and, concurrently, the founding director of the Public Governance Programme at Lingnan University. His major research areas include: Hong Kong's governance and institutional design, voting behavior and electoral politics, legislative studies, policymaking and public choice. He is the author of *Governing Hong Kong: Insights from the British Declassified Files* (管治香港：英國解密檔案的啟示) (Oxford University Press [Hong Kong] 2012).

Percy Luen-Tim LUI is an assistant professor in the School of Arts and Social Sciences at Hong Kong Metropolitan University. His research interests include public policy analysis, bureaucratic responsibility, and comparative public administration.

NG Mee Kam is the director of the Urban Studies Programme, associate director of the Hong Kong Institute of Asia-Pacific Studies at the Chinese University of Hong Kong. She is a fellow of the Royal Town Planning Institute (RTPI), a fellow of the Academy of Social Sciences in the UK, and a fellow of the Hong Kong Institute of Planners (HKIP). She has published widely on planning and sustainability issues in Pacific-Asia. Her publications have earned her seven HKIP Awards and the 2015 Association of European Schools of Planning (AESOP) Best Published Paper Award. She has been consultant to the UN and the EU.

Stephan ORTMANN is an assistant professor in the School of Arts and Social Sciences at Hong Kong Metropolitan University. He has worked on various issues related to political change and protest movements in Hong Kong, Singapore, China, and Vietnam. His publications have appeared in many reputable journals including *Asian Survey, Asian Studies Review, Administration and Society, China Quarterly, Journal of Democracy, Government and Opposition, and Pacific Review*. He is the author of *Politics and Change in Singapore and Hong Kong: Containing Contention* (Routledge 2010) and of *Environmental Governance in Vietnam: Institutional Reforms and Failures* (Palgrave Macmillan 2017).

SING Ming has been the author or editor of six books and over forty articles. His refereed publications can be found in the *Journal of Politics, Journal of Democracy, Democratization, Government and Opposition, Social Indicators Research*, and *Communist and Post-Communist Studies*, among others. He is the author of *Hong Kong's Tortuous Democratization* (Routledge 2004) and the coeditor of *Taking Back Our Future: An Eventful Sociology of the Hong Kong Umbrella Movement* (Cornell University Press 2019). His research interests include the comparative study of democracy and democratization, political culture, civil society, quality of life, and Hong Kong politics. He was associate professor at the Division of Social Science, Hong Kong University of Science and Technology.

TING Wai is professor emeritus in the Department of Government and International Studies, Hong Kong Baptist University (HKBU). Formerly a research fellow at the Institute of Southeast Asian Studies in Singapore, he was lecturer in politics at the Department of Communication and then professor of international relations at HKBU. His areas of research include domestic and foreign policies of China, and theories of international relations. After retiring in September 2019, he served as a part-time research fellow at the Advanced Institute for Contemporary China Studies of HKBU until its closure in June 2021. He was president of the Hong Kong Association for European Studies from 2006 to 2017.

WONG Hung is an associate professor (teaching) of the Department of Social Work, associate director of the CUHK Institute of Health Equity, and former director of the Yunus Social Business Centre@CUHK at the Chinese University of Hong Kong. His research interests include poverty, social security, and labor issues. He has also conducted research on marginal workers, unemployed youth, homeless people, and poor residents in old urban areas. He has actively advocated for community economic development and the setting up of a universal pension scheme in Hong Kong.

Mathew Y. H. WONG is an associate professor in the Department of Applied Social Sciences, Hong Kong Polytechnic University. His research interests include comparative politics and political economy, income inequality, and politics of East Asia. He is also the author of *Comparative Hong Kong Politics* (Palgrave Macmillan 2017).

Wilson WONG is founding director and associate professor of Data Science and Policy Studies Programme, Faculty of Social Science, the Chinese University of Hong Kong. He is also a fellow at Stanford University and the lead area editor of *Data & Policy*, a journal by Cambridge University Press focusing on data and policy interactions. His core research areas include digital governance, public management, public budgeting and finance, and comparative public policy. His works have been published in major journals of public administration such as *Governance, Journal of Public Administration and Research and Theory, Policy Studies Journal*, and *Public Administration Review*.

Raymond YUEN is a political specialist focusing on political development, policy trends, and cross-cutting issues in relations to Hong Kong and its role in China and the global political economy. He has taught at major universities in Hong Kong on global studies, political science, and public management. He received his BSSc and PhD in politics from the Chinese University of Hong Kong, as well as MSc in public policy from the University of Bristol, UK. He was a fellow of the Higher Education Academy in the UK and the Asia Pacific Leadership Program at the East-West Center in the US.

1
Political Context

Lam Wai-man

Following the Qing dynasty's military defeat in the first and second Opium Wars (1839–1842 and 1856–1860) (Pletcher 2023), Great Britain ruled Hong Kong as a colony for over 150 years. On 1 July 1997, China resumed its sovereignty over Hong Kong in accordance with the 1984 Sino-British Joint Declaration. During British colonial rule, Hong Kong had experienced World War I, World War II, postwar refugee influxes, the embargo on young Communist China in the 1950s, two significant riots in the 1960s, an economic upswing in the 1970s, growth of a local identity since the 1980s, and democratization and political transition in the 1990s. By the time of the handover in 1997, Hong Kong had become one of the world's leading cosmopolitans.

Sino-British Negotiations and the Basic Law

Negotiations between China and Britain over the sovereignty transfer of Hong Kong began after Hong Kong governor Murray MacLehose made an official and landmark visit to Beijing in 1979 (Foreign and Commonwealth Office n.d.). In 1984, the two countries signed a Joint Declaration stating that British administration of Hong Kong would end in 1997 and that Hong Kong would become Hong Kong Special Administrative Region (HKSAR) under Chinese sovereignty. According to the Joint Declaration, the policies stated, such as the existing socioeconomic systems of Hong Kong, its lifestyle, rights, and freedoms, would "remain unchanged for 50 years" after the handover (*Official Publication* 1984: 144). In 1990, the Basic Law was promulgated (Box 1.1). The general framework of governance laid down in the Basic Law mainly maintains that of the colonial government, namely, executive-led government, laissez-faire economic policy, capitalistic way of life, protection of individual freedoms, and limited democracy (Box 1.2). The belief enshrined in the Basic Law is that the colonial legacy, which includes clinging to the social goals of stability and prosperity, administrative efficiency, political neutrality of the civil servants, the rule of law, and gradual political reforms, could remain unchanged for some years.

With the promulgation of the Basic Law and subsequent handover arrangements, it was hoped that the stability and continuity in both pre-handover and post-handover Hong Kong would be ascertained. However, Chris Patten, after becoming the Governor of Hong Kong (1992–1997), made significant political and administrative reforms in response to citizens' demands for quality governance (Chapter 7 of this volume). China was alarmed with all these democratic reforms. As tensions heightened, the Preparatory Committee for the HKSAR passed a decision on the establishment of the Provisional Legislative Council (PLC) that would operate from 1997 to 1998 (Chen 1997: 6). The PLC soon reversed Patten's prodemocratic reforms after the handover, such as reintroducing appointed seats to the post-handover municipal councils and District Boards, and reinstating the repressive provisions of the Societies Ordinance and the Public Order Ordinance (Lau 2002a: xii–xiii).

While the initial questions for the post-1997 governance were the implementation of "one country, two systems" and the extent of its success under the colonial legacy and the constraints of the Basic Law, the focus in recent years has shifted to how the frameworks of "one country, two systems" and the Basic Law should evolve for better governance in Hong Kong.

The Rocky Path to 2023

As of 2023, in the 26 years of HKSAR governance, there are five Chief Executives (CE) of different backgrounds: Tung Chee-hwa, Donald Tsang Yam-kuen, Leung Chun-ying, Carrie Lam Cheng Yuet-ngor, and John Lee Ka-chiu. Hong Kong has also experienced seven District Council (DC) elections (1999, 2003, 2007, 2011, 2015, 2019 and 2023) and seven Legislative Council (LegCo) elections (1998, 2000, 2004, 2008, 2012, 2016 and 2021), with the latest LegCo elections postponed from 2020 to 2021 due to the COVID-19 pandemic, and the seventh District Council elections scheduled in December 2023 (Burns 2023). Over the years, the Standing Committee of the National People's Congress (SCNPC) had interpreted the Basic Law five times; namely, on the right of abode in 1999, the election method of the CE in 2004, the term of the CE in 2005, state immunity in 2011, and the requirement of legislators to take an oath in 2016. Such interpretations had aroused some public suspicion in Hong Kong. Further, in 2014, the State Council of China published a white paper on *The Practice of the "One Country, Two Systems" Policy in the HKSAR* (The State Council 2014), stating the principle of comprehensive jurisdiction. These developments were criticized by the opposition as breaching the Basic Law and sparked social discontents (Chapter 15 of this volume).

Beijing further adjusted its policies on Hong Kong after the Anti–Extradition Law Amendment Bill Movement (Anti-ELAB Movement) in 2019. Set to restore social order, the National Security Law (NSL) for Hong Kong that criminalizes secession, subversion, terrorism, and foreign interference came into effect on 30 June 2020. The provisions of the NSL are perceived by some people as having unfathomable, chilling effects (Westbrook 2020). Along with this was the Decision on Improving the Electoral System of the HKSAR, adopted by NPC on 11 March 2021, which drastically altered the election methods of Election Committee (EC) subsector elections and the LegCo elections in 2021, and the CE election in 2022 (HKSARG 2021a). With the in-depth analysis of the development of the executive, legislature, civil service, judiciary, and the District Councils in Chapters 2 to 6 of this volume, the following sections aim only to outline the general context of political changes in Hong Kong after 2012.

Over the years, the governing ideologies in Hong Kong have changed from maintaining the status quo in the local polity, to soft authoritarianism by the HKSAR, to Beijing-led comprehensive jurisdiction. As analyzed in Chapter 15 of this volume, comprehensive jurisdiction depicts the central authority's decision to assert its power over Hong Kong, which significantly indicates the evolution of the Mainland–Hong Kong relationship since 2014. The different governance ideologies rendered by the CEs under the guidance of the CPG have thus molded and transformed the city in different periods.

Key events during the governance of Tung and Tsang

The first CE, Tung Chee-hwa, delivered the HKSAR administration with grand development plans for the city, such as the pledge to provide 85,000 housing flats per year, the Chinese medicine port and the science park, and producing commitments to these plans while instituting longer-term visions for a city renowned for transience and pragmatism. To augment his leadership, Tung pioneered the Accountability System for Principal Officials (ASPO) in 2002, which significantly altered the tradition of political neutrality and hierarchical system of the civil service. Also, Tung stepped up civic education to allow youngsters to better understand China, "one country, two systems," and the Basic Law. Nevertheless, various crises—ranging from economic, such as the Asian Financial Crisis, and epidemiological (the 2003 SARS outbreak)—had plagued the city during his term. People accused the government of missteps causing Hong Kong's economic decline, deterioration of the rule of law, and sluggish development of democratization. Among all, the controversies over the national security bill (Article 23 of the Basic Law) tabled in the LegCo heightened social discontent and culminated in a demonstration on 1 July 2003 attracting half a million turnouts (Lau 2002b). Incidentally, in March 2005, Tung resigned on grounds of health reasons.

4   Political Context

The second CE, Donald Tsang, a former civil servant, succeeded Tung in 2005 and served until 30 June 2012, the end of his second term. Tsang was renowned for his pragmatic governance. In varying degrees, Tsang achieved strong governance, Hong Kong–Mainland integration, economic and trade expansion, large-scale infrastructural projects, community building and social harmony, and dialogue with the democratic camp and constitutional reforms. During most of his term, Hong Kong's economy started to recover from the 2008 financial crisis. On political development, the SCNPC in 2004 issued its interpretation to Annex I and Annex II of the Basic Law, the 6 April Decision prescribing a mechanism for amending the electoral method for selection of the CE, and the method for the formation of the LegCo and its procedures for voting on bills and motions. In January 2010, five democratic LegCo Members resigned to campaign for universal suffrage and the abolition of the FCs. The resignation was intended to achieve the effect of a *de facto* referendum in the subsequent territory-wide by-elections. In the same year, Tsang's second constitutional reform proposal managed to obtain the LegCo's support, which resulted from a compromise to modify the proposal by incorporating the Democratic Party's proposal of creating the District Council (Second) Functional Constituency in the LegCo and the additional five seats to be elected by over three million elec-torate (*SCMP* Reporters 2017; Chapters 6 and 7 of this volume). Nevertheless, the incident significantly affected the cohesion of the democratic camp in Hong Kong ever since (Cheng 2013).

On social cohesion, one of Tsang's key infrastructures in his *2007 Policy Address*, the Guangzhou-Shenzhen-Hong Kong Express Rail Link, triggered the Anti–Express Rail Protest in 2009 and 2010. The funding request of the rail link was passed in the LegCo, which made the protestors disillusioned with electoral politics; they realized that people's livelihood would not be improved without parallel political reforms. To this end, the new social movements and new democratic movements ushered in the growth of Hong Kong localism and direct-action activism. Alongside this, Tsang's expansion of the political appoint-ment system (ASPO) to add deputies and political assistants further politicized the civil service (Cheng 2013).

Key events during the governance of Leung, Lam, and Lee

During Leung's term, Hong Kong had become increasingly politicized. There was also increasing disharmony between the government and the people, and among the people. A notable event during the administration of the third CE, Leung Chun-ying, was the controversial 2012 Moral and National Education Curriculum Guide (Primary 1 to Secondary 6), which was criticized by some people as brainwashing. The Protest against National Education Curriculum led by some social organizations and the Scholarism (2011–2016), established by Joshua Wong and some young students, gathered momentum and successfully forced the government to withdraw the proposed curriculum. The protest signified heightened student and youth activism, growth of direct-action advocacy, and vocal demands for a slower pace of Hong Kong–China integration and protection of Hong Kong's autonomy (Chapter 9 of this volume).

In a 2012 interview with *TIME*, Leung seemed to have captured the signs of the time and told the journalist that one of the three things that Hong Kong needed most was "community building" (*TIME* Staff 2012). Notably, the "zero quota" policy by which all public hospitals would not accept any bookings by non-local pregnant women for delivery in Hong Kong had won some applause for the government (Press Releases, HKSARG: 28 December 2012). Nevertheless, in 2013, the Executive Council's rejection of licensing Hong Kong Television Network sparked a public outcry, with many questioning whether the decision was fair. In addition, in Leung's *2015 Policy Address*, he singled out a special issue entitled "Hong Kong Nationalism," and a cover story entitled "Hong Kong people deciding their own fate" published by *Undergrad*, a student publication of the University of Hong Kong's Student Union, as advocating Hong Kong to "find a way to self-reliance and self-determination" (Leung 2015: 3). Some, however, opined that there was utterly no such claim among the youngsters who had no established political views.

In twists and turns, in September 2014, the Occupy Central Movement (OCM) initiated by Reverend Chu Yiu-ming, Benny Tai, and Chan Kin-man demanding universal suffrage after the announcement of the 8.31 Decision eventually developed into the relatively decentralized and student-led Umbrella Movement (UM). The 8.31 Decision refers to the SCNPC's decision on universal suffrage of the CE elections announced on 31 August 2014. The SCNPC decided that if the election of the CE is implemented by the method of universal suffrage, the nominating committee will be formed in accordance with the number of members, composition, and formation method of the EC. The nominating committee could nominate two to three candidates, and each of them must receive the support of more than half of the members of the nominating committee (*Xinhua Net* 2014; Chapters 7 and 9 of this volume).

The 2016 Mong Kok riots triggered by the discontents with the government's restriction on unlicensed street hawkers during Chinese New Year further accelerated social tensions. Later in the year, the Electoral Affairs Commission implemented a new measure by which all candidates were obliged to sign an additional "confirmation form" to declare their acknowledgment of Hong Kong as an inalienable part of China. Those who refused to sign, such as Chan Ho-tin, convener of the pro-independence Hong Kong National Party, were barred from running in the LegCo elections. Those who signed—Agnes Chow, cofounder of

Demosistō, and Edward Leung of Hong Kong Indigenous—were still disqualified from the LegCo elections as their intent was doubted. The LegCo elections ended up returning two very popular localist legislators: Sixtus Chung-hang Leung and Yau Wai-ching of Young Inspiration. When assuming office, the manner in which they took the oath was heavily criticized by some pro-establishment figures. With an urgent judicial review application before the Court of First Instance, the CE and Secretary for Justice sought to disqualify Leung and Yau as legislators and crush the LegCo president's decision to allow the legislators to retake the oath. On 7 November, the SCNPC issued an interpretation of Article 104 of the Basic Law, which stated the requirements for a valid oath of office. On 15 November, the Court of First Instance rendered its judgment and the two legislators-elect were disqualified from being members of the LegCo. They were followed by four other legislators who were also subsequently disqualified for their improper oath-taking behavior (Zhu and Chen 2019; Chapters 3 and 8 of this volume).

During CY Leung's term, active promotion of Hong Kong's integration with the Mainland was underway. Hong Kong was incorporated into the national development strategy of China's 12th Five-Year Plan (2011–2015). This was repeated in the 13th and the 14th Five-Year Plans (2016–2020) (Chapter 15 of this volume). Moreover, Leung promoted Hong Kong's role in the "One Belt, One Road Initiative" and the Pearl River Delta region. He also encouraged practicing *nei jiao* (internal diplomacy) to develop a managed relationship between Hong Kong and the Mainland.

The term of office of the fourth CE, Carrie Lam, ran from 2017 to 2022. Her election campaign slogans, such as "we connect," were attempts to heal social divisions. When elected, she vowed to "heal the divide and to ease the frustration," and to "unite our society to move forward" (Press Releases, HKSARG: 26 March 2017). The first two policy addresses of Lam issued in 2017 and 2018 covered a wide range of subjects, from good governance and a livable city to connecting with young people (Chapters 12, 13, and 14 of this volume), though the emphasis was more on economic development and improving people's livelihood than on constitutional reforms. Amid the Anti-ELAB Movement and subsequent political tensions in Hong Kong, the 2019 and 2020 policy addresses put a heavy emphasis on restoring law and order, economic recovery, reframing the understanding of "one country, two systems," and deepening the integration of Hong Kong into the Mainland.

Lam's term has witnessed the culmination of political tensions and drastic changes in the governing ideologies and framework, as well as the civil society in Hong Kong. Politically, her term witnessed disqualifications of election candidates and banning of pro-independence political parties. For instance, Demosistō candidate Agnes Chow and the ousted legislator Lau Siu-lai were disqualified for running in the 2018 LegCo by-election for vacancies left by the disqualified legislators. Chow was disqualified because her political party had called for "self-determination," while Lau was accused of advocating for "self-determination." In 2019, Chow eventually succeeded in challenging the disqualification.

In 2018, the Hong Kong National Party was banned under the Societies Ordinance, which was considered necessary as preventive measures because the party could pose a threat to national security (*BBC* 2018). While these signified heightened social tensions, the Anti-ELAB Movement in 2019 further dampened the government-public relationship in Hong Kong and the relations between Hong Kong and the Mainland. The incident had turned rhetorical slogans of a few individuals into local pro-autonomy and pro-independence movements. The incident started with the introduction of a bill to amend the Fugitive Offenders Ordinance, which spurred worries that Hong Kong residents may be extradited to the Mainland. Protestors demanded the withdrawal of the bill, the resignation of Lam, and an independent inquiry into police conduct in handling the protests. Although Lam suspended the bill in June, she did not withdraw it until September and made no concession to the other demands of the protesters. In October, amid the protests, Lam invoked the Emergency Regulations Ordinance to prohibit "face covering" in public assemblies. The clashes between the protesters and police had continued to escalate, which eventually resulted in more than 10,000 arrests (C Lam 2020: 73) and over 2,300 prosecutions that year (C Lam 2020: 14). Building on the momentum of the protests, democrats and localists registered a landslide victory of 388 out of 452 seats in the DC elections in November 2019 (Chapters 6, 7, and 9 of this volume).

In June 2020, the National Anthem Ordinance, which criminalizes insults to the national anthem of China, came into effect alongside the NSL. After the promulgation of the NSL, there were various prosecutions of democrats and localists for joining or organizing a 4 June commemoration and a 1 October protest in 2020 not approved by the police, participation in the primaries organized by the pan-democratic camp for the 2020 LegCo elections (postponed to 2021 due to the COVID-19 pandemic), and publication of seditious materials. Furthermore, the police raided the offices of *Apple Daily* and *Stand News*. As of 26 July 2021 in Lam's term, the police had arrested or ordered the arrest of at least 138 people in relation to the NSL (Amnesty International 2021). The Anti-ELAB Movement and the implementation of the NSL have aroused international attention and unprecedented challenges to Hong Kong's external relations, such as the United States government's implementation of the Hong Kong Human Rights and Democracy Act of 2019 and the Hong Kong Autonomy Act of 2020, and Britain's offer to nearly three million British national overseas (BNO) Hong Kong residents the chance to settle in Britain and ultimately apply for citizenship (Chapter 16 of this volume).

Since 2020, all civil servants are required to swear allegiance and sign a pledge declaring that they would uphold the Basic Law, bear allegiance to the HKSAR, and be responsible to the HKSAR government. With the passing of the oath-taking requirement bill in the LegCo in 2021, the mandatory oath of allegiance has been extended to cover all DC members and personnel hired on non-civil service terms. This led to the resignation of over 200 District Councilors as of 2021. Furthermore, as stated above, the electoral system reform for Hong Kong has drastically altered the election methods for the EC subsector elections and the LegCo elections in 2021, the CE election in 2022, and the status of DCs (HKSARG 2021a; Chapters 2, 3, 5, 6, and 8 of this volume).

All these signify the challenges to the implementation of the principle of "one country, two systems," with a growing emphasis on the importance of "one country" in the principle. Lam's government had reiterated that Hong Kong's unique strengths and robustness came from "one country, two systems." To this end, Lam oversaw Hong Kong to uphold the "one country" principle (C Lam 2018: 3), stay committed to the basis of "one country" and leverage the benefits of "two systems" (C Lam 2018: 33), and comprehensively and accurately implement the principles of "one country, two systems," "Hong Kong people administering Hong Kong," and a high degree of autonomy (e.g., C Lam 2020: 6).

Lam commented that the CE was responsible to both the HKSAR and the CPG, and that she has "specific roles and functions to play in respect of the exercise of powers and functions by the legislature and the judiciary of Hong Kong." Lam helped redefine the executive-led framework that the powers of the executive authorities, the legislature, and the judiciary were "individually positioned" with a division of work (C Lam 2020: 8) and not a separation of power modelled on Western democracies.

Regarding the integration of Hong Kong into China, the Guangzhou-Shenzhen-Hong Kong Express Rail Link and the Hong Kong-Zhuhai-Macao Bridge were both opened in 2018. The plan to implement the colocation arrangement at the Western Kowloon Station of the Express Rail Link caused concerns about breaching Article 18 of the Basic Law, which stipulates that "National laws shall not be applied in the Hong Kong Special Administrative Region except for those listed in Annex III to this Law. The laws listed therein shall be applied locally by way of promulgation or legislation by the Region" (HKSARG 2021b; Chapter 4 of this volume). Lam denied this criticism. Moreover, Lam had actively promoted and involved Hong Kong in the "One Belt, One Road" Initiative and the Guangdong-Hong Kong-Macao Greater Bay Area development. In her *2020 Policy Address*, Lam encouraged the people, especially youngsters, to work and pursue their career in the Greater Bay Area, and promised to launch the Greater Bay Area Youth Employment Scheme to recruit university graduates to work there (C Lam 2020: 78).

The reconstitution of the local identity was another emphasis of Lam's *Policy Address*. Since the 2018–2019 school year, Chinese history was taught as an independent compulsory subject at the junior secondary level (C Lam 2017: 44). In her *2020 Policy Address*, Lam stressed that students shall be trained to become law-abiding, to respect different opinions, and adapt to social life as a responsible member of civil society (C Lam 2020: 72). Moreover, it is important to cultivate students' understanding of the country's development, the Basic Law, the implementation of "one country, two systems," and the importance of national security, and to teach them to respect and preserve the dignity of the national flag and the national anthem, as well as develop in them a sense of identity, belonging and responsibility towards the country, the Chinese race, and our society (C Lam 2020: 74). Amid complaints that Liberal Studies had encouraged students to participate in protests, the subject was reconstituted as Citizenship and Social Development from 2022 onward.

The term of CE John Lee started on 1 July 2022. While it is still early to make a definitive comment on Lee's governance style, it is noticeable that his government has sought to boost Hong Kong's economic and social development through active promotion of the city's integration into the national development alongside ensuring its social stability, patriotism, and national security. The economic, social, and urban policies of Lee's government would be of great interest (Chapters 12 to 14 of this volume). For instance, Victoria Harbour improvement work involving reclamation of less than 0.8 hectares will be exempted from the "public need test" required by the Protection of the Harbour Ordinance passed in 1997. Moreover, Lee has announced several measures to combat high housing prices, such as building private residential units and Light Public Housing. The government also plans to take forward three major road schemes and three strategic railway projects to drive Hong Kong's economic development. Parallel to the plans of snatching overseas global talents, the government has earmarked a coinvestment fund to attract overseas businesses back in. Regarding promotion of patriotism, the government has made a passing grade in the Basic Law and the NSL Test an entry requirement for civil service jobs requiring degree or professional qualifications from July 2022 onward. Last but not least, implementing security legislation under Article 23 of the Basic Law would be one of the top priorities of Lee's government (Lee 2022).

The Big Framework Redefined

For a very long time, people believed that China would use soft strategies to "win the hearts and minds" of the Hong Kong people, and that Hong Kong would continue to be a showcase of "one country, two systems" for Taiwan. Indeed, from 1997 to the early 2010s, Hong Kong people's trust in the CPG was high, and even amid the Article 23 controversies in mid-2003, the CPG still enjoyed a satisfaction rate of 57 percent (Civic Exchange 2004: Table 38). China had been highly self-restrained in ruling Hong Kong in the early post-handover years, and criticisms of the HKSAR government were not from the CPG but rather from pro-Beijing elites in Hong Kong and a few individual Chinese officials.

Nevertheless, the relationship between Hong Kong and China was one of mutual testing of limits and accommodations. Since the massive 1 July demonstrations in 2003, the CPG has become more involved in Hong Kong's affairs. Meanwhile, the integration of Hong Kong into China has been quickened, such as with the signing of the Closer Economic Partnership Arrangement (CEPA) and others (Geng and Chung 2022).

There was a significant reshuffle of China's personnel in Hong Kong since 2012. For instance, Zhang Xiaoming replaced Peng Qinghua as the director of the CLO in 2012. In the same year, SCNPC chairperson Zhang Dejiang took over the leadership of the Central Coordination Group on Hong Kong and Macao Affairs, while Li Yuanchao became the deputy. In 2014, a high-level think tank, the Chinese Association of Hong Kong and Macao Studies, was formed. In February 2020, Xia Baolong, vice-chairperson of the Chinese People's Political Consultative Conference (CPPCC), was appointed as head of the Hong Kong and Macao Affairs Office (HKMAO), which has thus added weight to the role of the office in governing Hong Kong (Cheung 2018; Lam 2020). From 2020 to 2023, Luo Huining, a senior member of the Chinese Communist Party, was appointed the director of the CLO. Luo was then succeeded by Zheng Yanxiong in 2023. Also in 2023, it was announced that a new overarching body called the Hong Kong and Macao work office of the CPC Central Committee would be formed based on the existing HKMAO. The new body will answer to the party's Central Committee instead of the State Council, while the original HKMAO will still be retained (Wong and Cheng 2023; Chapter 15 of this volume).

Indeed, the "new Hong Kong policy" of the Mainland embarked roughly around the OCM (Cheung 2018) with several characteristics. First, as discussed above, there is an emphasis to promote a correct understanding of the power of the central authorities and the importance of "one country" in the "one country, two systems" framework. For instance, in the 18th National Congress of the CCP in 2012, the then-political leader Hu Jiantao stated, "The underlying goal of the principles and policies adopted by the central government concerning Hong Kong and Macao is to uphold China's sovereignty, security and development interests and maintain long-term prosperity and stability of the two regions" (China.org.cn 2019). According to the white paper published in 2014, "the high degree of autonomy of HKSAR is subject to the level of the central leadership's authorization. There is no such thing called residual power" (The State Council 2014) (more examples in Chapter 15 of this volume).

Second, there is an increasing emphasis on Hong Kong's political system as an executive-led system with an overriding power of the CE over the legislative and judicial branches, rather than a separation-of-power system instituted in the last colonial years. For instance, it was reported that during his visit to Hong Kong in 2008, Xi Jinping stated that there should be mutual understanding and support among the executive, the legislature, and the judiciary, which had aroused public concerns (Press Releases, HKSARG: 27 January 2010). In the white paper published in 2014, "judges of the courts at different levels and other judicial personnel" are referred to as "those who administrate Hong Kong" and have "the responsibility of correctly understanding and implementing the Basic Law, of safeguarding the country's sovereignty, security and development interests, and of ensuring the long-term prosperity and stability of Hong Kong" (The State Council 2014).

Third, Chinese authorities are increasingly involved in Hong Kong's governance, particularly regarding national security concerns. Territorial integrity and sovereignty have been the uncompromised priorities for Beijing. For instance, after promulgation of the NSL for Hong Kong, the SCNPC has also clarified the allegiance requirements for Legislative Councillors. Meanwhile, researchers observed that pro-establishment organizations and coalitions became more and more active, and there has been an increasing number of native and neighborhood united front groups (Lo et al. 2019; Cheng 2020; Yuen 2020; Lam 2020).

Fourth, the economic incorporation of Hong Kong into China's overall developmental plans has accelerated. For instance, Hong Kong has continued to serve as an important center of China's financial networks and her window to global capital (Meyer 2018; Chapter 16 of this volume). Nevertheless, Hong Kong's growing economic dependence on China is also increasingly evident in the patterns of direct investment in Hong Kong. Over the years, the proportion of the Mainland's total inward direct investment in Hong Kong has manifested radical increases (Ting and Lai 2012). As of 2021, the proportion of Mainland China constituted 27.7 percent (HK$4,227.6 billion) of the total inward direct investment of HK$15,263.5 billion in Hong Kong, and that of the British Virgin Islands constituted 30.9 percent (HK$4,715.9 billion) (Census and Statistics Department 2022: Table 2, p. 15).

Some people claim that enterprises set up nonoperating companies in offshore financial centers, such as the British Virgin Islands, for channeling direct investment funds back to Hong Kong and avoiding tax (Holland 2016). The patterns of Hong Kong's outward direct investment have also exhibited the same trends. Over the years, most of the outward investment had gone to the Mainland (Ting and Lai 2012). As of 2021, the Mainland constituted 40.3 percent (HK$7,680.7 billion) of Hong Kong's total outward direct investment (HK$15,591.7 billion). There were also funds channeled via places like the British Virgin Islands before they arrived at the final destination in the Mainland. In 2021, British Virgin Islands constituted 30.3 percent (HK$4,720.7 billion) of the total outward direct investment (Census and Statistics Department 2022: Table 4, p. 21). Regarding Hong Kong's domestic exports, as of 2022, 37.1 percent went to Mainland China (Trade and Industry Department 2022a). Also, the Mainland took up the largest proportions in reexports (57.0 percent) (Trade and Industry Department 2022b) and imports (42.2 percent) in 2022 (Trade and Industry Department 2022c). On top of all these, Hong Kong is still China's leading offshore RMB center.

Fifth, patriotic education and social and cultural integration between Hong Kong and the Mainland have remained a strong emphasis of the authorities. Since the handover, the Hong Kong government has cultivated nationalism among the people of Hong Kong and promoted the public's sense of community by introducing nationalism as a correlate of ideal citizenship (Lam 2005). For example, since 1998, Putonghua, the national language of China, has been taught in all primary schools in Hong Kong (Morris et al. 2000: 249). China tours for Hong Kong students and youngsters, and cultural exchanges between students from Hong Kong and the Mainland, have been highly encouraged. In 2011, the government proposed the subject of moral and national education for primary and secondary schools but was met with strong protests and withdrew the proposal. In 2021, the Education Bureau announced that "Citizenship and Social Development (CS) will replace senior secondary Liberal Studies (LS) starting from Secondary Four in the 2021/22 school year" (Press Releases, HKSARG: 25 August 2021). The subject promotes a balanced understanding of Hong Kong with the themes of "one country, two systems," our country since reform and opening up, and interconnectedness and interdependence of the contemporary world, and requires all secondary school students to go to the Mainland for a study tour (Curriculum Development Council and the Hong Kong Examinations and Assessment Authority 2021).

As illustrated by the above analysis, under the Greater Bay Area development plans, Hong Kong will increasingly merge with Guangdong. Hong Kong people are highly encouraged to work and live in the Greater Bay Area (C Lam 2020: 4, 29 and 78; Constitutional and Mainland Affairs Bureau 2018; Chapter 12 of this volume). The Guangdong-Hong Kong-Macao Greater Bay Area Hong Kong Youth Internship Scheme launched under the Funding Scheme for Youth Internship in the Mainland has been expanded to cover all Greater Bay Area cities since 2019. To assist young people in exploring opportunities in the Greater Bay Area, the Youth Development Fund has rolled out a new funding scheme to help them develop their businesses in both Hong Kong and Greater Bay Area cities in the Mainland. The scheme sponsors NGOs in organizing youth entrepreneurship projects, which provide capital funding to youth entrepreneurial teams and relevant start-up and development support services to young people (Press Releases, HKSARG: 4 November 2020).

Youth work is also emphasized so that young people can learn about China's achievement through cultural exchanges. In recent years, the Education Bureau has implemented programs to foster the exchange between Hong Kong and Mainland schools, students, and teachers. For instance, researchers showed that the cumulative number of students receiving government subsidies for Mainland Exchange Programmes from 2007 to 2016 totaled 334,737, and the total government expenditure was HK$430 million (Fong 2017: Table 3). Besides, the Mainland–Hong Kong Teachers Exchange and Collaboration Programme aims at fostering the exchange and collaboration between Mainland and Hong Kong kindergarten teachers in designing and implementing music, visual arts activities, and so forth (Education Bureau 2020). The Sister School Scheme provides recurrent grant and professional support for about 900 pairs of local schools and their counterparts in the Greater Bay Area (Education Bureau 2021). Since the 2017–2018 school year, the Education Bureau has provided about 100,000 exchange quotas every year, which is sufficient for every student to join at least one Mainland exchange program in both the primary and secondary stages. These programs cover 22 provinces, four autonomous regions and four municipalities in the Mainland. Meanwhile, the Home Affairs Bureau also subsidizes NGOs to organize Mainland exchange projects for young people through the Funding Scheme for Youth Exchange in the Mainland. In 2018–2019, about 15,000 local young people benefited from the Scheme. In addition, the Home Affairs Bureau also collaborates with scientific research and cultural institutions in the Mainland as well as major corporations in Hong Kong to implement the Thematic Youth Internship Programmes to the Mainland and the Scheme on Corporate Summer Internship on the Mainland and Overseas. In 2019, altogether 4,000 young people were offered Mainland internship opportunities through these three internship schemes (Press Releases, HKSARG: 4 November 2020). In December 2022, the Hong Kong government released the Youth Development Blueprint that outlines the overall vision and guiding principles of youth work in the future (Press Releases, HKSARG: 20 December 2022). It is expected that the government will continue to push youth work forward.

Change of Regime Nature and Institutions

The redefined framework of "one country, two systems" discussed above has a lot of repercussions. One notable change happens in the regime nature of the Hong Kong government. Many have argued that, before the handover, Hong Kong was a liberal authoritarian regime (or liberal autocracy) in which people enjoyed social and economic freedoms, but their election rights were constrained. After the handover, it was noted that the HKSAR government had increasingly adopted soft authoritarian practices (So and Chan 2002: 380–381; So 2002: 413–417).

In recent years, scholars have noticed the change in the regime nature of the Hong Kong government towards greater authoritarianism. For instance, Brian Fong observed that Hong Kong has been juggling between liberal authoritarianism and electoral authoritarianism (Fong 2017: 739). Electoral authoritarianism manifests a trend of manipulating elections, such as distributing spoils among voters, maneuvering voter rolls, creating fake opposition, attacking opposition and pressuring opposition supporters, and manipulating the media. Some others saw Hong Kong as a competitive authoritarian regime (Levitsky and Way 2010), in which there is room for opposition groups to contest the ruling factions in elections in a largely suppressed environment with limited civil liberties (Wong 2014; Wong 2018: 711).

In what follows, the evolvement and features of the executive, legislature, judiciary, and the DCs will be outlined to illustrate the changing regime nature of Hong Kong.

The executive-led principle and the executive structure

Since 1997, the executive-led principle has remained a major governing ideology of the Hong Kong government. Article 48 of the Basic Law entrusts the CE with the power to sign bills, sign budgets, decide on government policies, appoint or remove holders of public offices and judges in accordance with legal procedures, and so on. Also, the CE could veto laws passed by the LegCo or dissolve the LegCo only once in each term of his or her office, in case of deadlocks between the LegCo and the CE (Articles 49 and 50 of the Basic Law). Nevertheless, if the LegCo passes the law again, the CE would have to adopt the law or dissolve the LegCo, and if the reconstituted LegCo passes the bill again by a two-thirds majority, the CE must resign (Article 52). The LegCo also has the power to impeach the CE (Article 73).

In realpolitik, the manifestation of an executive-led government appears as an interplay among the CE, ExCo, and civil service. At times, it could mean a government led by the CE and civil servants, with members of the ExCo only as advisors. This was very much the executive-led principle during colonial times of leadership by the governor and civil servants. In other times, it could mean a government led by the CE and ExCo, with an apolitical civil service responsible for policy implementation. This is a more presidential style of executive government (Cheung 2002). During CE Tung's time, we often saw governance by the CE and ExCo assisted by principal officials especially after the introduction of ASPO in July 2002.

After taking office in 2005, CE Tsang restructured the ExCo in November 2005 by appointing some new nonofficial members, including Anthony Cheung, an academic who was once active in both the Meeting Point, one of the earliest political groups formed in Hong Kong during the political transition, and the Democratic Party. To achieve his goals of strong governance and social harmony, Tsang also reintroduced the position of ExCo convener for better communication within the council. In 2008, Tsang further developed the political appointment system by adding undersecretaries and political assistants to assist bureau secretaries. In this direction, Tsang, a civil servant for many years, had continued the type of executive-led framework from CE Tung's time and consolidated the importance of political appointees and senior civil servants in the policy process (Cheng 2013).

Besides the evolvement of the executive structure toward a political appointment system, there have been different views about whether Hong Kong's system is better to be executive-led or modeled on the principle of separation of powers. Nevertheless, in 2007, then-NPC chairman Wu Bangguo stressed that the most important feature of the HKSAR's political system is that it is executive led. In 2015, Zhang Xiaoming, then director of CLO, opined that Hong Kong has an executive-led system with the CE at the core (*SCMP* Staff 2015). Zhang's view aroused a lot of debates and arguments throughout the entire term of CE Leung.

The assumption that the executive design of the HKSAR is modeled on the principle of separation of powers was grossly criticized in CE Lam's term. As stated, "In addition to leading the executive authorities, the Chief Executive has specific roles and functions to play in respect of the exercise of powers and functions by the legislature and the judiciary of Hong Kong. This demonstrates the HKSAR's adherence to the executive-led structure under the core leadership of the Chief Executive, who is directly accountable to the CPG" (C Lam 2020: 8). Furthermore, the article of Teresa Cheng, the former Secretary for Justice, pointed out that "the Basic Law envisages an executive-led system in the administration of the HKSAR. One should not just refer to a label, but should objectively review the substance of the Basic Law in ascertaining what the political structure of HKSAR entails—an executive-led system, with the executive authorities, the legislature, and the judiciary performing constitutionally designated roles with a division of work and complementing each other" (Cheng 2020).

As of 2023, the executive structure of the Hong Kong government has remained largely the same. With the inclusion of political appointees to lead various branches and departments, the governance of the HKSAR is still headed by the CE, assisted by ExCo and principal officials, and executed by the civil service. Regarding the election of the CE, in 2016, it was returned by the 5th EC of 1,200 members. The 2021 electoral system reform for Hong Kong expands the 6th EC to 1,500 members but reconstitutes its composition to reduce the number of eligible voters for the 1,500 members. The reconstitution includes (1) removing individual sectors from the First Sector (industrial, commercial, and financial sectors); (2) replacing individual voters with corporate voters, and adding ex officio and nominated members in the Second Sector (the professionals); (3) adding two new subsectors of "grassroots associations" and "associations of Chinese fellow townsmen" in the Third Sector (grassroots, labor, religious, and other sectors); (4) replacing the subsectors of DCs by members of Area Committees, District Fight Crime Committees, and District Fire Safety Committees, and adding representatives of associations of Hong Kong residents in the Mainland in the Fourth Sector (LegCo Members and representatives of district organizations); and (5) creation of the Fifth Sector, which will include (a) the subsector of Hong Kong deputies to the NPC and Hong Kong members of the CPPCC National Committee, (b) the subsector of representatives of Hong Kong members of related national organizations. Each of the five sectors has 300 members (HKSARG 2021a; Chapter 2 of this volume).

With the reform, the electoral base of the EC Subsector Ordinary Elections conducted in September 2021 was significantly reduced. Also, changes to the LegCo elections, as will be analyzed below, would further enhance the CE's power over the legislature and the executive-led nature of the government entrenched. The 2021 electoral system reform undoubtedly changes the patterns of political interaction to assure "patriots ruling Hong Kong" and broaden the Mainland's influence on the CE.

The legislature

The normal term of office for the LegCo is four years. The HKSAR's first LegCo lasted from 1998 to 2000 and comprised 60 seats, including 20 directly elected seats returned by GCs, 30 FC seats, and 10 seats returned by members of the 400-member Selection Committee. In the second LegCo (2000–2004), the number of GC seats increased from 20 to 24, while the size of the EC expanded to 800 members returning only six legislators. The number of FC seats remained unchanged. The third LegCo (2004 to 2008) and the fourth LegCo (2008 to 2012) had the same size of 60 seats with 30 GC seats, 30 FC seats and zero EC seat. The fifth LegCo (2012 to 2016) and the sixth LegCo (2016–2021) had increased the total seats to 70 with still half GC and half FC seats. It was meant to be a gradual process of democratization in the LegCo electoral system. However, the seventh LegCo, from January 2022, is composed of 90 members with 40 members returned by the EC, 30 members by FCs, and 20 members by GCs.

The post-1997 LegCo in Hong Kong has operated within two restrictions on Members' bills and separate voting mechanisms stipulated in the Basic Law. Since 1997, legislators can present private members' bills except in areas that involve public expenditure, issues of political structure, or operation of government, while other policy bills require written consent from the CE (Article 74 of the Basic Law). Researchers pointed out that between 1991 and 1997, the private members' bill was a powerful tool for legislators to push for substantial policy change. However, the number of private members' bills significantly decreased after the handover (Sing 2003: 30–32; Ma 2007: 117–118). Legislative power is further constrained by the separate voting mechanism. The post-1997 LegCo before 2022 was divided into two blocks: GC and FC members. Legislators proposing bills, moving motions or amendments to government bills required a simple majority from both the GC and FC members present (Annex II [7] of the Basic Law). For motions, bills, or amendments to bills raised by the executive, separate voting did not apply, and passage only required a simple majority of all members present. FC legislators, who in general are conservative in their political outlook, tended to represent sectoral interests. The constraints placed on the legislature had hindered not only the effectiveness of GC members channeling grassroots interests for policy reform but also the cooperation among legislators and political camps, in addition to the legislative-executive relationship.

In essence, until 2020, the post-1997 LegCo had witnessed increasing divisions into the pro-democracy, pro-local, pro-establishment, and non-affiliated camps competing for public support and engaging in confrontations, mutual name-calling and filibustering. Democratic legislators constantly pushed for the abolition of the FCs and democratization of the political system in Hong Kong. The Hong Kong government, the pro-establishment camp, and the Chinese authorities had sought to augment the leadership of the executive via different means, such as restatement of the executive-led governing principle in Hong Kong and making amendments to the LegCo's Rules of Procedure. An example is the 2011 amendment empowering chairpersons of all the LegCo committees to ask legislators whose conduct is grossly disorderly to withdraw immediately from the meeting. This power was previously exclusive to chairpersons of the standing and select committees and the LegCo president (LegCo 2011; 2023).

The 2021 electoral system reform for Hong Kong was intended to put an end to the lingering executive-legislative tensions by fabricating a cooperative legislature. The reform increased the total number of LegCo seats from 70 to 90 but changed its composition as stated above. Regarding the separate voting mechanism, the passage of motions, bills, or amendments to government bills introduced by individual legislators still requires a simple majority of votes of each of the two groups of members present, i.e., members returned by the EC, and those returned by FCs and by GCs through direct elections. Besides, the Candidate Eligibility Review Committee has been established to assess and validate if a candidate complies with the legal requirements and conditions for upholding the Basic Law and bearing allegiance to the HKSAR. This candidate eligibility review mechanism applies to LegCo elections, the EC formation, and the CE election. Alongside, LegCo candidature requires two to four nominations from each of the five sectors of the EC, on top of other statutory requirements for standing for election (HKSARG 2021a; Chapter 3 of this volume). This means that the restructured EC will also influence who can run in the LegCo elections.

The judiciary

Like other institutions in Hong Kong, the judiciary and the rule of law have witnessed significant changes. "Judicial independence" has acquired a renewed understanding in the redefined big framework since 2012. Apart from the saying that judges and other judicial personnel are a part of those who administrate Hong Kong discussed above, another notable development is that the SCNPC has asserted its higher power over Hong Kong courts. According to Article 158 of the Basic Law, the SCNPC has the power of final interpretation of the Basic Law. The courts must follow the SCNPC's interpretations in its future rulings on cases that involve the related provisions. For instance, in the oath-taking incident in 2016, before the Court of First Instance gave the ruling on the judicial review filed by CE Leung and the Secretary for Justice, the SCNPC preemptively issued an interpretation of Article 104 of the Basic Law leading to the subsequent disqualification of the legislators (Zhu and Chen 2019).

Another example is the colocation arrangement; some people queried whether it was compatible with Article 18 of the Basic Law. In 2017, the SCNPC ruled a green light for the colocation arrangement long before any judicial reviews on the subject were possible (Press Releases, Department of Justice, HKSARG: 26 March 2017). Furthermore, in the adjudication of *Apple Daily* proprietor Jimmy Lai's bail application, the Court of Final Appeal ruled in favor of the Department of Justice, which had challenged the High Court's bail decision for Lai. Lai's bail application was denied. The case is considered important as it signals how Hong Kong courts interpret bail conditions under the NSL (Chen and Wang 2021; Young 2021). Overall, it appears that the judiciary has been trapped between different expectations (Chapter 4 of this volume).

Local government

At the local government level, the period since 1997 saw the abolition of two municipal councils (the Urban and Regional Councils) amid public controversies. Before the abolition in December 1999, the councils were valuable venues for public participation, and served as the second tier of government administration between the first tier (the executive, the legislature, and the judiciary) and the third tier (the District Boards, renamed the DCs in 1999). The DC elections are held at four-year intervals. The first post-handover DCs lasted from 2000 to 2003, and the present one was elected in December 2023.

The constitutional reform in 2010 had empowered DCs to secure six seats in the LegCo election and 117 seats in the EC for electing the CE. With all these changes, the political importance of the DCs had been boosted. The landslide victory of democrats and localists taking 388 out of 452 seats in the 2019 DC elections, and thus controlling 17 out of 18 DCs, had alarmed the authorities. The 2021 electoral system reform replaces the subsectors of DCs by representatives of other government-appointed district organizations. Also, since a mandatory oath of allegiance had been imposed on District Councilors, over 200 of them had resigned as of 2021, and some others of them were disqualified. The previous DCs were composed of 452 elected members and 27 ex officio members (chairpersons of Rural Committees). The DCs formed after the December 2023 elections are composed of 470 members with 88 seats returned through popular vote, 179 seats directly appointed by the CE, 176 seats filled by members of Area Committees, District Fight Crime Committees, and District Fire Safety Committees, and the remaining 27 seats reserved for the ex officio members (chairpersons of Rural Committees) (Chapter 6 of this volume).

In reviewing the overall development of government institutions since 1997, the core questions are what sort of governance the political authorities have intended to achieve, and whether the political institutions in Hong Kong have developed in a way that helps achieve such governance. These questions will be addressed more fully in the chapters that follow.

The Media, Political Culture, Civil Society, and Global Relations

While the first half of the HKSAR governance was a period that went from maintaining the status quo to transiting to soft authoritarianism, the latter half witnessed increasing clashes between the "two systems," prompting the authorities to emphasize the principle of "one country" and asserting comprehensive jurisdiction over Hong Kong. Sovereignty and national security have become the overriding concerns for the authorities.

Some researchers have demonstrated that there have been increasing trends of self-censorship in the media, and growing affiliation of the Hong Kong media owners with various authorities in China both economically and politically, dampening media autonomy (Lee and Lin 2006; Chan and Lee 2012; HKJA Annual Report various years). The arrests of *Apple Daily* proprietor Jimmy Lai, top managers, and editors for violating the NSL have had serious, chilling effects on the media. Regarding Radio Television Hong Kong (RTHK), a government-funded radio station that produced many programs critical of government policies, critics accused the government of implementing measures to interfere with its editorial direction. The Governance and Management of Radio Television Hong Kong Review Report criticized the RTHK for multiple inadequacies (Press Releases, HKSARG: 19 February 2021). Amid public concern for editorial independence for the RTHK, the government announced in March 2021 the appointment of Patrick Li, an administrative officer who had no media experience, as the new Director of Broadcasting after the retirement of Director of Broadcasting Leung Ka-wing.

Despite the many problems that the HKSAR has confronted since 1997, its civil society had remained vibrant, especially in the 2010s, until recent years. Several trends were evident in its development. First, the participation of the public, social, and professional groups in politics had significantly increased to the extent that some call it "total mobilization from below" (Cheng et al. 2022). Second, strategies adopted by people to express their political views had become more diverse, action-oriented, and confrontational. Third, the younger generations in particular had become very active political actors since the protests against the demolition of the Star Ferry clock tower in 2006. Fourth, forms of political participation had expanded. Besides ordinary means such as demonstrations, voting in elections, and lobbying government officials, the past years witnessed growing popularity of online political participation on various social media platforms, especially during the UM in 2014 and the Anti-ELAB Movement in 2019. Digital activism via Facebook, Twitter, Instagram, personal blogs, YouTube channels, citizen journalism, and live journalism had rapidly developed as alternative means of political articulation and mobilization. Fifth, there was growing articulation and intense division between liberal, democratic values and the Hong Konger identity on the one hand, and pro-stability, conservative and patriotic sentiments on the other. Nevertheless, as analyzed in Chapters 7 to 11 of this volume, the media, civil society, and political participation in Hong Kong have undergone significant changes since 2019.

The increase in the number of political parties and groups in the first ten years of the HKSAR was fading. With the promulgation of the NSL and the electoral system reform, pro-autonomy and pro-independence political parties have disbanded while traditional pro-democracy political parties have been marginalized. The pro-establishment camp, on the contrary, has grown in number, influence, and political power (Chapter 8 of this volume).

Even after 1997, the world maintains an active interest in Hong Kong because of its economic and strategic value. The United States passed the *Hong Kong Policy Act* in 1992, which reiterated US support for democratization and pledged an active role in maintaining Hong Kong's confidence and prosperity. A *Hong Kong Policy Act* report is periodically prepared by the US Department of State. Similarly, in Britain, the government presents reports to Parliament every six months on the implementation of the Joint Declaration in Hong Kong. The

Anti-ELAB Movement and the implementation of the NSL have brought international attention on Hong Kong to another climax since 1997, causing unprecedented changes to Hong Kong's external relations (Chapter 16 of this volume).

Structure of This Book

In the chapters that follow, we aim to provide a comprehensive and critical analysis of Hong Kong's government and politics since the 1997 handover and particularly after 2012. Like the previous editions, this volume consists of four main topic areas: political institutions, mediating institutions and political actors, policy environment, and political environment. On each topic, this volume analyzes the developments in each topic area, and the implications of the governance and the "one country, two systems" model. This book is timely as it provides a valuable account of the Hong Kong from the past moving into the post-2020 paradigm. Hong Kong has been integrated into national development. In every step of the way, Hong Kong will either become more like an ordinary Chinese city or reidentify its uniqueness as well as role and relevance in China and the world.

Part I: Political Institutions contains five chapters. Besides this chapter, Chapter 2 examines the establishment and functions of the executive, its relations with the LegCo, and the challenges ahead. Chapter 3 discusses LegCo's history, composition, powers and functions, constraints, and effectiveness, as well as impacts of political developments on its future functioning. Chapter 4 reviews the challenges faced by the judiciary in post-1997 Hong Kong and analyzes the development of the relationships of the sovereign and the judiciary. Chapter 5 examines the distinctive features of the Hong Kong civil service, traces the development of civil service reform over the post-handover years, and offers an evaluation of its overall effectiveness. Chapter 6 examines the development, contribution, and significance of the DCs, advisory bodies and statutory bodies to governance and their limitations.

Part II: Mediating Institutions and Political Actors contains five chapters. Chapter 7 traces the development of the democratic movement in Hong Kong since 2003. It further examines the problems encountered by the movement and its possible future under the influence of the NSL. Chapter 8 traces the development of political parties and the electoral system in Hong Kong and analyzes the problems that have confronted their development. Chapter 9 studies the characteristics of civil society and social movements in Hong Kong and examines their contributions and challenges. Chapter 10 traces the development of the political identity, culture, and participation in Hong Kong after the handover, notably since the UM. Chapter 11 provides an analytical account of the concept of public opinion, and the media's role and performance in the process of public-opinion formation in Hong Kong.

Part III: Policy Environment contains three chapters. Chapter 12 traces the development of economic policy in Hong Kong since 1997 and explores the economic challenges confronting the government. Chapter 13 introduces the basics of social policy and investigates the main features of Hong Kong's social policy and their development. Chapter 14 examines the development of urban policy in Hong Kong with reference to the New Urban Agenda and sustainable development goals.

Part IV: Political Environment contains two chapters. Chapter 15 examines the key changes of Beijing's strategy toward Hong Kong and provides observations about the prospect of this relationship. Chapter 16 studies the changing international role and status of Hong Kong after 1997 and evaluates its future external relations by reviewing possible challenges and their implications for the world.

The concluding chapter presents a summary evaluation of Hong Kong governance since 1997 and provides a reflection of possibilities for achieving a more effective, fair, and legitimate governance for post-2020 Hong Kong.

Box 1.1: One country, two systems

The principle of "one country, two systems" was proposed by the late Chinese leader Deng Xiaoping during the Sino-British negotiations in the 1980s over the future political arrangement for Hong Kong. It stipulates that Hong Kong shall continue to practice capitalism with a high degree of autonomy for 50 years after 1997, and that its basic way of life shall remain intact. The interpretation and implementation of the framework have undergone changes as discussed in this chapter.

Box 1.2: The Basic Law

The Basic Law is the constitutional document for the HKSAR. It was promulgated by the National People's Congress of the People's Republic of China in 1990 and came into effect on 1 July 1997, when Hong Kong, formerly a British colony, was returned to China. The Basic Law consists of nine chapters with 160 articles and three annexes. The enshrined principles include "one country, two systems," "a high degree of autonomy," and "Hong Kong people ruling Hong Kong." Also, it stipulates the systems practiced in Hong Kong, such as the continuation of its capitalist system and way of life, and protection of the rights and freedoms of its residents.

Questions

1. How would you describe the overall political context in Hong Kong after the handover in 1997 and especially since the 2010s?
2. Which areas (e.g., government institutions, governing ideologies, the rule of law, local political culture, civil society, relations with the CPG) deserve particular attention with respect to improving the governance of Hong Kong?

Bibliography

Amnesty International 2021, "Hong Kong: First National Security Law Conviction Is 'Beginning of the End' for Freedom of Expression," 28 July, viewed 1 August 2021, https://www.amnesty.org/en/latest/news/2021/07/first-nsl-conviction-beginning-of-the-end-freedom-of-expression

BBC 2018, "Hong Kong National Party: Move to Ban Pro-Independence Group 'Concerns' UK," *BBC*, 18 July, viewed 20 March 2023, https://www.bbc.com/news/world-asia-44870238

Burns, J 2023, "Hong Kong District Councils: Where Has Public Opinion Gone?" *Hong Kong Free Press*, 14 May, viewed 14 May 2023, https://hongkongfp.com/2023/05/14/hong-kong-district-councils-where-has-public-opinion-gone

Census and Statistics Department, HKSARG 2022, *External Direct Investment Statistics of Hong Kong 2021*, viewed 21 March 2023, https://www.censtatd.gov.hk/en/data/stat_report/product/B1040003/att/B10400032021AN21B0100.pdf

Chan, JM & Lee, FLF 2012, "Mass Media and Public Opinion," in WM Lam, PLT Lui & W Wong (eds), *Contemporary Hong Kong Politics* (Expanded Second Edition), Hong Kong University Press, Hong Kong, pp. 223–246.

Chen, AHY 1997, "The Provisional Legislative Council of the SAR," *Hong Kong Law Journal*, vol. 27, no. 1, pp. 1–11.

Chen, Q & Wang, W 2021, "Jimmy Lai Denied Bail in 'Landmark Ruling Signaling HK Common Law System Adapting to National Security Law'," *Global Times*, 9 February, viewed 9 May 2023, https://www.globaltimes.cn/page/202102/1215373.shtml

Cheng, EW 2020, "United Front Work and the Mechanisms of Counter Mobilization in Hong Kong," *The China Journal*, vol. 83, January, pp. 1–33.

Cheng, EW, Lee, F, Yuen, S & Tang, G 2022, "Total Mobilization from Below: Abeyance Networks, Threats and Emotions in Hong Kong's Freedom Summer," *The China Quarterly*, vol. 251, pp. 629–659.

Cheng T 2020, "An Executive-led System, with the Executive, Legislature and Judiciary Performing Constitutionally Designated Roles," 9 September, viewed 1 June 2021, https://www.doj.gov.hk/en/community_engagement/speeches/20200909_sj1.html

Cheng, JYS 2013, "Has He Got the Job Done? An Evaluation of Donald Tsang Administration," in JYS Cheng (ed), *The Second Chief Executive of Hong Kong SAR: Evaluating the Tsang Years 2005-2012*, City University of Hong Kong Press, Hong Kong, pp. 1–30.

24   Political Context

Cheung, ABL 2002, "The Changing Political System: Executive-Led Government or 'Disabled' Governance?," in SK Lau (ed), *The First Tung Chee-hwa Administration: The First Five Years of the Hong Kong Special Administrative Region*, the Chinese University Press of Hong Kong, Hong Kong, pp. 41–68.

Cheung, TYP 2018, "In Beijing's Tightening Grip: Changing Mainland-Hong Kong Relations amid Integration and Confrontation," in BCH Fong & TL Lui (eds), *Hong Kong 20 Years after the Handover: Emerging Social and Institutional Fractures after 1997*, Palgrave Macmillan, Basingstoke, pp. 255–286.

China.org.cn 2019, "Full text: Report of Hu Jintao to the 18th CPC National Congress," 19 November, viewed 22 June 2021, http://www.china.org.cn/chinese/18da/2012-11/19/content_27152706_11.htm

Civic Exchange 2004, *Listening to the Wisdom of the Masses: Hong Kong People's Attitudes toward Constitutional Reform*, viewed 22 June 2021, http://www.hkbu.edu. hk/~hktp/listening/listening_e.pdf

Constitutional and Mainland Affairs Bureau, HKSARG 2018, "Greater Bay Area," viewed 22 March 2023, https://www.bayarea.gov.hk/en/home/index.html

Curriculum Development Council and the Hong Kong Examinations and Assessment Authority, HKSARG 2021, Citizenship and Social Development Curriculum and Assessment Guide (Secondary 4–6), viewed 17 May 2023, https://www.edb.gov.hk/attachment/en/curriculum-development/renewal/CS/CS_CAG_S4-6_Eng_2021.pdf

Education Bureau, HKSARG 2020, "Mainland-Hong Kong Teachers Exchange & Collaboration Programme," 30 September, viewed 21 June 2021, https://www.edb.gov.hk/en/edu-system/preprimary-kindergarten/sch-based-support-for-kindergar-tens/mainland-hk-teachers-exchange-collaboration-programme.html

Education Bureau, HKSARG 2021, "Sister School Scheme," 21 July, viewed 30 July 2021, https://www.edb.gov.hk/en/sch-admin/admin/about-sch/sister-sch-scheme/sister-sch-scheme-index.html

Fong, B 2017, "In-between Liberal Authoritarianism and Electoral Authoritarianism: Hong Kong's Democratization under Chinese Sovereignty, 1997–2016," *Democratization*, vol. 24, issue 4, pp. 724–750.

Foreign and Commonwealth Office n.d., "Visit of Sir Murray MacLehose, Governor of Hong Kong, to China, March–April 1979," FCO 40/1052, viewed 10 May 2023. https://discovery.nationalarchives.gov.uk/details/r/C11514187

Geng, C & Chung, Y 2022, "Hong Kong's Economic Integration with Chinese Mainland: An Index and Cointegration Analysis of Socio-economic Indicators," *Asia Pacific Business Review*, vol. 28, no. 5, pp. 740–764.

HKSARG 2021a, "Improving Electoral System (Consolidated Amendments) Bill 2021," 3 June, viewed 30 June 2021, https://www.cmab.gov.hk/improvement/en/bill/index.html

HKSARG 2021b, "Basic Law - Chapter II - Relationship between the Central Authorities and the Hong Kong Special Administrative Region," 26 August, https://www.basiclaw.gov.hk/en/basiclaw/chapter2.html

Holland, T 2016, "How Hong Kong Makes It Easy for Wealthy Chinese to Launder Billions of Dollars," *HKFP*, 6 April, viewed 30 June 2021, https://www.hongkongfp.

com/2016/04/06/how-hong-kong-makes-it-easy-for-wealthy-chinese-to-launder-their-money

Hong Kong Journalist Association (HKJA) various years, *Annual Report*.

Lam, C 2017, 2018, 2019 & 2020, *Policy Address*, HKSAR Government, Hong Kong.

Lam, WM 2005, "Depoliticization, Citizenship, and the Politics of Community in Hong Kong," *Citizenship Studies*, vol. 9, no. 3, pp. 309–322.

Lam, WM 2020, "China's Changing Ruling Strategies on Hong Kong and Their Implications," *Contemporary Chinese Political Economy and Strategic Relations: An International Journal*, vol. 6, issue 3, December, pp. 953–992.

Lau, SK 2002a, "Chronology," in SK Lau (ed), *The First Tung Chee-hwa Administration: The First Five Years of the Hong Kong Special Administrative Region*, the Chinese University Press of Hong Kong, Hong Kong, pp. xi–xxxiv.

Lau, SK 2002b, "Tung Chee-hwa's Governing Strategy: The Shortfall in Politics," in SK Lau (ed), *The First Tung Chee-hwa Administration: The First Five Years of the Hong Kong Special Administrative Region*, the Chinese University Press of Hong Kong, Hong Kong, pp. 1–39.

Lee, FLF & Lin, AMY 2006, "Newspaper Editorial Discourse and the Politics of Self-Censorship," *Discourse & Society*, vol. 17, no. 3, pp. 331–358.

Lee, JKC 2022, *The Chief Executive's 2022 Policy Address*, viewed 18 March 2023, https://www.policyaddress.gov.hk/2022/en

Legislative Council, HKSAR 2011, *Resolution of the Legislative Council* (L.N. 87 of 2011), viewed 17 May 2023, https://www.elegislation.gov.hk/hk/2011/ln87!en

Legislative Council, HKSAR 2023, "Rules of Procedure" (44. Decision of the Chair, and 45. Order in Council and Committee), viewed 17 May 2023, https://www.legco.gov.hk/en/legco-business/useful-information/legco-procedures/rules-of-procedure-i.html#45

Leung, CY 2015, *Policy Address*, HKSAR Government, Hong Kong.

Levitsky, S & Way, LA 2010, *Competitive Authoritarianism: Hybrid Regimes after the Cold War*, *Cambridge University Press*, New York, 2010.

Lo, SSH, Hung, SCF & Loo, JHC 2019, *China's New United Front Work in Hong Kong: Penetrative Politics and Its Implications*, Palgrave Macmillan, Singapore.

Ma, N 2007, *Political Development in Hong Kong: State, Political Society, and Civil Society*, Hong Kong University Press, Hong Kong.

Meyer, DR 2018, "Hong Kong: China's Global City," in TL Lui, SWK Chiu & R Yep (eds), *Routledge Handbook of Contemporary Hong Kong*, Routledge, London, UK, pp. 414–429.

Morris, P, Kan, F & Morris, E 2000, "Education, Civic Participation and Identity: Continuity and Change in Hong Kong," *Cambridge Journal of Education*, vol. 30, no. 2, pp. 243–262.

Official Publication: Sino-British Joint Declaration on the Question of Hong Kong, 7 Loy. L.A. Int'l & Comp. L. Rev. 139 (1984), viewed 10 May 2023, https://digitalcommons.lmu.edu/ilr/vol7/iss1/6

Pletcher, K 2023, "Opium Wars," *Britannica*, 28 April, viewed 10 May 2023, https://www.britannica.com/topic/Opium-Wars

Press Releases, HKSARG 2010, "LCQ2: The Relationship Among the Executive Authorities, the Legislature and the Judiciary," 27 January, viewed 15 May 2023, https://www.info.gov.hk/gia/general/201001/27/P201001270155.htm

Press Releases, HKSARG 2012, "Government Reaffirms Its Strict Enforcement of the 'Zero Quota' Policy," 28 December, viewed 10 May 2023, https://www.info.gov.hk/gia/general/201212/28/P201212280415.htm

Press Releases, Department of Justice, HKSARG 2017, "Response of the HKSAR Government on Co-location Arrangement," 26 March, viewed 16 May 2023, https://www.doj.gov.hk/en/community_engagement/press/20171229_pr2.html

Press Releases, HKSARG 2017, "Opening Remarks by CE-elect," 26 March, viewed 25 May 2021, https://www.info.gov.hk/gia/general/201703/26/P2017032600607.htm

Press Releases, HKSARG 2020, "Youth Exchange and Internship Activities on the Mainland," 4 November, viewed 25 May 2021, https://www.info.gov.hk/gia/general/202011/04/P2020110400517.htm

Press Releases, HKSARG 2021, "Government Releases Review Report on Governance and Management of RTHK," 19 February, viewed 25 May 2021, https://www.info.gov.hk/gia/general/202102/19/P2021021900420.htm

Press Releases, HKSARG 2021, "LCQ7: Subject of Citizenship and Social Development," 25 August, viewed 25 May 2023, https://www.info.gov.hk/gia/general/202108/25/P2021082500280p.htm

Press Releases, HKSARG 2022, "Government Releases Youth Development Blueprint," 20 December, viewed 22 March 2023, https://www.info.gov.hk/gia/general/202212/20/P2022122000592.htm

Sing, M 2003, "Legislative-Executive Interface in Hong Kong," in C Loh & Civic Exchange (eds), *Building Democracy: Creating Good Government for Hong Kong*, Hong Kong University Press, Hong Kong, pp. 27–34.

SCMP Reporters 2017, "'Someone I Admire': Three Letters of Mitigation for Convicted Former Hong Kong Leader Donald Tsang," *SCMP*, 21 February, viewed 20 March 2023, https://www.scmp.com/news/hong-kong/law-crime/article/2072520/someone-i-admire-three-letters-mitigation-convicted-former

SCMP Staff 2015, "Zhang Xiaoming's Controversial Speech on Hong Kong Governance: The Full Text," *SCMP*, 16 September, viewed 17 May 2023, https://www.scmp.com/news/hong-kong/politics/article/1858484/zhang-xiaomings-controversial-speech-hong-kong-governance

So, AY & Chan, MK 2002, "Conclusion: Crisis and Transformation in the Hong Kong SAR—Toward Soft Authoritarian Developmentalism?," in MK Chan & AY So (eds), *Crisis and Transformation in China's Hong Kong*, M.E. Sharpe, Armonk, New York, pp. 363–384.

So, AY 2002, "Social Protests, Legitimacy Crisis, and the Impetus toward Soft Authoritarianism in the Hong Kong SAR," in SK Lau (ed), *The First Tung Chee-hwa Administration: The First Five Years of the Hong Kong Special Administrative Region*, the Chinese University Press of Hong Kong, Hong Kong, pp. 399–418.

The State Council (PRC) 2014, *The Practice of the "One Country, Two Systems" Policy in the Hong Kong Special Administrative Region*, viewed 14 June 2021, http://english.www.gov.cn/archive/white_paper/2014/08/23/content_281474982986578.htm

TIME Staff 2012, "Q&A: Hong Kong's New Leader Is a Divisive Figure, but Aims to Build Bridges," *TIME*, 28 June, viewed 20 March 2023, https://world.time.com/2012/06/28/qa-hong-kongs-new-leader-is-a-divisive-figure-but-aims-to-build-bridges-2

Ting, W & Lai, E 2012, "Hong Kong and the World," in WM Lam, PLT Lui & W Wong (eds), *Contemporary Hong Kong Government and Politics* (Expanded Second Edition), Hong Kong University Press, Hong Kong, pp. 349–370.

Trade and Industry Department, HKSARG 2022a, "Hong Kong's Domestic Exports by Main Destination 2020," 17 May, viewed 22 March 2023, https://www.tid.gov.hk/english/aboutus/publications/tradestat/exdes.html

Trade and Industry Department, HKSARG 2022b, "Hong Kong's Re-exports by Main Destination 2020," 17 May, viewed 22 March 2023, https://www.tid.gov.hk/english/aboutus/publications/tradestat/rxdes.html

Trade and Industry Department, HKSARG 2022c, "Hong Kong's Imports by Main Suppliers 2020," 17 May, viewed 22 March 2023, https://www.tid.gov.hk/english/aboutus/publications/tradestat/imsup.html

Westbrook, L 2020, "National Security Law: Human Rights NGOs Dreading Impact of Legislation in Hong Kong Slammed for Fearmongering," *South China Morning Post*, 21 June.

Wong M 2018, "Selectorate Theory in Hybrid Regimes: Comparing Hong Kong and Singapore," *Government and Opposition*, vol. 53, issue 4, October, pp. 707–734.

Wong, N & Cheng, L 2023, "Beijing's Top Office on Hong Kong Affairs Gets Revamp with Wider Scope, Will Report Directly to Communist Party's Central Leadership," *South China Morning Post*, 16 March, viewed 20 March 2023, https://www.scmp.com/news/hong-kong/politics/article/3213778/beijings-key-office-hong-kong-affairs-answer-directly-chinas-top-communist-party-leadership

Wong, SHW 2014, "Resource Disparity and Multi-level Elections in Competitive Authoritarian Regimes: Regression Discontinuity Evidence from Hong Kong," *Electoral Studies*, vol. 33, pp. 200–219.

Xinhua Net 2014, "Full Text of NPC Decision on Universal Suffrage for HKSAR Chief Selection," *Xinhua Net*, 31 August, viewed 20 March 2023, https://web.archive.org/web/20140831212741/http://news.xinhuanet.com/english/china/2014-08/31/c_133609238.htm

Young, S 2021, "Hong Kong's Highest Court Reviews the National Security Law—Carefully," *Lawfare*, 4 March, viewed 9 May 2023, https://www.lawfareblog.com/hong-kongs-highest-court-reviews-national-security-law-carefully

Yuen, S 2020, "Native-Place Networks and Political Mobilization: The Case of Post-Handover Hong Kong," *Modern China*, 3 July, online.

Zhu, H & Chen, AHY 2019, "The Oath-Taking Cases and the NPCSC Interpretation of 2016: Interface of Common Law and Chinese Law," *Hong Kong Law Journal*, vol. 49, no. 1, pp. 381–415.

Useful Websites

Basic Law
https://www.basiclaw.gov.hk/en/index

HKPORI
https://www.pori.hk

Hong Kong SAR Government
http://www.gov.hk/en/residents

Hong Kong University Public Opinion Poll
http://www.hkupop.hku.hk

Further Reading

Chan, MK 2008, *China's Hong Kong Transformed: Retrospect and Prospects beyond the First Decade*, City University of Hong Kong Press, Hong Kong. This book is a good introduction to the changes and development of Hong Kong politics and society after the handover.

Cheng, EW 2020, "United Front Work and the Mechanisms of Counter Mobilization in Hong Kong," *The China Journal*, vol. 83, January, pp. 1–33. This article critically examines how Chinese Communist Party apparatuses have penetrated Hong Kong, and how the pro-government united front alliance was utilized in the Anti-ELAB Movement.

Lau, SK (ed) 2002, *The First Tung Chee-hwa Administration: The First Five Years of the Hong Kong Special Administrative Region*, the Chinese University Press of Hong Kong, Hong Kong. This book contains an analysis of various areas of governance in Hong Kong up to 2001.

Lo, SSH, Hung, SCF & Loo, JHC 2019, *China's New United Front Work in Hong Kong: Penetrative Politics and Its Implications*, Palgrave Macmillan, Singapore. This book provides a comprehensive investigation of the dynamics of China's new united front work and its latest development in Hong Kong.

Ma, N & Cheng EW 2019, *The Umbrella Movement: Civil Resistance and Contentious Space in Hong Kong*, Amsterdam University Press, Amsterdam, Netherlands. This edited volume examines the dynamics of the protestors, the regime, and the wider public in the Umbrella Movement.

Miners, N 1998, *Government and Politics of Hong Kong*, 5th ed., with post-handover update by James T. H. Tang, Oxford University Press, Hong Kong. This book provides a comprehensive review of government and politics in colonial Hong Kong.

Part I: Political Institutions

2
The Executive

Li Pang-kwong

The election of John Lee as the sixth Chief Executive (CE) of the Hong Kong Special Administrative Region (HKSAR) in 2022 marks the first time Hong Kong has a CE coming from a local disciplinary force. On top of the deep-seated socioeconomic problems—such as rocketing property price, wealth polarization, low social mobility, and so on—the new CE also faces the challenge of a politically polarized society and the brain drain issue, which are the result of the political antagonism left behind by the controversy over the *Fugitive Offenders and Mutual Legal Assistance in Criminal Matters Legislation (Amendment) Bill 2019* since March 2019. Successive CEs have tried very hard to address these problems but have had limited success. From the governing point of view, this may have its roots in the governing system in general and the institutional design for selecting the CE and forming the executive in particular. This chapter therefore first examines the establishment and functions of the executive of the Hong Kong government, and then the way the CE and the executive operate and interact with the Legislative Council (LegCo) in terms of general policymaking and budgetary decision-making processes. Lastly, various challenges faced by the executive are considered.

Role and Functions of the Executive

Every political system has an executive branch to act as the central policymaking mechanism. While other branches of government are involved in the policymaking process in one way or another, the executive enjoys an edge because of its critical institutional position. The executive holds the upper hand in initiating policy, shaping the public mood in favour of its proposals, aligning resources for effective implementation, and achieving the intended objectives. The other two main branches of government, the legislature and the judiciary, tend to play a passive role. It is no exaggeration to say that anything other than legislation, budget approval, and adjudication of conflicts may fall within the jurisdiction of the executive.

The executive is usually headed by a single individual who is supported by a group of ministers or secretaries in policy formulation and decision-making. Each minister or secretary is empowered to coordinate and supervise departments with responsibility for policy implementation and law enforcement. Positions in the executive are usually filled by politicians, while departments are usually staffed by civil servants or bureaucrats. In practice, however, their roles often overlap. Nevertheless, politicians are ultimately responsible for a policy's success or failure. However, Hong Kong is unusual in that there was no clear demarcation between the roles of politicians and bureaucrats (Box 2.1) before the introduction of the Accountability System for Principal Officials (ASPO) in July 2002. The design of the British colonial and immediate post-1997 political system allowed bureaucrats to play political roles, which eventually led to the misconception of the functions of politicians and bureaucrats, and the domination of the executive by bureaucrats.

The political system of Hong Kong is somewhat peculiar: it is a subsystem of the Chinese communist political system but has been allowed to have a different political and institutional arrangements from that of her local counterpart on the Mainland because of the principle of "one country, two systems." For example, the formation of the Hong Kong government and the selection/appointment of its executive head are different from those of municipal/provincial governments and their mayors/governors on the Mainland. Having said that, the Central People's Government (CPG) holds the ultimate powers that have usually been enjoyed by the central government in the unitary state.

The Hong Kong Executive: Positions, Offices, and Functions

Hong Kong's executive branch is headed by the CE, who is assisted administratively by the Chief Executive's Office. The CE's work is supported by the principal officials (three senior secretaries and fifteen bureau secretaries), who are responsible for policy formulation and the supervision of subordinate executive departments within their portfolios. During the temporary absence of the CE, the chief secretary for administration (CS), the financial secretary (FS), or the secretary for justice (SJ) deputies are prioritized in the above order. Among the principal officials, the CS and the FS each maintain a sizable office to assist them in carrying out their duties. Under each policy bureau are a number of executive departments or agencies that are responsible for policy implementation, law enforcement, and delivery of government services.

The CE is returned by an election committee and is appointed by the CPG. The membership of the CE Election Committee (EC) varies over the years: 400

members in the first Selection Committee formed in 1996, 800 members in the second and third EC formed in 2000 and 2006, and 1,200 members in the fourth and fifth EC formed in 2011 and 2016. With the decision made by the National People's Congress on improving the electoral system of the HKSAR on 11 March 2021, a brand new Election Committee of 1,500 members was formed in September 2021 with the following revamped formation arrangements: the removal of individual voters from the First Sector; the substitution of individual voters by corporate voters, and the inclusion of ex officio and nominated members in the Second Sector; the adding of two new subsectors (i.e., grassroots associations and associations of Chinese fellow townsmen) in the Third Sector; the substitution of the subsectors of Hong Kong and Kowloon District Councils and New Territories District Councils with representatives of members of Area Committees, District Fight Crime Committees, and District Fire Safety Committees of Hong Kong Island and Kowloon and the New Territories, and the adding of representatives of associations of Hong Kong residents in the Mainland in the Fourth Sector; and the creation of the Fifth Sector, consisting of "HKSAR deputies to the NPC and HKSAR members of the CPPCC National Committee" subsector and "Representatives of Hong Kong members of relevant national organisations" subsector. After reconstitution, the new EC has five sectors with 300 members in each sector. Each sector is further divided into subsectors that return a certain number of members by anyone or a combination of the following methods: ex-officio members, nomination, or election (HKSARG 2021a and 2021b). On top of electing the CE, the new EC is also responsible for electing 40 (out of 90) LegCo members.

In the 2016 EC Subsector Elections (the fifth EC), there were 246,440 registered individual and corporate voters, except for those of the NPC subsector, the LegCo subsector, and the Religious subsector. The size of franchise varied from 120 corporate voters in the Hotel subsector to 80,643 individual voters in the Education subsector (HKSARG 2016). The number of EC members returned in each subsector also varied from 16 (in the subsectors of Employers' Federation of Hong Kong and Hong Kong Chinese Enterprises Association) to 60 (in the subsector of New Territories District Councils and all the subsectors of the Third Sector). On top of the 1,034 EC members elected by 35 subsectors, there were 106 ex officio members (36 Hong Kong deputies to the NPC and 70 LegCo members) and 60 members nominated by the Religious subsector (Chief Executive Election Ordinance [Chapter 569, Laws of Hong Kong] Schedule).

However, the number of registered voters of the new EC formed in September 2021 decreased to 7,971 with the implementation of the revamped formation arrangements mentioned above. The size of franchise varied from 18 corporate voters in the Employers' Federation of Hong Kong subsector to 1,083 individual voters in the subsector of Representatives of Members of Area Committees,

District Fight Crime Committees, and District Fire Safety Committees of Hong Kong and Kowloon (HKSARG 2021c). The number of EC members returned in each subsector also varied from 15 (in the subsectors of Employers' Federation of Hong Kong, and Small and Medium Enterprises) to 190 (in the subsector of HKSAR deputies to the NPC and HKSAR members of the National Committee of the CPPCC). According to the methods of returning these 1,500 EC members, 362 are "ex-officio member[s] for which no election is required," 156 are nominated by eligible bodies of specific subsectors, and 982 are elected by corporate and individual voters of the subsectors (of which 293 are elected in four subsectors comprising individual voters only) (HKSARG 2021d). Given the changes of formation arrangements as indicated above, the political dynamics of the CE elections would have been affected.

Starting from the 2022 (sixth-term) CE Election, a candidate must secure nomination from at least one-eighth of the EC members (i.e., 188 members in the 2022 CE election) with no less than 15 from each of the five sectors; and be confirmed by the Candidate Eligibility Review Committee (its members are appointed by the CE), with the inputs from the Committee for Safeguarding National Security of the HKSAR (its chairperson is the CE) as to whether a candidate meets the legal requirements and conditions of upholding the Basic Law of the HKSAR of the PRC and swearing allegiance to the HKSAR of the PRC. There was only one valid nomination in each of the 2002, 2005, and 2022 CE elections: Tung Chee-hwa in 2002, Donald Tsang in 2005, and John Lee in 2022. However, there was more than one valid nomination in each of the 2007, 2012, and 2017 CE elections: Donald Tsang and Alan Leong in 2007; Leung Chunying, Henry Tang, and Albert Ho in 2012; and Carrie Lam, John Tsang, and Woo Kwok-hing in 2017. After the election, the elected CE must be formally appointed by the CPG before assuming office. In other words, the elected CE is required to go through the acceptance test conducted by the CPG.

The CE enjoys a wide variety of powers in governing Hong Kong. Some are constitutional and are defined in the Basic Law and other constitutional and legal documents. Others are partisan and generated by the support base in the CE's governing coalition, for instance in the LegCo (Mainwaring and Shugart 1997; Shugart and Mainwaring 1997). The CE's constitutional powers can be further subdivided into legislative powers, including introduction of legislation, budgetary powers, package veto (override) and decree power, and non-legislative powers, including nomination of principal officials, and dissolution of the legislature. The exercise of some constitutional powers by the CE may need the approval or endorsement of the CPG (e.g. appointment of principal officials) or the legislature (e.g. annual budget).

The CE is assisted by the CE's Office, which in March 2023 had an estimated establishment of five directorate posts and 98 non-directorate posts (HKSARG

2022a, Head 21). The work of the CE's Office includes providing support to the CE on policy formulation and pledges delivery, planning and implementing CE's public engagements, coordinating a mass media and public relations strategy, and managing the CE's office building, the Government House, and the CE's Fanling lodge. The office also provides administrative support to the Executive Council (ExCo).

Other than the support rendered by the CE's Office, the CE is assisted by the principal officials in policy formulation and in supervising the daily operations of the executive departments and agencies. The CE is empowered to nominate candidates, and the CPG reserves the right of appointment. Principal officials are politically appointed and are employed on non-civil-service terms, and their term of office should not be longer than that of the CE. Within their own portfolio, they are accountable to the CE for policy success and failure and may have to step down for serious policy failure or grave personal misconduct. The three senior secretaries are the CS, the FS, and the SJ. The 15 bureau secretaries cover the civil service; constitutional and Mainland affairs; culture, sports and tourism; education; environment and ecology; health; home and youth affairs; labor and welfare; security; commerce and economic development; development; financial services and the treasury; housing; innovation, technology and industry; and transport and logistics.

Before the adoption of the ASPO in July 2002, the CE did not have a direct line of command to the bureau secretaries. The bureaus were divided into two groups headed and supervised either by the CS or the FS. The CE's policy agenda would only be effectively implemented if it was shared by the CS and the FS, especially the former. In view of the fact that the policy proposals from the bureaus were required to be tabled and discussed by the CS's Committee in which the CS was the chairperson, it was difficult, if not impossible, to further process any policy proposal without the CS's endorsement. On the one hand, the CS's Committee thus served as the coordination hub within the Government Secretariat and provided bureau secretaries and department heads with a place to review and assess policy progress, consider policy proposals and mediate their policy conflicts, and discuss current public concerns that may have an impact on policy planning (Miners 1998: 90). On the other hand, the CS's Committee was a screening mechanism in which the CS could push or defer any policy proposal that had come before the Committee. The role of the CS and the CS's Committee in the policy approval process will be maintained so long as the CE is satisfied with the policy screening works done by the CS. Unfortunately, the reality suggests otherwise during the era of Tung Chee-hwa.

The repeated policy and personality clashes between CE Tung Chee-hwa and CS Anson Chan since 1997 provided the catalyst for the introduction of the ASPO in July 2002, which was designed to assert the power of the CE. Since

2002, the CE has gained direct supervision over the bureau secretaries at the expense of the CS and the FS, as indicated by a new solid command line connecting the CE and the bureau secretaries, and a new dotted line (a solid line before 2002) connecting the CS and the FS on the one hand and the bureau secretaries on the other in the organization chart of the Hong Kong government. As a result, the CS and the FS may coordinate the work of certain policy areas "as and when delegated by the CE" (HKSARG 2002: note 1). The power of the CS is further cut down by the fact that the previously powerful CS's Committee (currently called the Policy Committee) no longer enjoys veto power over policy proposals submitted by the bureau secretaries. Instead, the bureau secretaries can submit policy proposals to the ExCo even without the Committee's support (Burns 2004: 80).

Even though the restriction put on the supervisory role of the CS and the FS has been removed, and the dotted line between the CS and the FS on the one hand and the bureau secretaries on the other has been replaced by a solid line since July 2007, the direct supervision of the bureau secretaries by the CE remains intact (HKSARG 2007a and 2018). The resumption of the previous role of the CS and the CE has signified the emergence of a more cohesive governing team at the highest level after Donald Tsang's reelection in 2007. However, since the CE maintains a direct supervisory role, the division of labor between the CE on the one hand and the CS and the FS on the other in supervising the bureau secretaries may be an interactive one, depending on the degree of policy consensus between them.

According to Articles 54 and 56 of the Basic Law, the CE is required to make policy decisions in ExCo meetings (CE-in-Council), "[e]xcept for the appointment, removal and disciplining of officials and the adoption of measures in emergencies" (Box 2.2). If the CE chooses to ignore a majority view of the ExCo, he is required to minute the reason(s) for doing so. On 7 June 2005, Donald Tsang revealed to the press during his CE by-election campaign that there were no more than five times that the governor or the CE had failed to accept the advice of ExCo members since his own involvement dating back to 1995. The ExCo's role is equivalent to that of a cabinet; however, not every ExCo member can fully participate in the whole policymaking process. Indeed, some nonofficial ExCo members with party representation in the LegCo have complained publicly that they are only allowed access to policy information just before the ExCo meeting. In addressing this issue, Donald Tsang announced in his first Policy Address in October 2005 that the nonofficial members could participate in the initial stage of policy formulation of all the policy bureaus and even put forward policy proposals. Although the ExCo is operated in accordance with the principles of collective responsibility and confidentiality, some members have expressed in public their own views, which are different from the prevailing government policies over the years.

For many years, only the three senior secretaries served as ex officio ExCo members. However, since the adoption of ASPO in July 2002, principal officials have been appointed to serve concurrently as official members of the ExCo. Initially, this diluted the influence of nonofficial ExCo members and allowed the policy consensus arrived at, if any, in the Policy Committee to dominate the ExCo debate. However, in November 2005, the nonofficial majority in the ExCo was restored when CE Donald Tsang appointed eight additional nonofficial members, bringing their total number to 15. At the same time, the official ExCo members "can opt to attend [ExCo meetings] only when items on the agenda concern their portfolios," to allow more participation for the nonofficial members (2005–2006 Policy Address: para. 16). In addition, the nonofficial members have been allowed to participate in individual policy areas through division of labor among themselves since then. Currently, with the creation of the Deputy CS, Deputy FS and Deputy SJ, and two bureau directors by CE John Lee in July 2022, the ExCo has 21 official members and 16 nonofficial members.

Regarding policy research and advocacy, the CE has been supported by the CE's Policy Unit (CEPU), which was formed in December 2022. The CEPU is led by a head with the support of three deputy heads. The CE is also advised by the CE's Council of Advisers on "the strategic development of Hong Kong, leveraging on opportunities from national and global developments." Currently, the Council has 34 members who are organized along three streams: economic advancement and sustainability, innovation and entrepreneurship, and regional and global collaborations.

Regarding the 15 bureaus, each of them is headed by a politically appointed bureau secretary who is supported by a political team of an undersecretary and a political assistant (except Civil Service Bureau), and a group of civil servants led by one or more permanent secretaries. Those secretaries who are not former civil servants may have difficulty working with their colleagues in the bureau because of possible personality or policy clashes. Still more important is the lack of a cohesive policy package owned by the whole governing team. Internal conflicts over policy priority and resource alignment are thus inevitable. The major reason for this is the fact that the CE forms their governing team only after the election. The short time span allowed to form the governing team has condensed the training, mixing-and-matching evolution process into an ad hoc hit-and-go exercise. This also points to the fact that Hong Kong is lacking the kind of environment and infrastructure that facilitates the nurturing of political leaders on a systemic basis.

The number of permanent secretaries in a bureau depends on its policy portfolio. For example, there is only one permanent secretary in the Constitutional and Mainland Affairs Bureau, while there are two in the Development Bureau. The post of permanent secretary was created only after the introduction of the ASPO in July 2002. Their major functions include: assisting the principal officials in formulating policies and securing public and legislative support; steering and coordinating the executive departments under their portfolios and liaising with other bureaus for effective policy implementation; assisting in acquiring and deploying resources; and monitoring public needs and aspirations and propose changes to existing policies if necessary (Constitutional Affairs Bureau 2002).

An executive department is one level down from the bureau. At the end of 2021, there were 56 executive departments and agencies. Of these, 53 departments are reported to their relevant bureau and the remaining three are reported either to the CE (the Audit Commission), the FS (the Hong Kong Monetary Authority), or the SJ (Department of Justice) (Information Service Department 2022: 11). Each bureau supervises a number of executive departments or agencies, depending on its portfolio. For example, there is one executive department for the Housing Bureau to supervise, while there are nine for the Development Bureau (HKSARG 2022b). These executive departments or agencies are headed by a senior civil servant and are responsible for policy implementation, service provision, and law enforcement.

The Executive in Action

Policy initiatives can come from the CE and the politically appointed secretaries. In addition, CE Tung in 1997 designated three nonofficial ExCo members to lead policy reforms in housing, elderly services, and education. The arrangement was extended in October 2005, when CE Tsang allowed nonofficial members to have a focus of policy area(s) and be briefed by the bureau secretaries concerned throughout the policy formulation process. Policy initiatives proposed by bureaus need to be submitted to the Policy Committee before they are put before the ExCo for formal approval. If the proposed initiative needs legal advice or is a piece of legislation, the SJ and the Department of Justice will be consulted. Every policy has to be decided in an ExCo meeting. If a policy initiative involves budget and/or legislation, the LegCo's endorsement is required. After going through all the necessary procedures, approved policy initiatives are referred directly to the relevant bureau and/or department for implementation.

In the financial decision-making process, the FS has a major role to play. When preparing the annual budget, the FS has to follow the direction set in the CE's policy agenda and by the Public Finance Ordinance. Suggestions for resource allocation and applications for resources from bureaus, executive departments, and agencies for the coming financial year are invited before a high-ranking resource allocation meeting is convened to decide on the matter.

After the resource allocation meeting, bureaus, executive departments, and agencies are required to prepare their own draft estimates, which are then scrutinized by the Treasury Branch. These budget requests, if endorsed, are consolidated to form the draft estimate. A public consultation on the raising of government revenue for the coming financial year, especially with LegCo members, is also scheduled before the formal decision. Afterwards, the Estimates of Revenue and Expenditure is laid before the LegCo by the FS, who will then deliver the annual budget speech, which contains the budgetary proposals and moves the adoption of the Appropriation Bill.

The Executive in the Legislative Council

Even though a long list of powers has been entrusted to the CE and the executive to establish new policies, or to maintain prevailing ones, successful exercise of these powers largely depends on the size of the CE's legislative support and the degree of responsiveness of LegCo members to the CE's policy preferences. Therefore, how to cultivate majority support in the LegCo is a critical issue for the CE, who is formally not allowed to have any party affiliation.

Taking advantage of the functional constituency elections and the proportional representation system adopted in the geographical constituency elections, the CE has been supported by a pro-government majority coalition in the LegCo since 1998. That means the pro-government coalition has won the majority seat after each LegCo election (41, 39, 35, and 37 out of 60 members after the 1998, 2000, 2004, and 2008 LegCo elections, respectively; 43 and 40 out of 70 members after the 2012 and 2016 LegCo elections). However, the number of pro-government LegCo members is only a general indicator of the CE's legislative support. The actual distribution of votes in a division over a specific bill or motion can be highly dependent on the subject matter. While nearly all the bills and budgets proposed by the executive have been supported and approved by the LegCo, a few cases indicate the vulnerable situation of the CE and the executive.

The first case was an on-street parking fee increase from HK$2 to HK$4 for 15 minutes proposed in the Revenue Bill of 1999 and deliberated by the LegCo on 8 July 1999. The division was 27 to 26 in favor of the fee increase. Given that 27 votes did not constitute an absolute majority of the 54 members present during the division, the item was rejected. Much the same happened in the election of the chairperson of the LegCo's Finance Committee on 6 October 2004. Emily Lau from the opposition coalition and Philip Wong from the pro-government coalition contested the position. Among 58 members present at the meeting, Emily Lau managed to get 30 votes, while Philip Wong got 28. The third case was the decision to defer the resumption of the second reading of National Security (Legislative Provisions) Bill on 7 July 2003. The decision was "forced" on the government by the Liberal Party's call for deferral following the historic march of half a million Hong Kong people on 1 July 2003, which deprived the government of eight Liberal Party votes. The fourth case was the FS's decision to do an about-turn on injections of HK$6,000 into Mandatory Provident Fund retirement schemes in the 2011–2012 Budget. In the face of mounting public opposition, the FS was "forced" to adopt a revised budget plan that distributes HK$6,000 cash to all adult permanent residents of Hong Kong. The lack of majority support from the LegCo in general and the pro-government LegCo members in particular had been attributed to the dramatic U-turn of the FS's budget plan. The fifth case was the "withdrawal" of the Fugitive Offenders and Mutual Legal Assistance in Criminal Matters Legislation (Amendment) Bill 2019 on 23 October 2019, after several waves of historic mass protests and street confrontations. Even though the pro-government LegCo coalition was in the majority, the concerns expressed by social and business sectors were so deep that they eventually forced the Hong Kong government to withdraw the bill.

The next two cases are related to those matters that required a two-thirds majority for approval—a number of seats that the pro-government LegCo coalition had never won from 1998 to 2021. The first one was the rejection of the motion put forth by the Hong Kong government to expand the number of EC members from 800 to 1,600 in the 2007 CE Election, and to add ten more LegCo seats (five for geographical constituencies and five for functional constituencies) in the 2008 LegCo elections, as proposed by the *Fifth Report of the Constitutional Development Task Force* published in October 2005. Given that the motion touched on the election methods of the CE and the LegCo, it required the support of a two-thirds majority (i.e., 40 members at that time) of the LegCo. However, only 34 members supported the motion, resulting in its defeat on 21 December 2005. Nevertheless, a similar motion with an expanded franchise for the five new LegCo's functional constituency seats was approved by more than the required two-thirds majority on 24 and 25 June 2010, after acquiring the support from an opposition party (i.e., the Democratic Party).

The second one was the rejection of the motion proposed by the Hong Kong government on 17 June 2015 to elect the CE among the two to three CE candidates endorsed by more than half of all the nominating committee members in 2017 by universal suffrage. The reform details stated in the motion were based on the Decision of the Standing Committee of the NPC on 31 August 2014. The motion was eventually put to a vote on 18 June 2015, with eight votes in support and 28 votes against.

In any case, the split of seat share may serve as an indicator of how vulnerable the motions, bills, or budgets proposed by the Hong Kong government are. The closer the opposition gets to holding a majority of seats or even only one-third of seats in the LegCo, the higher the probability of the blockage of the passage of ordinary and important motions, bills, or budgets proposed by the executive. Having said that, the CE can return the passed bill to the LegCo for reconsideration; and the CE can even dissolve the LegCo if the latter has passed the returned bill again by a two-thirds majority, or "refuses to pass a budget or any other important bill introduced by the government" (Articles 49 and 50 of the BL). The CE must resign if the new LegCo passed "the original bill in dispute" by a two-thirds majority and s/he still refuses to sign it, or the new LegCo still refuses to pass the budget or the important bill in dispute (Article 52 of the BL). In other words, the CE may choose to dissolve the LegCo and appeal directly to the support of voters in the new LegCo elections to break the deadlock with the LegCo. However, the CE has yet to choose for doing so, even in the cases mentioned above.

"Executive-Led Government" and Legislative Dynamics

The term "executive-led government" has been used widely in Hong Kong, but there has yet to be a clear conceptualization of it (Box 2.3). In the context of policymaking before 1997, and especially before 1985, the governor and the executive occupied an extraordinary position, with the prerogative to constitute the LegCo. It is therefore no surprise to learn that government-initiated bills and budgets were not challenged seriously in the LegCo up to the mid-1980s.

Under the Basic Law, the LegCo shall be constituted by election (Article 68). However, the CE and the executive have still held the upper hand in shaping policy decisions by having a nearly exclusive power to initiate policy and budgetary proposals; and by the fact that the LegCo members are not allowed to introduce bills relating to "public expenditure or political structure or the operation of the government," they are required to have the CE's written consent before introducing bills relating to government policies as stated in Article 74 of the Basic Law, and a passive and fragmented legislature that rarely opposed the executive's initiatives (Li 2001: 89–92). Given the separate formation of the executive and the legislature, and the possible presence of an opposition majority in the legislature, a new relation between the executive and the legislature has emerged. The traditional concept of "executive-led government" is no longer useful in understanding the political dynamics of Hong Kong, at least up to 2021. In order to capture the changing executive-legislature relationships, a typology aimed at differentiating "executive-led government" and "executive-driven government" using two criteria can be proposed: whether the legislature is constituted by the executive, and whether the pro-government coalition or the opposition is in a majority. The former criterion is defined by the constitution, while the latter is driven by the politics of the day.

42   The Executive

Under executive-led government, the executive is vested with the power to constitute the legislature, and the legislature is dominated by pro-government political figures by default. It is normal to expect that the executive will use its power to form a pro-government legislature. Even though the executive may appoint opposition leaders to the legislature, they will always be in a minority. This is the type of government that was present almost throughout British colonial rule, except from September 1991 onward, when the official and appointed members lost their majority position in the LegCo to those members elected by functional and geographical constituency elections.

However, the inability of the executive to constitute the LegCo after 1997 has signified the transformation of "executive-led government" into "executive-driven government." The Hong Kong government has to build up its majority coalition in the LegCo by persuasion and performance, not by institutional default anymore. Equipped with the nearly exclusive power of initiating policy and budget, the Hong Kong government can take the lead to break the policy status quo and to align public resources with its preferred programs and policies. Given its privileged constitutional position, the executive can still drive the government machine along its preferred route, but subject to the approval or endorsement of the LegCo.

A Variant Form of "Executive-Led Government" Emerged

Whether the voters will vote in a pro-government legislative majority and whether the legislative approval or endorsement of the executive's initiatives is forthcoming are highly dependent on the politics of the day. The political dynamics developed since the Anti-Extradition Law Amendment Bill Movement (Anti-ELAB Movement) in early 2019 have paved the way for the possible loss of the LegCo majority to the opposition camp. The early signal was the landslide victory of the opposition candidates and the exceptionally high turnout rate in the 2019 District Council elections. The adoption of the "35-plus" strategy (i.e., winning more than half of the LegCo seats) by the opposition camp in the then-upcoming 2020 LegCo elections further intensified the fear of the CPG and the Hong Kong government losing the majority position in the LegCo and political influence in the wider society.

In response, the Hong Kong government postponed the 2020 LegCo elections, and the CPG subsequently initiated a fundamental electoral reform aimed at ensuring "patriots administering Hong Kong" through the Decision of the National People's Congress on Improving the Electoral System of the Hong Kong Special Administrative Region, adopted on 11 March 2021. After the reform, the potential LegCo candidate is required to have two to four nominations from each of the five sectors of the EC, on top of meeting the general conditions on standing for election and other nomination thresholds. Given that the formation of the EC is both highly shaped by and reflective of the will of the CPG and the Hong Kong government, the above requirement has given the latter two a de facto power to accept or reject any potential LegCo candidates regardless of their political affiliation, and thus creates an asymmetric power relationship between the executive and the legislature. Furthermore, the eligibility of candidates is to be assessed and validated by the Candidate Eligibility Review Committee (its members are to be appointed by the CE) "whether a candidate complies with the legal requirements and conditions for upholding the Basic Law and bearing allegiance to the HKSAR of the People's Republic of China," following the advice provided by the Committee for Safeguarding National Security of HKSAR chaired by the CE and advised by a National Security Adviser appointed by the CPG. The new electoral arrangements put in place since 2021 have made room for the CE and the executive to judge and confirm the eligibility of LegCo candidates, and thus equip the CE with the ability to return a LegCo with a pro-government majority (maybe an overwhelming one) if s/he thinks fit. Indeed, the NPC's Decision in 2021 brought back a variant form of executive-led government to Hong Kong. Subsequently, the 2021 LegCo Election did return a legislature with an overwhelming pro-government majority (89 out of 90 LegCo members).

Challenges Ahead

Accompanying the sovereignty transfer from Britain to China in 1997 was the introduction of a new constitutional and political order established by and stipulated in the Basic Law. The extensive appointment system that the authoritarian colonial political system relied on has been replaced by an election system that serves as a new political rule of allocating political power. The political system has thus gone through a "revolutionary" reform, leading to the emergence of a new type of political order based on a more symmetrical power relationship among branches of government in Hong Kong. The rolling back of the executive (in terms of the formation and direct control of the LegCo by the executive) and the bringing back of the legislature (in terms of its veto power and the resulting political dynamics and legislative competition) into the political arena signify the transformation of the local political system. Whether intended or not, these systemic transformations have their own logic of development. From this perspective, three major challenges faced by the executive are noteworthy: the availability of professional politicians, the formation of a credible governing team, and the establishment of a stable ruling coalition.

The political appointment system that allows the CE to nominate senior and bureau secretaries (for the approval of the CPG), and to appoint undersecretaries and political assistants (upon the advice of the Appointment Committee) has been adopted since July 2002, but its acceptability and legitimacy have yet to be established because of the unpopularity of the CE on the one hand and the low social visibility and weak political credentials of most of, if not all, the political appointees on the other. The dominant role of bureaucrats and their "magnificent" accomplishments during British colonial rule have left little room for the public in general and the socioeconomic elites in particular to realize the indispensable role played by the politicians in the new political order of the Basic Law. Furthermore, the adoption of a political appointment system has been separated from the corresponding reforms of the political recruitment mechanism, which has caused a short supply of professional politicians. The roles and functions of civil servants (bureaucrats) and politicians are as different as the mindset and skill set required. In fact, the half-baked politicians have filled up many of the politically appointed posts, and their performance has been repeatedly questioned and regarded by the public as far from satisfactory. How to reform and transform the political recruitment mechanism so that an adequate supply of politicians can be secured, and how to establish a visible career path so that individuals of high caliber can be attracted to join the political profession, are the two critical issues that need to be addressed before the formation of a credible governing team becomes possible.

The formation of a governing team is not an easy task in many places and Hong Kong is no exception. But Hong Kong is rather peculiar in the sense that the governing team formation is not embedded in a political party system or its equivalent. The governing team formed by civil servants was the norm of British colonial rule. The bureaucracy has provided the institutional platform to nurture suitable administrative candidates for the top leadership posts. However, the logic and operation of elections and the political appointment system have required a different kind of institutional arrangements, which facilitate the recruitment of potential candidates as well as the building of an effective governing team.

The elected CEs so far have been hampered by individual upbringing and career training (as businesspeople, senior civil servants, and professionals), and by their limited reach and penetration in society and the political network. More alarming is the fact that the governing team formation is regarded as a one-person show and is seldom considered in a proper institutional context or from a systemic level. This rather individualistic governing team-building effort is not going to work well in the age of mass and party politics. These inadequacies can be compensated for by a more developed political party system that Hong Kong has to build from scratch. While employing the phrase "political party system" is secondary, this kind of political institution has served as a training ground and anchor of political talents, an arena for policy debate and competition, a platform for building common governing visions and cohesive policy programs, and so on.

Besides, the executive must face challenges from the legislature and society as well. How does the executive construct a governing coalition that can command the popular support of the wider society in general and the majority support of the legislature in particular? Not affiliated with any political party, the CE has to knit his/her supporting net by building a coalition with social and political groups in society and in the legislature as well. CE Tung formed a ruling coalition by way of appointing some leaders from those groups or parties that have a certain number of LegCo members to the ExCo. This was not so successful and has finally broken down because Tung was reportedly not that accommodating to the policy suggestions put forth by the ruling coalition players. CE Tsang seemed to adopt a different strategy of forming a rather ad hoc coalition on a case-by-case basis. This type of coalition is inefficient and is subject to the pressure of short-term political currents of the day. CE Leung was not that successful in drawing support from the rival political forces within the pro-government camp and in the wider society. Like her predecessors, CE Lam suffered from the lack of solid political allies inside and outside the legislature, not to mention the tremendous difficulties she encountered in handling various controversial issues and pieces of legislation.

Whatever the governing coalition may be, the partners in the coalition are relatively "small and numerous"—small in terms of popular support in society and seat share in the legislature commanded by each of the partners, and numerous in terms of the number of partners in the coalition. Given the "small and numerous" partners in the governing coalition, the presence of a coalition-wide policy consensus is called into doubt, not to mention a cohesive policy program. The fragmented legislature has also subjected the CE to the political pressure of "pivotal player(s)" in the legislature because only a handful of members can flip the result of a bill or resolution when there is a close vote. Furthermore, the CE's policy initiative can be kept at bay when the legislature is led by an opposition majority (Li 2008).

Without the availability of adequately credible and capable political leaders, and of a stable governing coalition, the CE and his/her governing team may have difficulty in transforming their policy visions and preferences into enforceable programs, even though they are equipped with a list of active constitutional powers as defined in the Basic Law. Missing from the CE is the partisan power in the LegCo and the popular support in the wider society, as well as an effective governing team and a stable governing coalition. But more important is the fact that these inadequacies have their roots in the contradictory institutional design of the political system in general, and the under-development of the political recruitment mechanism and political party system in particular.

With the NPC's Decision in 2021 and the growing supports from the CPG, the CE has been equipped with the ability to confirm the candidacy of LegCo

46   The Executive

elections and released from the pressure of losing the majority in the LegCo since then. However, the question of how to return a credible and capable CE with an effective governing team remains the pressing issue to be addressed, which is the core foundation of good governance.

Box 2.1: Accountability System for Principal Officials and further development of the political appointment system

With the support of the CPG, the Hong Kong government implemented the ASPO on 1 July 2002. The reform seeks to resolve the mismatch between the senior civil servants and bureau secretaries and the political demands and accountability put upon them. An equally important reason is to enable the CE to form his/her own governing team without the restriction of having to choose from inside the civil service. The ASPO applies to the posts of principal officials. With the reform:

- the CE can nominate candidates for these posts from within or outside the civil service, to be appointed by the CPG; the principal officials are employed on non-civil service terms and may leave office if required by the CE with one month's notice; their term of employment should not exceed that of the CE;
- the principal officials are accountable to the CE and are fully responsible for success and failure within their policy portfolios; they may even step down if there is a serious policy failure or grave personal misconduct;
- all the principal officials are appointed concurrently as official ExCo members.

After the release of the *Report on Further Development of the Political Appointment System* in October 2007 (Hong Kong government 2007b), two additional layers of political appointees were created in each policy bureau (except the Civil Service Bureau): undersecretary and political assistant. The undersecretaries are responsible for assisting the bureau secretaries "in undertaking the full range of political work," while the political assistants are responsible for "providing political support and input" to the bureau secretaries and conducting "the necessary political liaison" at the instruction of the bureau secretaries.

Box 2.2: The Chief Executive and ExCo

In making policy decisions, the CE is assisted by the Executive Council (ExCo). "Except for the appointment, removal and disciplining of officials and the adoption of measures in emergencies," the CE is required to consult ExCo "before making important policy decisions, introducing bills to the Legislative Council, making subordinate legislation, or dissolving the Legislative Council." Thus, all major policy decisions are made by "the CE in Council." If the CE chooses not to accept a majority view of ExCo, he/she is required to put on record his/her reason(s) (Article 56 of the BL). Members of ExCo are appointed by the CE from among "the principal officials of the executive authorities, members of the Legislative Council and public figures," who are both Chinese citizens and permanent residents of Hong Kong with no right of abode in any foreign country. These appointments do not require formal endorsement by the CPG. Their term of office cannot exceed that of the CE who appoints them (Article 55 of the BL). There is no fixed number for ExCo membership: there were 21 official and 16 nonofficial members as of March 2023. The 21 official members are the three senior secretaries, three senior deputy secretaries, and 15 bureau secretaries, while the 13 nonofficial members are leaders of political parties, trade unions, financial and business sectors, and prominent professionals.

Box 2.3: Executive-led government

"Executive-led government" describes the dominant position held by the executive in the governance of Hong Kong in general, and in executive-legislature relations in particular. The exact meaning of the term varies. It is a concept derived from the political system and institutional design of Hong Kong under British colonial rule from 1842 to 1997. The dominant position of the executive, headed by the governor, was supported by the fact that he was vested with the power to constitute the LegCo.

According to Clause VI of the Letters Patent and Clause XIII of the Royal Instructions, the LegCo was composed of the official and nonofficial members up to 1985. The official members were themselves government officials, while the nonofficial members were nominated by the governor and were appointed by the secretary of state in London. The official members were in the majority up to 1976 (including the governor, who was concurrently the president of the LegCo) and were required to support any initiative from the executive except when otherwise permitted by the governor. The nonofficial members seldom challenged the government's initiatives openly or unanimously because their continued service to the LegCo depended on the Crown's pleasure. Due to such a prerogative, the governor could impose his will on the LegCo if he wished to do so. However, with the growing numbers of elected LegCo members and the decreasing number of official and nonofficial LegCo members since 1985, the governor started to employ persuasion and negotiation as an instrument to build majority support in the LegCo. This is especially the case when the combined number of the official and nonofficial LegCo members was no longer in the majority after 1991.

48   The Executive

Questions

1. Are there any differences between bureaucrats and politicians in terms of their roles and functions in Hong Kong's policymaking process?
2. Discuss the pros and cons of the adoption of the ASPO in July 2002 and the expansion of the political appointment system in 2007.
3. Identify and discuss the major problems/difficulties for the CE to form his/her own governing term.
4. How accurate is the term "executive-led government" in describing the privileged position of the CE and the executive in Hong Kong's policymaking process?
5. Analyze whether the NPC's decision to improve the electoral system of the HKSAR in March 2021 brings back a variant form of executive-led government to Hong Kong.

Bibliography

Burns, JP 2004, *Government Capacity and the Hong Kong Civil Service*, Oxford University Press, Hong Kong.

Constitutional Affairs Bureau, Hong Kong government 2002, *Accountability System for Principal Officials* (Paper submitted to the Legislative Council on 17 April 2002), viewed 26 November 2023, https://www.cmab.gov.hk/cab/topical/doc/acc-e.pdf

Constitutional Affairs Bureau, Hong Kong government 2007, *Relationship between the Executive Authorities and the Legislature*, viewed 2 June 2021, https://www.legco.gov.hk/yr06-07/english/panels/ca/papers/ca0123cb2-900-1-e.pdf

Electoral Affairs Commission, Hong Kong government 2007, *Report on the 2007 Chief Executive Election*, viewed 26 November 2023, https://www.eac.hk/en/elections/chief/2007ce_election/report.html

HKSAR Government 2002, *Organisation Chart of the Government of the Hong Kong Special Administrative Region*, viewed 17 July 2002, http://www.info.gov.hk/govcht_e.htm

HKSAR Government 2007a, *Organisation Chart of the Government of the Hong Kong Special Administrative Region*, viewed 3 July 2008 http://www.gov.hk/en/about/gov-directory/govchart/index.htm

HKSAR Government 2007b, *Report on Further Development of the Political Appointment System*, viewed 26 November 2023, https://www.cmab.gov.hk/doc/issues/report_en.pdf

HKSAR Government 2016, *Distribution of Registered Voters by Election Committee Subsectors in 2016*, viewed 6 June 2021, https://www.voterregistration.gov.hk/eng/statistic20164.html

HKSAR Government 2021a, *Legislative Council Brief: Improving Electoral System (Consolidated Amendments) Bill 2021*, viewed 2 June 2021, https://www.cmab.gov.hk/improvement/filemanager/content/pdf/en/bill/LegCo-brief-IES(CA)Bil-2021.pdf

HKSAR Government 2021b, *Improving Electoral System (Consolidated Amendments) Bill 2021*, viewed 6 June 2021, https://www.elegislation.gov.hk/hk/2021/14!en

HKSAR Government 2021c, *Distribution of Registered Voters by Election Committee Subsectors in 2021*, viewed 9 October 2021, https://www.voterregistration.gov.hk/eng/statistic20214.html

HKSAR Government 2021d, *2021 Election Committee Subsector Ordinary Elections: Composition, Methods for Returning Members and Electorates of Sub-sectors*, viewed 9 October 2021, https://www.elections.gov.hk/ecss2021/eng/subsectors.html

HKSAR Government 2022a, *Estimates for the Year Ending 31 March 2023*, viewed 20 March 2023, https://www.budget.gov.hk/2022/eng/estimates.html

HKSAR Government 2022b, *Organisation Chart of the Government of the Hong Kong Special Administrative Region*, viewed 22 March 2023, https://www.gov.hk/en/about/govdirectory/govchart/index.htm

Information Service Department 2022, *Hong Kong 2021*, viewed 22 March 2023, https://www.yearbook.gov.hk/2021/en/

Li, PK 2001, "The Executive-Legislature Relationship in Hong Kong: Evolution and Development," in JYS Cheng (ed), *Political Development in the HKSAR*, City University of Hong Kong Press, Hong Kong, pp. 85–100.

Li, PK 2004, 「『合一政府』或『分掌政府』？香港行政立法關係的演變和發展」 ("Unified" or "Divided Government"? The Evolution and Development of Hong Kong's Executive-Legislature Relations), paper presented at the Conference on Lesson to Learn: Governing Hong Kong, organized by the Hong Kong Policy Research Institute, Civic Exchange and SynergyNet, 8 May 2004, Hong Kong. A modified version of the paper appeared in Ming Pao, 10 May 2004, p. A31.

Li, PK 2008, 「從『共識政治』到『否決政治』：香港行政立法關係的質變」 (From "Consensus Politics" to "Veto Politics": The Transformation of Hong Kong's Executive-Legislature Relations), *Hong Kong Journal of Social Sciences*, vol. 34, pp. 27–55.

Mainwaring, S and Shugart, MS 1997, "Conclusion: Presidentialism and the Party System," in S Mainwaring and MS Shugart (eds), *Presidentialism and Democracy in Latin America*, Cambridge University Press, Cambridge, pp. 394–439.

Miners, N 1998, *The Government and Politics of Hong Kong*, 5th ed., with post-handover update by JTH Tang, Oxford University Press, Hong Kong.

National People's Congress 2021, *Decision of the National People's Congress on Improving the Electoral System of the Hong Kong Special Administrative Region*, viewed 2 June 2021, https://www.cmab.gov.hk/improvement/filemanager/content/pdf/en/whatsnew/china-adpots-decisions-to-improve.pdf

Shugart, MS and Mainwaring, S 1997, "Presidentialism and Democracy in Latin America: Rethinking the Terms of the Debate," in S Mainwaring and MS Shugart (eds), *Presidentialism and Democracy in Latin America*, Cambridge University Press, Cambridge, pp. 12–54.

Standing Committee of the NPC 2004, *The Interpretation by the Standing Committee of the National People's Congress Regarding Annex I (7) and Annex II (III) to the Basic Law of the Hong Kong Special Administrative Region of the People's Republic of China*, viewed 26 November 2023, https://www.basiclaw.gov.hk/filemanager/content/en/files/basiclawtext/basiclawtext_doc16.pdf

50 The Executive

Useful Websites

The Basic Law of the Hong Kong Special Administrative Region
https://www.basiclaw.gov.hk/en/basiclaw/index.html

Hong Kong e-legislation
https://www.elegislation.gov.hk/

The budget of the HKSAR government
https://www.budget.gov.hk

Chief Executive's policy address
https://www.policyaddress.gov.hk

The Electoral Affairs Commission of the HKSAR
https://www.eac.gov.hk/en/about/chairman.htm

Government and related organizations of the HKSAR
https://www.gov.hk/en/about/govdirectory/govwebsite/alphabetical.htm

Hong Kong Yearbook
https://www.yearbook.gov.hk/

Improve electoral system
https://www.cmab.gov.hk/improvement/en/npc-decision/index.html

The Registration and Electoral Office of the HKSAR
https://www.reo.gov.hk/en/about/ceo_msg.htm

Further Reading

Chau, PK 2001, *Executive Accountability System in the United Kingdom, Germany, France and Hong Kong*, Legislative Council Secretariat, Hong Kong, http://www. legco.gov. hk/yr00–01/english/library/0001 in 14.pdf. An outline of the basic institutional features of the executive branch and its accountability system in the United Kingdom, Germany, France, and Hong Kong.

Cheung, ABL 2002, "The Changing Political System: Executive-led Government or 'Disabled' Governance?," in SK Lau (ed), *The First Tung Chee-hwa Administration*, the Chinese University Press, Hong Kong, pp. 41–68. An analysis of the working features of the political system of Hong Kong and its defects and limitations under the first Tung Chee-hwa administration, with discussion of the crises faced and the likely adoption of some kind of political ministerial system.

Cheung, CY 2011, "How Political Accountability Undermines Public Service Ethics: The Case of Hong Kong," *Journal of Contemporary China*, vol. 20, no. 70, pp. 499–515. A critical evaluation of the ASPO and the ways its institutional design undermines the neutrality and meritocracy of the Hong Kong civil service.

Li, PK 2008, 「從『共識政治』到『否決政治』：香港行政立法關係的質變」 (From "Consensus Politics" to "Veto Politics": The Transformation of Hong Kong's Executive-Legislature Relations), *Hong Kong Journal of Social Sciences*, vol. 34, pp. 27–55. An examination of the changing executive-legislature relations in the context of the Basic Law's political framework and the coalition dynamics in the legislature. The effects of "pivotal player" and "veto politics" on the executive in the legislature are also discussed.

Miners, N 1998, *The Government and Politics of Hong Kong*, 5th ed., with post-handover update by JTH Tang, Oxford University Press, Hong Kong, chapters 6–9. An authoritative introduction to the operation of the government machinery of Hong Kong before 1997 that remains a good reference book.

3
The Legislature

Percy Luen-tim Lui

Briefly, a legislature is an institution that represents the people in the governmental process. As direct democracy is not practical in today's complex society, people have no choice but to delegate the governing responsibilities to representatives whom they elect openly, freely, and regularly. The functions and powers of the legislature are usually enshrined in a constitutional document or constitutional conventions. In addition to representing the people in the governmental process, legislatures also make laws, control public finance, and monitor the performance of the executive branch.

This chapter looks in detail at the Hong Kong Special Administrative Region Legislative Council (LegCo). The first section examines the history of the LegCo and its current membership composition. The second section discusses how membership composition affects the LegCo's functioning and studies the functions and powers of the LegCo under the Basic Law. The third section reviews constitutional constraints on the capacity of the LegCo, and studies the sixth-term LegCo (2016–2021) to see how constitutional restrictions on its capacity affected its performance. With reference to political developments since the 2019 Anti–Extradition Law Amendment Bill Movement (Anti-ELAB Movement), the final section considers possible developments of the LegCo in the coming years.

The HKSAR Legislative Council

The LegCo was established under British rule in 1843, with four official members (including the governor, who was President and Member). It was mainly an advisory body to the governor (*History of the Legislature* 2023). As the years went by, the LegCo has developed into a modern institution that makes laws, controls public finance, and monitors the performance of the government. The LegCo's assertiveness (manifested in its determination to monitor the behavior of the government) was at its highest after the 1995 LegCo elections. The last colonial governor, Chris Patten, introduced constitutional reforms that practically opened all 60 seats of the LegCo for direct election. China's displeasure with Patten's unilateral political reform eventually led to the dismantlement of the LegCo on 1 July 1997.

In December 1996, China established the Provisional Legislative Council (PLC), which functioned as Hong Kong's legislature the minute China resumed sovereignty over Hong Kong. As nowhere in the Basic Law was the PLC being mentioned, its legitimacy and legality were in doubt, and it was subjected to several lawsuits brought by critics. Though the court later upheld the PLC's legality (on the grounds that its establishment was endorsed by the National People's Congress, the highest organ of state power), Beijing knew that it was not well received by the Hong Kong people. Hence the term of the PLC was limited to one year. The first term LegCo was constituted on 24 May 1998. The 1998 LegCo elections entrusted the legislature with the popular mandate and legitimacy that its predecessor, the PLC, was never been able to get.

Membership composition of the Legislative Council

Members of the LegCo, except in the PLC and the first-term LegCo (which was elected for only two years), are elected to a four-year term through different election methods. In the second-term LegCo (2000–2004), members served four-year terms and were returned through three different categories: geographical constituencies (GC) (24 in total, elected on a one-person-one-vote basis), functional constituencies (FC) (30 in total, elected on an indirect election basis), and the Election Committee (EC) (six in total, elected by the 800-member EC, which also elected the second-term Chief Executive). In the third- and fourth-term LegCo (2004–2008, 2008–2012), members were composed of GCs and FCs only; each category returned 30 seats. In the fifth- and sixth-term LegCo (2012–2016, 2016–2021), there were 70 members, with GCs and FCs each occupying 35 seats. The increase in the total number of LegCo members is a result of the passing of a constitutional reform resolution tabled by the government in the LegCo on 23 June 2010.

In March 2021, the Central People's Government (CPG) initiated a new round of reforms to the electoral systems for both the LegCo and the Chief Executive Office. For the seventh-term (2022–2026) LegCo elections, its number of seats are increased from 70 to 90. Moreover, not only is the EC (which was no longer entrusted with the function to elect legislators from the third-term LegCo onwards) reassigned with the duty to elect LegCo members, but it also elects the largest proportion of the LegCo seats. Forty out of the 90 (about 44.44 percent) seats of the seventh-term LegCo are elected by the EC. There are also changes to the number of seats returned by the FC and GC elections; the former

54   The Legislature

returns 30 seats while the latter returns 20 seats. In other words, the proportion of directly elected GC seats is 22.2 percent in the seventh-term LegCo, which is the lowest proportion in the history of the LegCo. More importantly, individuals who ran in the seventh-term LegCo elections or would like to run in any future LegCo elections must secure the nomination from "at least two but no more than four members from each sector of the Election Committee," and then secure the endorsement from the Candidate Eligibility Review Committee, which determines whether individual candidates are patriotic enough to run in the LegCo elections. In other words, those who are deemed unpatriotic by the Committee would be disqualified to run in the elections even if they got the required number of nominations from the EC. It would be fair for one to argue that under this new electoral system, the chances of success for candidates from the pan-democratic camp (not to mention those from the localist groups) running in the LegCo elections would be remote.

The seventh-term LegCo election was originally scheduled to take place in September 2020 but was postponed more than one year to December 2021 due to the COVID-19 pandemic. The following table (Table 3.1) includes the breakdown of the membership composition of the LegCo from 1997 to 2026.

Table 3.1: Membership composition of the LegCo (1997–1998, 1998–2000, 2000–2004, 2004–2012, 2012–2021, and 2022–2026)

Composition of the LegCo	1997–1998*	1998–2000	2000–2004	2004–2012	2012–2021	2022–2026
Geographical constituencies (GC)	0	20	24	30	35	20
Functional constituencies (FC)	0	30	30	30	35	30
Election Committee (EC)	60	10	6	0	0	40

* All 60 members of the PLC were elected by the 400-member EC, which also elected the first term CE of the HKSAR.

From Table 3.1, one might get the impression that political powers were equally distributed among the GCs and FCs for the third-, fourth-, fifth-, and sixth-term LegCo. However, when we examine the detailed breakdown of the composition of FCs, we notice that political powers were not equally distributed among different sectors; political powers were lying unproportionally in the business sectors. The business sectors exerted more influence than any other sectors in the public policymaking process through legislators returned by FCs (Table 3.2).

Table 3.2: Composition of the sixth-term LegCo (2016–2021) and the election methods

(a) Thirty-five members returned from geographical constituencies (voting system: list system of proportional representation): Hong Kong Island (6), Kowloon West (6), Kowloon East (5), New Territories West (9), and New Territories East (9).
(b) Thirty-five members returned from functional constituencies (voting systems: "first past the post" voting system applies to all functional constituencies, except for the four special functional constituencies marked with * where the "preferential elimination system of voting" is adopted). Each of the following functional constituencies has one seat, except for Labour, which has three seats, and District Council (Second), which has five seats: Heung Yee Kuk*; Agriculture and Fisheries*; Insurance*; Transport*; Education; Legal; Accountancy; Medical; Health Services; Engineering; Architectural; Surveying and Planning; Labour; Social Welfare; Real Estate and Construction; Tourism; Commercial (First); Commercial (Second); Industrial (First); Industrial (Second); Finance; Financial Services; Sports, Performing Arts, Culture and Publication; Import and Export; Textiles and Garment; Wholesale and Retail; Information Technology; Catering; District Council (First); District Council (Second).

Source: Adapted from "2016 Legislative Council Election—Facts about Election," https://www.elections.gov.hk/legco2016/eng/brief.html

It is no exaggeration to say that the composition of the LegCo is essential to its performance. In brief, the composition of the LegCo would determine how it positions itself and functions. The LegCo is more assertive when more democrats are elected, and vice versa. For example, in the 2004 LegCo elections, the pro-democracy camp won only 25 of the 60 LegCo seats. As a result, the flag-carrier of the pro-government and pro-Beijing political parties, the Democratic Alliance for the Betterment and Progress of Hong Kong (DAB, formerly Democratic Alliance for Betterment of Hong Kong, which merged with the Hong Kong Progressive Alliance on 16 February 2005), replaced the Democratic Party (DP), the main pro-democracy political parties, as the largest political party in the LegCo. The former Chief Executive (CE), Tung Chee-hwa (July 1997–March 2005) then commented that the result was "good and comfortable" (*South China Morning Post* 14 September 2004).

We can better understand the impact of a change in membership composition on the functioning of the LegCo when we compare the performance of the 1985 LegCo with the 1991 LegCo. Before the 1991 LegCo elections, appointed legislators and officials controlled 30 of the 57 seats. They could pass whatever measures the government wanted. However, among the 60 seats in the 1991 LegCo, the government could only control 22 (18 appointed members and four ex officio members). Naturally, the 1991 LegCo was more assertive than its predecessor. This was not only because of the increasing number of democrats, but also because it was the last term of the LegCo that still had appointed members. The appointed members who wanted to serve in the LegCo again in 1995 would need to appeal to the public instead of to the governor. Thus, they no longer needed to vote in line with the government's position. Understandably, the 1991 LegCo brought great frustration to senior civil servants, who were used to getting what they wanted without much difficulty from the LegCo (Cheek-Milby 1995: 180). In short, the change in the composition of the 1991 LegCo's membership began a new era in the history of the LegCo. Never before had the Hong Kong people seen so many open conflicts and disagreements between the government and the LegCo. Comments were even made that the government was facing a serious problem of ungovernability.

After the establishment of the HKSAR, the indirectly elected PLC maintained a harmonious relationship with the executive branch. This was so because among the PLC's 60 members, only four were from the moderate democratic political party, the Hong Kong Association for Democracy and People's Livelihood. The rest of the PLC members were mostly pro-government. As Sonny Lo (1998: 79) observes, the PLC was "more an arm of the administration than a watchdog of the government." The first item of business of the PLC soon after its swearing in on 1 July 1997 was the suspension of a number of ordinances (primarily on labor rights) passed by the democratically elected 1995 LegCo at the eleventh hour of British rule.

The Hong Kong government knew that it would be harder to accomplish these unpopular policy agendas when the first-term LegCo was constituted in 1998. By then, democrats and government critics would most likely be elected to the LegCo. The government was right in its prediction. A record high turnout rate (53.29 percent) helped the pro-democracy camp win 15 of the 20 GC seats. This change in the membership composition of the LegCo, as witnessed in the 1991 LegCo, again transformed the LegCo from the submissive PLC to one that was willing to confront the executive branch when necessary.

Powers and functions of the HKSAR Legislative Council

Constitutionally, the Basic Law grants a wide range of powers to the legislature to carry out its functions, including the powers to enact, amend, or repeal laws; to examine and approve government budgets; to approve taxation and public expenditure; to debate the CE's policy addresses and issues of great public interests; to raise questions on the work of the government; to endorse the appointment and removal of the judges of the Court of Final Appeal and the Chief Judge of the High Court; to receive and handle complaints from the public; to impeach the CE; and to summon persons.

The LegCo also has informal powers that are not stipulated in the Basic Law, such as influence on government policies and finance. Such influence can be manifested in the following two scenarios:

(i) When the LegCo has the support of public opinion and when major political parties are united. For example, in October 2008 the government was forced to shelve a proposal to introduce a "means test" mechanism to the old age allowance (OAA) scheme. In his 2008 Policy Address, the CE said that the government would consider increasing OAA payments on the one hand, and study the possibility of introducing a means test mechanism on the other hand. The rationale behind the means test is that elders who can support themselves should be excluded from the OAA scheme. The general public and major political parties in the LegCo were all opposed to the proposal. The government knew that without the support of the major political parties, the proposal would not stand a chance of becoming law. Subsequently, on 24 October 2008, the CE announced that: "Having assessed the latest situation, I have decided to shelve the idea for a means test for OAA" (*CE's remarks on Old Age Allowance* 2008).

(ii) When the pan-democratic camp occupies the number of seats that reaches the threshold of the so-called "critical minority," which would allow it to block the Hong Kong government's major legislation proposals such as constitutional reform proposals. In the fifth-term LegCo (2012–2016), the pan-democratic camp occupied 27 of the 70 LegCo seats. In other words, it has reached the threshold of critical minority. The government needs to get a "yes" vote from at least 47 of the 70 LegCo members (i.e., two-thirds of the total number of LegCo members) to pass any constitutional reform proposal. This was exactly what the government failed to secure when it tabled an electoral reform proposal in the LegCo in June 2015. The government's electoral reform proposal was rejected by the LegCo on 18 June 2015 by a vote of 28 to eight.

The core duty of the LegCo is to represent the people in the governmental process. Specifically, major functions of the LegCo are: enacting laws, controlling public expenditure, and monitoring the government's performance.

Enacting laws

Legislation is enacted in the form of bills. Both the government and legislators may introduce new legislation into the LegCo, or bills to amend or repeal existing legislation. Though legislators can initiate legislation through the mechanism of private member's bills, they are only allowed to introduce bills that do not relate to public expenditure, the political structure, or the operation of the government (Article 74 of the Basic Law). As almost any change in the existing law would involve additional public expenditure, or affect the operation of the government, an absolute majority of the bills considered by the LegCo in the past 25 years were not initiated by legislators but by the government.

The process of enacting laws consists of three readings of a bill in the LegCo. The First Reading is a formality, with the Clerk to the LegCo reading the short title of the bill. During the Second Reading of the bill, the LegCo, through a bills committee, will examine the bill clause by clause, and make amendments to it if necessary. When all the clauses have been thoroughly examined, and amendments, if any, made, the bill is read a third time. The Third Reading is usually a formality. When a bill has been given three readings and signed by the Chief Executive, it becomes a piece of enacted law. Unless a later date has been specified, it may take effect after it is signed by the CE and promulgated in the Gazette (for details, see "Bills" Legislative Council, https://www.legco.gov.hk/general/english/bills/bill_1620.htm).

Controlling public expenditure

The power of the purse rests with the LegCo, which, through its Finance Committee, approves or rejects government funding requests or new taxation proposals. The Finance Committee consists of all members of the LegCo except the President. The chairperson and deputy chairperson of the Committee are elected by and from among its members. The power of the LegCo is apparent when it scrutinizes the government's annual budget and funding requests. In March, the Financial Secretary prepares and submits to the LegCo the government's annual budget, which is then examined carefully by the LegCo's Finance Committee. When the budget is approved by the LegCo, the government has the money to finance its programs. If government departments have underestimated their expenditure in a given financial year, or if unforeseen causes of additional expenditure have arisen, they have to turn to the LegCo again for additional appropriation. The Finance Committee is an effective tool for the LegCo to check on the government because it can reject the government's funding requests and/or reduce the overall budget to a particular item in the budget. Put simply, if the LegCo has the will to monitor the government's performance seriously, it also has the means to do so.

Monitoring the government's performance

The LegCo has the constitutional duty to monitor the government's performance. Article 64 of the Basic Law stipulates that the HKSAR Government "must abide by the law and be accountable to the Legislative Council of the Region: it shall implement laws passed by the Council and already in force; it shall present regular policy addresses to the Council; it shall answer questions raised by members of the Council; and it shall obtain approval from the Council for taxation and public expenditure." The spirit of Article 64 is in line with the practice found in liberal democracies where monitoring every act of the government is the solemn duty of the legislature. The LegCo relies on the following means to discharge its watchdog function.

(i) Private members' bills

A private member's bill is the only tool that legislators have in initiating legislation. Before the handover, the private member's bill was an effective tool that legislators could use to participate in or influence the policymaking process. However, since the handover, constraints stipulated in Article 74 and Annex II of the Basic Law have greatly weakened the utility of this tool. For a private member's bill to become law, it needs to go through the same process as a government bill; that is, with first, second, and third readings, and the signature of the CE. However, unlike a government bill, which only requires a simple majority vote of the members of the LegCo present, the passage of a private member's bill requires a simple majority of votes of each of the two groups of members present; that is, members returned by the Election Committee, and those returned by functional constituencies and by geographical constituencies through direct elections (Clause 7, Annex II). Moreover, Article 74 of the Basic Law prohibits legislators from putting forward bills that affect public expenditure, political structure, or government operations unless the CE has given his/her written consent to the introduction of the bills.

(ii) Debates, motions, and questions

Debates, motions, and questions (including the CE's Question and Answer Session, during which legislators ask the CE about government policies and various public issues) are means through which legislators raise questions regarding government policies; urge the government to follow-up on issues of great public concern; check against the performance of the government, and so forth. In every session, the LegCo holds numerous debates on the CE's policy proposals for administering Hong Kong (Policy Address Debate), the government's annual revenue and expenditure proposals (Budget Debate), and all the motions moved at LegCo meetings (Other Debates).

What exactly is a motion? Motions are the mechanism through which most of the LegCo's business is transacted. For instance, amendments to bills are effected by way of motions. Of course, not all motions have legislative effect. Legislators may move motions that do not have legislative effect. For example, during the

2022 LegCo session, the LegCo debated 34 motions moved by its members that did not have any legislative effect (*Motions not intended to have legislative effect, Year 2022*, available at the LegCo web page, https://www.legco.gov.hk/en/legco-business/council/members-motions.html?2022#schedule&cm20220119).

During the debate on the motion, legislators can express their views on public issues or call on the government to take certain actions to address issues of great public concern. Another way for the LegCo to monitor the government's performance is through "Questions." Legislators may ask government officials questions at Council meetings. In general, questions are aimed at seeking information on government actions on specific problems or incidents and on government policies. They are also raised for the purpose of monitoring the effectiveness of the government. No more than 22 questions, excluding urgent questions that may be permitted by the President of the LegCo, may be asked at any one Council meeting. Replies to questions may be given by designated public officers orally or in written form. For questions seeking oral replies, supplementary questions may be asked by any legislator to elucidate the answer (Questions, available at the LegCo web page, https://www.legco.gov.hk/en/legco-business/council/questions.html?2023#about).

(iii) Committees, select committees, and panels

The LegCo performs its functions of scrutinizing bills, controlling public expenditures, and monitoring the work of the government through a system of committees and panels. Unlike legislatures in Western democracies, the LegCo does not rely on a well-developed system of standing committees to carry out its work. Instead, it depends on 18 nonpermanent panels. The LegCo has three standing committees, namely the Finance Committee, Public Accounts Committee, and Committee on Members' Interests (for details on the duties of these committees, see *Legislative Council Annual Report 2022*: Chapter 3). In performing its watchdog function, the most powerful tool of the LegCo is the "select committee." The LegCo may by resolution appoint one or more select committees for in-depth consideration of matters or bills referred by the Council. Select committees, where so authorized by the LegCo, may summon—as required when exercising its powers and functions—persons concerned to testify or give evidence.

A select committee is a very powerful tool because it has the power to summon officials to testify. If summoned, an official must appear before the committee and testify under oath, unless the CE decides that in light of security and vital public interests, that official should not testify or give evidence before the LegCo or its committees (*Rules of Procedure of the Legislative Council of the Hong Kong Special Administrative Region*, 80[b]). Put differently, the select committee has the power to obtain answers that would not be made available under normal

LegCo meetings. For example, in November 2016, the LegCo established a select committee to investigate the matters relating to the agreement signed between the former CE Leung Chun-ying and the Australian firm UGL Limited after Leung assumed the office of the CE (for more information, see *Select Committee to Inquire into Matters about the agreement between Mr. Leung Chun Ying and the Australian firm UGL Limited*, available at the LegCo web page, https://www.legco.gov.hk/yr16-17/english/sc/sc_lcyugl/general/sc_lcyugl.htm).

The major mechanism that the LegCo depends on in discharging its duties is panels with nonpermanent status. In the current LegCo, 18 panels are established to monitor, examine, and discuss in detail issues relating to the policy areas of their corresponding bureaus (Table 3.3). These panels give views on major legislative or financial proposals before their formal introduction into the LegCo or the Finance Committee. A panel may appoint subcommittees (e.g.,

Table 3.3: Panels of the seventh-term LegCo (2022–2026)

	The 18 LegCo Panels
1	Administration of Justice and Legal Services
2	Commerce, Industry, Innovation and Technology
3	Constitutional Affairs
4	Development
5	Economic Development
6	Education
7	Environmental Affairs
8	Financial Affairs
9	Food Safety and Environmental Hygiene
10	Health Services
11	Home Affairs, Culture, and Sports
12	Housing
13	Information Technology and Broadcasting
14	Manpower
15	Public Service
16	Security
17	Transport
18	Welfare Services

Source: "Panels of the Legislative Council," https://www.legco.gov.hk/en/legco-business/committees/panels-and-subcommittees.html.

Panel on Transport Subcommittee on Matters Relating to Railways) to study specific issues and report back to the LegCo if necessary. Each panel is headed by a chairperson elected by and from among its members (*Legislative Council Annual Report 2022*: 41). The chairperson holds a casting vote, making this an important position.

The HKSAR Legislative Council in Action

This section examines constraints that the Basic Law has imposed on the LegCo, and then reviews the performance of the sixth-term LegCo. However, the period under review would be only from October 2016 to June 2019, as the functioning of the LegCo—and in fact, the normal routines of the whole of Hong Kong—was seriously disrupted by the Anti-ELAB Movement that started in June 2019. We will return to this movement later when we discuss what lies in the future for the LegCo in the final section.

The following review will focus on three main dimensions: initiating legislation that challenges the government's policy agenda; controlling public finance; and monitoring the performance of the government.

Restrictions on the powers of the HKSAR Legislative Council

Two major restrictions on the powers of the LegCo are Article 74 of the Basic Law and the separate vote count system stipulated in Annex II of the Basic Law. Article 74 practically forbids legislators to propose any bills of political significance without the prior consent of the CE. Naturally, no CE would approve the tabling of private members' bills if they posed a serious challenge to government policies or forced the government to act against its will. While the government's inclination to uphold its authority is understandable, it is equally the case that the legislature has a solemn duty to see that the government is acting in the best interests of the people. A restriction on legislators' capacity to initiate private members' bills weakens the capability of the LegCo to perform its functions.

The second restriction on the capability of the LegCo concerns the vote count system stipulated in Annex II of the Basic Law. The separate vote count system, requiring separate majorities on private members' bills among both GC and FC members, makes it very difficult for such bills to pass. To defeat an initiative taken by any legislator, all it takes is 18 votes out of the 35 votes of either group of legislators, which should not be a difficult threshold for the major political parties to reach (the amendments made to this separate vote count system by the CPG in March 2021 did not change this fact). Predictably, a weak legislature, rather than a strong one, results from this vote count system.

Performance of the sixth-term HKSAR Legislative Council

Initiating alternative legislation proposals

The restrictions on private members' bills have weakened legislators' ability to effectively put forward alternative legislation proposals to challenge the government's policy agenda. With reference to how legislators used the private member's bill to challenge the government's policy agenda in the 1995–1997 LegCo, it is fair to say that a private member's bill is no longer an effective tool of the LegCo after the handover. In 1995–1997, 53 private members' bills were tabled and 26 were passed. The 53 private members' bills made up 23.2 percent of all the bills tabled in the LegCo (228) in 1995–1997 (Ma 2002: 355). By contrast, from October 2016 to June 2019, legislators tabled a total of four private members' bills, which was only about 3 percent of the total bills (132) tabled. More importantly, all four private members' bills concerned only the operation of non-profit-making or charitable organizations and did not challenge any government policy. In short, the observation made by Ma Ngok (2002: 356) decades ago is still valid—private members' bills ceased to be a policy tool of the LegCo after the 1997 handover.

Article 74 and Annex II also made it very difficult for members of the LegCo to successfully amend government legislation proposals. Among the 143 bills passed in the period under review, only two were passed with amendments moved by legislators (a success rate of 1.5 percent). Members' amendments had a much higher success rate before the 1997 handover. For example, in the last colonial LegCo (i.e., 1995–1997), members' amendments had a success rate of 71 percent. It is beyond doubt that the success rate has dropped drastically ever since the 1997 handover. The success rate was 14.7 percent and 5 percent in the first (1998–2000) and second-term (2000–2004) LegCo, respectively (all the performance figures of the second-term LegCo are the author's own calculation, information from the LegCo's website, https://www.legco.gov.hk/general/english/timeline/council_meetings.htm). It is worth noting that among the 87 members' amendments vetoed in 1998–2000, 17 of them in fact received simple majority support but were vetoed because of the separate vote count system (Ma 2002: 357). In sum, the LegCo performed poorly from October 2016 to June 2019 in terms of initiating legislation that could challenge the government's policy agenda.

Controlling public finance

The LegCo has the constitutional power to approve or reject the government's plans to spend or raise money. Without the approval of the LegCo, the government would not be able to fund its projects, and it would have no legal authority to raise any new money. When the major political parties in the LegCo are united in opposing the government's funding requests, they can force the government to make policy concessions. For example, the government was forced to reconsider its information technology (IT) education policy after it was criticized by legislators during an Education Panel meeting in January 2008. In its original proposal, the government did not include grants to support schools to hire permanent IT support staff. However, legislators asserted that the government should fund schools to hire permanent IT support staff to maintain expensive IT hardware. As expected, the government had no choice but to reconsider its IT education policy (*South China Morning Post* 19 January and 2 February 2008). More recently, the LegCo rejected a proposal by the government to provide interest-free loans totaling HK$1.4 billion to four international schools to "ease their cash flow" amid the COVID-19 pandemic (*The Standard* 8 May 2020). Overall, the LegCo is more effective in monitoring the government's expenditure and revenue-raising plans than in challenging the government's policy agenda.

It is worth pointing out that not everyone agrees that challenging the government's policy agenda should be a major function of the LegCo. For example, it is clear that the CPG and the HKSAR Government believe that in an executive-led polity like the HKSAR, the authority to initiate public policy is vested with the HKSAR Government, not the LegCo.

Monitoring the performance of the government

Other than initiating alternative policies and controlling public funding, the LegCo also relies on committees, panels, questions, motion debates, and sometimes select committees to monitor the performance of the government. However, the institutional design of these two mechanisms has weakened their capacity to effectively monitor the work of the executive branch. As for select committees, they were seldom used by the LegCo. Unless there were cases of great public concern that had escalated into protracted controversies, the resolution to set up a select committee could be easily voted down by pro-government legislators. In the sixth-term LegCo, only one select committee was set up (The Select Committee to Inquire into Matters about the agreement between Mr. Leung Chun Ying and the Australian firm UGL Limited).

The sixth-term LegCo (the reviewing period is from October 2016–July 2019) members asked 1,847 questions (both oral and written). If we compare the number of questions asked in the earlier LegCo terms—say the third-term (2004–2008) LegCo, when members asked 2,482 questions (both oral and written)—we witness a decrease (about 25.6 percent) in the number of questions asked. The effect of such a decrease in the number of questions asked is difficult to quantify. However, the upward trend in the number of questions asked in LegCo meetings in the 1990s was discontinued with the second-term (2000–2004) LegCo.

As far as motion debate is concerned, 86 motion debates without legislative effect were moved by the sixth-term LegCo members. Motion debates, as Ma (2002: 360) points out, are an ineffective means of pressuring the government. This is because the separate vote count system has made it difficult for LegCo members to pass substantial and controversial motions. For example, the motion debate moved by Leung Kwok Hung (New Territories East) on 5 July 2017 urging the government to establish a universal retirement protection system was voted down by members from the FCs. Likewise, the motion debate moved by Gary Fan (New Territories East) on 21 March 2019 on reforming the immigration and admission policies was also voted down by members from the FCs. Overall, other than inflicting humiliation on the government, a motion debate is not an effective tool to check the behavior of the government.

Thus far, we have reviewed the performance of the sixth-term LegCo and concluded that it did not perform well in terms of initiating alternative legislation proposals and monitoring the performance of the government. Obviously, if measures were not taken to strengthen the capacity of the LegCo, it would not be able to make much improvement in discharging its duties. Three measures to strengthen the performance of the LegCo are conceivable. First, to empower the legislature to function properly, restrictions that Article 74 of the Basic Law has imposed on the LegCo's power should be removed. Second, the LegCo's committee and panel systems should be reformed. Third, the LegCo's staff support system (mainly the LegCo Secretariat) should be strengthened (for those who are interested in details of these measures, please see Lui 2012). However, discussing how these measures should be implemented makes little sense in the post-2019 Anti-ELAB Movement Hong Kong. The political context within which the seventh-term LegCo was formed was drastically different from the earlier terms of the LegCo. As a result, whether the seventh-term LegCo has the same degree of assertiveness as the previous terms LegCo to discharge its duties is in doubt. As such, in the following section, I will not discuss measures to strengthen the performance of the LegCo. Instead, I will examine developments in the political contexts of Hong Kong since June 2019 and make a logical guess of what lies ahead for the seventh-term LegCo.

Hong Kong after the 2019 Anti–Extradition Law Amendment Bill Movement

Indeed, there was a rather dramatic change in Hong Kong's political context at the very beginning of the sixth-term LegCo. For the first time in the history of the HKSAR LegCo, six legislators (all were from the pan-democratic camp) were disqualified and ceased to be members of the sixth-term LegCo because they committed acts specified in Article 79 of the Basic Law. The following paragraphs will examine three key changes to the political context within which the sixth-term and future terms of LegCo operate: (i) Disqualifying legislators: Round 1 (November 2016 and July 2017); (ii) the Anti-ELAB Movement (June 2019–early 2020), the enactment of the National Security Law (NSL) (July 2020), the COVID-19 pandemic, and disqualifying legislators: Round 2 (November 2020); and (iii) reforming the LegCo's electoral methods (March 2021).

Disqualifying legislators: Round 1 (November 2016 and July 2017)

The sixth-term LegCo election, held on 4 September 2016, returned several young legislators who had their roots in the 2014 Umbrella Movement, a movement that aimed at protesting against the 8.31 Decision made by the Standing Committee of the National People's Congress (SCNPC) in 2014 (to the pan-democratic camp, the Decision imposed a very restrictive framework for Hong Kong's democratic reform in 2017).

A noted characteristic of these newly elected young legislators is that they "all advocate greater independence or Hong Kong's right to self-determination with varying degrees of radicalism" ("Hong Kong election: Who are the new faces in politics?" *BBC News*, 6 September 2016). Among these "young and radical" legislators are Sixtus Chung-hang Leung and Yau Wai-ching from the Youngspiration, a vocally pro-independence organization. Leung and Yau used the oath-taking ceremony on 12 October 2016 (the inaugural meeting of the sixth-term LegCo) to express their political stance. They shouted a derogatory term for China and showed a "Hong Kong is not China" flag during their oath-taking ceremony ("What is Hong Kong's political controversy about?" *BBC News*, 7 November 2016). Likewise, four other legislators from the pan-democratic camp (though not all of them are young and radical)—including Nathan Law (a former Umbrella Movement leader), Lau Siu-lai (a former Umbrella Movement protestor), Leung Kwok-hung (who was first elected to the LegCo in 2004), and Yiu Chung-yim (representing the Architectural, Surveying, Planning and Landscape functional constituency)—also took their oath in a way that was regarded as improper by the Hong Kong government. To the government, these legislators failed to meet the requirement stipulated in Article 104 of the Basic Law, which states that, "When assuming office, the Chief Executive, principal officials, members of the Executive Council and of the Legislative Council . . . need to swear allegiance to the Hong Kong Special Administrative Region of the People's Republic of China." As a result, the government filed judicial reviews challenging the LegCo President's decision to allow Leung and Yau to retake the oath and to disqualify Leung and Yau from assuming office as a member of the LegCo.

Before the court ruled on the case, the SCNPC issued its interpretation of Article 104. Clause 2(3) of the interpretation states that "[a]n oath taker is disqualified forthwith from assuming the public office specified in the Article if he or she declines to take the oath . . . or takes the oath in a manner which is not sincere or not solemn, shall be treated as declining to take the oath. The oath so taken is invalid and the oath taker is disqualified forthwith from assuming the public office specified in the Article" (Instrument 27, *The Basic Law of the Hong Kong Special Administrative Region of the People's Republic of China*, May 2021 edition). All levels of courts in Hong Kong are abided by the SCNPC interpretation of Article 104. Subsequently, through a series of court rulings in 2016 and 2017, the above six elected pan-democratic legislators lost their seats for failing to take a valid oath of office. In addition to previously mentioned acts performed by Leung and Yau when they took their oath, acts such as inserting pro-democracy declarations before, in the middle of, or after the prescribed oath were deemed by the courts as having "declined" to take the oath, which in turn justified their "automatic" disqualification (i.e., no opportunity to retake the oath is to be granted). As a result of this disqualification, the voice of 185,727 voters was written off and the pro-democracy camp lost its veto power in the LegCo (Leung 2019: 221–222). The loss of veto power by the pan-democratic camp allows the pro-establishment camp to amend the Rules of Procedure of the LegCo, which has a long-lasting impact on the functioning of the LegCo. As Yu (2018) points out, the pro-establishment camp was successful in introducing major amendments to the Rules of Procedure in early 2018, which, among other things, allow the LegCo president to resume the council meeting shortly after its adjournment, thereby putting an end to the previous attempt by the pan-democrats to mount filibusters or force the adjournment of meetings.

The Anti–Extradition Law Amendment Bill Movement (June 2019–early 2020); the enactment of the National Security Law (2020) and the COVID-19 pandemic; and disqualifying legislators: Round 2 (November 2020)

Though it is too early for anyone to fully comprehend the ramifications of the 2019 Anti-ELAB Movement, one thing is for certain: the almost year-long, large-scale movement is among the most significant—if not the single most important—events in the history of the HKSAR. It has forever changed Hong Kong and its politics. The following paragraphs will examine the Anti-ELAB Movement and subsequent developments in Hong Kong politics.

The Anti–Extradition Law Amendment Bill Movement (June 2019–early 2020)

As Vukovich (2020: 1) aptly points out, "2019 will prove to be a watershed moment for Hong Kong politics and society . . . There may be no going back from such a violent and shocking event as the recent protests, which have for much of, though not of all the city's population, transformed the police–society relationship into one of open antagonism, fully exposed people's fear and loathing of the mainland and their local government." The magnitude of this public sentiment was vividly reflected in the November 2019 District Council elections.

Even though the government had officially withdrawn the amendment to the extradition law on 23 October 2019, protesters continued their regular demonstrations. This was not a surprise, as the bill's formal withdrawal met only one of five key demands emphasized by many protesters, who had chanted "five demands, not one less" in Hong Kong's streets ("Hong Kong formally scraps extradition bill that sparked protests" *BBC News*, 23 October 2019). It is fair to conclude that the Anti-ELAB Movement evolved into a wider pro-democracy movement. The rationale behind such a change in the focus of the Anti-ELAB movement is understandable; people believed that a more democratic political system would empower the public to hold the government accountable, which in turn, would minimize chances for the government to propose bad policies like the amendments to the extradition law. Against this backdrop, it was widely expected that pro-establishment politicians and political parties would do poorly in the 2019 November District Council elections. Put differently, the pan-democratic camp would have good chances to win big in the District Council elections. A record high voter turnout rate (71.23 percent) helped the pan-democratic camp and localist groups secure a landslide victory in the District Council elections. As Purbrick (2020: 472) observes, "the results were a major vindication of the popular dissatisfaction with the Government as pro-democracy and localists gained control of 17 of the 18 District Councils. The pro-establishment and pro-PRC parties won only 60 seats, compared to 292 in the last elections in 2015. The pro-democracy parties won 392 seats compared to 116 in 2015. The large voter turnout, over 70 per cent, contributed to what was a defeat for the Government, the establishment, and China."

This landslide victory was a strong boost to the morale of the pan-democratic camp, which subsequently aimed at winning big in the upcoming September 2020 LegCo election. Benny Tai, one of the initiators of the 2014 Umbrella Movement, Andrew Chiu, convener of Power for Democracy, and several District Council chairpersons revealed at a press conference on 9 June 2020 that they planned to hold primaries among five directly elected geographical constituencies, five "super district councilor" seats, as well as the health services sector. The sole purpose of the primaries is to come up with lists of candidates that the whole pan-democratic camp agrees on. By so doing, the pan-democratic camp can concentrate its resources to contest the LegCo elections to achieve the objective of winning more than 35 LegCo seats (the so-called 35+ plan). By controlling the majority of LegCo seats, some participants of the primaries believed that they would be more effective in asserting pressure on the government to respond to the demands of the pan-democratic camp and the Anti-ELAB protestors.

Naturally, the government was alarmed by this move and warned that organizing and holding primaries may violate the NSL, which was enacted at 23:00 on 30 June 2020. In an interview with *Oriental Daily* published on 9 July 2020, Secretary for Constitutional and Mainland Affairs Erick Tsang said that those who took part in organizing, planning, or participating in the primary elections may violate Articles 20, 22, and 29 of the NSL. These Articles concern secession, subversion, and collusion with a foreign country (*The RTHK* 9 July 2020). Indeed, in January 2020, about 50 members who participated in the primaries were arrested and eventually 47 of them were charged with various offences of subversion.

Let us now move on to examine the impacts of the NSL on Hong Kong politics.

The enactment of the National Security Law (June 2020), the COVID-19 pandemic (December 2019–early 2023), and disqualifying legislators: Round 2 (November 2020)

As earlier mentioned, the NSL was enacted an hour before the 23rd anniversary of the establishment of the HKSAR. The timing of the enactment of the NSL is symbolic. Whether it symbolizes the end of the principle of "one country, two systems" or the restoring of law and order to Hong Kong depends on one's political orientation. For the pan-democratic camp, the NSL is a draconian law that does not fit with Hong Kong's common law tradition. This kind of concern is commonly shared among activists who have actively participated or even organized campaigns against the government in the Anti-ELAB Movement. On 30 June 2020, hours before the promulgation of the NSL, activists such as Joshua Wong, Nathan Law, and Agnes Chow quit a pro-democracy group that they helped found—the Demosistō—and disbanded it. Likewise, pro-independence groups Studentlocalism and Hong Kong National Front disbanded their local branches. Some pro-democracy shops and businesses removed notices and other material supporting the anti-government protest movement ("One month in, the impact of national security law on Hong Kong," *Reuters*, 31 July 2020).

Amid all these political developments is a public health care crisis that effectively "put a brake" to all kinds of activities, not just in Hong Kong but across the globe—the outbreak of the COVID-19 pandemic. The first batches of COVID-19 cases were first reported in Wuhan, China, on 27 December 2019, and the first two confirmed cases in Hong Kong were reported on 23 January 2020. Ever since, Hong Kong, like everywhere in the world, was hit hard by the COVID-19 pandemic. To prevent the spread of COVID-19, large parts of the world ground to a standstill as countries closed their borders and international travel was halted. Hong Kong was no exception. A direct impact of the pandemic on the LegCo was the postponement of the seventh-term LegCo election. The government announced on 31 July 2020 that "the Chief Executive in Council has decided to postpone the 2020 Legislative Council (LegCo) General Election, originally scheduled for September 6, 2020, for a year to September 5, 2021, in order to protect public safety and public health as well as ensure elections are conducted openly and fairly" (Press Releases, the HKSAR Government, 31 July 2020). On 11 August 2020, the NPCSC responded to the request from the Hong Kong government and decided to extend the sixth-term LegCo for one more year. All the incumbent legislators (including four pan-democratic legislators who were disqualified from running again in the seventh-term LegCo election) could stay in office during the extended term.

However, the harmonious atmosphere created by the NPCSC decision soon disappeared. On 11 November 2020, at the request of the Hong Kong government, the NPCSC clarified "allegiance" requirements for Hong Kong legislators and announced its Decision on "the "legal requirements and preconditions" for running for or assuming the office of a LegCo member" (*NPC Observer* 11 November 2020). Based on various legal authorities, including Article 104 of the Basic Law (and the NPCSC's 2016 interpretation of the Article) and the newly enacted NSL, the Decision lists acts that would be deemed detrimental to national security and thus would be regarded as violating the "legal requirements and preconditions" for serving as LegCo members. Specifically, these acts are: advocating or supporting the notion of "Hong Kong independence; refusing to recognize China's sovereignty or exercise of sovereignty over Hong Kong; seeking foreign or overseas forces to interfere in Hong Kong affairs; and otherwise endangering national security."

Hours after the announcement of the NPCSC Decision, the Hong Kong government announced that four pan-democratic incumbent legislators, namely Alvin Yeung, Kwok Ka-ki, and Dennis Kwok of the Civic Party, and Kenneth Leung of the Professional Commons (these four were disqualified by the Hong Kong government from running in the seventh-term LegCo election earlier in June 2020) were immediately disqualified from being LegCo members, as they had violated the acts stipulated in the Decision. In response, to keep their pledge to quit the LegCo if the CPG ousted any members of their camp, the 15-remaining pan-democratic legislators resigning en masse on 12 November 2020. From

1 December 2020 onward, for the first time in the history of the HKSAR LegCo, there has been nearly no opposition legislators in the LegCo. This is the most dramatic change in the membership composition of the LegCo that one has ever witnessed. However, for supporters of the pan-democratic camp, the worse had yet to come. To this, let us now turn to the CPG's decision to amend the election method of the seventh-term LegCo.

Reforming the LegCo's electoral methods (March 2021)

The mass resignation of the pan-democratic legislators did not deter the CPG from making its next move in Hong Kong's political affairs. At a legal summit on the 30th anniversary of the promulgation of the Basic Law, Zhang Xiaoming, a deputy director of the Hong Kong and Macao Affairs Office of the State Council, said that "patriots governing Hong Kong has now become a legal norm" (*Xinhua Net* 17 November 2020). As such, designing measures to ensure that Hong Kong would only be governed by patriots becomes the focus of Hong Kong politics. A few months later, on 11 March 2021, the NPC announced its Decision on "Improving the Electoral System of the Hong Kong Special Administrative Region." The Decision includes changes to the electoral systems of both the CE and LegCo elections. The following points are worth mentioning: "(i) The HKSAR is to establish an Election Committee that is broadly representative . . . The Election Committee is responsible for such matters as electing the Chief Executive-designate and part of the members of the Legislative Council, as well as nominating candidates for the office of the Chief Executive and for members of the Legislative Council; (ii) Each Legislative Council of the HKSAR is to be composed of 90 members. They are to be respectively elected through elections by the Election Committee, elections by functional constituencies, and direct elections by geographical constituencies; and (iii) There is to be established a HKSAR Candidate Qualification Review Committee, responsible for reviewing and confirming the qualifications of candidates for Election Committee members, the Chief Executive, and Legislative Council members" ("Decision of the National People's Congress on Improving the Electoral System of the Hong Kong Special Administrative Region," 11 March 2021).

Critics (especially those from the pan-democratic camp) believe that under the new electoral system, there is virtually no chance for the pan-democratic camp's candidates to run in future LegCo elections. They contend that the sole purpose of the Candidate Eligibility Review Committee is to ensure that candidates running for the Chief Executive, LegCo seats, and the Election Committee itself, are patriots. Thus, one should not be surprised to hear that the Committee is not hesitant to disqualify candidates from the pan-democratic camp to stand for LegCo elections on the grounds that they are unpatriotic.

Conclusion

This chapter has discussed how changes to the membership composition of the LegCo would affect its functioning and performance. From the experiences of the 1991, 1995–1997 LegCo, the PLC (1997–1998), and the first- (1998–2000) and second-term HKSAR LegCo, one can observe that the more democrats were elected to the LegCo, the higher its degree of assertiveness, and vice versa. The higher its degree of assertiveness, the greater its determination to check and balance the behavior and performance of the Hong Kong government. This is so because membership composition determined how LegCo positioned itself. The most telling example was the PLC. Since its membership was mostly composed of pro-government legislators, it was more like an arm than a watchdog of the government. As the seventh-term LegCo comprises an overwhelming majority of pro-government legislators (though whether it would act like the PLC remains to be seen), it is fair to assert that it would not be as assertive and aggressive as the third-, fourth-, fifth-, and sixth-term LegCo in checking the behavior and performance of the Hong Kong government.

This chapter has also assessed the performance of the sixth-term LegCo. The assessment shows that the LegCo's capacities to discharge its duties were weakened by restrictions stipulated in the Basic Law, most notably Article 74 and Annex II. Article 74 has made it very difficult for the legislature to initiate alternatives that challenge the government's policy agendas. Likewise, the separate vote count mechanism stipulated in Annex II has made it very hard for legislators to initiate amendments to government-proposed legislation.

Box 3.1: Article 74, Annex II, and Private Members' Bills

Article 74 of the Basic Law reads as follows: "Bills which do not relate to public expenditure or political structure or the operation of the government may be introduced individually or jointly by members of the Council. The written consent of the Chief Executive shall be required before bills relating to government policies are introduced." It is no exaggeration to say that Article 74 forbids legislators from proposing any bills of political significance without the prior consent of the CE. Naturally, no CE would approve the tabling of private members' bills if they posed a serious challenge to government policies or forced the government to act against its will. Even if a private member's bill is being tabled in the LegCo, the government and the pro-establishment camp can still defeat it via the separate vote count system stipulated in Annex II. It is fair for one to argue that the separate vote count system was adopted to make it more difficult for the liberal legislators to propose and pass private members' bills that the government would like to block, or to amend the government's legislation against its will. In the previous terms of the LegCo, there have been many occasions in which legislators from the functional constituencies have blocked a member's initiative, although most of the legislative councillors were in favor. Overall, it is beyond question that these restrictions on legislators' capacity to initiate private members' bills and amend government bills have weakened the capability of the LegCo to monitor the performance of the government, and to participate effectively in the policymaking process.

Box 3.2: Committee systems and panels

Around the world, different kinds of committee systems are utilized to help legislatures cope with their ever-increasing workloads. Legislators can develop specialized knowledge of policy areas by participating in committee activities of their choice. This specialized knowledge in turn enhances a legislature's capacity vis-à-vis the executive branch. Specifically, with the help of committee systems, legislatures can discharge their duties more effectively. Legislatures around the world have shown that strong committee systems are indispensable for them to operate competently. However, the LegCo's current committee system is far from strong, as it has only three standing committees that enjoy permanent status. The assertion that the current panel system is adequate in assisting the LegCo to discharge its duties is not well grounded. At the beginning of a new LegCo session, its House Committee will recommend the number and terms of reference of panels to the whole council for approval. The problem with the panel system is its lack of a permanent status. Put differently, the existence of panels is anything but certain. This is undesirable, as experiences elsewhere have demonstrated that "strong committee systems tend to be mainly permanent, while weaker committee systems tend to have a larger ad hoc component" (Shaw 1979: 380).

Questions

1. What are the major functions of a legislature? Which of these functions do you think are most important for a legislature? Why?
2. Among the major functions of the legislature, which do you think does the Hong Kong LegCo perform the best? Why?
3. What are the implications of changes to the membership of the Hong Kong LegCo for its functioning?
4. Discuss in what ways do the existing constitutional restrictions imposed on the Hong Kong LegCo affect its functioning.

5. Do you think the seventh-term LegCo, constituted by the new electoral system (2021), can still assertively and effectively discharge its major functions? Support your answer with examples.

Bibliography

CE's Remarks on Old Age Allowance, 2008, viewed 20 July 2023, http://www.info.gov.hk/gia/general/200810/24/P200810240231.htm

Cheek-Milby, K 1995, *A Legislature Comes of Age: Hong Kong's Search for Influence and Identity*. Hong Kong: Oxford University Press.

Hong Kong Legislative Council 2023, *History of the Legislature, 2023*, viewed 29 July 2023, https://www.legco.gov.hk/en/about-legco/history-art-and-architecture.html#history-of-the-legislature

Hong Kong Legislative Council 2023, *Legislative Council Annual Report, 2022*, viewed 29 July 2023, https://www.legco.gov.hk/general/english/sec/reports/2022/files/textversion.pdf

Leung, JHC 2019, "Interpretive Violence and the 'Nationalization' of Hong Kong Law: Notes on the Oath-taking Controversy," *Law & Literature*, vol. 31, no. 2, pp. 221–238.

Lo, SSH 1998, "The Changing Dimensions of Executive-Legislative Relations: The Case of Hong Kong," *Public Administration and Policy*, vol. 7, no. 2, pp. 73–103.

Lui, PLT 2012, "Legislature," in WM Lam, PLT Lui & W Wong (eds) *Contemporary Hong Kong Government and Politics*, Expanded Second Edition, Hong Kong University Press, Hong Kong, pp. 45–65.

Ma, N 2002, "Executive-Legislative Relations: Assessing Legislative Influence in an Executive-Dominant System," in SK Lau (ed), *The First Tung Chee-hwa Administration: The First Five Years of the Hong Kong Special Administrative Region*, the Chinese University Press of Hong Kong, Hong Kong, pp. 349–374.

Purbrick, M 2020, "Hong Kong: The Torn City," *Asian Affairs*, vol. 51, no. 3, pp. 463–484.

Shaw, M 1979, "Conclusion," in JD Lees and M Shaw (eds), *Committees in Legislatures: A Comparative Analysis*, Durham, NC: Duke University Press, pp. 361–434.

Vukovich, D 2020, "A City and a SAR On Fire: As If Everything and Nothing Changes," *Critical Asian Studies*, vol. 52, no. 1, pp. 1–17.

Yu, KY 2018, "Pro-Beijing Camp Not Keen on Further Amending LegCo Rules," *Ejinsight*, 26 October, https://www.ejinsight.com/eji/article/id/1975724/20181026-pro-beijing-camp-not-keen-on-further-amending-legco-rules

Useful Websites

The Hong Kong Legislative Council
https://www.legco.gov.hk/index.html

Hong Kong government website
http://www.gov.hk/en/residents/

Further Reading

Hong Kong Legislative Council 2023, *Legislative Council Annual Report, 2022*, available at https://www.legco.gov.hk/general/english/sec/reports/2022/files/textversion.pdf. This annual report is full of information on the functions, activities, organization, and records motions of the LegCo during the period 1 January 2022 to 10 January 2023.

Ma, N 2002, "Executive-Legislative Relations: Assessing Legislative Influence in an Executive-Dominant System," in SK Lau (ed), *The First Tung Chee-hwa Administration: The First Five Years of the Hong Kong Special Administrative Region*, the Chinese University Press of Hong Kong, Hong Kong, pp. 349–374. This book chapter examines the executive-legislative relationship in Hong Kong after 1997. It discusses the various channels that the Hong Kong LegCo may utilize to influence the governance of Hong Kong. Ma's article points out that a weak legislature is harmful for the future of governance in Hong Kong.

Rules of Procedure of the Legislative Council of the Hong Kong Special Administrative Region, available at https://www.legco.gov.hk/general/english/procedur/content/rop.pdf. This document details regulations that govern how the Hong Kong LegCo should conduct its business. These regulations also apply to those who attend LegCo meetings.

4

The Judiciary[1]

Lai Yan-ho

A robust, independent judiciary is often regarded as the cornerstone of the rule of law, which has been recognized by both the government and society of Hong Kong as one of the city's core values for decades. As a famous global financial hub, Hong Kong was ranked nineteenth out of 139 countries and jurisdictions for its adherence to the rule of law in the *World Justice Project's Rule of Law Index®* in 2021. However, local surveys revealed that public confidence toward the rule of law continued to decline when the courts became a contested site between political authorities and defendants who engaged in the pro-democracy movement in recent years. In a 2019 public opinion telecommunication survey, more than half of the respondents (i.e., 1,003 individuals following random sampling) were displeased with the overall situation of the rule of law, and "prevention of the abuse of power by the government" has ranked at the bottom since 2017 (Bauhinia Foundation Research Centre 2019).

The rule of law has been highlighted as a necessary and indispensable condition of democratization and democratic consolidation (Linz and Stepan 1996; Diamond and Morlino 2015). An independent judiciary is a cardinal institution to implement and safeguard the rule of law by defending political rights and democratic procedures (O'Donnell 2004). However, literature on authoritarianism also reveals that laws and courts are capable of serving as instruments for autocratic and hybrid regimes to empower repressive agencies and crack down on their political enemies with facades of legality and judicial independence (Box 4.1) (Ginsburg and Moustafa 2008; Rajah 2012; Moustafa 2014).

Since the handover in 1997, Hong Kong's judiciary certainly falls in between the two models above. On the one hand, the Hong Kong courts were regarded

---

1. Part of this chapter draws from the author's published article, "Securitisation or Autocratisation? Hong Kong's Rule of Law under the Shadow of China's Authoritarian Governance," *Journal of Asian and African Studies*, vol. 58, issue 1, pp. 8–25, 2023.

as an impartial and robust arena for justice and protection of basic rights (Chan 2007; Yap 2007). On the other hand, as this chapter will show, the sovereign state, i.e., the People's Republic of China (PRC) and the Hong Kong Special Administrative Region (HKSAR) governments, which are not fully democratized, have been making use of laws and courts to consolidate its governances. Although Hong Kong has been praised by the global commercial and legal communities for its common law system (Box 4.2) and independent judiciary, this chapter also examines how the recent developments of the legal and political environments of Hong Kong have impacted the capacities and performances of the judicial institutions. This chapter begins with an overview of the colonial origin of the judiciary in Hong Kong and its development since 1997. Then, the challenges that the courts in the second decade of the HKSAR are discussed, especially in areas of constitutional review, criminal justice, and national security.

Origins and Establishment of the Rule of Law and Judiciary in Hong Kong

A common understanding of the rule of law is that it rejects "rule by man," where a single ruler or a group of individuals can exercise political power freely and arbitrarily without any constraints. The idea of the rule of law is also different from "rule by law," as the latter concept does not necessarily limit the government's arbitrary use of power. Thus, a foundational concept of the rule of law is that everyone, including both the government and citizens, is subject to the law, ensuring that the principles of "equality before the law" and "no men are above the law" are realized (Dicey 1982 [1885]: 114). Laws, regulations, and legal institutions should be capable of limiting the dominant political power from intruding into the rights of the ruled (Thompson 1975: 266). Laws should be certain, accessible, predictable, and fairly enforced to ensure that people can easily comply with the laws and that any abuse of laws and courts be prevented (Chan 2015: 5–7). External checks and balances, such as establishment of an independent judiciary or the elected legislature, are thus essential institutions to limit and regulate executive power to ensure that it acts in accordance with the law. Today, the concept of the rule of law has been tied to democracy and expanded to safeguard the rights and dignity of individuals by public authorities—a result of international human rights conventions becoming a general norm in the postwar international community (Davis 2015; U.N. Secretary-General 2009).

A comprehensive concept of the rule of law, therefore, comprises both procedural and substantive elements that guarantee fair and democratic procedures of governmental acts, as well as protection of civil, political, and socioeconomic rights of citizens, subject to the level of cultural and institutional development of the rule of law in a particular historical context (Tamanaha 2004: 91; Tai 2017:

152). If legal and judicial institutions cannot be supported by principles of equality before the law, effective checks against and prevention of misuse of power by the government and the safeguarding of basic rights and freedoms of individuals, laws, and courts will only become instruments of the state. The state can use laws to combat its political enemies by criminalizing their words and deeds, and laws will merely become tools of consolidating the prerogative powers of the ruling regime (Fraenkel 1941).

The early days of Hong Kong's legal system did not meet the above requirement of the rule of law. During the era of colonial administration, Hong Kong was transplanted with a common law system like other former British colonies. When Hong Kong Island and Kowloon were ceded by the Qing authorities to Britain in 1841, the colonial authority guaranteed that traditional Chinese laws and customs would continue to take effect (Wong 2020: 21–22). Yet at the same time, a colonial criminal justice system was also established when a Chief Magistrate of Hong Kong was appointed in the same year. Archives reveal that jury trials were implemented by the magistrates at that time (Norton-kyshe 1971: 16–17). Two years later, the colonial government continued to transplant judicial bodies and codified laws and statutes incrementally. The laws of England were fully in force in 1843, and a Supreme Court with a Chief Justice in Hong Kong was established in 1844, but the power of final appeal remained with London's Judicial Committee of Privy Council (Munn 2019: 2–3). The jurisdiction also extended to the New Territories, which was occupied by the British colonizers in 1898. However, the administration of justice at that time was accused of arbitrariness and serious deficiencies, and legal discrimination against Chinese people was a norm (Tsang 2004: 45). Moreover, various codified laws were enacted to consolidate colonial rule by implementing deportation, repression against anti-colonial activism, and censorship of the press. Between the 1910s and 1960s, the governor was also empowered with emergency powers, such as the Public Order Ordinance, the Seditious Publication Ordinance, and the Emergency Regulation Ordinance (Munn 2009 and 2017; Ng 2016 and 2017).

Only in the 1970s did the colonial government start to refrain from employing those laws intensively and introduced some reforms to improve the legal system. Apart from the establishment of the new Independent Commission Against Corruption (ICAC), judicial reforms were also introduced in the same decade, including the establishment of the Labour Tribunal and government legal aid system to strengthen public access to justice (Jones 2006). Other tribunals were also set up to handle different kinds of disputes.

Prior to the handover in 1997, the Bill of Rights Ordinance (BORO) was enacted in 1991 to institutionalize safeguards of basic rights and freedoms according to provisions of the International Covenant on Civil and Political Rights (ICCPR), which is also applicable in the new era of Hong Kong since

1997 through protection under the Basic Law of HKSAR (Tai 2012). As Wong suggests, BORO was regarded as a legacy of the British colonial government to safeguard the implementation of the ICCPR in Hong Kong's political and legal system, and as an attempt to regain public confidence toward Hong Kong's handover to PRC, which drastically declined in the aftermath of the Tiananmen incident in 1989 (Wong 2017).

Since 1997, provisions of the Basic Law ensure that most of Hong Kong's judicial structure and institutions would remain unchanged, except the establishment of the Court of Final Appeal (CFA), which replaced the Judicial Committee of the Privy Council of the UK and exercises the power of final adjudication in the local regime (Table 4.1). Provisions of the Basic Law also promise judicial independence (Articles 2, 19, 85), equality before the law (Article 25), access to justice and administrative review (Article 35), safeguarding of civil rights and liberties in accordance with the ICCPR (Article 39), continuity of the previous practice of jury trial (Article 86), and judicial immunity as well as a well-defined process of judicial appointment by the Chief Executive (CE) (Article 88). The Judicial Officers Recommendation Commission, which consists of the Chief Justice, the Secretary for Justice (SJ), and the CE's appointed members from legal and nonlegal communities, was set up to advise and give recommendations to the CE regarding the appointment of judicial officers. The Legislative Council also takes part in the appointment or removal process of judges, as the CE must obtain an endorsement from the legislature to appoint judges of the CFA and the Chief Judge of the High Court and report the appointment or removal to the Standing Committee of the National People's Congress (SCNPC) (Article 90) (Box 4.3). In 2021, the judiciary established a two-tier mechanism for handling complaints against judicial conduct and appointments to the "Advisory Committee on Complaints against Judicial Conduct," which is headed by the Chief Justice and composed of judges, lawyers, and nonlegal members, to further enhance judicial accountability. The next sections introduce the institutions and practices of judicial review in Hong Kong's courts.

Constitutional Review and the Relationship between Local Courts and the Sovereign State

Judicial review by the courts consists of administrative review and constitutional review. Administrative review refers to the judicial authority to review administrative decisions and acts and thus invalidate those that are not made according to law, while constitutional review refers to the judicial authority to review legislative or executive acts on their compatibility with the constitution (Tai 2012: 68–69). The stalemate of democratization in Hong Kong has made judicial review a practical way for activists and marginalized groups to defend constitutional

Table 4.1: Structure and jurisdiction of the HKSAR courts (by 2023)[1]

Name	Jurisdiction
Court of Final Appeal (CFA)	Hears appeals on civil and criminal matters from the Court of Appeal and the Court of First Instance. Has the power to seek an interpretation of Basic Law provisions, which are relevant to a case to be judged, from the Standing Committee of the National People's Congress.
Court of Appeal (CA)	Hears appeals on all civil and criminal matters from the Court of First Instance and the District Court. Also hears appeals from Lands Tribunal and various Tribunals and Statutory Bodies. Together with the Court of First Instance, they form the High Court.
Court of First Instance (CFI)	Has unlimited jurisdiction in both civil and criminal matters. Also hears appeals from Magistrates' Courts, the Small Claims Tribunal, the Obscene Articles Tribunal, the Labour Tribunal, and the Minor Employment Claims Adjudication Board. For criminal trials, life imprisonment can be imposed, and judges of the Court of First Instance sit with a jury of seven or nine on the special direction of the Judge. Jury trial can be removed in cases of offences under the National Security Law of 2020 if the Secretary for Justice issues a certificate to request a no-jury trial under certain condition(s).
District Court	Hears civil disputes valued between $75,000 and $3 million. Criminal jurisdiction is limited to seven years' imprisonment.
Magistrates' Court	The seven Magistrates' Courts (Eastern, Kowloon City, Kwun Tong, West Kowloon, Fanling, Shatin, Tuen Mun) exercise criminal jurisdiction over a wide range of indictable and summary offences meriting up to two years' imprisonment and a fine of $100,000.
The Family Court	Deals mainly with divorce cases and related matters, such as maintenance and the welfare of children.
The Lands Tribunal	Deals with cases arising from tenancy disputes and matters in relation to building management. Also hears applications for the determination of compensation caused by land resumption, appeal against the assessment of ratable value/government rent, or market value of property under the Housing Ordinance.
The Labour Tribunal	Hears cases concerning employment where the amount of claim exceeds $8,000 for at least one of the claimants in a claim, or where the number of claimants in the claim exceeds 10. Other claims are dealt with by the Minor Employment Claims Adjudication Board. Hearings are informal and no representation by lawyers is allowed.

(continued on p. 81)

Table 4.1 (continued)

Name	Jurisdiction
The Small Claims Tribunal	Hears claims of up to $75,000 within its jurisdiction. Hearings are informal and no representation by lawyers is allowed.
The Obscene Articles Tribunal	Determines and classifies whether an article or other matter publicly displayed is obscene or indecent.
The Coroner's Court	Conducts inquests into unusual circumstances causing death.
The Juvenile Court	Hears charges against children and young persons under the age of 16, except in cases of homicide. Also has the jurisdiction to make care and protection orders in respect to young persons under the age of 18.

1. This table is updated based on Tai, B.Y.T. 2012, "The Judiciary," in W. M. Lam, P. L. T. Lui and W. Wong (eds), *Contemporary Hong Kong Government and Politics*, Expanded Second Edition, Hong Kong University Press, Hong Kong, p. 70.

rights, check the excesses of state administration, and strive for policy change (Kapai 2011: 49; Kong 2012: 588; Tam 2012). This phenomenon has been labeled as either "the politicization of the judiciary" or "the judicialization of politics and public policy" (Cheung and Wong 2006: 117; Chan 2007: 407). While the use of judicial review to challenge the government's administrative decisions is popular in the HKSAR, others criticize these measures as a misuse of the law and censure such actions as politicization of the judiciary. These criticisms of the judiciary and citizens exercising their legal rights were revealed in cases against Link REIT's privatization of shopping malls in public housing estates, rights of abode of foreign domestic helpers, housing rights of the Mainland new arrivals, as well as social and economic rights of LGBTQ couples in Hong Kong.

While constitutional reviews on socioeconomic rights and minority rights did not spur resistance from the sovereign state, the central authorities constrained the local courts' power to review the constitutionality of legislations, policies, and executive decisions related to Mainland–Hong Kong relations. In these cases, Hong Kong's independent judiciary had even been labeled as exercising "judicial sovereignty" against the executive government and the central authorities (Jiang 2015: 173). Since 2014, the central authorities took initiative to constrain the judicial authority in ideological and practical ways. This chapter mainly focuses on the tensions between the sovereign power and the Hong Kong judiciary on the latter's exercise of constitutional review.

Tensions between Hong Kong's rule of law and China's "rule-based governance"

One of the key elements of Hong Kong's rule of law has been the safeguarding of basic freedoms and rights in accordance with international human rights conventions under the Basic Law, along with principles of the common law, shared with at least some Commonwealth jurisdictions that uphold the integrity of law. Values like equality before the law, protection of basic rights and freedoms, and limiting the powers of the government are well appreciated in the Bill of Rights Ordinance (BORO) as well as some provisions of the Basic Law. In contrast, the PRC has often interpreted the rule of law as "rule-based governance" (依法治國), while at the same time "socialist rule of law" and "party leadership" are emphasized as being complementary to each other to achieve "rule-based governance" (Trevaskes 2019: 251). It means the law and judicial institutions in the PRC are subject to the Chinese Communist Party (CCP), instead of the other way round. Therefore, serving the political goals of the party-state is the fundamental mission of the socialist Chinese legal institutions (Chan 2018: 374).

Judicial independence following the principle of separation of powers does not exist in the Mainland justice system. Rather, the judicial system in China is supervised by the Central Political and Legal Affairs Commission of the CCP. Also, unlike the common law system, where the courts have sole power to interpret the law publicly, the power of interpreting the law in the Mainland justice system is vested in different political institutions, in particular the SCNPC; the interpretation is also done by a closed process (Chan 2015: 17). One year after Xi Jinping became the leader of the CCP in 2012, an internal government document was leaked to the public. The document requested that seven liberal ideas from the West, including "judicial independence," be banned in Mainland universities. The document was labeled by the press as "7 Ideas that You Should Not Talk" (七不講) (Li 2013). This official paper is evidence that the CCP has its own notion of judicial independence—one that is distinct from Western models. In recent years, the central authorities have repeatedly claimed that they would not follow the "Western model" of "judicial independence," which is embedded with ideas of constitutional democracy and separation of powers, in the PRC (Reuters 2017). Although Hong Kong enjoys a separate judicial system from the Mainland, when the central authorities have imposed more direct or indirect control over Hong Kong; the latter lacks ability to resist the exercise of power by the sovereign.

The release of the *White Paper on the Practice of the "One Country, Two Systems" in the HKSAR* by the State Council of the PRC in June 2014 is one example of the sovereign state's attempt to impose direct control over the local courts' exercise of the power of constitutional review. The White Paper serves both as an ideological and theoretical framework to justify imposing a political mission on Hong Kong judges. First, the idea of "overall jurisdiction" of central authorities over HKSAR was introduced, asserting that the NPC, SCNPC, the President of PRC, the CPG, and the Central Military Commission can directly exercise jurisdiction over Hong Kong according to the Constitution of PRC and the Basic Law of Hong Kong. The White Paper also stressed that such overall jurisdiction is sourced from the nature of the PRC as a unitary state. Hence, Hong Kong's high degree of autonomy shall not be read as a "full autonomy" nor an exercise of residual power like a federal state but shall be subject to the central leadership's authorization. Second, the White Paper explained the state's expectations of the political duty for Hong Kong judges. It described judges of the courts at different levels and other judicial personnel as part of Hong Kong's administration and says that they shall be "patriotic" and "love the country." The White Paper also asserted that loving the country is "the basic political requirement" for judges, and that judges are required to safeguard the country's sovereignty, security, and development interests, as well as guarantee the long-term prosperity and stability of Hong Kong. Last but not the least, judges shall bear "the responsibility of correctly understanding" the Basic Law (State Council of PRC 2014).

The White Paper led to controversy, particularly from the legal community. The Hong Kong Bar Association issued a statement to reiterate that judges and judicial officers of the HKSAR are not part of Hong Kong administration or the governance team; judges do not need to learn or take any "definitive correct meaning of the Basic Law from anyone else" when adjudicating cases (Hong Kong Bar Association 2014). Around 1,800 lawyers, lawmakers, and even former judges hosted a silent march to express their disagreement with the White Paper. Later, the first Chief Justice of HKSAR, Andrew Li, also publicly disapproved of the notion of judges as administrators and expressed concerns regarding the notion of patriotism, which is generally perceived as supporting and cooperating with the political authorities as well as protecting the latter's interests (So 2014). Regarding the Law Society, when the President openly uttered his support for the White Paper and the rule of the CCP in a radio program, he attracted wide criticism from the community of solicitors afterwards. On 15 August 2014, members of the Law Society called for an emergency general meeting and passed a motion of no confidence against the President, who later resigned from the Council of the Law Society.

The strong reactions from the legal profession and former judges signified their worries that the conventional practice of judicial independence in Hong Kong would be damaged through the direct and literal implementation of the White Paper into the judicial system. Under the common law tradition of Hong Kong, judicial independence is recognized as a way for upholding good

84   The Judiciary

governance through exercising checks and balances over other branches of government under the principle of "separation of powers"—a principle of that has been rejected by the central authorities on many occasions. Judges and the public will also be confused by the vague and broad notions of safeguarding "the country's sovereignty, security, and development interests" and of ensuring the "long-term prosperity and stability" of Hong Kong, which are political require-ments imposed on Hong Kong judges through the White Paper. Consequently, whether judges can still uphold impartiality and act as guardians of human rights when adjudicating judicial reviews or criminal trials related to anti-government protests became questionable. Although the central authorities did not make any further attempts to promote the political requirements of judges in public, the SCNPC continued to expand its influence on local courts by directly exercising powers to interpret provisions of the Basic Law and making decisions over issues concerning the Basic Law, to restrict Hong Kong's judicial autonomy under the sovereign state. As explained in the later section of this chapter, the implementa-tion of the White Paper became ostensibly effective following the imposition of the national security law by the central authorities in 2020.

Interpretations of the Basic Law by SCNPC

Under the Basic Law, the courts of the HKSAR have the power to interpret pro-visions of the Basic Law in adjudicating cases, and the CFA enjoys the power of final adjudication. Yet, Article 158 of the Basic Law also requires the CFA "seek an interpretation of the relevant provisions from the Standing Committee of the National People's Congress" if the provisions of the Basic Law in question concern affairs that are the responsibility of the central authorities or concern the relationship between the central authorities and HKSAR. The provision did not entitle either the CE or the Legislative Council to have the power to seek SCNPC's interpretation of the Basic Law (Tai 2002: 193). In other words, although the CFA enjoys powers of interpretation of laws and of final adjudication, where provi-sions of the Basic Law are concerned, the SCNPC enjoys the ultimate authority to interpret the Basic Law, which would consequentially affect local adjudication.

The first direct clash of the adjudication power between courts of the HKSAR and the Chinese authorities occurred in 1999. In *Ng Ka Ling and another v. The Director of Immigration*, a constitutional review was held concerning the right of abode among children of Hong Kong permanent residents born in Mainland China (29 January 1999). The CFA ruled in favor of the applicants by stressing the right of family union under Article 23 of the ICCPR. Furthermore, the court stated that the Hong Kong courts "do have jurisdiction to examine NPC's laws and acts which affect the region" (paragraph 71). The court's judgment received criticism from Mainland legal experts who were involved in the drafting of the

Basic Law, criticizing the CFA as challenging the absolute authority of the NPC; officials in Beijing also commented that the court ruling should be reversed (Tai 2002: 196). One month after that ruling, the CFA released a "number 2" judgment of the same case (26 February 1999). This action was unprecedented in Hong Kong's judiciary and very unusual in the common law tradition. This second judgment stated that the courts of Hong Kong "cannot question that authority" of the NPC or SCNPC "to do any acts in accordance with the provisions of the Basic Law and the procedure therein" (paragraphs 3 and 4). Finally, upon the request of the CE, SCNPC pronounced its first interpretation of the Basic Law on the matter of right of abode in June 1999, which in effect overruled the decision of the CFA.

The power of final adjudication of the CFA in constitutional review is de facto in the hands of the SCNPC, as shown by the exercise of power by the SCNPC in interpreting the Basic Law to overrule the decision of the highest level of court in Hong Kong. Moreover, the CE's request for interpretation of the Basic Law from Beijing, which is not prescribed in the condition of Article 158 of the Basic Law, also appears to undermine the rule of law and judicial independence in Hong Kong. After the first interpretation of the Basic Law, the SCNPC continued to interpret the Basic Law on four occasions between 2004 and 2021. Three of them were related to domestic constitutional order, and one concerned state immunity. Only the case of state immunity was initiated by the CFA. The rest of the interpretations were either sought by the CE or directly issued by the SCNPC. These interpretations of the Basic Law brought about a change in the procedure of political reform, clarified the length of term of the succeeding CE, and justified disqualifications of electoral candidates and lawmakers due to disapproval of various forms of oath-taking for public office. Although the SCNPC enjoys the absolute power to interpret the Basic Law under the Chinese constitutional framework, some of the interpretations were seen as controversial by the local community, and worries began to build up as to whether judicial autonomy and due process in courts can still be upheld.

The oath-taking saga in 2016 is the most recent case showing how, after the publishing of the White Paper, the SCNPC exercised its power of interpretation of the Basic Law to diminish judicial autonomy in Hong Kong. In the Legislative Council elections of 2016, two young activists from the localist group Youngspiration, Sixtus Leung and Wai-ching Yau, were elected as lawmakers. During the oath-taking session before assuming their office in the LegCo, which is required by the Oaths and Declarations Ordinance and Article 104 of the Basic Law, Leung and Yau displayed a flag declaring "Hong Kong is not China." Yau then swore the oath by using a derogatory term that the Japanese used to refer to the Chinese during wartime, and the pronunciation was interpreted as being offensive to the Chinese people. Leung and Yau's behavior led to wide criticisms from the pro-government camp as damaging national sentiment (Steger 2016). As a result, the President of the Legislative Council ruled that their oaths were invalid, but they were also allowed to retake the oath.

Nevertheless, the CE and the SJ filed court proceedings against Leung and Yau, who were ready to retake their oaths. The SJ argued that the President of the Legislative Council had no power to allow them to retake the oath, as Leung and Yau had refused to take the mandatory legislative oath already (Chan 2018: 378). The case was heard in the Court of First Instance (CFI), and the judge adjourned the case for judgment. Prior to the court giving judgment, the SCNPC pronounced its interpretation of Article 104 of the Basic Law. Officials asserted that upholding the Basic Law of Hong Kong and bearing allegiance to Hong Kong and China are the "legal requirement and preconditions for standing for election" as well as for taking up public office; any oath-taker who does not read out the oath "sincerely and solemnly" will be disqualified from assuming public office (SCNPC 7 November 2016). The CFI, though stating that it did not take the SCNPC's interpretation of Article 104 of the Basic Law into account in making its decision, decided the oaths of Leung and Yau were invalid and thus removed them from their seats in the legislature (*Chief Executive of the HKSAR v. President of the Legislative Council*). Leung and Yau also failed in their appeal at the Court of Appeal, and the CFA refused to grant them leave to a final appeal (*Yau Wai Ching v. Chief Executive of the HKSAR*).

After the SCNPC's pronouncement of the interpretation of Article 104 of the Basic Law, the CE and the SJ issued court proceedings against four other lawmakers, challenging their oaths as invalid. The court accepted the CE and the SJ's arguments, and, giving full effect to the SCNPC's interpretation, held that the oaths taken by the four lawmakers were invalid and disqualified them from their offices in the legislature (*Secretary for Justice v. Nathan Law Kwun Chung*).

The NPCSC's interpretation of Article 104 of the Basic Law was regarded as an unprecedented move from Beijing, as the interpretation was announced when a litigation case was still in progress (Chan 2018: 379). Although the CFI did not refer in its reasoning to the SCNPC's interpretation of the Basic Law, the SCNPC's act of interpretation was affirmed by the Court of Appeal to have binding power on the court (*Chief Executive of the HKSAR v. President of the Legislative Council*). Later, in *Secretary for Justice v. Leung Kwok Hung*, the Court of Appeal also reaffirmed the CFA's position that the SCNPC's interpretation of the Basic Law has retrospective effect, meaning that the interpretation of Article 104 of the Basic Law could be used by the authorities to challenge the validity of oaths taken by lawmakers before the release of that interpretation.

The SCNPC's interpretation of the Basic Law in 2016 disrupted due process of a constitutional review and disproportionately took away the right to political participation of individual citizens. In this sense, the action of the sovereign state, though backed by its legality, did not fit the standard of the rule of law that embraces values of democracy and human rights; it also weakened judicial independence in Hong Kong. A total of six pro-democracy lawmakers who were elected in the 2016 Legislative Council elections were disqualified due to the new requirements set out in the interpretation. Between 2018 and 2020, the interpretation was also applied by the government returning officers and the courts to invalidate election candidates and to dismiss election petitions respectively, with a total of at least 17 pro-democracy candidates unable to convince the authorities of their willingness to uphold the Basic Law and allegiance to the PRC.

Decisions on the Basic Law by SCNPC

Besides interpreting the Basic Law, the SCNPC also passes "decisions" to justify certain acts and policy implementations as being compatible with the Basic Law and its constitutional arrangement in Hong Kong. As of 2019, the SCNPC had made 20 decisions in relation to the HKSAR, including issues of the election of deputies to the NPC, deletion of the list of national laws applicable to the region, constitutional development, and the establishment of port areas at Mainland–Hong Kong transportation hubs (Chan 2020b). Most of these decisions were pursuant to the Basic Law and SCNPC interpretation, but some were not. One of the key SCNPC decisions over constitutional development was made on 31 August 2014, when SCNPC announced that a tight screening mechanism for candidates shall be put in place for CE elections carried out by universal suffrage. When a student activist filed an application for judicial review on the matter, the court refused to give her leave to challenge the validity of the SCNPC's decision (*Leung Lai Kwok Yvonne v. The Chief Secretary for Administration and Others*, HCAL 31/2015).

Another SCNPC's decision about the practice of the Basic Law occurred in 2017, when the "colocation arrangement" became a heated debate in society. "Colocation arrangement" refers to the system by which both Hong Kong and Mainland authorities colocate their clearance facilities in the same terminal at an Express Railway Station in West Kowloon of Hong Kong (Cheung 2020b). In 2010, the Legislative Council approved a budget to construct the Guangzhou-Shenzhen-Hong Kong Express Rail Link (XRL). Then in 2017, the Hong Kong government released a proposed colocation arrangement inside the XRL West Kowloon Station stating that Chinese personnel can enforce Chinese laws on clearance procedures in the Mainland Port Area inside the station. However, this joint checkpoint proposal was regarded by members of the legal community as well as opposition lawmakers as a violation of the Basic Law, as Article 18 of the Basic Law disallows the application of national laws in the territory of HKSAR unless listed in Annex III of the Basic Law or when a state of emergency is declared by the SCNPC (Huang 2017). In response to the criticisms, the government asserted that the arrangement did not contravene the Basic Law, which does not define the border of HKSAR in detail; the government also hinted that it would seek a resolution from the SCNPC (Tong 2017). Five months later, the SCNPC announced by way of a decision that the colocation arrangement complies with the Basic Law and that the decision should be given effect in Hong Kong by way of domestic legislation (Ng 2017a).

Prior to the SCNPC's decision, no domestic legislative procedures and public consultations were carried out in Hong Kong to ensure due process and scrutiny of the constitutionality of the joint checkpoint arrangement. When Deputy Secretary General of SCNPC Li Fei announced the decision in a press conference, he used a Chinese proverb—"one word is as heavy as nine tripods" (一言九鼎)—to justify the reasoning of the decision, claiming that the decision was final as well as absolute and could not be questioned (Ng 2017b). A year after the SCNPC decision, the High Court confirmed in a judicial review ruling that the SCNPC can exercise supervisory power on any arrangement and issue decisions under the PRC Constitution and was thus in compliance with the Basic Law; therefore, the SCNPC decision was compatible with the Basic Law (*Leung Chung Hang, Sixtus v President of Legislative Council & Secretary for Justice*). In 2021, the Court of Appeal reaffirmed that the colocation arrangement is compatible with the Basic Law, recognizing the SCNPC's decision as having "a highly persuasive weight in the courts' construction of the Basic Law." However, the court did not give a direct ruling over the constitutional status of the SCNPC decision (*Kwok Cheuk Kin v Secretary for Justice*).

The decision on colocation arrangement in 2017 became a landmark case, signifying that the SCNPC was now eager to issue any decision to justify its new practices or interpretations over Hong Kong and the Basic Law when the matters concerned are affecting Mainland–Hong Kong relations, even if such decision is not made pursuant to or under any provision of the Basic Law or SCNPC interpretation. So far, local courts have much less autonomy to review such decisions that are not made in accordance with provisions of the Basic Law but rather has taken the stance of avoiding answering the question of constitutionality. In 2020, the SCNPC passed two decisions in August and November, postponing the Legislative Council election and providing national security causes as justifications for the disqualification of lawmakers by the local government. The executive branch of the government was empowered to bypass judicial procedures to remove any lawmakers with retrospective power, further reducing the jurisdiction of local courts as well as the legislature.

This exercise of SCNPC's decision over Hong Kong also implicitly transplanted provisions of the PRC Constitution and laws to be directly implemented in Hong Kong, although Article 5 of the Basic Law states that the socialist system and policies are not applicable in Hong Kong. Mainland laws are now applied in part of the territory of Hong Kong under the 2017 SCNPC decision, whereas Articles 52 and 54 of the PRC Constitution that address the obligations of Chinese citizens in safeguarding national security were cited as a source of the SCNPC decision in November 2020 (Lam 2020). It appears that the court will have little chance of claiming jurisdiction to determine the validity or constitutionality of matters involving the direct application of the PRC Constitution like in the past, and its role of safeguarding the civil and political rights under the ICCPR has diminished under the expanding influences of the central authorities.

Criminal Justice and Weaponization of Laws

The criminal justice system was a subject of less concern in the policy agenda and public debate in early post-handover Hong Kong. Some activists have been arrested and charged by public order laws in protests (Ku 2007 and 2017). In fact, after 1997, various draconian laws remained in force or were even further amended to enhance social control and limit citizens' rights of free speech, assembly, and association, such as the national security provisions in the Societies Ordinance and the revival of public assembly notification system in the Public Order Ordinance. Nevertheless, with the rise of contentious politics in Hong Kong since 2014, where confrontational street protests and mass mobilizations emerged to promote political and legislative reforms as well as resistance, mass arrests in demonstrations and prosecutions of political activists became a common response of the government, paving the way for politicizing the courts, particularly the judicial spaces of criminal trials.

The Public Order Ordinance, which was enacted to restore law and order during the 1967 Riot, was repeatedly used to repress protestors since the handover, particularly after 2014. While the offence of rioting has been used by the authorities to prosecute protestors committed in various degrees and forms of violence, peaceful protestors were also charged with offences of incitements of organizing or attending an unlawful or unauthorized assembly in which a letter of no objection from the police commissioner was absent. Between 2014 and 2020, there were two major protests that fundamentally challenged the democratic backslide in Hong Kong, and the courts became the eye of the storm when protestors and activist leaders became criminals. In the Umbrella Movement in 2014, which was a 79-day occupation of major hubs in Hong Kong to call for the implementation of universal suffrage without a screening mechanism by the SCNPC, at least 102 citizens were prosecuted, and more than one-third of the defendants were charged with contempt of court, as they did not comply with injunction orders to leave the protest sites (Ma 2020: 37–41).

90   The Judiciary

The Hong Kong court became a center of attention for local and foreign media as well as the public when student activists and prominent figures in the Umbrella Movement were put on trial. Two years after the Umbrella Movement, three student activists—Nathan Law, Alex Chow, and Joshua Wong—were convicted of participating in and inciting others to participate in an unlawful assembly. They were given sentences of community service orders or suspended sentences at that time. However, in August 2017, the Department of Justice—which is headed by the SJ, a politically appointed principal official in Hong Kong—applied for a review of the sentences, and the Court of Appeal ruled in the government's favor, sentencing the activists to jail for six to eight months. Prior to that ruling, another 13 activists also had their sentences reviewed by the court pursuant to the application of the Department of Justice and were sent to jail as well. The reviews of sentences initiated by the government as well as the rulings of the Court of Appeal were widely criticized as retributions against student activists. Although the CFA reversed the decision of the CA on the basis of non-retrospectiveness in applying new sentencing guidelines, observers worried that the CFA had nonetheless set new precedent, providing guidance to lower courts in handling protest cases that involve "the relatively low degree of violence" that occurred, resulting in harsher sentences in the future (Davis 2020: 45; Human Rights Watch 2018).

One example is a case of unauthorized assembly in June 2019, as part of the Anti–Extradition Law Amendment Bill Movement (Anti-ELAB Movement). In this case, three activists—Agnes Chow, Joshua Wong, and Ivan Lam—took part in a peaceful assembly outside the headquarters of the Hong Kong Police Force. The assembly was not given a letter of no objection from the police commission. The three were later convicted of inciting, organizing, and participating in an authorized assembly, and then sentenced to jail for between 10 and 13.5 months. The court ruled that even though that assembly was nonviolent, immediate imprisonment became the "only option" that would achieve deterrence, as the court judged there were "potential risks" that the assembly could have turned violent as well as the fact that the three activists were challenging the authority of the police (*HKSAR v. Wong Chi Fung, Lam Long Yin, and Agnes Chow*). This case illustrates that in cases subsequent to the 2018 ruling, the courts have extended the guidelines to peaceful assembly, creating a deterrent effect by imprisoning protesters just because they attended nonviolent but illegal protests (Chan, Lai, and Kellogg 2023: 46–47).

After the 2018 ruling, the courts continued to be a contentious space between activists and the government when nine Umbrella Movement activists were taken to trial beginning on 19 November 2018. They were charged with the common law offences of "incitement to commit public nuisance," "incitement to incite public nuisance" and "conspiracy to commit public nuisance." The nine activists included former lawmakers, student activists, and the "Occupy Central Trio": law professor Benny Tai, sociologist Chan Kin-man, and 75-year-old pastor Chu Yiu-ming. They initiated the civil disobedience campaign in early 2013. During the trial, defense lawyers and their witnesses presented evidence and statements recollecting their experiences in the 2014 movement. Many of the defendants gave speeches to explain their motives and aspirations for engaging in the democratic movement and defending the rule of law, reminding the public of the imagination of democratization and the meaning of civil disobedience (Chan 2019). In the end, all defendants were convicted. Benny Tai and Chan Kin-man were sentenced to 16 months in jail; Chu Yiu-ming was given a two-year suspended sentence. The rest were either sentenced to jail for several months or received suspended sentences or community service orders (Ma 2020: 37).

Although the defendants went on to appeal their convictions and sentences, the Court of Appeal refused their leave to appeal in 2021, arguing that the occupy protests on 28 September 2014, despite not operating as planned by the Occupy Trio, remained "a determined and sustained effort to paralyze the main arterial roads in the very center of Hong Kong for weeks on end in order to pressure the Government into changing its mind" and "went far beyond a matter of inconvenience for ordinary citizens going about their business and trying to earn their living" (*HKSAR v. Tai Yiu Ting and others*). In the court's view, the charge of public nuisance in this case was justified, even though the defendants disagreed and saw it as leading to heavier sentencing than offences in the Public Order Ordinance that covered similar activities and as setting precedents to criminalization of peaceful protests. That said, as of April 2023, the defendants had not applied to appeal at the CFA.

The prosecution used draconian laws to criminalise a few leading activists in the Umbrella Movement that involved thousands of citizens. Together with the government's applications to the court for reviews against sentence, resulting in heavier sentences against the activists, the government's acts delivered a signal to both civil society and the courts that the government is willing to enforce draconian law, exercise prosecutorial power to a tough extent, make use of the right to appeal in criminal trials to restore "law and order" like in colonial times, and seek retaliation and heavy punishment against activists.

These practices became more prominent in the Anti-ELAB Movement in 2019. The movement was originally a resistance to an extradition agreement between the HKSAR and the PRC, but later evolved into a six-month long anti-authoritarian movement that demanded independent investigation of alleged police brutality in policing protests as well as full universal suffrage in Hong Kong (Lee et al. 2019). At the same time, uncivil disobedience also emerged, when vandalism and vigilantism became common forms of violent clashes in the city (Tai 2021: 173). The movement resulted in a high number of protestors being arrested by the police. As of April 2021, more than 10,200 citizens had been arrested, with more than 600 being convicted; more than 2,500 of them had undergone or were undergoing judicial proceedings, including 720 charged with rioting (Ng 2021). Other offences with which protestors have been commonly charged include unauthorized assembly and unlawful assembly. Amid this movement, the government enacted anti-mask regulations, invoking its powers under the Emergency Regulation Ordinance, a wide-ranging power existing since colonial days. The criminal justice system has become overburdened due to mass prosecutions, with waiting times for trial of up to four years (*The Standard* 2021).

In terms of judicial functioning, the local court was put under extreme stress as it started to deal with the hundreds of criminal prosecutions stemming from the Anti-ELAB protests. Some of Hong Kong's legal professionals foresaw that the unprecedented wave of new criminal cases would challenge the courts as never before and could impact the quality of the judicial process. In his speech at the 2020 ceremony of the opening of the legal year, then-Bar Chairman Philip Dykes called on the DOJ to consider the broader public interest—including the interest of the public in having a functioning judiciary that is not overwhelmed by protest cases—in its prosecutorial decisions (Dykes 2020). In fact, according to the annual reports of the judiciary, from 2019 to 2021, the waiting time for criminal trials at all levels of the court system have increased dramatically. For instance, the average waiting time for all criminal cases at the District Court, where all rioting cases have been tried, has increased by 50 percent between 2019 and 2021, to a full 287 days. This waiting time is almost three times longer than the targeted average waiting time of 100 days set by the judiciary itself. These developments demonstrate that the local court is overburdened under the weight of the massively increased caseload (Chan, Lai, and Kellogg 2023: 39–40).

That said, as of 2022, the Department of Justice and law enforcement declined to take up the suggestions of reducing caseloads by discharging cases or discontinuing investigations related to the Anti-ELAB Movement. Rather, the Department of Justice has been seeking to file appeals for sentencing review against convicted protestors in that movement. As of July 2021, 20 appeals had been filed by the Department of Justice for review of sentencing, all of which were granted by the court. In all 20 cases, these appeals have resulted in more punitive sentencing against those convicted. Moreover, in some cases, the Department of Justice has also appealed against not guilty verdicts. In one case, the DOJ appealed the acquittal in 2020 of eight people accused of rioting (香港特別行政區 訴 余德穎及另七人). The appeal was finally heard in January 2023, i.e., more than two years after the acquittal. In the end, the Court of Appeal ruled in favor of the Department of Justice and ordered retrial as the court saw the previous acquittal as "plainly wrong." Consequently, the Department of Justice's decisions to file appeal for reviews of sentencing and acquittal create a long waiting time for appeal hearings, creating new legal burden for protestor defendants even if they have already been acquitted (Chan, Lai, and Kellogg 2023: 65–67).

Judicial independence was also under pressure in the Anti-ELAB Movement. On the one hand, the central authorities repeatedly emphasized cooperation of powers between the three governmental branches to end violence and resume public order, which should be a "common responsibility for Hong Kong's executive, legislative and judicial bodies" (Ting 2019). The courts appear to have been imposed with a task to ally with the political means to handle the protests. Furthermore, after the CFI released a judgment ruling that the anti-mask law was unconstitutional during the Anti-ELAB Movement, an intense backlash was seen from SCNPC and the Hong Kong and Macao Affairs Office of the State Council, which stated that the Emergency Regulation Ordinance complies with the Basic Law and that the court ruling challenged the authority of both the SCNPC and the CE of the HKSAR (Myers 2019). The first Chief Justice of HKSAR, Andrew Li, had to come out to defend the local court's jurisdiction of constitutional review in Hong Kong (*The Standard* 2019). The active response from SCNPC showed that it is hard for the courts to ignore the central authorities' view on the matter with respect to these sensitive political cases. However, there are still cases that show the courts' view against the government, such as the ruling that the non-displaying of distinctive identification numbers by riot police was unconstitutional (*Yeung Tsz Chun v. Commissioner of Police*); the ruling against the improper use of joint enterprise principle in rioting cases (*HKSAR v. Lo Kin Man*); and the ruling that overturned an offensive weapon conviction that involved the possession of zip ties (*HKSAR v. Chan Chun Kit*).

As there are many pending trials related to the Anti-ELAB Movement, it is important to wait and see how the verdicts and sentences might impact the criminal justice system, judicial independence, and the overall rule of law in Hong Kong. Nevertheless, given the introduction of a new national security law in Hong Kong by the SCNPC in 2020, the enjoyment of judicial autonomy and the agency of the courts to defend constitutional rights are perceived to be further restricted.

The New National Security Law: Securitizing Constitutional Review and Criminal Justice of Hong Kong's Court

In May 2020, the NPC decided to establish new legal institutions and enforcement agencies to safeguard national security in HKSAR, despite the fact that Article 23 of the Basic Law requires the SAR government to introduce local legislation on offences that endanger national security by itself. The new *Law of the People's Republic of China on Safeguarding National Security in the Hong Kong Special Administrative Region* (National Security Law, NSL) is a national law imposed by SCNPC, which was delegated by the NPC to draft and promulgate the law within a month. Civil society organizations, pro-democracy lawmakers, and the Hong Kong Bar Association were not given a chance to provide their opinions in advance, as the drafting process was not open to public and the SCNPC's consultation only included selected representatives. The NSL is an unprecedented institutional measure to impose a new legal architecture on Hong Kong's common law system (Chan 2021: 13–14).

During the drafting process, two issues related to the local judiciary arose. First, whether the CE can designate judges to deal with national security cases; second, whether the central authorities can exercise jurisdiction in Hong Kong in some exceptional cases. The first Hong Kong Chief Justice of the HKSAR, Andrew Li, publicly commented that the CE's power of designating judges would be "detrimental to the independence of the Judiciary," whereas defendants would be denied the safeguards of the local judicial process if the central authorities can request that local defendants be tried in Mainland courts, thus undermining the independent judicial power of Hong Kong courts (Cheung 2020a). Li's viewpoints were immediately rebutted by Zhang Yong, the Deputy Director of SCNPC's Legislative Affairs Commission. Zhang argued that judicial independence only refers to judges being free from any interference to exercise their powers independently in trials; it does not relate to issues of jurisdiction and the power of adjudication (Chung and Cheung 2020). Such a perspective, however, is incompatible with the common law principle and would further undermine Hong Kong's independent judiciary if the CE can handpick as well as prohibit some judges from trying national security cases, as stated by law professor Johannes Chan SC (Chan 2020a).

The question over upholding the conventional practices of judicial independence under NSL has yet to be solved, as the SCNPC decided to ignore the reservations of Andrew Li and went on to implement the law that criminalizes acts of subversion, secession, terrorism, and collusion with foreign forces or external elements. The new law also tightens control over the jurisdiction of the courts. Article 12 states that a Committee for Safeguarding National Security of HKSAR (CSNS) is established by the SAR government to oversee affairs related to safeguarding national security in Hong Kong and is accountable to the CPG. Headed by the CE and supervised by a Mainland official appointed by the central authorities, the CSNS is not subject to judicial review under Article 14. This provision unprecedentedly narrows the jurisdiction of local courts to review the constitutionality of decisions by CSNS.

Although Article 4 of NSL gives assurance to protections of rights and freedoms under the ICCPR and ICESCR, and Article 5 warrants presumption of innocence in trial, other provisions introduce new mechanisms in the judiciary and would create tensions with the rights to a fair trial and due process in conventional ways of proceeding in Hong Kong. Article 42 twists the principle of presumption of bail in criminal proceedings by declaring that no bail shall be granted to a defendant unless the judge has "sufficient grounds for believing that the defendant will not continue to commit acts endangering national security." Article 44 confirms the power of the CE to designate judges to handle national security cases, and any judge shall not be designated to take those cases if he/she "has made any statement or behaved in any manner endangering national security." Article 46 empowers the SJ to issue a certificate directing a national security case to be tried by a panel of three judges at the CFI instead of a jury, if the protection of state secrets, involvement of foreign factors in that case, and/or the protection of the personal safety of jurors and their families are concerned. Article 47 also gives power to the CE to issue a certificate to certify "whether an act involves national security" when such question arises in the adjudication of a trial, and the certificate has binding power on the courts. The courts are unable to defend a variety of rights prescribed in the BORO in national security cases as Article 62 declares that NSL prevails over local laws that are inconsistent with the NSL. Furthermore, under the schedules of the Implementation Rules of Article 43 of NSL, the law enforcement authorities can search places without a court warrant if the Assistant Commissioner of Police or other senior officers regard it as necessary; and the Secretary for Security can also freeze assets of anyone suspected of endangering national security prior to the CFI's review.

NSL also affirms the jurisdiction of the central authorities in the local national security regime. The Office for Safeguarding National Security of the Central People's Government (OSNS) is set up in Hong Kong under Article 49 and is subject to supervision under national supervisory authorities only in Article 50. Article 55 allows OSNS to exercise jurisdiction in Hong Kong under three conditions: (1) the case involves a foreign country or external elements, and hence it becomes difficult for local authorities to exercise jurisdiction over the case; (2) a serious situation arises where the local government fails to enforce NSL; and (3) a major and imminent threat to national security has happened. Article 56 further requests that, in the aforementioned circumstances, OSNS can investigate into the case, and a criminal suspect shall be prosecuted by the Supreme People's Procuratorate and then be tried by the Mainland's court designated by the Supreme People's Court. Last but not least, Article 65 asserts that the power of interpretation of NSL is vested in the SCNPC.

The implications of these new measures are threefold. First, the local judiciary is now subject to greater executive influences in operation, as the CE is empowered to designate judges to try national security cases, to certify any act as involving national security or state secrets, whereas the SJ is entitled to remove a jury trial from a national security case at the High Court. The Implementation Rules of NSL also widen the powers of the Security Bureau and the police to search for evidence and freeze assets without a court warrant. The autonomy of judges trying national security cases is much narrower than in ordinary criminal cases. Second, the establishment of CSNS and OSNS has become a substantial way to circumcise the functions of the judiciary, i.e., checking and limiting the executive power from acting ultra vires, as courts are barred from hearing judicial review cases concerning the constitutionality as well as the behavior of these new institutions. Third, under the above-stated exceptional scenarios, Mainland political/legal institutions can directly exercise jurisdiction in Hong Kong to handle national security cases, meaning that local courts, which are supposed to exercise full jurisdiction of adjudication of criminal cases in Hong Kong, will now be unable to try those cases.

Given the new powers bestowed on the executive branch of the government in the OSNS and judicial settings, as well as the power of Mainland agencies to take over national security cases, whether criminal suspects under NSL can be fairly tried by an independent judiciary in accordance with conventional common law practices in Hong Kong is still in doubt. Between July 2020 and December 2022, 227 political activists, candidates of pro-democracy camp's primaries for Legislative Council elections, journalists, and ordinary citizens were arrested for violating NSL; 135 of them were charged and 92 of these charged individuals were remanded in pretrial detention (*ChinaFile* 13 March 2023). On 30 July 2021, Tong Ying Kit, the defendant of the first national security trial, was convicted of inciting others to commit secession and of terrorist act, and was sentenced to nine years' imprisonment (Davidson 2021; Lai and Kellogg 2022). His case is also a precedent of trial without a jury under NSL (Kellogg and Lai 2021).

The process of diminishing jurisdiction of local courts continued in March 2021, when the SCNPC introduced drastic reforms to the composition and selection of the Election Committee and the Legislative Council elections of Hong Kong, to safeguard electoral security in the eyes of the central authorities. The most fundamental change to the electoral system is the introduction of a Candidate Eligibility Review Committee (CERC), which is headed by principal officials of the local government to validate nominations of candidates with reference to the investigation and reports from CSNS and the national security department of the Hong Kong police. Again, any nomination decisions made by CERC are immune from election petitions and judicial review by the courts (Lai 2021). Overall, both NSL and the election overhaul constitutes an establishment of a national security regime in Hong Kong's legal and political system, and the judiciary is unavoidably embedded in the new system and has compromised on the autonomy it enjoyed before. In light of this new judicial environment, four of the 14 foreign judges serving on the CFA (James Spigelman, Brenda Hale, Robert Reed, and Patrick Hodge), decided to resign. Although Spigelman and

Hale did not go public with their substantive reasons for leaving Hong Kong's court, they expressed their concerns on the content of NSL in other public occasions (Torode and Pandey 2020; Torode 2021). Reed and Hodge, as presiding judges at the Supreme Court of the UK, made a public statement to explain their resignations, stating that remaining on the court would be seen as an endorsement of Hong Kong's departure "from values of political freedom, and freedom of expression" (Lai 2022). Although the remaining foreign judges have declared that they would stay in the CFA, whether the departure of the four foreign judges from the CFA will affect the future appointment of foreign judges alongside the overall confidence of the rule of law and judicial independence in Hong Kong are worth noting.

Another noteworthy trend is the use of sedition law by national security authorities to criminalize individuals if they were considered to be acting out of "seditious intent." After the imposition of the NSL, the NSD redeployed the sedition law in the Crimes Ordinance that had been unused since the 1970s to charge activists, unionists, and civilians for making "seditious" speeches and publishing or disseminating "seditious" publications. Since the CFA considered sedition crimes to be part of the offences endangering national security in Hong Kong, the provision of bail under NSL becomes applicable to cases of sedition (*HKSAR v. Lai Chee Ying*; *HKSAR v. Ng Hau Yi Sidney*). For instance, in 2022, five unionists of the General Union of Hong Kong Speech Therapists were convicted of conspiracy to "printing, publishing, distributing or displaying seditious publication" for publishing a series of illustration books that allegedly promoted disaffection and hatred against the government and the courts. At the end of 2021, the sedition law was employed to criminalize two media outlets: *Stand News* and *Apple Daily*. Their former directors or owners were arrested, their editors were charged, and the companies' assets were frozen under the Implementation Rules for the NSD operation (Lai 2023a). As of October 2023, the trials against *Stand News* and *Apple Daily*, as well as appeal of the convicted speech therapist unionists above, had not yet completed. It will be important to observe how the courts rule in these cases in light of the right to free expression and free press following the HKSAR's commitment to international human rights protections under the Basic Law.

Conclusion

As legal scholars suggested, the "one country, two systems" formula for Hong Kong reveals a tension between the central and local authorities, as it tests whether a common law system can be accommodated within a socialist civil law system of the sovereign state and whether a liberal jurisdiction can survive within a nation embedded in socialist ideology (Chan, C 2019; Chan, 2019: 88).

In light of such tension, the judiciary in Hong Kong faces a dilemma. While the courts wish to regain trust from the sovereign state, which has a different notion of judicial independence and has adopted various measures to diminish judicial autonomy and jurisdiction of the local courts, any obvious dependence on the authority of the central authorities in adjudication may be seen as compromising judicial independence of the common law by the public, who may lose confidence in the judiciary. Although judges pledging allegiance to the nation-state and upholding an independent judiciary are not necessarily mutually exclusive, in the context of post-handover Hong Kong, the judiciary is sandwiched between the expectations of the central authorities and of the public, due to the fundamental differences of the understandings of the rule of law and judicial independence between the two jurisdictions.

After the enactment of the 2020 NSL, citizens have become less confident in the rule of law and judicial independence that have been vital in safeguarding free speech and peaceful political participation in Hong Kong. A public opinion survey from Path of Democracy, a local think tank founded by Ronny Tong, a member of the Executive Council of the HKSARG, illustrates that people's ranking of the independent judiciary in Hong Kong dropped from 4.52 (out of 10) in August 2019 to 4.00 in January 2021; the ranking of freedom of speech also declined from 4.80 in August 2019 to 3.92 in January 2021 (Path of Democracy March 2021, Figure 4.1). Other longitudinal surveys from Hong Kong Public Opinion Research Institute (PORI) also illustrate a significant decline of public confidence toward the rule of law and the judiciary 23 years after the handover. Public rating of the rule of law in Hong Kong has dropped from 6.9 out of 10 at the beginning of the handover to 4.5 in July 2021 (Hong Kong Public Opinion Research Institute 2021, Figure 4.2). Public appraisal of the degree of fairness of the judicial system decreased from 6.7 in July 1997 to 4.3 in February 2021, and impartiality of the courts from 6.9 in July 1997 to 4.4 in February 2021 (Hong Kong Public Opinion Research Institute 2021: Figures 4.3–4.4).

As of August 2023, several NSL cases have completed; either the defendants pleaded guilty or the court convicted them. Trial hearings of some famous NSL cases, such as the subversion case against participants of a citywide civil voting known as "pro-democracy camp's primaries," as well as the case of inciting subversion against organizers of the annual commemoration vigil for the June Fourth Incident are still ongoing (Lai 2023b). Furthermore, the SCNPC made its inaugural interpretation of the NSL in December 2022, empowering the CSNS to make judgments and decisions on the question of whether national security is involved, even if a judicial decision has been made, such as whether overseas lawyers without full qualification in the HKSAR could be legal representatives in cases related to offences endangering national security (China Law Translate 2022). Meanwhile, the court also made several rulings to deal with the tensions between implementing the NSL and enforcing the common law principles and practices in Hong Kong, such as the relationship between sentence reduction and guilty plea in NSL cases (*HKSAR v Lui Sai Yu*). In light of the rapidly changing legal and judicial environment of Hong Kong, it would be a crucial but challenging task for the judiciary and the governments of both HKSAR and PRC to rebuild public trust in the judiciary.

Table 1 : Index (A): Public Opinion
表 1：指數（A）：民意調查

	2019.8	2019.10	2019.12	2020.6	2021.1	
Average 平均分	3.98	3.26	3.53	3.39	3.37	
Original ways of life 原有生活方式	5.34	4.28	4.55	4.39	4.41	
Independent judiciary 獨立司法權	4.52	3.93	4.27	4.16	4.00	
Freedom of speech 言論自由	4.8	4.04	4.36	4.04	3.92	
Independent legislature 獨立立法權	4.21	3.34	3.75	3.71	3.62	
Self-conduct of administrative affairs 自行處理行政事務	3.98	3.31	3.49	3.40	3.34	
Democratisation 民主政制發展	3.61	2.90	3.21	3.08	3.01	
'Hong Kong people administering Hong Kong' and 'high degree of autonomy' principles 「港人治港、高度自治」原則	3.48	2.78	2.99	2.82	2.77	
Full implementation of 1C2S 全面落實「一國兩制」	2.95	2.30	2.53	2.37	2.70	*
Resolving differences via dialogue and negotiation 對話協商解決矛盾	2.9	2.46	2.63	2.53	2.59	

Figure 4.1: Path of Democracy's "one country, two system" index

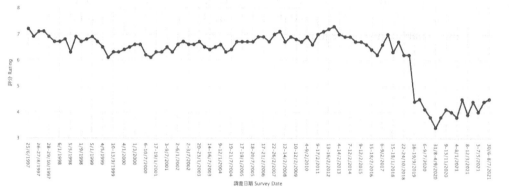

Figure 4.2: PORI's appraisal of degree of compliance with the rule of law (6/1997–7/2021)

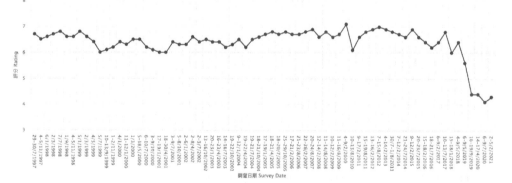

Figure 4.3: PORI's appraisal of degree of fairness of the judicial system (6/1997–2/2021)

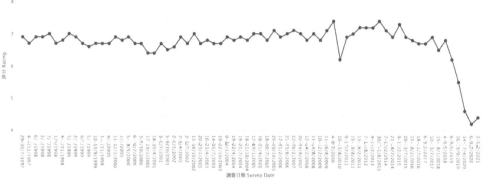

Figure 4.4: PORI's appraisal of degree of impartiality of the courts (6/1997–2/2021)

Box 4.1: Judicial independence

The judiciary is independent from the executive authorities, legislature, and all external bodies so that it can make decisions impartially. To ensure judicial independence, the procedure to appoint, promote, and dismiss judges must also be protected from external influence. The terms of service of judges must be secure and attractive enough to discourage corruption or pressure. The judiciary also needs to have financial autonomy to maintain its integrity.

Box 4.2: Common law

Common law is a legal method and a set of principles and values developed by the British courts. The legal method is to rely on precedents and adversarial procedures of adjudication. The principles cannot be summarized in a few sentences, but values such as the rule of law, individual rights, fair procedure, and equity are incorporated into common law. Common law has been exported to many other legal systems, where modifications to the method and values of common law have evolved and developed.

102   The Judiciary

Box 4.3: National People's Congress and the Standing Committee of the National People's Congress

The National People's Congress (NPC) is the highest constitutional organ in the People's Republic of China. Executive, legislative, and judicial powers all originate from the NPC. The term of the NPC is five years, and it meets annually. Only the NPC has the power to amend the Basic Law. The Standing Committee of the National People's Congress (SCNPC) exercises various powers when the NPC is not in session. It has the power to interpret laws, including the Basic Law. It can return any law enacted in the HKSAR if it considers the law is in contravention of certain provisions of the Basic Law. National laws can also be made applicable to the HKSAR by the SCNPC, such as the National Security Law of 2020. It can also propose an amendment to the Basic Law.

Note: The boxes are adapted from Tai, BYT 2012, "The Judiciary," in WM Lam, PLT Lui and W Wong (eds), *Contemporary Hong Kong Government and Politics*, Expanded Second Edition, Hong Kong University Press, Hong Kong.

Questions

1. What is the relationship between the rule of law and judicial independence?
2. How does the Basic Law realize the principle of judicial independence?
3. What kind of impact does the power of interpretation of the Basic Law by the SCNPC have on judicial autonomy in the HKSAR?
4. How does the new National Security Law change the conventional practices of the judicial system in Hong Kong?
5. What is the prospect for judicial independence in the HKSAR?

Bibliography

Bauhinia Foundation Research Centre 2019, *Survey on Public Perceptions towards the Rule of Law in Hong Kong* (18 December), http://www.bauhinia.org/index.php/english/research/106, viewed 9 July 2020.

Chan, C 2019, "Thirty Years since Tiananmen: China, Hong Kong, and the Ongoing Experiment to Preserve Liberal Values in an Authoritarian State," *International Journal of Constitutional Law*, vol. 17, pp. 439–452.

Chan, J 2007, "Basic Law and Constitutional Review: The First Decade," *Hong Kong Law Journal*, vol. 37, no. 2, pp. 407–447.

Chan, J 2015, "Human Rights, the Rule of Law and Democracy: Recent Experience of Hong Kong and China," University of Hong Kong Faculty of Law Research Paper No. 2015/039, https://ssrn.com/abstract=2641332

Chan, J 2018, "A Storm of Unprecedented Ferocity: The Shrinking Space of the Right to Political Participation, Peaceful Demonstration, and Judicial Independence in Hong Kong," *International Journal of Constitutional Law*, vol. 16, no. 2, pp. 373–388.

Chan, J 2019, "A Shrinking Space: A Dynamic Relationship between the Judiciary in a Liberal Society of Hong Kong and a Socialist-Leninist Sovereign State," *Current Legal Problems*, vol. 72, no.1, pp. 85–122.

Chan, J 2020a, "National Security and Judicial Independence: A Response," *HKU Legal Scholarship Blog*, last updated 30 July 2020, https://researchblog.law.hku.hk/2020/07/johannes-chan-on-national-security-and.html.

Chan, J 2020b, "Reconciliation of the NPCSC's Power of Interpretation of the Basic Law with the Common Law in the HKSAR," *Hong Kong Law Journal*, vol. 50, part 2, pp. 657–684.

Chan, J 2021, "Judicial Responses to the National Security Law: HKSAR v Lai Chee Ying," *Hong Kong Law Journal*, vol. 51, part 1, pp. 1–14.

Chan, J, Lai, EYH & Kellogg, TK 2023, *The Hong Kong 2019 Protest Movement: A Data Analysis of Arrests and Prosecutions*, Center for Asian Law, Georgetown University Law Center, Washington DC.

Chan, K (ed) 2019, *A Trial of Love and Peace: Statements of the Umbrella Movement* (審判愛與和平: 雨傘運動陳詞), Step Forward Multimedia, Hong Kong.

ChinaFile 2023, "Tracking the Impacts of Hong Kong's National Security Law," last updated 13 March 2023, https://www.chinafile.com/tracking-impact-of-hong-kongs-national-security-law

China Law Translate 2023, "Interpretation by the Standing Committee of the National People's Congress of Article 14 and Article 47 of the PRC Law on Safeguarding National Security in the Hong Kong Special Administrative Region," *China Law Translate*, last updated 30 December 2022, https://www.chinalawtranslate.com/en/18902-2

Chung, K & Cheung, G 2020, "Judges with 'Dual Allegiance' Because of Foreign Nationality Should Not Handle National Security Cases, Beijing Says," *South China Morning Post*, last updated 24 June 2020, https://www.scmp.com/news/hong-kong/politics/article/3090400/hong-kong-national-security-law-citys-leader-must-have

Cheung, ABL & Wong, MW 2006, "Judicial Review and Policy Making in Hong Kong: Changing Interface between the Legal and the Political," *Asia Pacific Journal of Public Administration*, vol. 28, no. 2, pp. 117–141.

Cheung, G 2020a, "Hong Kong National Security Law: Former Chief Justice Expresses Concern over Provisions of Legislation," *South China Morning Post*, last updated 23 June 2020, https://www.scmp.com/news/hong-kong/politics/article/3090120/hong-kong-national-security-law-former-chief-justice

Cheung, G 2020b, "The Co-location Arrangement of the Guangzhou-Shenzhen-Hong Kong Express Rail Link," The Division of Public Policy, Institute for Public Policy, and Leadership and Public Policy Executive Education at the Hong Kong University of Science and Technology, viewed 12 August 2021, https://ppol.ust.hk/public_uploads/2020011C_Co_location_Arrangeme.pdf

Davis, M 2015, "The Basic Law, Universal Suffrage and the Rule of Law in Hong Kong," *Hasting International and Comparative Law Review*, vol. 38, no. 2, pp. 275–298.

Davis, M 2020, *Making Hong Kong China: The Rollback of Human Rights and the Rule of Law*, Association for Asian Studies, Michigan.

Davidson, H 2021, "Hong Kong Jails Man, 24, for Nine Years under National Security Law," *Guardian*, last updated 30 July 2021, https://www.theguardian.com/world/2021/jul/30/hong-kong-jails-man-24-nine-years-under-national-security-law-tong-ying-kit

Diamond, L & Morlino, L 2015, "The Quality of Democracy," in L Diamond (ed), *In Search of Democracy*, Routledge, New York, pp. 33–45.

Dicey, AV 1915 [1885], *Introduction to the Study of the Law of the Constitution*, Liberty Classics, UK.

Dykes, PJ 2020, "Speech Given at the Opening of the Legal Year by the Chairman of the Hong Kong Bar Association," *Hong Kong Bar Association*, last updated 13 January 2020, https://www.hkba.org/uploads/20200113%20-%20Speech%20of%20Chairman%20at%20Opening%20of%20Legal%20Year%202020%20(Eng).pdf

Ernst, F 1941, *The Dual State: A Contribution to the Theory of Dictatorship*, Oxford University Press, New York.

Hong Kong Bar Association 2014, "Response of the Hong Kong Bar Association: White Paper on the Practice of 'One Country, Two Systems' Policy in the Hong Kong Special Administrative Region" dated 11 June 2014, https://www.hkba.org/sites/default/files/White_Paper_Response_eng_0.pdf

Hong Kong Public Opinion Research Institute 2021, "The Rule of Law, Fairness of the Judicial System, Impartiality of the Courts – Combined Charts," https://www.pori.hk/pop-poll/rule-law-indicators-en/g-combined.html?lang=en

Huang, J 2017, "Critics: Hong Kong Sets Bad Precedent with Mainland Police in Rail Station," *Voice of America*, last updated 28 July 2017, https://www.voanews.com/a/hong-kong-mainland-police-high-speed-rail/3962653.html

Human Rights Watch 2018, "Hong Kong: Student Leaders' Sentences Overturned," last updated 6 February 2018, https://www.hrw.org/news/2018/02/06/hong-kong-student-leaders-sentences-overturned

Jiang, S 2015, "Jurisdiction in 'Peaceful Revolution': From the Case of Ma Wai Kwan and Ng Ka Ning to the Struggle of Judicial Sovereignty under the Transformation of Constitutional Order" (「和平革命」中的司法管轄權：從「馬維騉案」和「吳嘉玲案」談香港憲政秩序轉型中的司法主權之爭), in AHY Chen and PX Zhou (eds), *Multiple Facets of the Hong Kong Basic Law* (香港基本法面面觀), Joint Publishing, Hong Kong, pp. 151–188.

Jones, C 2006, "Politics Postponed: Law as a Substitute for Politics in Hong Kong and China," in K Jayasuriya (ed), *Law, Capitalism and Power in Asia: The Rule of Law and Legal Institutions*, Routledge, London, and New York.

Kellogg, TE & Lai, EYH 2021, "Death by a Thousand Cuts: Chipping Away at Due Process Rights in HK NSL Cases," *Lawfare*, last updated 28 May 2021, https://www.lawfare-blog.com/death-thousand-cuts-chipping-away-due-process-rights-hk-nsl-cases

Kong, K 2012 "Adjudicating Social Welfare Rights in Hong Kong," *International Journal of Constitutional Law*, vol. 10, no. 2, pp. 588–599.

Ku, A 2007, "Constructing and Contesting the 'Order' Imagery in Media Discourse: Implications for Civil Society in Hong Kong," *Asian Journal of Communication*, vol. 17, no. 2, pp. 186–200.

Ku, A 2017, "From Civil Disobedience to Institutional Politics: Conflict over the Public Order Ordinance in 2000," in MHK Ng and JD Wong (eds), *Civil Unrest and Governance in Hong Kong: Law and Order from Historical and Cultural Perspectives*, Routledge, New York, pp. 163–178.

Lai, E (YH) 2021, "Ask the Experts: Has Democracy in Hong Kong Come to an End?," *China Dialogues, LSE*, last updated 26 May 2021, https://blogs.lse.ac.uk/cff/2021/05/26/ask-the-experts-has-democracy-in-hong-kong-come-to-an-end

Lai, YH 2022, "Hong Kong: British Judges Leaving Top Court is a Strong Condemnation of the End of Civil Liberties," *Conversation*, last updated 4 April 2022, https://theconversation.com/hong-kong-british-judges-leaving-top-court-is-a-strong-condemnation-of-the-end-of-civil-liberties-180375

Lai, YH 2023a, "Securitisation or Autocratisation? Hong Kong's Rule of Law under the Shadow of China's Authoritarian Governance," *Journal of Asian and African Studies*, vol. 58, issue 1, pp. 8–25.

Lai, E (YH) 2023b, "Hong Kong's Democratic Primary Trials Show a Dark Truth," *Diplomat*, last updated 4 February 2023, https://thediplomat.com/2023/02/hong-kongs-democratic-primary-trials-show-a-dark-truth

Lai, YH & Kellogg, TK 2022, "Departure from International Human Rights Law and Comparative Best Practice: HKSAR v Tong Ying Kit," *Hong Kong Law Journal*, vol. 52, part. 2, pp. 466–486.

Lam, CY 2020, "Beijing Takes Action to Implement Patriots Administering Hong Kong, Rejecting Separation of Powers and Targeting the Judiciary," *Central News Agency (CAN)*, last updated 23 November 2020, https://www.cna.com.tw/news/acn/202011230122.aspx

Lee, FLF, Yuen, S, Tang, G & Cheng, E 2019, "Hong Kong's Summer Uprising: From Anti-Extradition to Anti-Authoritarian Protests," *China Review*, vol. 19, no. 4, pp. 1–32.

Li, R 2013, "Seven Subjects off Limits for Teaching, Chinese Universities Told," *South China Morning Post*, last updated 10 May 2013, https://www.scmp.com/news/china/article/1234453/seven-subjects-limits-teaching-chinese-universities-told

Linz, JJ & Stepan, A 1996, *Problems of Democratic Transition and Consolidation—Southern Europe, South America, and Post-Communist Europe*, the Johns Hopkins University Press, Maryland.

Ma, N 2020, *The Resistant Community* (反抗的共同體), Rive Gauche Publishing House, Taiwan.

Munn, C 2009, *Anglo-China: Chinese People and British Rule in Hong Kong, 1841–1880*, Hong Kong University Press, Hong Kong.

Munn, C 2017, "Our Best Trump Card': A Brief History of Deportation in Hong Kong 1857–1955," in MHK Ng and JD Wong (eds), *Civil Unrest and Governance in Hong Kong: Law and Order from Historical and Cultural Perspectives*, Routledge, New York, pp. 26–45.

Munn, C 2019, *A Special Standing in the World: The Faculty of Law at the University of Hong Kong, 1969–2019*, Hong Kong University Press, Hong Kong.

Myers, SL 2019, "In Warning to Hong Kong's Courts, China Shows Who Is Boss," *New York Times*, last updated 20 November 2019, https://www.nytimes.com/2019/11/20/world/asia/hong-kong-protests-china-courts.html

Ng, E 2017a, "China's Top Legislature Approves Joint Checkpoint Plan; Says It Complies with Hong Kong Constitution," *Hong Kong Free Press*, 27 December 2017, https://www.hongkongfp.com/2017/12/27/chinas-top-legislature-approves-joint-checkpoint-plan-says-complies-hong-kong-constitution

Ng, E 2017b, "Beijing's 'Distortion' of Hong Kong Basic Law Greatly Undermines Rule of Law, Legal Experts Warn," *Hong Kong Free Press*, 28 December 2017, https://hongkongfp.com/2017/12/28/beijings-distortion-hong-kong-basic-law-greatly-undermines-rule-law-legal-experts-warn

Ng, HKM 2016, "Rule of law in Hong Kong History Demythologised: Student Umbrella Movement of 1919," *Hong Kong Law Journal*, vol. 46, no. 3, pp. 829–848.

Ng, HKM 2017, "When Silence Speaks: Press Censorship and Rule of Law in British Hong Kong (1850s–1940s)," *Law and Literature*, vol. 29, issue 3, pp. 425–456.

Ng, J 2014, "Law Society President Ambrose Lam Resigns after Historic No-Confidence Vote," *South China Morning Post*, 19 August 2014, https://www.scmp.com/news/hong-kong/article/1576791/law-society-president-ambrose-lam-resigns-following-historic-no

Ng, K 2021, "Hong Kong Protests: More Than 10,200 Arrested in Connection with Unrest Since 2019, Government Tells Lawmakers," *South China Morning Post*, last updated 9 April 2021, https://www.scmp.com/news/hong-kong/politics/article/3128836/hong-kong-protests-more-10200-arrested-connection-unrest

Norton-kyshe, JW 1971, *The History of the Laws and Courts of Hong Kong from the Earliest Period to 1898*, 2 vols., Vetch and Lee, Hong Kong.

O'Donnell, GA 2004, "Why the Rule of Law Matters," *Journal of Democracy*, vol. 15, no. 4, pp. 32–46.

Path of Democracy 2021, *"One Country, Two Systems" Index*, March 2021, http://pathof-democracy.hk/wp-content/uploads/2021/05/PoD_Index_2021_March_online.pdf

Puja, K 2011, "A Principled Approach towards Judicial Review: Lessons from *W v Registrar of Marriages*," *Hong Kong Law Journal*, vol. 41, pp. 49–74.

Reuters 2017, "China's Top Judge Warns Courts on Judicial Independence," *Reuters*, last updated 16 January 2017, https://www.reuters.com/article/us-china-policy-law-idUSKBN1500OF

So, P 2014, "Judges Don't Need to Be Patriots, Says Former Top Judge Andrew Li," *South China Morning Post*, last updated 15 August 2014, https://www.scmp.com/news/hong-kong/article/1573867/judges-dont-need-be-patriots-andrew-li

Standard 2021, "Legco Rioting Case Set for Trial in May 2023," *Standard*, last updated 26 March 2021, https://www.thestandard.com.hk/breaking-news/section/4/168348/Legco-rioting-case-set-for-trial-in-May-2023

Standing Committee of the National People's Congress of the People's Republic of China 2016, "Interpretation of Article 104 of the Basic Law of the Hong Kong Special Administrative Region of the People's Republic of China by the Standing Committee of the National People's Congress," dated 7 November 2016, https://www.basiclaw.gov.hk/en/basiclawtext/images/basiclawtext_doc27.pdf

State Council of the People's Republic of China 2014, *White Paper on the Practice of the "One Country, Two Systems" Policy in the Hong Kong Special Administrative Region*, dated 10 June 2014, http://www.fmcoprc.gov.hk/eng/xwdt/gsxw/t1164057.htm

Steger, I 2016, "Beijing Is Determined to Keep Defiant, Pro-independence Lawmakers out of Hong Kong's Legislature," *Quartz*, last updated 19 October 2016, https://qz.com/812500/hong-kongs-government-and-beijing-are-determined-to-kick-pro-independence-lawmakers-out-of-the-legislature

Strait Times 2016, "Hong Kong Lawyers March in Silence to Condemn China's Interpretation of Basic Law," *Strait Times*, 8 November 2016, https://www.straitstimes.com/asia/east-asia/hong-kong-lawyers-march-in-silence-to-condemn-chinas-interpretation-of-basic-law

Tai, BYT 2002, "Chapter 1 of Hong Kong's New Constitution: Constitutional Positioning and Repositioning," in MK Chan and AY So (eds), *Crisis and Transformation in China's Hong Kong*, Hong Kong University Press, Hong Kong.

Tai, BYT 2012, "The Judiciary," in WM Lam, PLT Lui, and W Wong (eds), *Contemporary Hong Kong Government and Politics*, Expanded Second Edition, Hong Kong University Press, Hong Kong.

Tai, BYT 2017, "Civil Disobedience and the Rule of Law," in MHK Ng and JD Wong, (eds) *Civil Unrest and Governance in Hong Kong: Law and Order from Historical and Cultural Perspectives*, Routledge, New York, pp. 141–162.

Tai, BYT 2021, "Authoritarian Rule of Law in Hong Kong," in BC Jones(ed) *Democracy and Rule of Law in China's Shadow*, Hart Publishing, Oxford, pp. 149–178.

Tam, WK 2012, *Legal Mobilization under Authoritarianism: The Case of Post-Colonial Hong Kong*, Cambridge University Press.

Tamanaha, BZ 2004, *On the Rule of Law: History, Politics, Theory*, Cambridge University Press, Cambridge.

Thompson, EP 1975, *Whigs and Hunters: The Origin of the Black Act*, Penguin Books, UK.

Ting, V 2019, "As Hong Kong Protests Rage On, Barristers Hit Back at Beijing's Comments on the City's Judiciary and Its Responsibilities," *South China Morning Post*, last updated 9 November 2019, https://www.scmp.com/news/hong-kong/politics/article/3037054/hong-kong-protests-rage-barristers-hit-back-beijings

Tong, E 2017, "'Basic Law Doesn't Define Hong Kong's Borders': Justice Sec. Defends Mainland Rail Checkpoint," *Hong Kong Free Press*, last updated 25 July 2017, https://hongkongfp.com/2017/07/25/basic-law-doesnt-define-hong-kongs-borders-justice-chief-defends-mainland-rail-checkpoint

Torode, G 2021, "Hong Kong Judiciary Says British Judge to Step Down from City's Top Court," *Reuters*, last updated 4 June 2021, https://www.reuters.com/world/china/hong-kong-judiciary-says-british-judge-step-down-citys-top-court-2021-06-04

Torode, G and Pandey, S 2020, "Australian Judge Quits Hong Kong Court, Citing National Security Law," *Reuters*, last updated 18 September 2020, https://www.reuters.com/article/us-hongkong-security-judges-australian-judge-quits-hong-kong-court-citing-national-security-law-idUSKBN26912R

Trevaskes, S 2019, "Socialist Law," in C Sorace, I Franceschini and N Loubere (eds) *Afterlives of Chinese Communism: Political Concepts from Mao to Xi*, ANU Press and Verso Books, pp. 251–256.

108   The Judiciary

Tsang, S 2004, *A Modern History of Hong Kong*, Hong Kong University Press, Hong Kong.

UN Secretary-General 2009, "Guidance Note of the Secretary-General on Democracy," *United Nations*, viewed 2 November 2021, https://www.ohchr.org/Documents/Issues/RuleOfLaw/UNSGGuidance_Note_Democracy-EN.pdf

Wong, MWL 2017, *Re-ordering Hong Kong: Decolonisation and the Hong Kong Bill of Rights Ordinance*, Wildy, Simmonds and Hill Publishing, UK.

Wong, MWL 2020, *Chinese Marriage and Social Change: The Legal Abolition of Concubinage in Hong Kong*, Springer, Singapore.

World Justice Project 2021, *WJP Rule of Law Index 2021*, viewed 2 November 2021, https://worldjusticeproject.org/sites/default/files/documents/WJP-INDEX-21.pdf

Yap, PJ 2007, "Constitutional Review under the Basic Law: The Rise, Retreat and Resurgence of Judicial Power in Hong Kong," *Hong Kong Law Journal*, vol. 37, part 2, pp. 449–474.

Case Law

Ng Ka Ling and another v. The Director of Immigration (1999) 2 HKCFAR 4

Ng Ka Ling and another v. The Director of Immigration (1999) 2 HKCFAR 141

Leung Lai Kwok Yvonne v. The Chief Secretary for Administration and Others (unreported, HCAL 31/2015, 5 June 2015, Hon Au J)

Chief Executive of HKSAR v. President of Legislative Council (unreported, HCAL 185/2016, 15 November 2016, Hon Au J)

Chief Executive of HKSAR v. President of Legislative Council [2017] 1 HKLRD 460

Secretary for Justice v. Nathan Law Kwun Chung [2017] 4 HKLRD 115

Secretary for Justice v. Leung Kwok Hung [2019] HKCA 173

Yau Wai Ching v. Chief Executive of the HKSAR (2017) 20 HKCFAR 390

Leung Chung Hang, Sixtus v. President of Legislative Council & Secretary for Justice [2019] 1 HKLRD 292

Kwok Cheuk Kin v. Secretary for Justice [2021] 3 HKLRD 140

Yeung Tsz Chun v. Commissioner of Police [2020] 5 HKLRD 653

HKSAR v. Wong Chi Fung, Lam Long Yin, and Agnes Chow [2020] HKMagC 16

HKSAR v. Tai Yiu Ting and others [2021] 2 HKLRD 899

香港特別行政區 訴 余德穎及另七人 [2020] HKDC 992

HKSAR v. Lo Kin Man (2021) 24 HKCFAR 302

HKSAR v. Lai Chee Ying (2021) 24 HKCFAR 33

HKSAR v. Lui Sai Yu (2023) HKCFA 26

HKSAR v. Ng Hau Yi Sidney (2021) 24 HKCFAR 417

HKSAR v. Chan Chun Kit (2022) 25 HKCFAR 191

Useful Websites

HKU Legal Scholarship Blog
https://researchblog.law.hku.hk/

Hong Kong Judiciary
https://www.judiciary.hk/en/home/index.html

Hong Kong Public Opinion Research Institute Rule of Law Indicators
https://www.pori.hk/pop-poll/rule-law-indicators.html?lang=en

Implementation Rules for Article 43 of the Law of the People's Republic of China on Safeguarding National Security in the Hong Kong Special Administrative Region
https://www.elegislation.gov.hk/hk/A406A!en

International Covenant on Civil and Political Rights (ICCPR)
https://www.ohchr.org/en/professionalinterest/pages/ccpr.aspx

International Covenant on Economic, Social and Cultural Rights (ICESCR)
https://www.ohchr.org/en/professionalinterest/pages/cescr.aspx

The Basic Law of the Hong Kong Special Administrative Region of the People's Republic of China
https://www.basiclaw.gov.hk/en/basiclaw/index.html

The Hong Kong Bar Association
https://www.hkba.org/

The Law Society of Hong Kong
https://www.hklawsoc.org.hk/

The Law of the People's Republic of China on Safeguarding National Security in the Hong Kong Special Administrative Region
https://www.elegislation.gov.hk/fwddoc/hk/a406/eng_translation_(a406)_en.pdf

World Justice Project Rule of Law Index
https://worldjusticeproject.org/our-work/wjp-rule-law-index

Further Reading

Chan, C & de Londras, F (eds) 2020, *China's National Security: Endangering Hong Kong's Rule of Law?* Hart Publishing, Oxford. This edited volume provides multiple perspectives of institutionalizing the national security regime in Hong Kong.

Chan, J 2022, "National Security Law in Hong Kong: One Year On," *Academia Sinica Law Journal*, 2022 Special Issue, pp. 39–101. This article provides a comprehensive account of the constitutional, legal, and social impact of the new National Security Law in the HKSAR, and its effects on the "one country, two systems" constitutional model in the HKSAR.

Chan, J & Lim, CL (eds) 2021, *Law of the Hong Kong Constitution*, 3rd Edition, Sweet & Maxwell, Hong Kong. This edited volume introduces the implementation of the PRC-HKSAR constitutional order and protections of various human rights in accordance with international human rights treaties in Hong Kong since the handover.

Chan, JMM, Fu, HL & Yash, G (eds) 2000, *Hong Kong's Constitutional Debate: Conflict Over Interpretation*, Hong Kong University Press, Hong Kong. This edited volume discusses the legal and constitutional consequences of the first SCNPC's interpretation of the Basic Law provisions in 1999.

Chen, AHY 2021, *The Changing Legal Orders in Hong Kong and Mainland China: Essays On "One Country, Two Systems,"* City University of Hong Kong Press, Hong Kong. This monograph is a collection of Albert Chen's writings on the "one country, two systems" of Hong Kong and its constitutional relationship with the PRC in recent years.

Davis, MC 2024, *Freedom Undone: The Assault on Liberal Values and Institutions in Hong Kong*, Association for Asian Studies, Michigan. This is the latest monograph that explains how liberal constitutional institutions of separation of powers that provide legal checks and public accountability are undone in the case of post-handover Hong Kong.

Fu, HL & Hor, M (eds) 2022, *The National Security Law of Hong Kong: Restoration and Transformation*, Hong Kong University Press, Hong Kong. This is the latest edited volume that comprehensively examines the laws and practices of the new National Security Law in Hong Kong in light of international and comparative best practices.

5

The Civil Service

Institutional Conscience, Politicization, and Capacity-Building

Wilson Wong

The civil service, a critical component of all modern governments, plays an extraordinarily important role in the politics and governance of Hong Kong (Burns 2004; Cheung 1998; Miners 1998; Scott 2010). Different from its counterparts in Western democracies, it is responsible for much more than policy advice and implementation. Many senior civil servants, particularly administrative officers, are policymakers with substantial power and influence. Two of the four Chief Executives (CEs) in Hong Kong and many principal officers are former civil servants.

Before 1997, the Hong Kong political system was designed by the British colonial regime to be not only executive-led, but also bureaucrat-dominated. After the 1997 handover, however, the governing role of the civil service is challenged by many changes. The power of bureaucrats has been checked by the rise of two opposing forces: political control by business interests, the pro-establishment camp, and the Central People's Government (CPG) on the one hand and the demand for a more democratic and efficient administration from citizens on the other hand. For the former, politicization of the civil service through mechanisms such as the Accountability System for Principal Officials (ASPO) and the new requirement of oath-taking are major means to reduce the influence and autonomy of the civil service especially after 2020 (Wong and Yuen 2022). Structurally, the civil service has also been subject to New Public Management (NPM) reforms based on the private sector model, undermining many of its traditional strengths and core values.

Senior civil servants in general and administrative officers (AOs) specifically are still given a major role in governance, but they must adjust to the new political environment of shared power, cope with conflicting forces of public accountability and political control, and develop new capacities associated with the progress and further development of Hong Kong. This chapter examines the changing role of the civil service in the governance of Hong Kong in the post-1997 era, including a focus on the post-2020 paradigm with the recent sociopolitical development. It first examines the special role of the civil service in the governance of Hong Kong. Then, it looks at structural and systemic features of the civil service and discusses how they contribute to its function of institutional conscience for the public interest. Finally, it examines how changes and reforms, including politicization and the new environment under the National Security Law (NSL), affect the autonomy and role of the civil service and underscore the need for developing new capacities.

The British Colonial Legacy: Pure Administrative State

Before 1997, civil servants occupied a very unusual and highly important role in the governance of Hong Kong. Without democracy, senior officials were not simply public servants; they were actually the masters of the colonial political system (Cheung 1998; Lau 1987). Until democratization reforms were introduced in the 1980s, Hong Kong was ruled mainly by civil servants. With the exception of Chris Patten, the 28th and also the last governor of Hong Kong (1992–1997), the governors themselves were civil servants of the British system. The political system in the colonial period was basically made up of four key institutions or actors: the governor, the civil service, the Executive Council (ExCo), and the Legislative Council (LegCo). The civil service was a key part of this system (Box 5.1). Like the ExCo of the HKSAR, the colonial ExCo was mostly advisory in nature. Although the governor was constitutionally required to consult the ExCo on all important matters, he was never obligated to follow its majority opinion (Miners 1998: 74–75). The LegCo often served as little more than a rubber stamp, as the governor held the ultimate power of appointment.

Under the leadership of the governor, many major policy decisions were formulated by civil servants who served as policy secretaries. It was obvious that the political system was actually a bureaucrat-dominated system with only bureaucrats and no politicians. The absence of "politics" was often taken as one of the major characteristics of the politics of Hong Kong in the colonial era. Pre-1997 Hong Kong was often described as a "pure administrative state"—a state with only administration but no "politics" (Harris 1988)—or a "bureaucratic polity"—a political system run mainly by bureaucrats (Lau 1982). In effect, it was a liberal government under an authoritarian system, or a form of "soft authoritarianism" (So and Chan 2002). The function of the pure administrative state was to replace democracy so as to reduce the demand for democratization (Wong 2004).

One of the key objectives of the Basic Law drafters was to preserve the features of the British colonial government as much as possible to maintain the stability and advantages of the system after the handover (Ghai 1999). In the formal system prescribed by the Basic Law, most of the power is still concentrated in the hands of the CE and the executive branch headed by him/her, which is called an "executive-led system," and this has become one of the major features that the CPG has strongly defended in the political development of post-1997 Hong Kong. Therefore, the use of bureaucracy to replace or delay democratization has been a major feature of the governance of Hong Kong, not only in the pre-1997 era but also in the post-1997 era.

Despite the transfer of sovereignty and the related challenges, it is argued that the civil service is still one of the powerful actors in the post-1997 era. It is true that the influence of the civil service has been undermined by the rise of new policy actors such as the business tycoons, pro-Beijing forces or the CPG itself, and other social forces, but civil servants continue to maintain a significant political position. First, "business-politicians" or politicians without a civil service background are still greatly outnumbered by civil servants in the government apparatus. Before the political appointment system was introduced, the CE, as an "outsider" in government, often found himself incapable of mastering the entire bureaucracy with the help of just a few advisors in his office and the ExCo. Even after the further development of the political accountability system, the number of political appointees is still a small figure, and they could not replace civil servants at every major layer of government to perform all the essential functions of governance. Besides, without a full democracy, much of the decision-making power is still reserved inside the bureaucracy. Owing to their valuable expertise and experience, civil servants are often irreplaceable in policymaking, which can be indicated by the fact that former civil servants are still occupying many key positions among principal officials or even serving as the CE.

Administrative grade: Replacing democracy with bureaucracy

For the CPG, an administrative state model is an attractive option for governing post-1997 Hong Kong. With memories of the British colonial legacy in mind, it is often believed by both Chinese officials and many citizens in Hong Kong that one of its most appealing strengths is being capable of governing an active civil society and an advanced economy, with good protection of freedoms and rights. All this is done under an authoritarian political structure, where formal constitutional power and the ultimate right of intervention is reserved by the bureaucrat-dominated government as self-restraint becomes the major check on its power. In other words, under the administrative state model, the British successfully replaced democracy with bureaucracy in the sense that a closed, elitist, and hierarchical bureaucratic system could deliver similar policy outputs to a democratic system (Wong 2004 and 2013).

In the administrative state model, the key policymakers are AOs. Bureaucracy (Box 5.2) is a very hierarchical organizational structure, and not all civil servants are equal. AO is a grade in the civil service—the most elitist and superior group. In the government structure, there are two layers of organization: policymaking bureaus and executive departments. Executive departments, responsible for implementing the policies set by the bureaus, are grouped under their related bureaus. For example, the Customs and Excise Department, the Hong Kong Police Force, the Fire Services Department, the Immigration Department, and the Correctional Services Department, are all grouped logically under the Security Bureau. Under the administrative-officer-dominated administrative state model, the AOs occupy all major policymaking positions, except those political appointments, in a policy bureau. The AOs also head many of the departments under the bureaus.

Like other grades in the civil service, the AO grade is in general a closed system in which there is little built-in lateral entry and no formal bridging system from other grades. Advocated by the Civil Service Reform (1999), in 2001, a direct recruitment exercise at the rank of Senior Administrative Officer (SAO) was introduced for the AO grade. However, due to fierce opposition from the AO grade and other reasons, the outcome of the recruitment was not satisfactory, with only four candidates being selected (Burns 2004: 139). No further exercise of open recruitment at the nonentry level has been conducted since then. With limited lateral entry, most AOs are recruited at the entry level and then promoted to the senior ranks (Box 5.3).

In theory, there is "in-service recruitment" for the AO grade, to which the officers in other grades may apply. However, it may not be taken as a real "bridging" system because officers in other grades applying through "in-service recruitment" can only be exempted from part of the written examination (Burns 2004: 120–121). Like the external candidates outside the government, in-service applicants still have to go through most of the selection process and be evaluated independently by the selection panel, made up mostly of AOs themselves. Bridging among different grades is also uncommon and difficult. Even though such a mechanism does exist, bridging is usually only allowed under special and restricted conditions and operates on a limited scale. As of 31 March 2022, there were a total of 747 AOs and seven ranks or levels of hierarchy in the grade (Table 5.1).

Table 5.1: Administrative Officer Grade: Grade structure and establishment

The Administrative Officer Grade comprises the following seven ranks, and the establishment as of 31 March 2022 is as follows:

Rank	Number of Posts*
Administrative Officer Staff Grade A1 (D8)	19
Administrative Officer Staff Grade A (D6)	16
Administrative Officer Staff Grade B1 (D4)	28
Administrative Officer Staff Grade B (D3)	64
Administrative Officer Staff Grade C (D2)	219
Senior Administrative Officer	235
Administrative Officer	166
Total	747

* Includes permanent posts and supernumerary posts, except those created on a temporary basis to accommodate replacement for officers on various types of leave, or to be held against vacant permanent posts.

Source: Civil Service Bureau, HKSAR Government.

Governance model: Civil servants as guardian of the public interest

The administrative state model in Hong Kong closely reflects one particular model of governance. In their study of the relationship between politicians and bureaucrats, Aberbach, Putnam, and Rockman (1981) discuss two completely different models of governing: the governance model and the politics model. The politics model endorses a pluralistic conception of the public interest and affirms the legitimacy of conflicts among different social groups. It also takes contest among competing forces and divergent groups as an inevitable and healthy pathway toward defining and realizing the public interest. Under this model, elected politicians in a pluralistic democracy should be entrusted with the task of governing. By contrast, the governance model entrusts bureaucrats with the governing role. It holds that only rulers who are "above politics" and free from short-term electoral pressure can understand and protect the real and long-term public interest (Polidano 2001). It therefore endorses an elitist and even authoritarian approach to policymaking in which career and nonelected bureaucrats, as an elite group and an intellectual class, serve as the guardians of the public interest.

Hong Kong traditionally tilts more toward the governance model in the spectrum, as officers in the administrative grade are groomed to be statespersons. Although AOs are not elected, to a large extent they function as politicians in performing the political roles of interest aggregation and interest articulation in society. They are expected to be extremely sensitive to public opinion and even able to predict citizen demands to prevent political mobilization and reduce the public urge for faster democratization.

As part of the British colonial legacy, it is generally believed that there are at least two major advantages in AO governing. First is their ability to balance competing and different sectoral interests in society. Backed by the civil service system, AOs are not directly connected with particular interests in society and are relatively free from either political pressure outside the government or managerial pressure within the government. This ensures that they will not be biased in their judgment. Second, AOs are trained as "generalists" rather than "specialists" (Box 5.4) and are frequently rotated among different bureaus and departments in their career (Scott 1988). This safeguards that they will not form a "tunnel vision" in formulating policies by viewing policies from the specific and partial perspective of a particular bureau. It helps them develop a broader horizon in public policies and builds up their loyalty to the entire government, not a particular policy, department, or profession.

Combining these two advantages means that AOs or the "AO party" is probably the only group of policy actors in Hong Kong that can develop a long-term vision of the public interest without being biased by any particular interests and views, pressured by short-term and frequent elections, or at the same time being given the authority to fulfil such a vision (Cooper and Lui 1990). That is the reason why Anson Chan—the former Chief Secretary for Administration and one of the most popular political figures in Hong Kong, who is also a former member of the AO grade—is widely known as "Hong Kong's conscience."

The AO system, together with other strategies like the "administrative absorption of politics" (King 1975), in which many social and business elites are co-opted into a big web of advisory committees, plus the principle of limited social and economic intervention and the underdevelopment of political parties in Hong Kong, has helped to contribute to the British colonial legacy of having political stability in an era of unprecedented economic growth (Goodstadt 2000; Lau and Kuan 2000). However, institutional incongruity, the mismatch between contexts and institutions, is one of the major sources of governance crises in post-colonial Hong Kong (Lee 1999). It is questionable whether the governance model is still suitable or the best for Hong Kong, given its more advanced social and economic development after its gradual but continued democratization reforms since the 1980s (Sing 2001; Wong and Kwong 2017). Moreover, one of the significant challenges in the administrative state model is ensuring that powerful bureaucrats do not abuse their authority in the absence of institutional checks and balances (Tsang 2017).

Institutional Conscience: Systems and Mechanisms

The civil service is often seen as the "conscience" of Hong Kong. But it should be seen as an "institutional conscience," as a major part of the conscience is built on an institutional level by the civil service system. The civil service system is designed and constructed to serve the objective that civil servants can make the best decisions based on their own expertise and judgment, without being threatened or biased by both internal and external pressures (Peters and Pierre 2004).

The civil service system consists of several essential and interrelated features (Rosenbloom, Kravchuk and Clerkin 2014: chapter 5). Firstly, civil servants are granted tenure, and working in the civil service is seen as a career, not a job. Tenured civil servants are given high job security and cannot be removed unless they have committed serious mistakes. Due process following major legal principles and procedures must also be adhered to before any disciplinary action can be taken. With the protection of tenure, civil servants are more likely than employees in the private sector to speak truth to power without the fear of having their job threatened.

The idea of seeing working in government as a lifelong career also enhances the development of the "institutional conscience." Civil servants are often recruited at the entry level and at a young age, when they do not have any substantial experience of working outside government. Once they join the civil service, they are expected to spend the rest of their working lives inside the government, meaning going straight to retirement after leaving the government without joining the private sector. All these factors minimize the connection civil servants can have with sectoral interests and help to ensure they will not make decisions during their tenure as civil servants with the intention of benefiting their previous or future employers.

Another feature constituting the institutional conscience is the emphasis on merit in the recruitment, promotion, and other management functions of the civil service (Ingraham 1995). Only the best person for the position will be hired or promoted in the civil service, and all other factors except the suitability and ability of the person in mastering the job should not be considered. The emphasis on merit is meant to attain the highest level of efficiency in the operation of government machinery. This also leads to the depoliticization of the civil service and the limitation of managerial discretion in government (Hood 1991). The supremacy of the principle of merit implies that the operation of the civil service should not be tainted by political pressures from other branches of government. An independent monitoring authority, the Public Service Commission (PSC), is set up to ensure that the principles of merit are followed properly in the daily functioning of the civil service. Another important office playing a significant role in ensuring the integrity and corruption-free nature of the civil service is the Independent Commission Against Corruption (ICAC).

However, depoliticization of the civil service is not equivalent to political neutrality. The political neutrality of the civil service is a myth or rhetoric rather than a reality in Hong Kong. As most of the senior civil servants are policymakers themselves, they are not politically neutral in the sense that they do have to decide who would gain and who would lose when making policies. In Hong Kong, the term "political neutrality" is sometimes used or intentionally misused by civil servants themselves to fend off political interference and challenges from other branches of policymaking to maintain the high autonomy of civil servants in the administrative state model of governing in Hong Kong. At the same time, the popularity of using the term "politically neutral" to describe the civil service also reflects the positively perceived role of the civil service in serving as "Hong Kong's conscience," in which the civil service is trusted to be "above politics" and to always act in a nonpartisan manner in policymaking to serve the public interest.

The limitation of managerial discretion, meaning that the public managers in government enjoy much less power than their counterparts in the private sector, is another major feature of the civil service system (Kettl 1997). This feature ensures that civil servants can make decisions based on the best of their expertise without the fear of managerial pressure coming from the top of government. In the civil service, there is actually very little room for managers to manage, and decisions on pay, recruitment, promotion, and many other managerial functions are often made out of the direct control of managers by well-established mechanisms based on the principles of merit, objectivity, and scientific rationality. For this reason, traditionally in the public administration literature, managers in the public sector are called "administrators," not managers, as they are often taken to be responsible for administrating the system following well-defined procedures and standards, without being allowed to exercise their own judgment and personal views.

One outstanding example of the limitation of managerial discretion in the civil service is its disciplinary system. It is never adequate and appropriate to discipline a civil servant based on the decision and discretion of the managers. Instead, the civil servants needed to be proved "guilty" by well-defined and legally based procedures. Due process and procedural justice, following legal principles including the rights of hearing and appeal of the civil servants and presumption of their innocence, must be followed before any disciplinary action can be taken. Under this legally oriented disciplinary system, which places a high value on the protection of the rights of civil servants, very few civil servants are actually dismissed each year. In 2021–2022, in the civil service of an establishment of more than 190,000 people, only 35 were dismissed or had their service terminated, which was even fewer than the 112 civil servants who died in service during the same period.

The limitation of managerial discretion, which is essentially done by taking power away from the managers, has helped to build up the institutional conscience, though it is hard to deny that tolerance of inefficient and ineffective employees may be higher in government due to the difficulty of disciplinary action. In addition, there is little doubt that the civil service system has contributed to the extraordinarily high stability of the civil service. In 2022–2023, although the rate of resignation significantly increased after 2020, still only 3,863 civil servants chose to resign from the government, which represented a very low drop-out rate of about two percent.

Weberian bureaucracy: Structural features in government

Bureaucracy, the organizational form proposed by German sociologist Max Weber (Gerth and Mills 1958), is a useful concept for understanding the structure of modern governments including the HKSAR government. According to Weber, bureaucracy is the best form of organization for maximizing efficiency, control, and reliability. There are a few key structural features in an "ideal type" bureaucracy (Rosenbloom, Kravchuk, and Clerkin 2014: chapter 4): high formalization, high centralization, and high complexity. High formalization refers to the high extent to which the structure of an organization and its procedures are formally established in written rules and regulations. The government in Hong Kong is highly formalized, as it mainly operates via rules and regulations, which are often backed up by legislation. In addition, written communication is often preferred inside the government for being considered as the "official" record. The second structural feature of bureaucracy is high centralization, which means a large degree of power and authority is concentrated in the higher levels of the hierarchy. The third distinctive feature of bureaucracy is its high complexity, which is measured in terms of the number of subunits, levels, and specializations. There are two dimensions of organizational complexity: horizontal differentiation (the specialized division of labor across subunits and individuals) and vertical differentiation (the number of hierarchical levels in an organization, or the "tallness" or "flatness" of the organization).

The HKSAR government is a highly complex organization on both horizontal and vertical dimensions. Horizontally, there are 15 policy bureaus and more than 60 departments and major offices. All of them are highly specialized by policy area or function. Grades in the civil service are also highly specialized. With the exception of a few generalist grades—including the administrative grade, executive officer grade, and clerical grade, which are more mobile across tasks and departments and more multiskilled—most grades in the government are specialists, such as police officers and firemen, assigned to a single department or required to conduct one particular well-defined task. Under the concept of bureaucracy, specialization can generate expertise and efficiency, as each department or each grade is focused only on a single task it should excel at.

Vertically, many departments are tall organizations, with many levels of hierarchy in the organizational chart. An advantage of being tall is minimizing the span of control, which is the ratio between the supervisor and his or her subordinates in each layer of the hierarchy, to enhance both control and overall efficiency in the department. For example, this vertical complexity is observed in the seven-rank structure of the administrative grade.

Typically, a civil servant will join the public bureaucracy via an open and competitive process, which typically includes written examinations and interviews. But instead of joining the civil service as a whole, an individual needs to apply for a specific grade, as all positions in the government are classified by grade. As each grade is separated into different ranks, after successfully joining the grade, the civil servant will spend the rest of his/her career climbing up the rank ladder in a specific grade. How much salary the civil servant earns depends on grade, rank, and seniority, which are usually measured by years of service. For those who are lucky and outstanding, they may one day reach the highest rank in their grade. For the AO grade, it is "administrative officer staff grade (A1)." However, as each grade is a closed system, civil servants cannot be easily transferred to a different grade, regardless of their performance.

Ironically, while bureaucracy had been seen as the best form of organization for enhancing efficiency in the past, it was considered more of a problem rather than a solution in the modern era (Welch and Wong 2001; Kettl 1997). When a task is highly predictable and there is a stable organizational environment, the most efficient way of accomplishing the task can be specified in rules and regulations, which are then enforced by the bureaucracy. In recent decades, the rise of globalization and the postindustrial economy has generated rapidly changing tasks and a dynamic environment demanding high adaptability from an organization, which a bureaucracy is very poor at due to its structural constraints (Wong 2013). The structural features of a bureaucracy—the rigid rules, lack of horizontal communication, and slow decision-making process in dealing with exceptions and uncertainties—make it hard to cope with changes and crises in the new environment. These inherent weaknesses, together with poor government performance in handling major crises during the first few years immediately after the handover—such as the economic downturn brought by the Asian Financial Crisis of 1997–1998, the bird flu of 1998, and the SARS crisis of 2003— had dramatically reduced the faith of the public in the bureaucrat-dominated administrative state. Although problems in policymaking and weak political leadership are also factors in those failures, the legacy of the bureaucracy is doubted by the public.

The Weberian civil service of Hong Kong is facing pressure to change from multiple fronts. In addition to performance issues, there are demands from politicians to reduce their autonomy and power as well as expectations from society for more democratic accountability and opportunities for public participation in the policymaking process. They trigger many reforms and changes in the post-1997 era. As these forces are further intensified by the growing state-society tension and social movements since 2014, major impacts have been generated on the fundamental values and features of the civil service (Lee 2020; Cheng 2013 and 2020; Lau 2002).

Reforms, Changes, and Impacts

Major reforms have been made to target the political and administrative roles of the civil service since the 1997 handover, which was further intensified in the post-2020 era (Wong and Yuen, 2022). One of the most important political reforms of the civil service, not only for the post-1997 era but also in the political development of Hong Kong, is the politicization of the civil service, including the introduction of a political appointment system that has shaken the role of the administrative grade in the governance of Hong Kong and weakened the autonomy of the civil service. On the administrative front, NPM reforms based on the private-sector model are pushed aggressively by the government, but resisted strongly by civil service unions. NPM reforms belong to the larger new right movement in western industrial countries, which is anti-bureaucracy, anti-big government, anti-welfare state, pro-business, and pro-market (Pollitt and Bouckaert 2017; Kettl 1997; Hood 1991).

Political appointment system

The political accountability system was introduced in two major phases. It was first adopted by the first CE, Tung Chee-hwa, in 2002 as the Accountability System for Principal Officials (ASPO). The major content of the system is using political appointees by the CE to replace civil servants, mainly AOs, as the principal officials who head the policy bureaus. The political accountability system was further expanded by CE Donald Tsang in 2008 to introduce undersecretaries and political assistants into the layer of political appointment on the top of the civil servants.

The official reason for the adoption of the ASPO is to enhance the political accountability of the principal officials, and this is exactly the reason for terming it an "accountability system" (Burns 2005). It was stated that, as civil servants are protected by the civil service system and permanently in employment, they could not be removed for taking responsibility. If they were replaced by political appointees, those appointees would be more responsive to the policy direction and more accountable to the public, as they could be removed if they were found responsible for any policy failure.

In reality, it was widely believed that one of the major reasons for Tung to introduce the ASPO was to enhance his political influence by reducing the power of the administrative grade in policymaking. Before ASPO, it was standard practice to appoint civil servants as principal officers; non-civil servants were appointed only when such talent was not available inside the government. Thus, Tung was a lonely outsider in government, as most of the policymaking positions were occupied by the AOs who were permanent civil servants and could not be easily removed by him.

Tung often found it difficult to implement policy initiatives unless he got the support of the "AO party." Unfortunately, it did not take long for him to realize that there were many fundamental differences between him and the AO party in policies (Lo 2001). Nevertheless, to pacify the AOs, the new political appointees under ASPO did not replace them literally, as they are added as an additional layer on the top of the organizational structure of the policy bureaus, with the original AO heading the bureau being retitled as "permanent secretary."

ASPO has broken the monopoly of the AOs in policymaking by shifting more power to the CE. However, it is questionable whether ASPO can really enhance political accountability. Although ASPO does in theory allow the CE to remove unpopular principal officials, many politically appointed officials with little public support continue to serve in the government. ASPO is actually a form of the ministerial system that has been practiced in almost all democratic countries (Burns 2005). Nevertheless, unlike all those countries, in Hong Kong, the CE is not popularly elected and the LegCo plays no role in the appointment and removal of the principal officials. There is no institutional safeguard to ensure that the principal officials will be accountable to the public, not just to the CE. The question of "accountable to what" also poses a problem. In practice, there is no clear division of areas of accountability and responsibility between the political appointees and the AOs after ASPO. Many AOs still need to attend LegCo meetings on behalf of principal officials to defend government policies and take criticisms after the adoption of ASPO. ASPO also had a negative impact on the morale of AOs and increased its drop-out rate. The recent appointment of a former police officer as the Chief Secretary for Administration, the most powerful position in the administration under the CE, has broken the principle of "generalists on top" and undermined the influence of the AOs in its already diminishing role in the governance of Hong Kong.

The effect of ASPO on governance is equally unclear and ambivalent. Although it allows the CE to select individuals who share his/her own visions and are loyal to him to be the principal officials, the party system is weak and underdeveloped in Hong Kong. This makes it extremely difficult for the CE to find individuals who think alike and have a strong connection with the LegCo to become principal officials, to ensure policy coordination and a smooth executive-legislature relationship in enhancing governance (Scott 2000). While the appointment of undersecretaries and political appointees can be taken as a natural expansion of the political appointment system, its effect on enhancing governance is similarly uncertain. Because the whole process of selection and appointment is not transparent, the expansion is frequently viewed as a practice of political favoritism and patronage. Its effect on training political talent is also doubted.

Further politicization: Trickle-down and ripple effects

Although there was no further expansion of the ASPO after 2008, it does not mean the politicization of the civil service has stopped. Further politicization of the civil service is seen under the two Administrations by Leung Chun-ying and Carrie Lam through the trickle-down effect and ripple effect (Wong and Yuen 2020). "Trickle-down politicization" refers to situations and incidents in which political appointees are able to politically influence the nonpolitical layer of the bureaucracy, including lower-level career civil servants, through their formal and informal powers. Selective enforcement by the police in handling protestors of different political stances in the Umbrella Movement of 2014 is one of the most cited instances of this problem (Wong and Chu 2017).

Trickle-down politicization works in two different modes. In addition to top-down political pressure, it also encourages bottom-up politicization from bureaucrats to bypass their bureaucratic superiors to receive political hints and orders from political appointees. That can happen because some bureaucrats may show political loyalty and obedience to the political appointees, even at the risk of violating commands from their immediate civil service supervisors, to fast-track their own careers, especially if they are also interested in taking up political appointments in the future.

A concern about trickle-down politicization lies in its hidden and subtle nature because, under its effect, many of the politicized decisions are made by civil servants themselves, either in the fear of political retaliation from the political appointees or in the hope of winning the favor of their political masters. Many of those incidents are suspected by the public in the daily operation of the civil service. Candidates with anti-government platforms in elections are disqualified by constituency returning officers, who are administrative officers of the civil service. The staff of the Leisure and Cultural Services Department (LCSD) deleted the term "national" from "National Taiwan University" in an event booklet due to concerns of "political incorrectness" (i.e., Taiwan should not be recognized as a "nation" or "country"). The Food and Hygiene Department forbade some political parties or groups from operating stalls at the city's largest Lunar New Year fair in Victoria Park, Causeway Bay. Those decisions by the civil service were seen by many as a violation of the freedom of speech of the citizenry.

While trickle-down politicization works vertically inside the bureaucracy, the ripple effect of politicization works horizontally to influence the advisory, consultative, and statutory bodies and committees, which are the extended arm of the bureaucracy in governing. Although these committees and organizations are not strictly part of the bureaucracy, they have been an extension of it since the era of bureaucratic polity, playing a critical function in policymaking. The administration adopted the strategies of actively managing and heavily securitizing the appointment of members in those agencies and organizations, and creating new committees and agencies with the effect of bypassing the civil service for advice and leadership (Wong and Yuen 2020). The latter strategy is highly related to the concept of "externalization" of the policy advisory system, which is "the relocation of advisory activities previously performed inside government organizations to places outside of government" (Veselý 2013: 200).

Due to the upheaval caused by the Anti–Extradition Law Amendment Bill (Anti-ELAB) Movement of Hong Kong of 2019, the CPG has been determined to tighten its control on the civil service significantly to stabilize the unrest in society. Under the NSL of Hong Kong enacted in July 2020, all public officials have to take an oath to uphold the Basic Law and swear allegiance to the HKSAR. This new oath-taking measure becomes a powerful and effective tool to amplify the trickle-down effect of politicization to hold all civil servants and government employees legally accountable for political loyalty, not simply merit and performance only as before.

Public sector reform and civil service reform

There are two major types of NPM-oriented administrative reforms in Hong Kong. The first, "public sector reform," is more about reducing the size and scope of government to make market or private sector-like organizations the major mode of resource allocation in society and agents of production and delivery for public services. The second, "civil service reform," holds that management systems and skills used in the private sector should be introduced in operating the government so that the government itself can learn from business, which is supposed to be more efficient and superior. Both reforms have created changes and impacts throughout the post-1997 period.

Table 5.2: Hong Kong civil service: Strength and the 12 largest departments (as of 31 March 2020)

Department	Strength	(%)
Hong Kong Police Force	33,245	(18.7)
Fire Services Department	10,695	(6.0)
Food and Environmental Hygiene Department	10,524	(5.9)
Leisure and Cultural Services Department	9,516	(5.4)
Housing Department	9,131	(5.1)
Immigration Department	8,817	(5.0)
Customs and Excise Department	7,112	(4.0)
Correctional Services Department	6,631	(3.7)
Department of Health	6,526	(3.7)
Social Welfare Department	6,229	(3.5)
Education Bureau	5,466	(3.1)
Post Office	4,866	(2.7)
Others	58,898	(33.2)
Total	177,656	(100.0)

Source: Civil Service Bureau, HKSAR Government.

The essence of public sector reform is redefining the role of the public sector and the private sector and deciding the best form of government intervention, whenever it is deemed necessary (Sankey 2001). For functions that should be more appropriately taken up by the private sector, the government should offload them, which often leads to the downsizing of government through privatization (Scott 2010). Table 5.2 shows some of the largest government departments in Hong Kong in 2020 according to the strength of their workforce. It is clear that the HKSAR government has played a major role in providing critical services to the public. Many of those services, such as law and order, will not be normally provided by the private sector. Besides, for services like education and housing, if the government does not provide them, the poor will have no or very limited access to the services, as they will usually find similar services provided by the private market unaffordable.

Under the lens of public sector reform, the role of the public sector in providing services, particularly those that are available in the market and can be produced more cheaply by it, is not only reexamined but also put under much stricter scrutiny. Even for policy areas in which the government has a role to play, the form of government intervention may vary. For example, the Social Welfare Department has contracted out many of its services to the nonprofit sector.

The public sector reform report of 1989 also classified three different types of services (core services, support services, and commercial services), three types of pricing strategy (free, partial cost recovery, full cost recovery), and four types of executive agency (traditional departments, trading fund departments, public corporations, and non-departmental public bodies). In general, the more a service moves towards the nature of commercial services, the more its cost should be recovered by a user fee and the less control government should have over it. Over the years, there is also a trend of agencification—the creation of autonomous government bodies such as the Hong Kong Monetary Authority and Urban Renewal Authority to perform public functions under the assumption that better efficiency and effectiveness can be achieved with less government control and political influence (Pollitt et al. 2004).

While public sector reform is well-intentioned in terms of maximizing efficiency, there are many controversies in terms of its impact (Kettl 1997). How to balance the concerns for efficiency and equity in the reform is always a tough act. The government is often criticized for using public sector reform as a means to retrench the welfare state in Hong Kong and step back from its obligations of providing good quality but reasonably priced services to the public. Another major problem of public sector reform is the diffusion of responsibility and the weakening of public accountability when major public services involving the public interest are transferred to nontraditional government departments (Pollitt and Bouckaert 2017). Many become irresponsive to the government but at the same time are not subject to market discipline, as they are often the monopolistic supplier of a service in the market. The toll hike of a privately owned cross-harbour tunnel and the resulting traffic jam is one example of how private gain can be maximized at the expense of public interest.

The claim that public sector reform can reduce the size of government is not supported fully by empirical evidence. The size of the civil service can be illusory in measuring the size of government, as it does not count people hired by the government under non-civil service terms, or people hired by government contractors but not by the government directly, or the overall budget of the government. This implies that the reform itself may not necessarily make government smaller. It can replace it with a "hollowed out" state in which services are provided by contractors rather than civil servants (Milward 1996).

In 1999, the Civil Service Bureau issued a consultation document—"Civil Service Reform: Civil Service into the 21st Century"—outlining the blueprint and the major directions for reforming the civil service. Following the NPM approach, many of the proposed reforms were almost the direct opposite of the ideals of the civil service system in order to "reinvent government" (Osborne and Gaebler 1992). Major reform initiatives include using contracts to replace tenure, which would severely weaken the permanent nature and job security of the civil service. The reforms became controversial as the downside of directly transplanting private sector systems and techniques to the public sector, especially the negative impact on the "institutional conscience," did not seem to be carefully thought through by the reformers (Wong 2004). In 2019, more than 10,000 employees working inside the government are non-civil service contract (NCSC) staff, without tenure protection and the offering of a career. In 2023, there is a proposal to streamline the disciplinary system, including making it easier to terminate the employment of civil servants.

The rise of managerial discretion or even political will in managing the civil service can eventually dismantle and deinstitutionalize many of the existing mechanisms governing it (Wong 2013). A well-known example of deinstitutionalization is the use of legislation to bypass the pay review mechanism to cut civil service pay in 2003 (Cheung 2005). In the same way, the idea of allowing lateral entry to let staff go in and out of government more freely and frequently, which is also a concern in the political appointment system, can induce the serious problem of a "revolving door," leading to a serious conflict of interest in balancing the competing sectoral interests in society. In this regard, Rafael Hui, the former Chief Secretary for Administration (2005–2007) was charged with corruption related to business-government collusion and given a seven-year imprisonment sentence in 2014.

By making politicization of the civil service its top agenda, many important issues including building up the capacities of the civil service in new and pressing areas have been neglected by government leaders. With regard to digital governance, many public services are now delivered conveniently through the internet, but there is still room for improvement in tapping the potential of information and communication technologies (ICTs) in enhancing citizen engagement and public participation on new interactive platforms such as social media (Holliday and Kwok 2004; Wong and Chu 2020). Mastering emerging and disruptive technologies is critical for attaining the vision of a smart city in which ICTs and new technologies such as big data, AI, and the Internet of Things (IoT) are deployed and integrated to provide seamlessly connected and personalized public services. In addition, under the "improved electoral system" in the new era of the NSL, as the component of direct election of the legislature is reduced, the principle of "using bureaucracy to replace democracy" is restored. Under these new but familiar circumstances, the civil service would be expected to strengthen its function in assessing public opinions and forming a partnership with society, implying that it must also enhance its abilities in avant-garde knowledge areas such as design thinking and collaborative governance (Emerson, Nabatchi, and Stephen 2011; Peters and Pierre 1998).

128   The Civil Service

Conclusion

This chapter has reviewed the major features of the civil service system and the transformation of the role of the civil service in the governance of Hong Kong. It also discusses the major reforms of the civil service in the post-1997 era including the post-NSL era since 2020. The leading role of the civil service has been constantly challenged since the handover and most recently by the NSL, which is reflected by its redefined character and having its autonomy as symbolized by institutional conscience eroded by a trend of politicization, including the political appointment system and the new oath-taking measure. With the trickle-down and ripple effects, the effect of politicization is extended from the top to the bottom of the bureaucracy and also from the core government apparatus to the agencies and organizations with government functions, affiliation, and influence.

Despite its diminishing power, as long as no full democracy is attained, it is clear that the civil service in general and AOs specifically would continue to assume the role of politicians by default and remain as one of the key political actors. With the delayed if not denied democratization of Hong Kong under the "improved electoral system," the CPG is expected to restore the principle of "using bureaucracy to replace democracy" and resort to the administrative state model of governance of the colonial legacy. On the capacity-building of the civil service, there is little disagreement that reforms are necessary, but it is doubtful whether NPM reforms are really the solution. Recognizing the reduced role of direct election in the political system, the state-society tension after the social movements, and the need to make use of emerging technologies to continuously improve public services, the civil service should invest much more aggressively in areas including collaborative governance, digital governance, and smart city to strengthen its capacities to cope with the new circumstances and challenges.

Box 5.1: Civil service

This term is sometimes used interchangeably with bureaucracy, but there are actually some marked differences between the two. "Civil service" is generally used to refer to the people who work for the government and are managed under the civil service system. It is a special personnel system with the main purpose of ensuring that civil servants can maintain professionalism and objectivity in decision-making without being subject to pressures from within or outside the government.

Box 5.2: Bureaucracy

Bureaucracy is a form of organization which is often associated with government, as many government departments adopt this organizational form, though it can also be found in the private sector. According to Max Weber, a famous German sociologist, bureaucracy has the major features of high formalization, high differentiation, and high centralization. Its key advantage is the maximization of efficiency and control. But many contemporary scholars contend that bureaucracy only maximizes efficiency under certain contingencies.

Box 5.3: Grade and rank

In the HKSAR government, all positions can be classified by both grade and rank. Grade refers to the type of position. Rank refers to the level of the position within the organizational hierarchy. For example, AO is a grade and within that grade there are seven ranks. In general, grades in the government are closed, with no bridging between them, which means that each grade recruits at the entry level, promotes from within, and no direct personnel transfer is allowed between different grades.

Box 5.4: Generalists and specialists

Grades in the government can be classified into two types: generalists and specialists. Generalists, including AO, executive officer, and clerical officer, can serve in different departments, while specialists, due to their specialized nature, usually can only serve in one department. Because of the governing philosophy of "generalist on top, expert on tap," many leading positions in the government are taken up by administrative officers, who are generalists.

Questions

1. How does the role of the civil service in the governance of Hong Kong change after the 1997 handover? What are the factors leading to the change?
2. What is the relationship between institutional conscience and politicization of the civil service? What are its implications on the overall governance of Hong Kong?
3. What are the roles and functions of the civil service under the new environment of the post-2020 paradigm, including the development of smart city and "improved electoral system"? What capacities should the civil service develop to fulfil them?

Bibliography

Aberbach, J, Putnam, R & Rockman, B 1981, *Bureaucrats and Politicians in Western Democracies*, Harvard University Press, Cambridge, MA.

Burns, J 2004, *Government Capacity and the Hong Kong Civil Service*, Oxford University Press, Hong Kong.

Burns, J 2005, "Enhancing 'Executive Accountability' in the Hong Kong Government," in A Cheung (ed), *Public Service Reform in East Asia*. Hong Kong, the Chinese University Press of Hong Kong, Hong Kong, pp. 125–156.

Cheng, JY 2013, "Has He Got the Job Done? An Evaluation of Donald Tsang Administration," in JY Cheng (ed), *The Second Chief Executive of Hong Kong SAR: Evaluating the Tsang Years 2005–2012*, The City University Press, Hong Kong, pp. 1–30.

Cheng, JY 2020, "Overall Evaluation of the C. Y. Leung Administration," in JY Cheng (ed), *Evaluation of the C. Y. Leung Administration*, The City University Press, Hong Kong, pp. 1–30.

Cheung, A 1998, "The Transition of Bureaucratic Authority: The Political Role of the Senior Civil Service in the Post-1997 Governance of Hong Kong," in PK Li (ed), *Political Order and Power Transition in Hong Kong*, the Chinese University Press of Hong Kong, Hong Kong, pp. 79–108.

Cheung, A 2005, "Civil Service Pay Reform in Hong Kong: Principles, Politics and Paradoxes," in A Cheung (ed), *Public Service Reform in East Asia*, the Chinese University Press of Hong Kong, Hong Kong, pp. 157–192.

Cooper, T & Lui, T 1990, "Democracy and the Administrative State: The Case of Hong Kong," *Public Administration Review*, vol. 50, no. 3, pp. 332–344.

Emerson, K, Nabatchi, T & Stephen, B 2011, "An Integrative Framework for Collaborative Governance," *Journal of Public Administration Research and Theory*, vol. 22, no. 1, pp. 1–29.

Gerth, H & Mills, W (eds and trans) 1958, *From Max Weber: Essays on Sociology*, Oxford University Press, New York.

Ghai, Y 1999, *Hong Kong's New Constitutional Order: The Resumption of Chinese Sovereignty and the Basic Law*, 2nd ed., Hong Kong University Press, Hong Kong.

Goodstadt, L 2000, "China and the Selection of Hong Kong's Post-colonial Political Elite," *China Quarterly*, vol. 163, September, pp. 721–741.

Harris, P 1988, *Hong Kong: A Study in Bureaucracy and Politics*, Macmillan, Hong Kong.

Holliday, I & Kwok, R 2004, "Governance in the Information Age: Building E-government in Hong Kong," *New Media and Society*, vol. 6, no. 4, pp. 549–570.

Hood, C 1991, "A Public Management for All Seasons," *Public Administration*, vol. 69, no. 1, pp. 3–19.

Ingraham, P 1995, *The Foundation of Merit*, Johns Hopkins University Press, Baltimore, MA.

Kettl, D 1997, "The Global Revolution in Public Management: Driving Themes, Missing Links," *Journal of Policy Analysis and Management*, vol. 16, no. 3, pp. 446–462.

King, A 1975, "The Administrative Absorption of Politics in Hong Kong," *Asian Survey*, vol. 15, no. 5, pp. 422–439.

Lau, SK 1982, *Society and Politics in Hong Kong*, the Chinese University Press of Hong Kong, Hong Kong.

Lau, SK 1987, *Decolonization Without Independence: The Unfinished Political Reforms of the Hong Kong Government*, Occasional Paper No. 19, Center for Hong Kong Studies, Institute of Social Studies, the Chinese University of Hong Kong, Hong Kong.

Lau, SK 2002, "Tung Chee-hwa's Governing Strategy: The Shortfall in Politics," in SK Lau (ed), *The First Tung Chee-hwa Administration*, the Chinese University Press of Hong Kong, Hong Kong, pp. 1–40.

Lau, SK and Kuan, HC 2000, "Partial Democratization, 'Foundation Moment' and Political Parties in Hong Kong," *China Quarterly*, vol. 163, no. 1, pp. 705–720.

Lee, E 1999, "Governing Post-colonial Hong Kong: Institutional Incongruity, Governance Crisis, and Authoritarianism," *Asian Survey*, vol. 39, no. 6: pp. 940–959.

Lee, F 2020, "Solidarity in the Anti-Extradition Bill Movement in Hong Kong," *Critical Asian Studies*, vol. 52, no. 1, pp 18–32.

Lo, SH 2001, *Governing Hong Kong: Legitimacy, Communication and Political Decay*, Nova, New York.

Milward, B 1996, "The Changing Character of the Public Sector," in J Perry (ed), *Handbook of Public Administration*, 2nd ed., Jossey-Bass, San Francisco, CA, pp. 77–92.

Miners, N 1998, *The Government and Politics of Hong Kong*, 5th ed., Oxford University Press, Hong Kong.

Osborne, D & Gaebler, T 1992, *Reinventing Government: How the Entrepreneurial Spirit is Transforming the Public Sector*, Addison-Wesley Publishing Company, Reading, MA.

Peters BG & Pierre, J (eds) 2004, *The Politicization of the Civil Service in Comparative Perspective—A Quest for Control*, Routledge, New York.

Peters, G & Pierre, J 1998, "Governance without Government? Rethinking Public Administration," *Journal of Public Administration Research and Theory*, vol. 8, no. 2, pp. 223–243.

Polidano, C 2001, "Don't Discard State Autonomy: Revisiting the East Asian Experience of Development," *Political Studies*, vol. 49, no. 3, pp. 513–527.

Pollitt, C & Geert, B 2017, *Public Management Reforms: A Comparative Analysis*, 4th ed., Oxford University Press, UK.

Pollitt, C, Talbot, C, Caulfield, J & Smuellan, A 2004, *Agencies: How Governments Do Things Through Semi-Autonomous Organizations,* Palgrave Macmillan, New York.

Rosenbloom, D, Kravchuk, R, & Clerkin, R, 2014, *Public Administration: Understanding Management, Politics and Law in the Public Sector*, 8th ed., McGraw-Hill, New York.

Sankey, C 2001, "An Overview of Public Sector Reform Initiatives in the Hong Kong Government Since 1989," in A Cheung and J Lee (eds), *Public Sector Reform in Hong Kong: Into the 21st Century*, the Chinese University Press of Hong Kong, Hong Kong, pp. 3–28.

Scott, I 1988, "Generalist and Specialist," in I Scott and J Burns (eds), *The Hong Kong Civil Service and Its Future*, Oxford University Press, Hong Kong, pp. 17–49.

Scott, I 2000, "The Disarticulation of Hong Kong's Post-handover Political System," *China Journal*, no. 43, January, pp. 29–53.

Scott, I 2010, *The Public Sector in Hong Kong*, Hong Kong University Press, Hong Kong.

Sing, M 2001, "The Problem of Legitimacy for the Post-handover Hong Kong Government," *International Journal of Public Administration*, vol. 24, no. 9, pp. 847–867.

So, A & Chan, M 2002, "Crisis and Transformation in the Hong Kong SAR—Toward Soft Authoritarian Developmentalism?," in M Chan and A So (eds), *Crisis and Transformation in China's Hong Kong*, M. E. Sharpe, New York, pp. 363–384.

Tsang, S 2007, *Governing Hong Kong: Administrative Officers from the Nineteenth Century to Handover to China, 1862–1997*, Hong Kong University Press, Hong Kong.

Welch, E & Wong, W 2001, "Effects of Global Pressures on Public Bureaucracy: Modeling a New Theoretical Framework," *Administration and Society*, vol. 32, no. 4, pp. 371–402.

Wong, W 2004, *From A British-Style Administrative State to A Chinese-Style Political State: Civil Service Reforms in Hong Kong After the Transfer of Sovereignty*, Brookings Working Paper, Center for Northeast Asian Policy Studies (CNAPS), Brookings Institution, Washington, DC.

Wong, W 2013, "The Search for a Model of Public Administration Reform in Hong Kong: Weberian Bureaucracy, New Public Management or Something Else?," *Public Administration and Development*, vol. 33, no. 4, pp. 297–310.

Wong, W & Chu, M 2020, "Digital Governance as Institutional Adaption and Development: Social Media Strategies between Shenzhen and Hong Kong," *China Review*, vol. 20, no. 3, pp. 43–69.

Wong, W & Kwong, YH 2017, "Political Marketing in Macao: A Solution to the Legitimacy Gap for a Hybrid Regime?," *Asian Survey*, vol. 57, no. 4, pp. 764–789.

Wong, W & Yuen, R 2022, "Hong Kong," in CM Park, Y Han, & Y Chang (eds), *Civil Service Systems in East and Southeast Asia*, Routledge, UK, pp. 80–97.

Wong, W & Yuen, R 2020, "Politicisation of the Civil Service under the C. Y. Leung Administration: Unprecedented Control," in JY Cheng (ed), *Evaluation of the C. Y. Leung Administration*, The City University Press, Hong Kong, pp. 31–60.

Useful Websites

Civil and Miscellaneous Lists, HKSAR Government
http://www.info.gov.hk/cml/

Civil Service Bureau, HKSAR Government
http://www.csb.gov.hk/hkgcsb/index.jsp

Efficiency Office, HKSAR Government
https://www.effo.gov.hk/en/index.html

Joint Secretariat for the Advisory Bodies on Civil Service and Judicial Salaries and Conditions of Service, HKSAR Government
http://www.jsscs.gov.hk/

Name List of Principal Officials, Permanent Secretaries, and Heads of Government Departments
https://www.gov.hk/en/about/govdirectory/pshd.htm

Office of the Government Chief Information Officer
https://www.ogcio.gov.hk/en/

Organizational Chart of the HKSAR Government
https://www.gov.hk/en/about/govdirectory/govchart/index.htm

Panel on Public Service, The Legislative Council
https://www.legco.gov.hk/general/english/panels/yr08-12/ps.htm

Public Service Commission, HKSAR Government
https://www.psc.gov.hk/

Further Reading

Civil Service Bureau, HKSAR Government 1999, *Civil Service Reform: Civil Service in the 21st Century*, Hong Kong Government Secretariat, Hong Kong (available at: http://www.info.gov.hk/archive/consult/1999/reforme.pdf). A consultation paper that reviews the traditional civil service system and outlines a blueprint for reform.

Cheung, A & Lee, J (eds) 2001, *Public Sector Reform in Hong Kong: Into the 21st Century*, the Chinese University Press of Hong Kong, Hong Kong. A resourceful book on public sector reform in Hong Kong that examines both its theoretical foundation and the critical issues involved.

Hong Kong SAR Government 2020, *Hong Kong Smart City Blueprint 2.0*, Office of the Government Chief Information Officer, Innovation and Technology Bureau, Hong Kong. A key policy document of the smart city and digital governance initiatives of Hong Kong, in which the civil service plays a major role in steering and facilitating.

OECD 2017, *Skills for a High Performing Civil Service*, OECD Public Governance Reviews, Organization for Economic Cooperation and Development Publishing, Paris. A guide to the major skills and capacities required for the civil service.

OECD 2017, *Engaging Public Employees for a High-Performing Civil Service*, OECD Public Governance Reviews, Organization for Economic Cooperation and Development Publishing, Paris. A timely report on how to enhance public commitment of the civil service during a critical period of crises and changes.

Page, EC & Wright, V 2000, *Bureaucratic Elites in Western European States*, Oxford University Press, New York. A good examination of the role and functions of bureaucratic elites in policymaking in Western democracies.

6
District Councils, Advisory Bodies, and Statutory Bodies

Rami Hin-yeung Chan

Public participation is an important aspect of governance, especially in a society without universal suffrage like Hong Kong. Since Hong Kong's political system does not allow the government to fully represent and reflect views and demands from the public as it did in the colonial era, the government is aware of how crucial it is that public voices get heard. In this regard, the District Councils (DCs), advisory bodies, and statutory bodies in Hong Kong are playing supplementary and supportive roles in the governance process. They serve as communication channels to link up the government and the general public. They are created by the government to make sure that public views have been received and are being taken into consideration, and on the other hand, that messages and rationales behind government policies and decisions have been accurately delivered to the public. They also serve as a platform to solicit support from the community to ensure a smooth and stable administration.

The mechanism of getting the relevant local elites to act as key opinion leaders to facilitate governance was best described as "administrative absorption of politics" by Ambrose Yeo-chi King (1979). As the Hong Kong polity before the 1980s can be described as "politics without politicians," the consultative system is playing a very important role for the bureaucrats to measure public support and acceptability of the government's major policy decisions. Consensus politics is indeed a significant feature of Hong Kong politics. Apart from the partial representation by directly (and indirectly) elected members in the Legislative Council (LegCo), political consensus-building is also partly contributed by the DCs, advisory bodies, and the statutory bodies. Consensus politics has been duly emphasized as the governing principle to maintain political stability and long-term prosperity in Hong Kong.

In recent years, the demand for universal suffrage in Hong Kong has transformed the nature of the consultative system. The public is no longer satisfied by the advisory function of these consultative bodies. Political and democratic demands have shocked the executive-led consultative system. With more politicized agendas in play, DCs were becoming battlefields among various political blocs, including the government and the pro-establishment parties themselves. Advisory and statutory bodies have also been criticized as another form of spoil system that fully housed the government's supporters and allies, hence resulting in a loss of credibility. Reviews and reforms of the DCs, advisory bodies, and the statutory bodies were undertaken to refine the consultative system.

The political role of DCs has been controversial in the past decade. It turns out that the 2010 political reform in Hong Kong has empowered the DCs by creating the District Council (Second) Functional Constituency (aka Super District Council, Box 6.1) in the LegCo as well as a significant increase in memberships of the CE Election Committee (EC) returned from the DCs sector. However, the electoral reform decided by the National People's Congress in 2021 has almost removed all the political influence of the DCs in the name of reinforcing DCs to align their status as not an "organ of political power" according to the Basic Law. The decision is also to be seen as the aftermath of the overwhelming victory of the pan-democrats in the 2019 DC elections due to the outbreak of the Anti–Extradition Law Amendment Bill (Anti-ELAB) Movement. In this chapter, the changing roles and functions of the DCs, advisory bodies, and statutory bodies will be analyzed in the context of political reforms and changes in Hong Kong.

District Boards: Early Development

In Hong Kong, public direct participation in local affairs can be traced back to the establishment of the Sanitary Board in 1883 (later the Urban Council, generally referred to as the municipal councils together with the Regional Council). The 1888 Sanitary Board election was the first recorded election in Hong Kong in which only very few and selective elites could vote (with only 669 eligible voters). In that election, two unofficial members were elected to the Board. However, the Sanitary Board and the later municipal councils were regarded as part of the central (territorial-wide) administration, as they managed a wide range of urban services from a more territorial perspective (i.e., the Urban Council was responsible for Hong Kong Island and Kowloon, while the Regional Council was responsible for the New Territories). They were not regarded as a district administrative organization since their decision-making and operations were generally centralized (Wang 2017). For over a century, local or district administration in Hong Kong was under the jurisdiction of the bureaucracy. The City District Officers (CDO) scheme was an initiative assigned after the 1967 Riots to ensure that Administrative Officers (senior bureaucrats) could put themselves in daily contact with the local Chinese community. The government expected the CDOs to act as a bridge to link up the public and the government. To be more specific, the CDOs aimed at explaining government policies to the people and initiating proposals that served the needs of the public (Tsang 2017).

However, district administration in Hong Kong had nothing to link with democracy until the government announced the *White Paper on District Administration* in 1981. This sudden and dramatic move was seen as a negotiation strategy, as it occurred when Britain was discussing with China the future of Hong Kong after 1997. According to the White Paper, even though the newly proposed District Boards (DBs) would remain advisory in nature, the introduction of direct elections carry the symbolic implication that the people will be "counted" in the government decision-making process (Lau 1982). Apart from giving advice on various local administrative matters—such as provision and use of public facilities and services, adequacy and priorities of government programs, and the use of public funds for local public works and community activities—the DBs were also authorized to undertake minor environmental improvements and promotion of recreational and cultural activities within the district that achieved a certain degree of decentralization. This laid the foundation for the further development of District Councils (DCs) as an important element of local administration in Hong Kong, as the major role and function did not change significantly until 2023.

In April 1981, the first DB was set up in Kwun Tong. As a transitional arrangement, no election had been organized. The democratization in Hong Kong had moved one step forward in 1982 when elections to the 18 DBs were held for the first time; one-third of the membership of the DBs—132 members—had returned through elections. At the beginning, the District Officers (who were Administrative Officers from the bureaucracies) had served as chairpersons of the DBs. From 1985 onward, the DB members would elect the chairman among themselves, and the government officials would no longer serve as members. More importantly, ten members of the LegCo had returned from the DBs. This was the first time that the DBs influenced the "central" authority.

With regard to the composition, the membership of Urban Council members on the DBs in Hong Kong and Kowloon were abolished in 1991, which reflects the separate functions of the two entities. During Governor Chris Patten's last term of office, part of his initiatives was a constitutional reform package to further democratize the political system, as the appointed membership of DBs was abolished in 1994. As a transitional arrangement, the Provisional District Boards (1997–1999), which were set up by the HKSAR government after the handover of Hong Kong to China in 1997, consisted of all appointed members. From 2000 onwards, the arrangement of appointed members (along with elected members) was retained until 2016. The District Boards were officially renamed as District Councils in 2000 when the two municipal councils (Urban Council and Regional Council), which were responsible for making decisions on environmental hygiene and recreational affairs, were abolished. The abolition of the two municipal councils created new room for expansion of responsibilities to the DCs, since they are the only elected chambers below the LegCo to represent public opinions.

Table 6.1: Number of District Council (Board) members (1982–2023)

Term	Elected Member	Appointed Member	Ex Officio Member	Urban Councillor	Official Member	Total
1982–1985	132	134	27	30	167	490
1985–1988	237	132	27	30	–	426
1988–1991	264	141	27	30	–	462
1991–1994	274	140	27	–	–	441
1994–1997	346	–	27	–	–	373
1997–1999*	–	469	–	–	–	469
2000–2003	390	102	27	–	–	519
2004–2007	400	102	27	–	–	529
2008–2011	405	102	27	–	–	534
2012–2015	412	68	27	–	–	507
2016–2019	431	–	27	–	–	458
2020–2023	452	–	27	–	–	479

Source: Hong Kong SAR Government 2006; data expanded by the author.
* Provisional District Councils (1/7/1997–31/12/1999).

The Empowerment of District Councils: The 2001 and 2006 Reviews

The Basic Law of Hong Kong does not define the role and function nor mention the terminology of "District Councils." Instead, under Section 5 District Organizations, Article 97 defines "district organizations" as non-organs of political power. They are "to be consulted by the government on district administration and other affairs, or to be responsible for providing services in such fields as culture, recreation and environmental sanitation." Currently, in line with Article 98 of the Basic Law, which stated that "The powers and functions of the district organizations and the method for their formation shall be prescribed by law," the District Council Ordinance defined the functions of a district council as follows:

(a) To advise the government:

i.   on matters affecting the well-being of the people in the district; and
ii.   on the provision and use of public facilities and services within the district; and
iii.   on the adequacy and priorities of government programs for the district; and
iv.   on the use of public funds allocated to the district for local public works and community activities; and

(b) Where funds are made available for the purpose, to undertake:

i.   environmental improvements within the district;
ii.   the promotion of recreational and cultural activities within the district; and
iii.   community activities within the district.

District organizations are being defined as not "organs of political power" in accordance with the historical background of drafting the Basic Law. It was mainly because of the two relatively independent and powerful municipal councils (i.e., the Urban Council and the Regional Council) in the colonial era. The two municipal councils—with their directly elected councillors, independent budget, and decision power—oversaw roughly the matters currently managed by the Food and Environmental Hygiene Department (FEHD) and Leisure and Cultural Service Department (LCSD) before the end of 1999.

The abolishment of the two municipal councils has made the DCs the only formal district organization under the LegCo, especially from the perspective of election politics. The DCs have also become the important arena for training the next generation of politicians of major parties (before taking part in the LegCo elections). With high expectations from society, the government completed a review of the role and functions of the DCs in 2001 and made five major recommendations: (a) enhancing the role and functions of DCs and providing additional funding for them; (b) enhancing the communication between the DCs and the administration; (c) enhancing the participation of DC members in the policymaking process; (d) strengthening support for DC Members; and (e) enhancing the accountability and efficiency of DCs.

In the *2004 Policy Address*, the Chief Executive (CE) decided to further strengthen the cooperation between the government and the DCs and to review DCs' functions and composition. An interdepartmental working group was set up in January 2005. In 2006, the government had conducted a comprehensive review of the role, functions, and composition of the DCs with a view to enhance the functions of DCs and improve government work in districts. In the *Policy Address of 2005–2006*, the CE had announced an initiative to allow the DCs to participate in the management of some district facilities within the limits of the existing institutional framework. The CE also announced that the role of District Officers and the coordination function of District Management Committees would be enhanced. Therefore, the DCs' role in district administration would be strengthened and district needs would be promptly met.

The 2006 review focused on strengthening the role and function of DCs mainly in four areas: (a) the involvement of DCs in the management of district facilities, (b) enhancement of the work of the administration in districts, (c) composition of the DCs, and (d) matters related to the DC elections. For the involvement of DCs in management of district facilities, the government aimed at enhancing the role of DCs to better meet local needs in the scope of district facilities like public libraries, community halls, and sports venues, etc.; however, territory-wide or regional facilities such as museums will not be included. The DCs, through their District Facilities Management Committee (DFMC), would take a more active role in managing district facilities. In most cases, the proposals that were considered and endorsed by DFMCs would be followed or taken into serious considerations by LCSD or the Home Affairs Department (HAD) on matters including (a) operations, management, and maintenance of the facilities, (b) programs and activities held in district facilities, (c) facility improvement and upgrading works (no more than $15 million each), and (d) design and details of facility improvement and upgrading works.

The government aimed at enhancing communications between the government and the DCs and institutionalizing the support for District Officers and District Management Committees. The government has built a closer relation with DCs by setting up the Steering Committee on District Administration with direct access to policy committees to resolve cross-department issues. The department heads are expected to regularly attend the DCs' meeting. Also, the government would also encourage the DCs to partner with other social sectors or community organizations to create programs with district features and characteristics. Moreover, the remunerations of DCs' members have been increased, and a financial assistance scheme for DC election candidates at the rate of $10 per vote was implemented. All these initiatives marked the enhanced role and function of the DCs in Hong Kong district affairs.

Intensified Political Battles of District Council Elections

Elections of the DCs have been political battlegrounds for various political parties to gain influence. Many junior party members debuted their political career at the DCs as a "community officer" in the office of a current DC member. By gaining valuable experience to serve the community while also developing networks with local residents, the DCs have been treated as training grounds in the hope that junior party members can enter the LegCo sometime in the future.

The DC elections are also used by political parties in consolidating their supporters through the utilization of resources of the DCs. All these local connections and networks among local organizations would in return play an important role in the LegCo elections. Given the continuous exposure and contact with the residents in various districts, political mobilization through local units is essential for soliciting community-wide support. The DCs have become political platforms for political parties to disseminate their political views and ideology. As the DCs were taking a more important role in governmental matters including political reforms, government policies, and even sensitive issues concerning relationship with Beijing, the DCs have become political venues for political parties and politicians to pit one another against each other.

Indeed, platforms and campaigns of the DC elections have been focused on political matters, principles, and ideology, alongside local district issues. Political colours have been added to the DC elections, and political dynamics within the DCs have been complex. From previous elections, we can see that political debates and controversies did affect the returns of seats of various political parties. The 2003 election was a good example as the pan-democrats earned a lot of seats from the pro-establishment bloc. However, the advantage brought by people's dissatisfaction toward the government that led to the 1 July rally were not sustained in the election in 2007 in which the pan-democrats could only retain two-thirds of their seats as compared to 2003. In general, in contrast with the LegCo, voters in DC elections are more focused on members' effort on "district work." Appealing purely to ideology and political controversies may not sustain voters' support in the next election; thus many high profile candidates could not be reelected for a second term because they failed to express enough concern to their constituents.

Although the focus of the 2010 electoral reforms was on the election methods and composition of the LegCo and the CE (via Election Committee), the amendments had a large impact on the DCs, which unleashed the "golden era" of DCs in extending their political influence. The very direct changes were the introduction of the District Council (Second) Functional Constituency (aka Super District Council) in the LegCo with five new seats added. The amendments had returned the five seats by providing proportional representation with popular vote for almost 3.2 million registered voters who did not have a "second vote" in any functional constituency previously. This move brought two major implications. First, the newly elected LegCo would consist of at least six DC members (together with the original one seat in functional constituency retuned by DCs), with other possible "dual councillors" (members who are serving on the LegCo and DC at the same time). This would enlarge the political influence of the DCs by bringing district administrative issues to the LegCo and most likely create an impact on the government's agenda. Second, the newly established "Super

Table 6.2: Seat distribution of major parties in District Council elections after 2000

Major Pro-establishment Political Parties*	2003	2007	2011	2015	2019
Democratic Alliance for the Betterment and Progress of Hong Kong (DAB)	62	115	136	119	21
Hong Kong Federation of Trade Unions (HKFTU)	–	1	7	27	5
Liberal Party (LP)	12	14	9	9	5
New People's Party	–	–	4	26	–
BPAHK (Economic synergy, New Kowloon New Dynamic)	–	–	1	13	5
Roundtable	–	–	–	–	2
Pro-establishment Total (Includes Nonpartisan Candidates)	239	302	299	298	63

Major Pan-democratic Political Parties*	2003	2007	2011	2015	2019
Hong Kong Association for Democracy and People's Livelihood (ADPL)	25	17	15	18	19
Civic Party	–	6	7	10	32
Civic Passion	–	–	–	–	2
Democratic Party (DP)/The Frontier	101	62	47	43	91
Hong Kong Confederation of Trade Unions (HKCTU)	–	–	–	–	–
League of Social Democrats (LSD)	–	6	–	–	2
Labour Party	–	–	–	3	7
Neighbourhood and Worker's Service Centre (NWSC)	4	4	5	5	4
Neo Democrats (ND)	–	–	8	15	19
People's Power	–	–	1	–	1
Youngspiration	–	–	–	1	–
Pan-democratic Total (Includes Nonpartisan Candidates)	161	106	103	126	388

* Parties that were represented in the LegCo through geographical constituencies.

District Council" has become the largest constituency in terms of the number of voters. Since these five seats will be returned by proportional representation, which makes the whole of Hong Kong into one single constituency, they draw much public attention; both the pro-establishment and pan-democrats would like to get the third seat, as the general supporting ratio between the two blocs has been always more or less 4:6 to 4.5:5.5. To secure the third seat, different voting and promotion strategies were used in the 2012 and 2016 LegCo elections. Some parties adopted a vote allocation strategy while some parties put all the candidates into one single list to capture all the supporting votes. In both elections, the pan-democrats successfully obtained three seats. Once the candidates were running for the "Super District Council," the whole election campaign was manpower- and resource-intensive, as the whole "party machine" was involved with the aids of district level branches, offices of DC members, and various community organizations. This new constituency is also being seen as a "thermometer" of government popularity given its large voter base, which covers the entire Hong Kong.

The 2019 DC elections: Power dynamics within the government

The 2019 DC elections gave birth to the first DCs in Hong Kong to be dominated by pan-democrats (17 out of 18). As an aftermath of the Anti-ELAB Movement, the 2019 DC elections recorded the highest turnout rate ever—71.23 percent (2.9 million votes)—in the electoral history (i.e., popular vote) of Hong Kong. With 57.44 percent of the vote, the pan-democrats obtained 388 out of 452 DC seats, compared to 59 seats (41.32 percent) for the pro-establishment. By looking into individual DCs, except the Islands DC, the pan-democrats controlled all other 17 DCs, while the Wong Tai Sin DC achieved 100 percent control. After securing a majority, the pan-democrat councillors tried their best to challenge the status quo and attempted to make some "breakthrough" on various local livelihood matters, as well as pushing forward their political ideologies via different means. As DCs have to work closely with various government departments, given the highly politicized environment after the Anti-ELAB Movement, bureaucrats are being placed at the front line to deal with all the "challenges" brought by the DCs. In this regard, the role of DCs has created great tension with various government departments, especially the Home Affairs Department, over different issues.

In general, by reviewing all the confrontations between the DCs and the government, three major types can be identified: budget rejection, service rejection, and meeting rejection. Budget rejection includes but is not limited to reimbursement requests made by particular DC members who were being rejected, or their requests for public funding were turned down by the HAD. Some of these requests were being rejected due to political reasons, such as the expenses for the "Go Hong Kong Go" thematic festival lighting decoration and "a peaceful life" "red banner" for the Chinese New Year. The government argued that these products carried inappropriate political messages that will "affect social harmony" and "cause public anxiety." The delay in providing certain resources and materials can also be regarded as budget rejection. An example is the delay in distributing face masks during the COVID-19 outbreak, while at the same time prohibiting DC members from using public funding to buy face masks. The government explained that coordination was in progress.

Meeting rejection occurred when some of the agenda items were being removed by the HAD (in their capacity as the DCs' Secretariat) for various reasons. For example, the HAD removed the agenda items of a Yau Tsim Mong DC meeting on discussing the "Hong Kong Story" exhibition at the Hong Kong History Museum, as the item deviated from the functions of DC as stated in the Cap 547 District Councils Ordinance. Another agenda item on discussing a policeman pointing a gun at the protesters in Tsuen Wan was also rejected by the HAD, as they claimed that the item had "no relation to the local residents."

Service rejection refers to the refusal of various government departments (other than HAD) to communicate, act upon, or simply ignore the request from DCs. In a broader sense, it also applies to various forms of noncooperative government departments. The most dramatic case happened during the Central and Western DC meetings held in January 2020, during which Chris Tang, in his capacity as Police Commissioner, attended a DC meeting for the first time. During the meeting, critical questions were raised toward the performance of the police during the Anti-ELAB Movement in 2019. The meeting ended by a censure motion in which Tang and other officials from HAD walked out of the meeting room. Apart from direct confrontation, government departments were also found to be less likely to take suggestions and comments from DCs into consideration. On the occasion of the naming of the Tuen Mun-Chek Lap Kok Tunnel and its linkage roads, the Tuen Mun DC passed a new proposal on naming in September 2020, but the final decision made by the government was the same as the one that was originally tabled by the Lands Department. Many DC members argued that the consultation (with DC) acts like a formality without any real meaning.

The "new order": Confirmation form, swearing in, and the National Security Law–related controversies

All the controversies regarding the loyalty of elected officials toward the Basic Law can be traced back to the 2016 LegCo elections in which all the candidates, for the first time, were being asked to sign a Confirmation Form declaring that they would "uphold the Basic Law and pledge allegiance to the Hong Kong

Special Administrative Region." Later, similar practices were also being applied to DC elections. In the 2019 DC election, eight candidates had been disqualified, as the Election Officer of the Hong Kong government did not believe that those candidates were "truly loyal" to the Basic Law, although some of them had signed the Confirmation Form.

In fact, the Standing Committee of the National People's Congress reinterpreted Article 104 of the Basic Law in November 2020. The aim was to clearly state the swearing-in requirements and the possible consequences of not properly doing so. However, according to the Basic Law, Article 104 does not cover DC members. Thus, until the end of 2020, the Confirmation Form is the only "checkpoint" on DC candidates' loyalty to the Basic Law. Swearing in was not required at the time when those elected took their seats at the DCs. The pan-democrats' sliding victory in the 2019 DC Election, in which they had secured more than 80 percent of the seats with majority control in 17 of 18 DCs, had raised the concern of Beijing. Officials of the Central Government, on various occasions, insisted that public offices should be in the hands of the patriots and that the DC (resources) cannot be served as the fuel of any anti-China and Hong Kong (government) attempts.

The legislation of the National Security Law (NSL) enacted in June 2020 has facilitated the further enforcement of loyalty requirements for the DC members. In Part 2, under Chapter III of the NSL, subversion is defined as "seriously interfering in, disrupting, or undermining the performance of duties and functions in accordance with the law by the body of central power of the People's Republic of China or the body of power of the Hong Kong Special Administrative Region." In March 2021, some pan-democratic DC members were charged by the police as they participated in the preliminary election of the LegCo originally scheduled for September 2020. They were accused of planning to jeopardize the Hong Kong government by rejecting the government budget (if they could secure a majority), which may lead to a possible dismissal of the LegCo by the CE. Since according to the Basic Law, the CE must resign if the reelected LegCo votes down the budget for the second time.

Article 104 of the Basic Law states that five categories of public officers (i.e., the CE, principal officials, members of the Executive Council and of LegCo, judges of the courts at all levels, and other members of the judiciary) in Hong Kong must swear to uphold the Basic Law and swear loyalty to the Hong Kong Special Administrative Region (HKSAR) when assuming office. Apart from the abovesaid five categories of public officers, Article 6 of the NSL specifies that a resident of Hong Kong who stands for election or assumes public office shall confirm in writing or take an oath to uphold the Basic Law and swear allegiance to the HKSAR in accordance with the law.

To align with the legal requirement of the NSL, the Public Offices (Candidacy and Taking Up Offices) (Miscellaneous Amendments) Ordinance 2021 was passed by the LegCo in May 2021. The ordinance clearly explains the meaning of a reference to "upholding Basic Law and bearing allegiance to HKSAR." At the same time, it introduces the oath-taking requirement for members of the DCs; specifies oath-taking requirements; standardizes arrangement of oath administrators; enhances the mechanism to deal with breach of oaths; and introduces restrictions on participation in public elections for related situations.

After the ordinance came into effect, the DC seats of Lester Shum, Tiffany Ka-wai Yuen, Fergus Leung, and Tat-hung Cheng, who were disqualified for running for the LegCo in 2020, were all vacant. Among them, Fergus Leung and Tat-hung Cheng had resigned earlier, whereas Lester Shum and Tiffany Ka-wai Yuen were sentenced to more than three months in prison for involvement in the June Fourth rallies. Thus, they lost their seats as district councillors accordingly. As of July 2021, before the scheduled oath-taking ceremony organized by the Home Affairs Bureau, more than 100 DC members had resigned or lost their seats for various reasons. The majority of them had been involved in the pre-election campaign for the LegCo elections in 2020, which put them at high risk of being "disqualified" by the government.

The Politics of District Councils

2010 electoral reform vs. 2021 electoral reform

In 2010, the government officially approved the methods (ratified by the National People's Congress) of selecting the CE and forming the LegCo in 2012. There were two major changes that increased the political influence of DCs. First, regarding the formation of the LegCo, seats will be increased to 70 (from 60). Both the number of seats to be returned by geographical constituencies through direct elections and those returned by functional constituencies are to be increased to 35. The five new seats from the functional constituencies will be returned by (nearly) popular election (i.e., those without a "second vote" in any other functional constituencies previously). Second, for the election of the CE, it was proposed to increase the number of members of the Election Committee to 1,200, and more importantly, to increase the proportion of elected DC members in the Election Committee. Eventually, 117 out of 1,200 Election Committee members are returned through election by DC members from among themselves. Since the system of block voting (Box 6.2) is applied in electing the Election Committee members, the political bloc with majority control on DCs will technically secure all the 117 seats. With a 15 percent threshold on CE candidate nominations still in place, the DCs will become a very important sector (117 out of 1,200 seats, equal to 9.75 percent) among all Election Committee sectors for possible candidates to run for the CE election.

Before the 2019 DCs elections, the pro-establishment parties had always secured a majority in the membership of DCs. Thus, from the perspective of DCs, the most controversial element of the 2010 electoral reform was about the method of selecting these five new "functional constituencies" seats. According to the original proposal of the government, these five new seats, together with the original seat of DC representatives in the LegCo, shall be returned through election among DCs members. Technically, taking into consideration past electoral results, all the seats shall be under the control of pro-establishment parties. However, after a series of negotiations between the government (including Beijing's representatives in Hong Kong) and the pan-democrats (especially the Democratic Party), the finalized reform package allowed the new five functional constituency seats to be returned by popular vote under a proportional representation system; as such, the five new seats have become the "functional constituencies" with the largest voter base since all eligible votes without affiliation with any functional constituencies will automatically be eligible to vote in these five new functional constituencies. Given such a large voter base, these five new seats soon became an important battlefield in future LegCo elections, and the term "Super District Councils" was created to describe these five new functional constituency seats. It also creates an alternative pathway for "rising stars" in various DCs to enter the LegCo, as only DCs members are eligible to compete for these new seats.

After the 2010 reform was implemented, there was no major change for almost ten years. There was no big change in terms of the composition of DCs after the 2011 and 2015 elections, in which the pro-establishments controlled most of the seats. However, the social unrest and intense public dissatisfaction brought by the Anti-ELAB Movement led to the historical, overwhelming victory of the pan-democrats in the 2019 DCs Election. It triggered Beijing's intention to further revise the political system of Hong Kong, in which one of the major concerns is on playing down the political role of DCs controlled by opposition parties. At the National People's Congress General Meeting held in March 2021, the National People's Congress adopted a decision to further revise Hong Kong's political system to ensure that Hong Kong is being ruled by "patriots." For amendments related to the DCs, Beijing reinforced that the DCs are not part of the "organ of political power." Thus, significant involvement and participation of DC representatives in the LegCo and the Election Committee (to elect CE) was deemed inappropriate.

The decision, according to the National People's Congress, was seen as "another major step taken by the state to improve the HKSAR's legal and political systems" since the NSL was adopted in June 2020. There are two major changes that would affect the DCs. First, the restructured Election Committee will comprise 1,500 members from five sectors: (1) industrial, commercial, and financial sectors; (2) the professions; (3) grassroots, labour, religious, and other sectors; (4) LegCo members and representatives of district organizations; and (5) Hong Kong deputies to the National People's Congress, Hong Kong members of the National Committee of the Chinese People's Political Consultative Conference, and representatives of Hong Kong members of related national organizations. In this regard, all the 117-seat DC subsectors on the committee would be eliminated and replaced by "representatives of members of area committees," including members of the government-appointed District Fight Crime Committees and the District Fire Safety Committee, as well as representatives of the pro-Beijing associations of Hong Kong residents in the Mainland.

Second, for the LegCo, the new structure comprises 90 (instead of 70) Members in each term. Members of the LegCo include Members returned by the Election Committee (40 seats), those returned by functional constituencies (30 seats), and those by geographical constituencies through direct elections (20 seats). The total number of functional constituency seats is down from 35 to 30, representing 28 sectors, with more than two-thirds of the sectors elected by corporate or organizational voters. The five seats being phased out are the District Council (Second) Functional Constituency seats (aka Super District Councils), which were introduced by the government in its political reform package in 2010 after it had reached a consensus with some of the pan-democrats. The amendments to the two Basic Law annexes came into effect on 31 March 2021. Many comments suggested that the main reason is to avoid allowing the pan-democrat-controlled DCs to have any influence on future CE election, as according to the original arrangement, the pan-democrats should unsurprisingly secure all 117 seats (out of 1,200) in the Election Committee through the bloc vote system. The 2021 reform apparently aims at avoiding any possibility that an overwhelming victory of the pan-democrats (together with the political influence generated from their majority) would happen again in any level of election. It is fair to say that the big win by pan-democrats in the 2019 DC elections led Beijing to tighten the control of Hong Kong electoral system. From a regime stability perspective, if the election method of DCs remains unchanged, the minimization of their political role and influence will be the only way out.

Disputes on drawing electoral boundaries

A study conducted by Stan Hok-wui Wong in 2017 tried to investigate the possibility of gerrymandering in Hong Kong DC elections. Introduced by the Americans, *gerrymandering* is a term that refers to the practice of drawing the boundaries of electoral districts in a way that gives one political party an unfair advantage over its rivals, or that dilutes the voting power of members of minority groups. Wong's (2017) studies observed three patterns. First, the Hong Kong government is more likely to redraw the boundaries of constituencies controlled by pro-democracy opposition parties. Second, there is little evidence that redistricting can deter opposition incumbents from seeking reelection. And third, although there is no negative effect on the incumbent's voting share, the government's redistricting plans have an adverse impact on opposition incumbents' reelection rate.

Wong (2017) suggested that there are two major reasons behind the utilization of gerrymandering in DC elections. The first reason is to diminish the opposition parties' financial and political resources. As the opposition party does not receive regular donations, elected officials have become the major income source for them. Losing in the DC election means losing stable income as well as their connection to the constituents. The second reason is to disrupt the opposition parties' electoral coordination at the LegCo level. As the proportional representation system (adopted in the geographical constituency elections of the LegCo) requires coordination to maximize the outcome, district councillors can contribute to the calculation, as they have firsthand information on their constituents' voting preferences. More DC seats means better coordination in the LegCo elections. Regarding the two reasons for employing gerrymandering in DC elections, political resources, as suggested in the first reason by Wong, should be given more attention because political resources also connect to the LegCo election campaigning. As the DCs can also serve as a path in nurturing the next generation of politicians and building long-term support from the local community, the importance of the political resources DC seats can bring should not be overlooked.

Moreover, Wong's (2017) study assumed that electoral fraud is not common in Hong Kong. While there are reported cases in every election, gerrymandering may be used along with other plots. There have long been accusations of various electoral frauds in every election, and they are all governed under the Cap. 554 Elections (Corrupt and Illegal Conduct) Ordinance. However, there are always gray areas, such as "palm thunder" (a little paper to "remind" voters about their voting preference) and de facto "vote buying" behavior through providing "welfare" to supporters continuously. In recent years, political parties, via their DC members, have begun setting up their own community-based organizations to reward their supporters by allocating resources obtained from the DCs (Lee 2012). Soon before the election period, in the name of welfare distribution, some DC members who are running for another term would provide festival gifts or organize short trips to the residents via those community-based organizations to avoid potential legal consequences. There are also some reported cases of candidates arranging vehicles to "deliver" voters (most are elderly) to the polling stations. All these practices may not be illegal (like using the name of community-based organizations) but apparently are carried out with an intention to maximize the chances to win the elections.

Advisory and Statutory Bodies

The Hong Kong government, in the broadest sense, placed advisory and statutory bodies under the Home Affairs Bureau under the category of "District, Community and Public Relations." However, advisory bodies and statutory bodies, legally speaking, are very different entities; the latter are normally established by an ordinance that authorizes the legal power to perform specific duties and executive functions, such as the Airport Authority (Cap. 483) and the Hospital Authority (Cap. 113), whereas the former is less formal. Most of these statutory bodies are placed under a specific policy bureau while they are not under the management of the HAB in daily operation. Each of these statutory bodies should be governed by an independent board and employs staff members to perform various duties that are usually outside the civil service system. In contrast, advisory bodies that normally exist in a less formal manner can be committees—advisory boards of a government department that usually aim to obtain "the best possible advice on which to base decisions . . . by consulting interested groups and individuals in the community" (HAB 2021). In most cases, advisory bodies do not carry out daily operations or function on their own; they exist to give advice on various matters that may have no direct impact on government decisions.

Currently, there are around 500 advisory and statutory bodies. Usually, these bodies consist of both government officials and members of the public (appointed by the government). According to the HAB data in 2022, more than 4,600 members of the public have been appointed to serve on about 450 bodies and hold around 7,100 posts (some serve on more than one body). All in all, the Hong Kong government takes these bodies as a platform for public participation in the initial stage of policymaking and public service planning, as a wide cross section of the community and other relevant organizations can also participate.

Principles of Appointments to Advisory and Statutory Bodies

In general, the government claims that the appointment to advisory and statutory bodies is based on a merit system, which means that an individual's ability, expertise, experience, integrity, and commitment to public service are taken into consideration. For sure, bodies with specific functions would recruit members from relevant industries or sectors. The government tries to ensure equal opportunities in public affairs participation. As stated by the Home Affairs Bureau, there are four major concerns in the appointment to advisory and statutory bodies. First, under the so-called "six-year rule," a nonofficial member should not be appointed to serve on the same body in the same capacity for more than six years, to ensure a healthy turnover of members of advisory and statutory bodies. Second, under the "six-board rule," a person should not be appointed to serve as a nonofficial member on more than six advisory and statutory bodies at any one time, to ensure a reasonable distribution of workload. Third, in January 2004, the Hong Kong government set the "25 percent gender benchmark" as an initial working target, meaning at least 25 percent of appointed nonofficial members of advisory and statutory bodies should be either male or female. As of June 2022, 36.1 percent of appointed nonofficial post-holders of advisory and statutory bodies were female. Fourth, in her *2017 Policy Address*, the then-CE Carrie Lam announced that the government will appoint more young people to various government boards and committees, with the aim of increasing the overall ratio of young members (i.e., persons who are aged between 18 and 35) to 15 percent. As of June 2022, 15.7 percent of the appointed nonofficial post-holders with age information were aged 35 or below on their first appointment to the relevant advisory and statutory bodies. The Member Self-recommendation Scheme for Youth (MSSY, Box 6.3) will be detailed in later chapters.

Meeting the needs of the community is the top priority of the government. Composition and operation of the advisory and statutory bodies will be reviewed regularly. There have been increasing public concerns about the turnover of membership as well as the transparency of these bodies. Appointment of new members to these bodies usually attracts wide discussion on whether the government would ensure the inflow of new ideas and balance the participation from different political spectrum. At the same time, government transparency measures—including issuing press releases, holding press briefings, opening meetings to the public, and providing public access to meeting materials and documents and uploading the relevant information to the internet—have not instilled much confidence in the public around the effectiveness of these bodies at bringing public views into the government's decision-making process. The membership appointment is always the top concern of the public in judging the openness of the government to different views (i.e., anti-government views).

For many years, advisory bodies were skeptically seen as being so full of pro-establishment people that it affected their function as a platform to hear concerns from the public. In Carrie Lam's term of office, the government tried to invite candidates from a more diverse background in which some party members from the pan-democrats were being appointed. Apart from that, many new faces with various backgrounds were being appointed to some important bodies. For instance, in March 2018, the government appointed Senia Ng, a Democratic Party member, "Ngai Yuen," a former premiership coach of a local professional soccer team, and Julia Poon, a former television news anchor, to the Youth Development Commission.

However, the outbreak of the Anti-ELAB Movement in 2019 seriously damaged the relationship between the government and the pan-democrats. Many pan-democrat appointees decided to quit or not to extend their appointment to serve on advisory bodies. In contrast, the government has also significantly decreased appointing pan-democrats to those bodies. Normally, LegCo Members will concurrently serve on many bodies, but it is now not the practice for those pan-democrats as they were not being invited (reappointed) to serve.

Member Self-recommendation Scheme for Youth (MSSY)

To provide more opportunities for young people to participate in policy discussions and understand government operation, the Home Affairs Bureau launched the Member Self-recommendation Scheme for Youth (MSSY), which aimed at recruiting self-nominated people between the ages of 18 and 35 to become members of specified government advisory committees through the scheme. The MSSY aimed to recruit young people, under the principle of meritocracy, who have the commitment to serve the community. Candidates who are able to contribute to the committees concerned will be recommended to the relevant government departments for consideration of appointment. In the assessment process, the government looked for candidates to serve the community with the attributes of strong commitment, good understanding of the policy area concerned, and good analytical and communication skills.

The Pilot Scheme started in 2017, as stated in the *2020 Policy Address*. The scheme aimed to provide more opportunities for youth to participate in public affairs, so that the government can better understand their views and suggestions and take them into account. Despite the fact that many appointees were found to have a close relationship with various pro-establishment parties, think tanks, and organizations, the background (and the average age) of the appointees were being more diversified as the government, at the same time, appointed other notable celebrities and professionals (outside MSSY) from various sectors to the advisory bodies and committees.

Controversies related to the selection of appointees

Technically speaking, the CE, as the head of the Hong Kong government, would have the final decision on the appointment of the members of advisory and statutory bodies. Compared to advisory bodies, which normally do not carry any executive function, appointment to statutory bodies would be more important and influential, as they will typically impact government decision-making

152   District Councils, Advisory Bodies, and Statutory Bodies

Table 6.3: Committees applicable to the Member Self-recommendation Scheme for Youth (MSSY)

Pilot Scheme
- Youth Development Commission
- Committee on the Promotion of Civic Education
- Environmental Campaign Committee
- Committee on Innovation, Technology, and Re-industrialization
- Action Committee Against Narcotics

Phase I
- Advisory Committee on Enhancing Self-Reliance Through District Partnership Programme
- Lantau Development Advisory Committee
- Food Wise Hong Kong Steering Committee
- Joint Committee on Student Finance
- Transport Advisory Committee
- Committee on Community Support for Rehabilitated Offenders
- Community Sports Committee
- Advisory Committee of the Partnership Fund for the Disadvantaged
- Council for Sustainable Development
- Community Investment and Inclusion Fund Committee

Phase II
- Ping Wo Fund Advisory Committee
- Commission on Poverty
- Committee on the Promotion of Racial Harmony
- Hong Kong Advisory Council on AIDS
- Aviation Development and Three-Runway System Advisory Committee
- Committee on Home-School Co-operation
- Animal Welfare Advisory Group
- Museum Advisory Committee
- Advisory Committee on Gifted Education
- Working Group on Green Burial and Related Matters

Phase III
- Fight Crime Committee
- Advisory Committee on Mental Health
- Telecommunications Users and Consumers Advisory Committee
- Culture and Promotion Working Group of the Chinese Temples Committee
- Board of Management of the Chinese Permanent Cemeteries
- Panel on Manpower Development, the Hong Kong Council for Testing and Certification
- Hong Kong Film Development Council
- Advisory Committee on Enhancing Employment of People with Disabilities
- Country and Marine Parks Board
- Public Libraries Advisory Committee

Source: Home Affairs Bureau.

and operations, especially when it comes to the use of public money. Thus, the appointment of the head (usually the chairperson) of these statutory bodies draws wide public attention. If we review the list of chairpersons of various statutory bodies, most of them have a business background, either as an entrepreneur (business owner) or as senior management in listed companies. This practice can be traced back to the colonial era, as the colonial Hong Kong government used to invite local Chinese elites to participate in public affairs, believing that local Chinese elites (mostly businessmen and some professionals) would serve as opinion leaders for the entire local Chinese community. Scholars or professionals serving a leadership role in statutory bodies are relatively rare, even for advisory bodies, and only those with a very technical expertise, such as medical-related bodies, would be chaired by a registered doctor. Sometimes, these positions are held by the presidents of public universities, who are definitely not "outsiders" from the general public.

Some of these appointments have received a wide range of criticism from the public. For example, Barry Cheung, former chairman of the Urban Renewal Authority, had been serving his tenure since 2007 and was renewed for another two years in 2013 (for a total of eight years), which violated the "six years rule." Many media reported his close relationship with the then-CE Leung Chun-ying. In fact, Barry Cheung was the chairman of Leung's CE election campaign team back in 2012. The close relationship between the appointee and the CE would affect the creditability of the bodies because once scandals emerge, the government or their representatives often serves as a proxy for the public's anger. It may be accused of failing to ensure that there were sufficient checks and balances over the organization (Scott 2010).

Another controversy was about the then-CE Carrie Lam appointing Lau Ming-wai as the chairman of the Commission on Youth and later the vice-chairman of the Youth Development Commission (restructured from the Commission of Youth; the Chief Secretary of Administration serves as the ex officio chairman). Later, Lau was also appointed as the chairman of Ocean Park in July 2020, where he had to lead Ocean Park out of serious deficits due to social incidents and the pandemic. Being the second generation of a well-known businessman, Lau was widely criticized as failing to understand the needs and demands of the younger generations, especially those from grassroots families. At the same time, his legal and finance background was deemed a mismatch to the nature of Ocean Park, a theme park that belongs to the cultural and creative industry. Lau's ability to run Ocean Park was highly questioned, especially when compared to his predecessor, Allan Zeman, a very successful entertainment operator and property developer who is well known as the "father of Lan Kwai Fong."

Concluding Remarks on Future Development

The aftermath of Anti-ELAB Movement has created a very different polity that affects every aspect of the political community. In general, there are three major potential challenges that the DCs (and their members) have to face. First, the implementation of NSL would seriously narrow the space for DC members to promote their political agenda. Obviously, claims and attempts that target or potentially threaten the "regimes" (both the Central and Hong Kong governments) would no longer be legally acceptable. The commemoration of the June Fourth Incident or the demonstration related to the fight for universal suffrage has not been seen since 2020, despite the fact that the social gathering ban was removed in early 2023. Second, the Public Offices (Candidacy and Taking Up Offices) (Miscellaneous Amendments) Ordinance 2021 clearly states that persons who have been disqualified from entering political office because they declined or neglected to take an oath, breached an oath, or failed to fulfill the legal requirements and conditions around "upholding the Basic Law and bearing allegiance to the HKSAR" would be disqualified from being nominated or elected in relevant elections for five years. It is questionable how pan-democrats can participate in future DC elections under such requirements.

After the introduction of the oath-taking requirement for DC members, a significant number of DC members were "disqualified," especially those who have been highly critical of Hong Kong and Chinese governments over the years. As of March 2023, more than 330 seats (of 479) were vacant due to various reasons. Third, according to the National People's Congress decisions on amending Hong Kong's electoral systems, the District Council (Second) Functional Constituency in the LegCo, as well as the DC sector within the CE Election Committee, has been removed. Obviously, the political influence of DCs would be significantly reduced (or even totally removed) to align with the Basic Law, which has positioned "district organizations" not as an "organ of political power."

The government announced the proposals on improving governance at the district level in May 2023 with the following major changes. First, instead of electing among the DCs members themselves, District Officers, who are civil servants, will serve as DC chairmen and lead the work of DCs. Second, the composition of DCs and the corresponding methods of filling those seats will be changed significantly. DCs will comprise (1) appointed, (2) District Committees Constituency (DCC), (3) District Council Geographical Constituency (DCGC) and (4) ex officio members, with appointed, DCC, and DCGC members accounting for about 40 percent, 40 percent, and 20 percent of the total number of members, respectively, plus 27 ex officio members. The total number of seats will be comparable to the current term (i.e., 479 seats). Third, an eligibility review mechanism will be introduced to ensure that all candidates participating in the election, as well as appointed and ex officio members, uphold the Basic Law of the HKSAR and bear allegiance to the HKSAR of the People's Republic of China. Fourth, a monitoring mechanism of DC members' performance will be introduced. It includes investigating DC members whose behavior falls short of public expectations and imposing appropriate sanctions proportionate to the severity of the shortfalls. The "District Councils (Amendment) Bill 2023" was passed by the Legislative Council on 6 July 2023. The next DCs election (with all the new arrangements) will be held in December 2023. There are some debates on the positioning of the DC, as many community-related functions of the DC have been taken up by various community-based bodies, such as the new District Services and Community Care Teams (Care Teams) proposed in the *2022 Policy Address*. The new reform on DCs also rationalized the division of labor and collaboration among DCs, the District Fight Crime Committees, the District Fire Safety Committees, the Area Committees, and Care Teams.

When electoral politics cannot reflect public views effectively, supposedly the advisory and statutory bodies should play a more active and significant role in channeling public views. However, with a narrowing political environment, the role and function of advisory and statutory bodies will be in question, as the government may avoid the involvement of people with different voices to make these bodies apolitical. When political loyalty becomes a priority in the selection and appointment of membership, it will further affect the creditability of these consultative bodies.

Box 6.1: "Super District Council"

The District Council (Second) (usually called the "Super District Council) was a functional constituency with five seats in the elections for the LegCo of Hong Kong. It was created in 2012 based on the constitutional reform package approved in 2010. The candidates had to be in-service DC members who had secured at least 15 nominations among the DC members. It was the largest constituency in the LegCo (with 2 million registered voters) returned by those who were not eligible to vote in the other functional constituencies. However, these five seats were being phased out in the 2021 electoral reform.

> **Box 6.2: Block voting system**
>
> A block voting system is an electoral system in which a voter can select as many candidates as there are open seats. The candidates with the greatest number of votes are elected. This system is sometimes also referred to as plurality-at-large voting or multiple non-transferable voting. In practice, political parties can win all the seats if they can secure minor support from the voters. It happened to the DC sector in the Chief Executive Election Committee, in which the pro-establishment bloc won all the seats through a block voting system as they controlled the DCs.

> **Box 6.3: Member Self-recommendation Scheme for Youth (MSSY)**
>
> To provide more opportunities for young people to participate in policy discussions and understand government operation, the Home Affairs Bureau has launched the Member Self-recommendation Scheme for Youth (MSSY), which aims to recruit self-nominated people between the ages of 18 and 35 to become members of specified government advisory committees through the Scheme. The MSSY is targeted, under the principle of meritocracy, at recruiting young people who have the commitment to serve the community and the ability to contribute to the committees concerned, for recommending to the relevant government departments for consideration of appointment.

Questions

1. Should DCs exert political influence?
2. To what extent should the DCs remain mainly as advisory bodies?
3. To what extent should advisory and statutory bodies be independent from the administration?
4. Should advisory and statutory bodies be accountable to the LegCo?

Bibliography

HKSARG 2003, *Review of the Role and Functions of Public Sector Advisory and Statutory Bodies*, Government Printer, Hong Kong.

HKSARG 2006, *Review on the Role, Functions and Composition of District Councils*, Government Printer, Hong Kong.

HKSARG 2021, *Public Offices (Candidacy and Taking Up Offices) (Miscellaneous Amendments) Bill 2021 Gazetted Today*, Press Release, February, Government Printer, Hong Kong.

Home Affairs Bureau, HKSARG 2021, *Member Self-recommendation Scheme for Youth*, Government Printer, Hong Kong.

Hong Kong Government 1981, *District Administration in Hong Kong*, Government Printer, Hong Kong.

King, A 1979, "Administrative Absorption of Politics in Hong Kong," *Asian Survey*, vol. 15, no. 5, pp. 422–439.

Scott, I 2010, *The Public Sector in Hong Kong*, Hong Kong University Press, Hong Kong.

Lau, SK 1982, "Local Administrative Reform in Hong Kong," *Asian Survey*, vol. 22, no. 9, pp. 858–873.

Lee, E 2012, "Civil Society Organizations and Local Governance in Hong Kong," in S Chiu and SL Wong (eds), *Repositioning the Hong Kong Government: Social Foundations and Political Challenges*, Hong Kong University Press, Hong Kong, pp. 147–164.

Legislative Council Constructional Affairs and Home Affairs Panels 2006, *District Council Review*, Government Printer, Hong Kong.

Tsang, S 2007, *Governing Hong Kong Administrative Officers from the Nineteenth Century to the Handover to China, 1862–1997*, Hong Kong University Press, Hong Kong.

Wong, S 2017, "Gerrymandering in Electoral Autocracies: Evidence from Hong Kong," *British Journal of Political Science*, vol. 49, pp. 479–610.

Wang, F 2017, *History of Hong Kong's Political System (1843–2015)*, Chung Hwa Book, Hong Kong.

Useful Websites

District Councils
http://www.districtcouncils.gov.hk

Home Affairs Bureau: Advisory and Statutory Bodies
http://www.hab.gov.hk/en/related_departments_organizations/asb.htm

Home Affairs Bureau: Member Self-recommendation Scheme for Youth
https://www.hab.gov.hk/en/policy_responsibilities/District_Community_and_Public_Relations/selfrecommendation.htm

Home Affairs Department
https://www.had.gov.hk

Further Reading

Cheung, F 2003, "A Study on the Advisory and Statutory Bodies in Hong Kong, Hong Kong Democratic Foundation, Hong Kong." This is an original study on the operation of the advisory and statutory bodies in Hong Kong.

King, A 1979, "Administrative Absorption of Politics in Hong Kong," *Asian Survey*, vol. 15, no. 5, pp. 422–439. This provides a very good conceptual framework to understand elite co-option and integration in Hong Kong.

Wong, S 2015. *Electoral Politics in Post-1997 Hong Kong: Protest, Patronage, and the Media*, Springer, Singapore. This book offers a novel framework to help understand Hong Kong's lengthy democratic transition by analyzing the electoral dynamics of the city's competitive authoritarian political system.

Yuen, S & Cheng, W 2020. "Deepening the State: The Dynamics of China's United Front Work in Post-Handover Hong Kong," *Communist and Post-Communist Studies*, vol. 53, no. 4, pp. 136–154. This paper suggests that united front work has involved a steady organizational proliferation of social organizations coupled with their increasingly frequent interaction with Mainland authorities and the Hong Kong government.

Part II: Mediating Institutions and Political Actors

7

Democratic Development in Hong Kong

Lai Yan-ho and Sing Ming

Hong Kong, a global metropolis and a glamorous Asian financial center, has been well known for its outstanding economic development since the 1960s. Hong Kong was categorized as a high-income society by the World Bank as early as 1987, when Japan was the only other Asian society classified under the same category (Sing 2004). Hong Kong was ranked the most globalized society in the world by the 2012 Globalization Index (The World Bank 2021). Based on the Fraser Institute's assessment for the 25-year period up to 2018, Hong Kong has remained the world's freest economy for 25 consecutive years (Fraser Institute 2020). The dazzling economic achievement of Hong Kong was also recognized in 2019, when the World Bank ranked Hong Kong's GDP per capita, measured in purchasing power parity, 13th in the world.

Despite these spectacular economic achievements, Hong Kong's democratic development has been dwarfed when compared with those of other similarly prosperous liberal democratic societies around the world. Hong Kong's limited democratization has been repeatedly reversed and blocked since the transfer of Hong Kong from Britain to China in 1997. While the Basic Law of Hong Kong—that is, its "mini-constitution"—promises Hong Kong a path to universal suffrage in electing the Chief Executive (CE) and the legislature (Articles 45 and 68), there has been repeated procrastination by Chinese authorities to make this a reality, and Hong Kong's rule of law and civil liberties have been diminished as a result (Qiao 2004; Zhang 2016). Hence, Hong Kong continues to be classified as only a partly-free society (Freedom House 2020).

This chapter will elaborate on how different stakeholders perceive Hong Kong's democratization, and how the stalemate of democratic development has unfolded since Hong Kong's colonial era. The following discussion will be divided into four parts. The first part reviews the nature and dynamics of democratization in Hong Kong before 2014, emphasizing how the strategic bargaining of different actors at the domestic, national, and international levels

162 Democratic Development in Hong Kong

have shaped democratization since the handover. The second part examines the political conflicts over democratic reform in 2014, during which the government in Hong Kong proposed what were widely perceived as pseudo-democratic reforms, leading to unprecedented public protests that became known as the Umbrella Movement. The third part discusses the consequences that followed this vetting of political reform, when civic space and freedom were diminished. The fourth part concludes with observations about Hong Kong's mass protests in 2019, the subsequent introduction of the National Security Law (NSL), and the implications of this for the prospect of Hong Kong's political liberalization and democratization.

Interplay of International Politics and Domestic Mobilization in Hong Kong's Democratization (1949–2010)

Despite the presence of multiple meanings of democracy, there is great consensus that a genuine democratic institution entails the existence of meaningful political competition, free and fair elections, and a high degree of civil liberties (Dahl 1971; Diamond 2002; Diamond and Morlino 2016; Schumpeter 1947). Democratization refers to the process of establishing democratic institutions. Political Science scholars have developed different theories to explain democratization. Among them, the "bargaining model" explains democratization as an outcome of negotiation, transaction or bargaining, and finally, pact-making among different political actors or forces, as found in the "third wave" of democratic transitions since the early 1970s (O'Donnell 1986: 3–18; Share 1987; Huntington 1991: 165–174; Przeworski 1991: 24). During the third wave of global democratization, governing elites are conventionally viewed as key players during democratic transitions (Collier 1999: 6). However, cross-national studies have revealed that civil society and political society are important in fostering democratic transitions from authoritarian rule (Chou and Nathan 1987; Chung 1990; Kim 1996; Kamrava and Frank 1998, 893–894; Manuel 1998: 133; Diamond 1999: 234; Peruzzotti 2001). In addition, the domestic political culture, which shapes the level of public support for democracy, and the interplay of international pro-democracy and anti-democracy forces can also play significant roles in democratization (Lipset and Turner 1986: 12–13; Whitehead 1991 and 1996; Lipset 1994; Pridham and Vanhanen 1994; Klingemann and Fuchs 1995; Rose 1998; Inglehart 1997; Diamond 1999 and 2001; Norris 1999; Shin 1999; Welzel and Inglehart 2001). The bargaining power of the above forces lies in their capacity to menace the interests of their opponents (Sing 2004: 24).

Two major issues in the literature of democratization that may shed light on Hong Kong pertain to the path of democratization of subnational states and democratic backsliding or autocratization (Frantz 2018). Despite the categorical claim of Linz and Stepan that the democracy of a non-sovereign sub-polity is not achievable under a non-democratic sovereign state (1996), Hong Kong, as a Special Administrative Region of China, may serve as an acid test for the above notion. Scholars have contended that many democracies or hybrid regimes have experienced democratic backsliding or autocratization when civil liberties and political opposition are dampened, when the executive power becomes arbitrary without effective checks, and when laws and courts are weaponized for the political ends of the state (Fong 2017; Ginsburg and Huq 2018; Scheppele 2018). In the case of post-handover Hong Kong, not only does it fall into the category of a hybrid regime between 1997 and 2019, but recent developments seem to suggest that the city is undergoing a rapid process of autocratization. Such a process can be attributed to both local and external factors, as the sovereign state has shaped the electoral institutions and the rule of law (Lai 2019; Ma 2017).

The post–Second World War history of Hong Kong demonstrated the nature of Hong Kong's democratization as a process of bargaining among multiple actors at various levels (Sing 2004: 19). Unlike other British colonies, Hong Kong did not enjoy decolonization through independence nor transition to full democracy after the Second World War for two reasons. First, in 1958, the new People's Republic of China made it clear that it would perceive any move by the British to establish a "Dominion status" or "self-government" in Hong Kong as "a very unfriendly act," and threatened to invade Hong Kong, Kowloon, and the New Territories to have them "liberated" (UK FCO/40/327). Second, in 1972, the Chinese government pressured the United Nations to remove Hong Kong from the UN List of Non-Self-Governing Territories. Thus, the United Nation's Declaration on the Granting of Independence to Colonial Countries and Peoples could not be applied to Hong Kong, implying that it could not enjoy the right to self-determination under international law (Miners 1998: 6; Wong and Ngo 2016).

When formal negotiations on the post-colonial future of Hong Kong commenced in 1982, the democratic development of Hong Kong continued to be dictated by bargaining between the Chinese government and other international players alongside internal forces in Hong Kong. A Joint Declaration between China and Britain was signed in 1984 to confirm the transfer of sovereignty of Hong Kong to China in 1997, which included the implementation of "one country, two systems" to preserve its market economy, the continuation of the common law system, and a high degree of government autonomy for Hong Kong. The treaty also stated that "the Chief Executive will be appointed by the Central People's Government on the basis of the results of elections or consultations to be held locally" (Article 4). During the political transition between 1984 and 1997, the British government progressively promoted several democratic reforms for Hong Kong. During this period, the Chinese government repeatedly impeded those democratic reforms with well-publicized economic and political threats and mass mobilizations.

To understand the dynamics of this bargaining process, it is of pivotal importance to grasp the major interests of the Chinese Communist Party (CCP) with respect to Hong Kong. Globally speaking, besieged with economic and political crises, the Leninist state of the Soviet Union resorted to political liberalization and economic reform by the early 1990s. By contrast, the CCP, though also modeled along the Leninist structure keen on complete political control, followed a different path. The Chinese government endeavored to achieve economic liberalization without political liberalization, for a fully democratized Hong Kong could inspire Mainlanders in China to strive for democracy and challenge the CCP's monopoly of power (Sing 2004: 152). Besides preserving the hegemony of the CCP, the Chinese government also has a strong interest in maintaining Hong Kong's economic contribution to China.

The Chinese government has, however, made moderate concessions in Hong Kong's democratic development after witnessing the colossal, broad-based, and strenuous mass mobilization in support of Hong Kong's democratization amid the public protest against the crackdown on the Tiananmen incident in 1989 (Sing 2004). The crackdown plunged Hong Kong into a most severe confidence crisis. If the Chinese government had ignored the growing public demands for democratization completely, it might have risked greater capital flight and exodus of talented people, threatening Hong Kong's political stability and economic contribution to China (Sing 2003). Despite the moderate concessions of the Chinese government regarding Hong Kong's democratization and its official promise in the Basic Law that Hong Kong could commence political reform as early as 2007 (Annexes I and II), legislation on national security was expanded in the same constitutional document, with tougher conditions against challenging the authorities to prevent Hong Kong from turning into a "subversive base against China" (Kuan 1991; Sing 2004; Tai 2019). China's national security concerns and the majority of public aspiration to achieve full democracy in Hong Kong have been intertwined ever since, especially when the mutual skepticism between the Chinese authorities and the majority of people in Hong Kong continued (Chan 2019).

From the CCP's perspective, the launching of the democratic reforms in 1992 by Chris Patten, the last British governor of Hong Kong, could undercut the Chinese government's future control over Hong Kong. The 1989 student movements in Tiananmen had already inspired a robust and widespread "anti-China sentiment." It also abetted the pro-democracy activists' sweeping victory during the 1991 legislative election. Against the backdrop of the belated British campaign for democratization and the breakdown of the Soviet Union, Patten's reform intensified the siege mentality of the Chinese Communist Party. The speedy and unequivocal backing of Patten's reform by the American, Canadian, Australian, and Japanese governments only heightened the Chinese leaders' concerns that the reform represented a Western ploy of encirclement. Consequently, the CCP not only reiterated that it would demolish the semi-democratic structure immediately after the handover, but also endeavored to set itself up as a second power center prior to 1997 (Sing 2003).

Dynamics of Bargaining for Democracy in Post-colonial Hong Kong (1997–2012)

After Hong Kong's transfer of sovereignty, the locus of the bargaining process over Hong Kong's democratization gradually shifted from the Chinese government versus the international forces to the domestic sphere. Pro-democracy parties and civil society figured as crucial forces in advancing democracy by engaging in partially democratic elections and a raft of social mobilizations amid Beijing's growing reluctance to progressively grant full democracy to Hong Kong after 1997. Beijing worried that a fully democratic Hong Kong would engender a demonstration effect in Mainland China, prompting demands for democratic reforms there and challenging the survival and legitimacy of the CCP. The CCP has repeatedly rejected any suggestion of democratizing its one-party rule (Lin 2004). Some of the CCP's leaders also expressed concern that Hong Kong's democratic movement would be a lever for the United States to influence the Chinese government (Overholt 2004). Therefore, immediately after the transfer of sovereignty, the Chinese government reversed the partial democracy in Hong Kong and hindered further democratic reforms. The size of the enfranchised population was reduced from over 2 million to around 200,000 voters for the elections of the nine new legislative seats dedicated to different professional sectors. A proportional representation system was introduced for selecting the directly elected seats to prevent pro-democratic forces from gaining a majority in the legislature (Sing 2009: 298).

Even so, popular aspiration for democracy continued to grow, especially amid the escalating threats to Hong Kong's rule of law, civil liberties, and democracy arising from the unsuccessful attempt to impose national security legislation in Hong Kong in 2003. Despite its promises of "Hong Kong people ruling Hong Kong," a "high degree of autonomy" under "one country, two systems," and a transition to full democracy, in 2004, the CCP asserted that only "patriots" could run for public elections and govern the city, paving the way for a tougher line against democratization in Hong Kong. In March 2004, the Standing Committee of the National People's Congress (SCNPC) reinterpreted the Basic Law (Gazette Ext. no.5/2004), ruling out the possibility of universal suffrage in Hong Kong's elections for the CE and legislature in 2007 and 2008, respectively. The SCNPC required that the CE submit a report to it for any political reform, and that any proposed reform could only proceed with the approval of the SCNPC. In 2007, the SCNPC announced that universal suffrage for the CE and legislative elections could be implemented in 2017 and 2020, respectively, while the implementation of universal suffrage in 2012 was rejected.

In response to Beijing's procrastination, local pro-democracy parties progressively adopted more aggressive tactics to push for democratization. In 2010, five lawmakers from the Civic Party (CP) and the League of Social Democrats (LSD) jointly resigned to activate a by-election to galvanize public backing for universal suffrage and abolition of functional constituencies. The by-election ended in a low turnout rate of 17.1 percent due to the boycott of the pro-establishment camp and the tactical disagreement from the moderate flank of the pro-democracy movement, including the Democratic Party (DP) (Sing 2020: 155). Later, the DP reached a pact with the Beijing government to introduce electoral reform in the legislature, expanding the size of five additional occupation-based functional constituencies to all electorate who did not have a vote in traditional functional constituencies. The 2010 political reform proposal was thus passed with the support of the DP and other moderate pan-democrats, although the method of the CE election remained unchanged, and no timeline of abolishing functional constituency was fixed. The passage of the reform divided the pro-democracy movement and the DP, as well as other moderate pan-democrats, who were reprimanded by the party's radical flank for compromising (Ma 2011). The serious split also weakened the bargaining power of civil society groups and the entire political opposition, triggering further radicalization of the democratic movement led by the younger generation, who were deeply frustrated with the mild tactics and poor performance of the traditional pro-democracy camp.

Confrontations between the state and civil society in Hong Kong continued—as reflected in the mass campaign against the introduction of a patriotic national education curriculum in 2012. In this context, in late 2013, the Hong Kong SAR government (HKSARG) put forth a proposal to advance elections for Hong Kong's legislature in 2017 and for the CE in 2020. However, given the objections from Beijing in Hong Kong's democratization since the early 1980s, the pro-democracy activists were far from certain that the promised elections in 2017 and 2020 would be truly democratic. The contest between those activists and the HKSARG soon surfaced in 2013.

Political Reform Package and Bottom-up Mobilization (2013–2015)

A six-month consultation commenced in December 2013 by the HKSARG in response to the proposal for electoral reform. Although the consultation focused on both the CE and legislative elections, the method of electing the CE in 2017 became a major controversy. According to Article 45 of the Basic Law:

> The method for selecting the Chief Executive shall be specified in the light of the actual situation in the Hong Kong Special Administrative Region and in accordance with the principle of gradual and orderly progress. The ultimate aim is the selection of the Chief Executive by universal suffrage upon nomination by a broadly representative nominating committee in accordance with democratic procedures. (Article 45(2))

Therefore, the composition and method of selecting a nominating committee became the focus of the debate. Prior to public consultation, the pro-democracy camp had already commenced a campaign to advocate for genuine universal suffrage in 2017. The "Occupy Central" Movement (OCM) was initiated by two scholars and a pastor in March 2013 to rally public support for electing the CE by universal and equal suffrage in 2017. In the end, without the endorsement of the ultra-radical wing, the OCM decided to include 15 proposals of constitutional reform—representing the different positions of pro-democracy forces—in the last round of deliberations and voting by participants of the deliberation days. The top three proposals chosen by the participants of the deliberation days were put forward for all eligible voters in Hong Kong to choose, alongside the government's proposal, in a citywide "civic referendum" (OCM Organizers 30 April 2014).

The major differences in the proposals lie in the inclusion or exclusion of "civic nomination" mechanisms, in which registered voters would be allowed to nominate candidates for the CE elections (Box 7.1). Advocates of civic nomination, such as those of the Scholarism group, stressed that civic nomination was a necessary tool, which enabled the average public to "seize the government back" (Scholarism 2013; Wong 2013). The pro-democracy parties such as the DP and the CP did not endorse any proposal with a single channel of nomination by petition, but instead proposed a "three-track" nominating mechanism that included nomination by a committee as prescribed in the Basic Law, as well as that by political parties. Ultra-radicals like the Civic Passion, which did not participate in the OCM's campaign, challenged the legitimacy of the Basic Law and called for ignoring the existing framework of the Basic Law in advancing democratization (Yuen and Chung 2018:29). Ultimately, three proposals that included civic nomination were selected in the last round of OCM's deliberation. All other proposals that excluded civic nomination proposed by moderate democrats were excluded from the civic referendum.

While most of the pro-democracy groups endorsed civic nomination, such a mechanism was rejected by Beijing and the pro-establishment camp, arguing that it contravened the Basic Law (Hong Kong Policy Research Institute 2013).

In the face of popular demand for full universal suffrage and the controversy of civic nomination, the CCP took two steps to reject civic nomination and other channels of nomination in addition to a nominating committee. On 10 June 2014, the State Council of China released the *White Paper on the Practice of the "One Country, Two Systems" Policy in the HKSAR*, in which the CCP asserted that Beijing was entitled to have "comprehensive jurisdiction" over Hong Kong. The White Paper also stated that all people working in the HKSARG, including judges, should be "patriotic" in the sense that they must safeguard "the country's sovereignty, security, and development interests" (State Council of the People's Republic of China 2014). The White Paper sparked backlash from the public and the pro-democracy forces, who regarded it as a symbol of Beijing's hard-lined policy against Hong Kong. The White Paper also signaled that any proposals for nominating procedures in future CE elections that could be open to "unpatriotic" candidates would be rejected for national security reasons. Despite the political pressure generated by the White Paper, 792,808 voters, out of 3,507,786 eligible voters in Hong Kong participated in the OCM's civic referendum challenging the notion of nomination contained in the White Paper. The proposal of ATD, which suggested a "three-track" nominating channel that included civic nomination, received the most votes. In addition, 87.5 percent of voters in the civic referendum supported a motion that lawmakers should veto any government proposal that does not comply with the principles of universal suffrage in accordance with the Universal Declaration of Human Rights and the International Covenant on Civil and Political Rights of the United Nations, which allowed genuine choice by electors (HKUPOP 26 June 2019). The result of the referendum revealed the palpable clash between the hard-lined stance of Beijing and the popular demands for a genuine democratic reform.

Tensions between Beijing and the pro-democracy camp flared up after the SCNPC's decision on universal suffrage of the CE elections was released on 31 August 2014. The SCNPC decided that if popular elections were to be held: (i) the number of members, composition, and formation method of the nominating committee shall be arranged in accordance with the practices of the existing Election Committee (Box 7.2), (ii) the nominating committee could only nominate two to three candidates for the CE elections, and (iii) each candidate must be endorsed by more than 50 percent of all the members of the nominating committee (SCNPC 31 August 2014). The SCNPC's move, also called the "8.31 Decision," would secure the dominance of pro-Beijing forces in the future nominating committee. Following this decision, the right to a fair and equal nomination, as well as to equal participation in political elections in Hong Kong, would be undermined as the decision does not comply with the aforementioned international standards. Agitated by the CCP's breach of its promise of installing full democracy in Hong Kong, an occupy movement, dubbed the Umbrella

Movement, broke out in late September 2014. The movement was orchestrated as civil disobedience that aimed at pressuring Beijing to withdraw the "8.31 Decision" and concede on democratization through a large-scale occupation outside government headquarters.

As shown by a public opinion survey, the movement mobilized 1.2 million Hong Kong citizens to join, which constituted 20 percent of the city's population between the ages of 15 and 65, turning the protest into the largest civil resistance in Hong Kong's history (Sing 2018). A survey also revealed that 87 percent of participants in the Umbrella Movement were primarily motivated by their desire for genuine universal suffrage (Cheng and Yuen 2014). Nonetheless, Beijing did not withdraw the "8.31 Decision". The Umbrella Movement was ended by the clearance of protest sites under civil injunctions issued by the courts (Davis 2016).

In April 2015, the HKSARG released a constitutional reform package, suggesting future CE elections will be subject to the 8.31 Decision. Further democratization in the legislative election was not included (HKSAR Government 2015). The constitutional reform package was predictably vetoed by the pro-democracy lawmakers (Kwok and Lee 2015). In short, the bargaining process for democratic reform between pro-democracy forces and the state at this stage was much more confrontational.

Resistance Movement (2016–2019)

The rule of law is one of the "indispensable conditions" of democratization and lays a foundation for all other qualities that constitute democracy (Linz and Stepan 1996: 10; Diamond and Morlino 2015: 36). Rule of law refers to, under the minimalist understanding, the idea that both government officials and citizens abide by and are bound by laws that constrain the arbitrary power of the state from intruding upon citizens' rights (Thompson 1975; Cole 2001; Tamanaha 2007 and 2012). While the rule of law is widely perceived as a warrant of protection of civil liberties and judicial independence in Hong Kong and as a constituent to future democratization, citizens' enjoyment of civil liberties and the rule of law in Hong Kong have been diminished from 2015 onward, as the government found ways to prevent another outbreak of pro-democracy mass mobilization. However, these tactics only sowed seeds for an unprecedented citywide movement in defense of the rule of law and civil liberties in 2019 and revived the popular demand for full democratization in Hong Kong.

Elections between 2016 and 2018

To prevent both the old and the newborn opposition forces that arose in the aftermath of the Umbrella Movement from gaining political power in the legislature, the Hong Kong and Chinese governments decided to screen out progressive or radical pro-democracy figures from elections. Disqualifying candidates as well as elected lawmakers from running for office became a major way to scupper the political opposition. Between 2016 and 2018, there were three waves of political disqualifications against such candidates and lawmakers in Hong Kong.

The first wave commenced in the beginning of the nominating period for the 2016 Legislative Council elections, when the HKSARG introduced a "confirmation form" for all candidates requiring them to uphold the Basic Law, including provisions of Hong Kong "as an inalienable part of the People's Republic of China" (Article 1 of the Basic Law) and "as a local administrative region . . . directly under the Central People's Government" (Article 2 of the Basic Law), and stating that "no amendments of this (Basic) Law shall contravene the established basic policies of the People's Republic of China regarding Hong Kong" (Article 159(4) of the Basic Law) (Electoral Affairs Commission 2016). The confirmation form enabled officials to examine whether the "words and deeds" of candidates in the public sphere complied with their declaration of "upholding the Basic Law and allegiance to the HKSAR." In the end, six candidates in the legislative election were invalidated for their nominations by the government's returning officers, who claimed they were not convinced that the candidates would genuinely uphold the Basic Law. Among them, Edward Tin-kei Leung, a localist figure who got more than 60,000 votes in a previous by-election of the Legislative Council, made clear to the public and signed the confirmation form with a "resounding no" to Hong Kong independence. Yet his declaration was not approved by the officials, and his nomination was rejected (Cheng 2016).

The second wave of political disqualification targeted newly elected lawmakers in 2016 with the SCNPC's reinterpretation of the Basic Law. Following the rise of youth activism in the Umbrella Movement and the "Fish Ball Revolution," where violent clashes between police and localist protestors occurred during the first night of the Lunar New Year in 2016, two localist figures and four activists who advocated for "self-determination" were elected to the legislature. During the oath-taking ceremony, the two localist lawmakers, Sixtus Leung and Yau Wai-ching, displayed a flag with the slogan "Hong Kong is not China." Yau pronounced "China" as "Shina" during her oath-taking, which was a derogatory term used by the Japanese to refer to the Chinese during World War II (*Hong Kong Free Press* 16 October 2016). Other lawmakers, such as Lau Siu-lai, Edward Yiu, Nathan Law, and "Long-hair" Leung Kwok-hung also took their oath by either very sluggish murmuring or adding clauses on their spoken statements. After the oath-taking, Sixtus Leung and Yau were condemned by the pro-government camp for humiliating the Chinese people in their oaths, and the CE asked the court to review the constitutionality of their oath-taking. Before the court gave a verdict in November 2016, the SCNPC reinterpreted Article 104 of the Basic Law, requiring Hong Kong's elected lawmakers to take their oath of office "sincerely and solemnly," or else they would be disqualified from taking the office as members of the legislature (Williams 2016). In confirming their dismissal from office, the Court of First Instance relied solely on the local legislation and did not apply that interpretation to rule against Yau and Leung. In contrast, the Court of Appeal applied the interpretation to confirm the decision of the Court of First Instance. The other aforementioned pro-democracy lawmakers subsequently faced lawsuits by the HKSARG for their oath-taking and were dismissed from office in August 2017, following the court's ruling (Table 7.1).

Table 7.1: Electoral profiles of disqualified legislators in 2016 and 2017

Legislator	Political Affiliation	Constituency	Votes Gained	Vote Share in the Constituency
Baggio Leung	Youngspiration	New Territories East	37,997	6.5%
Yau Wai-ching	Youngspiration	Kowloon West	20,643	7.3%
Nathan Law	Demosistō	Hong Kong Island	50,818	13.3%
Lau Siu-lai	Democracy Classroom	Kowloon West	38,183	13.5%
Edward Yiu	The Professional Guild	Architecture, Surveying, Planning and Landscape	2,491	43.4%
Leung Kwok-hung ("Long-hair")	League of Social Democrats	New Territories East	35,595	6.1%

Source: Electoral Affairs Commission (2016).

The third wave of disqualification happened during the by-election of the Legislative Council in 2018, which was held to fill the vacancies left in four constituencies due to the oath-taking saga. Agnes Chow, a member of the pro-democracy party Demosistō, submitted the nomination form alongside the confirmation form but was rejected by the government on 27 January 2018. In the explanation, the relevant official claimed that Agnes Chow's nomination was invalid as she promoted "self-determination" given her party affiliation and thus has failed to "uphold the Basic Law and pledge allegiance to the HKSAR." Chow was not given an opportunity to respond to questions on her political affiliation about self-determination prior to disqualification (*South China Morning Post* 29 January 2018). In total, three candidates were banned from running for the by-elections due to their political background. Although Chow's disqualification was overturned in 2019, the High Court's ruling reaffirmed that the returning officer has the power to decide whether the candidate's statement of upholding the Basic Law and pledging allegiance to the HKSAR is genuine and to invalidate the nomination of candidates.

The three waves of disqualifying electoral candidates and lawmakers between 2016 and 2018 revealed that the opposition camps were scrutinized on a three-pronged basis. At first, the government targeted new pro-democracy parties and organized political groups such as Demosistō and Youngspiration, in which the young leaders addressed new demands of self-determination and Hong Kong independence, respectively. The second group pertained to new progressive political activists who emerged after the Umbrella Movement, such as Lau Siu-lai and Edward Yiu, who had been robustly advocating democratic reforms. Lastly, veteran radical leaders in the traditional pro-democracy camp were disqualified, such as "Long-hair" Leung Kwok-hung, a party figurehead in the LSD. Consequently, both fresh and veteran progressive leaders for democracy were prevented from gaining power and resources in the legislature. The same tactic was also deployed in the Rural Representative Elections for Rural Committees in December 2018. The nomination of pro-democracy lawmaker Eddie Chu was invalidated due to his claim that Hong Kong's independence was "an option for Hong Kong people" when replying to the question from the returning officer (Chu Hoi Dick's Facebook Page 2 December 2018). Similarly, in the 2019 District Council elections, the nomination of Joshua Wong of Demosistō was declared invalid by a returning officer on the grounds of Wong's political platform (Hong Kong Election Observation Project 2019).

In addition to the loss of seats and resources in the legislature, the disqualification also enabled the government and the pro-government legislators to drastically undermine the veto power of the pro-democracy camp by amending the legislature's rules and procedures. For major legislative amendments, the veto power is exercised by a majority in both the geographical constituency and the functional constituency. Before the disqualification of the six pro-democracy and localist lawmakers, the pro-democracy camp remained the majority in the geographical constituencies in the legislature. After the disqualification, the pro-democracy camp lost both its status as the majority and the subsequent veto power in the same constituencies (Table 7.2).

Table 7.2: Composition of the Sixth Legislative Council after six legislators were disqualified in 2016 and 2017

	Geographical Constituency (GC)		Functional Constituency (FC)	
	Pro-establishment camp	Democrats and localists	Pro-establishment camp	Democrats and localists
Before disqualifications	16	19	24	11
After disqualifications	16	14	24	10
Majority camp before disqualifications	Non-establishment		Pro-establishment	
Majority camp after disqualifications	Pro-establishment		Pro-establishment	
Total seats	35		35	

Source: Archive on the website of the Legislative Council of Hong Kong, https://www.legco.gov.hk/index.html.

The minority position of the pro-democratic legislators in the legislature has enabled the government to amend the rules and procedures of the legislature. Amendments were proposed and passed in December 2017 to diminish the legislature's capacity to check the executive branch and to block filibustering, which was repeatedly deployed by the democrats to resist or delay the passage of controversial or unpopular bills or the annual government budget. Some of the most controversial amendments include the following: First, the quorum requirement for a general meeting was reduced from 35 to 20, making filibustering more difficult by calling for quorum counts. Second, the minimum number of signatures by lawmakers required to form an investigating committee was raised from 20 to 35, making it nearly impossible to successfully set up any investigation committee in the absence of support from the pro-government legislators. Third, the power of the President of the legislature was raised to the extent that he or she can combine or reject amendments from lawmakers, to curb the democrats' tactic of tabling piles of amendments for filibustering (*Hong Kong Free Press* 15 December 2017).

Freedom of the press and of expression

Freedom of the press is a crucial pillar in enhancing democratization and consolidating democratic accountability. Furthermore, the freedom to publish news, opinions, and printed matters without political censorship plays a pivotal role in safeguarding freedom of expression in the public sphere (United Nations Human Rights Committee 2011). However, since the aftermath of the Umbrella Movement, the Hong Kong and Chinese governments have tightened their control over media firms and publishers in Hong Kong, and self-censorship in media outlets has been increasing, as reflected by a series of dismissals of editors and columnists (HKJA 2019).

Freedom of speech was also challenged in 2016, when five booksellers who sold books on Chinese politics were allegedly abducted or lured from Hong Kong to the Mainland and were later detained in China (HKJA 2016). One of the booksellers, Lam Wing-kee, who returned to Hong Kong after eight months of disappearance, revealed that he and the other booksellers were kept in custody involuntarily by Mainland agents and suffered forced confession and interrogation without due process. This incident was widely covered by the local and international media, as Lam's and other booksellers' stories raised deep concerns about Beijing's extrajudicial contravention of personal liberty and free speech in Hong Kong, and the fragility of basic rights and freedoms of Hong Kong citizens (*BBC News* 16 June 2016; HKJA 2016).

Another incident that raised concerns about freedom of expression was the revocation of a work visa from Victor Mallet in 2018. Mallet, the *Financial Times* Asia editor and the first vice president of the Foreign Correspondents' Club in Hong Kong, was refused renewal of his work visa after hosting a talk with the leader of the Hong Kong National Party, an organization that was declared an unlawful association by the police (HKJA 2019). This incident was a shock to the international community, and the governments of the UK, Canada, Australia, and the US issued statements about their serious concerns regarding press freedom and freedom of speech in Hong Kong (*CNN World* 10 October 2018).

Arresting and charging pro-democracy activists

After the Umbrella Movement, the government repeatedly resorted to the laws to suppress political activists. While judicial independence in Hong Kong has been globally reputable, laws inherited from British colonialism were used to arrest and charge leading figures of the Umbrella Movement and other protests. The use of laws began in 2016, when student leaders, the OCM troika, lawmakers, and activists were charged for their engagement in the occupying movement.

In August 2016, three student leaders of the Umbrella Movement—Alex Chow, Joshua Wong, and Nathan Law—were convicted of inciting unlawful assembly under the Public Order Ordinance and were sentenced to community service (*New York Times* 16 August 2016). However, the Secretary of Justice appealed to the court for a review of their sentencing. In August 2017, the Court of Appeal mandated harsher sentencing guidelines and revised the sentences to include six to eight months of imprisonment for the three young men. A few months after, the Court of Final Appeal reversed the sentence based on the non-retrospective principle when applying the new sentencing guidelines (Davis 2020: 45).

In December 2018, nine pro-democracy activists, including the OCM trio, were brought to trial for allegedly breaching the law of "incitement to incite public nuisance" and "conspiracy to commit nuisance." The choice of charges by the public prosecution was controversial because they imposed the charge of public nuisance not under statutory law, carrying a maximum penalty of three months' jail sentence and a fine, but under common law, which carries a maximum sentence of seven years in prison and a fine. As the famous legal scholar J. R. Spencer has argued, the offence of public nuisance is "vague and infinitely extensible" (Spencer 1989: 83). The charge of public nuisance under common law is often ambiguous and abstract in comparison with statutory law (Amnesty International 16 November 2018). Thus, the charges and convictions of public nuisance could curtail the public exercise of the right to free speech, free expression, and free assembly (Hom 2019).

In the end, the District Court of Hong Kong convicted all the defendants. Two prominent scholars of the movement, Benny Tai and Chan Kin-man were sentenced to 16 months in jail; the third, 75-year-old pastor Chu Yiu-ming, was given a two-year suspended sentence. For the rest of the convicted, two were sent to jail for eight months, three got eight months' imprisonment (suspended for two years), and one got a sentence of 200 hours of community service (Ma 2020). In the defendants' appeal against their convictions and sentences, the Court of Appeal ruled that the occupy protests paralyzed the main arterial roads in Hong Kong for weeks for the sake of pressurizing the government, going far beyond creating mere inconvenience for local people. In the Court of Appeal's view, the charge of public nuisance under common law as well as the heavy sentences imposed in this case were justifiable (Chapter 4 of this volume).

That said, the use of laws above against activists in peaceful protests, and as well as the appeal for heavier sentencing has become more frequent, and morphed into the attempted extradition law of 2019.

The 2019 Anti–Extradition Law Amendment Bill (Anti-ELAB) Movement

The Anti–Extradition Law Amendment Bill (Anti-ELAB) Movement in 2019 was originally an attempt to resist the passage of the amendments to the extradition law in Hong Kong, which proposed allowing fugitives to be transferred to China. The bill was unpopular in Hong Kong, not only because of people's lack of confidence in fair trials and protections of human rights in the Chinese legal system, but also because of the HKSARG's reluctance to hold an extensive public consultation (Lai and Sing 2020: 46). Furthermore, the controversial proposal made civil society groups, the business sector, and even judges worry about how the passage of the bill would damage Hong Kong's judicial independence and its rule of law (*Reuters* 28 May 2019). Despite the fact that 66 percent of the respondents disapproved of extraditing Hong Kong citizens to the Mainland for trial, as reflected in a citywide survey conducted in early June (*Ming Pao* 6 June 2019), and the fact that more than a million citizens joined a rally on 9 June 2019 against the passing of the bill, the government did not budge in its attempt to pass the legislation through quickly. Only after a violent clash between riot police and protestors, who attempted to block the legislators in the Legislative Council Complex from passing the bill on 12 June 2019, did the government announce the postponement of the legislation. However, the government's refusal to withdraw the bill entirely resulted in another large-scale protest on 16 June 2019. The organizer of the rally, the Civil Human Rights Front, announced that 2 million citizens joined the rally (Lai and Sing 2020: 50).

The government's refusal to withdraw the extradition bill, alongside a police crackdown on the protest outside the Legislative Council Complex on 12 June that was perceived as brutal where at least 72 people were injured, spurred citizens to broaden their demands (Li 2019). Protesters demanded an independent investigation into police's use of force during the handling of the protests, release of all peaceful protestors from the June clashes, removal of the label of "riot" to describe the protests on 12 June, and the resignation of the CE. The demands were both substantial and symbolic, taken from a banner unfurled by protester Leung Ling-kit before his fatal fall from a building (Lee et al. 2020: 29). The Anti-ELAB Movement evolved and transformed into a pro-democracy movement when protestors stormed the Legislative Council Complex on 1 July 2019 and vocally demanded universal suffrage (Lee et al. 2020: 30). At the same time, violence had continued to escalate during the Anti-ELAB Movement when police employed more severe crowd-controlling equipment to quell the protest and when some protestors deployed more violent tactics. However, the causes of the escalation of the protesters' violence were intertwined with the state's responses to the protests. The escalation of violence among some protesters since July 2019 could be attributed to the pervasive public anger with allegedly widespread state-sponsored police violence and to protestors' increasing grief with the suicides of some protesters. The widely perceived collusion between the police and the counter-protesters in the latter's attacks on protesters had also intensified the protesters' violence against the police and the government (Tang 2022).

Despite the violent protests, support for the aforementioned "five demands" of the movement remained strong. According to a public opinion survey conducted by the Chinese University of Hong Kong, the demand for reactivating political reform for universal suffrage had increased from nearly 75 percent in August 2019 to more than 80 percent in October 2019 (Table 7.3). In the District Council elections held on 24 November 2019, candidates who supported the movement gained 57 percent of the popular votes and won 391 of 452 seats, which enabled them to hold the majority seats in 17 of 18 District Councils (Hui 2020: 297). However, neither the landslide victory in elections nor the sustained pro-democracy mass protests in 2019 fostered improvements of the rule of law or protections of civil liberties. Instead, as the concluding section suggests, 2020 brought a backlash against freedom and democratic development in Hong Kong.

Table 7.3: Public support for universal suffrage in CE and legislative elections during the Anti-ELAB Movement

	7–13 August 2019 (%)	5–11 September 2019 (%)	8–14 October 2019 (%)
Support for universal suffrage	629 (74.8)	462 (74.2)	611 (81.3)
Opposed to universal suffrage	105 (12.5)	93 (14.9)	72 (9.6)
No opinion/no answer	108 (12.8)	68 (10.9)	69 (9.1)
Total	842 (100.0)	623 (100.0)	751 (100.0)

Source: Centre for Communication and Public Opinion Survey 2019.
Note: The surveys were commissioned by *Ming Pao* between July and November 2019. The original survey question was, "Should the government re-activate political reform and implement universal suffrage (in both executive and legislative branches)?".

Hong Kong's Democratic Development under the National Security Law

In late June 2020, the NPC directly promulgated and implemented the National Security Law (NSL) in Hong Kong, bypassing Hong Kong's consultation and legislative process. The Hong Kong judiciary has no jurisdiction to review and question the constitutionality of such a law imposed by Beijing. The NSL was widely criticized for having violated basic human rights and judicial independence (Amnesty International 28 June 2020). Many Western countries and some Hong Kongers also saw it as the final straw in turning Hong Kong into "one country, one system" and breaching the Joint Declaration of 1984 (*BBC News* 30 May 2020; James 1 July 2020; *The Irish Times* 12 November 2020).

As of December 2022, 227 individuals in Hong Kong had been arrested by the national security police, and 135 of them were charged with offences under the NSL (*ChinaFile* 2023). Further alarm was raised with the very first trial related to national security offences, in which the jury was removed at the request of the HKSARG, generating wider fear over whether courts can uphold due process and have fair trials for the political opposition (Kellogg and Lai 28 May 2021).

Since the implementation of the NSL, localists' and pro-independence parties were disbanded, and the nominations of 12 candidates to the 2020 Legislative Council election were invalidated based on allegations of opposing the NSL, soliciting foreign intervention, and proposing a budget veto in the legislature (Civil Rights Observer 2020). The HKSARG postponed the legislative election of 2020, ascribing the decision to the outbreak of the COVID-19 pandemic. In November 2020, the SCNPC promulgated its decision to extend the term of office of the Legislative Council for at least one year. Four pro-democracy lawmakers, who were disqualified from taking part in the 2020 election, were disqualified from office by the CE, leading to an en masse resignation of the pro-democracy lawmakers from the legislature.

In March 2021, after the prosecution of 47 pro-democracy candidates who campaigned in the democrats' primaries of 2020 for subverting the state, Beijing announced that it would implement the principle of "patriots administering Hong Kong." Beijing would also "improve the electoral system of Hong Kong" by setting up the Candidate Eligibility Review Committee to scrutinize candidates at all levels of elections (*Xinhua News* 11 March 2021). In the end, the authorities resurrected seats for Election Committee members in the legislature that were abolished in 2004 and authorized the National Security Department of the Hong Kong Police Force to provide assessments of candidates for the Candidate Eligibility Review Committee's consideration. With the overhaul of the electoral system, the total number of seats in the legislature rose from 70 to 90. However, the number of directly elected seats in the geographical constituencies was significantly diminished from 35 to 20, whereas the seats returned by elections in functional constituencies was reduced from 35 to 30, with the abolition of "super District Council" constituencies. The remaining 40 seats were returned by Election Committee members. The aforementioned scrutiny marked a further blow to Hong Kong's democratic development, especially when the screening of election candidates' background will be institutionalized and performed by the loyalists to Beijing (Karimi 2020).

The HKSARG took a further step to criminalize any public call for casting blank votes to prevent boycotting campaigns against the new electoral system (Ho 2021a). The new electoral system, combined with the prosecution of the 47 pro-democracy candidates, discouraged the major pro-democracy political parties from running for the Legislative Council election rescheduled for December 2021. In the end, all seats of the Legislative Council were occupied by the pro-Beijing candidates, except one who claimed to be a "pro-democracy" lawmaker, though he has not been endorsed by the major pro-democracy parties in Hong Kong (Ng and Cheng 2021).

The HKSARG also expanded political screening in District Councils. Following the aforementioned victory of the pro-democracy camp in the District Council elections of 2019, the HKSARG proposed legislative amendments in February 2021. The bill requires all District Councillors to take an oath to "uphold the Basic Law and pledge allegiance to the SAR government." The new amendment proposes that those who violate the oath, including District Councillors, will be criminalized and prohibited from running for election for five years. The government further proposed a list of criteria that would be regarded as complying or breaking the oaths. For instance, anyone who commits acts of endangering national security, advocating Hong Kong independence or self-determination, soliciting foreign intervention in Hong Kong affairs, or forcing the CE to step down by obstructing government functions are considered to be breaking their oaths and will therefore be immediately suspended from duties (Cheng 2021).

Even though the proposal did not specify its retrospective effect, the government made clear that past behavior may be considered by the commissioner of oath-taking. The commissioner, as a senior member of the executive government, will have absolute power to determine whether the oath-taker has complied with the requirement of oath-taking and the validity of the oath. The Secretary for Justice can also bring proceedings against any District Councillor at any time during their term of office if they are suspected of breaking the oath. If so, their office will also be suspended until a verdict is given by the court (Ho 2021b).

The introduction of the oath-taking requirement can be read as the government's response to the support for pro-democracy candidates by a majority of voters in 2019, when the popularly elected District Councillors faced a long list of restrictions. The new requirement acts as a Sword of Damascus, dampening organized efforts of pro-democracy politicians and parties to push for greater democratization via various means. Consequently, following the passage of the bill in May 2021, more than 250 pro-democracy district council seats became vacant due to resignation, disqualification by the government, or incarceration under NSL charges (Lam 2021).

Conclusion

This chapter provided an overview of the path of democratization in Hong Kong since the colonial era. Despite the promises of full democracy prescribed in the Basic Law, Beijing's blockade of a fair and open process for nominating future candidates in the CE elections in 2014 was a watershed in Hong Kong's crusade for democracy. It contributed to the outbreak of the largest occupying movement in the city's history. The Umbrella Movement has been followed by the state-led sapping of Hong Kong's civil liberties, media censorship, and political repression. Despite the state's strenuous efforts to control Hong Kong, the resistance to the extradition law and the clamor for democracy throughout the Anti-ELAB Movement have challenged Beijing in terms of its policy imperatives for Hong Kong. In response, the CCP adopted a tougher line in governing Hong Kong more directly. As of April 2023, more than 100 civil society organizations and trade unions have been shut down or dissolved following the implementation of the NSL since 2020, and many trials against pro-democracy media and pro-democracy leaders, including the 47 pro-democracy candidates, are still ongoing. The dramatic and rapid transition from a hybrid to an authoritarian political system in Hong Kong has decimated the public aspiration of democratization as reflected in the following public opinion polls. Popular confidence about democracy in Hong Kong dropped from 6.11 on a scale of 10 in February 2015 to 3.56 in May 2021; confidence in the rule of law in Hong Kong suffered a palpable dive from 6.67 in February 2015 to 4.01 in May 2021, and confidence in freedom also experienced a sharp fall from 7.16 in February 2015 to 4.56 in May 2021 (Hong Kong Public Opinion Research Institute 18 May 2021). Despite the ratings of public confidence in democracy, the rule of law and freedom in Hong Kong in February 2023 slightly increased to 5.25, 6.14, and 6.22, respectively (Hong Kong Public Opinion Research Institute 2023), after the NSL was imposed. This may be explained by the rapid decline in freedoms resulting in pro-democracy citizens becoming less likely to respond to political polls and more likely engage in preference falsification and underreport some potentially sensitive past behavior, leading to the underrating of the public discontent with the autocratic or autocratizing states (Kobayashi and Chan 2022:5). Regardless of the validity of the latest polls, the widely perceived rapid transition of Hong Kong has been detrimental to any renewed mass mobilization for democratic reforms that commenced in the early 1980s.

Despite the disappearance of pro-democracy forces in the last few years, history reveals that geopolitics has played a pivotal role in shaping the destiny of democratization in Hong Kong and many other societies. The Anti-ELAB Movement of 2019 captured global attention and sympathy for human rights and the impasse in the democratic development of Hong Kong. The sharply escalating economic conflicts between China and Western democracies, the intense economic and technological competition between China and the US, the concerns among liberal democracies over human rights in Mainland China, and the Western condemnation over China's promulgation of the NSL in Hong Kong herald the new levels of geo-political conflict in which Hong Kong remains engulfed. It is likely that the political future of Hong Kong will not simply hinge on Beijing, but also on the interaction between China and the West. The support for greater democracy among Hong Kong citizens in the last few decades is unlikely to evaporate entirely, given the decades-long intense yearnings for freedom and democracy among the public. Those yearnings have been vindicated in the pervasive and determined mass participation during the recent Anti-ELAB and previous pro-democracy movements unfolded since the 1980s. The interplay between the CCP, the domestic pro-democracy forces, and other major powers around the globe will continue to shape the development of democratization or autocratization in this postcolonial metropolis.

Box 7.1: Civic nomination

The proposal of "civic nomination" was first introduced by the Scholarism in 2013, which suggested that enfranchised individuals in the public at large should have the right to nominate candidates running for the CE elections. The governments of Hong Kong and China opposed civic nomination on the grounds that it contravened Article 45 of the Basic Law, which stipulates that only a nominating committee with broad representativeness should be allowed. The civil society and political activists, however, put forth a variety of civic nomination mechanisms during the heated debates around constitutional reform between 2013 and 2014, ranging from setting up a minimum requirement of signed endorsement from 1 percent of the registered voters to 100,000 registered voters as a step to fulfill the Basic Law.

Box 7.2: The Election Committee (EC)

Between 1997 and 2007, the EC for selecting the Chief Executive was a committee composed of 1,200 members, which had an electoral base of four sectors with 300 votes from each. The First Sector included the industrial, commercial, and financial subsectors; the Second Sector comprised the professional subsectors; the Third Sector included labor, social services, religious, and other subsectors; and the Fourth Sector consisted of members of LegCo, members of District Councils, representatives of the Heung Yee Kuk, Hong Kong deputies to the

National People's Congress, and representatives of Hong Kong members of the National Committee of the Chinese People's Political Consultative Conference. In 2021, the National People's Congress decided to expand the size of the EC to 1,500 members, reorganizing the electoral base of sectors in the EC, and drastically cutting the potential number of voters from 257,992 (registered voters as of 2020) to 7,971 (registered voters as of 2021). In the newly reformed LegCo, 40 seats are returned by the EC, while 30 seats are returned by the Functional Constituencies, and 20 seats are returned by Geographical Constituencies. Furthermore, under the new election overhaul, the EC now enjoys the power of nomination in each constituency of the LegCo.

Questions

1. How has the China factor affected democratic development in Hong Kong since the handover?
2. What have been the major factors affecting the rule of law and civil liberties since 2015?
3. Was the government's proposed method of electing the CE in line with the democratization of Hong Kong? Why?
4. Has the Anti-ELAB Movement consolidated the democratic movement in Hong Kong? Why?

Bibliography

Amnesty International 2018, "Umbrella Movement: End Politically Motivated Prosecutions in Hong Kong," last updated 16 November 2018, https://www.amnesty.org/en/documents/asa17/9379/2018/en/

Amnesty International 2020, "China: National Security Law for Hong Kong Risks Turning City into Police State," last updated 8 June 2020, https://www.amnesty.org/en/latest/news/2020/06/china-national-security-law-for-hong-kong-risks-turning-city-into-police-state/

BBC News 2016, "Hong Kong Bookseller: China TV Confession was 'Forced,'" last updated 16 June 2016, https://www.bbc.co.uk/news/world-asia-china-36549266

BBC News 2020, "Trump Targets China over Hong Kong Security Law," last updated 30 May 2020, https://www.bbc.co.uk/news/world-us-canada-52856876

Chan, C 2019, "Thirty Years from Tiananmen: China, Hong Kong, and the Ongoing Experiment to Preserve Liberal Values in an Authoritarian State," *International Journal of Constitutional Law*, vol. 17, no. 2, pp. 439–452.

Cheng, E & Yuen, S 2014, "Post-Umbrella Movement: A Farewell to the Age of Political Apathy" (後雨傘運動：告別政治冷感的年代), *Ming Pao*, last updated 29 November 2014, https://news.mingpao.com/pns/%E8%A7%80%E9%BB%9E/article/20141129/s00012/1417197542046/%E5%BE%8C%E9%9B%A8%E5%82%98

%E9%81%8B%E5%8B%95-%E5%91%8A%E5%88%A5%E6%94%BF%E6%B2%BB
%E5%86%B7%E6%84%9F%E7%9A%84%E5%B9%B4%E4%BB%A3

Cheng, K 2017, "Hong Kong Legislature Passes Controversial House Rule Changes Taking Powers from Lawmakers," *Hong Kong Free Press*, last updated 15 December 2017, https://hongkongfp.com/2017/12/15/legislature-passes-controversial-house-rule-amendments-taking-powers-lawmakers/

Cheng, K 2016, "Edward Leung Has Not Genuinely Switched from Pro-Independence Stance, Says Election Official," *Hong Kong Free Press*, lasted updated 2 August 2016, https://hongkongfp.com/2016/08/02/edward-leung-not-genuinely-switched-pro-independence-stance-says-election-official/

Cheng, S 2021, "Hong Kong to Require District Councillors to Swear Allegiance to Gov't—Violators Face Election Ban," *Hong Kong Free Press*, last updated 23 February 2021, https://hongkongfp.com/2021/02/23/breaking-hong-kong-to-require-district-councillors-to-swear-allegiance-to-govt-or-face-election-ban/

Cheung, T & Lam, J 2018, "Hong Kong Democracy Activist Edward Yiu Cleared to Run in Legco By-election," *South China Morning Post*, last updated 29 January 2018, https://www.scmp.com/news/hong-kong/politics/article/2131043/hong-kong-democracy-activist-edward-yiu-cleared-run-legco

ChinaFile 2023, "Tracking the Impact of Hong Kong's National Security Law," *ChinaFile*, last updated 13 March 2023, https://www.chinafile.com/tracking-impact-of-hong-kongs-national-security-law

Chou, YS & Nathan, AJ 1987, "Democratizing Transition in Taiwan," *Asian Survey*, vol. 27, pp. 277–299.

Chung, ES 1990, "Transition to Democracy in an Authoritarian Regime: A Case Study of South Korea," PhD thesis, City University of New York.

Cole, DH 2001, "'An Unqualified Human Good': E.P. Thompson and the Rule of Law," *Journal of Law and Society*, vol. 28, no. 2, pp. 177–203.

Collier, RB 1999, *Paths Towards Democracy: The Working Class and Elites in Western Europe and South America*, Cambridge University Press, Cambridge.

Constitutional and Mainland Affairs Bureau 2004, "Speech by Qiao Xiaoyang, Deputy Secretary-General of the Standing Committee of the National People's Congress," Press Release, last updated 26 April 2004, https://www.cmab.gov.hk/cd/chi/media/s042604-1.htm

Dahl, R 1971, *Polyarchy: Participation and Opposition*, Yale University Press, New Haven, CT.

Davis, M 2016, "Promises to Keep: The Basic Law, the 'Umbrella Movement,' and Democratic Reform in Hong Kong," in M Monshipouri (ed), *Information Politics, Protests, and Human Rights in the Digital Age*, Cambridge University Press, pp. 239–266.

Diamond, L and Morlino, L 2016, "The Quality of Democracy," in L Diamond (ed), *In Search of Democracy*, Routledge, pp. 33–45.

Diamond, L 1999, *Developing Democracy: Toward Consolidation*, Johns Hopkins University Press, Baltimore, MD.

Diamond, L 2001, "How People View Democracy: Findings from Public Opinion Surveys in Four Regions," paper presented to the Stanford Seminar on Democratization, Stanford, January.

Diamond, L 2002, "Elections without Democracy: Thinking about Hybrid Regimes," *Journal of Democracy*, vol. 13, no. 2, pp. 21–35.

Electoral Affairs Commission 2016, "Press Statement by EAC on 2016 Legislative Council Election," last updated 14 July 2016, https://www.info.gov.hk/gia/general/201607/14/P2016071400441.htm

Electoral Affairs Commission 2019, "2019 District Council Ordinary Election," last updated 10 March 2020, https://www.eac.hk/en/distco/2019dc_elect.htm

Fong, BCH 2017, "In-between Liberal Authoritarianism and Electoral Authoritarianism: Hong Kong's Democratization under Chinese Sovereignty, 1997–2016," *Democratization*, vol. 24, no. 4, pp. 724–750.

Frantz, E 2018, *Authoritarianism: What Everyone Needs to Know*, Oxford University Press.

Ginsburg, T & Huq, AZ 2018, *How to Save a Constitutional Democracy*, University of Chicago Press, Chicago.

Griffiths, J 2018, "Hong Kong Leader Defends Journalist's Expulsion as FT Says Will Appeal," *CNN World*, last updated 10 October 2018, https://edition.cnn.com/2018/10/09/asia/ft-hong-kong-victor-mallet-visa-intl/index.html

HKU Public Opinion Programme, "Results of 6.22 Civil Referendum," viewed 6 March 2021, https://www.hkupop.hku.hk/chinese/release/release1164.html

Ho, K 2021a, "Urging People to Spoil or Cast Blank Ballots in Elections to Become a Crime in Hong Kong," *Hong Kong Free Press*, last updated 13 April 2021, https://hongkongfp.com/2021/04/13/just-in-urging-people-to-spoil-or-cast-blank-ballots-in-elections-to-become-a-crime-in-hong-kong/

Ho, K 2021b, "Hong Kong Lawmakers Pass Bill Requiring Public Officers to Pledge Allegiance to Gov't," *Hong Kong Free Press*, last updated 12 May 2021, https://hongkongfp.com/2021/05/12/hong-kong-lawmakers-pass-bill-requiring-public-officers-to-pledge-allegiance-to-govt-four-district-councillors-to-be-ousted/

Hom, S 2019, "The 'Occupy Central 9' Cases: Rule of Law or Rule by Law in Hong Kong?," *JURIST*, last updated 30 April 2019, https://www.jurist.org/commentary/2019/04/haron-hom-central-9-rule-of-law-hong-kong/

Hong Kong Bar Association 2014, "Consultation Document on Methods for Selecting the Chief Executive in 2017 and for Forming the Legislative Council in 2016: Submission of the Hong Kong Bar Association," 28 April 2014, https://www.hkba.org/sites/default/files/2-HKBA-ConstDev%20Submission%20final_0.pdf

Hong Kong Journalist Association and Independent Commentators Association 2016, "Shocked by the Termination of Lian's Column, Increasing Worries over Free Speech" (記協、評協：對《信報》停練乙錚專欄表震驚 對言論自由情況越感憂慮), *Stand News*, last updated 29 July 2016, https://www.thestandnews.com/politics/%E8%A9%95%E5%8D%94%E8%A8%98%E5%8D%94%E5%B0%8D%E4%BF%A1%E5%A0%B1-%E5%81%9C%E7%B7%B4%E4%B9%99%E9%8C%9A%E5%B0%88%E6%AC%84%E8%A1%A8%E9%9C%87%E9%A9%9A-%E5%B0%8D%E8%A8%80%E8%AB%96%E8%87%AA%E7%94%B1%E6%83%85%E6%B3%81%E8%B6%8A%E6%84%9F%E6%86%82%E6%85%AE/

Hong Kong Policy Research Institute 2013, *Research Report on Nomination by Petition*, 19 September, http://www.hkpri.org.hk/storage/app/media/report/20130919.pdf

Hong Kong Public Opinion Research Institute 2021, "Press Release on May 18, 2021: POP Releases Five Core Social Indicators," viewed 29 June 2021, https://www.pori.hk/wp-content/uploads/2021/05/pr_2021may18.pdf#page=4

HKSARG 2014, *Report on the Public Consultation on the Methods of Selecting the Chief Executive in 2017 and for Forming the Legislative Council in 2016*, viewed 6 March 2021, http://www.2017.gov.hk/filemanager/template/en/doc/report/consultation_report.pdf

HKSARG 2015, *Method for Selecting the Chief Executive by Universal Suffrage: Consultation Report and Proposals*, viewed 6 March 2021, http://www.2017.gov.hk/filemanager/template/en/doc/report_2nd/consultation_report_2nd.pdf

Hui, VTB 2020, "Beijing's Hard and Soft Repression in Hong Kong," *Orbis*, Spring, pp. 289–311.

Huntington, SP 1991, *The Third Wave: Democratization in the Late Twentieth Century*, University of Oklahoma Press, Norman, OK.

Inglehart, R 1997, *Modernization and Postmodernization*, Princeton University Press, Princeton, NJ.

Irish Times 2020, "The Irish Times View on Hong Kong: One Country, One System," last updated 12 November 2020, https://www.irishtimes.com/opinion/editorial/the-irish-times-view-on-hong-kong-one-country-one-system-1.4407759

James, W 2020, "UK Says China's Security Law is Serious Violation of Hong Kong Treaty," *Reuters*, last updated 1 July 2020, https://www.reuters.com/article/us-hongkong-protests-britain-idUSKBN2425LL

Kamrava, M & Mora, F 1998, "Civil Society and Democratisation in Comparative Perspective: Latin America and the Middle East," *Third World Quarterly*, vol. 19, pp. 893–915.

Karimi, N 2020, "Iran Disqualifies Thousands from Running for Parliament," *AP News*, last modified on 14 January 2020, https://apnews.com/article/44ad5910fa3e1a297d6c0b5ad6c3c59f

Kellogg, T & Lai, EYH 2021, "Death by a Thousand Cuts: Chipping Away at Due Process Rights in HK NSL Cases," *Lawfare*, 28 May, https://www.lawfareblog.com/death-thousand-cuts-chipping-away-due-process-rights-hk-nsl-cases

Kim, S 1996, "Civil Societies in South Korea: From Grand Democracy Movements to Petty Interest Groups?," *Journal of Northeast Asian Studies*, vol. 15, pp. 81–97.

Klingemann, HD & Fuchs, D 1995, *Citizens and the State*, Oxford University Press, Oxford.

Kobayashi, T & Chan, P 2022, "Political Sensitivity Bias in Autocratizing Hong Kong," *International Journal of Public Opinion Research*, vol. 34, pp. 1–7.

Kuan, HC 1991, "Power Dependence and Democratic Transition: The Case of Hong Kong," *China Quarterly*, vol. 128, December 1991, pp. 774–793.

Kwan, CH 2014, "71 Assembly for Formulating Constitution by the People Calls for Re-formulating the Basic Law" (七一全民制憲大會 推動重寫《基本法》), *Passion Times*, last updated 2 July, http://www.passiontimes.hk/article/07-02-2014/17376

Kwok, D & Lee, Y 2015, "Hong Kong Vetoes China-Backed Electoral Reform Proposal," *Reuters*, last updated 18 June 2015, https://www.reuters.com/article/us-hongkong-politics-idUSKBN0OY06320150618

Lai, YH 2019, "Lady Justice or the Golden Calf? The 'China Factor' in Hong Kong's Legal System," *Social Transformations in Chinese Societies*, vol. 15, no. 2, pp. 178–196.

Lai, YH & Sing, M 2020, "Solidarity and Implications of a Leaderless Movement in Hong Kong: Its Strengths and Limitations," *Communist and Post-Communist Studies*, vol. 53, no. 4, pp. 41–67.

Lam, J 2021, "Explainer|Hong Kong's District Councils: With Opposition Members Resigning in Droves as Oath Looms, What Happens Next to These Local Bodies?," *South China Morning Post*, last updated 16 July 2021, https://www.scmp.com/news/hong-kong/politics/article/3141388/why-are-hong-kongs-district-councillors-resigning-droves

Lee, F, Tang, G, Yuen, S & Cheng, E 2020, "Five Demands and (Not Quite) Beyond: Claim Making and Ideology in Hong Kong's Anti-Extradition Bill Movement," *Communist and Post-Communist Studies*, vol. 53, no. 4, pp. 22–40.

Li, DK 2019, "At Least 72 Injured in Violent Hong Kong Protests over Extradition Bill," *NBC News*, last updated 12 June 2019, https://www.nbcnews.com/news/world/least-72-injured-violent-hong-kong-protests-over-extradition-bill-n1016866

Lin, CL 1988, "The Mass Basis of the Kuomintang and the Democratic Progressive Party: A Comparative Analysis of the Party Support from the Voters in Taiwan (1983–1986)," Master's dissertation, National Taiwan University (in Chinese).

Linz, JJ & Stepan, A 1996, *Problems of Democratic Transition and Consolidation—Southern Europe, South America, and Post-Communist Europe*, Johns Hopkins University Press.

Lipset, SM 1994, "The Social Requisites of Democracy Revisited," *American Sociological Review*, vol. 59, pp. 1–22.

Lipset, SM & Turner, FC 1986, "Economic Growth and Democratization: The Continuing Search for Theory," paper presented at the Seminario sobre Cultura Política en las Nuevas Democracias, Madrid, April 1986.

Lo, S 2016, *Hong Kong's Indigenous Democracy: Origins, Evolution and Contentions*, Palgrave Macmillan, London.

Ma, N 2017, "The China Factor in Hong Kong Elections: 1991 to 2016," *China Perspectives*, no. 3, pp. 17–26.

Ma, N 2020, *The Resistant Community* (反抗的共同體), Rive Gauche Publishing House, Taiwan.

Manuel, PC 1998, "Civil Society and Democratization in Europe: Comparative Perspectives. Introduction," *Perspectives on Political Science*, vol. 27, pp. 133–134.

Ming Pao 2019, "Fugitive Offenders Regulations, Hong Kong University Poll: If Extradition of Hong Kong People for Trial in The Mainland, more than 40% of Hongkongers Intend to Emigrate" (學者民調：倘港人可引渡內地46%擬移民), 7 June 2019.

Ng, E & Cheung, S 2021, "Pro-Beijing 'Patriots' Sweep Hong Kong Election with Record Low Turnout," *Reuters*, last updated 20 December 2021, https://www.reuters.com/world/china/hong-kong-patriots-only-election-draws-record-low-turnout-2021-12-19/

Norris, P (ed) 1999, *Critical Citizens: Global Support for Democratic Governance*, Oxford University Press, Oxford.

Occupy Central with Love and Peace 2014, "Summaries: Proposals on Nomination and Electoral Procedures for Election of Hong Kong's Chief Executive by Universal Suffrage," viewed 6 March 2021, http://oclp.hk/index.php?route=occupy/discussthree/detail&discuss_id=3

O'Donnell, GA, Schmitter, PC & Whitehead, L (eds) 1986, *Transitions from Authoritarian Rule: Comparative Perspectives*, Johns Hopkins University Press, Baltimore, MD.

Overholt, WH 1984, "Hong Kong and the Crisis of Sovereignty," *Asian Survey*, vol. 34, pp. 471–484.

Peruzzotti, E 2001, "The Nature of the New Argentine Democracy: The Delegative Democracy Argument Revisited," *Journal of Latin American Studies*, vol. 33, pp. 133–155.

Peterson, CJ 2018, "Prohibiting the Hong Kong National Party: Has Hong Kong Violated the International Covenant on Civil and Political Rights," *Hong Kong Law Journal*, vol. 48, pp. 789–805.

Pridham, G & Vanhanen, T 1994, *Democratization in Eastern Europe: Domestic and International Perspectives*, Routledge, London.

Puddington, A et al. (eds) 2016, *Freedom in the World 2016: The Annual Survey of Political Rights and Civil Liberties*, Archives, Freedom House, viewed 6 March 2021. https://freedomhouse.org/sites/default/files/2020-02/Freedom_in_the_World_2016_complete_book.pdf

Radio Television Hong Kong, "Hong Kong Connection: The Book Merchant," YouTube Video, last updated 9 November 2018, https://www.youtube.com/watch?v=XrMc4le3k0w

Rose, R, Mishler, W and Haerpfer, C 1998, *Democracy and its Alternatives: Understanding Post-Communist Societies*, Johns Hopkins University Press, Baltimore, MD.

Scholarism 2013, "6.23 Statement on Political Reform: Universal Suffrage for All People, Nomination by the People, Seizing Back the Government" (學民思潮623政改聲明：全民普選 全民提名 重奪政府), Facebook, last updated 23 June 2013, https://www.facebook.com/notes/學民思潮-scholarism/623政改聲明全民普選-全民提名-重奪政府/596808673684876/

Schumpeter, J 1947, *Capitalism, Socialism and Democracy*, 2nd ed., Harper, New York.

Share, D 1987, "Transitions to Democracy and Transition through Transaction," *Comparative Political Studies*, vol. 19, pp. 525–548.

Przeworski, A 1991, *Democracy and the Market: Political and Economic Reforms in Eastern Europe and Latin America*, Cambridge University Press, Cambridge.

Scheppele, KL 2018, "Autocratic Legalism," *University of Chicago Law Review*, vol. 85, no. 2, pp. 545–583.

Shin, DC 1999, *Mass Politics and Culture in Democratizing Korea*, Cambridge University Press, Cambridge.

Sing, M 2003, "Governing Elites, External Events and Pro-Democratic Opposition in Hong Kong (1986–2002)," *Government and Opposition*, vol. 38, no. 4, pp. 456–478.

Sing, M 2004, *Hong Kong's Tortuous Democratization: A Comparative Analysis*, Routledge.

Sing, M 2009, "The Quality of Life in Hong Kong," *Social Indicators Research*, vol. 92, no. 2, pp. 295–335.

Sing, M 2020, "How Students Took Leadership of the Umbrella Movement: Marginalization of Prodemocracy Parties," in CK Lee and M Sing (eds), *Take Back Our Future: An Eventful Sociology of the Hong Kong Umbrella Movement*, Cornell University Press, pp. 144–166.

Spencer, JR 1989, "Public Nuisance – A Critical Examination," *Cambridge Law Journal*, vol. 48, no. 1, pp. 55–84.

Tai, Benny 2019, "30 Years After Tiananmen: Hong Kong Remember," *Journal of Democracy*, vol. 30, no. 2, pp. 64–69.

The World Bank 2021, "GDP Per Capita, PPP (Current International $)," viewed 6 March 2021, https://data.worldbank.org/indicator/NY.GDP.PCAP.PP.CD?most_recent_value_desc=true

Standing Committee of the National People's Congress of the People's Republic of China 2014, *Decision of the Standing Committee of the National People's Congress on Issues Relating to the Selection of the Chief Executive of the Hong Kong Special Administrative Region by Universal Suffrage and on the Method for Forming the Legislative Council of the Hong Kong Special Administrative Region in the Year 2016*, 31 August, viewed 6 March 2021, http://www.2017.gov.hk/filemanager/template/en/doc/20140831b.pdf

The State Council of the People's Republic of China 2014, *White Paper on The Practice of the "One Country, Two Systems" Policy in the Hong Kong Special Administrative Region*, viewed 6 March 2021, http://english.www.gov.cn/archive/white_paper/2014/08/23/content_281474982986578.htm

Tamanaha, BZ 2007, "A Concise Guide to the Rule of Law," *Legal Studies Research Paper Series*, Paper 07-2282, pp. 3–7.

Tamanaha, BZ 2012, "The History and Elements of the Rule of Law," *Singapore Journal of Legal Studies*, pp. 232–247.

Tang, TY 2022, "The Evolution of Protest Repertoires in Hong Kong: Violent Tactics in the Anti-Extradition Bill Protests in 2019," *China Quarterly*, vol. 251, pp. 660–682.

Thompson, EP 1975, *Whigs and Hunters: The Origin of the Black Act*, Penguin Books, England.

Torode, G & Pomfret, J 2019, "Exclusive: Hong Kong Judges See Risks in Proposed Extradition Changes," *Reuters*, last updated 29 May 2019, https://www.reuters.com/article/us-hongkong-politics-extradition-judges-idUSKCN1SZ09U

UN Human Rights Committee 2011, "General Comment No. 34: Article 19: Freedom of Opinion and Expression," United Nations ICCPR, 12 September, https://www2.ohchr.org/english/bodies/hrc/docs/gc34.pdf

Welzel, C and Inglehart, R 2001, "Human Development and the 'Explosion' of Democracy: Variations of Regime Change across 60 Societies," unpublished conference paper presented in Berlin, April.

Whitehead, L 1991, "The International Dimension of Democratization: A Survey of the Alternatives," paper presented at the 15th World Congress of the International Political Science Association, Buenos Aires, July.

Whitehead, L (ed) 1996, *The International Dimensions of Democratization: Europe and the Americas*, Oxford University Press, New York.

Williams, W 2016, "Elected Hong Kong Leaders to Appeal Disqualification for 'Insincere' Oaths," *Christian Science Monitor*, last updated 15 November 2016, http://www.

csmonitor.com/World/Asia-Pacific/2016/1115/Elected-Hong-Kong-leaders-to-appeal-disqualification-for-insincere-oaths

Wong, J 2013, "Seize the Government Back" (重奪政府), *Ming Pao*, 6 July.

Wong, L & Kellogg, T 2021, "New Data Show Hong Kong's National Security Arrests Follow a Pattern," *ChinaFile*, last updated 22 June 2021, https://www.chinafile.com/reporting-opinion/features/new-data-show-hong-kongs-national-security-arrests-follow-pattern

Xinhua News 2021, "China Adopts Decision to Improve Hong Kong Electoral System," last updated 11 March 2021, http://www.xinhuanet.com/english/2021-03/11/c_139802279.htm

Yeung, C 2018, "How Does the Liaison Office Engaging in Publication Industry Comply with One Country, Two Systems?" (中聯辦辦出版　如何符合一國兩制？), *Citizen News*, last updated 30 May 2018, https://www.hkcnews.com/article/12486/%E4%B8%89%E4%B8%AD%E5%95%86-%E4%B8%AD%E8%81%AF%E8%BE%A6-%E6%9B%B8%E5%BA%97-12486/%E4%B8%AD%E8%81%AF%E8%BE%A6%E8%BE%A6%E5%87%BA%E7%89%88-%E5%A6%82%E4%BD%95%E7%AC%A6%E5%90%88%E4%B8%80%E5%9C%8B%E5%85%A9%E5%88%B6%EF%BC%9F

Yuen, C 2016, "Over 44,000 Sign Petition against Youngspiration's Yau Wai-ching amid 'Chee-na' Oath Fallout," *Hong Kong Free Press*, last updated 14 October 2016, https://hongkongfp.com/2016/10/14/over-44000-sign-petition-against-youngspirations-yau-wai-ching-amid-chee-na-oath-fallout/

Yuen, S & Chung, S 2018, "Explaining Localism in Post-Handover Hong Kong: An Eventful Approach," *China Perspectives*, vol. 3, pp. 19–29.

Zhang, Z & Chung, YW 2016 (eds), *Hong Kong Three Years* (香港三年), Oxford University Press, Hong Kong.

Useful Websites

ANTI-ELAB Research Data Archive
https://antielabdata.jmsc.hku.hk/

Centre for Communication and Public Opinion Survey, the Chinese University of Hong Kong
http://www.com.cuhk.edu.hk/ccpos/en/

Full Text of PRC's Constitution and the Hong Kong Basic Law
https://www.basiclaw.gov.hk/en/basiclawtext/index.html

Hong Kong Journalist Association
https://www.hkja.org.hk/en/

Public Opinion Research Institute
https://www.pori.hk/

Further Reading

Chan, JMM 2018, "A Storm of Unprecedented Ferocity: Shrinking Space for Political Rights, Public Demonstrations and Judicial Independence in Hong Kong," *International Journal of Comparative Constitutional Law*, vol. 16, no. 2, pp. 373–388. It discusses how the aftermath of the Umbrella Movement and the oath-taking saga following the 2016 Legislative Council elections had unprecedented impacts on Hong Kong's political rights, the rule of law, and judicial independence in Hong Kong.

Davis, MC 2020, *Making Hong Kong China: The Rollback of Human Rights and the Rule of Law*, the Association for Asia Studies, USA. This monograph provides an analytical overview of Hong Kong's democratic movement since its handover to China, as well as preliminary observations of the political and legal significance of the Anti-ELAB Movement and the implementation of the NSL in Hong Kong.

Lee, CK & Sing, M (eds) 2019, *Take Back Our Future: An Eventful Sociology of the Hong Kong Umbrella Movement*, Cornell University Press, New York. This edited volume offers an in-depth study of the Umbrella Movement in 2014, including different facets of the movement in relation to democratization in Hong Kong.

Tai, B 2019, "30 Year After Tiananmen: Hong Kong Remembers," *Journal of Democracy*, vol. 30, no. 2, pp. 64–69. This article reflects how Hong Kong's democratic movement evolved from the social mobilization in support of the student movement in Beijing in 1989 until the eve of the Anti-ELAB Movement in 2019.

Tong, J & Sing, M (eds) 2020, "Special Section on Hong Kong Protests," *Communist and Post-Communist Studies*, vol. 53, no. 4, pp. 2–154. This Special Section of the journal comprises seven articles that examine multiple aspects of the outbreak alongside the process of the Anti-ELAB Movement in 2019.

Wasserstrom, J 2020, *Vigil: Hong Kong on the Brink*, Columbia Global Reports, New York. This brief report highlights the key aspects of Hong Kong's democratic development since the 1980s.

8
Political Parties and Elections

Kwong Ying-ho and Mathew Y. H. Wong

Political parties are regarded as indispensable to a well-functioning democracy. In modern politics, they can be found in most political systems. By definition, a political party is "an autonomous group of citizens having the purpose of making nominations and contesting elections in the hope of gaining control over governmental power" (Huckstorn 1984: 10). A political party is distinct from an interest group (Box 8.1) in that, among other things, it aims to acquire the power to govern. Parties can exist in most political systems, including democratic and nondemocratic states, while they mostly seek power through elections, ranging from competitive to noncompetitive ones. Theoretically, political parties have an important role in representing society and facilitate the formation of government. Ultimately, party politics aims to coordinate policymaking within the government, within society, or between the government and society (Katz 2014). In general, it is believed that party politics encourages competition with diversified political ideologies and enhances the legitimacy of the whole political system. However, the experience in Hong Kong is inconsistent with this theoretical perspective.

This chapter aims to provide an overview of party politics and elections and highlight the dynamics among the Chinese government, the Hong Kong Special Administrative Region (HKSAR) government, pro-Beijing, pro-democracy, and localist parties in Hong Kong.

Theoretical Review

Party politics in the post-handover era were characterized by emerging tensions and contradictions, due to institutional and political constraints. Constitutionally, political parties in Hong Kong can compete for some elections, but elections do not serve to legitimize the governance of the Hong Kong government authorities. Starting in 2004, half of the seats in the Legislative Council (LegCo) and over 400 seats in District Councils are directly elected. Paradoxically, Hong Kong's system of governance has traditionally been described as an "executive-dominant system" (Cheung 1997). The Chief Executive (CE) has supposed to maintain such an executive-led style of governance since 1997, with nonpartisan affiliation. Currently, the CE is nominated and elected from the 1,500-member Election Committee, which in turn is formed by uncontested seats and a limited franchise of around 4,900 pro-China, business, professional, and political elites (the turnout rate of the Election Committee is around 90 percent). The election of the CE is largely cut off from political parties, while none of the CE hold party affiliation before they are elected.

Existing literature on political parties and elections mostly focuses on the level of sovereign states, and it is largely assumed that parties compete at the national level (Diamond 2002; Levitsky and Way 2002). However, Hong Kong's party politics is an important exception to the existing literature due to its autonomous status. Hong Kong is a SAR of China based on the principles of "one country two systems" and "Hong Kong people ruling Hong Kong." According to the general principles of the Basic Law (Chapter 1), Hong Kong enjoys a high degree of autonomy and shall be an autonomous region of China for 50 years. The formation of the HKSAR retains a hybrid regime and maintains a limited electoral franchise with a certain level of civil liberties. With the consideration of its hybrid regime and autonomous status, Hong Kong's experience is unique in comparative studies and can be classified as a "sub-national hybrid regime" (Fong 2017; Kwong 2018). It is admitted that center-periphery cleavage has been widely studied in the European context, but the mainstream studies focus on the dynamics between democratic central government and democratic peripheral authorities. Spain and Catalonia as well as the United Kingdom and Scotland are some textbook examples (e.g., Colomer 2017; Jeffery 2009). Thus, before the electoral reform in 2021, the uniqueness of Hong Kong was a multiple party system with multiple cleavages, including "localism vs. patriotism" (arising from one country, two systems), "pro-democracy vs. pro-Beijing" (arising from the democratization process), and "pro-labor vs. pro-capitalist" (arising from Hong Kong's economic structure). However, based on the existing executive-dominant system, the power of the executive branch is guaranteed while the legislature is given relatively limited power, resulting in a fragmented legislature. This setting also brings low popular support for political parties, so party politics remains weak and its development is stagnant regardless of political spectrums.

Historical Review

Party politics in Hong Kong has a relatively short history. Its development was parallel to the gradual democratization of Hong Kong in the 1980s and the beginning of direct elections in the LegCo in 1991. The origins of political parties can be traced to a series of student and interest group movements in the 1970s, such as the "Fight Corruption, Arrest Godber Campaign" and the movements to recognize Chinese as an official language and to defend the Diaoyu Islands. The movements were mostly organized by ad hoc interest groups, while the issue usually had a single-issue focus (Ma 2007). Subsequently, many leaders of the movement in the 1970s became leaders of the democracy movements in the 1980s and leaders of the political parties in the 1990s. This development has gone through several stages.

The first stage was during the Sino-British negotiations over the future of Hong Kong in the early 1980s. At that time, the negotiations were politicized around not only the transfer of sovereignty but also the potential transformation from capitalism to socialism (Fong 2015). Some political groups were formed to take part in the political debates and join the District Board and the two Municipal Councils (Urban Council and Regional Council) elections, such as the Meeting Point (founded in 1983), the Hong Kong Affairs Society (founded in 1984), and the Association for Democracy and People's Livelihood (founded in 1986). Those groups were an embryonic form of parties with limited resources and solid support.

The second stage was the extension of cooperation between the pro-democracy groups in the mid-1980s (Ma 2007). In response to democratic reforms after the handover, the Joint Committee on the Promotion of Democratic Government was formed by 95 pro-democracy political and social groups from different sectors to fight for the introduction of direct election of the LegCo in 1988 and a more democratic design in the Basic Law. The Tiananmen crackdown was the most important turning point of the origin of party politics and increased the demands for democracy in Hong Kong. This incident further prompted the democrats to strengthen their better cohesion in preparation of the 1991 LegCo elections. In April 1990, the United Democrats of Hong Kong, the first political party in Hong Kong, was formed.

The third stage was from 1991 to 1997, which was a period of growth for political parties. The landslide victory of pro-democracy parties showed the possibilities of an organized party in campaigning, and Hong Kong people generally accepted party politics to a certain extent (Lam 1997). Also, the abolishment of appointed seats in the LegCo had created more opportunities to run direct elections and organize parties. This attracted more elites to form and join parties with the consideration of a potential career path. The political debates over Chris Patten's reforms polarized local politics and drove more politicians to join political parties.

The United Democrats of Hong Kong and the Meeting Point merged in 1994 to form the Democratic Party (DP), the largest pro-democracy party, which represented a further consolidation of pro-democracy forces. The most significant change was the rise of pro-Beijing parties to extend their political influence. In 1992, some pro-Beijing and pro-business politicians formed the Cooperative Resource Centre, which was subsequently reorganized to become the Liberal Party (LP) in 1994. To counter the rising influence of pro-democracy parties, pro-Beijing politicians and leaders from the Hong Kong Federation of Trade Unions (HKFTU) formed the Democratic Alliance for the Betterment of Hong Kong (DAB) in 1992.

The Traditional Pro-democracy and Pro-Beijing Divide

In most societies, political parties are distinguished by their ideological orientation, which refers to the left-right spectrum (Heywood 2019). The left-right spectrum summarizes the different attitudes adopted by various political parties toward economics and the role of the state. In short, this divide is based on the ideology of welfare distribution: the left generally supports more state intervention and collectivism, while the right generally favors free markets and individualism. The left-right spectrum is still widely use in modern politics.

Given the unique situation in Hong Kong, political parties are not primarily distinguished along the left-right spectrum but are divided into two major camps based on their political ideologies around the issue of democratization and their attitudes toward Beijing. Parties in the pro-democracy camp include the DP, the Civic Party (CP), the Labour Party, the League of Social Democrats (LSD), and People's Power (PP). In general, the pro-democracy parties advocate a more progressive attitude toward democratization (Wong 2020). They emphasize the early implementation of universal suffrage for the CE and the LegCo and protect the electoral rights of all Hong Kong people. Also, they adopt a more critical attitude toward the Chinese and the Hong Kong government against its misadministration. They demand the protection of civil liberties such as human rights, rule of law, and a higher level of autonomy for Hong Kong. In contrast, the pro-Beijing parties adopt a more conservative approach toward democratization. Generally, the pro-Beijing parties put more emphasis on the respect for the decisions of the Beijing and Hong Kong governments around democratic reforms. The consideration of expanding electoral rights should put the interests of the Chinese government as a top priority. Also, they stress a more cooperative relationship with the Chinese and the Hong Kong governments and tend to legitimize the decisions of both authorities (Wong 2020). Values such as stability and propriety are emphasized more than the issue of civil liberties. Parties such as the DAB, HKFTU, LP, and the Business and Professionals Alliance (BPA) are some examples.

Events such as the Umbrella Movement in 2014 and the veto of the proposal on universal suffrage of the CE in 2015 can best illustrate the ideological divide between the two camps. On 31 August 2014, the Standing Committee of the National People's Congress announced that the electoral method for the CE in 2017, according to Article 45 of the Basic Law, would require majority support from a nominating committee, thus enabling the Chinese government to control the candidates under universal suffrage. The proposal limited the number of candidates to two or three who could first win majority support from a China-dominant Nomination Committee with 1,200 members and put all candidates up for a general election afterward. It aimed to fulfill the constitutional commitment under the Basic Law for "the selection of the CE by universal suffrage," but the Chinese government could still manipulate the candidates at the same time. This decision led to a massive confrontation in the Umbrella Movement against the decision, while protesters blocked main roads in Hong Kong for 79 days. Pro-democracy parties mostly supported and were involved in the campaigns to fight for democracy and freedom, while pro-Beijing parties opposed it as a violation of the law and condemned the occupations to protect the economic property of Hong Kong. The proposal failed to obtain support of two-thirds of all 70 LegCo Members; all 27 pro-democracy legislators voted against the proposal and 39 pro-Beijing legislators claimed to vote for it, even though only at least eight of them voted.

Localism: A New Focal Point or Short-Term Exception?

This status quo was challenged through the rise of localism and the formation of a new group of political organizations. This had realigned the party competition to a new spectrum between "pro-establishment" (pro-Beijing) and "non-establishment" (consisting of the original pro-democracy parties plus the new localist groups). This shift reflected the emerging social debate on the acceptance and rejection of greater integration with China and the recognition of the national Chinese identity (vis-à-vis the local Hong Kong identity). Although the pro-democracy parties have been criticized by the pro-Beijing camp since the 1990s, many of them still affiliated themselves with Chinese identity. They emphasized their opposition to the intervention of the Chinese Communist Party but respected the sovereignty of China over Hong Kong (Ma 2015). Some pro-democracy parties also considered protests in Hong Kong as parts of China's democratic movement, while Hong Kong people could make use of its political freedom to fight for democratization and human rights protection in Mainland China. The annual June Fourth candlelight vigil was a typical example of such ideas.

In recent years, the negative feelings toward the Chinese government, Mainland tourists, and even new immigrants nurtured new political sentiments. These new sentiments can be summarized by four main factors, including (1) the fear of the erosion of Hong Kong's autonomy (Wu 2016), (2) increasing affirmation of Hong Kong identity against Chinese identity (Lam 2020), (3) the increasing daily conflicts between Hong Kong people and Mainland tourists (Ma 2015), and (4) growing dissatisfaction with the traditional advocacy of the existing pro-democracy camps (Kwong 2016). The most significant turning point was the failure of the Umbrella Movement. When the Movement failed to bring concrete political concessions, many pro-democracy supporters realigned with the localist camp in order to seek new resistance advocacies (Cheng 2016; Fong 2017).

Localism, according to Madanipour and Davoudi (2015), is defined as a movement based on a desire to struggle for self-determination, to protect local autonomy, and to fight against the external forces attempting to integrate a locality into larger political units. In the political context of Hong Kong, localism refers to a political movement that stands for the Hong Kong identity and resists excessive control by the Chinese government (Kwong 2018). As a political movement, the localism brand incorporates a wide range of parties and groups with a diverse set of ideas, including the maintenance of existing autonomy, the fight for self-determination by referenda, or even a fundamental change to the relationship between Hong Kong and Mainland China. While some localist parties advocate non-violent strategies such as protests and assemblies, many do not shy away from adopting radicalism such as violent clashes with the authorities. Examples of localist groups were Youngspiration and Demosistō.

In fact, public attention to localism was not very high initially, as the focus of political debate has been placed on democratization. In recent years, with the growing fears about political intervention by the Chinese government, the rise of localism is more notable (Kwong 2018). Crucial events included the anti-parallel trading protests in 2015 and the Mong Kok Riots 2016. While these events led to a strong debate on whether Hong Kong people should fight for the rights for self-determination and whether violent methods were acceptable in social movements, localist parties performed strongly in subsequent years. This new wave gained much public support and created new opportunities for the localist parties in the LegCo elections in 2016. However, notwithstanding their promising performance with substantial public support in the District Council elections in 2019 and primaries for the non-establishment camp in July 2020, the emergence of localism as a mainstream political ideology was undermined by the disqualification of elected localist legislators (Chapter 3 of this volume). The National Security Law (NSL) implemented in 2020 poses a profound challenge for them not only in terms of electoral disqualifications but also prosecution. As a result, most localist parties are either dissolved or largely inactive. The suppression also extended to the pro-democracy camp. Altogether, 47 opposition figures from both pro-democracy and localist camps who took part in internal primaries have been charged with subversion under the NSL. The recent electoral reforms further impose political screening on the opposition by granting powers to the police force to ban the opposition. The passing of the NSL and the electoral reforms provide more electoral seats to the pro-Beijing camp because of more "controllable" vacancies and less competition from the opposition. The dynamics among pro-Beijing, pro-democracy, and localist camps remain important for further observations.

People's Skepticism toward Political Parties

Although the competition among different camps becomes intense, Hong Kong people generally have a strong skepticism about party politics, while many studies have argued that the term "political parties" is quite negative. For instance, based on the data from a public poll in 2016 (Hong Kong Institute of Asia-Pacific Studies 2022), more than half of respondents revealed that they are nonpartisan; that is, none of the political parties could represent their interests. In the latest data in 2022, people who claim they are nonpartisan further increased to around 77 percent due to the heavier political restrictions. The endorsement of all pro-democracy (e.g., DP and CP) and pro-Beijing parties (e.g., DAB and LP) dropped significantly from around 20 percent in 2016 to 0.7 percent in 2022, and from 18 percent to 0.9 percent, respectively, as shown in Figure 8.1.

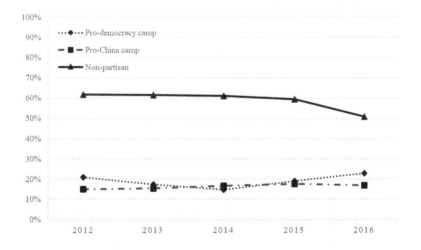

Figure 8.1: Self-identified affiliation of participants

This negative impression is closely related to strategies of the Chinese government in Hong Kong. First, political parties were unable to exercise the theoretical functions of political parties, such as representation and facilitating governance. The actual influence of political parties is still limited due to the executive-dominant system. The resources are still dominated by the executive branches while the bargaining power of political parties, even among pro-Beijing parties, is obviously weak (Fong 2014). Second, the major political parties continuously engaged in either legitimating the government's proposals or criticizing every decision of the government. The "demonstration vs. anti-democratization" divide and "pro-China vs. anti-China" divide would continue to define the major political polarization between parties in Hong Kong. More struggles within the legislature are observed that hinder the governance of Hong Kong (Wong 2014). Third, the NSL and the electoral reforms painted a pessimistic outlook for party politics in the future. Pro-democrats and localists were not involved in elections, while pro-Beijing parties could gain a large number of seats from the functional constituencies and the Election Committee even without geographical direct elections. People's voting and support to parties have become less influential.

To summarize, weak political parties in Hong Kong have failed to channel the interests of people and facilitated the formulation of policy suggestions, further widening the gap between the government and society. The lack of an effective ruling party points to the fact that the Hong Kong government has no effective political machine to mobilize public support from pro-Beijing parties but faces more criticisms from the opposition camp (Fong 2014). The recent electoral reforms provide opportunities for the pro-Beijing parties to monopolize the LegCo with little or no objection. In the short run, the government can enact laws, make policies, and approve budgets with no difficulties. Whether the reforms can facilitate the governance of Hong Kong in the long run requires more observation.

The Electoral System in Hong Kong

The LegCo was first established in 1843, and all seats were appointed by the colonial governors until 1985. As part of its strategy to ensure an "honorable retreat" from Hong Kong, the British government decided to introduce various reforms to democratize the political system in the final years of its rule (Ma 2007). The first wave was the incorporation of 12 functional constituency seats; twelve seats from the electoral college were formed by members of the District Board and the Urban and Regional Councils. Shortly after that, direct elections were first introduced in 1991, with 18 of 60 seats returned by geographical constituencies.

The LegCo adopts a combined electoral system. In March 2021, the National People's Congress approved a decision to amend the electoral system (Annex

II of the Basic Law) of Hong Kong to ensure "patriots governing Hong Kong." Currently, based on the electoral reform approved in Hong Kong in May 2021, 70 seats in the LegCo have been expanded to 90. Altogether, 35 seats in geographical constituencies have been reduced to 20, 35 seats in functional constituencies have been decreased to 30 (five seats from District Council (Second) elected by all voters are removed), and 40 seats are returned by the 1,500-member Election Committee. In the early stage of the handover, the 60 Members of the LegCo were elected through three different categories: geographical constituencies through direct elections; functional constituencies through indirect elections by corporations, organizations, and professional elites; and the Election Committee (Table 8.1). The seats of the Election Committee were elected by a committee, while its composition was the same as the 800 member CE Election Committee from business, professional, social welfare, and labor, as well as political sectors. The Election Committee elected 10 legislators in 1998 and six legislators in 2000 and was abolished in 2004. Those representatives were mostly elected by corporations, associations, and professionals that were criticized as being "small-circle elections" and biased in favor of business and professional interests (Fong 2015). The majority of the Election Committee was formed by pro-Beijing members to ensure the pro-Beijing camp dominated the LegCo and the CE in the early stage.

Table 8.1: Composition of the Legislative Council of Hong Kong, 1998 to 2020

	Geographical Constituencies (GC)	Functional Constituencies (FC)	Election Committee (EC)	Total
1998–2000	20	30	10	60
2000–2004	24	30	6	60
2004–2008	30	30	0	60
2008–2012	30	30	0	60
2012–2016	35	35	0	70
2016–2020	35	35	0	70
2021–present	20	30	40	90

With the abolishment of the Election Committee in 2004, the geographical constituencies took up 30 seats to balance the seats with functional constituencies (Box 8.2). Starting in 2012, the seats of geographical constituencies have increased to 35. Hong Kong is divided into five constituencies, with each constituency electing five to eight legislators in 2016 according to the population distribution. The seats in geographical constituencies are elected by the proportional representation (PR) (Box 8.3) system formula, adopting the Largest Remainder method with a Hare quota. The PR system allows candidates to form a list to attend the election and allocates seats to parties or candidates according to the proportion of vote they garner in the election. In theory, this system discourages large parties from winning the election, which is different from the "single-member plurality system" but encourages smaller parties to be represented in accordance with their small vote share. The Largest Remainder method with a Hare quota is commonly considered a method to encourage a multiparty system with diversified representation in the legislature. This electoral method was reformed in May 2021. The seats from geographical constituencies were reduced to 20 and the PR system was withdrawn. The boundaries of five constituencies were changed to 10 with a "binomial voting system" (also known as "two seats, single vote" system) which favors large pro-Beijing parties.

The functional constituencies have been adopted in the colonial era since 1985. The original formula of this system was to guarantee the representation of business and professional leaders who were appointed by the colonial governors and could win the seats again by a newly adopted method of election. This political formula of returning business and professional elites continued by the Chinese government when the Beijing leaders designed the electoral system of the legislature during the transitional period (Goodstadt 2009). Starting in 2012, seats of functional constituencies increased to 35. All registered electors are formed from bodies such as associations and corporations and individuals such as registered professionals. In the LegCo elections in 2016, about 15,800 bodies and around 225,000 individuals were registered as electors, excluding all voters of the District Council (Second). By 2016, the majority of functional constituencies represented only about 240,000 voters, compared to 3.5 million voters in geographical constituencies (Registration and Electoral Office 2016).

In particular, the composition of functional constituencies can be classified into four major methods: (1) umbrella organization by corporates or individuals in a particular umbrella organization, such as "Commercial (First) from members of the Hong Kong General Chamber of Commerce"; (2) corporates by companies in that particular business sector, such as Insurance; (3) representative bodies by major representative bodies, such as labor sectors from labor unions; and (4) professionals by registered professionals under relevant legislation, such as education sector by teaching-related staff. Since most business seats are elected by only several hundred to several thousand voters, most of them are elected by corporate voting with a very limited electoral basis. Thus, the legislators from functional constituencies are commonly considered to have a close connection with local business tycoons and large corporations, which are criticized as "small-circle elections" (Fong 2015). This narrow electoral basis with substantial influence of functional constituencies creates endless political debates in society. Table 8.2 compares elections at different levels in Hong Kong.

Table 8.2: Elections in Hong Kong (prior to 2021)

	District Councils in 2019	Geographical Constituencies of LegCo in 2016	Functional Constituencies of LegCo in 2016*	Chief Executive in 2017
Number of Seats	452	35	35	1
Number of Voters	4,132,000	3,779,000	240,000	1,200 elected by 232,000 voters
Voter Participation	All	All	Restricted	Highly restricted
Competitiveness	High	High	Relatively low	Low
Electoral Formula	Plurality	Proportional representative	Mixed methods	Simple majority
Terms of Office	4 years	4 years	4 years	5 years

Note: Adapted and updated from Wong (2014); voters of District Council (Second) constituency are excluded.

Election Results

The China factor is one of the most important factors of local political development. In the 1991 and 1995 LegCo elections, candidates' attitudes toward the Tiananmen crackdown and democratic reforms after the handover were the deciding factor (Ma 2007). Democrats who criticized the crackdown and supported fast-paced democratization in Hong Kong received overwhelming support. After 1997, while the significance of historical events might have waned, the attitude toward China remained the most crucial factor in determining the electoral results.

There were six elections from 1997 to 2016. In the early stage, when the fading out of the Tiananmen Incident was accompanied by the Asian financial crisis, Hong Kong people turned more attention to employment and economic issues. But the outbreak of the July 2003 protest triggered a return of political affairs. Attitudes toward the Hong Kong government and democratization remained the major dividing line between parties. The political spectrum between the pro-democracy and pro-Beijing camps had become more important in the first five elections until 2012. The votes for pro-democracy parties reflected the endorsement of taking a more anti-government position for better autonomy in Hong Kong. The votes for pro-Beijing parties implied the endorsement of adopting a more constructive position for the government and more integration with China. With the rise of localism in the LegCo elections in 2016, the votes reflect a more criticizing position to both the intervention of China and the advocacy styles of traditional pro-democracy parties with new localist ideas and tactics.

Results in Geographical Constituencies and Functional Constituencies

An analysis of vote shares of the three political camps in geographical constituencies showed that the pro-democracy camp had long obtained a stable and major share of about 60 percent of the popular vote since 1991, while the pro-Beijing camp got about 40 percent (Figure 8.2). In the 2016 LegCo elections, the vote shares of pro-democracy parties rapidly declined from 56 percent in 2012 to 36 percent, with the rise of the localist camp getting about 19 percent. The total vote shares of the opposition camp totaled 55 percent and the pro-Beijing camp gained 40 percent. In terms of the number of seats, the pro-democracy parties obtained 13 and localist parties won six, while the pro-Beijing parties garnered 16 seats. The opposition camp took a large portion of the votes and seats and earned a safer majority in direct elections than the pro-Beijing camp. With the new electoral restrictions, most pro-democracy parties were not involved in the election in 2021, whereas only a few pro-democracy independents joined. The votes for the opposition camp dropped to around 3 percent, with the pro-Beijing camp winning around 93 percent of votes. The pro-Beijing camp is favorable of dominating under the current reformed electoral system.

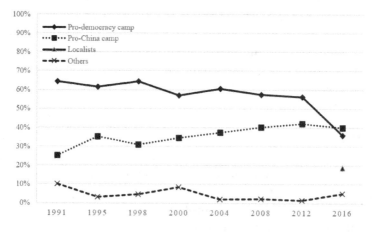

Figure 8.2: Vote shares of different camps, 1991 to 2016

Table 8.3 indicates the partisan distribution of the LegCo. The DP, the largest party in 1998 with 13 seats, dropped its seat number to nine in 2004 and 2009 with the rise of the CP and other new pro-democracy parties. In 2016, the DP obtained five seats in geographical constituencies and two seats in the functional constituencies from the District Council (Second). More new pro-democracy parties and localist parties could gain the seats. Under the new electoral system, none of the pro-democracy and localist parties are able to get a seat in the Legislative Council. The DAB is the largest political party with 19 seats (21 percent). The HKFTU also increased the seats from five in 2016 to eight in 2021. The new binomial voting system makes it easier for large pro-Beijing parties to gain at least one seat in each constituency. With coordination among the pro-Beijing camp, such an electoral system encourages more small and new pro-Beijing parties, such as New Prospect for Hong Kong and Kowloon West New Dynamic, to take part in the election. It is believed that the intention of the new system design was that the more popular pro-Beijing parties would be able to win a greater majority of geographical constituencies, while the less established ones would also be able to obtain a sizable share of votes in the elections.

Table 8.3: Partisan distribution of the LegCo

	1998–2000	2000–2004	2004–2008	2008–2012	2012–2016	2016–2020	2021–2025
DP	13	12	9	9	6	7	0
CP	–	–	6	5	6	6	0
Other Pro-Democracy Parties	5	6	6	8	12	11	0
Other Localist Parties	–	–	–	–	–	6	0
DAB	10	9	10	10	13	12	19
HKFTU	–	3	4	4	6	5	8
LP	10	8	10	3	5	4	4
BPA	–	–	–	–	7	8	7
Other Pro-Beijing Parties	13	13	6	10	4	5	19
Pro-Beijing Independents	9	9	9	11	11	6	32
Total	60	60	60	60	70	70	89*

* Tik Chi-yuen, an independent from neither the pro-democracy camp nor the pro-Beijing camp, is not included in the table.

The results in the functional constituencies election were more complicated. About one-third of the seats, such as Insurance and Tourism, would usually be uncontested. These typically belonged to the business sectors that adopted corporate voting. The endorsement of the related corporate and business chambers determined the winner and at the same time discouraged any potential challengers. Pro-democracy parties could mostly compete in the professional sectors, which have a wider electoral franchise on an individual basis. In the 2004 elections, democrats successfully captured two new seats in the medical and accountancy sectors, taking seven seats out of nine professional sectors. In 2008, the democrats faced setbacks with four seats, as the party affiliation affected the sectors with limited franchise. In 2016, the pro-democracy parties gained seven seats again with the failure of coordination within the pro-Beijing camp. Overall, the Hong Kong government enjoyed the majority in functional constituencies, winning over 70 percent of the seats. Under the new electoral reform, the pro-democracy parties have been further marginalized while pro-Beijing parties/independents have gained all the seats. Even in those seats from traditional professional sectors (e.g., the education and legal sectors) that were dominated by the pro-democracy camp, no pro-democracy parties/independents took part in the election.

Strategies of the Chinese Government over Party Development in Hong Kong

In general, political parties in Hong Kong have remained weak and even been marginalized in terms of political influence, resources, and mobilization since the handover. Although political parties grew significantly in the 1990s, their influence declined after 1997. The strategies of the Chinese government introduced several factors that hinder the party politics involved in the executive and legislative branches.

Institutional constraints: Nonpartisan advantages through institutional designs

To begin with, the Chinese government has always been unfavorable to party development in Hong Kong, especially the formation of a ruling party (Lau and Kuan 2002; Ghai 1997; Ma 2007). A strong ruling party with mobilization and mass support would be difficult to control and might cultivate more local politicians who can confront the influence of the Chinese government over Hong Kong. The constraints of party politics in the executive can be observed by the institutional design. The Chinese government is intended to develop a nonpartisan CE, neither from pro-Beijing nor pro-democracy parties, in the name of balancing the interests among different political forces (Fong 2014). The CE Election Ordinance Section 31 declares that the CE cannot be a member of any political party during his/her tenure, which intentionally discourages the formation of a single and strong ruling party. Furthermore, the CE is also restrained from appointing party politicians to take key executive positions (at least until the recent decade). This situation formally continues despite the introduction of the Principal Officials Accountability System in 2002 and its further expansion in 2008. Under the system, all principal officials—including secretaries of departments, directors, deputy directors, and assistants to directors of bureaus—need to withdraw or freeze their party memberships before taking their positions. When most of the key executive positions are not open for electoral contestation, thus discouraging party membership, it is difficult for political parties to compete for power positions through elections. As political parties have little chance to share executive power, party politicians are forced to run for the positions in the LegCo that are relatively powerless under the executive-dominant system. This also makes it more difficult for parties to nurture future leaders for governance.

Also, the institutional designs of the LegCo discourage the development of party politics. Although political parties tend to participate in the geographical constituencies, half of the seats in the LegCo are still elected by functional constituencies, which are dominated by pro-Beijing business chambers, companies, and organizations (Wong 2015). With very limited franchise, politicians running for the functional constituencies, especially in those business sectors, usually do not require the party support for mobilizing voters, while candidates count on the support of relevant business chambers and corporations. Party affiliation may even lose voter support in a particular sector when voters believe the advocacies may oppose sectoral interests (Kwong and Wong 2020). Members of functional constituencies need to defend their interests to survive and put political compromises within the party as a low priority. As a result, party affiliation limits the room for development of party politics; in fact, a certain number of the legislators of functional constituencies are pro-Beijing independents. This logic can further be extended to the recent electoral reforms. Since pro-democracy and localist parties have faced many restrictions to take part in the election, pro-Beijing parties are capable of dominating geographical constituencies. Party affiliation is still important to gain popularity and seats in general elections. However, for the seats with limited voters from functional constituencies and the Election Committee, party affiliation may not facilitate the elections but would still be considered burdens for sectoral interests. Thus, pro-Beijing "independents" are expected to keep a significant number of seats under the new reforms (Table 8.3).

Political constraints: Support for pro-Beijing parties and repression of the opposition

Political parties tend to be more actively involved in geographical constituencies. The Chinese government has adopted different strategies to support pro-Beijing parties to win elections over pro-democracy parties. Pro-Beijing parties have gradually expanded their voter base by making use of their resource advantages for distributing material rewards (Fong 2017). While pro-democracy parties tend to struggle to secure business donations due to the close partnership between the Chinese government and pro-Beijing business sectors, some pro-Beijing parties, especially DAB and BPA, made use of their close ties with the Liaison Office and pro-Beijing businessmen to establish a clear resource advantage. The Liaison Office can even mobilize the pro-Beijing businessmen to donate a large amount of money to support the parties. Due to the huge amount of donations and sponsorships, pro-Beijing parties extensively distribute spoils to grassroots voters, for example by providing free meals and gifts. By doing so, the pro-Beijing parties have successfully built stronger district networks, especially in the District Council elections, and better coordination in the LegCo elections (Wong 2014).

On the other hand, the Chinese government has long utilized many repression strategies to stunt the development of pro-democracy parties. With the rise of localism, the Chinese government has intensified its effort to suppress localist groups (relative to other pro-democracy parties) (Kwong 2018). In response to the Anti–Extradition Law Amendment Bill (Anti-ELAB) Movement in 2019–2020, the Chinese government further enacted the NSL in June 2020, criminalizing any act of secession, subversion, terrorism, or collusion with foreign forces. In response, some localist parties or groups promptly disbanded prior to the enactment. Initially, pro-democracy parties that support the autonomous status quo and democratic reforms have become moderate in Beijing's eyes, as they do not touch Beijing's "red line." However, 47 opposition figures from both democrats and localists involved in the primaries have been prosecuted under the NSL. Some prosecuted figures announced their retirement from politics, quit their parties, and even urged the party to disband for the safety of its members. The repression of the opposition further extends to both radicals and moderates.

After the Umbrella Movement in 2014, the pro-democracy and localist parties invariably confronted resistance tactics. In the Mong Kok riots in February 2016, the conflict peaked when the pro-democracy parties openly criticized the violent and radical actions of localist parties. During the Anti-ELAB Movement in 2019, there was a high degree of solidarity between the moderate and radical flanks. The solidarity has contributed to the movements' sustainability and all opposition camps, including both pro-democracy and localist parties, frequently use movement slogans such as "brothers climbing mountains, each offering one's efforts" and "no splitting and no severing of ties" to release the internal struggles (Lee 2020). As the newly adopted NSL in 2020 targeted both localist parties and moderate pro-democracy parties, the Neo Democrats, a moderate pro-democracy party, has announced it is disbanding due to the security law and the "tight" political environment. It is expected that most pro-democracy parties will be excluded from the political system for a long period of time.

Strategies of the Chinese Government over Elections in Hong Kong

Starting in 2016, the Chinese and Hong Kong governments started disqualifying candidates in the LegCo elections. After the Mong Kok riots, the localist sentiment reached a peak during the LegCo New Territories East by election in February 2016. Edward Leung, the founder of Hong Kong Indigenous and a key figure in the incident, won 15.4 percent (66,524 votes) in the election, while the candidates of pro-democracy parties won 37.2 percent and pro-Beijing parties got 34.8 percent. This result took the Chinese government by surprise, as the localist camp has become the "respectable third" compared to pro-democracy and pro-Beijing parties. As it was estimated that Edward Leung would gain one seat in the LegCo elections in September 2016, the Chinese government made use of the administrative process to ban Leung and other localist activists from the elections (Kwong 2018).

During the nomination period of the 2016 LegCo elections, the government required all candidates to either sign an additional declaration form declaring their acceptance of Hong Kong as an inalienable part of China or face disqualification. Previously, the system only required candidates to sign a declaration to uphold the Basic Law and pledge allegiance to Hong Kong. In the face of these measures, the pro-democracy and localist parties responded differently in 2016. Nearly all pro-democracy parties, such as DP and CP, refused to sign the declarations on the belief that they had no legal basis, yet all candidates were still permitted to compete in the election. Some localist parties also refused to sign but were given candidacies. However, at least five nominations from the localist camp, including Edward Leung (who nonetheless signed the declaration) and Chan Ho-tin (who refused to sign), were disqualified by the Electoral Officers with claims that the candidates had "no intention to uphold the Basic Law."

The electoral disqualifications were further expanded in the LegCo elections in 2020. In late July 2020, citing the NSL and previous calls for foreign governments to sanction the Chinese and Hong Kong authorities as reasons, election officers invalidated 12 electoral candidates, including those from localist parties, such as Joshua Wong, and pro-democracy parties, such as Cheng Tat-hung from CP. Four sitting legislators including Alvin Ngok-kiu Yeung and Dennis Kwok from CP were also included. The mass disqualifications can be summarized as the returning officers believed that disqualified candidates had no intention to support, promote, and embrace the Basic Law. Basically, three reasons can be summarized: (1) candidates objected to the NSL, (2) candidates would seek to veto the government budget, and (3) candidates appealed to foreign governments to impose sanctions on Hong Kong (*South China Morning Post* 30 July 2020). In May 2021, the LegCo approved the electoral reforms and granted the national security police new powers to screen and ban candidates who represent potential threats to national security. Regardless, under the reformed system, virtually none of the opposition parties and candidates could clear the nomination threshold to contest in recent elections.

Conclusion

In all political systems, parties have an important role to articulate voters' views and facilitate the formation of governments. The stronger the capacity of the government to command major political parties, the higher the degree of government to legitimate policy decisions, and vice versa. From this perspective, the experience in Hong Kong was largely inconsistent with the literature and failed to facilitate the governance of the Hong Kong government. Party politics in Hong Kong can be traced to the 1990s, when the colonial British government implemented partial elections. While the Chinese government decided to maintain the executive-dominant system after 1997 and has since installed a pro-Beijing majority in the LegCo, the opposition camp, with strong public endorsement, kept challenging the legitimacy of the Hong Kong government.

Party ideology in Hong Kong is not distinguished along the established left-right spectrum but is based on political ideologies toward democratization and the Chinese and Hong Kong authorities. Traditionally, party politics involved the struggle between pro-democracy and pro-Beijing parties over the divide between democratic progression and civil liberties. Subsequent to the Umbrella Movement in 2014, more people hoped for a new way out and joined localist parties that aimed at novel resistance tactics and new demands, including, for example, the rights of self-determination. In the 2016 LegCo elections, the pro-democracy parties and localist parties obtained 35 percent and 19 percent of the vote, respectively, while the pro-Beijing camp gained 40 percent in the geographical constituencies. It is generally recognized that the political spectrum in Hong Kong has shifted to the divide between "non-establishment" (making up the traditional pro-democracy parties plus the new localist parties) and "pro-establishment" (pro-Beijing), in terms of the more contentious issues of China–Hong Kong relations and acceptance or rejection of national identity. However, the non-establishment camps can be marginalized by the functional constituencies and the Election Committee, as the oppositionists are largely unable to lay their hands on the functional constituencies that are mostly elected by bodies and corporate voting.

Indeed, the Chinese government exercised many measures, such as the NSL, against those opposition parties and disqualifications of candidates. Many significant figures from opposition parties are prosecuted and banned from taking part in the coming elections, while some opposition parties and groups have been dissolved due to the heavy political pressure. Thus, it is expected that the pro-Beijing camp will continue to hold the majority in the LegCo. Whether the authorities will intensify the efforts of suppression, whether this newly elected pro-Beijing camp can facilitate the governance of the HKSAR, and whether the pro-democracy parties will participate in political affairs in the future remain important questions not only for researchers in Hong Kong politics but for everyone interested in the ongoing development and governance of Hong Kong.

Box 8.1: Interest groups

Interest groups are organizations that aim to influence the policies or actions of government. There are four characteristics to distinguish between political parties and interest groups (Katz 2014): (1) parties aim to win government office while interest groups aim to influence policies, (2) parties are organized with a formal membership while interest groups have a less formal structure, (3) parties adopt a broad focus on issues while interest groups have a single-issue focus, and (4) parties emphasize a shared ideology while this may not be important in interest groups.

Box 8.2: Functional constituencies

Functional constituencies (FCs) represent business, professional, labor, and professional sectors in the legislature. The electoral system in Hong Kong ensures the formation of the LegCo by a pro-Beijing majority. Those legislators returned by functional constituencies provide stable support and votes to the Chief Executive in the legislative process. Also, FCs limit the political influence of those opposition legislators returned by geographical constituency (GC) elections.

210   Political Parties and Elections

Box 8.3: Proportional representation

A proportional representation system is an electoral system that allocates seats roughly according to the proportion of votes obtained by each party/list. A list that obtains 30 percent of the vote should get approximately 30 percent of the seats under the system. The proportionality of the system (i.e., how close the two percentages are) depends on the number of seats being distributed.

Questions

1. What are the major differences in positions among political parties in Hong Kong?
2. What are the factors that hinder the development of political parties in Hong Kong? How does this relate to the "executive-led" model of governance?
3. What are the major features of the electoral system of Hong Kong?

Bibliography

Cheng, W 2016, "Street Politics in a Hybrid Regime: The Diffusion of Political Activism in Post-colonial Hong Kong," *China Quarterly*, no. 226, pp. 383–406.

Cheung, A 1997, "The Transition of Bureaucratic Authority: The Political Role of the Senior Civil Service in the Post-1997 Governance in Hong Kong," in PK Li (ed), *Political Order and Power Transition in Hong Kong*, the Chinese University Press of Hong Kong, Hong Kong, pp. 79–108.

Colomer, JM 2002, "The Venturous Bid for the Independence of Catalonia," *Nationalities Papers*, vol. 45, no. 5, pp. 21–35.

Diamond, L 2002, "Thinking about Hybrid Regimes," *Journal of Democracy*, vol. 13, no. 2, pp. 21–35.

Fong, B 2014, "Executive-Legislative Disconnection in Post-colonial Hong Kong: The Dysfunction of the HKSAR's Executive-Dominant System, 1997–2012," *China Perspectives*, no. 1, pp. 5–14.

Fong, B 2015, *Hong Kong's Governance under Chinese Sovereignty: The Failure of the State-Business Alliance after 1997*, Routledge, Oxon.

Fong, B 2017, "In-between Liberal Authoritarianism and Electoral Authoritarianism: Hong Kong's Democratization under Chinese Sovereignty, 1997–2016," *Democratization*, vol. 24, no. 4, pp. 724–750.

Ghai, Y 1997, *Hong Kong's New Constitutional Order: The Resumption of Chinese Sovereignty and the Basic Law*, Hong Kong University Press, Hong Kong.

Goodstadt, F 2009, *Uneasy Partners: The Conflict between Public Interest and Private Profit Interest in Hong Kong*, Hong Kong University Press, Hong Kong.

Hong Kong Institute of Asia-Pacific Studies 2022, "Survey Findings on Evaluations of Political Parties in Hong Kong Released by Hong Kong Institute of Asia-Pacific

Studies at CUHK," viewed 3 March 2023, https://www.hkiaps.cuhk.edu.hk/wd/ni/20220901-105127_1.pdf

Heywood, A 2019, *Politics*, 5th ed., Macmillan International Higher Education/Red Globe Press, London.

Jeffery, C 2009, "Devolution in the United Kingdom: Problems of a Piecemeal Approach to Constitutional Change," *Publius: The Journal of Federalism*, vol. 39 no. 2, pp. 289–313.

Katz, R 2014, "Political Parties," in D Caramani (ed), *Comparative Politics*, 3rd ed., Oxford University Press, Oxford, pp. 199–215.

Kwong, YH 2016, "The Growth of 'Localism' In Hong Kong: A New Path for the Democracy Movement?" *China Perspectives*, no. 3, pp. 63–68.

Kwong, YH 2018, "Political Repression in a Sub-national Hybrid Regime: The PRC's Governing Strategies in Hong Kong," *Contemporary Politics*, vol. 24, no. 4, pp. 361–378.

Kwong, YH & Wong, YH 2020, "One Formula, Different Trajectories: China's Coalition-Building and Elite Dynamics in Hong Kong and Macau," *Critical Asian Studies*, vol. 52, no.1, pp. 44–66.

Lam, J 1997, "Party Politics in Hong Kong during the Political Transition," *American Asian Review*, vol. 15, no. 4, pp. 71–95.

Lam, WM 2020, "Hybridity, Civility and Othering: In Search of Political Identity and Activism in Hong Kong," in T Gold & S Veg (eds), *Sunflowers and Umbrellas: Social Movements, Expressive Practices and Political Culture in Taiwan and Hong Kong*, University of California Press, Berkeley, pp. 65–98.

Lau, SK & Kuan, H 2002, "Hong Kong's Stunted Political Party System," *China Quarterly*, no. 172, pp. 1010–1028.

Lee, F 2020, "Hong Kong Solidarity in the Anti–Extradition Bill Movement in Hong Kong," *Critical Asian Studies*, vol. 52, no. 1, pp. 18–32.

Levitsky, S & Way, L 2002, "The Rise of Competitive Authoritarianism," *Journal of Democracy*, vol. 13, no. 2, pp. 51–65.

Ma, N 2007, *Political Development in Hong Kong: State, Political Society and Civil Society*, Hong Kong University Press, Hong Kong.

Ma, N 2016, "The Making of A Corporatist State in Hong Kong: The Road to Sectoral Intervention," *Journal of Contemporary Asia*, vol. 46, no. 2, pp. 247–266.

Ma, N & Choy, C 2003, "The Impact of Electoral Rule Change on Party Campaign Strategy – Hong Kong as a Case Study," *Party Politics*, vol. 9, no. 3, pp. 347–367.

Ma, N 2015, "The Rise of 'Anti-China' Sentiments in Hong Kong and the 2012 Legislative Council Elections," *China Review*, vol. 15, no. 1, pp. 39–66.

Madanipous, A & Davoudi, S 2015, "Localism: Institutions, Territories, Representations," in S Davoudi & A Madanipour (eds), *Reconsidering Localism*, Routledge, London, pp. 11–29.

Registration and Electoral Office 2016, "Voter Registration Statistics: Functional Constituency 2016," viewed 8 January 2021, https://www.voterregistration.gov.hk/eng/statistic20163.html

South China Morning Post 2020, "Hong Kong Elections: What Does It Mean to Be Disqualified, Who Decides, and How Have Hopefuls Been Barred in the Past?"

30 July, viewed 9 January 2020, https://www.scmp.com/news/hong-kong/politics/article/3095215/hong-kong-elections-what-dq-or-disqualification-who-decides

Wong, YH 2015, "Party Models in a Hybrid Regime: Hong Kong 2007–2012," *China Review*, vol. 15, no. 1, pp. 67–94.

Wong, YH 2020, "Party Competition and Ideology in Hong Kong: A New Manifesto Coding Dataset," *Journal of East Asian Studies*, vol. 20, no. 2, pp. 207–230.

Wong, HW 2014, "Resource Disparity and Multi-Level Elections in Competitive Authoritarian Regimes: Regression Discontinuity Evidence from Hong Kong," *Electoral Studies*, no. 33, pp. 200–219.

Wu, RR 2016, "The Lilliputian Dreams: Preliminary Observations of Nationalism in Okinawa, Taiwan and Hong Kong" *Nations and Nationalism*, vol. 22, no. 4, pp. 686–705.

Useful Websites

Business and Professionals Alliance
https://en.bpahk.org/

Civic Party
https://www.civicparty.hk/en/

Democratic Alliance for the Betterment and Progress of Hong Kong
https://www.eng.dab.org.hk/

Democratic Party
https://www.dphk.org/index.php?route=eng/about_us

Electoral Affairs Commission
https://www.eac.hk/en/about/chairman.htm

Liberal Party
http://liberal.org.hk/en

Further Reading

Cheng, YS 2005, "Hong Kong's Democrats Stumble," *Journal of Democracy*, vol. 16, no. 1, pp. 138–152. This article provides a historical review of party politics after the protests against Article 23 in 2003 and the Legislative Council elections in 2004.

Kwong, YH 2016, "State-Society Conflict Radicalization in Hong Kong: The Rise of 'Anti-China' Sentiment and Radical Localism," *Asian Affairs*, vol. 47, no. 3, pp. 428–442. This article explores the rise of radical localist parties after the Mong Kok riots in 2016.

Lau, SK & Kuan, HC 2000, "Partial Democratization, 'Foundation Moment' and Political Parties in Hong Kong," *China Quarterly*, no. 163, pp. 705–720. This article offers a pioneering study of party politics in the 1980s and the early post-colonial era.

Loh, C & Civic Exchange 2006, "Functional Constituencies: A Unique Feature of the Hong Kong Legislative Councils," Hong Kong University Press, Hong Kong. This book is one of the pioneering studies to offer a comprehensive analysis of party politics and functional constituencies.

Wong, YH 2017, *Comparative Hong Kong Politics: A Guidebook for Students and Researchers*, Palgrave Macmillan, Singapore. This book offers some comparative insights into the development of political parties and electoral systems in Hong Kong.

Zhang, B 2011, "Democratizing Hong Kong: Functional Representation and Politics of Institutional Change," *Pacific Affairs*, vol. 84, no. 4, pp. 643–664. This article provides an in-depth analysis of the origin, challenges, and opportunities of functional constituencies.

9

Civil Society

Stephan Ortmann

Writing a chapter on civil society during a time of great political change is a treacherous endeavor, as the characteristics are likely to shift significantly in the process. With the introduction of the National Security Law (NSL) on 30 June 2020, the Chinese government fundamentally altered the regime dynamics of the once liberal authoritarian enclave, with far-reaching consequences for civil society. There are an increasing number of red lines that are difficult to determine. Many activists were arrested and a number of organizations came under attack. This chapter will briefly revisit the emergence of civil society, then take stock of the situation after 1997, with a view toward the united front effort to provide an alternative to civil society, and finally focus on the period from 2014 until today. While the Umbrella Movement was widely described as a watershed event that heightened civil society activism (Lam and Cooper 2018), the Anti–Extradition Law Amendment Bill (Anti-ELAB) Movement of 2019–2020, which saw unprecedented mobilization and unrest, may well be considered its culmination. The chapter will then discuss the impact of the NSL on civil society. The massive efforts to curtail any form of dissidence suggest that the ultimate goal is to replace the activist civil society with compliant social organizations, including pro-government mass organizations in which a few weak, depoliticized nongovernmental organizations can exist within the very narrow confines of the state.

Defining Civil Society

Civil society is a term that has been much debated in academic literature, with rival concepts that diverge to such an extent that readers need to be mindful of which definition has been used (Box 9.1). For the analytical discussion, civil society is usually conceptualized as a sphere separate from state and market but still closely tied to both. Outside of a realm of private interests, civil society is characterized by freedom of association of individuals who come together due to shared norms to pursue similar interests. People are free to become members of any association as well as leave. Civil society achieves two basic aspects of liberal democracy. First, to maintain the pluralism that is necessary for collective expressions and ensure the free deliberation of ideas. This in turn is necessary for the ability of government to determine the collective will beyond regular elections. Second, civil society also teaches people the basic principles and rules of modern democracy. By participating in society, people get firsthand collective experience fighting for the common good (Box 9.2). Naturally, these expressions of civil society idealize civil society as a separate sphere, when in fact there are numerous areas in which society overlaps with the state and the market. Corporate interest groups, for instance, can be seen partially in civil society, but their financial strength and market interests clearly separate them from notions of the public good (Jensen 2006).

As the concept of civil society is deeply tied to democracy, it has been difficult to apply it to authoritarian regimes. Hong Kong has, however, been characterized as a liberal authoritarian regime—an anomaly in the world—because of constitutionally guaranteed civil liberties in the absence of a democratically elected government. This had been the case from the 1970s onward, when there was a slow process of liberalization (Fong 2016). As this regime form, however, is inherently unstable, Case (2008) argued that it was maintained by various factors, including a demobilized population, economic performance legitimacy, a growing sense of Chinese nationalism, the incorporation of local elites into central government consultative organs, and the prospect of repression. Over time, the population became increasingly empowered, as I will show below, while the economic legitimacy has eroded and support for the Chinese nation declined. As only part of the elite is co-opted, the threat of repression has given way to repression and thus eroded the liberal elements of the hybrid regime.

In order to understand the transformation in Hong Kong, it is necessary to briefly discuss how scholars have studied civil society in Mainland China, where civil society technically cannot exist. Despite the barriers, the number of small organizations outside the party-state has increased significantly. They have even become "fairly autonomous," while the state has become more willing to use indirect control (Teets 2013: 20). Nevertheless, social organizations in China usually have maintained a close relationship with the state; they rarely act as a check on government power, nor do they necessarily strive for greater autonomy and freedom. Instead, for instance, nongovernmental organizations are mainly service providers for the government, even if some of them are actively trying to influence government decisions (Dai and Spires 2018). Since the rise of Xi Jinping in 2012, the relatively relaxed environment of the reform period has been replaced with greater control as more activists have been arrested, censorship has been tightened, and new laws have been enacted that greatly limit nongovernmental activities. This has also affected Hong Kong, where the liberal civil society appears destined to be supplanted with government-controlled mass associations and tightly controlled nongovernmental organizations.

The Emergence of Civil Society in Hong Kong

In the early colonial period, the Hong Kong government greatly limited its involvement in society. The deeply ingrained racism meant that the Chinese and European societies were largely separate from each other. The colonial power mainly sought to maintain order and thus co-opted some societal leaders through the establishment of social organizations. This arrangement only slowly fell apart, and after World War II there was growing pressure to localize the British societies. The civil war on the Chinese Mainland entailed competing social organizations, which either followed the Nationalist Party (KMT) or the Communist Party. This separation would leave deep marks in society and had lasting consequences during colonial rule that are still visible today. None of these organizations, however, could be described as the kind of civil society found in modern states. In particular, they were not deeply rooted in the political system of Hong Kong, which was still predominantly colonial.

The situation only changed in the 1970s, as the colonial government accelerated the localization trend in the aftermath of two riots in 1966 and 1967. These violent incidents revealed significant discontent with the social situation in the colony. The 1967 riots were moreover driven by pro-Communist organizations, which sought to weaken British colonial rule. In response, the government established the City District Officer Scheme in 1968 to reach out to ordinary people. It was, however, only with the arrival of Governor Murray MacLehose in 1971 that things slowly turned around. Unhappiness over corruption fermented in 1973 when a British chief superintendent, Peter Godber, fled to England to escape prosecution. Protests were successful in bringing about one of the most consequential institutions ever: the Independent Commission Against Corruption (ICAC), which was established in 1974. Empowered to prosecute anyone accused of corruption, the ICAC strengthened the rule of law. This and other reforms of the 1970s such as the introduction of nine years of compulsory education, a ten-year public housing program, and reforms to the health care system transformed the role of the government but also strengthened the community and fostered a Hong Kong identity. The government also recognized the need for a community spirit or a sense of citizenship, which included setting up civic organizations to achieve cleanliness and fight crime (Ip 1997). As a consequence, activists focused increasingly on local affairs, and Chinese nationalism slowly lost relevance (Carroll 2007).

This change in the governance fostered the rise of new social organizations, which for the first time could actually be called civil society both in terms of being a space for public debate and an intermediary sphere between government and the people. The roots of the liberal civil society can be found in the rise of pressure groups, such as the Hong Kong Observers, a group of middle-class professionals who had come together in 1975 to discuss public issues affecting Hong Kong. Its goal had been to "supervise and criticise the government through objective research exerting pressure on the government by influencing public opinion" (cited in Cheng 1989: 3). As such, they regularly commented on public affairs in local newspapers, making them part of a budding civil society. Some elected Urban Councillors also considered themselves representatives of the people and played an important role in linking civil society to the rudimentary electoral system. These events challenged the notion that Hong Kongers were politically apathetic (Lam 2015).

The decision in 1984 to transfer power from British to Chinese control in 1997 raised the need for a stronger civil society. Few people had envisioned a transfer of power to the Communist government, while the majority wanted to retain the status quo of British control (So 1993). However, Hong Kongers had not been consulted about their future, and a growing number of activists believed that their voice needed to be heard. A number of activists believed the "one country, two systems" framework could only be effectively implemented if Hong Kong people were ready to defend local autonomy. Only if democratic elections were implemented could the promise of Hong Kong people ruling Hong Kong be realized. They sought to influence the British government to allow more fundamental reforms prior to the handover and to allow the Chinese government to enshrine universal suffrage and necessary liberties for an active civil society in the Basic Law.

The year 1989 was pivotal in many ways. For the first time, hundreds of thousands of people joined a mass movement. They supported the pro-democracy movement across China in the hope that a more democratic China would make the integration of Hong Kong easier. More than a million people participated in mass rallies that summer. Many Hong Kongers also donated money to the cause, and some students even went to Beijing in support of the pro-democracy protesters (So 1997). Meanwhile, the Chinese government grew concerned about the political activism and added language to Article 23 of the Basic Law that made it more restrictive and widened its scope. The final version required the post-handover government to "enact laws on its own to prohibit any act of treason, secession, sedition, subversion against the Central People's Government, or theft of state secrets, to prohibit foreign political organizations or bodies from conducting political activities in the Region, and to prohibit political organizations or bodies of the Region from establishing ties with foreign political organizations

218   Civil Society

or bodies." Problematic for civil society, in 2003 "the government proposed a broadening of existing laws, while further empowering both the local government and the national government in Beijing to infringe on the rights of the people of Hong Kong" (Kellogg 2004: 311). Civil society resisted, but it was only a matter of time before the restrictions were put in place.

Different Forms of Civil Society Organizations

At least until the introduction of the NSL, civil society in Hong Kong could be categorized into two basic forms of organization: traditional societal organizations and contemporary grassroots organizations. This distinction entails weak horizontal linkages between the different types of organizations although there was some cooperation. The most important issues of civil society are related to heritage, poverty, migration, environmental protection, and universal suffrage. An overview of different sectors can be found in Box 9.3.

First, there are traditional nongovernmental and nonprofit organizations that pursue special interests akin to those in many other countries. These organizations can be divided into affiliates of international organizations, territory-wide organizations, and regional organizations. The first captures a wide spectrum of organizations that may not only be interested in local issues but also deal with global or regional concerns. As Hong Kong had been more open to the creation of non-governmental organizations, the territory used to provide a good location to deal with issues related to China and other Asian countries. When handling local issues, these nonprofit and other formal nongovernmental organizations tend to be very careful and seek to avoid any confrontation with the government. In the environmental field, there are for instance World Wide Fund for Nature Hong Kong (WWF), Friends of the Earth (HK), or the Conservancy Association, which are deeply involved in government projects. WWF for instance manages the Mai Po Marshes on behalf of the Agriculture, Fisheries and Conservation Department. Despite a certain institutionalization of these organizations, the legal framework is relatively loose, and thus it is difficult to determine the size and composition of this sector (Lam and Perry 2000). This form of organization has been encouraged by the government for the voluntary provision of services to help the government with problems (Chan 2012).

Outside of these formal organizations, there are many grassroots organizations which are more closely tied to society and far less rigidly organized. Many of them are not even registered with the government because of the onerous registration process and the unwillingness of being subjected to government control. These usually short-lived, cash-strapped organizations allow for quick mobilization of activists against unpopular government policy. Some of them are ad hoc alliances of different organizations, sometimes involving traditional organizations that work together with more activist groups. This form of organization is usually created with a press conference that draws attention to the organization and its issues. It has been at the forefront of defending the autonomy of civil society, which could be maintained by keeping a distance from the government. This part of civil society has been called vibrant and pluralistic but also lacking in political influence, due to weak organizational resources and limited linkages with more institutionalized and less political groups (Ma 2009). In the environmental sector, there are many such small groups, including the Living Islands Movement, Lantau Buffalo Association, or Lantau Society. To counter massive development in Lantau—including the projected Lantau Tomorrow Vision, which will cost an estimated HK$500 billion—various groups and individuals have joined the Save Lantau Alliance, which is a flexible cooperation that relies entirely on voluntary participation.

United Front

To influence the local society and to counter first the Nationalists (KMT) and later the rising liberal civic groups, the Chinese government has sought to penetrate society through its own united front organization. Under strict hierarchical control, the united front in Hong Kong has formed a vast network of conservative groups, such as pro-establishment parties, the traditional leftist trade unions, many business elites, newly created counterprotest organizations, hometown associations, and neighborhood organizations to provide a counterbalance to liberal civil society (Cheng 2020). It is an effort to transform Hong Kong's societal structure closer to those in the Mainland, which are controlled mainly by mass organizations. There are many associations that formally appear to be part of civil society but operate under the umbrella of these organizations. These include organizations such as Voice of Loving Hong Kong, Caring Hong Kong Power, and Hong Kong Youth Care Association, which were created in 2012 in support of then-Chief Executive (CE) Leung Chun-ying. With the passing of the NSL in 2020, the Chinese government has further strengthened the oversight and influence of these groups.

The united front organizations appeal to conservative residents, including those who hold strong Chinese nationalist sentiments. To some extent, at a formal level, the united front has filled the gap of neighborhood organizations. This dates back to 1985, when the Xinhua News Agency (established in Hong Kong in 1947) opened three branches in Hong Kong's different districts (Cheng 2014). Through it, the Chinese government controlled the leftist newspapers and other front organizations whose goal was to spread propaganda and co-opt local elites. Although they suffered a setback as a consequence of the Tiananmen Incident in 1989, they have since been able to recover. In 2000, Xinhua was replaced by the

Liaison Office of the Central People's Government, and one of its main functions became connecting with Hong Kong society to strengthen the exchange between the territory and the Mainland (Hong Kong Government 2020).

Part of the strategy has been the attempt to co-opt business leaders, through the appointment to consultative institutions of the central government, such as the Chinese People's Political Consultative Conference. Access to the Mainland market and the promise of maintaining capitalism has ensured their compliance (Cheng 2020). For instance, during the 2019 Anti-ELAB Movement, large businesses either explicitly or implicitly supported the government because they were worried about the economic consequences. In the aftermath, companies have been forced to publicly express support for the government. For instance, in June 2020, HSBC publicly backed the NSL following criticism by the former CE Leung Chun-ying. This demonstrates the attempt to include these elites in closely knit networks to make them dependent on the central government. Tycoons or their proxies have readily accepted this in the hope of maintaining influence over political decisions that could affect them. It has, however, also been extended to include societal organizations that are normally part of civil society. The approach here is to co-opt as well as to reorganize societal organizations, such as local federations, hometown associations, and service-oriented non-governmental organizations, to incorporate them in mass organizations similar to the state corporatist structure in place in Mainland China (Cheng 2020).

The united front effort not only aimed to penetrate Hong Kong society but also sought to promote the idea that love for the country was synonymous with love for the Chinese Communist Party, which is a key aspect of the party's legitimacy on the Mainland. The goal was to ensure the smooth transfer of Hong Kong from British to Chinese control. As anyone opposed to the CCP and its local regime was potentially a traitor to the Chinese nation, it had significant consequences for civil society, which has no space in a Communist system. At the same time, concepts such as universal suffrage or the rule of law have been redefined to justify illiberalism (Lam and Lam 2013). Naturally, this approach aims to only strengthen organizations within the united front while eventually marginalizing any other social organizations. Part of this effort has been the attempt to stigmatize activists as overly radical and as traitors, which has widened the societal divide (Cheng 2020). This applied especially to young activists such as Joshua Wong and Agnes Chow in Scholarism (founded in 2011 and merged into Demosistō in 2016, dissolved in 2020), Sixtus Leung, the convener of Youngspiration (founded in 2015), or Ray Wong of Hong Kong Indigenous (founded in 2015).

Increasingly Contentious Politics under Chinese Control

When British authorities handed over power in 1997, many in society remained worried about the potential impact. But for the first few years, civil society was largely unaffected by the change in power. There was cautious optimism that "one country, two systems" would be able to accommodate a separate political system that guaranteed civil liberties and provided sufficient political space for civil society. This would, however, change six years later when in 2003 CE Tung Chee-hwa introduced a National Security Bill under Article 23, which many saw as a fundamental threat to the civil and political liberties of Hong Kongers (Cheung 2005). On 1 July 2003, an estimated 500,000 people poured into the streets to demonstrate their opposition to the proposed legislation. As a consequence as well as concern from the Liberal Party leader James Tien, the bill was eventually shelved. This appeared to be a significant victory for civil society at the time but eventually proved to be only short lived.

The protest revealed the ability of civil society to come together on a single issue. As Ma Ngok stated, it constituted "an unprecedented awakening of civil society, with priests, barristers and journalists leading the charge, joined by party politicians and social activists, in a struggle against the state" (Ma 2005: 465). Participation in the protest had raised political awareness, although participants in a study still exhibited concern over being too active in politics, which was perceived in negative terms (Lee and Chan 2008).

For years afterward, the Hong Kong government was careful not to trigger another similar protest. The number of participants in annual protest marches declined when there were no major issues. Protesters were also concerned whether their participation made any difference. Popular sentiments about China peaked in 2008 with the Olympic Summer Games in Beijing, which were followed with great interest in Hong Kong. The growing sense of Chinese nationalism, however, did not last, as an increasing number of Hong Kongers grew concerned over increasing Chinese control as well as unhappiness about livelihood issues. Hong Kong's notorious high living costs were exacerbated by increasingly wealthy and skilled Chinese migrants who competed on the housing and job market. In addition to the wealthy migrants, there have also been up to 150 migrants daily on a one-way permit scheme, placing a possible strain on public services such as health care and public housing. The human rights organization Society for Community Organization (SoCO), however, has defended the migrants, arguing that they work hard and do not drain social services. Meanwhile, a small but devoted group of activists had rallied around the preservation of heritage and local culture. This included the movement to preserve Queen's Pier in 2006–2007 and the movement to save Choi Yuen Village (also known as the Anti–Hong Kong Express Rail Link Movement) in 2009–2010.

222   Civil Society

The next major protest movement emerged in 2012 with proposed Moral and National Education, which many saw as an attempt to use propaganda to shape the minds of students in Hong Kong or as the "brainwashing" of children. Thirty organizations joined in a march that according to their own estimates drew 90,000 people on 29 July. Among the protesters were many parents and their children. The movement gave rise to Scholarism, a group of secondary school students that occupied the government headquarters on 30 August, when three of its members started a hunger strike. On 7 September, an estimated 120,000 people joined a mass rally in front of government headquarters. One day later, CE Leung Chun-ying announced the temporary withdrawal of the subject. At the time, this was another victory for the protesters. While civil society was already considered vibrant at the time, Scholarism alone started to mobilize people to join the protest, even though it eventually profited greatly from the resources of the pan-democratic camp. The movement then brought in many new people, especially youth, who were self-initiated due to the rising concern over a textbook that suggested the authoritarian "China model" was superior to democracy. A great number of concern groups were subsequently founded. As Wang (2017) noted, the movement constituted the preparatory stage in terms of resources and tactical repertoires for the Umbrella Movement, which is the focus of the next section.

The Umbrella Movement: Embryonic Civil Society on the Street

While protests had appeared from time to time since 2003, no one was prepared for the massive 79-day occupation of three major streets in central districts that took place in the latter part of 2014. The idea to occupy the streets originated with the Occupy Central with Love and Peace Movement initiated by Professor Benny Tai, Professor Chan Kin-man, and Reverend Chu Yiu-ming on 27 March 2013, with the goal to use civil disobedience to pressure the Chinese government to allow universal suffrage according to international standards. Following a summer of workshops discussing the risks of a street occupation, students initiated a class boycott and at the end of it clashed with police over occupying Civic Square (the East Wing Forecourt of the Central Government Offices) on 27 September. Thousands of people joined the protest. Early on Sunday, the street occupation had officially begun. The police cordoned off Tim Mei Avenue, and the growing number of citizens seeking to support the movement was increasingly blocking traffic on the large highway between the Admiralty MTR station and the government complex. In the afternoon, the police decided to clear the road with tear gas and protesters stood their ground with umbrellas, which eventually gave the movement its name. The public's shock over the level of police response would have lasting effects.

The protest had been in response to a Chinese government electoral reform proposal that would have limited the ability of pan-democrats to contest any future CE election. The so-called "8.31 Decision" asserted that any candidate must be endorsed by a nominating committee, which would be heavily stacked in favor of pro-Beijing politicians to ensure that only candidates who support the central government (i.e., "love the country") would be selected. Instead, the pro-democratic activists sought to have "real universal suffrage" that would allow all Hong Kongers to contest and vote in future elections. In the summer of 2014, there had been an unofficial referendum that had asked people to choose between different electoral reform proposals. Altogether, 792,808 people had participated in the event, which was harshly criticized by the regime. For instance, CE Leung Chun-ying asserted that the referendum constituted an anti-Chinese act: "Nobody should place Hong Kong people in confrontation with Mainland Chinese citizens" (cited in Kaiman 2014). Although the question of universal suffrage is a political issue related to the administration of the territory, the leader sought to reframe it as a societal conflict.

While the Umbrella Movement failed to lead to any compromise between the protesters and the government, it did create a flourishing civil society that sought to protect the city through civic actions. A strong participatory Hong Kong identity was forged in the streets, leading many young people to become much more concerned in local affairs than before (Ortmann 2021). The Admiralty protest site became a city in itself with many tents, a study area, religious sites, art displays, and a small garden, to name a few. Protesters maintained order on the site. Crossings were erected that showed the direction of walking. The nearby toilet was kept clean and the women's toilet even provided all kinds of toiletries. There was also free wireless internet. People made soup and distributed it to others inside the protest sites. Volunteers offered free tuition for students. There were regular religious services. And perhaps most important, there were speeches and debates, as well as a democracy classroom to exchange ideas. While the movement drew heavily on existing organizations like pan-democratic parties, a significant number of people who did not have any connection to existing groups joined for the first time. This strengthened the organizational basis of civil society at the time.

The lack of progress, however, also laid seeds for disagreements. The decision to strictly maintain a peaceful movement irked some protesters who felt that more radical actions were needed. They felt unhappy that the leaders of the movement sidelined their views, which was reflected in slogans like the "Hong Kong Federation of Students does not represent us," which refers to the alliance of student organizations that was seen as a leader of the movement. When the decision was finally made to increase pressure by retaking Tim Wa Avenue, the protesters failed to achieve their objective, which radicals blamed on the timidity of peaceful protesters. The long-lasting occupation also gradually lost support from the population. Many saw it as futile to continue occupying the roads without a sign of progress. A Chinese University of Hong Kong survey showed a growing sense (from 67.4 percent in November to 76.2 percent in December) that protesters should vacate the occupied sites even though a majority (52.8 percent) felt that the government should make political concessions to the protesters' demands. In late November, the government started clearing the streets in Mong Kok. In the Admiralty site, injunctions were used to remove the barricades on 12 December. In the end, the protesters remained true to the peacefulness, as they did not put up a struggle. Instead, more than 200 activists remained at the sites to be arrested by the police.

The outcome of the protests had long-term consequences for civil society. On the one hand, peaceful protests lost support as fewer people joined various annual protest activities from the 1 July march to the Tiananmen vigil on 4 June. But activism did not stop, as the newly politicized people searched for new ways to actively participate in the city's development. This gave rise to new localist groups with more radical goals—for instance, some now even demanded full independence for Hong Kong—and propagated more extreme tactics. While there was growing peaceful activism in the community, during the Lunar New Year in 2016, protesters seeking to defend unlicensed food hawkers in Mong Kok clashed with police in a night of social unrest that proved pivotal for activism. Supporters of the protest called it the Fishball Revolution, while the government condemned it as a violent riot. Meanwhile, many liberals were shocked by the level of violence in the streets. The radicals, however, saw it as a success because the government conceded to their demands. Hawking during the Lunar New Year would continue to be tolerated. The clash seemed to confirm to radicals that moderate and peaceful strategies were useless against the government. At the time, however, most members of civil society condemned the violence, and peaceful resistance returned to be the norm.

To counter the rising contention, pro-establishment activists sought to mimic the approach to mobilize support. When protesters used a yellow ribbon as a symbol of the movement, opponents responded with blue ribbons. The color was meant to show support for the police, but it also implicitly represented repression of the street occupation using force; for instance, by using tear gas to clear the streets or arresting protesters. This had the unfortunate side effect of politicizing the police force, which in the past had been a neutral part of the administrative state. The "blue ribbon movement," in addition to existing pro-establishment organizations, also included new actors such as the Alliance for Peace and Democracy, which was formed by 40 pro-Beijing groups and scholars in 2014 in response to the Occupy Movement. Robert Chow, the leader of the pro-Beijing organization Silent Majority for Hong Kong, became its spokesperson.

As such, it was meant to provide an alternative to the pro-democracy movement that was supportive of the government but not part of it. It allowed criticism of the government if it was meant to be "constructive," which bears resemblance to the consultative authoritarianism in Mainland China (Teets 2013).

The Anti–Extradition Law Amendment Bill Movement

The year 2019 proved to be critical for civil society in Hong Kong. On 9 June, an estimated 1 million people (according to the organizer) joined the largest mass protest since 2003. The impetus was an extradition bill that would allow the government to send criminals to Mainland China. The turnout was much larger than expected. The mass protest revealed the strong mobilization capacity of society, which was largely driven by social media platforms such as LIHKG and Telegram. They provided like-minded individuals a basis for lively debates about protest goals and tactics while facilitating the division of labor between different activists. Protesters showed a high degree of creativity and even created a protest anthem titled "Glory to Hong Kong," which contributed to the cohesion in the movement. They shared deep-seated concerns about the growing influence of Communist China over the local state and society. Fear of China's legal system—which lacks many of the protections of Hong Kong's rule-of-law system, such as an independent judiciary, as well as the absence of forced confessions, torture, and secretive detentions—was the driving factor at the outset of what would become an extended period of social unrest that has shaken society to the core. While society was relatively unified at the start, the prolonged movement and protest violence reinforced the societal divide between the so-called yellow ribbons, who either actively or passively support the movement for democracy, and the blue ribbons, who are opposed to protests and either support or accept authoritarian controls. As the former tend to be younger and the latter older, it indicated a generational divide and split many families internally.

Despite the massive opposition, CE Carrie Lam refused to withdraw the bill and asserted that opposition to the bill was the result of a misunderstanding. While she rejected the notion that the Chinese government had forced her to support the law, the pro-Beijing press made it clear that there was strong support from the central authorities. The unwillingness to concede, however, motivated some activists to escalate protest action, which led to the first clash between protesters and police on 12 June 2019 following a smaller picnic protest in Tamar Square, which had been organized through social media. As that day was the scheduled second reading of the bill, protesters had called for a general strike. Unions such as the Hong Kong Confederation of Trade Unions (HKCTU) and the Hong Kong Professional Teachers' Union (HKPTU) had asked their members to join a protest gathering. In the early morning, many protesters reoccupied the

226   Civil Society

roads that had been blocked during the Umbrella Movement in 2014. By 11 a.m., the reading of the bill had been postponed. However, not everyone believed it, and protesters sought to block roads to prevent legislators from reaching the building.

The first clashes between protesters and police took place after some protesters broke through the barriers at Tim Wa Avenue and the police responded with pepper spray. Some protesters also sought to charge the Legislative Council building and were met with tear gas. As protesters refused to clear the road, the police continued to use tear gas, rubber bullets, and beanbag shots in an effort to forcefully end the protest. Some protesters responded by throwing plastic bottles and other items. A crowd of peaceful protesters were also trapped at CITIC Tower. Altogether, 72 people were injured, including two seriously. As a consequence of this incident and others, the police were accused of using excessive force against protesters and bystanders. Meanwhile, protests continued into the night and for the rest of the week.

The government declared the incident a "riot," which would come with long prison terms for those found guilty. Carrie Lam used strong rhetoric against the protesters by asserting that the clash was "unacceptable for any civilized societies" (cited in *BBC News* 12 June 2019). While she severely criticized the actions of activists, she refrained from equally chiding police violence. The next day, 200 members of the CE Election Committee called on the leader to resign and withdraw the bill. Further discussions of the controversial bill were postponed again. On 15 June, Lam decided to suspend the bill indefinitely but still refused to withdraw it, arguing, "I believe that we cannot withdraw this bill, or else society will say that this bill was groundless" (cited in Bradsher and Stevenson 2019). The statement indicated that she believed the bill was in the interest of society, which only had to be better convinced of its need. Her paternalistic attitude thus denied any role for bottom-up civic participation.

Appalled by the leader's attitude, an even larger crowd protested peacefully on the following Sunday, 17 June. Protest organizers claimed over 2 million people had joined the rally from Victoria Park to Central. The angry crowd now not only demanded the withdrawal of the extradition bill but also a change to the classification of the previous protest as a riot, the unconditional release of protesters who had participated on 12 June, and an independent investigation of police actions. To this, protesters added "genuine universal suffrage," the rallying cry of the 2014 protests, which together became the "five demands" that united the movement afterward. While many also called for the resignation of the CE, this did not become part of the five demands.

Despite broad opposition to the government, Carrie Lam remained firm in her support of the extradition bill until she withdrew it on 4 September, when anger over police violence had become the main issue. At the time, she was adamant not to concede to any of the five demands, even though they were purposefully reform-oriented. Not surprisingly, protests persisted. A turning point came on 1 July, when the annual protest march organized by the Civil Human Rights Front became another mass protest against the extradition bill. This time, however, a leaderless group of spontaneous protesters had decided to storm the Legislative Council, which they successfully achieved. Inside the chamber, some of the protesters posted pro-independence slogans and flags, which indicated the growing desire to break with the authoritarian regime on the Mainland. While they were all masked, one protester daringly showed his face and communicated the protest message to the media. He argued "that this was not just mob action but to register the accumulated frustrations of an unfair electoral system" (cited in Lum 2019).

During the unrest that followed, an alliance between peaceful protesters and radicals was formed, which bridged the divide between pan-democrats and localists that had been deepened by the Umbrella Movement in 2014. The act of transgression and vandalism caused much debate on social media platforms, but the intransigence of the regime left little room for opposition. Liberal activists, who would normally oppose such radical tactics, decided that this would lead to internal splits in the movement, resulting in inevitable failure. This was reflected in protest slogans such as "No snitching, no severing of ties." The five demands became the main rallying cry even as new demands emerged. The unprecedented unity was strengthened through the collective memory of the protests in which people had participated, as well as the harsh response people received from the police. Most protesters and many residents had, for instance, experienced exposure to tear gas, which had caused significant discomfort or even panic. As protests took place in residential areas, many ordinary people perceived the police to act with excessive as well as indiscriminate violence (Lee 2020). When protesters later vandalized pro-government offices and businesses, there was little opposition from liberal civil society.

The flexibility of the protest tactics promoted by the idea of "be water" made it difficult for the police to effectively crack down on protesters, who were quick to evade the repressive tools. Tear gas, water cannons, pepper spray, and other forms of nonlethal weapons became increasingly frequent and impacted passersby and residents. Live streams of the protests showed the police using large amounts of tear gas into what appeared to be empty spaces. At other times, tear gas was used without warning on people. When the police arrived, the situation quickly escalated into battles between protesters and police officials, relying on an increasing arsenal of weapons. For instance, the police acquired water cannons, which sprayed high powered water and coloring agents on protesters to better identify them. Protesters also increased their repertoire, including Molotov cocktails, bows and arrows, as well as catapults. The battles grew increasingly dangerous. At one point, the police decided to use real bullets, which caused serious anger in society.

The most serious incident was the attack on passengers at Yuen Long Station on 21 July 2019 by a white-clad mob armed with sticks. As they beat up passengers, the police failed to respond immediately to the violence despite numerous calls for help; it took 39 minutes for them to arrive at the scene. No arrests were made during the night. As a consequence, many protesters suspected collusion between the mob and police, which was expressed in protest slogans and banners. When police entered Prince Edward Station on 31 August and sealed the station, video later showed them using disproportionate force on unarmed protesters, which increased public anger even further. Following confusion about the number of injured people, some protesters started to believe that the police had killed protesters. They demanded the CCTV video and turned a station entrance into a shrine. It became obvious that trust in the police had seriously deteriorated. The government, however, resisted allowing an independent investigation that could have, at least partially, restored trust in the police.

The Hong Kong identity, which had already greatly contributed to the Umbrella Movement, also motivated protesters and in turn was strengthened by participation in various forms of resistance. There was a great sense that Hong Kongers should fight for their own city and defend it from the growing influence of the Communist Party-state on the Mainland. This was also expressed in protest slogans, such as "Fight for Freedom" and "Stand with Hong Kong." Over time, the urgency increased, which was reflected in slogans. For instance, "Hong Kongers, add oil" first changed to "Hong Kongers, resist" and then "Hong Kongers, revenge." The last one arose in response to the deaths of protesters, such as Chow Tsz-lok, who fell from a building during a protest, and a girl who had protested and whose death was declared a suicide after her naked body was found in the ocean. The protests climaxed when students barricaded university campuses and the police entered them with tear gas. While the Chinese University of Hong Kong became a battlefield, the Polytechnic University eventually turned out to be a trap for protesters who were arrested after a harrowing siege.

The onset of the COVID-19 pandemic in early 2020 provided the government with an opportunity to limit further acts of contentious politics. Under the guise of safety measures, the government cracked down on the movement. As of May 2021, more than 10,000 people had been arrested in connection with the protests. No protests have been permitted since then, including the vigil for the June Fourth Incident, which many had regarded as a sign of the existence of civil liberties. Trust in the government has eroded, though, which was reflected in the wearing of masks despite government's initial advice that only sick people should wear them. The masks became a symbol of resistance because the government sought to ban them during the 2019 protest movement. While the solidarity in wearing masks helped contain the spread of infection, distrust in the government eventually inhibited interest in vaccinations once it became possible in 2021.

The Impact of the National Security Law

The NSL enacted on 30 June 2020 in response to the protests poses the most fundamental challenge for civil society and threatens its very existence. The new law—which was introduced directly into the Basic Law, thus avoiding the legal process prescribed in the Basic Law—includes a wide scope of crimes, such as secession, subversion, terrorism, and collusion with foreign powers. People convicted of such crimes face life sentences. International human rights organizations have raised serious concerns that the law could be arbitrarily used against any form of independent activism. For instance, Amnesty International asserted that the law is "dangerously vague and broad," which has created widespread fear. Not only is the law used against activists, it also affects the basis of civil society, including freedom of speech and the rule of law.

The many developments since the law was introduced clearly indicate that its ultimate goal is to undermine the active and independent civil society. The space for political dissent has narrowed significantly and is enforced by a massive new state apparatus targeting violations of national security. The Chinese government has set up an Office for Safeguarding National Security of the Central People's Government in Hong Kong Special Administrative Region. It stands outside of the jurisdiction of Hong Kong's legal system and thus is beyond any legal constraints in the territory. The Hong Kong government has also established a Committee for Safeguarding National Security of the Hong Kong Special Administrative Region, which is not subject to any interference by other institutions or to judicial review. Moreover, the police force has also established a special unit tasked with prosecuting violations of the National Security Law. This has eroded the safeguards of the rule of law that once protected civil society in Hong Kong.

The new supralegal institutions have been used in a very short time since the new law was enacted. Already, on 1 July 2020, 10 people were apprehended under the new law. By June 2021, at least 128 people had been arrested, and more than half had been charged under the law. On 6 May, five suspected members of a student group called Returning Valiant were detained, and the police seized Hong Kong independence flags and an air gun. Although some of them are secondary school students, a source told the *South China Morning Post (SCMP)* that "[t]heir comments left on social media could constitute the offence of subversion under the national security law" (cited in *SCMP* Reporter 2021). On 23 June 2021, the first case of a protester, who had a banner that read "Liberate Hong Kong" with him when he was arrested under the NSL for allegedly driving his motorcycle into a group of police officers, went to court without a jury. Such cases have created widespread fear among democracy activists and their supporters.

Many activists in Hong Kong have been prosecuted. In January 2021, 53 pan-democratic politicians and activists were arrested for subverting state power under the NSL. They had organized a primary in July 2020 with the aim of selecting a powerful team of opposition candidates and avoiding three-cornered fights, which in the past had often weakened pan-democratic candidates. The primaries took place in the aftermath of the 2019 District Council elections, which had not only seen a record turnout but also led to a landslide victory for the pan-democratic camp. This had come as a surprise for the pro-Beijing parties, who had thought that Hong Kong people would vote against the democrats due to the ongoing political unrest. To prevent another election upset as in 2019, the government passed an electoral reform law in May 2021 that will make it harder for pan-democrats to contest and win seats. The new electoral system is meant to ensure that only "patriots" are elected.

Besides political activists, the government has also targeted the loosely organized part of civil society. By June 2022, 58 organizations had either disbanded or ceased operation. One of the most prominent groups had been the Civil Human Rights Front (CHRF), which had emerged as a form of cooperation between civil society organizations in the 2003 campaign against a proposed national security law. It had played a crucial role in organizing many mass protests, including the annual 1 July marches. Following rumors that the organization was under investigation for national security concerns, many prominent pan-democratic organizations such as the Democratic Party and the Hong Kong Professional Teachers' Union left the alliance. This deprived it of the most prominent supporters and raised questions about its ability to survive. In addition, the police had launched an investigation into its funds, while asserting that the organization was illegal because it had continued to exist even though it had been deregistered in 2006, two months after it had been registered. The convener, Figo Chan Ho-wun, refused to fully cooperate with the police. Under pressure, the organization disbanded on 15 August 2021, while the government asserted that legal actions would still be forthcoming. This incident indicates the possibility that the government may consider any concerted or united effort to object to government policy as a violation of the NSL, posing serious additional obstacles for collaboration within civil society. Forming alliances such as the Save Lantau Alliance may face additional barriers in fighting against government development plans if the government considers such activism contrary to the national interest. This obviously erodes the already weak horizontal linkages within society.

While some groups have directly been targeted by the state, others face difficulties from other parts of society. For instance, this is the case for student organizations, which have often been especially vocal critics of the government. They have been targeted by university administrators, with many of them cutting relations with the student unions. In February 2021, the Chinese University of Hong Kong cut ties with the student union after it disagreed with statements made by the newly elected leadership. The election platform of Syzygia had accused the university of "kowtowing to the regime." It had also sharply criticized the NSL, which students saw as an infringement on basic human rights and freedoms (*The Standard* 26 February 2021). In response, the newly elected student leaders resigned and withdrew their election manifesto. They even cited death threats when making the decision. The University of Hong Kong also cut ties with its student union in late April because the student union brought "legal risks to the university" (cited in *Hong Kong Free Press* 30 April 2021). This came after the union had criticized the university's plans to implement national security education. It had also opposed the electoral reform proposal. This indicated that the space for political discourse had narrowed significantly. For the student unions, this means an uncertain future because of the administrative difficulties of collecting membership fees and maintaining space for student activities. The Chinese University of Hong Kong Students' Union has become the first to disband (on 7 October 2021) after it had been asked to register as an independent society.

The law has also been used against the pro-democratic press, challenging the right to freedom of expression. Jimmy Lai, the founder of the now defunct pro-democratic paper *Apple Daily*, has been put on trial, and his assets and shares have been frozen, threatening the survival of the paper. Moreover, the government plans new laws aimed at doxxing and "fake news." The police commissioner, Chris Tang, asserted that such a law would "assist national security and make Hong Kong safer" (cited in Wong and Lam 2021). This followed a news report in the paper that had placed a picture from the police actions in Prince Edward next to National Security Day photos in which children played with toy guns in a mock MTR station. As a consequence of allegations that a number of articles had violated the National Security Law and the freezing of the company's funds, *Apple Daily* was forced to close down and published its last copy on 24 June 2021. Moreover, the government has removed a growing number of books written by activists from public libraries. The international media has also been subject to serious rebuke. Following strong criticism of the conviction of Bao Choy, who had produced an award-winning documentary about the Yuen Long incident in 2019, the Foreign Correspondents' Press Club in Hong Kong was accused of being a foreign force meddling in China's internal affairs, a criticism that the Chinese government has often leveled against journalists and foreign governments.

The accusation of foreign interference has also become a potential concern for international nongovernmental organizations, especially when their activities involve potentially sensitive topics, such as political and human rights. On 24 September 2021, the Chinese government released a list of supposed American interference in Hong Kong's affairs, which included many public meetings between activists and US officials, revealing that the definition of what the Chinese government considers interference is very broad. Some international political rights groups have already decided to leave the territory. For instance, the German liberal democratic Friedrich Naumann Foundation closed its office in Hong Kong in November 2020. The organization stated that the National Security Law "gives the government in Beijing free reign to take criminal action against foreign organizations operating in Hong Kong as well as against their partners and employees" and that they could not "do our work there without endangering partners and staff" (Paqué 2020). Amnesty International also decided to close its offices by the end of 2021 for similar reasons. So far, other organizations have not yet announced whether they will stay. However, it is uncertain how long this will continue to be possible, and organizations need to constantly assess the possible risks for their own employees as well as partners in Hong Kong. As the Chinese government has implemented a Foreign NGO Law in 2017, which has reduced both the number and the scope of activities of international NGOs in China, there is now a distinct possibility that this could also happen in Hong Kong at some point in the future.

The growing repression has motivated many to emigrate or even flee from Hong Kong. This "exit" option is obviously a problem for civil society, which loses an important "voice" (Hirschmann 1970). Prominent activists as well as ordinary people have slowly left the city. This includes famous names, such as former student leader Nathan Law and former lawmaker Ted Hui, as well as the former leader of the Hong Kong Baptist Church, who had supported the protest movement. It is yet unclear how many people will choose this path. The Chinese government seems to be worried about a mass exodus as it has sought to curtail the use of the British National Overseas (BNO) travel document after the British government had made it possible for Hong Kongers to emigrate to the United Kingdom. Moreover, changes to the immigration law in April 2021 raised fears that under the vague new legislation people could be barred from leaving the city, which would be similar to exit bans placed on dissidents in Mainland China. Twelve people who were trying to escape by boat to Taiwan in August 2020 were also caught by the Chinese Coast Guard, which triggered a campaign to free them.

While most of the repression so far has focused on the democracy movement, there are signs that traditional societal organizations will also be affected. For instance, the Bar Association has faced serious criticism. Anger was directed at its chairman, Paul Harris, after he had suggested the need for modifications to the National Security Law. The Liaison Office not only harshly criticized the chairman but also asserted that the legal organization could face serious consequences if it did not drop its chairman. One member told the *SCMP*: "Some senior counsels are asking if there is going to be a complete wipeout, a total annihilation" (cited in Lau and Wong 2021). Opposition to official policies such as the NSL and electoral reform has become risky. Moreover, not all the repression has been directly linked to the National Security Law. Shortly after the Chinese press called the 90,000-member Hong Kong Professional Teachers' Union—one of the oldest civil society groups founded in 1973—a "tumor" that must be eradicated, the Hong Kong government cut all ties with the union, and as a consequence the union disbanded on 10 August 2021. Moreover, on 3 March 2023, the Hong Kong Women Workers' Association cancelled the first planned protest march that had been approved by the police since the start of the COVID-19 pandemic. Members of the League of Social Democrats had been informed by the police that they would be arrested if they participated in the march. Moreover, Dennis Cheng Wai-kin, a police superintendent, asserted that "violent groups" had indicated their interest in the march, without providing any examples or evidence (Cheung 2023). The first march that was eventually allowed on 26 March finally required protesters to wear numbered badges and was strictly cordoned off by the police. Only about 80 people participated in the protest against land reclamation near Tseung Kwan O. These events suggest that the space for protest marches has significantly declined since the introduction of the NSL. Finally, the government's suggestion that ill-defined "soft resistance" will be regulated in the future under Article 23 legislation suggests that more repression could come in the future.

Initially, there were signs that supporters of the pan-democratic movement intended to continue their activism. The Yellow Economic Circle, which is driven by a strong local identity and aims to support pro-democratic businesses, had continued to draw many customers to support pro-democratic businesses. When the government raided a number of AbouThai stores in early 2021, scores of people queued at branches to buy products from the pro-democratic supermarket chain. This illustrates that there are still many people who are deeply unhappy with the political developments. Even without civil society mobilization, they are ready to support the democratic cause. However, the government has also sought to make it more difficult for businesses to side with pro-democracy activists. For instance, on 6 May 2021, a Chickeeduck branch displaying protest related items was cordoned off by police. In 2023, AbouThai founder Mike Lam declared his decision to leave the economic circle, as he testified for the prosecution in a high-profile court case against 47 democrats accused of violating the NSL when they held a primary vote.

Conclusion

Until the introduction of the NSL in 2020, Hong Kong had a vibrant civil society with a growing number of people willing to contribute to the future of the territory. They shared a strong sense of belonging and were no longer refugees in a foreign land. However, this raised great concern in Beijing, which is deeply worried about any divisions in the country. A one-party state, the Chinese government does not tolerate dissent or independent opposition. In a context of increased recentralization since Xi Jinping's ascendance to power (Bulman and Jaros 2021), control over Hong Kong has also been increased. Following massive unrest in 2019, this has accelerated and space for different views has quickly narrowed. While repression has become common, self-censorship has also become more rampant, leading to an emasculated society. There might be still resistance against the government, but it has become less overt. People may support particular shops that they regard as pro-democratic. Some activists have fled Hong Kong and many others are considering leaving. It appears at this stage that Hong Kong has made the full transition from a liberal authoritarian to an illiberal authoritarian regime. This will have serious consequences for civil society, which cannot flourish in a climate of repression and fear.

Box 9.1: Definition of civil society

Civil society is a sphere separate from state and market. It is characterized by freedom of association of individuals, who come together based on shared norms to pursue similar interests.

Box 9.2: Definition of social movement

Social movement is a loose network of organizations and individuals engaged in a sustained pursuit of a social, cultural, economic, or political goal.

Stephan Ortmann   235

> **Box 9.3: Civil society sectors according to a 2004 study by the Central Policy Unit**
>
> 1. Education and Research
> 2. Professional, Industry, Business, and Trade Unions
> 3. District and Community-Based Organizations
> 4. Civic and Advocacy Organizations
> 5. Law and Legal Services
> 6. Politics
> 7. Welfare Services
> 8. Health Services
> 9. Environment
> 10. Sports
> 11. Arts and Culture
> 12. Religion
> 13. Philanthropic Intermediaries
> 14. International and Cross-Boundary
>
> Source: Chan 2012.

Questions

1. What are the biggest challenges and opportunities for civil society in Hong Kong?
2. What is the relationship between civil society and the united front?
3. How did the 2014 Umbrella Movement and the 2019 Anti-ELAB Movement affect civil society?
4. What is the future of civil society under the NSL?

Bibliography

BBC 2019, "Hong Kong Extradition Protests: Lam Criticises 'Organised Riots,'" *BBC News*, 12 June, https://www.bbc.com/news/world-asia-china-48615161

Bradsher, K & Stevenson A 2019, "Hong Kong's Leader, Yielding to Protests, Suspends Extradition Bill," *The New York Times*, 15 June.

Carroll, JM 2007, *A Concise History of Hong Kong*, Rowman & Littlefield Publishers, Lanham, MD.

Chan, E & Chan, J 2007, "The First Ten Years of the HKSAR: Civil Society Comes of Age," *Asia Pacific Journal of Public Administration*, vol. 29 no. 1, pp. 77–99.

Chan, EYM 2012, "Civil Society," in WM Lam, PLT Lui, & W Wong (eds), *Contemporary Hong Kong Government and Politics*, Hong Kong University Press, Hong Kong, pp. 179–198.

Cheng, EW 2020, "United Front Work and Mechanisms of Countermobilization in Hong Kong," *The China Journal*, vol. 83, no. 1, pp. 1–33.

Cheng, JY 1989. "Political Modernisation in Hong Kong," *Journal of Commonwealth & Comparative Politics*, vol. 27, no. 3, pp. 294–320.

Cheng, JYS 2014. "The Emergence of Radical Politics in Hong Kong: Causes and Impact," *The China Review*, pp. 199–232.

Cheung, ABL 2005, "The Hong Kong System under One Country Being Tested: Article 23, Governance Crisis and the Search for a New Hong Kong Identity," in JSY Cheng (ed), *The July 1 Protest Rally: Interpreting a Historic Event*, City University of Hong Kong Press, Hong Kong, pp. 33–70.

Cheung, E 2023, "Rights Group Abruptly Calls off Hong Kong's First Authorised Rally in 3 Years," *South China Morning Post*, 4 March, https://www.scmp.com/news/hong-kong/law-and-crime/article/3212383/rights-groups-abruptly-calls-hong-kongs-first-authorised-rally-3-years

Dai, J & Spires, AJ 2018, "Advocacy in an Authoritarian State: How Grassroots Environmental NGOs Influence Local Governments in China," *The China Journal*, vol. 79, no. 1, pp. 62–83.

Fong, B 2017, "In-between Liberal Authoritarianism and Electoral Authoritarianism: Hong Kong's Democratization under Chinese Sovereignty, 1997–2016," *Democratization*, vol. 24, no. 4, pp. 724–750.

Hirschman, AO 1970, *Exit, Voice, and Loyalty: Responses to Decline in Firms, Organizations, and States*, Harvard University Press, Cambridge.

HKSARG 2020, "Government Clarifies Functions of LOCPG in Hong Kong," *Press Releases*, 12 March, https://www.info.gov.hk/gia/general/202003/12/P2020031200740.htm

Ip, PK 1997, "Development of Civil Society in Hong Kong: Constraints, Problems and Risks," in PK Li (ed), *Political Order and Power Transition in Hong Kong*, the Chinese University Press of Hong Kong, Hong Kong, pp. 159–186.

Kaiman, J 2014, "Hong Kong's Unofficial Pro-Democracy Referendum Irks Beijing," *Guardian*, 25 June, https://www.theguardian.com/world/2014/jun/25/hong-kong-unofficial-pro-democracy-referendum-beijing

Lam, WM & Cooper, L (eds) 2018, *Citizenship, Identity and Social Movements in the New Hong Kong: Localism after the Umbrella Movement*, Routledge, London.

Lam, WM 2015, *Understanding the Political Culture of Hong Kong: The Paradox of Activism and Depoliticization*, Routledge, New York.

Lam, WF & Perry, JL 2000, "The Role of the Nonprofit Sector in Hong Kong's Development," *Voluntas: International Journal of Voluntary and Nonprofit Organizations*, vol. 11, no. 4, pp. 355–373.

Lam, WM & Lam, CY 2013, "China's United Front Work in Civil Society: The Case of Hong Kong," *International Journal of China Studies*, vol. 4, no. 3, pp. 301–325.

Lau, C & Wong, J 2021, "Does Hong Kong's Bar Association Need to Ditch Chairman Paul Harris to Reset Ties with Beijing? Or Is the Job a Poisoned Chalice?," *South China Morning Post*, 28 April, https://www.scmp.com/news/hong-kong/politics/article/3131333/does-hong-kongs-bar-association-need-ditch-chairman-paul

Lee, EW 2020, "United Front, Clientelism, and Indirect Rule: Theorizing the Role of the 'Liaison Office' in Hong Kong," *Journal of Contemporary China*, vol. 29, no. 125, pp. 763–775.

Lee, F 2020, "Solidarity in the Anti-Extradition Bill Movement in Hong Kong," *Critical Asian Studies*, vol. 52, no. 1, pp. 18–32.

Lee, FL & Chan, JM 2008, "Making Sense of Participation: The Political Culture of Pro-Democracy Demonstrators in Hong Kong," *The China Quarterly*, pp. 84–101.

Lum, A 2019, "'It Wasn't Violence for Violence's Sake': The Only Unmasked Protester at Storming of Hong Kong's Legislature Gives His Account of the Day's Drama," *South China Morning Post*, 4 July, https://www.scmp.com/news/hong-kong/politics/article/3017327/it-wasnt-violence-violences-sake-only-unmasked-protester

Ma, N 2005, "Civil Society in Self-Defense: The Struggle against National Security Legislation in Hong Kong," *Journal of Contemporary China*, vol. 14, no. 44, pp. 465–482.

Ma, N 2008, "Civil Society and Democratization in Hong Kong: Paradox and Duality," *Taiwan Journal of Democracy*, vol. 4, no. 2, pp. 155–175.

Ortmann, S 2021, "Hong Kong's Constructive Identity and Political Participation: Resisting China's Blind Nationalism," *Asian Studies Review*, vol. 45, no. 2, pp. 306–324.

Paqué, KH 2020, "Possibilities and Limits of Our Work," *Friedrich Naumann Foundation*, 26 November, https://www.freiheit.org/hongkong-possibilities-and-limits-our-work

SCMP Reporter 2021, "National Security Law: Hong Kong Police Arrest Five for Alleged Acts of Subversion on Social Media, Sources Say," *South China Morning Post*, 6 May, https://www.scmp.com/news/hong-kong/law-and-crime/article/3132457/national-security-law-hong-kong-police-arrest-3

So, AY 1993, "Hong Kong People Ruling Hong Kong! The Rise of the New Middle Class in Negotiation Politics, 1982–1984," *Asian Affairs: An American Review*, vol. 20, no. 2, pp. 67–86.

So, AY 1997, "The Tiananmen Incident, Patten's Electoral Reforms, and the Origins of Contested Democracy in Hong Kong," in MK Chan (ed), *The Challenge of Hong Kong's Reintegration with China*, Hong Kong University Press, Hong Kong, pp. 49–84.

Teets, JC 2013, "Let Many Civil Societies Bloom: The Rise of Consultative Authoritarianism in China," *The China Quarterly*, vol. 213, pp. 19–38.

The Standard 2021, "CUHK Cuts Ties with Student Union," 26 February, https://www.thestandard.com.hk/breaking-news/section/4/166332/CUHK-cuts-ties-with-student-union

Wang, KJY 2017, "Mobilizing Resources to the Square: Hong Kong's Anti-moral and National Education Movement as Precursor to the Umbrella Movement," *International Journal of Cultural Studies*, vol. 20, no. 2, pp. 127–145.

Wong, N & Lam, J 2021, "Hong Kong Police Chief Wants 'Fake News' Law as He Ramps Up Attacks on Newspaper He Accused of Inciting Hatred," *South China Morning Post*, 20 April, https://www.scmp.com/news/hong-kong/politics/article/3130348/hong-kong-police-chief-wants-fake-news-law-he-ramps-attacks

Useful Websites

Hong Kong Timeline 2019–2021: Anti-Extradition Protests & National Security Law
https://www.hrichina.org/en/hong-kong-timeline-2019-2022-anti-extradition-protests-national-security-law

List of NGOs at CT Goodjobs
https://www.ctgoodjobs.hk/ngo/ngo_list.asp

Lists of links for Non-Governmental Organizations in Hong Kong compiled by the US Consulate
https://hk.usconsulate.gov/our-relationship/ngo-hk/

Umbrella Movement collection in the CUHK library
https://archives.lib.cuhk.edu.hk/repositories/5/resources/455

Social indicators of Hong Kong: Strength of Civil Society
https://www.socialindicators.org.hk/en/indicators/strength_of_civil_society

Further Reading

Au, LY 2020, *Hong Kong in Revolt: The Protest Movement and the Future of China*. Pluto Press, London. This book provides a clear explanation for the development of the protest movement in Hong Kong from the Umbrella Movement in 2014 to the Anti-ELAB Movement in 2019. It is essential reading to understand the transformation of the civil society during this period.

Davis, MC 2020, *Making Hong Kong China: The Rollback of Human Rights and the Rule of Law*, Association of Asian Studies, Ann Arbor, MI. This book, written by a legal scholar, explains how Hong Kong's civil society was transformed by the protest movement and the NSL that was implemented in response to it.

Lo, SSH, Hung, SCF & Loo, JHC 2019, *China's New United Front Work in Hong Kong: Penetrative Politics and Its Implications*, Palgrave Macmillan, Singapore. This essential reading reveals how China has strengthened the United Front in Hong Kong as an alternative to the liberal civil society. It shows how these groups have sought to gain the support of Hong Kong people for the Chinese state.

Loh, C 2018, *Underground Front: The Chinese Communist Party in Hong Kong*, 2nd ed., Hong Kong University Press, Hong Kong. Although rarely visible to political observers in Hong Kong, the Chinese Communist Party has played a critical role behind the scenes to influence Hong Kong society. This book provides the most comprehensive discussion of this topic.

Ma, N and Cheng, EW (eds) 2019, *The Umbrella Movement: Civil Resistance and Contentious Space in Hong Kong*, Amsterdam University Press, Amsterdam. The Umbrella Movement was a watershed moment for Hong Kong's civil society, which blossomed on the streets. This book, written by many prominent scholars, provides the most eclectic discussion of the pro-democracy movement.

10
Political Identity, Culture, and Participation

Lam Wai-man

Political identity, culture, and participation in Hong Kong have undergone significant changes since the handover in 1997. This subject matter has garnered much attention amid the drastic political changes in Hong Kong, especially after 2012, the publication of the last edition of this book, and thus requires fundamental revisions of its assumptions. Indeed, the previous, long-held academic debate as to whether Hong Kong's political culture and participation are apathetic and passive is no longer relevant. Rather, there has been a general observation that, in the past ten years, the Hong Kong identity of sections of the population has shed much of its Chineseness and instead developed into a new Hong Konger identity, with consolidated cultural and value contents generating and sustaining political actions. Nevertheless, it is to be expected that political identity, culture, and participation in Hong Kong has changed in the post-2020 era after the promulgation of the National Security Law on Hong Kong.

This chapter aims to examine the developments of political identity, political culture, and political participation in Hong Kong after 2012, and to analyze the implications of these developments for the understanding of contemporary politics and governance in the city. The concepts of political identity, culture, and participation are linked closely with each other and are key to the study of political science (Boxes 10.1 and 10.2). Political identity of the people constitutes the broader political culture and forms their political participation; political behaviors thus impact the political environment and in turn shape the society's common beliefs around politics and the choice of political roles and actions. Since beliefs and attitudes are constantly influenced by various political factors, the contents of political identity, culture, and choices in the form of political participation are never fixed. Post-handover Hong Kong as analyzed below is a

240   Political Identity, Culture, and Participation

good example of a constantly remaking process of political identity, culture, and participation by the various political forces within the polity.

A Historical Review of Political Identity, Culture, and Participation before 1997

As analyzed in the previous edition of this book, the earlier portrayal of Hong Kong after the Second World War was as a borrowed place inhabited by many newly arrived migrants exhibiting a mixture of vague Chinese cultural identity and weak local citizen identity. The short-term political vision of these migrants had made the local political culture a refugee type of mentality characterized by political apathy, political passivity, and a strong sense of political powerlessness. People focused primarily on survival and livelihood of the family. Over the years they became submissive to paternalism, with a weak sense of citizen duty and little concern for public affairs (Hoadley 1973; King 1981).

With the postwar baby boom generation coming into adulthood in the 1960s, a distinct local identity embedded with a sense of belonging to Hong Kong and a stronger sense of citizen duty emerged. Previous studies have found that a local Hong Kong identity prevailed in the city especially after the 1966 and 1967 Riots (Scott 1989; Turner 1995; Matthew 1997; Ngo 1999). It was observed that with the colony's growing affluence in the 1970s and more speed-ily in the 1980s, more Hong Kong people came to identify themselves as Hong Kong Chinese or even "Hongkongese" instead of Chinese. The distribution of these three senses of identity had remained stable across the years that followed (Lau 1997). Prevalence of the Hongkongese identity well-illustrated the people's attachment to the colony vis-à-vis China; this identity was affective by nature rather than associative with political faiths or ideologies at the time. It signified people's emotional attachment to Hong Kong and acceptance of the local way of life as contrary to that of Mainland China. With the growing affluence of the city, the Hongkongese identity exhibited increasingly capitalistic characteristics rather than developing local ideals, political ideologies, or political actions. As depicted by Lau Siu-kai, Hong Kong was under the combined influence of tra-ditional Chinese culture and that of an affluent modern city culture, resulting in the prevalence of utilitarian familism. Under utilitarian familism, people put familial interests above the interests of society and saw societal issues as mate-rialistic and instrumental. Consequently, they prioritized social stability and economic prosperity and became desensitized toward political powerlessness, with low expectations in the government. Political participation in Hong Kong, as argued by Lau, was characterized by aloofness, usually minimal in extent and nonideological in nature, and carried little political impact due to its ad hoc and sporadic character (Lau 1982; Lau and Kuan 1988).

Over the years, only a few challenges were raised in the academic circle against the above observations of Hong Kong's political culture and participation as apathetic or aloof and non-ideological. Arguably, Hong Kong's political identity, culture, and participation had appeared much more dynamic than any academic has recognized. Truly in the postwar decades, political activism, if any at all at the time, was checked by a depoliticized culture that embodied a strong political sensitivity and fear of politics, as well as an emphasis on maintaining stability and prosperity. All these had resulted in a collective cultural disposition among the Hong Kong people to refrain from getting actively involved in politics and hence hindered massive collective mobilization (Lam 2004).

Importantly, the promulgation of the 1981 *White Paper on District Administration* marked a turning point in Hong Kong governance by introducing universal suffrage into Hong Kong's elections. According to the White Paper, the District Board (subsequently renamed the District Council) shall be established in each district and members directly elected to their post. An indirect election element was introduced to the territory-wide Legislative Council election in 1985 by giving members of the District Boards, the Urban and Regional Councils, and functional constituencies the right to return 24 out of the 56 Legislative Council seats. In 1991, the government further opened the Legislative Council to direct election, allocating 18 out of its 60 seats to be returned by geographical constituencies.

At the same time, noninstitutional politics flourished since the 1980s. There were three riots in the 1980s: two happened on Christmas Day of 1981 and New Year's Day of 1982 because of the high concentration of people celebrating the holidays; and the third was a road strike in 1984 when angry taxi drivers protested the increase in license fees. The period was also characterized by flourishing citizen movements involving various sectors of the public, namely workers, students, women, civil servants, professionals, and consumers. The concerns constituting these collective actions were diverse, ranging from the tangible to the ideological.

It was not until the late 1990s that Hong Kong's political culture and participation were seen in a new light in academic circles. As argued by Chiu Wing-kai and Lui Tai-lok (2000), without upsetting the political order, various old and new social movements in Hong Kong had posed serious challenges to the colonial government and opened political opportunities for future movements. Moreover, with a more inclusive definition of political participation in reexamining the political history of Hong Kong, Lam Wai-man (2004) found a substantial amount of political activism in Hong Kong informed by various but fragmented ideological traditions, including nationalism, liberalism, social equality and justice, the rule of law, and democratic ideals. In the years running up to the handover, Chris Patten, the last British-appointed governor (he arrived in 1992), implemented significant political and administrative reforms for quality governance. The Patten administration had aroused Beijing's suspicion in the transition politics but resonated with the local people's desire for democracy since the 1980s, with increased institutional participation and electoral politics.

Overall, political identity in Hong Kong, especially since the 1980s, had embodied a stronger sense of citizenship and become more ideological, with rising aspirations for contradictory political ideals, such as national integration, liberalism, social equality and justice, the rule of law, and democracy (Lam 2004). In the run-up to 1997, the different readings of Hong Kong's political identity, culture, and participation reflected different assumptions and observations of the character of Hong Kong society and its people in the transition politics. With the changing political situation after 1997, the issues of political identity, culture, and participation have also acquired new developments in Hong Kong.

Political Identity, Culture, and Participation in the First 15 Years of the Hong Kong Special Administrative Region

In the first 15 years after the handover, the underlying contradiction between the senses of Hongkongese and Chinese continued but appeared to be resolved with the prevalence of a dual identity of Hongkongese and Chinese. Polls found that the proportion of people who regarded themselves as only Chinese had gradually increased, with occasional fluctuations, while those who saw themselves as only Hongkongese had steadily decreased. Around 40 percent claimed a dual identity of Hongkongese and Chinese, which, nevertheless, started to drop after 2011 (HKPORIa various years; Lam 2012). Alongside these was the people's acquisition of a regional and global identity, with an awareness of Hong Kong's connection with the world. For instance, Hong Kong people's identity as an Asian and a global citizen had remained strong over the years (HKPORIa various years).

The above figures once indicated that Hong Kong people's identification with China or their own Chineseness had grown, demonstrating the results of the earnest attempts made by the Hong Kong government and Beijing to cultivate people's national identification. After the handover, patriotism was promoted in schools and the public sphere. For instance, Beijing-arranged astronauts and athletes' visits to Hong Kong successfully aroused nationalistic public sentiment in the city. Moreover, in the "patriotism debate" in 2003, some Mainland legal experts and local pro-Beijing figures claimed that the people of Hong Kong should serve the duty of "loving your country and loving Hong Kong," and Hong Kong should be ruled by patriots. Also, China tours for Hong Kong students and youngsters, and cultural exchanges between students from Hong Kong and the Mainland, were highly encouraged by both governments. In 2012, the controversial Moral and National Education Curriculum Guide (Primary 1 to

Secondary 6) was criticized by some people as brainwashing and triggered the Protest against National Education Curriculum.

Regarding political culture, political activism became a hallmark of Hong Kong. The earlier interpretations of a politically apathetic, aloof, and passive Hong Kong political culture had gradually subsided. A growing activist political culture characterized by people's lessened fear of politics, the articulation of their political beliefs and rights, and the readiness to uphold these values and assert these rights had quietly emerged. New norms and values of political action surfaced along with the expansion of new forms of political participation. There was an increasing amount of institutional and noninstitutional political participation. Discursive participation, digital participation, citizen journalism, and alternative media had become popular and prominent in the period. Meanwhile, some people started to relinquish conventional standards of social peace and order and employ physical tactics to capture public attention. Political activism had since been signified by growing use of radical tactics, until 2020.

Despite the growth of political activism during this period, the local political culture still embodied elements of political passivity. In the face of a strong government machinery and propaganda, people's feeling of political efficacy, which would significantly influence their readiness to get politically involved, remained low. In the 2000s, counterprotests or regimented participation mobilized and sponsored by pro-establishment figures and groups in support of government policies had gained ground. Furthermore, the efforts by the government and pro-establishment political figures to cultivate patriotic identity as the major political value in the political landscape of Hong Kong had moderated, downplayed, or even deterred political activism.

Political Identity since 2012

Many important political events had happened since 2012, which explained the significant changes in political identity, culture, and participation in Hong Kong in the previous years. Notable political events include the Protest against National Education Curriculum in 2012, the Umbrella Movement in 2014, the Protests against Parallel Trading between 2012 and 2015, the Mong Kok riots in 2016, and the Anti–Extradition Law Amendment Bill (Anti-ELAB) Movement in 2019.

Ethnic identity

Rapid consolidation of the new Hong Konger identity was a hallmark of the period. Table 10.1 demonstrates the relatively stable proportions of people claiming a dual identity from 2012 to 2022. Also, the proportions of those identifying as Hong Kongers had grown, whereas the number of those identifying as Chinese had decreased during the period until 2021.

Table 10.1: Ethnic identity in HKSAR

Date of Survey	% of Hong Konger	% of Chinese	% of Mixed Identity	% of Other	% of Don't Know
5–9/12/2022	32.0	20.5	45.9	0.3	1.3
31/5–5/6/2022	39.1	17.6	42.4	0.0	1.0
7–10/6/2021	44.0	13.2	41.7	0.6	0.5
4–1/6/2020	50.5	12.6	35.9	0.0	1.0
17–20/6/2019	52.9	10.8	35.8	0.0	0.5
4–7/6/2018	40.7	17.8	38.8	0.5	2.2
13–15/6/2017	37.3	20.9	40.0	1.4	1.0
10–16/6/2016	41.9	17.8	38.0	1.3	0.9
15–18/6/2015	36.3	22.1	40.5	0.3	0.8
6–12/6/2014	40.2	19.5	38.7	0.2	1.3
10–13/6/2013	38.2	23.0	36.3	1.1	1.6
13–20/6/2012	45.6	18.3	34.3	1.1	0.7

Sources: Data from HKUPOP website and PORI, "Identification of oneself as a Hong Konger / Chinese / mixed identity" (Chinese in Hong Kong or Hong Konger in China), https://www.pori.hk/pop-poll/ethnic-identity/q001.html.

Table 10.1 reveals notable trends in the development of political identity in Hong Kong. The respondents perceived their own Hong Kong identity as separate or distinct from the Chinese identity. The vague sense of cultural Chineseness prevalent among the older Hong Kong people had become much less obvious in this identity, to an extent that it might have harbored the ideas of protectionism and separatism. With hindsight, it was noticeable that the dichotomy of Hong Kong and the Mainland had prevailed since 2010 with the rising concerns that Mainlanders were depriving the locals of essential consumer goods and public services, such as the scramble for maternity beds and formula milk for infants, the access to public spaces and transport facilities, and the increasing inflation in local property prices. As the feelings of difference between Hong Kong and the Mainland grew stronger, separatism also grew, which fueled the strong sentiments of the Hong Konger identity and drove people to act to protect local interests and the perceived unique culture and values of Hong Kong from disruption. These added to people's growing discontent with the government.

Their perceived value clashes between the Mainland and Hong Kong eventually unleashed localism after the Umbrella Movement.

Localism and identity politics

The development of localism, which had been constituted by the overall local political culture in Hong Kong since the Umbrella Movement, signified landmark developments in the Hong Kong identity. Worthy of note, the meaning of the earlier version of localism that emerged after the Umbrella Movement was relatively broad. As such, it was open to various interpretations and had the potential to be politicized on various fronts. Table 10.2 shows the various understandings of localism in 2016 (Path of Democracy 2016; Lam 2018b).

Table 10.2: Understandings of localism as of 2016

What Do You Think "Protect the Local" Mean?	% of Yes
To protect Hong Kong's way of life, culture, and history.	60.8
Hong Kong people have priority over the resources of Hong Kong.	53.4
To implement the Basic Law in safeguarding a high degree of autonomy.	46.7
To abide by the core values of Hong Kong people.	43.0
To defend the autonomy and decision-making of various Hong Kong affairs.	39.6
To combat parallel trading and reduce the number of individual Mainland travelers.	19.8
Hong Kong interests over national interests.	16.1
The independence of Hong Kong.	10.2
To rectify China-Hong Kong economic integration.	4.6

Sources: Survey on Political Culture in Hong Kong (Path of Democracy 2016); Lam 2018b.

The later development of localism in Hong Kong had evolved into various brands. As found, localisms that developed after the Umbrella Movement had given rise to a tide of newly formed community-oriented organizations, professional organizations, and political organizations. Worthy of note is that these three types of localism had become embedded in the political culture of Hong Kong. First, there emerged the community-oriented localism promoted by activists serving at the community level. This localism was embedded with non-nativist demands for the attainment of greater social equality and better protection of Hong Kong's way of life, core values, and history. Second, there was a type of non-nativist civic localism informed by liberal and cosmopolitan ideals.

It strongly emphasized protecting Hong Kong's core values by upholding Hong Kong's political autonomy vis-à-vis China. It encouraged people to take political action to achieve their aims but was against violent means. Third, there was a type of nativist localism that promoted Hong Kong people's priority and rights over the resources of Hong Kong, and Hong Kong's interests over national interests. It encouraged people to take political action to achieve their aims and regarded political confrontations as an inevitable part of the process (Lam 2018a).

As Sebastian Veg analyzed, there was a shift after the Umbrella Movement from an ethnocultural mode to a civic mode of identification, giving rise to two types of localism in Hong Kong. The former was ethnic and cultural in nature, promoting a kind of Hong Kong chauvinism, nativism, and anti-Mainland xenophobia, while the latter was civic in nature, emphasizing democratic federalism and local autonomy to achieve genuine autonomy and reject Chinese nationalism for Hong Kong (Veg 2016). Amid the fine distinctions among the various types of localism is a common trait of a strong Hong Kong identity that testified to those people's search for an identity without China (Lam 2018a).

During the Anti-ELAB Movement in 2019 to 2020, a brand of localism in Hong Kong had taken an ideological and strategic turn into "civic nationalism," attempting to further consolidate a united Hong Konger identity for the local social movement to gear toward greater political autonomy for Hong Kong. According to Michael Ignatieff (1993), civic nationalism means a kind of nationalism which emphasizes people's civic identity rather than their ethnic identity. Civic nationhood is a political identity built around shared citizenship in a liberal-democratic state, which is a non-xenophobic form of nationalism compatible with the values of freedom, equality, tolerance, and rights. Contrary to ethnic nationalism, civic nationalism considers it unnecessary to unite people by commonalities of ancestral origins, ethnicity, or language and sees membership in the nation as voluntary and open. It is a form of national belonging based on individuals' personal choices rather than their ethnic origin. Practically, the civic nationalism at that time portrayed Hong Kong as an imagined nation in which people held shared and unique history and values (universal values). Hong Kong people were thus broadly defined as residents, local or immigrant, who embraced and shared the Hong Kong identity and values.

The development of political identity in Hong Kong has aroused a lot of academic discussions on the ideas of identity politics (Box 10.3). Indeed, identity-building is a process of meaning construction. According to Manuel Castells, there are three types of identity: legitimizing identity, resistance identity, and project identity. Legitimizing identity is introduced by the dominant authorities of a society to establish and maintain domination. Resistance identity, in negation of the legitimizing identity, is generated by the political actors who are being dominated or excluded. Lastly, project identity represents the new identity, with contents built by political actors to redefine themselves and their position in the society that guides their subsequent political actions. As such, identity building is a catalyst for social change and a form of activism (Castells 2010: 8). As seen in the case of Hong Kong, the Hong Kong political identity had grown over several significant political events after 2012, and a brand of it reached its climax in 2019 as resistance and project identities to counter the legitimizing identity promoted by the authorities. The territory-wide and enduring protests in 2019 superseded the deep-rooted divergences among the various brands of localism and had fostered unity, notably that between the pro-democracy and localist camps.

In combating the growth of localism, booming pro-Beijing mobilization and propaganda in support of government policies was prevalent (Cheng 2020; Yuen 2021). Understandably, there was a substantial proportion of people in Hong Kong who were loyal to their Chinese identity or secure in a dual identity (Table 10.1). The stepping-up efforts by the authorities to cultivate patriotism and the promulgation of the National Security Law have shaped and entrenched major political values and political participation in Hong Kong. Worthy of note, the political identity in Hong Kong after 2020 manifested decreasing proportions of the Hong Konger identity and increasing proportions of the Chinese identity and mixed identity (Table 10.1).

Political Culture since 2012

The rise of the Hong Konger identity and localism had transformed the political culture in the period. In spite of this, the political culture in Hong Kong still embodied elements of political passivity.

Political interest, efficacy, and trust

Table 10.3 indicates the levels of public interest in politics in the three recent waves of the Asian Barometer Hong Kong Survey in 2012, 2016, and 2021. Notably, only a relatively small proportion of the respondents in the surveys claimed that they were very or somewhat interested in politics.

The sense of political efficacy, which would significantly influence people's readiness to get politically involved, remained low. In 2007, the Asian Barometer Hong Kong Survey (wave two) showed that up to 89.6 percent of respondents felt incapable of participating in politics regardless of the experience of political empowerment for many of them during the 2003 protest against Article 23 (Lam 2012). In 2012, 2016, and the 2021 post–National Security Law Hong Kong, the respective surveys found that only 17.5 percent, 21.7 percent, and 17.1 percent of respondents agreed that they had the ability to participate in politics. Also, up to 74.9 percent, 67.5 percent, and 71.3 percent agreed with the statement that "People like me don't have any influence over what the government does."

Table 10.3: Political interest and political efficacy

Question	Response	2012 % (N)	2016 % (N)	2021 % (N)
How interested would you say you are in politics?	Very interested / Somewhat interested	26.7 (1,208)	27.3 (1,217)	29.3 (1,176)
I think I have the ability to participate in politics.	Strongly agree / Somewhat agree	17.5 (1,208)	21.7 (1,218)	17.1 (1,095)
People like me don't have any influence over what the government does.	Strongly agree / Somewhat agree	74.9 (1,208)	67.5 (1,216)	71.3 (1,164)

Sources: Weighted international data from Asian Barometer Hong Kong Survey wave 3 (2012) and wave 4 (2016) and weighted data from Asian Barometer Hong Kong Survey wave 5 (2021).
Note: "N" denotes the total number of responses.

Meanwhile, political trust had dwindled over the years. Table 10.4 shows the proportions of respondents who had a great deal or quite a lot of trust in various political institutions. All the proportions signified obvious decline, including the trust in the Chief Executive, the courts, the Central Government, local political parties, the Legislative Council, the civil service, the People's Liberation Army in Hong Kong, the police, newspapers, television media, and the Electoral Affairs Commission / Registration and Electoral Office. Significant decline in trust was witnessed on all fronts, including for various government institutions, the courts, and newspapers. The Anti-ELAB Movement in 2019 had evolved into calls for accountability of police power and genuine democracy. The decline of political trust to pathetic levels in 2021 demonstrates widespread mistrust in society after the protests. Nevertheless, a poll conducted in November 2022 found that trust in the Hong Kong government had increased to 49.7 percent, which substantially exceeded the proportions of distrust (34.1 percent) (HKPORIb various years).

Political activism

Despite the contradictory trends of low political interest, political efficacy, and political trust analyzed above, the political culture in Hong Kong had demonstrated an activist character, marked by some people's growing fundamental social and political demands and increased endorsement of radicalized and confrontational strategies. Table 10.5 indicates the levels of public acceptance for confrontational tactics in a survey conducted in 2016. The figures show that

Table 10.4: Political trust

Extent of Trust	% of a Great Deal of Trust / Quite a Lot of Trust (Total Number of Responses)		
	2012	2016	2021
The Chief Executive	65.3 (1,207)	39.3 (1,216)	12.6 (1,177)
The courts in Hong Kong	89.8 (1,207)	76.7 (1,218)	26.0 (1,170)
The Central Government	60.3 (1,207)	37.9 (1,218)	24.4 (1,079)
Political parties	43.4 (1,206)	28.5 (1,216)	14.3 (1,098)
Legislative Council	57.9 (1,207)	40.1 (1,216)	15.4 (1,158)
The civil service	83.4 (1,207)	65.6 (1,215)	24.1 (1,163)
People's Liberation Army in Hong Kong	76.8 (1,208)	44.7 (1,217)	24.1 (947)
The police	87.4 (1,206)	66.1 (1,216)	25.2 (1,135)
Newspapers	58.9 (1,206)	51.5 (1,218)	11.9 (1,096)
Television	67.9 (1,206)	54.8 (1,217)	16.7 (1,168)
Electoral Affairs Commission / Registration and Electoral Office	79.0 (1,207)	55.2 (1,216)	16.0 (1,077)

Sources: Weighted international data from Asian Barometer Hong Kong Survey wave 3 (2012) and wave 4 (2016) and weighted data from Asian Barometer Hong Kong Survey wave 5 (2021).

Table 10.5: Public acceptance of confrontational tactics as of 2016

To What Extent Are You Accepting the Following Confrontational Tactics?	% of Strongly Accepting / Accepting	% of Strongly Not Accepting / Not Accepting
Participating in rallies, petitions, marches, protests not approved by the police	33.0	64.1
Occupying public spaces	19.4	77.3
Occupying government buildings	16.1	80.7
Throwing objects at officials or those with opposing views	14.1	82.8
Striking government buildings	8.5	88.7
Calling on people to use provocative bodily tactics	7.9	89.4
Assaulting the police	7.0	89.9
Resorting to violence	6.9	90.4
Total no. of responses = 1,016		

Sources: Survey on Political Culture in Hong Kong (Path of Democracy 2016); Lam 2018b.

a significant number of respondents, ranging from 6.9 percent to 33 percent, were attitudinally strongly accepting or accepting the confrontational tactics of participating in protests not approved by the police, e.g., occupying public spaces, occupying government buildings, and so on (Path of Democracy 2016; Lam 2018b).

Indeed, the political culture in Hong Kong has undergone significant changes. As examined above, under British colonial rule, Hong Kong was depoliticized, and there was a popular and strong sense of political inefficacy. Scholars argued that the hallmark of the local political culture back then was political apathy rather than political activism, not to say political radicalism. To define, political activism signifies the readiness to participate in politics, which may or may not aim at bringing about fundamental social and political changes, whereas political radicalism entails the idea that political change is to come from the grassroots and through political action to target thorough social and political changes (Lam 2020a: 70).

Civility and the rule of law had long been seen as indispensable elements of the colonial order. In 2012, the culture of depoliticization was fundamentally questioned with the Protest against National Education Curriculum. The campaign had rallied 90,000 protestors outside government headquarters opposing the proposal to introduce moral and national education as a compulsory subject. Later, in 2014, the Occupy Central Movement proposed the use of civil disobedience to strive for genuine democracy in Hong Kong, which subsequently led to the Umbrella Movement. With hindsight, the above incidents—empowered by the Hong Konger identity and the aim to reclaim the city's democratic ideals—were posing significant challenges to the culture of political self-restraint and the belief in law and order in Hong Kong (Lam 2020a).

After the Umbrella Movement, which was largely a 79-day sitting in Admiralty with occasional violent clashes in other parts of the city, political activism diverged on resistance strategies and quickly dichotomized into *wo-lei-fei* (peaceful resistance) and *yong mo* activism (vigilant resistance). After the movement, the two camps had undergone internal divisions and were generally demoralized until 2019, when the Anti-ELAB Movement proclaimed the principle of cooperation (*wo-lei-but-fun*) among different groups and between the two camps. Part of the later developments of the 2019 protests had grown into an ideology of endgame resistance (*naam-chaau*) (Chan 2020). All of these various strategies (and camps) reflected important deviations in Hong Kong's political culture that had been underpinned by depoliticized inclinations and civility, and a dual identity of Hong Konger and Chinese (Lam 2020a). The changing political culture had enhanced institutional and noninstitutional participation, collective actions, and social movements in Hong Kong, which reached a climax in 2019 (Chapter 9 of this volume).

The vehement political activism analyzed above had met substantive counter political reactions. For instance, pro-Beijing organizations such as the Silent Majority had attempted to incite public dissent over the Occupy Central Movement and any attempts of political and social reforms labeled as disruptive of Hong Kong. The counter discourses that arose afterward all focused on the preservation of social stability and order, patriotism, national unity, and law-abidingness in Hong Kong, and the prevention of foreign influence in the internal affairs of Hong Kong and China (Lam 2020b). Civil society in Hong Kong had become very polarized between the pro- and anti-establishment political identities and political participation after the Umbrella Movement. This rift intensified during the Anti-ELAB Movement in 2019. With the introduction of the National Security Law in 2020 and the COVID-related restrictions that had been in place from 2020 to early 2023, social stability has been restored in Hong Kong. Political street activism has been put to a halt, whereas civil society is finding its new areas of focus and learning to operate behind the red line.

Political Participation since 2012

Institutional participation

Political participation in Hong Kong had witnessed rising levels, intensity, breadth, and depth of participation during this period, and noninstitutional participation was more popular than institutional participation before the promulgation of the National Security Law. Regarding institutional participation, it is significant to note the increases in voter turnout rates in District Council elections from 41.49 percent in 2011 and 47.01 percent in 2015 to a record high 71.23 percent in 2019. Whereas for the Legislative Council elections, voter turnout rates were 53.05 percent in 2012, 58.28 percent in 2016, and 30.2 percent in 2021. The 2021 Legislative Council elections, postponed by the Hong Kong government from 2020 and conducted after a new round of reforms to the electoral systems in March 2021 (Chapters 2–3 of this volume), had the lowest voter turnout rates.

The record-breaking turnout rates in the 2019 District Council elections—and the landslide victory of the pro-democracy camp and localist groups in capturing 388 of 452 seats and 17 of 18 District Councils—demonstrated an activist attempt of merging institutional participation with social movement tactics. Pro-democracy and localist District Councillors were entitled to return 117 subsector seats in the 1,200-member Election Committee to elect the Chief Executive of Hong Kong (Mok 2020). However, the District Councils formed after the December 2023 elections comprise 470 members, with only 88 seats returned through popular vote (Chapter 6 of this volume).

Despite the high voter turnout rates examined above, Table 10.6 indicates that participation in election campaigning was not common. The proportions of respondents who had attended a campaign meeting or rally, tried to persuade others to vote for a certain candidate or party, and volunteered or worked for a party or candidate running in the election were small, ranging only from 0.8 percent to 7.6 percent. The percentages remained almost the same over the years. Table 10.7 shows the findings on other types of institutional participation, including contacting elected officials or legislative representatives at any levels, contacting officials at higher levels, and contacting other influential people outside the government in 2012, 2016, and 2021. The percentages of respondents who had expressed concern or sought help via institutional channels in the past three years had remained small. Comparatively speaking, the more common

Table 10.6: Election campaigning

Question	% of Yes (Total Number of Responses)		
	2012	2016	2021
Attend a campaign meeting or rally	2.5 (1,208)	1.2 (1,216)	3.0 (1,167)
Try to persuade others to vote for a certain candidate or party	7.6 (1,205)	4.2 (1,218)	4.6 (1,169)
Do anything else to help, or work for a party or candidate running in the election	1.6 (1,208)	0.8 (1,217)	2.6 (1,174)

Source: Weighted international data from Asian Barometer Hong Kong Survey wave 3 (2012) and wave 4 (2016), and weighted data from Asian Barometer Hong Kong Survey wave 5 (2021).

Table 10.7: Expressing concern or seeking help via institutional channels in the three years prior to the survey

Questions	% of More than Once / Once (Total Number of Responses)		
	2012	2016	2021
Contacted elected officials or legislative representatives at any level	6.7 (1,207)	7.4 (1,217)	15.4 (1,176)
Contacted officials at higher level	4.9 (1,207)	–	–
Contacted other influential people outside the government	1.5 (1,208)	2.9 (1,217)	5.5 (1,168)

Sources: Weighted international data from Asian Barometer Hong Kong Survey wave 3 (2012) and wave 4 (2016), and weighted data from Asian Barometer Hong Kong Survey wave 5 (2021).

choice of channel was contacting elected officials or legislative representatives at any level. In 2021, the percentages had risen to 15.4 percent compared to 6.7 percent in 2012 and 7.4 percent in 2016. The findings of Table 10.6 and 10.7 together reflect that that institutional participation was not a popular form of political participation in this period. However, this phenomenon may change, as institutional participation has become a more acceptable form of participation in the new political order in Hong Kong since 2020.

Non-institutional participation and discursive participation

Table 10.8 demonstrates the findings on selected forms of noninstitutional participation during the period. Comparatively speaking, getting together with others to resolve local problems and attending a demonstration or protest march were more common choices of activities. Notably, the 2021 survey found that 16.6 percent of respondents had worked with others to resolve local problems, and 18.1 percent had attended a demonstration or protest. The proportion of respondents who had worked with others to raise an issue or sign a petition had increased from 5.5 percent in 2016 to 19.3 percent in 2021, while 21.6 percent of respondents had signed an online petition, according to the survey in 2021. Nevertheless, noninstitutional participation may decrease in the future, as it has become much less welcome and more politically risky in the new political order in Hong Kong since 2020.

Table 10.8: Expressing concern or seeking help via noninstitutional channels in the three years prior to the survey

Questions	% of More than Once / Once (Total Number of Responses)		
	2012	2016	2021
Contacted news media	1.9 (1,207)	2.7 (1,217)	3.7 (1,176)
Got together with others to try to resolve local problems	8.0 (1,207)	7.5 (1,217)	16.6 (1,160)
Got together with others to raise an issue or sign a petition	3.8 (1,208)	5.5 (1,217)	19.3 (1,159)
Signed an online petition	–	–	21.6 (1,163)
Attended a demonstration or protest march	5.2 (1,207)	9.7 (1,217)	18.1 (1,106)
Used force or violence for a political cause	0.4 (1,207)	2.8 (1,217)	3.7 (1,110)

Sources: Weighted international data from Asian Barometer Hong Kong Survey wave 3 (2012) and wave 4 (2016), and weighted data from Asian Barometer Hong Kong Survey wave 5 (2021).

Discursive participation had remained a popular form of political participation during the period. Table 10.9 indicates that it was common for respondents to closely follow news about politics and government, as well as major events in foreign countries. In terms of discussing political matters with family members or friends, the percentages had abruptly dropped from 61.5 percent in 2012 to 27.5 percent in 2016, and then went back up to 41.9 percent in 2021. The probable reason for the drastic drop in 2016 was the Mong Kok riots, which sparked an unprecedented controversy over physical strategies, and people simply avoided political discussions. In the post–National Security Law and COVID-19 Hong Kong, people had become even more attentive to news about politics and government. Up to 84 percent of respondents in the 2021 survey followed the news every day or several times a week.

Table 10.9: Discursive participation

Questions	Response	2012 % (N)	2016 % (N)	2021 % (N)
Follow news about politics and government	Everyday / Several times a week	71.6 (1,207)	62.9 (1,216)	84.0 (1,188)
Follow major events in foreign countries	Very closely / Somewhat closely	67.1 (1,208)	47.6 (1,216)	–
Discuss political matters with family members or friends	Frequently / Occasionally	61.5 (1,206)	27.5 (1,217)	41.9 (1,177)

Sources: Weighted international data from Asian Barometer Hong Kong Survey wave 3 (2012) and wave 4 (2016), and weighted data from Asian Barometer Hong Kong Survey wave 5 (2021). Note: "N" denotes the total number of responses.

Digital activism and citizen journalism

Along with discursive participation, the importance of digital and social media as participatory channels has become even more obvious in Hong Kong (Chapter 9 of this volume). According to the ABS Hong Kong survey in 2021, 36.8 percent, 12.6 percent, and 8.4 percent of the respondents used Facebook, Telegram, and LIHKG, respectively, many times per day or several times per day. These were notable channels of communication during the Anti-ELAB Movement in 2019. Without denial, people in Hong Kong have engaged deeply in digital activities.

Digital media has a significant impact on political participation in Hong Kong. The analysis of the Umbrella Movement by Francis L.F. Lee and Joseph M. Chan showed that the protesters were active in online expression, online debates, online explanatory activities, and mobile communication, which were positively related to their degree of involvement (Lee and Chan 2016). Meanwhile, researches also confirmed the significance of social media in promoting political participation in Hong Kong. It was found that social media was significant for political actors to share political information and connect with each other, which had significant impact on motivating support and participation in the Umbrella Movement (Lee, Chen and Chan 2017). Also, another survey of university students showed that students' participation could be explained prominently by exposure to shared political information on Facebook besides direct connection with political actors (Tang and Lee 2013). Regarding the effects of television on political participation, research found that the widely televised live broadcasts of police use of tear gas on protestors in the Umbrella Movement had generated "mediated instant grievances" in the viewing public, thus contributing to escalating the Umbrella Movement (Tang 2015). Overall, digital and social media have become part and parcel of political participation in Hong Kong.

Meanwhile, citizen journalism had continued to grow in Hong Kong and reached its peak in 2019. Research found that citizen journalists in Hong Kong had used online channels—such as SocREC, MyRadio, Passion Times, Resistance Live Media, InMedia, and CitizenNews—as their main conduit to publish reports. Additionally, they would also publish on their own websites and global online media channels, such as Facebook, YouTube, Twitter, Instagram, and Telegram. Citizen journalism played a particularly significant part in sharing information and shaping collective action and mobilization in political campaigning in Hong Kong, notably during the Anti-ELAB Movement (Darbo and Skjerdal 2019). Nevertheless, the chilling effect of the National Security Law on journalists, citizen journalists, and digital activism since its passing has been noticeable (Chapter 9 of this volume). For instance, key opinion leaders and people who regularly shared news and views about politics online have disbanded their programs or closed their social media accounts for fear of violating the law. Also, worthy of note, parallel to the above efforts to promote democracy, there also arose pro-establishment digital activism using different channels—such as Think Hong Kong, Speakout, and HKG Pao—to express counter opinions during the period.

Community, professional, and political organizations

As stated above, from 2014 and notably after the Umbrella Movement, there emerged a tide of community organizations formed by locals and driven by social consciousness, namely the former participants of the Umbrella Movement and young activists of other movements. Numerous community organizations, such as Fixing Hong Kong, Wan Chai Commons, and TaiPosunwalker were formed.

While some of the organizations ran in the District Council elections in 2016 and 2019, others were formed to arouse social concern, empower local residents, consolidate community spirit, and monitor the authorities through community work and public education (Lam 2018a).

Similar trends of mobilization also took place in the professional sectors in the post–Umbrella Movement period in Hong Kong. Numerous professional organizations were formed, including, for example, Progressive Lawyers Group, the Médecins Inspirés, and the ArchiVision. Like the community-oriented organizations analyzed above, the formation of these professional organizations signified the post–Umbrella Movement generation's striving for a genuinely democratic Hong Kong. Some of them ran in the Functional Constituencies (FCs) of the Legislative Council Elections in 2016 to challenge the dominance of pro-establishment professional and business forces in the sectors (Lam 2018a). Amid the Anti-ELAB Movement in 2019, there arose the pro-democracy new trade unionism, which promoted the formation of trade unions in different sectors. Examples included the Union for New Civil Servants, the General Union of Hong Kong Speech Therapists, and HA Employees Alliance. This had become a new form of community qua professional participation.

Since the promulgation of the National Security Law in 2020, the above community and professional activism has declined and most of the organizations have become dispersed and minimized in scale. A few new groups, such as Student Politicism, were formed with constrained scale but disbanded by 2020 and 2021. Meanwhile, the collaboration of "yellow" (pro-movement, contrasting pro-establishment "blue") restaurants and the formation and promotion of yellow circle consumption signified for a short period a new form of community qua economic participation. Nevertheless, as stated above, pro-establishment groups have also grown significantly for the consolidation of patriotic forces and mobilization of counter protests (Cheng 2020; Yuen 2021).

Alongside the above, over the period, there arose other political organizations promoting greater political autonomy for Hong Kong. They adopted a new Hong Konger identity, as well as activist and even confrontational political tactics. Notable examples included Hong Kong National Party, Demosistō, Hong Kong Indigenous, Youngspiration, Hong Kong Resurgence, the Hong Kong National Front and Studentlocalism (Lam 2018a). These organizations have disbanded, and some of the leaders were arrested or fled Hong Kong after the National Security Law was introduced in 2020.

Conclusion

This chapter traces the development of the features of political identity, culture, and participation in Hong Kong. It reviews the conflicting readings offered by scholars before and after the handover in 1997. The dominant views before the 1990s believed that Hong Kong people had adopted a vague Chinese identity, or a dual identity of Hongkongese and Chinese. They paid attention to news and politics but were nonetheless politically apathetic or aloof due to their refugee mentality and the capitalistic culture of Hong Kong. After the handover, the contradiction between the senses of Hongkongese and Chinese continued for a while, with people identifying themselvcs as Hong Kongers, Chinese, or both. Regarding the political culture in Hong Kong, political activism had become its hallmark, characterized by some people's awareness of their political values and rights, lessened fear of politics, and increasing willingness to challenge the political authority, the growing use of radical tactics, and the proactive challenges posed to fundamental and mainstream social and political values. At the same time, there were vivid attempts on the part of the government and pro-establishment political figures after the handover to shape a patriotic identity and other core values for Hong Kong's political culture. Notwithstanding that, political participation had been on the rise with an ever-expanding political sphere. Despite people's lingering sense of political powerlessness and passivity, various means of participation had emerged.

The subject matter of political identity, culture, and participation in Hong Kong has continued to garner much attention amid the drastic political changes in Hong Kong, especially after 2012. This chapter examines the developments of the subject matter after 2012 and analyzes the implications of these developments for the understanding of contemporary politics and governance in the city. It found that in the past 10 years, the Hong Kong identity of some sections of the population had shed much of its Chineseness and instead developed into a new Hong Konger identity, with consolidated cultural and value contents generating and sustaining political actions. Research showed that the vague sense of cultural Chineseness prevalent among older Hong Kong people had become less important in this new Hong Konger identity. The development of localism signified another landmark turns in the Hong Kong identity. Three types of localism had become embedded in the political culture of Hong Kong: community-oriented localism, civic localism, and a type of nativist localism that promoted Hong Kong people's priority and rights over the resources of Hong Kong, and political action to defend Hong Kong. Importantly, during the Anti-ELAB Movement in 2019 to 2020, localism in Hong Kong took an ideological and strategic turn, namely into "civic nationalism," gearing toward greater unity of the local social movements. Meanwhile, the development of political identity in Hong Kong has aroused a lot of academic discussions on the ideas of identity politics.

The rise of the Hong Konger identity and localism had transformed the political culture in the period until the promulgation of the National Security Law in Hong Kong in 2020. In spite of this, the political culture in Hong Kong still embodied elements of political passivity, such as low interest in politics and low sense of political efficacy. Meanwhile, political trust had dwindled over the years and especially after the Anti-ELAB Movement in 2019. Despite these factors, according to recent polls, the proportion of the Hong Konger identity has decreased alongside the increase in the proportions of the Chinese identity and mixed identity. Also, political trust in the Hong Kong government has risen.

During the period, the political culture in Hong Kong had largely maintained an activist character, marked by people's fundamental social and political demands and increased endorsement of radicalized and confrontational strategies, although civility and the rule of law had long been ascribed as indispensable elements of the colonial order. The changing political culture had enhanced institutional and noninstitutional participation, collective actions, and social movements in Hong Kong. Political participation in Hong Kong had witnessed rising levels, intensity, breadth, and depth of participation during the period, and noninstitutional participation was more popular than institutional participation. The increases in the voter turnout rates of District Council elections and the percentages of people who had worked with others to resolve local problems, had attended a demonstration or protest, and had signed a petition were valid proofs. Meanwhile, discursive participation had remained a popular form of political participation during the period, along with participation through digital and social media and citizen journalism. As discussed above, these phenomena have changed, as institutional participation, rather than noninstitutional participation, has become a more acceptable form of participation in the new political order of Hong Kong.

From 2014 and notably after the Umbrella Movement, there emerged a tide of newly formed community and professional organizations by locals driven by social consciousness, namely former participants of the Umbrella Movement and young activists of other movements. Alongside the above, over the period, there arose many other political organizations promoting greater political autonomy for Hong Kong. Nevertheless, after the promulgation of the National Security Law in 2020, the above organizational activism has declined, and most of these organizations have been dispersed, minimized in scale, or disbanded.

Acknowledgments

The author thanks the General Research Fund (Ref: 746812 and 14614815) and the Faculty Development Scheme (Ref: UGC/FDS16/H05/18) of the Research Grants Council of Hong Kong for the funding support for these projects.

Box 10.1: Political identity and culture

Political identity refers to the set of personal or behavioral characteristics including beliefs and attitudes by which an individual is recognizable as a member of a political community. It mainly comprises people's cultural or ethnic identity, national identity, and citizen identity, as well as associated beliefs and attitudes.

Following Gabriel Almond and Sidney Verba's study of civic culture (1963), political culture, in the most popular sense, has been taken to mean the overall patterns of political beliefs and attitudes of people. It is the aggregate of people's psychological orientation to political objects, such as government institutions, political parties, parliaments, and the constitution.

Box 10.2: Political participation

Political participation refers to activities undertaken by individuals to influence who governs and what the government decides to do (e.g., selection of government personnel and public policy aims). These include instrumental political acts (e.g., voting, signing a petition, and marching in a protest) and participation in political organizations for expressive purposes. The forms of participation can be classified into conventional and unconventional ones. Conventional political activities refer to the activities conducted through formal and institutional channels, such as voting, whereas unconventional ones are those attempting to influence the policy process from outside government institutions, such as demonstrations.

Box 10.3: Identity politics

Political identity does not arise from a vacuum. It is a process of meaning construction. According to Castells, identity is the process of "the construction of meaning on the basis of a cultural attribute or a related set of cultural attributes" (Castells 2010: 6). There are three types of identity: first, legitimizing identity introduced by the dominant institutions of a society establishes their authority and domination; second, resistance identity produced by the political actors who are being dominated, excluded, or stigmatized, leading to the formation of communities and resistance (religious fundamentalism falls under this category); and third, project identity representing the new identity and social movement built by political actors redefines their self-understanding and position in society and transforms society. Feminist and environmental movements are examples of this latter category (Castells 2010: 8; Lam 2018b: 75).

> As such, identity-building is a motor of social change. While dominant groups structure how subordinate groups see themselves and are seen by others, the subordinate groups are challenged to reshape their identity and assert their sense of pride and self-respect. Identity, as a form of politics, serves to help members of a certain sector of society explore, reshape, and foster their shared collective identity. It further mobilizes them to challenge and overthrow oppression by the larger part of society in terms of political-cultural self-assertion. Identity politics is thus a form of activism, functioning as both a political strategy and a cultural and political goal for the activists (Heywood 2013: 160–169; Bernstein 2005: 59–63; Lam 2018b: 75).

Questions

1. What are the reasons for the common perception of the mutual exclusivity of the identities of Hong Konger and Chinese in Hong Kong? How would you evaluate the possibilities for their integration with each other?
2. What is identity politics? How would you analyze the development of Hong Kong identity using this concept?
3. What are the main features of political culture and participation in Hong Kong? What would be their future development in your view? What are the possibilities for and constraints on their development?

Bibliography

Almond, G & Verba, S 1963, *The Civic Culture: Political Attitudes and Democracy in Five Nations*, Princeton University Press, Princeton, NJ.

Bernstein, M 2005, "Identity Politics," *Annual Review of Sociology*, vol. 31, pp. 41–74.

Castells, M 2010, *The Power of Identity*, 2nd ed., Wiley-Blackwell, Malden, MA.

Chan, SCK 2020, "Some Thoughts on the Endgame of Resistance: Ngo-yiu Naam-chaau as Terminal Reciprocity," *Inter-Asia Cultural Studies*, vol. 21, no. 1, pp. 99–110.

Cheng, EW 2020, "United Front Work and the Mechanisms of Counter-Mobilization in Hong Kong," *The China Journal*, vol. 83, January, pp. 1–33.

Chiu, SWK & Lui, TL 2000, *The Dynamics of Social Movement in Hong Kong*, Hong Kong University Press, Hong Kong.

Darbo, KN & Skjerdal, T 2019, "Blurred Boundaries: Citizens Journalists versus Conventional Journalists in Hong Kong," *Global Media and China*, vol. 4, no. 1, pp. 111–124.

Heywood, A 2013, *Politics*, 4th ed., Palgrave Macmillan, Basingstoke, pp. 60–169.

Hoadley, JS 1973, "Political Participation of Hong Kong Chinese: Patterns and Trends," *Asian Survey*, vol. 13, no. 6, pp. 604–616.

HKPORIa (various years), "Identification of Oneself as a Hong Konger / Chinese / Mixed Identity" (Chinese in Hong Kong or Hong Konger in China), viewed 30 May 2021, https://www.pori.hk/pop-poll/ethnic-identity/q001.html

HKPORIb (various years), "People's Trust in the HKSAR Government," viewed 20 March 2023, https://www.pori.hk/pop-poll/government-en/k001.html?lang=en

Ignatieff, M 1993, *Blood and Belonging: Journeys into the New Nationalism*, Farrar, Straus and Giroux, New York.

Lam, WM 2004, *Understanding the Political Culture of Hong Kong: The Paradox of Activism and Depoliticization*, M. E. Sharpe, Armonk, NY.

Lam, WM 2012, "Political Identity, Culture and Participation," 2nd ed., in WM Lam, PLT Lui & W Wong (eds), *Contemporary Hong Kong Government and Politics*, Hong Kong University Press, Hong Kong, pp. 199–221.

Lam, WM 2018a, "Hong Kong's Fragmented Soul: Exploring Brands of Localism," in WM Lam & L Cooper (eds), *Citizenship, Identity and Social Movements in the New Hong Kong: Localism after the Umbrella Movement*, Routledge, London, pp. 72–93.

Lam, WM 2018b, "Changing Political Activism: Before and After the Umbrella Movement," in BCH Fong & TL Lui (eds), *Hong Kong 20 Years After the Handover: Emerging Social and Institutional Fractures After 1997*, Palgrave Macmillan, pp. 73–102.

Lam, WM 2020a, "Hybridity, Civility and Othering: In Search of Political Identity and Activism in Hong Kong," in TB Gold & S Veg (eds), *Sunflowers and Umbrellas: Social Movements, Expressive Practices and Political Culture in Taiwan and Hong Kong*, University of California Press, Berkeley, pp. 68–95.

Lam, WM 2020b, "China's Changing Ruling Strategies on Hong Kong and their Implications," *Contemporary Chinese Political Economy and Strategic Relations: An International Journal*, vol. 6, no. 3, December, pp. 953–992.

Lau, SK & Kuan, HC 1988, *The Ethos of the Hong Kong Chinese*, the Chinese University Press of Hong Kong, Hong Kong.

Lau, SK 1982, *Society and Politics in Hong Kong*, the Chinese University Press of Hong Kong, Hong Kong.

Lau, SK 1997, *Hongkongese or Chinese: The Problem of Identity on the Eve of Resumption of Chinese Sovereignty over Hong Kong*, Hong Kong Institute of Asia-Pacific Studies, Hong Kong.

Lee, FLF & Chan, JM 2016, "Digital Media Activities and Mode of Participation in A Protest Campaign: A Study of the Umbrella Movement," *Information, Communication & Society*, vol. 19, no. 1, pp. 4–22.

Lee, FLF, Chen, HT & Chan, M 2017, "Social Media Use and University Students' Participation in a Large-Scale Protest Campaign: The Case of Hong Kong's Umbrella Movement," *Telematics and Informatics*, vol. 34, pp. 457–469.

Mathews, G 1997, "Heunggongyahn: On the Past, Present, and Future of Hong Kong Identity," *Bulletin of Concerned Asian Scholars*, vol. 29, no. 3, pp. 3–13.

Mok, CWJ 2020, "Why and How Umbrella Movement Participants Ran in the Authoritarian Elections in Hong Kong: Bringing Umbrellas Indoors," *Asian Survey*, vol. 60, no. 6, pp. 1142–1171.

Ngo, TW 1999, *Hong Kong's History: State and Society under Colonial Rule*, Routledge, London & New York.

Path of Democracy 2016, Survey on Political Culture of Hong Kong (unpublished).

Scott, I 1989, *Political Change and the Crisis of Legitimacy in Hong Kong*, Oxford University Press, Hong Kong.

Tang, G & Lee, FLF 2013, "Facebook Use and Political Participation: The Impact of Exposure to Shared Political Information, Connections with Public Political Actors, and Network Structural Heterogeneity," *Social Science Computer Review*, vol. 31, no. 6, pp. 763–773.

Tang, G 2015, "Mobilization by Images: TV Screen and Mediated Instant Grievances in the Umbrella Movement," *Chinese Journal of Communication*, vol. 8, no. 4, pp. 338–355.

Turner, M 1995, "Hong Kong Sixties/Nineties: Dissolving the People," in M Turner & I Ngan (eds), *Hong Kong Sixties: Designing Identity*, Hong Kong Arts Centre, Hong Kong, pp. 13–36.

Veg, S 2016, "Creating a Textual Public Space: Slogans and Texts from Hong Kong's Umbrella Movement," *Journal of Asian Studies*, vol. 75, no. 3, August, pp. 673–702.

Yuen, SWH 2021, "Native-Place Networks and Political Mobilization: The Case of Post-Handover Hong Kong," *Modern China*, vol. 47, no. 5, pp. 510–539.

Useful Websites

Asian Barometer
http://www.asianbarometer.org/

Hong Kong Institute of Asia-Pacific Studies, the Chinese University of Hong Kong
http://www.cuhk.edu.hk/hkiaps/index.html

Hong Kong Legal Information Institute
http://www.hklii.org

HKPORI
https://www.pori.hk/

In-media
http://www.inmediahk.net/about

The National Security Law
https://www.isd.gov.hk/nationalsecurity/eng/law.html

Further Reading

Ma, EKW 2003, "Hong Kong Remembers: A Thick Description on Electronic Memory," in Pun, N & Yee, LM (eds), *Narrating Hong Kong Culture and Identity*, Oxford University Press, Hong Kong, pp. 557–577. This book chapter provides an analytical account of the role of media in shaping our memory of the 1967 riots.

Sing, M (ed) 2009, *Politics and Government in Hong Kong: Crisis under Chinese Sovereignty*, Routledge, London & New York. This book provides a good analysis of the mass protests in Hong Kong in the 2000s, notably since 2003.

Lam, WM & Cooper, L (eds) 2018, *Citizenship, Identity and Social Movements in the New Hong Kong: Localism after the Umbrella Movement*, Routledge, London. The book analyzes the identity, political, and social cleavages that were expressed through the Umbrella Movement and that underpinned the development of localism. It uses a range of theories to understand these processes, including theories of nationalism, social identity, ethnic conflict, nativism, and cosmopolitanism.

Lee, CK & Sing, M (eds) 2019, *Take Back Our Future: An Eventful Sociology of the Hong Kong Umbrella Movement*, Cornell University Press, Ithaca, NY. This book gives a good outline of how the Umbrella Movement has spurred new political identities while consolidating and expanding civil society organizations and networks in Hong Kong.

Yuen, SWH 2021, "Native-Place Networks and Political Mobilization: The Case of Post-Handover Hong Kong," *Modern China*, vol. 47, no. 5, pp. 510–539. This article reveals that native-place associations in Hong Kong have formed a "cultural nexus" through which the Chinese state fosters political mobilization in support of its interests and policies.

11

Mass Media and Public Opinion

Joseph M. Chan and Francis L. F. Lee

Hong Kong is a media-rich society where news outlets proliferate. As far as news and public affairs media are concerned, Hong Kong residents are served by more than 10 local daily newspapers, a number of international or regional papers, three radio broadcasters, four free-to-air television broadcasters, and one pay-TV service. While most daily newspapers and broadcasters have internet versions, there are several dedicated online news services, including HK01, a general news portal, and The Witness, a website dedicated to court news. Political information of all types is transmitted via social media and the internet. Television and the internet are the most important sources of news for the Hong Kong public.

Most politicians and officials believe that the media play very important roles in Hong Kong politics and have substantial influence on public opinion. Indeed, most common citizens have very limited direct access to the political process. The political world in people's heads is constituted mainly by images and information from the media. On the other side, politicians and officials also rely at least partly on the media for information about events and problems in society and for feedback from people and different social groups. The politics of public opinion in contemporary societies is largely "mediated"—the media shape, represent, and communicate public opinion, constituting a platform for political actors to act out in search of public support.

This chapter discusses various aspects of this mediated politics of public opinion in Hong Kong. We begin by explaining the concept of public opinion itself. We then discuss the media's role, performance, and effects in the process of public opinion formation. It is followed by an examination of how the Hong Kong government tries to manage and shape public opinion through interacting with the media and performing on media platforms. We then move to the other side and consider how the citizens themselves and various social forces may shape the representation of public opinion in the media, especially through collective action. The passage of the National Security Law (NSL) in 2020 is a watershed legislation that redefines the autonomy of Hong Kong and resets the parameters of its politics of public opinion. We will therefore highlight the impact of the NSL throughout the text whenever appropriate.

Conceptions of Public Opinion

In many contemporary democracies, opinion polling is the dominant way to measure "public opinion." In Hong Kong, polling has prospered since the 1990s as the political system was gradually democratized. In its heyday, academics, commercial companies, media organizations, civic associations, political parties, and the government formed a polling industry, and polls constituted a regular feature of news (Lee 2006). The NSL introduced new uncertainties about whether polls about sensitive matters would still be conducted. The pro-establishment forces are often suspicious of polls that cast unfavorable light on the administrations in Hong Kong and China. The pressure for pollsters to self-censor in regard to the choice of survey themes, data interpretation, and the publication of results is expected to mount in post-NSL Hong Kong. There is also the emerging concern of whether citizens would self-censor when responding to polls (Kobayashi and Chan 2022). But as of April 2023, at the time of writing this chapter, surveys on citizens' evaluation of government leaders and policies are still regularly conducted.

There is no doubt that, with the proper use of sampling and other statistical techniques, and assuming that preference falsification is not a huge problem, opinion polls can provide us with important information about where citizens stand on various issues. Nevertheless, it is questionable if "public opinion" can simply be equated with poll findings. Conceptually, what a poll provides is *an aggregation of individual opinions on issues with fixed alternatives*. To equate public opinion with poll findings, therefore, is to adopt an *aggregative conception of public opinion* (Price 1992). Theorists of democracy have questioned whether this aggregative public opinion, which may not be informed or reasoned, is what a democratic government should follow (Althaus 2003). Besides, one can raise doubts over the assumption that individual opinion weighs equally in society. The actual influence of an opinion can vary a lot with the status of the holder and whether it is organized or not. Others have argued that opinion polling is mainly a means for political leaders to manipulate the public rather than for the public to express itself (Ginsberg 1986).

Despite these theoretical critiques, opinion polling prevails in democratic societies, largely because of the close connection between opinion polling and democratic elections: both define an "opinion" as a choice among a fixed set of alternatives; both involve anonymous opinion expression; both involve aggregation of expressed opinions; and both give everyone's opinions equal weight. The survey interview, in these senses, reproduces the context of the voting booth. Opinion polls thus mirror the kind of public opinion that is translated into actual political power through the electoral system in established democracies. Hence, political leaders concerned with getting elected or reelected have very high incentives to pay attention to polls.

Understood in this way, one of the most important limitations of opinion polling in Hong Kong is the underdevelopment of democratic elections. As the Chief Executive (CE) and about three quarters of the legislature is not democratically elected, opinion polling does not enjoy the privileged status it has in established democracies. Polls can still measure and reflect the views of individual citizens in the society, but public opinion as measured by polls has limited actual political influence in Hong Kong.

Certainly, polling is not totally irrelevant. It remains a method of organizing public expression, and poll results are often continually interpreted and reinterpreted in the public arena to support or refute different viewpoints and policy ideas. But the above considerations urge us to adopt a *discursive conception of public opinion*, which provides a broader framework for analyzing how public opinion is formed and may influence the government. Public opinion, in this conception, is *a symbolic representation resulting from a process of discursive struggles among strategic actors in the mediated public arena*. This conception emphasizes that public opinion is discursive in nature, with individuals and groups trying to advance their interests (interests of specific groups or of the public at large) through an open exchange of symbols. For instance, during the COVID-19 outbreak, government officials, politicians, and medical experts would offer their views on the pandemic and various response measures. In the process, claims about public opinion were often evoked by actors to justify their arguments.

Claims or representations of public opinion may be based on different methods of organizing opinion expression, such as polls, petition campaigns, or public rallies. Sometimes, politicians may articulate an idea of where public interests reside on a given issue. In other cases, politicians may invoke commonly accepted moral or cultural values. Obviously, politicians and officials often provide varying or even contradictory representations of public opinion and public interests. In this case, discursive struggles occur, as people and groups try to validate their own representations and invalidate others. When one representation dominates the public arena, it would be regarded as the consensual public opinion on the issue. This may have different degrees of correspondence to poll findings. But the effectiveness of such apparent consensus is not guaranteed, as the political actors may choose to act otherwise.

Regardless, in many cases, a consensual public opinion does not emerge. In fact, in a pluralistic society such as Hong Kong, people have different backgrounds and various kinds of affiliations. As a result, they often hold diverse values and interests. A consensus is very difficult to build. Public opinion is thus not singular but plural. But since the passage of the NSL and the implementation of policies to centralize power, Hong Kong has become less pluralistic politically, resulting in a reduced public space and range of public opinions.

Discursive struggles to represent public opinion occur mainly in an arena that is visible to the public and mediated by professional communicators. In modern societies, mass media are the most efficient channels for government leaders, politicians, and activists to speak to the public at large. The media constitute the most important public space in Hong Kong. But this public space is not equally accessible to everyone. Access to media and the content of media are mainly regulated by journalists who, as gatekeepers of information, decide who and what is to appear in the media. Both the media and journalists thus serve as the mediators of public opinion.

Media Role and Performance

Being mediators in the political communication process, most journalists are not politicians or political party activists. While they are professional communicators with their own sets of norms and values, they are susceptible to the influence of their employing news organizations, which in turn are situated within the larger political and economic structures of society.

Media roles and journalistic ideals

In two surveys of Hong Kong journalists in 2006 and 2011, respectively, we found that an overwhelming majority of them regarded "monitoring the government," "reflecting public opinion," and "providing forums for public discussion" as important media functions. In contrast, other functions included in the survey questionnaire—"providing suggestions for policy making," "promoting citizen-official communication," and "promoting social reform"—received substantially less emphasis.

In a general sense, what these findings suggest is that Hong Kong journalists hold a liberal democratic conception of the press. This conception emphasizes the provision of relevant and timely information about public affairs to citizens; a watchdog role for the media in monitoring political leaders and other power holders; and the provision of public forums for various opinions to compete in a "marketplace of ideas." The primary role of media professionals with regard to the formation of public opinion is that of a facilitator. The media should allow a plurality of politicians, social associations, and, sometimes, individual citizens to voice their views, so that different representations of public opinion can compete fairly with each other in the media. This will allow the public to form their own judgments. Relatively less important is to support specific policy proposals or political stances. When media organizations do have their own views on public matters, they should express them through editorials or commentaries. News coverage, on the other hand, should remain objective, neutral, and fair.

While the above outlines the ideal as conceived by the liberal democratic conception, the reality is complicated by several factors, including the existence of media outlets that do not subscribe to the ideal, structural, and organizational constraints affecting journalists' capabilities in fulfilling their ideals, internal tensions within the ideal itself, and the vagueness of several of its key elements. Journalistic objectivity, for example, is notoriously difficult to define. A news story exposing the wrongdoing of a government official can be regarded as "objective" in the sense that it is based upon facts, but it is certainly not "objective" in the sense that it has no value judgment. Neutrality and "reflecting public opinion" can also come into conflict when citizens overwhelmingly favor one side of a policy. For example, should the Hong Kong media be neutral when the interests of Hong Kong and of the Mainland come into conflict on specific matters? To what extent and in what senses should they be neutral when reporting on a protest movement supported by the majority of Hong Kong citizens? These are hard questions for the Hong Kong media.

Despite the lack of complete coherence, the liberal democratic ideal has been the "legitimating creed" for journalism in Hong Kong since at least the 1980s. A legitimating creed is the set of principles and ideas that not only guides but also justifies journalistic practices. Forming the core of media professionalism, these are the principles and ideas that can be used to explain media behavior and evaluate media performance. These are also the principles and ideas that journalists invoke when they are criticized. The latter include situations when political actors criticize the professional media, as well as when newsroom managers are criticized for exercising self-censorship. For example, during the Umbrella Movement in 2014, TVB News notoriously changed the voice-over of a news story showing police violence against a protester. When criticized for exercising self-censorship, the news director of the station argued that the change was based on the judgment that the wordings used in the original voiceover were not objective enough (Box 11.1).

But there are signs that media professionalism in post-NSL Hong Kong is declining. The top management positions in some news organizations have been replaced by journalists who are known for their pro-establishment political orientations. This results in the adoption of editorial policies that place less emphasis on professionalism. Self-censorship is not only tacitly done but sometimes blatantly practiced. The monitoring function of the news media is giving way to viewing them as a developmental tool of the powers that be. Such tendencies are not confined just to these media organizations; they apply in varying degrees to the media environment as a whole. Notwithstanding these trends, we have to stress that professionalism is still alive in individual media outlets, and at the level of journalists and public discourses.

Media performance and structural constraints

There is no perfect correspondence between what individual journalists believe and how media perform. Journalists, after all, are workers within organizations, and the organizations are in turn situated in a press system that relates in intricate ways to larger political and economic structures in society. Structural factors shape the operation of media organizations in Hong Kong, and in the process constrain journalists' capabilities in adhering to their professional ideals.

It is only possible to sketch the major factors that interact with each other in defining the operation of mainstream media outlets. Most local news organizations are business enterprises, with the exception of Radio Television Hong Kong (RTHK), which is publicly funded. Commercialism leads to at least three concerns about how media outlets operate. The first concern is ownership influence. The question is whether owners, who might regard the news outlets as their private property, would affect news decisions and news contents. At the same time, most media owners, in Hong Kong as well as in other places around the world, also own other businesses. Sometimes a media organization can belong to a large business conglomerate. As a result, scholars and observers are also concerned with the issue of whether media personnel might downplay negative news about their owners and mother corporations.

The second concern is advertisers' influence. Most media outlets obtain their largest share of revenue not through subscriptions or purchase, but through fees advertisers pay for the audience's attention. Advertisers can therefore exert influence by linking their decision to place ads in a certain media outlet to its content. In April 2011, an advertising agency working for the MTR Corporation sent letters to media organizations in Hong Kong, claiming that MTR would consider withdrawing their advertisements if the media organizations report negative news about the corporation. It resulted in heavy public criticism toward the advertising agency and MTR, forcing the latter to publicly apologize. This kind of publicized controversy is uncommon, since the tension between advertisers and news organizations would typically be resolved behind the scenes. But the example illustrates the point that advertisers would try to influence the news media, though media organizations do not always succumb to the influence of advertisers.

The third concern results from commercial media's need to appeal to a mass audience. Around the world, "market-driven journalism" is often marked by the displacement of serious political news by sensationalized human-interest stories. For many local observers, there has indeed been such a trend of "tabloidization" in the Hong Kong media since the 1990s, as indicated by the increasing prominence of celebrity-related news in even presumably serious newspapers. In the world of online news, many media tend to work on "internet hot topics," i.e., topics that attract a lot of online discussion and attention, despite their possible lack of true public relevance.

While economic forces could limit the range and depth of information and viewpoints available in the media, they could interact with political forces to further damage media performance and press freedom. This is because, as already mentioned, media owners seldom run media businesses only; they usually also own other businesses, and media owners are often interested in extending their business interests to the lucrative market in Mainland China. They understand that this possibility can be undermined if the Chinese government perceives a business or its owners as "unfriendly." As a matter of fact, most news organizations in Hong Kong are owned by business people who have vast business operations in Mainland China. Some of these media owners also hold formal political titles in the Chinese political system, such as being members of the Political Consultative Conference. Since the early 2010s, there has also been the trend of ownership of Hong Kong media by Mainland Chinese capital. Co-optation of media owners has long been the fundamental means through which the Chinese state exercises control over the Hong Kong press (Lee 2018).

Many of the above problems are difficult to document. It is because the mechanisms of these influences are likely to be behind-the-scenes and indirect. When media scholars argue that advertisers can influence news organizations, they do not mean that the representatives of the advertisers would simply call up the editors at the news organizations and ask them not to report negative news about their companies. In fact, attempts by the government or business corporations to overtly control the media could backfire because journalists, as professionals, value their autonomy highly.

Talking about the structural constraints on media performance, we should take note of the immense pressure imposed on Hong Kong media that was consequential to the passage of the NSL in 2020. The legislation of the NSL was the response of the Central People's Government (CPG) to the outbreak of the Anti–Extradition Law Amendment Bill (Anti-ELAB) Movement in 2019, which turned violent and socially eruptive as the government refused to accommodate the public demand for an independent investigation of the police's mishandling of the protests, among other factors. The NSL, shrouded in total secrecy before it was announced by the National People's Congress on 30 June 2020, gives China sweeping powers to prohibit with severe penalties any offenses of secession, subversion, terrorism, and collusion with foreign powers. It follows, for instance, that advocacy for Hong Kong independence and self-determination will be banned. Interfering in the exercise of powers by the Chinese and Hong Kong governments may be considered subversive. The requests for foreign agencies to enact policies against China and Hong Kong will be considered acts of collusion. While the extraterritorial reach of the law is worldwide, Beijing has the ultimate right to interpret the NSL in case of controversies.

The stringent and broadly defined NSL has thus cast a dark shadow over the practice of civil liberties and human rights in Hong Kong. In the months following the enactment of the NSL, it appeared to have been quite effective in subduing more critical voices and organizations. For instance, the election return officers, empowered by the NSL, expanded the disqualification of candidates to cover not only the explicitly pro Hong Kong independence activists but also veteran Legislative Councillors fielded by the Civic Party, a pro-democratic party for the middle class. The police readily declared a protest to be breaking the NSL at the slightest hint. The Hong Kong Professional Teachers' Union, the largest labor union in the city, was forced to close along with various nongovernmental organizations (NGOs).

The chilling effect was felt in the media sector, too. The most notable incident portending an omen for press freedom in Hong Kong was the arrests of Jimmy Lai, the proprietor of *Apple Daily*, and his top managers and sons for allegedly violating the NSL and other laws. *Apple Daily* was forced to stop its publication in June 2021. At the same time, the Hong Kong government stepped up measures to take control of the public broadcaster RTHK. Some professional commentators relocated to other places for fear that their advocacies may overstep the new red lines. The Hong Kong Journalists Association (HKJA) expressed concerns over the growing pressure on journalists to self-censor. Remarkably, the HKJA itself has also been subjected to criticisms by government officials, pro-government forces, and media.

To ensure the effectiveness of the NSL and to further centralize political power, the CPG decreed that Hong Kong's administrative and electoral systems would be overhauled to allow only "patriots" to take up the key positions of the executive, legislative, and judicial branches of the government, as well as statutory bodies. As Xia Baolong, head of the Hong Kong and Macao Office, explicated, anyone "who goes against China and disrupts Hong Kong" would be considered unpatriotic and would be barred from assuming such offices. This drastic revision represents a centralization of power that is redefining the parameters of the politics of mediated public opinion in Hong Kong, including its formation, expression, diversity, and effectiveness. In general, a society with a concentrated mode of power distribution often results in subdued freedom of expression, less diversity of information and opinions, and less accountability from the government (Chan and Lee 1991). It will be more often the case for the pro-establishment force to be formally and informally represented in the political structure and public discourses. The opinions so mediated will more often rhyme with official views and will be given more recognition by the powers that be. Meanwhile, the dissenting views or views deviating from official lines will be slighted and sidelined, even if they are held by a significant number of citizens. They will have to expend much greater effort if they are to get their voices heard.

To clamp down on the outspoken media, the Hong Kong government not only makes use of the NSL, but it has also revived the dormant colonial Sedition Law that outlaws incitement to violence, to disaffection, and to other offences against the government. The best-known case is the government's prosecution of Stand News for its publication of allegedly seditious reports and commentaries. Its editors-in-chief were arrested, the online operation ceased, and a large fund was withheld. Prior to the imposition of the NSL, it was legitimate for media to report on a wide range of views, including those severely critical of the Hong Kong and Beijing authorities. This is consistent with the emphasis on the media being a marketplace of ideas. But the government broke away from this tradition and charged Stand News with inciting hatred against the administration. The trial is ongoing at the time of this writing. Whatever the verdict, the prosecution of Stand News has sounded a serious warning to all commentators and news media. The legitimate sphere of controversy in Hong Kong is narrowed.

The problem of media self-censorship

In Mainland China, the government has direct and institutionalized control over the news media. As the ultimate owner of all major news media, the ruling party and the government hold the authority to license media and appoint its key personnel. News coverage is subject to directives from the Propaganda Department or other relevant government units. The more important or sensitive information is subject to censorship before it is dispatched.

At the time of the writing of this chapter, direct government control of media organizations and a prepublication censorship system do not exist in Hong Kong. However, consequential to co-optation efforts on the part of the Chinese and Hong Kong governments, shifting media ownership, changes of media personnel appointment, uses of favoritism by the power centers, and the new trend of "legalization" of press control (Lee and Chan 2022), the Hong Kong media have largely been politically tamed in favor of the establishment, resulting in prevalent self-censorship. Formally, self-censorship can be understood as "a set of editorial actions ranging from omission, distortion, change of emphasis, to choice of rhetorical devices by journalists, their organisations, and even the entire media community in anticipation of currying reward and avoiding punishments from the power structure" (Lee 1998). In the surveys of Hong Kong journalists mentioned earlier, the percentage of respondents saying that self-censorship was serious inside news organizations increased from 13.3 percent in 2001 to 39.0 percent in 2011. The figure is likely to have gone up further in the years since then, especially in the wake of the NSL.

This does not mean that many journalists as a rule self-censor when they have to handle sensitive stories. Neither does it mean that journalists are always asked explicitly by their superiors to self-censor. Self-censorship is produced within news organizations through several indirect mechanisms, as Lee and Chan (2009) have shown. First, superiors can assign "suitable journalists" to report on certain stories to ensure the "political correctness" of the report. Putting it concretely, a simple method to avoid having a journalist write a story critical of the government is to assign a journalist who is not at all critical of the government to write the story. Second, through interacting with superiors and colleagues constantly and observing editorial decisions on a daily basis, journalists can quickly learn the unstated, informal rules of their organizations regarding how certain issues are to be handled or whether there are any "taboo topics." Third, frontline journalists may occasionally receive ambiguous orders from their superiors when handling potentially sensitive stories. For instance, a journalist reported that he had once been asked by his superior "to be smart" when reporting on an anti-government protest. This kind of ambiguous command can induce doubts in the minds of journalists and affect their work. Fourth, questionable editorial decisions are sometimes couched in technical or even professional terms.

Since self-censorship is partly produced through such indirect mechanisms, frontline journalists can sometimes resist the pressure to self-censor. Daring frontline journalists can argue with their superiors by resorting to professionalism when the latter back their directives with technical or professional reasons. Commands couched in ambiguous language can be simply ignored. The organizational pressure to self-censor, in other words, is often met with resistance from journalists, which is fueled by the journalists' own sense of professionalism.

Nevertheless, such resistance has its own limitations. While resistance may slow the decline of press freedom in Hong Kong, it is unlikely to stop or reverse the trend unless there are major changes in the political system at large. Besides, as older generations of experienced journalists are replaced by younger journalists, the latter may not have an adequate amount of experience and skills to resist political control. In fact, measures of political control are likely to become the constitutive rules of newsroom operation, as veteran journalist Allan Au explicated in his book-length study (Au 2018). Moreover, the chilling effect of the NSL has served to further erode the resilience of journalistic professionalism. Many mid-level journalists have left the field, producing a gap and difficulties for young journalists to learn. Journalistic professionalism is expected to face a grave challenge when the parameters for mediated public opinion are reconfigured

Media Effects on Public Opinion

Whether media can influence public opinion has long been one of the most important questions for researchers and political leaders. In Hong Kong, the question of media effects had gained new relevance as social mobilization and protests increased in intensity and frequency after the early 2000s and up to the passage of the NSL in 2020. The development raised the issue of whether citizens were mobilized to protest by certain media outlets. In this context, media effects become not only an academic question but also a political one. Government officials tend to emphasize that the media have powerful effects on people. Intentional or not, this argument heaps additional pressure on the Hong Kong media to be "responsible."

The question of media effects does not allow a simple yes or no answer. Part of the problem is that the idea of media effects itself is complicated. In academic research, media effects are usually studied by examining whether exposure to media contents is followed by changes in individuals' attitudes, opinions, and behavior. This technical definition—effects as post-exposure changes—provides a convenient starting point for academic studies, but it tells us little about the actual role the media play in the public opinion process. Going beyond the conventional model of effects analysis as post-exposure attitudinal change, four general types of media effects can be highlighted as particularly pertinent to our understanding of discursive public opinion formation.

Agenda-setting effects

Agenda setting refers to the idea that the media influence what people in a society think and talk about. This follows from the everyday phenomenon that we tend to regard the issues addressed on the front page of newspapers, at the very beginning of a television newscast, or by the top news feeds online as the most important issues of the day. The top news stories also tend to generate the largest amount of public discourse. The setting of news agendas involves a very complicated process. Social and political organizations have an interest in pushing certain issues up (and others down) in the news agenda. They might promote their concerns actively. Journalists, on the other hand, are expected to use their professional judgment to determine how much coverage each issue deserves. Sometimes, downplaying an issue in the news agenda is an act of self-censorship.

Publicity effects

When a person knows that what he or she does is visible to others, that person is likely to behave differently. Some media scholars thus point out that the mere existence of the news media will influence what public figures do because of public visibility. Media publicity, presumably, provides incentives for politicians to try hard not to make mistakes. Media publicity also implies that political leaders have to regard the public at large as the addressee of what they say. In a democratic context, politicians have to publicly justify their words and deeds, and they have to refer to some understandings of "public interests" and/or widely accepted moral principles when doing so. The discursive struggles central to public opinion formation largely involve struggles to define the relevant public interests and moral principles at hand. In a more authoritarian environment, visibility may become a showcase of power. Political leaders' public performance can signal the degree to which they are in control.

Legitimation effects

Media professionals are gatekeepers who decide what and who will appear in the news. Media professionals have to ponder the question of who the legitimate spokespeople are on a given issue. At the same time, there is a tendency for news audiences, including common citizens and social and political elites, to regard groups and organizations appearing in the media as important and legitimate speakers on public affairs. Therefore, when a group gains constant access to the media, other groups and actors are likely to take it more seriously. Over time, its share of influence in public debates may increase.

Omission effects

Last but not least, media can influence the formation of public opinion not by what they report but by what they do not report. What is absent in the media can be as important as what is present. This, of course, is related to the concern over self-censorship and press freedom. Failure to provide certain key information and opinions when a public debate occurs may skew the formation of public opinion toward certain directions unjustifiably and with undesirable consequences.

In sum, as facilitators of public opinion formation, the media can have huge effects on public opinion, though not through "brainwashing" the public to adopt certain ideas. Decades of media research has shown that direct and simple persuasive power of the media is limited, but the media do influence public opinion, first and foremost by determining the range of relevant information and opinions available to the public. Normatively, the media should provide the full range of relevant information and opinions for public consideration.

Government and Mediated Public Opinion

Governments around the world—be they dictatorial, colonial, or democratic—all claim that they are responsive to public opinion, but they differ in the methods they use and develop to "listen to the public." By constitution, the Legislative Council and the District Councils are supposed to be the formal conveyors of public opinion in Hong Kong. At the same time, the government has established an elaborate network of consultation bodies for tapping public opinion. Within the government itself, the Home Affairs Bureau is charged with promoting communication between the government and the public. The channels for achieving this include site visits to districts by top leaders and sponsorship of exchange sessions between the CE and the public. Another important responsibility of the Home Affairs Bureau is to collect public opinion on given issues at the district level on a periodic basis, and conduct polls to monitor the movement of public opinion. Besides the Home Affairs Bureau, virtually all bureaus have commissioned the Census and Statistics Department or other research units to conduct surveys of the public to meet their specific needs. Also active in gathering public opinion is the government's "policy research arm," which used to be the Central Policy Unit in the early post-handover years but was reformed into the Policy Innovation and Co-ordination Office in 2018 and then to the Chief Executive's Policy Unit in late 2022.

However, these institutions and channels have various limitations. The effectiveness of democratically elected legislators within the legislature is severely compromised by the restrictive voting system of the legislature and the fact that only half of the legislators are directly elected. This constraint would be further enhanced by the 2021 electoral reform allowing only about 22 percent of legislators to be democratically elected. Besides, the pro-democrats holding or running for an office in the Legislative Council are subject to disqualification when the government finds them politically intolerable. The criteria for such political screening are not fully spelled out and are criticized as arbitrary. Meanwhile, as Hong Kong society became more complex and pluralistic, the number of advisory and statutory bodies proliferated. As of June 2020, the government's website included a list of 503 Advisory and Statutory Bodies. With a membership favoring the establishment, the representativeness of the consultation bodies and their effectiveness are doubtful. When the network of consultation bodies fails to carry out its presumed functions, how the Home Affairs Bureau can fulfill its mission of collecting public opinion is a question.

This is why government leaders and politicians remain heavily dependent on the media to inform them what the public thinks. Part of the mission of the Information Services Department (ISD) under the Home Affairs Bureau is to collect mediated opinions. One responsibility of ISD is to produce updated summaries of the news, editorials, and commentaries published in newspapers, selected television shows, and radio phone-in programs. The summary is distributed to senior government officials to inform them of the latest happenings and public reactions to various issues. The information officers dispatched to work under various government bureaus are required to browse online for news that is of interest to the leading bureau officials.

The Hong Kong media, in this sense, play a surrogate democracy function in Hong Kong; by monitoring the government and communicating public opinion, they help ensure governmental accountability and hence compensate for the lack of fully developed democratic institutions (Chan and So 2004). However, as the freedom of general expression is hampered in the post-NSL era, how well the surrogate democracy functions has become questionable.

The government's information and media management

How the government listens to the public is only one side of the story. Governments around the world, including democratic ones, would try to influence or sometimes even manipulate the public. And to influence the public, the government has to first influence the media. In Hong Kong, the media system is not state-owned. But the status of RTHK is ambiguous. As a government department, it is under the jurisdiction of the Commerce and Economic Development Bureau. However, it has evolved over the years from a publicity arm of the government to a public broadcaster. Aspiring to be the BBC of Hong Kong, RTHK tried to take an impartial approach to news reporting and serve as a forum for open public debate. While RTHK has been criticized by conservative politicians for its critical stance toward China and the Hong Kong government, it has received very high credibility ratings from journalists and the public (Box 11.2).

The role of RTHK as a public broadcaster was reversed as the NSL began to take effect in 2020. The government revamped RTHK first by replacing its incumbent director Leung Ka-wing, a veteran journalist, with an administration officer. The editorial and programming policies were subsequently harmonized in line with the government's policies. All these changes were in step with the government's professed intention to rectify the "serious inadequacies" of RTHK by overhauling its management, editorial operations and work culture. The thrust of the measures was to shrink the editorial autonomy once enjoyed by the media producers, journalists, and the editor-in-chief. It is fair to observe that

RTHK's role as a public broadcaster has been eroded to the extent that it assumes more of the traits of a government arm.

With or without its own media outlet or channel, the government exerts substantial influence on public discourse. If the media can set the agenda for society, then who sets the agenda for the media? In fact, the government is in a privileged position to make news because journalists tend to equate authority with newsworthiness (Bennett et al. 1985). If the government so desires, it can raise issues for the media and help shape public opinion. With the help of ISD, which has information officers embedded in each government bureau, the government can map out various communication strategies, such as holding press conferences and making announcements on public occasions. Through these methods, the government can frame issues in its preferred ways and prepare for anticipated queries from the press. More often than not, the government's messages are given prominent coverage. In this sense, government officials are in general the "primary definers" of reality, whereas journalists are the "secondary definers" (Hall 1978). This is not to say that the government monopolizes views on any issue. The media have the autonomy to follow up news in ways they deem fit, such as by including comments from other public figures who may not agree with the government's position. Yet what is clear is that the government has ready access to the media, even though it does not own them.

The government's access to media is facilitated by the operation of the ISD. To ensure that the media do not miss any government information, the ISD is connected to each newsroom through dedicated communication lines. Written by veteran ex-journalists, all government news releases are made instantly accessible to news organizations. Although media organizations seldom simply "reprint" the press releases, the releases remain important references in the process of news making.

The government can also indirectly influence the media through co-optation. We have noted the co-optation of media owners earlier. In practice, official honors were also granted selectively to media operators and professionals, and the government can play favoritism among media outlets; that is, providing important information only to "friendly" media organizations. The government can make news by granting exclusive interviews to selected journalists. There is a strong tendency for the media to give such stories prominent and faithful coverage, as journalists do not want to jeopardize the goodwill of the source. In December 2020, a leaked video showed that, during a break in a television interview, the former CE of Hong Kong, Carrie Lam, asked a journalist why his questions were "so mild." The journalist was mocked by his peers and the public. Although we cannot attribute motivations to the journalist in this case, the incident suggests how some journalists might fail to confront powerholders in the way they are expected to according to their professional ideal.

Anonymous background briefing is another important method at the disposal of the government in its attempt to influence public opinion. On occasions when the government wants to test the public response to a policy idea or to avoid political sensitivity, it may choose to meet with journalists on an "off-the-record" basis. The common practice is for journalists to attribute the resulting news to "a source close to the government" or "an informed source." Again, anonymity tends to work to the advantage of the government since the government is not formally held accountable, and hence it allows the government to have greater flexibility in framing its messages. Not all background briefings result in news reports, though. Some are simply meant to try out ideas on journalists. Exchanges of the latter kind also serve to build a rapport between officials and journalists which, in the long run, may result in more empathetic news reporting and commentaries.

Toward political public relations

The methods and strategies the government uses to manage and influence the media discussed in the previous section are conventional and have been in place since the colonial days. Since the handover, there has been much discussion among politicians, officials, and commentators on the need for the government to improve its "public relations" (PR) skills. In fact, the increasing incorporation of PR techniques into the running of government and politics in general is a worldwide trend (Davis 2002; Cottle 2003). "Having a good image" seems to have become more and more important to political leaders and governments. The continual proliferation of media channels and the development of new media technologies mean that information and images about important social events are transmitted throughout society with unprecedented speed and scope. Immediate and appropriate responses to breaking events and various kinds of crises have become more and more important. More generally, assuming media images have huge effects on public perception, political leaders and their advisors nowadays pay close attention to minute details of their own public appearances and how government actions are to be executed in public.

However, while government PR may indeed be necessary in contemporary society, it is also risky and can easily backfire. This is because the news media would react negatively if the government's attempt to manipulate them and the public becomes too obvious. For example, in summer 2010, some media and commentators criticized the Hong Kong government's attempt to practice what is sometimes called a "Friday news dump," i.e., to publicize a lot of negative news on Friday in the hope that the impact of the negative news will be diluted over the weekend, when many organizations and people who may otherwise criticize the government are at rest and when citizens are on their days off. As some commentators pointed out, Friday news dump is indeed a commonly used technique in the business world. Yet, when the government employs it, it faces the possibility of being accused of trying to manipulate the public. In other words, while part of government PR is aimed at minimizing negative news about the government and its negative impact, government PR practices themselves can become negative news.

The use of public relations strategies indicates that the Hong Kong government is concerned about its popularity and legitimacy. However, the location of public opinion in the political culture of Hong Kong has been marginalized in the wake of the passage of the NSL. In the first place, the Hong Kong public was not consulted in anyway before it came into law. Following its passage were various restrictive government measures that ranged from the disqualification of democrats for elections, the arrests of democrats, the transformation of liberal studies, the infringement of RTHK's editorial autonomy, to the disbanding of prominent NGOs. All the signs indicate that the government has decided to adhere to the CPG's tightened policy towards Hong Kong and implement all the measures deemed essential for gaining political control. Public opinion appeared to have been tamed when the CPG was restructuring Hong Kong in its image. As discussed earlier, the CPG has ruled that only "patriots" are allowed to assume key positions in Hong Kong governance. The major parameters in which public opinion operates will thus be redefined in favor of the establishment, implying that the force of public opinion will likely be reduced in terms of range, intensity, and effectiveness.

Social Mobilization, Collective Action, and Public Opinion

While media portray and represent public opinion in various ways and the government may attempt to influence the public, citizens are not passive. Instead, public opinion can be organized and expressed by citizens and groups within society. It is an understatement to say that Hong Kong, a pluralistic city of more than 7 million people, does not lack disagreements and contradictions. Indeed, conflicts and sociopolitical realignments abound as Hong Kong is being transformed. As a reflection of this social pluralism, Hong Kong is teeming with civil organizations representing groups of varying interests, be they religious, occupational, ethnic, political, or cultural in nature. These interest groups constitute a significant source of public opinion (Lo 2001). The Catholic Church, for instance, has for a period of time immediately after the handover assumed a rather active role in responding to sensitive issues, such as the right of abode, national security laws, and democratization. In the capitalist city of Hong Kong, business groups are in general more influential than other groups, especially their labor counterparts. By contrast, the less resourceful groups often form coalitions to press their demands. The Democratic Party and other pro-democracy groups are frequent users of this united-front tactic. The actions and views of all these interest groups are often translated into news that forms the guns and bullets of discursive contestations.

Collective actions constitute a particularly important form of "bottom-up" expression of public opinion. Such collective actions range from the more usual and conventional ones, such as peaceful protest marches and rallies, to those involving higher stakes, such as hunger strikes or violent protests.

Collective actions often constitute powerful expressions of public opinion because the actions demonstrate the intensity of the opinions held by the partici- pating citizens and their commitment to the cause. Different from answering a pollster's question at home, joining a protest requires time and effort on the part of the participants. Moreover, through collective actions, citizens' opinions are conspicuous and publicly expressed. The possible power of collective actions in Hong Kong was first demonstrated in the post-handover era by the huge rally on 1 July 2003, during which 500,000 people took to the streets to protest against the national security legislation and to make clear their frustration over the Hong Kong government's perceived ineffective governance. The protest succeeded in forcing the government to postpone the national security bill, and many observ- ers believed that the protest was partly responsible for Tung Chee-hwa's stepping down from the position of CE in 2005.

The rally can be considered a "critical event" that kick-started a new dynamic between China and Hong Kong, as well as among various political actors within the city (Lee and Chan 2011). The protest also heightened citizens' belief in their capability to effect social and political change when they act together. It should be noted that social movements in Hong Kong have a history dating back to at least the late 1960s (Chiu and Lui 2000), and around the time of the rally in 2003, collective actions had already been taking place in Hong Kong so often that the city was nicknamed "the city of protests." Yet after 2003, collective actions such as protests and rallies appeared to have been adopted by more and more groups and people to press a wider variety of claims. Besides more long-standing and traditional issues such as labor rights and democratization, new issues such as heritage protection were also put forward by social groups through collective actions (Box 11.3).

At the same time, common people seemed to have become more receptive to protest actions. In several representative surveys throughout the 2010s, more and more respondents said that there is a real chance they would join a protest in the future to express their views (Lee and Chan 2018).

Certainly, protests do not always lead to success or concrete outcomes. Part of the reason is that collective actions remain subjected to interpretations and representations by the media, and various groups and actors can contest the

282   Mass Media and Public Opinion

meanings of a specific protest. Social movement theorist Charles Tilly (2004) defined social movements as involving the display of worthiness, unity, number, and commitment through collective actions, but in practice each one of these four aspects of a movement can be subject to debate. The media may portray the protesters as lacking unity; people who disagree with the protesters' goal can question the worthiness of the cause; the police, the protest organization, and other groups can give different estimations of the number of participants involved in a collective action. For example, during the Umbrella Movement, while protesters called for genuine popular elections and justified their occupation of urban streets through the concept of civil disobedience, the state responded by framing the protest actions as breaching the rule of law, being backed by foreign forces, and causing public nuisance (Lee and Chan 2018). During the Anti-ELAB Movement in 2019, supporters of the movement interpreted the violent tactics as "understandable," if not necessarily justifiable, given the lack of responses to the protest demand despite huge rally turnout. The pro-government forces, in contrast, labeled the protesters as "black violence" and saw "the ending of violence and chaos" as what the city needed the most.

It should also be noted that social mobilization and collective actions are not restricted to people and groups who want to criticize the government or other power holders. In fact, the increasing prominence of social mobilization in the public opinion process in Hong Kong is even better illustrated by the fact that civil organizations and political parties would also mobilize *for* government causes. In fact, since the late 2000s, 1 July had been marked not only by the largely pro-democracy and anti-government protest organized by the Civil Human Rights Front in the afternoon, but also by the pro-government, celebratory rally organized by pro-government political parties in the morning. During the Umbrella Movement, citizens against the movement were also mobilized, sometimes resulting in confrontations between protesters and counterprotesters on the fringes of the occupied areas. In the Anti-ELAB Movement in 2019, several pro-government rallies were also organized in the early months of the movement. The countermobilization against the pro-democracy movement was part of the Chinese government's united-front efforts in Hong Kong (Cheng, 2020). In any case, the rise of both mobilization and countermobilization reflected and reinforced the polarization of public opinion in Hong Kong during the 2010s (Lee 2016).

The above analysis of collective action as an expression of public opinion should be reassessed in view of the impact of the NSL. Since the law's passage, the Hong Kong government has denied the applications for peaceful demonstrations or assemblies, sometimes in the name of keeping social distancing measures during the COVID-19 pandemic. Violators were hunted down and arrested. The police readily deter people from participation by readily declaring on-site a demonstration to be one suspected of violating the NSL. The complication of organizing a collective action in the post-NSL era is illustrated by the case of the Hong Kong Women Workers' Association (HKWWA), which had secured police approval to stage a march for more rights on International Women's Day in 2023—the first of its type since the ebbing of large-scale protests three years earlier. The announcement of the pending demonstration was met with numerous online posts calling for huge turnouts with a tone that violent protesters used during the Anti-ELAB Movement. People became even more perplexed to find that some posts originated from figures within the pro-establishment camp. HKWWA reluctantly called off the demonstration as uncertainty grew. Meanwhile, the League of Social Democrats, a pro-democracy group, disclosed that some of its members had been warned of arrest by the National Security Branch if they were to attend the rally as originally planned. This case indicates that the government is in general suspicious of collective actions that express political criticisms. It will not hesitate to take measures to demobilize. The NSL has undoubtedly raised the mobilization cost of all oppositional demonstrations. Mobilizers are expected to require greater determination and effort to overcome people's growing inertia for collective action, especially at a time when a strong sense of powerlessness reigns among the public.

The demobilization of protests is linked to the government's effort to disband what it views as dissenting and subversive organizations (Chan, Tang, and Lee 2022). One of the most notable illustrations is the folding of the Hong Kong Professional Teachers' Union, a popular institution known for its adherence to professionalism and social activism. At the same time, the government has pulled strings to tighten its general control over many civic organizations. In contrast, the mirror civic organizations supportive of the government are empowered. As the civil society loses its vibrancy in terms of quantity, independence, and proactiveness, the public can only speak with a weaker voice.

Conclusion

We would like to conclude by highlighting the characteristics of the model of public opinion in Hong Kong. First, public opinion is discursive in nature. This means that the media plays the role of a critical forum for participants engaging in discursive struggles. This role is enhanced as Hong Kong has been plagued by the absence of democracy, the frequent occurrence of social crises, and the deterioration of governance since the handover. Civic organizations and opinion leaders have to depend on the media to voice their opinions. The media, as a whole, provides a space for the mediation of social discourses. Measures that prevent the media from performing this function will deny Hong Kong a safety valve and may result in social tensions.

Second, by the dynamic nature of discursive struggles, public opinion in Hong Kong is best viewed as a social process. As various agents seek to shape public opinion in ways that best fit their interests and visions, it may shift in directions and intensity over time. Very seldom does it assume a static state. Given the internal pluralism of Hong Kong and the constitutional protection of press freedom under the scheme of "one country, two systems," it is fair to say that the expression and mediation of public opinion took place in a relatively free and independent manner in the first two decades after the handover. However, journalists in Hong Kong have often been criticized for their tendency to self-censor to appease the political and economic power centers. Media professionalism, as an occupational ideology, provides a symbolic resource for journalists to draw on in fending off pressure toward self-censorship.

Third, both polls and collective actions are important forms of public expression in Hong Kong. As an indispensable part of Hong Kong's political culture, polling is treated as a tool for social struggle, the source of social information and legitimation. Collective actions also stand out in Hong Kong's repertoire for the expression of public opinion. In this sense, public opinion does not merely comprise discursive activities; the organization and the alliances of social forces as manifested in collective actions also form a prominent and integral part of the public opinion system in Hong Kong. Having said this, we should add that both polls and collective actions that are critical of the establishment are susceptible to government pressure to self-censor. As such polls and collective actions dwindle, the expression of public opinion can only suffer.

Fourth, the expression of public opinion in Hong Kong is institutionalized through a semi-democratic system and an elaborate consultative network. During the colonial days, the consultative network was known to have succeeded in absorbing politics administratively. However, how effective such a system is in coping with growing social pluralism and rising aspirations for democracy has become a legitimate question. By the Basic Law, Hong Kong is to go through a democratization process that, if fully implemented, will mean that representational politics and party politics will assume a more significant role in the years to come. However, this trajectory is called into severe doubt as China seeks to revamp Hong Kong's administrative and electoral system to ensure what it sees as its national security is well protected.

Fifth, public opinion has become a key factor of governance in Hong Kong. Public response is increasingly recognized as a significant determinant of successful policymaking at the stage of policy formulation, consultation, and implementation. The rich resources and the unmatched authority that the government has at its disposal have given it an edge in setting the agenda and defining social reality for the media and the public. It often resorts to the use of public relations strategies with the help of experienced journalists and publicity experts. This edge, however, does not guarantee that public opinion is always on the side of the government. It is subject to social contestation of various sorts. After all, it is the interplay among media, social formations, and public opinion that matters most in the discursive politics of Hong Kong. But given the centralization of political power in various domains in post-NSL Hong Kong, the space for such discursive politics to play out has significantly reduced.

Sixth, the legislation of the NSL is a watershed event in post-handover Hong Kong. It has reconfigured the politics of public opinion in Hong Kong in favor of the establishment, with the repercussions continuing to be felt at the time of this writing. Essentially, it serves to curtail the relative autonomy of Hong Kong as promised in the Basic Law, giving the CPG the right to have a more direct control over the city in its governance. It follows that freedom of assembly, of speech, and of the press have become more restrained, resulting in a chilling effect marked by self-censorship in all social sectors.

Despite these trends toward tighter control, Hong Kong remains a relatively pluralistic and international city. The media and civic organizations are diverse enough not to speak in one voice. The politics of public opinion is in a state of flux, with the old often mixing with the new in social contestations. Only history will tell how the people of Hong Kong will respond to what appears to be a protracted transition and how the politics of public opinion will settle to assume a more permanent shape.

Box 11.1: Media professionalism

Journalists are "professionals" in a specific sense, and they are different from other professionals such as lawyers and doctors. First of all, a person must spend years systematically studying a body of professional knowledge (in law schools or medical schools) to become a lawyer or doctor. In contrast, a person majoring in any subject in a university can become a journalist. Anyone can become a journalist so long as a newsroom hires him or her. In addition, journalists are not required to have licenses. In Hong Kong, journalists also do not have the salaries and social status enjoyed by other professionals. In fact, some theorists have questioned whether journalists can be regarded as professionals at all. But what journalists do have, just as all kinds of professionals have, is a set of professional ethics and professional norms. Objectivity, accuracy, timeliness, and fairness are some of the more important codes of journalistic professionalism, which serve to guide and legitimize the behavior of journalists.

Box 11.2: Public broadcasting

Public broadcasting refers to a broadcasting model developed and adopted mainly in Western Europe, especially Britain, in the early twentieth century. Under this model, a broadcaster is established as a publicly funded entity. That is, it does not generate profits from the market but obtains funding from the government through taxes and/or license fees. The broadcaster, however, is not regarded as an arm of the government. Editorial autonomy is maintained. It aims to be a public service by providing serious and comprehensive programmes of public affairs, quality cultural programming and entertainment, educational programmes for young people and for citizens at large, and a diverse range of programmes for minority groups. Such programs are often less entertaining and thus less profitable in the market. The commercial media tend not to feature them in their regular programming. In Hong Kong, RTHK used to play the role of a public broadcaster for some decades (Lee 2014; Leung 2007). After repeated rows over the status of RTHK, the Hong Kong government decided in 2010 to keep it as a government department and promised it the editorial autonomy deemed necessary for its public broadcasting role. But the government has stepped up its pressure on RTHK not to overstep political and ideological boundaries since the passing of the NSL in 2020. There are concerns regarding the editorial autonomy of RTHK, and whether it will remain a public broadcaster or become an official mouthpiece.

Box 11.3: Internet and citizen self-mobilization

While the increasing prominence of protests in Hong Kong has many causes, one important development related to media and communication is the advance of new media technologies, especially the internet. The internet provides a platform for civic associations and groups to communicate with their supporters and the public at large without the need for passing through the mainstream media, which may not always be friendly and accommodating. Civic associations can also contact each other and coalesce into movement networks via new media technologies, making the organization and coordination of collective actions easier. In addition, the internet provides a means for people to share political information and messages with each other. The advancement of web 2.0 and the growth of social media have led to the proliferation of online media contents that are critical (and often in a satirical way) of the government. Last but not least, common people can call their fellow citizens or "netizens" to action by posting mobilizing messages on discussion forums, Facebook groups, and so on. In other words, the

> internet allows citizens to "self-mobilize." Citizen self-mobilization is particularly important in Hong Kong because many civic groups and social associations are not particularly resourceful and do not have large memberships.

Questions

1. In recent years, many Hong Kong people have criticized television broadcasters for exercising self-censorship when covering political news. Some people called TVB "CCTVB," suggesting that it is behaving like Chinese Central Television (CCTV). After the introduction of the NSL, there were major personnel changes in the news departments of TV broadcasters NOW TV and I-Cable, raising concerns about the further shrinking of professional journalism. What are your observations? In what ways are the broadcasters doing or not doing their job?
2. The media are at the service of the powerful in the last instance. Do you think this is true in Hong Kong?
3. In the more ideal situation, public contestation in the media should proceed based on mutual respect and be based on facts, reasoning, common sense, and good arguments. But some have observed that the arguments that "win" in the public arena often turn out to be those backed by power instead of those backed by facts and reason. What is your judgment of the public arena in contemporary Hong Kong in this regard? That is, to what extent are public debates governed by facts, reason, and common sense, or are they governed by the logic of power?
4. Do you think taking to the streets is a good strategy for people and groups to voice their demands? If you have joined public rallies or protest actions in the past, what do you think about the ways the mass media covered the activities that you joined? Do you think the media reported them fairly and accurately?
5. Besides mass media, common citizens nowadays often express their views on public matters via the internet—discussion forums, Facebook, a wide range of other social media sites, etc. What are the strengths and weaknesses of the internet as a channel for the communication and expression of public opinion?

Bibliography

Althaus, S 2003, *Collective Preferences in Democratic Politics*, Cambridge University Press, New York.

Au, A 2018, *Freedom under Twenty Shades of Gray*, in Chinese, the Chinese University Press of Hong Kong, Hong Kong.

Bennett, WL, Grissett, L & Haltom, W 1985, "Repairing the News: A Case Study of the News Paradigm," *Journal of Communication*, vol. 35, pp. 50–68.

Chan, JM & Lee, CC 1991, *Mass Media and Political Transition: The Hong Kong Press in China's Orbit*, Guilford Press, New York.

Chan, JM & So, CYK 2003, "The Surrogate Democracy Function of the Media: Citizens' and Journalists' Evaluations of Media Performance," in SK Lau, MK Lee, PS Wan & SL Wong (eds), *Indicators of Social Development: Hong Kong 2001*, Hong Kong Institute of Asia-Pacific Studies, the Chinese University of Hong Kong, Hong Kong.

Chan, CK, Tang, G, & Lee, LF 2022, *Hong Kong Media: Interaction Between Media, State and Civil Society*, Palgrave Macmillan, Singapore.

Cheng, EW 2020, "United Front Work and Mechanisms of Countermobilization in Hong Kong," *China Journal*, vol. 83, pp. 1–33.

Chiu, SWK & Lui, TL 2000, *The Dynamics of Social Movement in Hong Kong*, Hong Kong University Press, Hong Kong.

Cottle, S (ed) 2003, *News, Public Relations, and Power*, Sage, London.

Davis, A 2002, *Public Relations Democracy*, Manchester University Press, Manchester.

Ginsberg, B 1986, *The Captive Public*, Basic Books, New York.

Hall, S, Crutcher, C, Jefferson, T, Clarke J & Roberts, B 1978, *Policing the Crisis*, Palgrave Macmillan, London.

Kobayashi, T & Chan, P 2022, "Political Sensitivity Bias in Autocratizing Hong Kong," *International Journal of Public Opinion Research*, vol. 34 no. 4, edac028.

Lee, CC 1998, "Press Self-Censorship and Political Transition in Hong Kong," *Harvard International Journal of Press/Politics*, vol. 3, no. 2, pp. 55–73.

Lee, FLF 2006, "Poll Reporting and Journalistic Paradigm: A Study of Popularity Poll Coverage in Newspaper," *Asian Journal of Communication*, vol. 16, no. 2, pp. 132–151.

Lee, FLF 2014, *Talk Radio, the Mainstream Press, and Public Opinion in Hong Kong*, Hong Kong University Press, Hong Kong.

Lee, FLF 2016, "Impact of Social Media on Opinion Polarization in Varying Times," *Communication and the Public*, vol. 1, no. 1, pp. 56–71.

Lee, FLF 2018. "Changing political economy of the Hong Kong media," *China Perspectives*, no. 3, pp. 9–18.

Lee, FLF & Chan, CK 2022, "Legalization of Press Control under Democratic Backsliding," *Media, Culture & Society*, advanced online publication, doi: 10.1177/01634437221140525

Lee, FLF & Chan, JM 2009, "The Organizational Production of Self-Censorship in the Hong Kong Media," *International Journal of Press/Politics*, vol. 14, pp. 112–133.

Lee, FLF & Chan, JM 2011, *Media, Social Mobilisation and Mass Protests in Post-colonial Hong Kong*, Routledge, London.

Lee, FLF & Chan, JM 2018. *Media and Protest Logics in the Digital Era*, Oxford University Press, New York.

Leung, LKG 2007, "Public Service Broadcasting at Its Crossroads: A Political Model of Radio Hong Kong's Evolution," in Chinese, *The Chinese Journal of Communication and Society*, vol. 3, pp. 90–112.

Lo, SH 2001, *Governing Hong Kong: Legitimacy, Communication and Political Decay*, Nova Science Publisher, New York.

Price, V 1992, *Public Opinion*, Sage, California.

Tilly, C 2004, *Social Movements, 1768–2004*, Paradigm, London.

Useful Websites

Hong Kong Journalists Association
http://www.hkja.org.hk

Hong Kong Press Council
http://www.presscouncil.org.hk

Hong Kong Public Opinion Research Institute
http://pori.hk

Information Services Department of the HKSAR Government
http://www.isd.gov.hk/eng

Radio Television Hong Kong
http://www.rthk.hk

Further Reading

Au, A 2018, *Freedom under Twenty Shades of Gray*, in Chinese, the Chinese University Press of Hong Kong, Hong Kong. This book provides a detailed analysis of how censorship is produced by the reconfiguration of rules, routines, and practices in the news media. The author presents a range of mechanisms and practices that aim at taming professional journalists. Responses to the book after it was published suggest that the story told in the book could also shed light on how political control was exercised in various types of professional sectors and organizations in Hong Kong.

Chan, CK, Tang, G & Lee, FLF 2022, *Hong Kong Media: Interaction Between Media, State and Civil Society*, Palgrave Macmillan, Singapore. This book provides an overview of the development of the Hong Kong news media, mainly in the first two decades after the handover. It outlines how the Hong Kong media developed under the paradigm of integration under liberal exceptionalism and how the interactions of political, economic, and social forces shape the performance and power of the news.

Lee, FLF & Chan, CK 2022, "Legalization of Press Control under Democratic Backsliding," *Media, Culture & Society*, advanced online publication, doi: 10.1177/01634437221140525. This article is among the first academic publications addressing the media scene in Hong Kong after the establishment of the NSL. The article conceptualizes the notion of legalization of press control to make sense of how legal instrumentals were developed and employed for taming the news media, as well as the consequences on the practice of media self-censorship.

Lee, FLF & Chan, JM 2018, *Media and Protest Logics in the Digital Era*, Oxford University Press, New York. This book provides a book-length analysis of the role of media and communication in the processes of social mobilization during the Umbrella

Movement in 2014, but it also situates the Umbrella Movement against the historical background of the evolving relationship between media and social mobilization in Hong Kong since the 2000s.

So, CYK (ed) 2017, Special Issue on "Hong Kong Media and Politics Revisited: Twenty Years after the Handover," *Chinese Journal of Communication*, vol. 10, no. 4.

Part III: Policy Environment

12
Economic Policy

Wilson Wong and Raymond Yuen

Introduction: Toward Visible Hand and Budgetary Punctuation

Economic policy can be understood broadly as how government manages the overall economy through defining the role, size, and scope of the public sector and structuring its fiscal system; or narrowly as industrial policy, incentives, and strategies targeting specific industries and sectors in the hope of achieving structural change and substantiated growth of the overall economy. Regardless of the definitions, Hong Kong used to be seen as a city of small government and a big market. Milton Friedman (1982), a famous Nobel Prize laureate in Economics, described Hong Kong as the world's greatest experiment in laissez-faire capitalism. At first glance, the economic policy of Hong Kong can be characterized as almost "government-free," with Hong Kong well qualified to be the "capital of capitalism," a symbol of the triumph of the market.

However, it is a mistake to ignore the role of government and to overestimate the influence of the invisible hand of the market while underestimating the impact of politics on economic policy, for two reasons. First, the government in Hong Kong has always played a very important role in steering Hong Kong's economy, which becomes increasingly visible in the post-1997 due to a series of economic and financial crises (Fong 2022). As argued by Joseph Stiglitz, another Nobel Prize laureate in Economics, there is essentially no such thing as a pure market economy, as government is always a major actor in all modern economies (Stiglitz 2000: 4–5). In his view, a more appropriate term for describing advanced economies should be a "mixed economy." It is government, or more broadly speaking political forces and its institutional contexts, that determine resource allocation in society—deciding what, how much, and whose resources should go into the public sector and the market, respectively (Coyle 2020).

Second, owing to the new and major developments in Hong Kong's politics and governance—as highlighted by other chapters in this volume and including the advent of the post-2020 paradigm—there have been corresponding changes to expedite the shift from the approach of a relatively invisible hand in economic policy toward a more state-led approach of an increasingly visible hand. Major adjustments had been seen under Chief Executive (CE) Carrie Lam, when old doctrines of economic policy such as positive nonintervention and fiscal prudence with a balanced budget were given less adherence. This trend continued under the new administration of CE John Lee. The Chinese Central Government is playing a more proactive role in influencing the governance and policies of Hong Kong, making the economic policy more similar to that of the Mainland, which prefers a bigger and economically more active government. The stronger role of government and its emphasis on planning has been translated into an economic policy of the visible hand of government, with budgetary punctuations, higher public expenditure, and a deficit budget as the watershed.

Because of these changes, Hong Kong is losing its long-standing reputation as an exemplary city of economic freedom. Heritage Foundation, a US think tank in Washington, DC, that ranked Hong Kong as the freest economy in the world for 25 years in a row since it established its index of economic freedom, ranked Hong Kong at No. 2, behind Singapore, in its 2020 ranking. Even more dramatically, in 2021, it decided to drop Hong Kong in its ranking, contending that Hong Kong is almost indistinguishable from other Chinese commercial centers (Heritage Foundation 2021).

As an economic policy chapter in a book on the government and politics of Hong Kong, this chapter distinguishes itself from chapters in economics textbooks in terms of its approach to analysis. While it will still go through the basic concepts and institutions of economic policy, its primary aim is to adopt a political perspective to describe and discuss how politics and power have shaped the economic policy of Hong Kong, with the post-1997 era including the post-2020 period as its focus. It is divided into two major sections. The first section approaches economic policy from a macro perspective to examine the public finance system of Hong Kong, including its monetary policy and fiscal policy and its revenue and expenditure systems. Attention will be drawn to how its public finance system is structured by the power dynamics in Hong Kong. The second section approaches economic policy from a micro perspective to examine government policies targeting specific industries and the political difficulties the government faced in restructuring the economy. In both sections, emphasis will be placed on the interaction between politics and economics.

Public Finance in Hong Kong

Monetary policy and fiscal policy

According to Richard Musgrave (1989), a Harvard scholar and a founding father of the field of public finance, there are three major economic functions of the public sector: stabilization, allocation, and redistribution. Stabilization refers to the management of the economy to ensure its stable and continuous growth. Allocation refers to the provision of goods and services that are usually not available in the market due to its inherent and structural limitations—market failures. In re-distribution, government plays the role of "Robin Hood," transferring resources from the rich to the poor to achieve a more equitable distribution of wealth in society.

The stabilization function is usually accomplished through two major policy tools: fiscal policy and monetary policy. Fiscal policy follows the traditional Keynesian approach of using taxes and public expenditure to adjust the pace of economic growth (Mikesell 2011: 115). In general, it suggests that during economic downturns, government should have a budget deficit (spend more but tax less) to stimulate the economy. During economic growth, it should have a budget surplus (spend less but tax more) to prevent the economy from overheating. In recent decades, faith in fiscal policy has been shaken. It is more about the inability of government to implement the policy rather than the correctness of the theory itself. Public choice economists have cast doubts on whether government is truly capable of intervening through fiscal policy correctly and with perfect timing to stimulate the economy (Mikesell 2011: 117). They have argued that due to the political, clumsy, and time-consuming nature of decision-making in government, the government often fails to intervene at the right time. Instead, politicians and bureaucrats, using fiscal policy as an excuse, would abuse the use of a budget deficit to benefit themselves by expanding the size of government.

Monetary policy influences the growth of the economy through money supply. According to the monetary approach, the interest rate should be increased accordingly as the economy blooms and shows signs of overheating, such as high inflation. Higher interest rates increase the cost of borrowing. Accordingly, individuals and businesses will have a lower incentive to borrow money to start up new economic activities, and the economy will cool down gradually, accomplishing a "soft landing." On the other hand, the interest rate should be lowered during an economic downturn to encourage more economic activities to stimulate growth.

Instead of following the logic of fiscal policy in both the colonial era and most of the period of the handover, a balanced budget has been seen as the norm of public budgeting in Hong Kong. The importance of a balanced budget is taken so seriously that it was actually written into Article 107 of the Basic Law. Hong Kong's fiscal conservatism is further reflected by the large fiscal reserve. About five years ago, in Budget 2017–2018, the reserve was estimated as $1,091.9 billion on 31 March 2017—equivalent to about 41 percent of GDP and sufficient to cover public expenditures for more than 25 months. In addition, according to the Hong Kong Monetary Authority (HKMA), Hong Kong has a huge foreign reserve of US$491.6 billion as of the end of June 2021, which represents over six times the currency in circulation or about 47 percent of Hong Kong Money Supply M3—the total amount of money both in circulation and in all private sector bank deposits.

One may argue the absence of fiscal policy represents a key principle of prudent fiscal management: that one should live within his/her means. It can also be justified by the principle of "positive non-intervention," in which government should take a more passive role in the economy and would intervene only when necessary (Chiu 2004). Nevertheless, the prudent budgeting argument usually does not fit well when the unit of analysis is government (Rubin 2000; Li 2006). In general, government faces a much lower limited budget constraint, as it possesses unlimited power to tax and must fulfill a much broader set of objectives in society. During the Financial Crisis of 1998, there was a heavy government intervention in the stock market: billions of dollars in taxpayers' money was used to buy the stocks of major blue-chip companies to "stabilize" the stock market (Wong 2009). Similarly, generous relief measures have been provided by the government since 2008 during the fiscal years of surplus (Fong 2015). All these suggest that the old colonial policy of positive nonintervention does not always have a binding effect on the new Hong Kong Special Administrative Region (HKSAR) government.

An alternative interpretation is that the HKSAR government is willing to intervene or cease to intervene in the economy whenever the core interest of the politically powerful is at stake. A good example is the ceasing in 2003 of the Home Ownership Scheme (HOS), one of the major public housing programs that targeted at the marginal income group sandwiched by the upper-middle and lower classes. Despite the skyrocketing housing prices in those years and strong demands from the public for reintroducing HOS, it was not relaunched until 2011. This attempt to increase the demand for private housing by limiting the scale of public and government-subsidized housing has the effect of protecting the interests of big property developers. Political leaders often choose the economic ideology that can best legitimate their preferred order, rather than allowing the ideology to dictate their policy choices. No matter what the ideology is, it is inevitable that any expansion of the current scope of the public sector will require additional sources of revenue and more redistribution. Otherwise, the only way to finance the additional expenditure will be a deficit budget, the spending down of the fiscal reserve, and eventually relying on debt financing.

To a large extent, the HKSAR government has given up its monetary policy, too. With the pegging of its dollars to the US dollar, the HKSAR government is deprived of much of its ability to regulate its economy through monetary policy, as it has lost control of the interest rate (Li 2006: 232). Under the pegging, Hong Kong's interest rate is generally driven by the interest rate in the US, set by the US Federal Reserve Bank, rather than the HKMA. If there is a major difference between the interest rates in Hong Kong and the US, capital will flow to the one that offers the higher interest rate (Latter 2007). Given the export-driven and open nature of its economy, without both monetary policy and fiscal policy, Hong Kong's economy and its public finances are very vulnerable to external shocks in the world economy, which are very much beyond the control of the government.

It has been questioned frequently whether it still makes sense to peg the Hong Kong dollar to the US dollar. The pegging was made in 1983, 40 years ago, during one of the most volatile and uncertain periods in the history of Hong Kong, when the political future of Hong Kong was still undecided. More amazingly, the rate of pegging set at that time (one US dollar for 7.8 HK dollars) is still used today. With the long-term trend of the weakening of the US dollar due to the quantitative easing (QE) policy of the US government since the 2008 financial crisis (which is expected to be continued under the COVID-19 pandemic to stimulate the global economy), keeping the pegging at the existing rate could translate into a high possibility of major inflation in Hong Kong. However, due to the importance of economic stability to the political order in Hong Kong, there is little sign that the pegging will be undone or adjusted in the near future to enable Hong Kong to manage its monetary policy though the weakening of the economy in Hong Kong and China, and the rising tension between the US and China has cast some uncertainty over this.

Size and role of the public sector

There are always conflicts and trade-offs between the two remaining functions of the public sector: allocation and redistribution. Under allocation, government is performing no more than the role of a firm, except that it is providing goods and services that cannot be normally provided by the market. In the theory of public finance, these special types of goods and services that can only be provided by the government have the characteristics of public goods (Box 12.1) or externalities (Box 12.2). Public goods are non-rival in consumption and nonexclusive in nature, meaning that they can be jointly consumed by many people, but the provider cannot exclude the non-payer from enjoying the good. Public goods should be adequately provided by the government, as it has the authority to use coercive taxation to require all people to pay for them to prevent "free-riding"—enjoying the goods without paying. Defense, law, and order are some classic examples of public goods (Rosen 2005: 55–58).

Externalities refer to the impact on a party outside the market exchange and can be negative or positive. Taking social benefits into consideration, government should use its resources to increase the supply of goods and services that have positive externalities, of which basic education is a frequently quoted example. Meanwhile, action is needed from the government to discourage activities with negative externalities, such as pollution, because firms are not taking the full cost—the social cost—into consideration in their production (Rosen 2005: 82–84).

There are two limitations to the theory of allocative function of government. First, it is normative in nature in the sense that it only states what "should be" provided by government but is not descriptive in nature to explain what is actually provided by government. As economic policy is driven by more than economic theory, many goods and services provided by the HKSAR government actually have little relation with public goods or externalities. For example, the government provides and operates sports and leisure facilities, such as sports gyms, tennis courts, and swimming pools, which are not public goods and are widely available in the market. Second, the allocative function mainly concerns itself with complementing the market in the provision of goods and services but pays less attention to the fairness and equity problems created by market allocation.

With its emphasis on voluntary exchange and strong protection of private property rights to minimize excess burden (Box 12.3), the market itself is incapable of rectifying the unequal distribution of wealth in society. Making society more equitable through redistribution is the third function of government. Nevertheless, redistribution is often in conflict with allocation, as redistribution requires government to take an intervening approach to reallocate property rights, which will violate the principles of voluntary exchange and protection of property rights emphasized in allocation. Such conflict is known as the "equity-efficiency trade-off" (Box 12.3) in the theory of public finance.

To better visualize the size and scope of government in terms of the economic functions in HKSAR, one may look at Table 12.1, which shows public expenditure as a percentage of GDP in Hong Kong and other major advanced economies. Although Hong Kong still has a relatively small public sector from an international perspective, with public expenditure accounting for below 30 percent of its GDP, the table reveals a significant growth of its public sector in recent years when compared with the earlier period, which has successfully kept the figure around 20 percent. In the research of budgeting, this growth can be explained by the punctuated equilibrium theory (Baumgartner and Jones, 1993)

(Box 12.4), which states that sudden and major budgetary changes can be caused by shifts in governance paradigms and structures. As the functions of defense and foreign affairs in Hong Kong are the responsibilities of the Central People's Government (CPG), the increase in public expenditure shows that government has enlarged its role in society by taking up more domestic functions and responsibilities.

Table 12.1: Size of government: Public expenditure as percentage of GDP in Hong Kong and other major industrial countries

Countries	2000	2004	2008	2020
Hong Kong	21.1%	22.2%	19.8%	27%
Canada	41.1%	39.4%	39.6%	40.7%
Japan	38.3%	37.3%	36.4%	37.1%
New Zealand	35.1%	34.1%	42.6%	36.7%
Norway	42.7%	46.6%	40.5%	48%
Sweden	57.3%	57.1%	51.2%	48.4%
United States	34.2%	36%	38.6%	35.1%
United Kingdom	37.5%	44.1%	45.4%	38.3%

Source: International Monetary Fund; Hong Kong Government Budget and Yearbooks.

Some caution, however, should be exercised in interpreting the figures. First, although Hong Kong has a small public sector in a relative sense, it still means that each year almost 30 percent of new resources produced in society are under the command of government. Besides, the figure is an underestimation of the full influence of government on the economy. It does not count resources owned by organizations that are highly influenced by the government. Take the Mass Transit Railway (MTR) as an example. It was turned into a publicly listed company in 2000, but the government remains its largest stockholder.

In addition to direct monetary expenditure, government also influences the flow and use of resources in society through regulation and direct transfer of resources. For example, the Mandatory Provident Fund (MPF) Ordinance requires that all employers and employees each put aside 5 percent of the payroll as a contribution to the Fund. The government may also give out resources directly, including land, which is all possessed by the government in Hong Kong, and only the right of use with a leasing period is for sale. For example, in the controversial Cyberport project, an expensive piece of premium land at the south end of Hong Kong Island is given out directly to PCCW, a firm owned by Richard Li, son of the influential business tycoon Li Ka-shing, for its development. The practice of direct transfer of resources also enjoys the advantage of bypassing the oversight of the Legislative Council (LegCo), as no public money is directly involved. Importantly, as argued in the discussion of the fiscal system in Hong Kong below, the size of the public sector is itself a product of careful political consideration, which has struck a delicate balance between protecting the interests and wealth of the powerful and maintaining the basic stability of Hong Kong.

All these point to the fact that the government is playing a much more significant and active role than the official figure has suggested. The image of the market economy is often a myth constructed purposely by governments to create a less visible role in market intervention, making it easier to manage public expectations and demands. As shown in Table 12.1, many governments of democracy and capitalism are playing a major role in the economy, with public expenditure accounting for about 40 percent of their GDP. Despite having a mixed economy, creating an obscure role of government can have the political advantage of making it less accountable for the negative consequences caused by its mismanagement of the economy.

The fiscal system: Tax and public expenditure

The revenue and public expenditure systems in Hong Kong provide a good example of how inequalities in the political system are translated into fiscal inequity and echoed with the major theme in this chapter: that resource allocation is often a reflection of structural power dynamics in society.

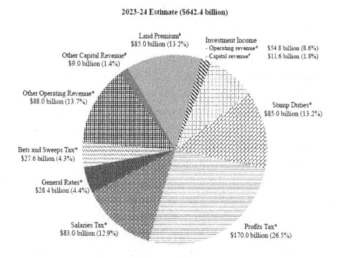

Chart 12.1: Major sources of revenue (2023–2024)
Source: Budget Speech 2023–2024, Hong Kong SAR Government.

Chart 12.1 shows the major revenue sources of Hong Kong. The total government revenue is HK$642.4 billion in 2023–2024. The two most important revenue sources in Hong Kong are profits tax and items directly related to investment and level of economic activities, which include investment income, stamp duties, and land premium. Altogether, they produce 63.3 percent of the total revenue. The current revenue structure has three major problems: lack of transparency, inequity, and instability (Wong 2009). Some of the major sources of revenue in Hong Kong, having the nature of tax, are often disguised as nontax revenues, creating the illusion for those who are shouldering the burden of financing public services that they are not being taxed. Land premium can be considered a land tax in disguise. Tax is defined as a compulsory payment from citizens to government, backed by government's coercive power, which is not for the direct exchange of goods and services. Using its authority, the government owns all land in Hong Kong and monopolizes the land supply. The government can make so much revenue from land sales because it deliberately controls its supply to set up a "high land price" policy. In buying the land, the property developers are paying a price that is much more than the true value of the land, as set by competitive market forces.

The tax incidence (Box 12.5) of many taxes in Hong Kong is heavily concentrated on the middle class, making them pay a higher percentage of their income for taxes, while the rich, who are more influential in the policymaking process including how the tax system is designed, are taxed at a much lower rate (Wong 2009). Tax incidence, the question of who has actually paid the tax, cannot be dictated by law and can be shifted to different parties (Rosen 2005: 274–278). Using the land tax above as an example, most of its tax incidence is believed to be shifted from property developers to the middle class. The middle class is not qualified for public housing programs because they are means-tested. Property developers, as owners of capital, have other options for investment of their capital. But the buyers of private housing, many of whom are members of the middle class, have nowhere to go to avoid the tax incidence unless they move out of Hong Kong.

The structures of salaries and profit taxes are also unfavorable to the middle class. Income and profit are defined very narrowly in the current tax system. For example, profit from the sale of capital assets including stocks is not considered "profit" or "income" under the present tax code. Similarly, there is also no capital gains tax. There is also no global taxation in Hong Kong, meaning that profit or income generated outside Hong Kong is not taxed, which has given the rich opportunities to legally avoid or reduce their taxes by manipulating the loopholes in the system. With the provision of a generous tax allowance by the government, most of the low-income class do not have to pay any salaries tax.

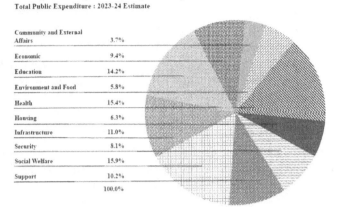

Chart 12.2: Public expenditure by function (2023–2024)
Source: Budget Speech 2023–2024, Hong Kong SAR Government.

Regarding instability, the revenue system is built for the era of economic boom, with a significant part of its revenue coming from sources extremely sensitive to economic fluctuations, such as land premium and investment income. This problem is one of the leading reasons the budget crisis of Hong Kong often perfectly coincides with the business cycle. Whenever there is an economic downturn, the unstable and inequitable nature of the tax system is exposed, which intensifies the politics of public budgeting in Hong Kong.

Chart 12.2 shows the breakdown of public expenditure by function. In 2023–2024, the total public expenditure is HK$810.5 billion. Reflecting the devastating impact of the COVID-19 pandemic, social welfare is the largest expenditure item (15.9 percent), followed by health (15.4 percent) and education (14.2 percent).

When the government really has to spend, much of its spending is concentrated on items of high economic return and items related to the promotion of social and economic development (Li 2006: 137). There is heavy government intervention in the sectors of education, health, and housing. Half of the population in Hong Kong lives in public or subsidized housing. Public hospitals had a market share of more than 90 percent in health care, and many major local universities are heavily funded by tax dollars in their core programs. Many of the large public programs, particularly housing and social welfare, are means-tested, targeting the lower-income group. Although many of the public programs are consumed by the lower-income group, it is not true that the public expenditure incidence (Box 12.5) is limited only to that group. In public housing, the construction business and property developers also benefit. Similarly, government-subsidized university education in professional programs can be viewed as a subsidization of training costs that benefit major businesses. The Government Public Transport Fare Concession Scheme, which allows the elderly to pay a fare of only HK$2, would also benefit the transport companies.

Even for those programs that are not means-tested, such as education, it is increasingly common to see the middle class and more well-off people opt for choices of higher quality in the private market. Combining the analysis of the tax system, it can be concluded that the biggest redistribution through the fiscal system in Hong Kong is from the middle class to the lower class. This does not exactly concur with the traditional view of the ability-to-pay principle of vertical equity in taxation that redistribution should be done from the highest income group to the lower income groups (Slemrod and Bakija 2004: 57–64). There are good political reasons for the design of this inequitable system. By protecting the rich from being taxed heavily, the system is protecting the business interests that have huge political clout in local politics. The lower-income group pays little tax but enjoys high services because the government does want to keep them pacified to stabilize society, while the middle class is often perceived as a more peaceful group who can afford to pay without strong protest. But this fiscal arrangement can have the undesirable side effect of encouraging more demand for public services from the lower-income group.

Tackling the problems of rising income inequality and poverty, which are intensified by factors including the digital divide and the COVID-19 pandemic, are going to be of prime concern in the public finance of Hong Kong. Although Hong Kong is economically robust in an aggregate sense, as reflected by the macroeconomic indicators such as GDP growth and unemployment rate before the arrival of COVID-19, many of its citizens are not. According to the Commission on Poverty, in 2020, without government intervention, 1.6 million people lived below the poverty line in Hong Kong, which represents 23.6 percent of the city's population (Government of Hong Kong Special Administration Region 2020). This means that without government welfare and subsidies, almost one in four people in Hong Kong would be living in poverty.

With a Gini Index (a measure of income inequality) of 0.54, Hong Kong has the highest income inequality among all countries or regions classified by the United Nations as having very high human development (UNDP 2020). With the sharp and significant rise of private housing prices in Hong Kong since the financial crisis of 2008, even the middle class, who are not eligible for public housing, have faced some tough times in livelihood issues as they find housing less and less affordable to them. The hard question faced by the HKSAR government is whether those severe problems can be resolved within the existing political parameters underlying its fiscal system. If any reform is necessary and inevitable, how can the interests of different groups in society be balanced without damaging its fiscal health?

Industrial Policy in Hong Kong

Rise of visible hand and interventionism

Government may provide specific incentives for a few chosen industries considered to be of strategic importance. This is often called "industrial policy" in which government plays an aggressive and interventionist role in the economy by picking winners among the industries (Pack and Saggi 2006; Rodrik 2008). Because of the close interaction between government and the economy, a completely noninterventionist approach to managing the economy seems to be unrealistic and impractical. However, before 1997, the British colonial government still tried its best to minimize the level of intervention and named it the doctrine of "positive nonintervention," meaning that the government would step in only when it was absolutely necessary. As a result, during the colonial regime, the absence of a strong industrial policy was seen as a major characteristic of the economic development of Hong Kong (Castells 1992; Tsui-Auch 1998; Wong and Ng 2001; Chiu 2004). The handover of Hong Kong from Britain to China in 1997 became a major political as well as economic watershed for Hong Kong (Cheung 2000). In economic policy, there is a shift toward more active intervention and a revival of the Asian Developmental State (Johnson 1982), the model behind the fast industrialization and economic miracles of major industrial economies such as Japan and South Korea in the last century.

While Hong Kong is gradually departing from its old doctrine with a more intervention-oriented approach—the rise of the visible hand—it is still struggling with the level of intervention and the functions and roles of government on its path of economic restructuring and transformation. During the term of office of CE Tung Chee-hwa, economically, the HKSAR economy was hard hit by the Asian Financial Crisis of 1997–1998. Facing this sudden, massive, and historic economic downturn—and with the ambition to prove his capacity and desire to establish a high-performance legitimacy for his new government, despite the open claim of maintaining the principle of "big market, small government"— the HKSAR government gradually deviated from the "positive nonintervention" approach to become much more interventionist in its industrial policy. Adopting this new approach, many major economic interventions were taken to diversify and restructure the economy, including injecting billions of dollars of taxpayer money into the stock market in 1998, directly picking the "winner" in economic development by granting specific industries and even a particular company exclusive terms and favorable conditions (e.g., the Cyberport project), and becoming a partner and the largest shareholder of Hong Kong Disney.

Due to the strong criticisms of government-business collusion in those high-profile projects involving strong government intervention, when Donald

Tsang succeeded Tung as the CE, he changed the course of industrial policy in Hong Kong to again make it less aggressively interventionist. However, the government still highlighted some traditional pillar industries—such as financial services, tourism, and logistics—in which Hong Kong should maintain its competitiveness, and six new industries—educational services, medical services, testing and certification, the environmental industry, innovation and technology, and cultural and creative industries—to be promoted for the further development and diversification of its economy.

In 2015, Chief Executive C. Y. Leung called for a shift from positive noninterventionism to the principle of "appropriately proactive" in economic policy. He also established the Innovation and Technology Bureau that same year. In the Carrie Lam administration, more policy initiatives were launched to develop the innovation and technology sector under national economic integration with the Greater Bay Area (Box 12.6). Despite the deliberate effort made so far, it does not seem capable of changing the fact that the economic base of Hong Kong is still narrow, and the restructuring project is far from being completed (Wong 2020).

Economic transformation: A political perspective

The economic troubles of HKSAR are not caused solely by political sources. Some of the roots of its economic problems were present well before the handover, including the gigantic bubble in the property market and the hollowing out of the industrial base—all obstacles for economic restructuring. Nevertheless, the HKSAR government cannot deny the charge that it has failed to take effective measures to create an economy for the era of knowledge and high technology.

There are several major political and institutional reasons for the HKSAR government's failure to successfully restructure the economy. First, although there is no clear consensus on whether an interventionist approach is preferred to a nonintervention approach as there are countries that accomplish fast economic growth under both approaches, it is widely recognized that the interventionist approach requires far more state capacity and state autonomy, which includes expertise from the bureaucracy and more precise information about the economy (Castells 1992; Lam 2000; Tsui-Auch 1998; Wong and Ng 2001). Unfortunately, in the case of Hong Kong, many policy-makers, including career bureaucrats, are "generalists" in nature who often lack the necessary professional training and expertise. Besides, bureaucratic-led economic development is often applied only to quicken the pace of industrialization in following the already-known path of development of Western countries (Chu 2016). As Hong Kong progresses toward the new economy, in which there are few proven models of success for emulation, it is getting more doubtful whether the bureaucracy should still serve as the commander in economic development in the new economic era.

Second, the "businessmen ruling Hong Kong" model is another reason for failing to upgrade and transform the economy. Without a real democracy, and with the lack of trust in a civil service trained and socialized under the British colonial government, the CPG adopted the "institutionalization of business in politics" after the handover by entrusting business leaders with the ultimate responsibility of government and co-opting business representatives into the political establishment (Chiu and Lui 2001). Former CE Tung Chee-hwa was recruited from the business community. The membership of the Executive Council, the highest decision-making center, has business well represented, and the LegCo is so arranged as to ensure business interests will dominate in the last resort (Petersen and Roberts 2003). As the number of directly elected seats in the LegCo has been reduced from 35 to 20 and the total number of LegCo seats is increased from 70 to 90, the influence and position of the business sector should remain relatively the same if not be further enhanced in the "improved electoral system" implemented in 2021.

The businessmen-ruling model has hindered the transformation of the economy by increasing and intensifying "rent-seeking" (Box 12.7) activities, using government influence for higher economic profit at the expense of the general public interest, typically by eliminating competition. Moreover, as it is often the big property developers who are politically most powerful, the government has the tendency to use all means to protect their interests, including reducing public housing supply to increase demand for private housing. Many of the new projects for restructuring the economy, such as the Cyberport and the controversial West Kowloon Cultural District project, are also criticized as no more than property development projects packaged with high technology and similar labels for the primary goal of benefiting the property developers.

The bias toward big property developers in economic policymaking and the growth of "crony capitalism" set up an unlevel playing field for competition, making Hong Kong less attractive for business, except for those who are politically connected. The monopolistic position of the major businesses in Hong Kong created by rent-seeking activities has also artificially inflated the prices of major production inputs, including land and energy, making Hong Kong less competitive as a place for investment and making it more difficult for new industries to emerge.

Furthermore, as property developers are themselves products of the property bubble under the old economy, they often have a vested interest in the status quo and are less interested in investing in the new economy. Their dominance in the economic policymaking of the HKSAR government would mean that the government itself is less enthusiastic about economic restructuring and upgrading, including the manufacturing and high-technology sectors. The trend of hollowing out industries continues, with the share of secondary production in GDP

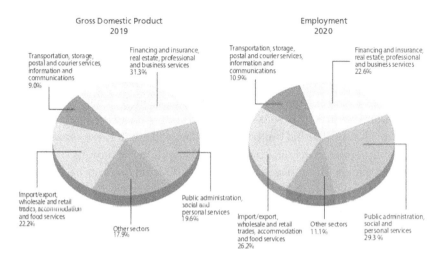

Chart 12.3: Gross Domestic Product (GDP) by sector and employment in Hong Kong
Source: *Hong Kong Yearbook 2020.*

decreasing dramatically: 23 percent in 1983, 11 percent in 1993, 4 percent in 2003, and 1 percent in 2019 (*Hong Kong Yearbook* 2020). As a result, the economy still depends on traditional engines, such as finance, trade, property, and tourism. Instead of starting a new technology base for future economic development, the share of the tertiary service sector in GDP increased dramatically from 67.4 percent in 1983 to 93 percent in 2019 (*Hong Kong Yearbook* 2020). Chart 12.3 shows both GDP and employment by sector in Hong Kong. They both show the overconcentration and overdependence of Hong Kong in the financial and service sectors, with manufacturing as a negligent component not shown individually in the charts. Together with the giving up of monetary policy, these factors make the economy of Hong Kong very vulnerable to external economic shocks and economic bubbles.

Economic bubbles, economic restructuring, and high technology

Although Hong Kong's economy appeared to be strong before the pandemic, this strength was related more to the economic bubble of the asset market and factors other than the successful transformation of its economy. Some of those major factors are the politically driven economic policy of Beijing and the inflow of hot money triggered by the QS policy of the US. The Closer Economic Partnership Arrangement (CEPA), Individual Visit Scheme, and economic integration under the Guangdong-Hong Kong-Macao Greater Bay Area are some examples. To the

CPG, maintaining Hong Kong's economic health can demonstrate the viability of "one country, two systems" and divert the strong demands for a faster pace of democratization (Sung 2005).

Economic integration between Hong Kong and China has deepened their link and interaction. China was Hong Kong's largest trading partner in 2020, accounting for more than half of the total trade value in Hong Kong (*Hong Kong Yearbook* 2020). At the same time, Hong Kong is the fourth largest trading partner of China—after the United States, Japan, and South Korea—accounting for about 6 percent of its total trade value. Hong Kong is the largest external investor in China. The cumulative value of its direct investment has exceeded US$1 trillion—more than half of the total direct investment in China. On the other hand, Hong Kong is also the largest destination for China's outward direct investment, which accounted for 58 percent of its total outward direct investment in 2019.

Depending too much on China economically is not without issues and concerns in the long term. A possible problem arising from the economic integration between the Mainland and Hong Kong is that competition, instead of complement, may lead Hong Kong to a less superior position (Cheung 2002). Using the cities in the Greater Bay Area as examples, Guangdong does not completely expect to rely on Hong Kong's service industry in the near future. It hopes to establish, modernize, and internationalize its own services industry in the next half-decade. Shenzhen is also one of Hong Kong's fiercest competitors in technology and innovation. Integration with China's economy would not replace the need for Hong Kong to complete its economic restructuring to reestablish its competitive edge in the global economy.

While China's active and policy-driven assistance and economic integration have helped Hong Kong recover economically from the previous crises, it also has had negative consequences. Aside from making Hong Kong more politically and economically dependent on China (Yeung 2002), it has masked the real problems of its economic structure and therefore reduced the incentives for policymakers to carry out effective reforms and may even mislead the development of Hong Kong's economy. For example, the HKSAR government puts too much emphasis on developing the tertiary service industries, especially tourism, and lets secondary industries, particularly the manufacturing industry, shrink even more, leading to a more concentrated and mismatched economy. Even Chinese officials in Beijing have frequently warned Hong Kong that its dependence on only a few sectors makes it vulnerable and sensitive to the risk of economic downturn. The large flow of hot money into Hong Kong since the 2008 financial crisis has also highly increased the risk of economic bubbles. The virtual economy driven by those bubbles does not benefit the real economy, which is more relevant to the livelihood of the general public and can be harmful to the real economy in the long run.

The lack of technological deepening and a vibrant sector of high technology make Hong Kong susceptible to economic volatility. Hong Kong's vulnerability to the financial crisis was due to the failure to upgrade local production, and the overwhelming dependence on finance and services (Chiu and Lui 2001). Since the early 1980s, deindustrialization has occurred in Hong Kong (Choy 2004). While the old low-end industries moved, Hong Kong has not, and it still has a long way to go in developing its technology-intensive high-end industries. As shown in Table 12.2, Hong Kong lags behind other newly developed Asian countries (NICs) in the general expenditure on Research and Development (R&D). In 2016, Hong Kong was only spending 0.79 percent of its GDP on R&D, while its competitors were spending a much higher percentage. For Singapore, it is spending 5.7 percent. For South Korea, it is 4.24 percent. The limited amount of resources makes it hard for Hong Kong to compete with other developmental Asian states, even if there is a clear and high-profile industrial policy.

Table 12.2: Research and Development (R&D) expenditure: Hong Kong, Singapore, and South Korea, 2005 to 2016

	Hong Kong		Singapore		South Korea	
	% of GDP	Share by Private Sector	% of GDP	Share by Private Sector	% of GDP	Share by Private Sector
2005	0.79	51.5%	2.4	65.2%	2.63	77.3%
2012	0.73	44.9%	7.2	61.1%	4.03	77.9%
2016	0.79	43.3%	9.5	60.2%	4.24	77.8%

Source: Chu (2020).

What is even more alarming and disappointing is, despite the claim of adopting an industrial policy to make technology and innovation one of its top initiatives in economic development, the proportion of resources spent by Hong Kong on R&D is actually quite stable across the entire period of 2005–2016, indicating a gap between the policy pledge and the fiscal commitment. Compared with Singapore and South Korea, Hong Kong has the lowest share of the private sector—less than 50 percent— in the general expenditure on R&D, which suggests the policies and measures adopted by Hong Kong have not been successful in creating new high-technology enterprises. Without continuous improvement in technology, Hong Kong would not be able to maintain its lead in skills,

310   Economic Policy

and outsourcing would only lead to a further hollowing out of the Hong Kong economy (Sung 2002; Chu 2020). According to the Global Competitiveness Report (World Economic Forum 2020), Hong Kong ranks among the Top 10 in the world on ICT adoption, flexible work arrangements, digital skills, and digital legal framework. It means Hong Kong is quite prepared in terms of digital infrastructure for economic transformation, so long as the government can take the lead with more investment and commitment on par with its competitors.

Conclusion: Economic Policy and Governance

A central theme in this chapter is that economic policy is shaped by more than economic forces. The mirage of a "market economy" constructed by the colonial government and some previous administrations of HKSAR government is revealed as more myth than reality when a critical look is taken in examining the role of government in the economy. Counting the resources it abstracts from society and the regulations it imposes on society, the impact of the HKSAR government on the economy is more important than what is commonly understood. Although the public sector in Hong Kong is still smaller in size than the international standard, this can also be taken as an outcome of governmental influence, instead of as evidence that the absence of government is closely related to the governing ideology of reducing the demand for government services and minimizing the need for redistribution. Importantly, there is a new trend of growing government intervention in the economy—the rise of a more visible hand, with budgetary punctuations in the form of higher expenditure, together with a deficit budget and debt financing. This trend is expected to be heightened in the post-2020 era with the latest political changes. In 2020, the budget deficit was HK$257.6 billion, the highest deficit ever recorded. Despite repeated efforts to stabilize the economy under the pandemic, in 2023, a deficit of HK$139.8 billion is estimated—the third deficit in the last four years—and the fiscal reserve will drop to HK$817.3 billion.

Adopting political logic in understanding economic policy, resource allocation in society can be conveniently understood as a reflection of the structural power dynamics in society. At the macro level of managing the economy, the two typical sets of policy tools are either severely constrained or absent in Hong Kong. To limit the commitment and obligation of government, fiscal policy is not seriously pursued in Hong Kong. The recent growth in public expenditure is more related to the shifting role of government to make a more visible and aggressive push to generate economic growth than to the active adoption of a fiscal policy. Some mega projects proposed include Greater Bay Area, Northern Metropolis Development Strategy, and Lantau Tomorrow Vision, which all involve long-term infrastructure development and huge fiscal commitments.

Regarding monetary policy, with the pegging of the Hong Kong dollar to the US dollar, Hong Kong has given away its capacity to manage the economy through money supply. The political importance of maintaining stability in society and the economy of Hong Kong has made the subject of unpegging an "untouchable" topic.

One of the examples of how governance and economic policy such as fiscal inequalities are correlated is its fiscal system. On the tax side, the tax incidence is highly concentrated on the middle class. The tax system is also very nontransparent in nature, disguising many tax items as non-tax revenue, making it harder to enforce fiscal discipline through public oversight. On the expenditure side, public spending is often concentrated on items promoting economic development, suggesting that big businesses, in addition to less well-off people, may also benefit from the expenditure incidence. Even for spending items targeting specifically the less well-off people—such as public housing, education, and health care—the expenditure incidence can also be shifted to the business sector by lowering its labor cost. Combined with the analysis of the tax system, it is interesting to see redistribution through the fiscal system in Hong Kong is not necessarily from the higher income group to the lower income group but also from the middle class to the lower income group.

At the micro level of economic policy, in terms of promoting and nurturing specific industries, the HKSAR government has gradually shifted from "positive nonintervention" of the colonial legacy to an active approach of interventionism. While a more active approach may be needed, problems in the HKSAR political system and governance—including its weak state capacity in areas such as expertise and knowledge about innovation and technology, weak state autonomy in terms of preventing rent-seeking activities and making decisions free from sectoral interests—have stalled the economic transformation. It is true that effort has been made in strengthening the technology and innovation sector, but when one closely examines the current economic base of Hong Kong, not much has changed. Compared with other industrialized Asian countries, Hong Kong is still lagging behind in its transformation to a new, creative, and high-technology economy. Hong Kong's economy continues to depend on the traditional pillars of finance, real estate, tourism, and services, which are quite vulnerable to business cycles, financial crises, and the pandemic.

Besides economic restructuring, the HKSAR government faces lots of acute problems, including balancing economic growth and social equity, and most recently a major economic downturn in both Hong Kong and the Mainland. It is often argued by both the HKSAR government and the CPG that Hong Kong should be an economic city, not a political city, focusing mainly on economic development in lieu of political development. This oversimplistic assumption about the separation between institutional political arrangements and economic

312   Economic Policy

performance has been rebutted by the analysis and discussion in this chapter. Given the inseparable linkage between economic policy and governance, the real challenge for the HKSAR government is in how it can coordinate the necessary changes and adjustments needed in economic policy with structural reforms in its governance system.

Box 12.1: Public goods

Public goods are goods that are non-rival in their consumption (i.e., many people can enjoy them simultaneously) and infeasible in exclusion (i.e., those who do not pay will also enjoy them). It is generally considered that government should be responsible for the provision of public goods, as only government has the author-ity to use coercive taxation to force people to pay for them.

Box 12.2: Externalities

Activities of a person or an entity affect the welfare of others who are outside the market exchange. Externalities can be positive—these are also called social ben-efits (e.g., education and immunization)—or negative, thereby generating social cost (e.g., industrial pollution and cigarette smoking).

Box 12.3: Excess burden and equity-efficiency trade-off

Economists believe individuals always make the best choice for themselves through voluntary exchange in the market, reaching a Pareto efficiency. Therefore, any change in individual choice caused by government policies will lead to a loss in welfare, also known as excess burden. As taxation, a nonvoluntary exchange, is often needed for reallocation, there is often a trade-off between equity and efficiency.

Box 12.4: Punctuated Equilibrium Theory

Punctuated Equilibrium Theory (PET) is a general theory, introduced by Baumgartner and Jones (1993), for explaining policy stability and change. According to PET, due to factors such as serial processing and long-term inatten-tion to a particular issue caused by bureaucratic bounded rationality, progressive institutional friction in a political system, and changes in governance structures, a period of policy stability would be punctuated by radical changes in budget allocation (budgetary punctuations), to be followed by another period of incre-mental changes.

Box 12.5: Tax incidence and expenditure incidence

Tax incidence refers to the question of "who pays the tax," and expenditure incidence refers to the question of "who benefits" from public expenditure. It is important to remember that tax incidence and expenditure incidence are determined not by law but by economic forces.

Box 12.6: Economic integration and the Greater Bay Area

Economic integration is when the barriers to business (either natural or institutional) between two economies are lowered. Since 2017, under the planning of the Chinese Central Government, the Guangdong-Hong Kong-Macao Greater Bay Area (Greater Bay Area)—which comprises two Special Administrative Regions (Hong Kong and Macao) and nine municipalities of the Guangdong Province (Guangzhou, Shenzhen, Zhuhai, Foshan, Huizhou, Dongguan, Zhongshan, Jiangmen, and Zhaoqing)—has become the key focus of economic integration between Hong Kong and the Mainland.

Box 12.7: Rent-seeking

Rent-seeking is the use of political power to seek economic benefit, mainly through eliminating competition. Rent-seeking is seen as a negative activity in economics for two reasons. First, it brings higher prices to consumers. Second, it is a waste of resources.

Questions

1. Does Hong Kong have a fair fiscal system? What should the government do to reform its fiscal system to address rising income inequalities and other social problems in Hong Kong?
2. What have been the major changes in budgetary allocations in recent years, including the post-2020 era? According to the punctuated equilibrium theory, what are the major factors leading to those changes?
3. What are the major problems in the economic structure of Hong Kong? What role should the government play in strengthening the innovation and technology sector?
4. How does Hong Kong's economic integration into the Greater Bay Area affect its economic and future development?

Bibliography

Baumgartner, FR & Jones, BD 1993, *Agendas and Instability in American Politics*, University of Chicago Press, Chicago, IL.

Castells, M 1992, "Four Asian Tigers with a Dragon Head: A Comparative Analysis of the State, Economy, and Society in the Asian Pacific Rim," in RP Appelbaum & J Henderson (eds), *States and Development in the Asian Pacific Rim*, SAGE Publications, Newbury Park, CA, pp. 33–70.

Cheung, A 2000, "New Interventionism in the Making: Interpreting State Interventions in Hong Kong after the Change of Sovereignty," *Journal of Contemporary China*, vol. 9, no. 24, pp. 291–308.

Cheung, PTY 2002, "Managing the Hong Kong-Guangdong Relationship: Issues and Challenges," in AGO Yeh, YSE Lee, T Lee & ND Sze (eds), *Building A Competitive Pearl River Delta Region: Cooperation, Coordination, and Planning*, Centre of Urban Planning and Environment Management, The University of Hong Kong, Hong Kong, pp. 39–58.

Chiu, SWK 2004, "Unravelling Hong Kong's Exceptionalism: The Politics of Laissez-Faire in the Industrial Takeoff," in KY Law & KM Lee (eds), *The Economy of Hong Kong in Non-Economic Perspectives*, Oxford University Press, Hong Kong, pp. 141–178.

Chiu, SWK & Lui, TL 2001, "The Hong Kong Model of Development Revisited," in PK Wong & CY Ng (eds), *Industrial Policy, Innovation & Economic Growth: The Experience of Japan and the Asian NIEs*, Singapore University Press, Singapore, pp. 431–459.

Choy, AHK 2004, "The Political Economy of Hong Kong's Industrial Upgrading: A Lost Opportunity (an extract)," in KY Law & KM Lee (eds), *The Economy of Hong Kong in Non-Economic Perspectives*, Oxford University Press, Hong Kong, pp. 141–178.

Chu, YW 2020, "Technology-based Development and Heightened Integration with Mainland China: C. Y. Leung's Economic Ambition," in YSC Cheng (ed), *Evaluation of the C. Y. Leung Administration*, The City University of Hong Kong Press, Hong Kong, pp. 329–360.

Chu, YW 2016, "The Asian Development State: Ideas and Debates," in YW Chu (ed), *The Asian Development State*, Palgrave Macmillan, New York, p. 1–26.

Coyle, D 2020, *Markets, State, and People: Economics for Public Policy*, Princeton University Press, Princeton, NJ.

Fong, B 2015, "The Politics of Budget Surpluses: The Case of China's Hong Kong SAR," *International Review of Administrative Sciences*, vol. 81, no. 1, pp. 134–157.

Fong, B 2022, *Hong Kong Budgeting: Historical and Comparative Analysis*, Palgrave Macmillan, Singapore.

Friedman, M 1982, *Capitalism and Freedom*, University of Chicago Press, Chicago.

Government of the Hong Kong Special Administrative Region, 2021, *Hong Kong Poverty Situation Report 2020*, Office of the Government Economist and Census and Statistics Department, Hong Kong.

Heritage Foundation 2021, *2021 Index of Economic Freedom*, Heritage Foundation, Washington, DC.

Information Services Department, HKSAR Government 2021, *Hong Kong Yearbook 2020*, Government Printer, Hong Kong.

Johnson, C 1982, *MITI and the Japanese Miracle*, Stanford University Press, Stanford.

Lam, NMK 2000, "Government Intervention in the Economy: A Comparative Analysis of Singapore and Hong Kong," *Public Administration and Development*, vol. 20, no. 5, pp. 397–421.

Latter, T 2007, *Hands On or Hands Off? The Nature and Process of Economic Policy in Hong Kong*, Hong Kong University Press, Hong Kong.

Li, KW 2006, *The Hong Kong Economy: Recovery and Restructuring*, McGraw-Hill, Singapore.

Mikesell, J 2011, *Fiscal Administration*, 8th ed., Thomson-Wadsworth, New York.

Musgrave, R & Musgrave, P 1989, *Public Finance in Theory and Practice*, 5th ed., McGraw-Hill, New York.

Pack, H & Saggi, K 2006, "Is There a Case for Industrial Policy: A Critical Survey," *World Bank Research Observer*, vol. 21, no. 2, pp. 268–291.

Petersen, D & Roberts, EV 2003, "The Hong Kong Business Environment since 1997," in R Ash, P Ferdinand, B Hook & R Porter (eds), *Hong Kong in Transition: One Country, Two Systems*, Routledge Curzon, London; New York, pp. 13–33.

Rodrik, D 2008, "Industrial Policy: Don't Ask Why, Ask How," *Middle East Development Journal*, vol. 1, no. 1, pp. 1–29.

Rosen, HS 2005, *Public Finance*, 7th ed., Irwin McGraw-Hill, New York.

Rubin, I 2000, *The Politics of Public Budgeting: Getting and Spending, Borrowing and Balancing*, 4th ed., Chatham House, Chatham, NJ.

Slemrod, J & Bakija, J 2004, *Taxing Ourselves: A Citizen's Guide to the Great Debate Over Tax Reform*, 3rd ed., MIT Press, Cambridge, MA.

Sung, YW 2002, "Hong Kong Economy in Crisis," in SK Lau (ed), *The First Tung Chee-hwa Administration*, the Chinese University Press of Hong Kong, Hong Kong, pp. 123–138.

Sung, YW 2005, *The Emergence of Greater China: The Economic Integration of Mainland China, Taiwan, and Hong Kong*, Palgrave Macmillan, Basingstoke; New York.

Tsui-Auch, LS 1998, "Has the Hong Kong Model Worked? Industrial Policy in Retrospect and Prospect," *Development and Change*, vol. 29, no. 1, pp. 55–79.

United Nations Development Programme (UNDP) 2020, *Human Development Report 2020*, UNDP, New York.

Wong, PK & Ng CY 2001, "Rethinking the Development Paradigm: Lessons from Japan and the Four Asian NIEs," in PK Wong & CY Ng (eds), *Industrial Policy, Innovation & Economic Growth: The Experience of Japan and the Asian NIEs*, Singapore University Press, Singapore, pp. 1–54.

Wong, SYS 2020, "Hong Kong's Economic Situation under C. Y. Leung," in YSC Cheng (ed), *Evaluation of the C. Y. Leung Administration*, City University of Hong Kong Press, Hong Kong, pp. 277–327.

Wong, W 2009, "The Days after the End of the Asian Miracle: The Budget Crisis of Hong Kong," in M Sing (ed), *Politics and Government in Hong Kong: Crisis under Chinese Sovereignty*, Routledge, London; New York, pp. 136–161.

316 Economic Policy

World Economic Forum 2020, *Global Competitiveness Report: How Countries are Performing on the Road to Recovery*. World Economic Forum, Switzerland.

Yeung, C 2002, "Separation and Integration: Hong Kong-Mainland Relations in a Flux," in SK Lau (ed), *The First Tung Chee-hwa Administration*, the Chinese University Press of Hong Kong, Hong Kong, pp. 237–265.

Useful Websites

Budget Speeches of the Financial Secretary
http://www.budget.gov.hk/

Census and Statistics Department
http://www.info.gov.hk/censtatd/home.html

Greater Bay Area
http://www.bayarea.gov.hk

The Economist Magazine
http://www.economist.com/index.html

Finance Committee of the Legislative Council
http://www.legco.gov.hk/english/index.htm

Hong Kong Economy
http://www.gov.hk/hkecon/

Hong Kong Monetary Authority (HKMA)
http://www.info.gov.hk/hkma/index.htm

Hong Kong Trade Development Council
http://www.tdctrade.com/

Hong Kong Yearbook
http://www.info.gov.hk/yearbook/

International Monetary Fund (IMF)
http://www.imf.org/

Organization for Economic Cooperation and Development (OECD)
http://www.oecd.org/home/

The World Bank
http://www.worldbank.org/

Further Reading

Fong, B 2022, *Hong Kong Budgeting: Historical and Comparative Analysis*, Palgrave Macmillan, Singapore. This book provides a good review of the budgeting systems and practices in Hong Kong from a historical and comparative perspective.

Latter, T 2007, *Hands On or Hands Off? The Nature and Process of Economic Policy in Hong Kong*, Hong Kong University Press, Hong Kong. This is a convincing work by a former top government official to dispel the myth of a noninterventionist and government-free approach in the economic policy of Hong Kong.

Mikesell, J 2017, *Fiscal Administration*, 10th ed., Cengage Learning, Boston. This is a good textbook on the important topics and reforms of public budgeting.

Rosen, H & Gayer, T 2013, *Public Finance*, 10th ed., Irwin McGraw-Hill, New York. This is a very good and widely adopted textbook on public finance written by a renowned Princeton economist.

Slemrod, J & Bakija, J 2017, *Taxing Ourselves: A Citizen's Guide to the Great Debate Over Tax Reform*. 5th ed., MIT Press, Cambridge, MA. This is a very accessible book written by top experts highlighting and discussing the major principles and issues in designing a good tax system.

Stiglitz, J & Rosenga, J. 2015, *Economics of the Public Sector*, 4th ed., Norton, New York. This is a good and thought-provoking book by a Nobel Prize Laureate in Economics. It points out that most economies are actually mixed and argues why government intervention is often needed to make the market work and to minimize its negative effects.

13

Changes in Social Policy in Hong Kong since 1997

Old Wine in New Bottles?

Wong Hung

Introduction

Many authors define social policy as the action of governments designed to promote welfare (Dorwart 1971; Wilding 2007). Contrary to this positive view on social policy, Jones (1990) treats social policy as an instrument of governments to regulate and manipulate people's social conditions. Jones defines social policy as "the involvement of government in systematic attempts to regulate and manipulate social conditions and life chances for sections of a given population" (Jones 1990: 3–4). In the context of Hong Kong, the government's social policy may promote, maintain, or even *damage* the welfare of certain sections of the population. We need to scrutinize the real impact of social policy on different sectors, especially on the vulnerable in society.

The laissez-faire economic policy and the so-called "positive noninterventionism" are regarded as two key cornerstones of Hong Kong's economic success in the postwar decades. They continue to be the fundamental framework guiding state policy and therefore also induce inertia that blocks major changes in the government's approach to launch new social policy initiatives.

Social policy in Hong Kong is not only framed in terms of the laissez-faire philosophy but is also restricted by the Basic Law. The Hong Kong Special Administrative Region (HKSAR) government is also restricted by its overall fiscal policy (such as low taxation), and the expectation of maintaining a financial surplus as required by the Basic Law.

In practice, Hong Kong has never claimed to be or committed to being a welfare state. On one hand, Hong Kong has limited welfare provisions—it has no universal pension, no unemployment benefit, and no minimum wage before 2011—compared to the welfare state in western countries. The implication of "noninterventionist" social policy is the persistent existence and intensifying problems of poverty for the elderly, the unemployed, and the working poor. The welfare of the "vulnerable" is indeed damaged by the residual nature and the inaction of social policy by the Hong Kong government. On the other hand, a large number of Hong Kong people have benefited from comprehensive public health care and low-rent public housing provisions. The scope and depth of such service provisions is astonishing—it is even comparable to the welfare states in the West. It is quite unique for Hong Kong to develop this pragmatic mix of passive inaction and active interventions by the state, which has been developed in adapting the political and economic environment of postwar Hong Kong.

The "big market, small government" principle of the HKSAR government was first stated by Tung Chee-hwa in his *2003 Policy Address* (Tung 2003: para. 16) and was restated by Donald Tsang in his *2009–10 Policy Address* (Tsang 2010: para. 6). In the *2013 Policy Address*, Leung Chun-ying introduced a new term— "appropriately proactive" government—to label the same idea; however, he failed to specify the meaning of "appropriately proactive" (Leung 2013: para. 20). In her *2017 Policy Address*, Carrie Lam, the next CE, proclaimed that "facilitator" and "promoter" are the new roles of the government; however, such roles were not really novel (Lam 2017: para. 9).

The current CE, John Lee, outlined his initiatives for Hong Kong development through his inaugural *2022 Policy Address* on 19 October 2022. He stated that "Hong Kong has achieved a major transition from chaos to order, and is now at the crucial stage of advancing from stability to prosperity." He will "lead the government team to unite and motivate all sectors of the community, and give full play to our fine traditions of inclusiveness, unity and respect for different viewpoints" (Lee 2022). Though Lee outlined a lot of old and new policy initiatives, he has not explicitly explained his social policy philosophy.

This principle of the Hong Kong government is indeed similar to the "positive noninterventionism" of its preceding colonial counterpart. It is just old wine in new bottles in two senses. First, the social policy of the Hong Kong government still has the economic pragmatism originating from its colonial past. The vague concepts of "big" and "small" make the new discourse as confusing as the old idea of "positive" vs. "noninterventionism." It gave much room for the government to interpret and manipulate what it should and should not do in specific moments and on specific issues. Second, the Hong Kong government is not a totally independent governance body; it has to follow the decisions of a higher political hierarchy—the colonial British government before 1997, and the Central People's Government (CPG) after 1997. Both governments have their own political interests, agendas, and considerations in determining their decisions over social policy in Hong Kong.

The economic-pragmatism origin of social policy in Hong Kong is not a special feature of Hong Kong; it is common in the East Asia region. Ian Holliday (2000: 708) claims that countries in East Asia—including Japan, Hong Kong, Singapore, South Korea, and Taiwan—are examples of "productivist welfare capitalism" in which "social policy is strictly subordinate to the overriding policy objective of economic growth." The economic-pragmatic characteristic of "productivist welfare capitalism" is minimal social rights with extensions linked to productive activity. However, after the 1997 Asian financial crisis, we witnessed welfare reforms in South Korea and Taiwan in which state institutions and the welfare state in particular were strengthened amid instability and flexibility in the globalized market (Kwon 2005). Other than economic considerations, cultural and political factors are also considered as the other key determining factors in shaping social policy in East Asia. Alan Walker and Wong Cheuk-ki (2002) contend that Chinese and East Asian states use "Confucianism" to justify their restrictive social policies.

In this chapter, factors shaping the development of social policy in Hong Kong will be explored, and the changes in social policy—including housing, health, and poverty alleviation policies from 1997 to 2020—will be investigated. We will also examine the policy formulation of the legislation of minimum wage to understand the political dynamics of the influence of the CPG.

The Old Wine: Laissez-Faire

Before 1997, social welfare in Hong Kong was residual in nature and acted as a safety net for the vulnerable and the unfortunate minority. It did not serve the purpose of redistributing resources. Chris Patten, the last governor of Hong Kong, stated in his final policy address in 1996, "Quite deliberately, our welfare system does not exist to iron out inequalities. It does not exist to redistribute income . . . we have a duty to provide a safety net to protect the vulnerable and the disadvantaged members of society, the unfortunate minority, who, through no fault of their own, are left behind by the growing prosperity enjoyed by the rest of Hong Kong" (Patten 1996: para 78).

The safety net function of social policy was echoed by Tung Chee-hwa, the first CE of the HKSAR government. In his *2000 Policy Address*, he said, "For those who have suffered setbacks, they should be given further opportunities to succeed" (Tung 2000: para. 48).

In the same policy address, there seemed to be some changes in social policy by the Hong Kong government, which stressed the government's responsibility for social development: to create an environment where participation and fair competition are open to all; to put in place a well-resourced basic safety net; to assist the disadvantaged with an emphasis on enhancing their will to be self-reliant; and to encourage the advantaged to participate in voluntary work to build a harmonious society. However, Tung admitted that "such a social policy, which stresses good will and equal opportunities as its fundamental values, is complementary to the laissez-faire economic policy we follow" (2000: para. 50). This clearly confirmed that although Hong Kong had entered the postcolonial period, the "old wines" were still liberalism and laissez-faire, whereas the emphasis on government responsibility for social development was just a "new bottle."

Donald Tsang, Tung's successor, also introduced a new term—"progressive development"—in his *2007–08 Policy Address*. However, his meaning of "progressive" is not really progressive but rather essentially conservative in nature. It really denotes promoting economic development as the government's primary goal, promoting economic development through infrastructure projects, promoting community development through the revitalization of historic and built heritage, and promoting social harmony under the concept of helping people help themselves (Tsang 2007). Again, "progressive development" is just a new bottle with no genuine changes in social policies.

It was Leung Chun-ying, the CE after Donald Tsang, who suggested that the government must be "appropriately proactive" in his *2013 Policy Address*. He upheld that the government should refrain from intervention when the market is functioning efficiently. Leung further argued that the government should proactively address the housing shortage and other pressing social problems.

Carrie Lam presented the idea that government should act as the facilitator and promoter. On the one hand, as a facilitator, the government should be a visionary and is duty bound to scrutinize existing policies, remove obstacles for industries, strengthen coordination across government bodies, and provide one-stop services to benefit the community. On the other hand, as a promoter, the government should strengthen the links between Hong Kong and the Mainland, as well as with other countries (Lam 2017). Actually, the facilitator has the administrative and coordinating role as a steward but not as a master. Meanwhile, the promoter only fulfils the function of a broker but does not act as an owner who manages the related functions. Both roles, however, do not address the role of the government in handling the well-being of the Hong Kong people, which is the key driver of social policy.

Social Policy Development since 1997

The Basic Law stipulates that Hong Kong has to maintain balanced budgets, and an increase in public expenditure is only possible when budget surplus is available (Chiu 2003). However, since 1997, Hong Kong has had budget deficits from 1998–1999 to 2004–2005. Financial deficits during these years restricted the Hong Kong government's new initiatives and expansion activities to welfare, health, and housing.

Education, health, housing, and social welfare have been the four major social policy areas that concerned the public and the government (Box 13.1). From Chart 13.1, which shows the current and capital expenditure of the government on these four policy areas from 1997–1998 to 2020–2021, we learn that there was a significant increase in expenditure on education from HK$47,027 million to HK$107,040 million in this period, with a significant increase since 2010–2011. The second social policy area that had a larger budget was social welfare, whose expenditure increased from HK$21,710 million to HK$98,046 million. The increase in health care has been similar with the social welfare from HK$27,982 million to HK$96,999 million. The housing area was the only policy area that recorded a decrease from 1999–2000 to 2007–2008, with a moderate increase after 2008–2009 to HK$35,151 million in 2020–2021.

Chart 13.2 shows the percentage of the expenditure on the four policy areas of GDP from 1997–1998 to 2020–2021. From 1997–1998 to 2003–2004, expenditure on education increased from 3.4 percent to 4.5 percent of Hong Kong's GDP; it decreased to 3.0 percent in 2014–2015 and eventually increased to 4.0 percent in 2020–2021. From 1997–1998 to 2003–2004, expenditure on social welfare significantly increased from 1.6 percent to 2.7 percent of Hong Kong's

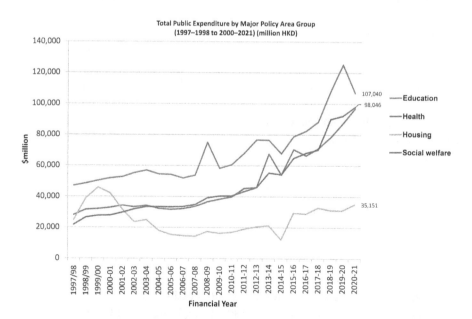

Chart 13.1: Current and capital expenditure of major policy area in Hong Kong dollars (million) (1997–1998 to 2020–2021)

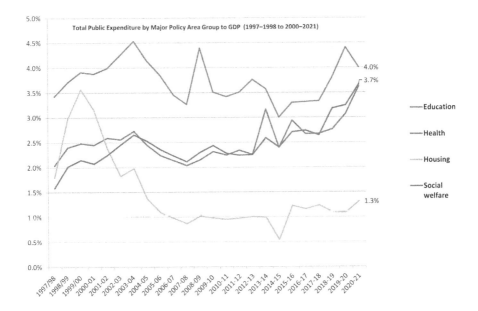

Chart 13.2: Major policy area expenditure as a percentage of GDP (1997–1998 to 2020–2021)

GDP; it decreased to 2.1 percent in 2007–2008 and subsequently increased to 3.7 percent in 2019–2020. Expenditure on health also increased from 2.0 percent to 2.7 percent from 1997–1998 to 2003–2004; decreased to 2.0 percent in 2007–2008 and increased to 3.6 percent in 2020–2021. Expenditure on housing notably decreased from 1.8 percent to 0.5 percent from 1997–1998 to 2014–2015 and slightly increased to 1.3 percent in 2020–2021. Following the sovereignty transfer in 1997, education received more attention and resources from the Hong Kong government. Meanwhile, public housing became less important compared to the 1970s and 1980s, which signified the retreat of the Hong Kong government's role in housing provision and even a retreat from the role to regulate the housing market. In the next section, we will examine the abrupt changes in housing policies in Hong Kong since 1997.

Housing

When Tung Chee-hwa assumed his post as the first CE of the HKSAR in 1997, the mounting cost of real estate became the hottest issue that deeply concerned the public. To address this rising concern, Tung set three targets on housing in his first Policy Address in 1997: to build at least 85,000 flats a year in the public and private sectors, to achieve a home ownership rate of 70 percent by 2007, and to reduce the average waiting time for public rental housing to three years (Hong Kong SAR Government 1997: para. 52). The "active" element among the "noninterventionism" or the "small" but "effective" government was a significant characteristic of this new housing policy after 1997, and a significant change from the housing policies before 1997.

However, the outbreak of the Asian financial crisis provoked the collapse of property prices in Hong Kong, which undermined Tung's housing policy strategy. Michael Suen, Secretary for Housing, Planning and Lands, announced a fundamental change in Tung's housing objectives and strategies in 2002. The new housing policy was remedial in nature, and its focus was to provide assistance to low-income families and minimize government intervention in the private property market (Suen 2002).

Suen proposed nine measures, including ceasing the production and sale of Home Ownership Scheme (HOS) flats indefinitely from 2003 onward. In 2005, the Housing Authority also ceased the Tenants Purchase Scheme (TPS) and stopped all publicly financed home-ownership schemes. The rationale behind the move was to address the overlapping between these subsidized flats and the private residential market; the immediate effect was the reduction of supply of publicly financed home-ownership schemes.

In 2007, the government objected to the recurring proposal of the public and LegCo members to relaunch the HOS and TPS. However, it did not think that property prices were at an extremely unreasonable level, making it difficult for the low and middle classes to purchase flats. The government argued that the overall property price level in 2007 was still lower than at the peak in 1997 by about 40 percent. Also, the government considered that the public had divergent views on whether or not the government should enter the market to build home ownership flats again (Transport and Housing Bureau 2007). Here we witness the passive essence of "noninterventionism" of the "small" government to give way to the "big" market of housing and real estate development, which in fact is the essence of the "old wine" of Hong Kong's social policy.

CE Donald Tsang announced in his *2012 Policy Address* at the end of his term that the Hong Kong government would relaunch the HOS. Thereafter, HOS flats were made available again in 2014, after a 12-year suspension since 2003. CE Leung Chun-ying considered the housing problem to be the first priority in his policy agenda. Under Leung's initiative, the Hong Kong government announced the Long Term Housing Strategy (LTHS) in 2014, which aimed to avert the supply-demand imbalance by building more public rental housing, providing more subsidized sale flats, and providing steady land supply and demand-side management measures. Though it represented a complete reversal of the previous housing policy, the supply of public rental housing remained stagnant after 2014. Only 6,000 public rental housing units were built in 2014, which increased to 10,000 in 2019. In addition, the subsidized sale flats (mainly HOS) increased from 0 in 2014 to 7,000 in 2019. Owing to the huge pressure to increase the supply of public housing, CE Carrie Lam announced in her *2020 Policy Address* that the Hong Kong government had already identified the 330 hectares of land required for providing 316,000 public housing units from 2020–2021 to 2029–2030, representing an increase of 44,000 units over the 272,000 units in the recent 10-year period.

Carrie Lam also announced the Lantau Tomorrow Vision in her *2018 Policy Address*. This project aimed to increase the supply of land and housing through the creation of a third core business district near Kau Yi Chau and Hei Ling Chau. This will be achieved by constructing an artificial island through massive land reclamation of the eastern waters of Lantau Island. The new reclamation area will be about 1,700 ha and will provide 260,000 to 400,000 housing units, of which 70 percent will be dedicated to public housing. The proposal created controversies. Many opposition forces—including individuals and groups—complained about its gigantic scale, huge financial burden, and negative environmental impacts.

Harmonious society and anti-rich sentiment

With limited supply, land in urban areas is considered a precious commodity in Hong Kong. The ever-increasing population and vibrant real estate development create a continuously rising demand for land in urban Hong Kong. To increase land supply in the city area, the Urban Renewal Authority was established to speed up the urban renewal process. Many local residents in this area were poor tenants, who were dependent on cheap accommodation and abundant supply of low-skilled jobs in the local economy. Redevelopment created a gentrified environment, which had a dampening effect on the concerned community. The poor viewed this phenomenon as a collusion between the Hong Kong government and real estate developers, who share a common interest in keeping the prices of land and real estate high at the expense of the people.

Under the urban redevelopment plan, *tong lau* (i.e., old buildings built in the 1950s and 1960s, most of which are three to nine stories but without a lift and are now in poor maintenance condition) in these poor urban areas were torn down, which cut the supply of flats suitable for cubicle flats or *tong lau* suites and made the rents for these flats extremely high. Aside from the poor, the younger generation also had a growing discontent with the government caused by the housing problem.

The term "post-80s" generation has become popular in Hong Kong since 2009. It was popularized in media to explain the outbreak of a social campaign by the opposition to the Guangzhou-Hong Kong Express Rail Link. During the campaign, a group of young activists vigorously promoted the preservation of living styles and memory in Hong Kong. Their anti-colonialism and ideological beliefs about sustainable development were radical in nature, which clashed with capitalistic mainstream values. However, the government interpreted that the discontent of these young activists originated from "their low upward social mobility and discrepancy between individual expectation and the objective reality" (Lau 2010). One discrepancy, according to the government, was that as university graduates, they expected to own a flat but could not afford to buy one, which nourished the "anti-rich" sentiment not only among the post-80s generation but across the lower and middle classes. As this "anti-rich" sentiment threatens social harmony, which may potentially be followed by instability, the Mainland and Hong Kong governments have to do something to handle and downplay the sentiment.

According to the survey by the Hong Kong Institute of Asia-Pacific Studies, more Hong Kong people think that Hong Kong is no longer a harmonious society. In 2010, only 26.5 percent of the respondents "agree" or "strongly agree" that Hong Kong is a harmonious society, which is significantly lower than 37.5 percent in 2008 and 37.8 percent in 2006. Among all conflicts, the conflicts between the rich and the poor are ranked as the most serious conflict in the surveys in 2006, 2008, and 2010 (HKIAPS 2010).

According to another survey conducted by the Hong Kong University Public Opinion Programme (HKUPOP), 88 percent of respondents consider "housing" problems to be the most pressing policy area to be addressed in the CE's *2010 Policy Address*. Public concern for housing is greater than economic development as well as labor and employment issues (HKUPOP 2010).

In his *2010 Policy Address*, Tsang responded to the public expectation and announced measures to alleviate the property market. One of the measures was the new "My Home Purchase Plan," which was intended to replace the HOS. It is a rent-to-buy scheme under which a total of 5,000 flats will be provided for lease to sandwich class home buyers at prevailing market rents for a maximum of five years. Tenants will be reimbursed half their rental fees to serve as down payments for their home purchase (Hong Kong SAR Government 2010).

However, the intervention of this plan, like many other government interventions, was too late and too small. The plan needs at least five to six years to benefit the first group of 1,000 home buyers. The plan is merely a cosmetic or window-dressing action of the Hong Kong government to demonstrate its half-hearted belief in regulating the housing market and property prices, and to do something to ease the "anti-rich" sentiment. This is a typical example of the recurring piecemeal and responsive actions of the government toward social sentiment. These actions can be seen as the ever-changing "new bottles" aim to extinguish hatred and prevent backlash against the government; however, the "old wine" is still the economic pragmatism consideration.

Health

In 1999, a consultancy report by the Harvard Team gave a highly critical analysis of the health care service in Hong Kong, particularly the absence of a coherent policy for health care service and financing (Harvard Team 1999). Nevertheless, the Hong Kong government did not adopt the recommendations but announced alternative proposals in 2000, without many implementation details (Health and Welfare Bureau 2000).

The outbreak of severe acute respiratory syndrome (SARS) in March 2003 was another critical incident for health policy development. The then-unknown virus infected 1,755 individuals and claimed the lives of nearly 300 people. The SARS outbreak turned a spotlight on the health care system and its inability to cope with an emergency (Gauld 2005). To a certain degree, the inability of the health care system and the lack of a coherent Health Policy and a Health Authority comprise the social policy of the government, which damages the welfare of the Hong Kong people. Wilding (2007) argues that these two issues— the Harvard Review and the SARS outbreak— neatly illustrate the ambivalence of the Hong Kong government's health policies. The government has long accepted responsibility for the provision of health services, but in a piecemeal, reactive, reluctant fashion (again, it is the old wine of social policy in Hong Kong). After the incident, the government's reaction was to establish a new Centre for Health Protection under the Department of Health in June 2004.

Another health policy move was the launching of the Elderly Health Care Voucher Pilot Scheme in 2008–2009. The scheme was a pilot trial for three years to annually provide five health care vouchers costing HK$50 each to elders aged 70 years and older to partially subsidize their use of private primary health care (PHC) services. The scheme aimed to provide additional choices for elders on top of the existing public PHC services, which also act as a model for subsidized PHC services in the future. Generally, the scheme was welcomed by the elderly; however, many of them thought the annual subsidy of HK$250 subsidy was too small to change their habit of choosing the PHC service provider. Many poor elderly still need to depend on the low-cost public PHC service. This move was again a "new bottle" to show the government's concern for the elderly and its intention to promote them to use the private primary health care.

In 2019, the government set up the District Health Centre (DHC) to change the current focus of Hong Kong's health care services regarding treatment, and to alleviate the pressure on public hospitals. Using the HK$100 million funding for DHC, the first center was launched at Kwai Chung District. Soon, more centers will be launched in other districts. The functions of the DHC are to enhance public awareness of disease prevention and their capability in selfmanagement of health through public-private partnership, medical-social collaboration support for the chronically ill, health promotion, health assessment, chronic disease management, and community rehabilitation. DHC is a new initiative, and its effectiveness and social impacts in delivering primary health care are as yet unknown.

Unswerving commitment: Safety net for all?

In 2008, the Hong Kong government proposed a package of reform proposals called "Your Health, Your Life," which stressed its "unswerving commitment to healthcare" to uphold the public health care system as the health care safety net for the whole population (Food and Health Bureau 2008). According to the reform package, more than HK$15 billion would be invested to improve health care infrastructure and enhance public health care services, including improving primary care, promoting public-private partnership in health care, developing electronic health record sharing, and strengthening the public health care safety net.

However, after the first stage of public consultation, the Hong Kong government found that the public had reservations about the mandatory supplementary financing options and instead preferred voluntary participation. Therefore, in October 2010, the government proposed a new Health Protection Scheme (HPS), which aims to make available government-regulated health insurance to provide better choices to those who prefer private health care services (Food and Health Bureau 2010). It also aims to "ease the pressure on public healthcare system by encouraging more people to use private healthcare on a sustained basis, and enhance the sustainability of the entire healthcare system."

According to this scheme, the government will set aside HK$50 billion over the next 25 years to subsidize 500,000 "high-risk" public health insurance policyholders, whose annual medical costs are more than 20 percent higher than those of a "normal, healthy individual." The subsidy fund will target the elderly, individuals with preexisting conditions, and young people to establish some form of private medical insurance coverage. In 2010, it was estimated that about 34 percent of the Hong Kong population had private health insurance, with only 4 percent of those over the age of 65 possessing coverage. One of the reasons is the rising premiums among the elderly. The insurance subsidy is intended to ease these barriers and attract more individuals to purchase medical insurance.

However, according to the comments of academic experts on HPS, there are considerable concerns about whether or not the incentives are sufficient to induce a critical mass of participants necessary to achieve the objective of enhancing access to private health care and relieving the burden on the public system. After nine years of consultation and preparation, the HPS was finally implemented as the Voluntary Health Insurance Scheme (VHIS) in April 2019.

Insurance companies participating in the VHIS offer individual indemnity hospital insurance plans that are certified by the Food and Health Bureau (FHB). Certified plans have some attractive characteristics, such as guaranteed renewal, despite changes to the health conditions of the insured, up to the age of 100; no "lifetime benefit limit"; and extension of coverage to include unknown preexisting conditions. Over 300,000 people had joined the VHIS by September 2019. About one-third were under the age of 30, and half of them were under the age of 40. As the expenditures for VHIS are tax deductible, it has become an attractive option to the taxpayers and younger population.

Nevertheless, VHIS as a new health policy initiative, like the "My Home Purchase Plan" as a new housing policy initiative, is a one-off commitment from the government to use a fixed amount of the budget to solve a pressing social problem. The commitment is too small and too narrow-minded without rational and long-term planning.

Poverty Alleviation

Amid a period of economic growth in Hong Kong, poverty not only remains but is on the rise. Between 1996 and 2009, Hong Kong's per capita GDP grew from HK$189,326 to HK$233,060; however, the number of people living in poor households increased from 0.84 million in 1996 to 1.26 million in 2010—an increase of 325,000. In 2010, the poverty rate stood at 18.1 percent (Hong Kong Council of Social Service 2010).

In the colonial era, the government's main strategy to deal with poverty was to ensure social stability by providing income support to poor households through the Comprehensive Social Security Assistance (CSSA) and Old Age Allowance to the elderly. After 1997, the Hong Kong government adopted the colonial government's view and believed that the best way to help poor households improve their conditions was to provide them with education and job opportunities.

CSSA is the major income support scheme in Hong Kong. Families that receive CSSA need to pass stringent income and assets reviews. As the most important safety net in Hong Kong's social security system, the recipients of CSSA can be regarded as constituting a core group of the abject poor in Hong Kong. In 1991, there were only 72,969 CSSA cases; whereas by 1997, the number of cases significantly increased to 186,932 and further to 289,139 by 2009. There were 282,623 CSSA recipients in 1997; the number of recipients grew tremendously in the early 2000s, and reached the highest figure at 522,456 individuals in 2004. Although the economic and poverty situation improved in the late 2000s, 482,001 persons still needed to live on CSSA in 2009.

It was only in 2000, the first time in contemporary Hong Kong, when Tung officially admitted that poverty was actually a serious problem. In his *2000 Policy Address*, Tung acknowledged that the Asian financial crisis did impact the community, particularly lower-income families, some of whom had suffered a substantial drop in their income. Tung pledged to focus on the plight of low-income families in the coming years (HKSAR Government 2000).

Many government officials still consider relative poverty as a necessary evil, a part of social reality, and a kind of hardship that can motivate the poor to work hard. Hence, after admitting the impact of the Asian financial crisis on low-income families in his *2000 Policy Address*, Tung emphasized, "Unfortunately, the wealth gap is an inevitable phenomenon in the course of economic development. It is not unique to Hong Kong." Finally, he established the Commission on Poverty before his resignation in 2005, a move that was hardly a major break from the misplaced strategies on poverty alleviation.

In his *2006 Policy Address*, Tsang restated, "[t]o assist those in need who are capable of working, our focus is not only on providing welfare, but also on enhancing their capability through education and training, and giving them proper employment assistance and support." The Commission on Poverty (CoP 2007) also explicitly states that support to low-income employees should not be focused on passive assistance but rather on proactive support, including the provision of training and employment assistance to help them enhance their capacities and overcome poverty.

Following the above assumption, most of the government's resources were allotted to establishing different training schemes to invest in the human capital of the poor. These schemes include Employee Retraining Schemes for unemployed middle-aged workers, and the Youth Pre-employment Training Programme and the Youth Work Experience and Training Scheme for unemployed youth. However, the major outcome measure of these programs was the employment rate of the participants. The wage level of the participants had not been included as an indicator of program outcomes. The poverty alleviation effects of these schemes have been far from satisfactory. As a result, the unemployment rate decreased and the problems of the working poor worsened.

It should be acknowledged that the Hong Kong government has taken several important initiatives in response to the escalating concern over poverty. These include establishing a minimum wage in 2010, reestablishing the Commission on Poverty (CoP) in 2012, and the launching of the Old Age Living Allowance (OALA) for the aged in 2013. Furthermore, the government introduced the Low-income Family Allowance (LIFA) in 2016, which was targeted at working poor families and their children. It was renamed the Low-income Working Family Allowance in 2018. These policy initiatives have raised the incomes of many low-income families, but so far have failed to significantly lower the headline poverty rate.

In 2012, after the reestablishment of the CoP, the overall poverty rates before and after government intervention were 19.6 percent and 15.2 percent, respectively. In 2019, the corresponding poverty rates slightly increased to 21.4 percent and 16.8 percent. Although the poverty rates have not increased significantly, the size of poor households increased substantially from 541,000 to 649,000 (+20 percent), while the poor population increased from 1,312,300 to 1,490,700 (+13 percent). In other words, alleviating poverty in Hong Kong, if not totally eradicating it, cannot be achieved by the government's misled poverty alleviation policies, with their highly selective criteria and overwhelming workfare philosophy.

The New Bottles: Decisions Made by the Masters

Colonial heritage

Many HKSAR government officials were civil servants under British rule before 1997. Many of them admire and always want to resemble the British colonial heritage. Regina Ip, an ex-HKSAR government senior administrative officer, states, "Hong Kong's colonial masters bequeathed the city an effective rule of law, open markets, plus predictable and transparent governance" (Ip 2010). Ip reports that the Hong Kong government had remained small, and its elitist administrative service, staffed mainly by British officers, did not undergo a significant expansion until 1973; she cites these as the specific reasons for the successful story of Hong Kong (Ip 2010). Since 1973, more Chinese administrative officers were recruited to join the Hong Kong government. However, the political and important decisions of the Hong Kong government were still made principally by British masters; most administrative officers of Chinese origin were only responsible for implementing and fine-tuning social policy and were not responsible for political decisions on social policy.

The influence of the CCP after 1997

After the CPG resumed sovereignty over Hong Kong in 1997, it intended to practice the concept of "one country, two systems," in which the Hong Kong government would enjoy a high degree of autonomy. Nevertheless, due to the underdevelopment of political leadership among the civil servants of the Hong Kong government, the senior leaders of the government maintained their apolitical and pragmatic consideration, as well as the "get the job done" mentality (the slogan of Donald Tsang's second election). Consequently, the CPG replaced the British colonial government to become the real master in the Hong Kong political arena and is responsible for resolving conflicts of different interests and making final political decisions. However, this political reality has been accepted by the Hong Kong people. The reasons behind this are the growing dependency of Hong Kong's economic prosperity on China and the rise of a powerful China on the international scene.

The Hong Kong Transition Project conducted a survey in 2007, which showed that Hong Kong people think the Chinese Communist Party (CCP) has a significant influence over the Hong Kong government. According to the survey, 44 percent of respondents were very satisfied or somewhat satisfied with the CCP's general performance; 50.9 percent said they were not worried about CCP interference with Hong Kong affairs; and 51.6 percent felt there was "a great deal of" or "somewhat" interference of CCP over Hong Kong government (Lok 2010). These figures reflect that Hong Kong people notice the CCP's interference in the Hong Kong government and, to a certain degree, recognize its existence. The legislation of the minimum wage is a concrete example of the decisive influence of the CPG on social policy decision-making in Hong Kong.

The legislation of minimum wage

After 1997, among different groups of poor people, the surge of poverty attracted more attention. In 2006, 13.1 percent of the working population (418,600 workers) earned less than half of the median income of the working population (Wong 2007). Since 1997, to alleviate rising working poverty, unions, NGOs, and political parties have jointly urged the Hong Kong government to introduce a statutory minimum wage (SMW). However, the response of the Hong Kong government was negative and argued that the government should not intervene in the free labor market under the "big market, small government" philosophy.

The pros and cons of minimum wage legislation had been debated passionately in Hong Kong. Economists were the major opponents of a minimum wage. Many economists and the business sector claimed that a minimum wage system would distort the price mechanism of the labor market and increase unemployment (disemployment effect) among the least-skilled workers.

In 1998, the Hong Kong Social Security Society recommended that the Hong Kong government follow Singapore's example expeditiously by creating a wages council, fixing the level of a minimum wage, ratifying the International Labour Convention on Minimum Wage, and establishing a system of minimum wages in Hong Kong. The Hong Kong government gave the LegCo an official response to this proposal, which stated that the Hong Kong government "does not consider it appropriate for the government to set up any form of minimum wage in Hong Kong. In fact, any move to tamper with private sector decisions on wage setting is bound to be counter-productive" (Education and Manpower Bureau 1998).

In April 1999, May 2000, and April 2002, using different wordings, LegCo member Lee Cheuk-yan, a unionist from the Hong Kong Confederation of Trade Unions, moved three motions urging the administration to establish a minimum wage system. However, all three motions were rejected by the LegCo. In November 2004, the Council again rejected a motion moved by Chan Yuen-han, another unionist from the Hong Kong Federation of Trade Unions, who also urged the creation of minimum wage legislation.

Under increasing pressure from unions and labor organizations, the Hong Kong government agreed to reexamine the issue. In November 2004, the Economic Development and Labour Bureau and the Labour Department gave an official response to LegCo. In the paper, the Hong Kong government asserted, "Hong Kong is well known for its flexibility and manpower resource is our most valuable asset. To retain our competitiveness, we must strike a balance between maintaining Hong Kong's strengths in this respect and safeguarding the rights and benefits of our workforce" (Economic Development and Labour Bureau and the Labour Department 2004). This pronouncement restated that economic consideration was the basic tone of the government. In response to the rising pressure, the Hong Kong government agreed to the feasibility and desirability of introducing a statutory minimum wage in Hong Kong and assessed fully the socioeconomic implications of the proposal, both in the short and long term, as well as its merits and demerits. The response of the government can be described as "half-hearted" and "proactive," without a solid will to implement minimum wage in a short period.

It was not until December 2005, at the first report session of new CE Donald Tsang to the CPG, when Premier Wen Jiabao said in front of the media that Hong Kong had "deep-rooted contradictions." However, Wen did not specify the contradictions publicly. Many commentators speculated that the deep-rooted contradictions were the structural contradictions in the political, economic, and social arenas. Two of them were the discontent of the grassroots and the widening gap between the rich and the poor.

Undoubtedly, the order of the CPG to solve the "deep-rooted contradictions" created intense pressure on the Hong Kong government to address the livelihood problem of the poor. The small concessions given in the past cannot really solve the deep-rooted problems. In 2006, the Hong Kong government suddenly changed its negative stand on minimum wage and agreed to launch the "Wage Protection Movement" (WPM), a wage protection campaign operating through the voluntary participation of employers. However, the coverage of WPM is limited and only involves cleaning workers and security guards.

After two years of experimenting with WPM, Tsang considered the situation of WPM as unsatisfactory in October 2008; the government agreed to introduce legislation on statutory minimum wage (SMW) for employees in all trades and industries in the 2008–2009 legislative session. According to the government, the main purpose of SMW is to forestall the payment of excessively low wages, thereby protecting vulnerable groups that are prone to exploitation. The government established the Provisional Minimum Wage Commission in February 2009, whose main task is to advise the CE on the initial statutory minimum wage rate.

In December 2009, in another report session of Tsang, Premier Wen Jiabao reiterated Hong Kong's "deep-rooted contradictions." In March 2010, Wen specified Hong Kong's contradictions in five areas, including developing Hong Kong's economic strength, key industries, and cooperation with Pearl River Delta; creating an inclusive and consensus-driven political atmosphere and livelihood of people; and developing education. Wen's pronouncement confirmed that people's livelihood is one of the deep-rooted contradictions seen by the CPG.

After extensive debate, the LegCo voted in July 2010 to introduce a minimum wage in Hong Kong. On 10 November 2010, an hourly rate of HK$28 was recommended by the Provisional Minimum Wage Commission and adopted by the CE-in-Council.

Conclusion

The concepts "big market, small government," "appropriately proactive," and "roles of promoter and facilitator," upheld by different CEs of the Hong Kong government, are really the old wine in a new bottle. Social policy of the Hong Kong government still has the same economic pragmatism origin as its colonial past. Moreover, the Hong Kong government had to follow the decisions of the British colonial government before 1997, and the Hong Kong government has to follow the guidelines of the CPG after 1997.

During the 1997 Asian financial crisis and the increasing demand for social services, the Hong Kong government's immediate response was to cut services and reduce benefits to balance the budget. This was a short-term, shortsighted measure that intensified the problems of health, housing, and poverty in Hong Kong. Consequently, the discontent of the poor and the middle class increased, and created the so-called "anti-rich" sentiment and other social unrests.

The Hong Kong government recognizes the growing discontent of Hong Kong people. However, it blames the society for lack of consensus on different policy suggestions to solve the discontent. Professor Lau Siu-kai, former head of the Central Policy Unit, summarizes the policy suggestions for solving the problem of intensified social conflicts: tax reform; land and housing policy changes; new economic growth engines; traditional industry support; faster democratization; improvement of government's governance; and increase in social welfare and social services. However, the public is also concerned with these social contradictions and stability problems. There is no consensus on how to handle the problems, which creates a feeling of being "confined in a worrisome city" (Lau 2010).

Are Hong Kong people or just the government officials confined in a worrisome city? Without a mission and vision of future development in Hong Kong, without a rational and systematic planning process, and without political leadership to handle conflicts, the social policy in Hong Kong maintains its piecemeal, pragmatic, and problem-solving nature as in the colonial past.

The Hong Kong government tends to wait for the CPG to take political leadership in handling the rising class conflicts. It is a shame because the CPG already has a pile of important and urgent problems and conflicts to handle. As the most developed city in China, Hong Kong has a low-cost health and public housing system and a well-developed social security system; moreover, it has a valuable strength and asset in its people, who should have confidence in themselves.

According to the principle of "one country, two systems," the Hong Kong government should have the will to govern. A more comprehensive, long-term, and people-oriented planning for social policy should be adopted with the greater participation of civil society to help Hong Kong people enjoy life with better health care, housing, and social security. The latest strategy of the Hong Kong government to further integrate Hong Kong into the development of the Bay Area and Mainland China can only offer a vague framework. To date, it remains unable to provide solid grounding for formulating a people-oriented social policy.

Box 13.1: Key social policy developments since 1997

Education	Education voucher for preschool children
	New 3.3.4 academic structure of senior secondary education
	Debate on small-class teaching
Health	Harvard Review and severe acute respiratory syndrome (SARS) test the system
	Elderly Health Care Voucher
	Health Protection Scheme–Voluntary Health Insurance Scheme (VHIS)
	District Health Centre (DHC)

Housing	Cease production and sale of Home Ownership Scheme (HOS)
	New rent-to-buy My Home
	Purchase Plan to replace HOS
	Relaunch HOS
	Long Term Housing Strategy (LTHS)
Social Welfare	Cutting of Comprehensive Social Security Assistance (CSSA) budget and promoting self-reliance
	Increasing poverty and gap between the rich and the poor; anti-rich sentiment
	Set up the Commission on Poverty
	Old Age Living Allowance (OALA)
	Low-income Working Family Allowance (LIFA) / Working Family Allowance (WFA)
Labor	Expansion of youth training and placement schemes
	Legislation of minimum wage

Questions

1. Does Hong Kong have a social policy? Have there been any changes in social policy since 1997?
2. What are the political, economic, and social factors that affect the development of social policy in Hong Kong? How do these factors interact with each other?
3. Will the CPG exert greater influence in determining social policy in Hong Kong? How would you see such influence?

Bibliography

Chiu, S 2003, "Local Policy in Global Politics: The Limit of Anti-Poverty Policy in Hong Kong," *Journal of Social Policy and Social Work*, vol. 7, no. 2, pp. 171–203.

Commission on Poverty 2007, *Report of the Commission on Poverty*, Commission on Poverty, HKSAR Government, Hong Kong.

Dorwart, RA 1971, *The Prussian Welfare State Before 1740*, Harvard University Press, Cambridge, MA.

Economic Development and Labour Bureau and the Labour Department 2004, *The Proposal for a Minimum Wage in Hong Kong*, paper resented in LegCo Panel on Manpower on 4 November 2004, Legislative Council, Hong Kong.

Education and Manpower Bureau 1998, *The Administration's Views on the "Proposal on Minimum Wage in Hong Kong" Put forward by the Hong Kong Social Security Society*, paper presented in LegCo Panel on Manpower on 29 October 1998, Legislative Council, Hong Kong.

Food and Health Bureau 2008, *Be Strong: Your Health, Your Life. The Healthcare Reform Consultation Document*, Food and Health Bureau, Hong Kong.

Food and Health Bureau 2010, *My Health My Choice: Healthcare Reform Second Stage Public Consultation Document*, Food and Health Bureau, Hong Kong.

Gauld, R 2005, "Exposing the Cracks: SARS and the Hong Kong Health System," *Journal of Health Organization and Medicine*, vol. 19, no. 2. pp. 106–119.

Harvard Team 1999, *Improving Hong Kong's Health Care System: Why and For Whom?* Hong Kong SAR Government, Hong Kong.

Health and Welfare Bureau 2000, *Lifelong Investment in Health: Consultation Document on Health Care Reform*, Health and Welfare Bureau, Hong Kong.

HKU Public Opinion Programme 2010, *Updated Report on Citizen's Expectation on Policy Address of the Chief Executive Donald Tsang*, 11 October, HKU Public Opinion Programme (in Chinese), Hong Kong.

Holliday, I 2000, "Productivist Welfare Capitalism: Social Policy in East Asia," *Political Studies*, vol. 48, no. 4, pp. 706–723.

Hong Kong Council of Social Service 2010, *Poverty Rate in Hong Kong*, http://www.poverty.org.hk/uploads/Poverty_Rate95-10_1stH.pdf

Hong Kong Institute of Asia-Pacific Studies, the Chinese University of Hong Kong 2010, *Result of the Opinion Poll about Social Harmony in Hong Kong*, 8 April, http://www.cuhk.edu.hk/cpr/pressrelease/100408_2.htm

Ip, R 2010, *Hong Kong after 1997—Agony and Ecstasy*, April http://www.hkjournal.org/archive/2010_summer/3.htm

Jones, C 1990, *Promoting Prosperity: The Hong Kong Way of Social Policy*, the Chinese University Press of Hong Kong, Hong Kong.

Kwon, HJ 2005, *Transforming the Developmental Welfare State in East Asia*, Social Policy and Development Programme, Paper No. 22, United Nations Research Institute for Social Development, Geneva.

Lam, C 2017, *The Chief Executive's Policy Address 2017: We Connect for Hope and Happiness*, Hong Kong SAR Government, Hong Kong.

Lau, SK 2010, "Comment on Opinion Poll about Social Harmony by CUHK," *Ming Pao*, 10 April, p. B14 (in Chinese).

Lee, J 2022, *The Chief Executive's Policy Address 2022: Charting a Brighter Tomorrow for Hong Kong*, Hong Kong SAR Government, Hong Kong.

Leung, CY 2013, *The Policy Address 2013: Seek Change, Maintain Stability, Serve the People with Pragmatism*, Hong Kong SAR Government, Hong Kong.

Loh, C 2010, *Underground Front: The Chinese Communist Party in Hong Kong*, Hong Kong University Press, Hong Kong.

Oxfam Hong Kong 2010, *Oxfam Poverty Report: Employment and Poverty in Hong Kong Families*, Oxfam Hong Kong, Hong Kong.

Patten, C 1996, *Hong Kong, Transition: The 1996 Policy Address*, Hong Kong Government Printer, Hong Kong.

Suen, M 2002, *A Statement on Housing Policy at the LegCo Housing Panel on 2 November 1992*, Legislative Council, Hong Kong.

Transport and Housing Bureau 2007, *Home Ownership Scheme and Tenants Purchase Scheme*, paper presented at LegCo Panel on Housing Legislative on 7 January 2008, Legislative Council, Hong Kong.

Tsang, D 2006, *The 2006-07 Policy Address: Proactive, Pragmatic, Always People First*, Hong Kong SAR Government, Hong Kong.

Tsang, DYK 2007, *The 2007-08 Policy Address: A New Direction for Hong Kong*, Hong Kong SAR Government, Hong Kong.

Tsang, D 2010, *The 2010-11 Policy Address: Sharing Prosperity for a Caring Society*, Hong Kong SAR Government, Hong Kong.

Tung, CH 1997, *The Policy Address 1997: Building Hong Kong for a New Era*, Hong Kong SAR Government, Hong Kong.

Tung, CH 2000, *The Policy Address 2000: Serving the Community, Sharing Common Goals*, Hong Kong SAR Government, Hong Kong.

Walker, A & Wong, CK (eds) 2005, *East Asian Welfare Regimes in Transition: From Confucianism to Globalisation*, Policy Press, Bristol, UK.

Wilding, P 2007, "Social Policy," in WM Lam, PLT Lui, W Wong and I Holliday (eds), *Contemporary Hong Kong Politics: Governance in the Post-1997 Era*, Hong Kong University Press, Hong Kong.

Wong, H 2007, "Misled Intervention by a Misplaced Diagnosis: The Hong Kong SAR Government's Policies for Alleviating Poverty and Social Exclusion," *China Review*, vol. 7, no. 2, pp. 124–147.

Useful Websites

Budget Speech Archive
http://www.budget.gov.hk/2010/eng/previous.html

Census and Statistics
http://www.censtatd.gov.hk/home/index.jsp

Government Information
http://www.gov.hk

Legislative Council
http://www.legco.gov.hk

Policy Address Archive
http://www.policyaddress.gov.hk/10-11/eng/archives.html

Poverty: Oxfam Hong Kong
http://www.oxfam.org.hk/en/default.aspx

Social Security: Hong Kong Council of Social Service
http://www.hkcss.org.hk/pra/list_of_recommendations_e.htm

Further Reading

J England & J Rear's *Industrial Relations and Law in Hong Kong* (Oxford University Press 1990) is a good introduction to the influence of British and Chinese politics on the development of postwar industrial relations and politics in Hong Kong.

For the background on the social policy system and issues before 1997, look at P Wilding et al. (eds), *Social Policy in Hong Kong* (Edward Elgar 1997). For the influence of colonial history on social security policy, look at CW Chan's book *Social Security Policy in Hong Kong* (Lexington Books 2011).

The more recent books that locate Hong Kong in the East Asian context include I Holliday and P Wilding (eds), *Welfare Capitalism in East Asia* (Palgrave Macmillan 2003); M Ramesh, *Social Policy in East and Southeast Asia* (Routledge Curzon 2004); and J Midgley and KL Tang (eds), *Social Policy and Poverty in East Asia: The Role of Social Security* (Routledge 2010).

For a comparison of the social policy systems of Hong Kong and other Chinese societies, refer to CK Wong, KL Tang and NP Ngai, *Social Policies in Comparative Perspective: How They Fare in Chinese Societies* (in Chinese) (the Chinese University Press of Hong Kong 2007).

For social development and social conditions, refer to R Estes (ed), *Social Development in Hong Kong: The Unfinished Agenda* (Oxford University Press 2005). For the governance of the HKSAR government, see M Sing, *Politics and Government in Hong Kong: Crisis under Chinese Sovereignty* (Taylor and Francis 2009).

For a detailed analysis of health care, look at Gauld's chapter in R Gauld (ed), *Comparative Health Policy in Asia Pacific* (Open University Press 2005), and G Leung and J Bacon-Shone (eds), *Hong Kong's Health System: Reflections, Perspectives and Visions* (Hong Kong University Press 2006).

For the historical development of housing policy, read YM Yeung and TKY Wong (eds), *50 Years of Public Housing: A Golden Jubilee Review and Appraisal* (Hong Kong Institute of Asia Pacific Studies, the Chinese University of Hong Kong 2003). On the relationship of social justice and housing policy, see B Yeung, *Hong Kong's Housing Policy: A Case Study in Social Justice* (Hong Kong University Press 2010).

For an analysis of social welfare in Hong Kong, look at CK Wong's "Squaring the Welfare Circle in Hong Kong: Lessons for Governance in Social Policy," *Asian Survey*, vol. 48, no. 2, 2008, pp. 323–342. On the impact of the financial tsunami on Hong Kong's social security system, look at KM Lee and KY Law's "The Financial Tsunami: Economic Insecurity and Social Protection in Hong Kong," *Development*, vol. 53, no. 1, 2010, pp. 83–90.

To understand the contributing factors to the situation of worsening poverty since 1997, see different reports of Oxfam Hong Kong and Hong Kong Council of Social Service, including H Wong and HW Chua, *An Exploratory Study on Termination and Reactivation of CSSA Cases* (Hong Kong Council of Social Service and Oxfam 1998); H Wong and KM Lee, *Exclusion and Future: A Qualitative Study of Marginal Workers in Hong Kong* (Oxfam 2001); Hong Kong Council of Social Service, *Growing Seriousness in Poverty and Income Disparity* (HKCSS 2004); and H Wong, *Employed, but Poor: Poverty among Employed People in Hong Kong* (Oxfam Hong Kong 2007).

14

Urban Policy

Governing Asia's World City—Ready for a Paradigm Shift toward People, Place, and Planet-Friendly Urban Development?

Ng Mee Kam

Introduction: New Urban Agenda, Sustainable Development Goals, and Hong Kong

The New Urban Agenda (United Nations 2017) was adopted by heads of state and government, ministers, and private sector and civil society delegates at the United Nations Conference on Housing and Sustainable Development (Habitat III) on 20 October 2016. The New Urban Agenda (Box 14.1) calls for a paradigm shift in urban planning, development, and management to achieve the Sustainable Development Goals (SDGs) (Box 14.2). The SDGs aim to transform the world by 2030, and it is a plan of action for people, planet, and prosperity through peace and partnership (UN 2015) (Figure 14.1). It invites transformative actions to solve the world's growing inequalities, the persistence of multiple forms of poverty and social and spatial vulnerability and marginalization (UN 2017). Numerous states, intergovernmental organizations, expert groups, NGOs, and networks participated in the shaping of the New Urban Agenda, and its adoption by many parties in Quito represents probably one of the strongest messages made so far in the twenty-first century: a vote of no confidence in the results of the human race's development pathway unleashed by the Industrial Revolution since the end of the eighteenth century. The carbon-intensive development has not only damaged the environment leading to climate crisis and global warming (IPCC 2014), but it has also produced polarized societies and less than healthy human beings in many parts of the world (Oxfam 2017). The New Urban Agenda, therefore, emphasizes "transformative actions."

Ng Mee Kam 341

Figure 14.1: The 17 SDGs
Source: Modified from UN 2015.

Similar to many other metropolises, Hong Kong, self-identified as Asia's World City, has been facing challenging urban issues. Many of these issues are related to its legacies as a British colony and a specific brand of "state-led liberal capitalism" that focuses on economic growth. To move from her current state toward the fulfilment of the New Urban Agenda, there is a need for concerted tripartite efforts by the now multilevel governments, the private sector, and the civil society to integrate ecological and social justice considerations during economic and spatial development.

The following outlines key dimensions extracted from the New Urban Agenda that aim to fulfil the 17 SDGs. Section 3 audits the work of the government of Hong Kong against the transformative commitments outlined in the New Urban Agenda (Section 2). A brief overview of the characteristics of Hong Kong's urban development—an urban biased mode of development bequeathed by the colonizers and the government's reliance on land and property-related revenue mean that some people, some places, and ecological concerns are being "left behind." Section 4 offers some bold suggestions to transform the urban policies to address the city's fundamental, structural spatial problems.

Implementing the SDGs in the New Urban Agenda

According to the IPCC (2014: 90), "urban areas accounted for 67–76% of global energy use and 71–76% of global energy-related CO2 emissions," and without mitigation, global mean surface temperature will increase from 3.7°C to 4.8°C by 2100 (2014: 8). Ever since the start of the industrial revolution, urban areas have released huge quantities of greenhouse gases through concentrated industrial and urban developments (Bulkeley et al. 2011). Indeed, it is reported that the average carbon footprint of "the richest 1% globally could be as much as 175 times that of the poorest 10%" (Raworth 2012: 5). About half of global carbon emissions are generated by only 11 percent of the world's population (Raworth 2012: 5). While cities are part of the climate change problem, they are also a key part of the solution if integrated policies are in place (IPCC 2014: 25; UN-Habitat 2011). The United Nations estimated that by 2050, urban population in Asia alone will increase by 61 percent; that is, 1.28 billion (2014: 12 and 36). Hence, the way these cities are built will be vital for humankind to combat the climate crisis.

Not only should we build more environmentally friendly cities, but it is also important for us to tackle the issue of socioeconomic polarization. According to Oxfam (2017: 2), "8 men . . . own the same wealth as the poorest half of the world." This latter group, the poorest half of the global population, received only 1 percent of the increase in global wealth, half of which went to the top 1 percent of the world population (Oxfam 2016: 2–3). It seems that we have been building an economy for the 1 percent, and it is all because of the increasing return to capital instead of productive labor work, thanks to the trends of globalization, neoliberalism, and deregulation, as well as the existence of a network of tax havens that "rob" states and poor countries of the resources for development (Oxfam 2016: 5–7). According to Raworth (2012: 5), "nearly 900 million people face hunger, 1.4 billion live on less than US$1.25 a day, and 2.7 billion have no access to clean cooking facilities."

These figures have a clear implication: there is a need to reframe and refine our value systems in urban development so that the goal of development is to eradicate poverty, bringing "everyone above the social foundation, and reducing global resource use, to bring it back within planetary boundaries" (Raworth 2012: 5). In other words, it is to use resources efficiently to satisfy people's needs and capability development (Nussbaum 1997–1998), leaving no one behind (United Nations 2017). The World Bank (2010: p.v) highlights the importance of governance in managing cities, mobilizing "a global array of stakeholders" to provide additional financing, foster partnership, and reform various policy sectors. The United Nations Development Programme (2009: 43) argues that governments continue to play a central role in establishing "the overall normative and regulatory framework" according to sustainability principles such as the precautionary principle and the principle of subsidiarity.

The New Urban Agenda, a result of concerted efforts by 193 United Nations member states and thousands of stakeholder organizations around the world, has three key principles: leaving no one, no place, and no ecology behind; that is, providing equal access for all to infrastructure and basic services, embracing sustainable and inclusive urban economies, and promoting environmental sustainability (United Nations 2017). This will require strong commitments in the planning, financing, development, governance, and management of cities to adopt sustainable, people-centered, age- and gender-responsive, inclusive and integrated approaches to socioeconomic and environmental urban and rural developments at different geographical scales (United Nations 2017: 3–7), and the purpose is to achieve the 17 SDGs.

To achieve the New Urban Agenda, it is important to build a supportive urban governance structure that can generate integrated multi-scalar territorial planning and development through inclusive, implementable, participatory, and integrated urban polices (United Nations 2017: 12). The New Urban Agenda also highlights the importance of the principle of subsidiarity in empowering local governments to work with different stakeholders to meet local needs through fiscal, political, and administrative decentralization (United Nations 2017: 12).

Integrated planning and its implementation are stressed in the New Urban Agenda. It is not just the urban areas that need planning. In fact, it is important to have sustainable urban and territorial planning that promotes "equitable growth of regions across the urban-rural continuum" (United Nations 2017: 13).

The New Urban Agenda prioritizes regeneration and retrofitting of urban areas rather than spatial segregation and gentrification (United Nations 2017: 13). Urban planning strategies should aim to provide safe, accessible, green, climate-proof, and quality public spaces that are friendly to local economies and communities (United Nations 2017: 14). It is important for cities to realize people's right to affordable housing, sustainable modes of transportation, water and sanitation utilities, energy services, and culture and heritage conservation (United Nations 2017: 14–17).

An enabling environment is required for implementing the New Urban Agenda. An integrated financing framework is required for implementing the plan—a framework that can capture the benefits of urbanization and is flexible enough to practice redistribution to achieve the SDGs and the New Urban Agenda (United Nations 2017: 18). One suggested best practice is to "capture and share the increase in land and property value generated as a result of urban development processes, infrastructure projects and public investments" (United Nations 2017: 18). Financial tools should be available to provide affordable housing, climate- and disaster-proofing, and capacity building at all levels and in different sectors (United Nations 2017: 19). The latter would require collaboration among governments at different levels—civil society organizations, the private sector, professionals, academia, and research institutions—to leverage knowledge exchange, science, technology, and innovation to practice and promote evidence-based governance and smart city development that "foster the creation, promotion and enhancement of open, user-friendly, and participatory data platforms" (United Nations 2017: 19–20).

In the face of increasingly uncertain climate conditions and progressively polarized socioeconomic realities, the adoption of the above measures in governing, planning, and managing urban development will hopefully foster the integration of natural, human, social, financial, and physical capital in cities, boosting their ability to mobilize resources to respond to changes and to transform into a more sustainable state (Maguire and Cartwright 2008: 10). However, as argued by Bulkeley et al. (2011: 30), such a reframing of the goal of development would require "the reconfiguration of socio-technical networks" that is bound to be "highly political and open to contestation and disruption." Existing vested interests may resist a paradigm shift toward an ecological and humane urbanism that allows the development of an economy for the 99 percent rather than the 1 percent (Oxfam 2016 and 2017). Hence, it is even more important for local communities to learn to work together and build up their capacities through, among other things, practicing procedural justice: respecting minority views, demanding access to information and decision-making processes, and acknowledging people's equal right to participation and decision-making (Pelling 2011: 77). In other words, the paradigm shift toward a more progressive and sustainable future demands a deep collective reflection on the existing development trajectory, challenging and reshaping its underlying values through social learning, mutual trust, and self-organizing socioeconomic and spatial experiments (Brown 2014; Pelling 2011; Wilkinson 2012).

Urban Policies in Hong Kong: "Leaving No One, No Place, and No Ecology Behind"?

Hong Kong's colonial past has bequeathed three characteristics that make the achievement of the New Urban Agenda difficult, if not impossible. The British colonial government had avoided strategic planning and development of the ceded New Territories, where the majority of Hong Kong land lies. The (colonial) government's reliance on land and property-related incomes has privileged certain economic sectors and sustained the problem of housing shortage. A growth-at-all-costs mentality has trivialized ecological concerns in the policy deliberation processes.

Urban bias: Concentrated development in former ceded territories during the colonial era

People's usual image of Hong Kong is a concrete jungle. Few realize that less than 25 percent of its land (comprising Hong Kong Island, Kowloon, and new towns), which houses 90 percent of its population, is used for development. This gives rise to a population density of about 26,000 per km^2 (Ng et al. 2021). Many would attribute such a high density to 40 percent of the land being zoned as country parks and other conservation areas. Yet a quick calculation naturally leads to a logical question: What has happened to the other 35 percent of the land? This 35 percent, or about 389 km^2 (38,900 ha) of land, is often referred to as the rural New Territories (with village-type settlements, brownfield sites [Box 14.3], agricultural land, and green belts, etc.). The rural New Territories is home to less than 10 percent of the city's population, giving rise to a population density of about 1,100 per km^2 (excluding country parks) (Ng et al. 2023). Why would "Asia's world city," where property price tops the world (Simpson 2020), allow most of its non-conserved land to be used so inefficiently?

Hong Kong's urban-biased policy has to do with its history as a British colony. Throughout its former colonial status, development had been confined to Hong Kong Island, Kowloon, and new towns. While the new towns were mostly built on reclaimed land along the coastal areas of the New Territories, Hong Kong Island and Kowloon were territories that had been ceded to the British government in two stages in 1841 and 1860 (Figure 14.2). The New Territories (occupying over 80 percent of land in Hong Kong), however, was leased to Britain

Figure 14.2: Hong Kong Island, Kowloon, and the New Territories

by China in 1898 for 99 years only; hence, the colonial government had largely avoided adopting strategic planning and development in the New Territories. The urban expansion of new towns into the New Territories through coastal reclamation was a necessary move for housing construction then, to pacify a rather restless society after the riots in 1966 and 1967. Throughout the postwar decades, the government worked with the Heung Yee Kuk (comprising heads of rural committees), a statutory advisory body representing established interests in the New Territories to govern its development.

Except for new towns or new development areas (Figure 14.2) that may sporadically affect land developments in the rural New Territories, the government has not undertaken holistic or comprehensive planning for the massive land resources there. In fact, urban planning was not extended to the New Territories until the 1990s. And as of today, about nine percent of land area in Hong Kong (mostly in the New Territories) is not planned. The lack of urban planning in the once rural New Territories could be understood then. The New Territories had very active farming activities in the postwar era up to the 1980s. In 1971, 50 percent of vegetables consumed in Hong Kong were produced in the New Territories (Chiu and Hung 1991: 32). However, this does not mean that the government had done nothing in the New Territories. To harness water resources, an important ingredient for the survival of the colony in the face of communist China, the government had implemented various water-related infrastructure projects throughout the New Territories (Lee 2014). In fact, over the years, active rural land uses such as farming have been shrinking due to the construction of reservoirs or water catchment areas (that diverted water supply), deepening of rivers (that reverse the flow of water from rivers to water the fields), pollution control (which led to the closure of chicken and pig farms), and, in recent decades, sprawling brownfield sites.

Also in 1972, when the government was actively planning to build new towns along coastal areas in the New Territories, the "small house policy" was introduced to pacify the indigenous population, as some of their land had to be resumed by the government to develop new towns. The small house policy allows every male descendant of the indigenous population (whose ancestors dwelled in the New Territories before the arrival of the British colonial government in 1898) to build a house of no more than 25 feet in height (up to three stories) and 700 ft^2 of covered area (Chan 1998: 64). These houses are exempted from the Buildings Ordinance, and if the villagers do not own land such as agricultural land that could be converted into housing sites, they could, once in their lifetime, apply for land on a private treaty grant and pay a concessionary premium of 2/3 of the full market value to build their "small house" (Goo 2014: 381). The small house policy has created a lot of controversies, as many have used this right for monetary gain (Goo 2014: 381) and a lot of land has been zoned in the rural New Territories for small house development. According to the official figures (Planning Department 2020), rural settlements cover 35 km^2 of land (housing less than 10 percent of the population), whereas private and public housing (mostly in urban areas) cover 42 km^2 of land (housing over 6.7 million people).

However, a major reason for the extension of urban planning to the once rural New Territories was not due to the water works or small house policy. Instead, it had to do with a court case related to land-use changes on farmland. The 1983 Melhado case involved the government's prosecution of the Melhado Company, which stored construction materials on farmland. The court ruled that the old "block crown lease" (now called "block government lease") (Box 14.4) had no land-use control function, and the ruling resulted in the mushrooming of "brownfield sites" in the New Territories (Hong Kong Case Law 2016). Thousands of hectares of agricultural land were then converted into storage grounds or dumping sites for containers, construction materials, etc., as China required an enormous amount of construction materials to fuel her industrialization and urbanization processes.

In 2019, a government-commissioned report estimated a total of 1,414 ha of brownfield sites in the New Territories (ARUP and Planning Department 2019: 19). And the conversion of agricultural land into brownfield sites has been increasing, especially in areas with accessible transportation networks. The current Chairman of the Heung Yee Kuk had suggested that the optimal use of "Tso-tong land" (housing or agricultural land owned by family and clan trusts that amounts to over 2,000 ha) in the New Territories was for public or private housing construction (Lau 2018). The existence of these different sources of land supply in the New Territories has not been discussed until recently (Task Force on Land Supply 2018). In a study that commenced in the 2010s, the government commissioned a consultant to identify suitable reclamation sites and rock cavern (through blasting hills) developments (CEDD and ARUP 2014), but nothing on the use of land in the New Territories. Why is the government so reluctant to adopt a more proactive approach to replan the New Territories? Besides the legacy of the New Territories as leased territory to the British colonial government, it has to do with a unique mode of financing and governance in Hong Kong.

Government: Growth-at-all-costs mentality with biased interests in land-related endeavors

The mode of governance in Hong Kong has not changed much, even though the postcolonial Special Administrative Region has been returned to Chinese rule for more than two decades. It is still very much an executive government-led polity supporting a "liberal" economy that has increasingly been dominated by the interests of property tycoons in a speculative economy (Goodstadt 2005; Poon 2005). Unlike some Western countries, Hong Kong has never developed into a welfare state, and hence discourses on the "rolling back" of the welfare state and the "rolling out" of neoliberal economic practices are quite irrelevant to the city's development. The government has always claimed that it has adopted a "small government, big market" approach and refrained from developing any socio-economic development strategy. However, in reality the 170,000 strong civil service has consumed about 30 percent of the government's operating expenditure. Another 30 percent is spent on capital works and "other charges" (possibly charges for consultancies) (Census and Statistics Department, various years). And on average, less than 30 percent of the government's budget is used to subvent education, health, social welfare, etc. (Census and Statistics Department, various years).

Even though for more than 20 years Hong Kong has been voted "the world's freest economy" (Heritage Foundation 2016), the city is under the hegemonic rule of the government and the private sector. For many years, about 20 to 30 percent of the government's revenue has come from land sales and property-related developments (Census and Statistics Department, various years), implying its necessary partnership with a super-rich "landlord" class (Ng 2015; Poon 2005). According to Parkes (2017):

> Hong Kong's wealthiest families, those almost mythical tycoons, dominate and collude on land ownership, local utilities, transport services and even the supermarkets.

And this can be done because of an undemocratic political setup at that time: the Chief Executive (CE) was elected by a 1,200-member Election Committee (dominated by the rich and powerful); the CE nominated all the principal officials and appointed the most important policymaking body, the Executive Council; and the Legislative Council election process was designed in such a way that 30 of its 70 seats were given to "functional constituencies" representing business and professional sectors, and their eligible voters made up only 6.2 percent of registered voters (Pepper 2016). Yet even this barely "democratic" system is disappearing. In China's 2021 National People's Congress, it passed a "Decision on Improving the Electoral System of the Hong Kong Special Administrative Region": the Election Committee was expanded to 1,500 members; Hong Kong's Legislative Council (LegCo) was expanded to 90 seats, comprising members elected by the Election Committee (40 seats) and those returned by direct election (20 seats) and functional constituencies (30 seats); and a new "Candidate Eligibility Review Committee" was set up to scrutinize candidates for CE, LegCo positions, and the Election Committee. The whole move is to ensure that Hong Kong is ruled by "patriots."

While the New Urban Agenda calls for stronger coordination within the government and between the government and the civil society, as well as the private sector, the political setup in Hong Kong is top-down and rather compartmentalized, with little devolution of power. There are 18 local District Councils with directly elected members, but these councils are only advisory in nature. With the mass resignation of district councillors after the introduction of the National Security Law in 2020, and the setting up of District Services and Community Care Teams in the 18 districts and the gazettal of the District Councils (Amendment) Bill in May 2023, it is very likely that the District Councils will be filled with "patriots" to aid the executive-led governance in Hong Kong. In any case, the amount of resources dedicated to the local level is very minimal, accounting for only 0.15 percent of the government's total operating budget (HKSAR 2020). As a result, the city does not practice the principle of subsidiarity, nor does it have a participatory mode of governance.

According to the New Urban Agenda, integrated urban and territorial planning can be instrumental in ensuring balanced and equitable spatial developments that cater to the needs of various socioeconomic, transportation, natural, and cultural conservation needs (United Nations 2017). However, administratively, the land-use planning system in Hong Kong is differentiated from the planning for transport, housing, environment, heritage conservation, or urban renewal. Unlike China, the city has no socioeconomic planning and the government can "hide" behind a facade of "small government, big market" rhetoric. In reality, the government has a vested interest in maintaining a high land price policy to sustain the public coffer. This may explain why the government has been very cautious in applying strategic planning in the New Territories, especially in releasing the development potential of its land resources, lest abundant land supply would disrupt the land market.

Yet, as mentioned, the government had initiated developments in the New Territories before. From the 1970s to the 1990s, Hong Kong underwent massive spatial restructuring as the then-colonial government tried to react to the riots in the 1960s and pacify a restless urban society with many social problems, especially poor housing conditions. A 10-year housing program was in place and was carried out via massive new town developments, primarily through reclaiming land from the sea along coastal areas in the New Territories. Land held by the indigenous villagers was resumed, turning many former farmers into urbanites. Since all land created on reclaimed land automatically belongs to the government, it has always been a preferred development option. New town development and urban redevelopment have led to continuous relocation of the local population in the past few decades, giving rise to the "eclipse of the local community" (Chui 2003).

All in all, it can be argued that the executive government-led undemocratic polity has been developing a property-led speculative economy centered around a psyche of land scarcity through restraining development in the New Territories, and the reclamation of land from the sea. Although there has been an awakening of civil society to reflect on the fundamental values of various development issues (Ku and Pun 2004; Chiu and Lui 1999; Ng, 2015, 2016, 2020), the momentum is not yet strong enough to reshape the underlying ethos of development. Under these contexts, we would like to conduct an audit of Hong Kong's urban development with reference to the New Urban Agenda.

Left behind in "Asia's world city": The poor and the old

Hong Kong is one of the most socioeconomically polarized cities in the world. In 2015, the post-social transfer and post-tax Gini Coefficient was 0.473 (Oxfam 2018: 16). In 2016, monthly household income of the top 1 percent was 43.9 times of that of the bottom 10 percent (Oxfam 2018: 11). According to the Census and Statistics Department (2020a: 21), after policy interventions, the total number of poor households was 287,400, with a total population of 641,500 or 9.2 percent of Hong Kong's population. As of October 2020, 319,300 people were recipients of the CSSA, and 76,700 households joined the Working Family Allowance scheme (Census and Statistics Department 2020a: 4). Poverty rates for the elderly after all policy interventions dropped from 32 percent (391,200) to 19.7 percent (Census and Statistics Department 2020a: 31, 36). In any case, 37 percent of the poor population in Hong Kong are the elderly (Census and Statistics Department 2020a: 37), and 32.5 percent of poor households are economically active (Census and Statistics Department 2020a: 38). Besides recurrent and non-recurrent cash allowances, in-kind benefits such as public rental housing have proven to be effective in reducing poverty, cutting the poverty rate by 3.7 percent (Census and Statistics Department 2020a: 36). While 35 percent of poor elders are living in public rental housing, only about 10 percent of poor households are living in such housing (Census and Statistics Department 2020a: 38, 47). In other words, about half a million of the poor population are not living in public rental housing, and it is highly likely that they are being left behind in terms of housing.

Given the government's "vested interests" in maintaining high land prices and property values, housing has always been a controversial issue in the city. On one hand, Hong Kong boasts a rather sizable public housing sector by international standards, housing 2.19 million (29.5 percent) in 834,200 public rental housing units and 1.14 million (15.4 percent) in 421,500 sales subsidized flats (HKHA 2020: 2; THB 2020: 2). In 2020, the number of applications for public rental housing was 153,000 (HKHA 2020: 5). On the other hand, the city has 226,340 people (about 3 percent) living in 100,943 sub-divided units within 29,897 quarters (THB 2021: 4). The majority of these quarters are in buildings over 50 years old, and about half do not have an owners' organization nor a property management company (THB 2021: 4). The median per capita floor area in these accommodations is 6.6m^2 (THB 2021: 4). The average rent per square foot (HK$41.7) they are paying is close to one-third higher than small domestic flats in the New Territories and Kowloon (from HK$30–37 per square foot), and landlords usually charge exorbitant fees for utilities, such as HK$13 per unit of water (when the highest tier of high water consumption is only $9.05 per cubic meter) and $1.5 per unit for electricity (when the utility companies are charging less than this) (THB 2021: 4–5). It was only in 2020 that the government set up a Task Force to study possible tenancy control of subdivided units. To ameliorate the dire housing needs of these people, the government has also committed to providing 15,000 transitional housing units (built by NGOs) in three years' time and 30,000 units of light public housing (built by government) in five years' time (Ng et al. 2023). Never has the government been so determined to tackle the housing issues of the inadequately housed households that amount to 122,000 (besides subdivided units, 21,600 households live in temporary structures, 5,600

352   Urban Policy

households live in non-residential buildings and 5,800 households live in shared units) (THB 2020: 4).

Given the dire housing situation in Hong Kong, it is interesting to note that in the government's Long Term Housing Strategy, it has planned to provide 1,430 units per year for buyers outside Hong Kong who do not sell or lease their units. And the city has done nothing with vacant units. According to the Housing Bureau (2022), in 2021, the number of public housing, subsidized sale flats, and private permanent housing units exceeded the number of households living in public housing, subsidized sale flats, and private permanent housing by 34,000, 25,000, and 236,000, respectively. While it is true that the government has tried to build "new development areas" in different parts of the New Territories (Table 14.1 and Figure 14.2), there continues to be a lack of holistic and comprehensive planning for the New Territories as a whole. Instead of rationalizing land uses in the New Territories where over 80 percent of the land resources lie, the government has pushed for the "Lantau Tomorrow Vision" involving the reclamation of a number of artificial islands (totaling 1,700 ha) outside the boundary of the Protection of the Harbour Ordinance (CEDD 2020). Reclamation of land from the sea, of course, incurs much less trouble compared to resuming land in the New Territories and a need to negotiate with different stakeholders.

The city also faces the challenging trend of an aging population. Besides the fact that more than a third of the poor population are elderly and two-thirds of them are not housed in public rental flats, it is estimated that the demand for long-term care services will increase from around 60,000 places in 2016 to 78,000 places in 2030, peaking at 2051 (125,000 places) (Elderly Commission 2017: 10). To meet the rising need of elderly care services, the Elderly Commission develops a model to encourage active aging, community support, community care, and, as the frailty and care needs increase, residential care and end-of-life care (Elderly Commission 2017: 16). In other words, concerted efforts are made to allow "aging-in-place" of the elderly population through the development of age-friendly environments, the promotion of retirement planning, strengthening community-based services, transitional care support, emergency placement services, day respite, support to family carers, quality residential care services, dementia care, and end-of-life care (Elderly Commission 2017: 22–31). To provide such services, there will be a need to maintain a quality workforce, supplemented by informal care providers (Elderly Commission 2017: 32–33). The Elderly Commission also revisits and reinstates planning standards for residential care and community care services, as well as their schedule of accommodation (Elderly Commission 2017: 35). Financing options and public-private partnerships among welfare, health care, and housing are also considered (Elderly Commission 2017: 39–41).

Table 14.1: New Development Areas (NDAs)

	Area (hectares)	Housing units	Population	Density (pop/km²)	Gross floor area for economic activities (m²)	Number of jobs
Hung Shui Kiu/ Ha Tsuen NDAs1	441	61,000 (51% public housing)	176,000	39,909	6,400,000	150,000
Kwu Tung North and Fanling North NDAs2	612	72,000 (70% public housing)	188,100	31,667	12 ha (business and technology park) 5.8 ha (research and development)	40,100
Yuen Long South NDA3	224	32,850 (68% public housing)	101,200	45,179	180,000 (commercial) 375,200 (storage and workshop) 14,000 (open storage)	10,500
Tung Chung NDA4	245	49,600 (63% public housing)	145,000	59,184	500,000 (office) 327,000 (retail) 50,000 (hotel)	48,2315

Source:
1. Development Bureau 2021a.
2. Development Bureau 2021b.
3. Development Bureau 2020.
4. Development Bureau 2021c.
5. CEDD 2015, p. 2.

According to government information, as of 31 March 2021, about 36,800 elderly people were on the waiting list for subsidized residential care services, and the waiting time of subvented homes was 42 months (versus eight months in private homes, the quality of which often varies and are much inferior to the subvented ones) (Social Welfare Department 2021).

Urban-rural divide, job-residence imbalance, and a skewed economic structure

The urban and rural divide has given rise to a serious job-residence imbalance in Hong Kong. Figure 14.3 shows that the working population with fixed workplaces (excluding those who worked in the same district) within the urban areas (including Kwai Tsing and Tsuen Wan) amounted to 1.274 million in 2016, and the number of establishments was 295,985, hiring 2.28 million people (CSD 2017). In the New Territories (including the new towns), the working population (excluding those who worked in the same district) was about 930,000 (73 percent of those in urban areas) in 2016, but the number of establishments was only 71,373 (24 percent of those in urban areas), hiring 548,842 people (24 percent of its urban counterpart) (CSD 2017). In other words, a sizable portion of the work force in the New Territories has to travel to the urban areas for employment opportunities, affecting the work-life balance of workers with long commutes (He et al. 2020).

According to the Trade and Industry Department (2020), about 98.4 percent of establishments in Hong Kong are small and medium-sized enterprises (SMEs), providing 44.5 percent of private sector employment. In 2019, there were a total of 374,830 establishments (CSD 2020b), and the number of employed persons was about 3.5 million (CSD 2020c). In other words, while 368,833 SMEs were hiring about 1.6 million workers (person employed per establishment was four), the other 6,000 enterprises were hiring about 2 million workers (persons employed per establishment was about 330) (CSD 2020b and 2020c). This skewed economic structure has given rise to many urban issues in the city. Although the government has introduced a two-tier profits tax regime in Hong Kong since 2018 to lower the profits tax rates of unincorporated businesses (from 8.25 percent to 7 percent for the first HK$2 million profits; and from 16.5 percent to 15 percent for more than HK$2 million profits) (KPMG 2018), the gap between the big corporations and SMEs is huge. The net profit of the international investments of eight major companies, including six big developers, "averaged up to 66% and 74% of the government's revenue and expenditure under the general revenue account from 2011 to 2016" (Ng 2020: 1458).

Hong Kong is a plutocracy where the rich have been privileged, whether in property development, utilities (gas, electricity), transport (buses and ferries),

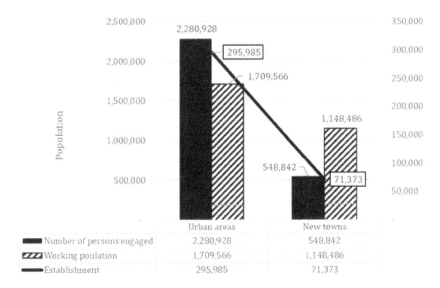

Figure 14.3: Disparities between number of establishments, persons engaged, and working population with fixed work places in the urban areas and new towns

and even supermarkets (Time Out Hong Kong 2016). As the government has to survive on a high land price policy, the big tycoons become their natural partners. In fact, Hong Kong topped the list of the *Economist*'s "crony capitalism" index[1] in 2014 (Keating 2014). On the other hand, the city has given minimal attention to the rights of workers. The minimum wage was not institutionalized until 2011 (at HK$28/hour, or US$3.59/hour), and as of May 2023, it was a meagre HK$40/hour (US$5.13/hour). This paltry amount needs to be "appreciated" against an absence of systemic retirement benefits. Indeed, according to the Mandatory Provident Fund Schemes Ordinance (Cap.485) begun in 2000, employers can use the accrued benefits of the contribution he/she made for an employee in a Mandatory Provident Fund scheme to offset the severance or long-service payment payable to the employee under the Employment Ordinance. It was only in the *2017 Policy Address* that a solution was suggested to end this malpractice. Yet this promise will not be realized until May 2025. This perhaps explains why in Oxfam's 2018 *Hong Kong Inequality Report*, it was reported that the monthly income of 37 percent of working poor households (about 300,000 in total) was

---

1. The index measures 'the wealth of a country's billionaires who are involved in a number of "industries that are vulnerable to monopoly, or that involve licensing or heavy state involvement", including utilities, ports, and airports, energy, infrastructure, investment banking and defense' (Keating 2014).

lower than the Comprehensive Social Security Assistance (CSSA). While they all would be eligible for CSSA, only 4.5 percent applied for it (Oxfam 2018: 23).

Although measures have been rolled out to support the SMEs (Trade and Industrial Department 2020: 3), the business environment in Hong Kong cannot live up to what the New Urban Agenda (UN 2017) has suggested; that is, as an enabling, fair, and responsible business environment supporting enterprises in the social economy. The promised provision of another 0.25 million jobs in the New Development Areas in the New Territories (Table 14.1) would help ameliorate job-residence imbalance, though these figures will only be realized if the market responds positively to the plans. Given the concentration of economic establishments (98 percent are in the service sectors) in urban areas, it remains unclear how these jobs will be delivered in the new development areas. Accordingly, plans have been made to extend mass transit to these new development areas, such as the Northern Link and Kwun Tung Station, Hung Shui Kiu Station, and Tung Chung West Extension (THB 2014: 22–23). The government has yet to produce plans to strengthen sustainable transport and mobility to enhance urban-rural interactions and connectivity, as recommended by the New Urban Agenda (UN 2017).

Ecology being left behind?

From a bird's eye view, Hong Kong is a very "green" city, as the government has zoned 40 percent of its land as legally protected country parks and conservation areas. Large stretches of land in the New Territories are left as woodland, shrubland, or grassland (Planning Department 2020). However, at the same time, the city's per capita open space standard is a mere $2m^2$ (the size of a toilet cubicle, as argued by Lai 2017), and even with such a humble standard, it is reported that "1.84 million Hong Kongers" (24.5 percent of the total population) lived in areas with outline zoning plans that fail to meet the standard (Planning Department 2020: 6).

Open space standards do not apply to the rural New Territories, where brownfield sites have proliferated in the more accessible parts of the city. According to ARUP and Planning Department (2019: 8), brownfield sites refer to:

> agricultural land in the New Territories converted into various operations and uses, including open storage, warehouse, workshop, logistics and freight operation, container storage, vehicle parking, vehicle repair yard and vehicle body building yard . . . brownfield sites are defined as *'primarily agricultural land in the New Territories which has been formed and occupied by industrial, storage, logistics and parking uses'*. (emphasis original)

A total of 1,579 ha of brownfield sites were found, and 1,414 ha were active brownfield sites (Planning Department 2019: 19, 37). About 70 percent and 23 percent of these active brownfield sites were located in northwest and northeast New Territories, respectively, generating about 50,600 full-time jobs (1.4 percent of total employments in Hong Kong) (Planning Department 2019: 24; CSD 2021). Among the 1,414 ha of active brownfield sites, the majority (83 percent) are on private land, and 234 ha (17 percent) are on government land (Planning Department 2019: 26). About 43 percent of these active brownfield sites fall within the boundaries of the new development areas (Planning Department 2019: 20). Over 20 percent of the active brownfield sites are on land zoned for conservation (5 percent), greenbelt (7.5 percent), and agriculture (11 percent) (Planning Department 2019: 27). The same report shows that 69 percent of the active brownfield sites exert a large to moderate scale of impacts on adjacent residential areas (Planning Department 2019: 38). It is obvious that ecologies have been left behind in these places.

Again, the government's high land price policy seems to be related to its reluctance to strategically, comprehensively, and ecologically replan the inefficiently used land resources in the New Territories. Otherwise, a proper understanding of existing land, socioeconomic, and cultural resources in the New Territories—coupled with people, place, and planet-centered planning and infrastructure development—will not only resolve housing and residence-job imbalance problems in the city but also lead it toward a much more sustainable future.

The government's lack of ecological literacy is also reflected in its treatment of the city's water resources. Although the government has resurrected the use of desalination for fresh water supply, 60 to 80 percent of the city's water will continue to be provided via Dongjiang from the Mainland (Water Supplies Department 2019: 26), giving rise to an "illusion of plenty" (ADM Capital Foundation et al. 2017). While Hong Kong "is more naturally water scarce than parts of the Middle East and Africa," it is argued that "water security is worryingly low on the Hong Kong government's agenda" (ADM Capital Foundation et al. 2017: 2).

The mismanagement of water, an extremely precious resource in Hong Kong, is rather frustrating. It is reported that in 2013, 17 percent of fresh water was squandered via poorly maintained government mains, and a further 15 percent was lost through leaks from private mains, illegal extraction, and inaccurate metering (ADM Capital Foundation et al. 2017: 5). The tariff system has a low pricing structure "facilitating increasing overconsumption," making Hong Kong one of the highest per capita water users in the world (ADM Capital Foundation et al. 2017: 6–7). Yet, despite the so-called Total Water Management Strategy (Water Supplies Department 2019), "no water policy has been advocated or established and little progress has been made in addressing long-term water security" (ADM Capital Foundation et al. 2017: 3).

The Environment Bureau has been very proactive to roll out policies and measures to minimize waste, recycling resources to promote a circular economy through the development of I-Park (integrated waste management), T-Park (treating sewage sludge), O-Park (recovering organic resources and treating food waste), Y-Park (for yard waste recycling), and EcoPark to recycle waste-paper (Environment Bureau 2021). The medium-term target is "to reduce per capita municipal solid waste disposal by 40 to 45% and to increase recovery rate to 55% of local yield" (Environment Bureau 2021: 3). The Environment Bureau published a Climate Change Action Plan in 2017, and in the *2020 Policy Address*, the government announced its goal to achieve carbon neutrality by 2050. The Environmental Protection Department has also set up a new community recycling network, supporting clean recycling. While the Waste Disposal (Charging for Municipal Solid Waste) (Amendment) Ordinance was passed in 2021, the scheme had not been implemented as of July 2023. Although the Environment Bureau (2016) published a strategic biodiversity action plan, it has endorsed the Lantau Tomorrow Vision project that aims to reclaim several artificial islands (totaling 1,700 ha) (Development Bureau and CEDD 2019). Recently, the government announced that three islands totaling 1,000 ha will be reclaimed to provide 190,000 to 210,000 residential flats (housing 500,000 to 550,000 people) and 270,000 jobs (Development Bureau 2022). These artificial islands are next to the 1,255-ha Central and Western District but with 2.3 times its population density.

New Territories Tomorrow? Alternative Development for the Well-Being of Planet, Place, and People

From a rational perspective, the pathway toward a future that will "leave no one, no place, and no ecology" behind in Hong Kong is to strategically reimagine and replan the rural New Territories where most of the land resources lie. This would require a reorientation of the government from reclaiming land from the sea to restoring and "reclaiming" land in the New Territories, practicing integrated planning that respects nature and promotes the conservation of tangible and intangible heritages. While the bureaucracy should have enough resources to undertake this challenge, the question is if they would have such a vision and mission. A practical concern of this "paradigm shift" from a growth-at-all-cost mentality is government revenue. If land and related revenue decreased, the government would need society's support to explore other revenue sources.

The expenditure on capital works and other charges (consultancy and outside services) may need to be channeled to the development of the rural New Territories. The government may take this opportunity to "recommon" rural land. Instead of getting a huge land premium up front, alternative business models can be explored to create a steady income stream for the government. Developing an ecological and humane rural New Territories will require engineering and professional work and support, too. These business sectors would not be worse off. Hopefully, with the development of the rural New Territories, more quality housing and land will be available to Hong Kongers. Not only would housing be more affordable, but there would also be more options for the SMEs and many other social enterprises that cannot afford the extremely high rents in the city.

Instead of developing the Lantau Tomorrow Vision that will cause self-inflicted vulnerabilities in the face of the climate crisis, an alternative New Territories Tomorrow Vision is preferred to restore places that have been damaged so that they can be used to create different types of affordable housing, provide spaces for economic activities to offer residents with dignified jobs, and a decent ecological environment that harmonizes with the historical and cultural contexts in the rural New Territories—a vision that will "leave no one, no place, and no ecology behind."

Box 14.1: New Urban Agenda

The New Urban Agenda, shaped and deliberated by thousands of networks across the globe, was endorsed by the United Nations in 2016. The Agenda calls for a transformative commitment to planning, designing, and implementing sustainable cities that will "leave no one, no place, and no ecology behind."

Box 14.2: Sustainable development goals

Sustainable development goals (SDGs) were endorsed by the United Nations in 2015 as a blueprint to achieve a more sustainable future for humankind. The target is to achieve all the 17 SDGs related to the flourishing of the planet (climate, environment, life on land in water), place (prosperity, infrastructure, sustainable cities, and communities), and people (poverty, inequality, peace, and justice) by 2030.

360   Urban Policy

Box 14.3: Brownfield sites

Brownfield sites normally refer to contaminated land previously used for industrial or commercial purposes. However, in Hong Kong, brownfields usually refer to formerly agricultural land now set aside for industrial, open storage, logistics, and parking uses.

Box 14.4: Block Government Lease

Formerly known as a Block Crown Lease, which was issued for each survey district (or demarcation district) in the New Territories in 1905. These survey or demarcation districts were classified and surveyed after the British colonial government leased the New Territories for 99 years. The original purpose was to collect rent from the landowners. The survey took three years (1899–1902) to complete, and according to the Land Registry (2021), a land court was set up in 1899 "to confirm land ownership and adjudicate disputes."

Acknowledgments

This research was supported by the Research Grants Council of the Hong Kong Special Administrative Region, China (project numbers: CUHK14604218 and CUHK14613320).

Questions

1. What is sustainable urban development in the twenty-first century?
2. To what extent has urban development in Hong Kong succeeded in "leaving no one, no place, and no ecology behind"?
3. Does Hong Kong have a land shortage problem? Please elaborate.
4. Compare and contrast the merits and problems of reclaiming artificial islands east of Lantau versus replanning and redesigning the New Territories.

Bibliography

ADM Capital Foundation, Civic Exchange and WYNG Foundation 2017, *The Illusion of Plenty: Hong Kong's Water Security, Working Towards Regional Water Harmony*, https://www.admcf.org/wp-content/uploads/2017/05/Illusion-of-Plenty-Hong-Kong-Water-Security.pdf

ARUP and Planning Department 2019, *Operation of Brownfield Sites in the New Territories—Feasibility Study. Final Report*, viewed 16 March 2021, https://www.

pland.gov.hk/pland_en/p_study/comp_s/Brownfield/Report/Brownfield%20Study_FR_ENG.pdf

Brown, K 2014, "Global Environmental Change I: A Social Turn for Resilience?," *Progress in Human Geography*, vol. 38, no. 1, pp. 107–117.

Bulkeley, H, Castan-Broto, V, Hodson, M & Marvin, S 2011, *Cities and Low Carbon Transitions*, Routledge, London.

Census and Statistics Department 2017, *2016 Population By*-census, https://www.bycensus2016.gov.hk/en/bc-mt.html

Census and Statistics Department 2020a, *Hong Kong Poverty Situation Report 2019*, viewed 17 March 2021, https://www.statistics.gov.hk/pub/B9XX0005E2019AN19E0100.pdf

Census and Statistics Department 2020b, *Table E010: Number of Establishments and Persons Engaged (Other Than Those in the Civil Service) Analysed by Industry Division and District Council District*, https://www.censtatd.gov.hk/en/EIndexbySubject.html?scode=452&pcode=D5250007

Census and Statistics Department 2020c, *Table E003: Number of Employed Persons by Industry and Occupation*, https://www.censtatd.gov.hk/en/EIndexbySubject.html?pcode=D5250003&scode=200

Census and Statistics Department 2021, "Employed Persons by District Council District," *General Household Survey 2020*, figures purchased from Census and Statistics Department on 5 May 2021.

Census and Statistics Department (various years), *Table 194: Government Expenditure (General Revenue Accounts and the Funds)*, https://www.censtatd.gov.hk/en/web_table.html?id=194#

Chan, KS 1998, "Negotiating the Transfer Practice of Housing in a Chinese Village," *Journal of the Hong Kong Branch of the Royal Asiatic Society*, vol. 37, pp. 63–80.

Chiu, SWK & Hung, HF 1997, *The Colonial State and Rural Protests in Hong Kong*, Hong Kong Institute of Asia-Pacific Studies, the Chinese University of Hong Kong, Hong Kong, http://www.hkiaps.cuhk.edu.hk/wd/ni/20181024-094705_1_hkiaps_op59.pdf

Chiu, SWK & Lui, TL 1999, *The Dynamics of Social Movements in Hong Kong*, Hong Kong University Press, Hong Kong.

Chui, E 2003, "Unmasking the 'Naturalness' of 'Community Eclipse': The Case of Hong Kong," *Community Development Journal*, vol. 38, no. 2, pp. 151–163.

Civil Engineering and Development Department (CEDD) and ARUP 2014, *Enhancing Land Supply Strategy: Reclamation Outside Victoria Harbour and Rock Cavern Development: Executive Summary on Final Report for Rock Cavern Development*, viewed 23 March 2021, https://www.cedd.gov.hk/filemanager/eng/content_961/4/Executive_Summary_on_Final_Report_for_Rock_Cavern_Development.pdf

Civil Engineering and Development Department (CEDD) 2015, *Tung Chung New Town Extension. InfoWorks Model User Manual*, Appendix 6.2.pdf (epd.gov.hk).

Civil Engineering and Development Department (CEDD) 2020, "Lantau Tomorrow Vision," https://www.lantau.gov.hk/en/lantau-tomorrow-vision/index.html

Development Bureau 2020, *Planning and Engineering Study for Housing Sites in Yuen Long South*, viewed 7 April 2021, https://www.yuenlongsouth.hk/links/ES_Revised_RODP_er.pdf

Development Bureau 2021a, *Hung Shui Kiu / Ha Tsuen New Development Area*, viewed 7 April 2021, https://hsknda.hk/

Development Bureau 2021b, *Kwun Tung North / Fanling North New Development Areas*, viewed 7 April 2021, https://www.ktnfln-ndas.gov.hk/en/index.php

Development Bureau 2021c, *Tung Chung New Town Extension*, viewed 7 April 2021, https://www.tung-chung.hk/about.php

Development Bureau 2022, *Kau Yi Chau Artificial Islands*, viewed 17 March 2023, https://www.centralwaters.hk/pdf/KYCAI%20-%20PE%20booklet.pdf

Development Bureau and Civil Engineering and Development Department (CEDD) 2019, *Lantau Tomorrow*, https://www.lantau.gov.hk/filemanager/content/lantau-tomorrow-vision/leaflet_e1.pdf

Elderly Commission 2017, *Elderly Services Programme Plan*, https://www.elderlycommission.gov.hk/en/download/library/ESPP_Final_Report_Eng.pdf

Environment Bureau 2016, *Hong Kong Biodiversity Strategy and Action Plan 2016–2021*, https://www.afcd.gov.hk/english/conservation/Con_hkbsap/files/HKBSAP_ENG_2.pdf

Environment Bureau 2017, *Climate Change Action Plan 2030+*, https://www.enb.gov.hk/sites/default/files/pdf/ClimateActionPlanEng.pdf

Environment Bureau 2021, *Waste Blueprint for Hong Kong 2035*, viewed 20 March 2021, https://www.enb.gov.hk/sites/default/files/pdf/waste_blueprint_2035_eng.pdf

Goo, SH 2014, "The Small House Policy and Tso and Tong Land," Chapter 15, in H Fu & J Gillespie, *Resolving Land Disputes in East Asia*, Cambridge University Press, Cambridge, UK.

Goodstadt, LF 2005, *Uneasy Partners: The Conflict Between Public Interest and Private Profit in Hong Kong*, Hong Kong University Press, Hong Kong.

He, SY, Tao, S, Ng, MK & Tieben, H 2020, "Evaluating Hong Kong's Spatial Planning in New Towns from the Perspectives of Job Accessibility, Travel Mobility, and Work-Life Balance," *Journal of the American Planning Association*, vol. 86, no. 3, pp. 324–338.

Heritage Foundation 2016, *Hong Kong: Economic Freedom Score*, viewed 17 January 2017, http://www.heritage.org/index/pdf/2016/countries/hongkong.pdf

Hong Kong Case Law 2016, *Attorney General v. Melhado Investment Ltd.*, *Hong Kong Case Law*, last modified 29 November, https://www.hongkongcaselaw.com/attorney-general-v-melhado-investment-ltd/

Hong Kong Housing Authority (HKHA) 2020, *Annual Report 2019/20: Work Together for Quality Public Housing*, viewed 17 March 2021, https://www.housingauthority.gov.hk/mini-site/haar1920/en/dlpdf.html

Hong Kong Special Administrative Region (HKSAR) 2017, *Policy Address 2017*, Government Printer, Hong Kong.

Hong Kong Special Administrative Region (HKSAR) 2020a, *The Chief Executive's 2020 Policy Address: Striving Ahead with Renewed Perseverance*, https://www.policyaddress.gov.hk/2020/eng/pdf/PA2020.pdf

Hong Kong Special Administrative Region (HKSAR) 2020b, "LCQ21: Allocation of funding to District Councils," *Press Releases*, https://www.info.gov.hk/gia/general/202001/08/P2020010800391.htm?fontSize=1

Housing Bureau 2022, *Housing in Figures*, viewed 17 March 2023, https://www.hb.gov.hk/eng/publications/housing/HIF2022.pdf

IPCC 2014, *Climate Change 2014: Mitigation of Climate Change: Working Group III Contribution to the Fifth Assessment Report of the IPCC*, Cambridge University Press, New York.

Keating, J 2014, "The World's 'Freest' Economy is also the Most Plutocratic," *SLATE*, https://slate.com/news-and-politics/2014/03/economist-crony-capitalism-index-the-world-s-freest-economy-hong-kong-is-also-the-most-plutocratic.html

Knowledge Transfer Project (KTF) Sustainable Communities for People's Multifaceted Well-Being Team 2021, *Sustainable Communities for People's Multifaceted Well-being*, CUHK Social Innovation, Institute of Future Cities, Urban Studies Programme, the Chinese University of Hong Kong; Community Living Room; and Collaborate Hong Kong, Hong Kong.

KPMG 2018, "Hong Kong Introduces Two-Tiered Profits Tax Rate Marking a Push towards a More Competitive Tax Environment," https://home.kpmg/cn/en/home/insights/2018/01/tax-alert-1-hk-introduces-two-tiered-profits-tax-rate.html

Ku, AS & Pun, N 2004, *Remaking Citizenship in Hong Kong*, Routledge Curzon, London, U.K.

Lai, C 2017, *Unopened Space: Mapping Equitable Availability of Open Space in Hong Kong*, Hong Kong: Civic Exchange, https://civic-exchange.org/wp-content/uploads/2017/04/20170224POSreport_FINAL.pdf

Land Registry 2021, "Block Government Lease," https://www.landreg.gov.hk/en/about/block.htm

Lau, YK 2018, "Restructuring the Planning Direction: Revitalising Land in the New Territories," *Think Hong Kong*, 18 September, viewed 16 March 2021, https://www.thinkhk.com/article/2018-09/18/29596.html

Lee, KK 2014, "Changing Nature of Border, Scale, and the Production of Hong Kong's Water Supply System since 1959," *International Journal of Urban and Regional Research*, vol. 38, no. 3, pp. 903–921.

Maguire, B & Cartwright, S 2008, *Assessing a Community's Capacity to Manage Change: A Resilience Approach to Social Assessment*, Bureau of Rural Sciences, Australian Government.

Ng, MK 2015, "Planning in Hong Kong as an Undemocratic Post-colonial Chinese Capitalist Society: Negotiating the Roles of Technocrats, Traditional Public Intellectuals and Reflective Practitioners," in J Hillier &J Metzger (eds), *Connections: Exploring Contemporary Planning Theory and Practice with Patsy Healey*, Ashgate, Surrey, England, pp. 113–126.

Ng, MK 2016, "From Xinhai Revolution (1911) to the Umbrella Movement (2014): Insurgent Citizenship, Radical Planning and Chinese Culture in the Hong Kong SAR," in H Rangan, MK Ng, J Chase, & L Porter, *Insurgencies and Revolutions: Reflections on John Friedmann's Contributions to Planning Theory and Practice*, Routledge, New York, pp. 279–288.

Ng, MK 2020, "Transformative Urbanism and Reproblematising Land Scarcity in Hong Kong," *Urban Studies*, vol. 57, no. 7, pp. 1452–1468.

Ng, MK 2023, "Hot Topics: Will Hong Kong's 'Light Public Housing' Scheme Really Help Low-Income Groups? Here's What You Should Know," *South China Morning Post*, 13 February, viewed 17 March 2023, https://www.scmp.com/yp/discover/news/hong-kong/article/3209814/hot-topics-will-hong-kongs-light-public-housing-scheme-really-help-low-income-groups-heres-what-you

Ng, MK, Lau, YT, Chen, H & He, S 2021, "Dual Land Regime, Income Inequalities and Multifaceted Socio-economic and Spatial Segregation in Hong Kong," in van M Ham, T Tammaru, R Ubrarevichiene, and H Jansesen (eds), *Urban Socio-Economic Segregation and Income Inequality: A Global Perspective*, Springer, https://link.springer.com/book/10.1007%2F978-3-030-64569-4

Ng, MK, Yeung, TC, Cheng, CH & Ma, NY 2023, "Hong Kong: One City, Three Spatial Forms and Two Possible Fates?," in R Hu (ed), *Routledge Handbook of Asian Cities*, Routledge, New York and London, pp. 87–103.

Nussbaum, MC 1998, "Capabilities and Human Rights," *Fordham Law Review*, vol. 66, 1997–1998, pp. 273–300.

Oxfam 2016, *An Economy for the 1%: How Privilege and Power in the Economy Drive Extreme Inequality and How This Can Be Stopped*, 210 Oxfam Briefing Paper Summary, 18 January 2016, https://www.oxfam.org/sites/www.oxfam.org/files/file_attachments/bp210-economy-one-percent-tax-havens-180116-summ-en_0.pdf

Oxfam 2017, *An Economy for the 99%: It's Time to Build a Human Economy That Benefits Everyone, not just the Privileged Few*, Oxfam Briefing Paper—Summary, January 2017, https://www.oxfam.org/sites/www.oxfam.org/files/file_attachments/bp-economy-for-99-percent-160117-summ-en.pdf

Oxfam 2018, *Hong Kong Inequality Report*, viewed 7 April 2021, https://www.oxfam.org.hk/f/news_and_publication/16372/Oxfam_inequality%20report_Eng_FINAL.pdf

Parkes, D 2017, "The Myth of Hong Kong's 'Free' Economy," *Time Out*, 6 June, viewed 23 March 2021, https://www.timeout.com/hong-kong/blog/the-myth-of-hong-kongs-free-economy-060817

Pelling, M 2011, *Adaptation to Climate Change: From Resilience to Transformation*, Routledge, London and New York.

Pepper, S 2016, "The Complex Design of Hong Kong's Legislative Elections Ensure That Nothing Will Change," *Hong Kong Free Press*, 27 August, viewed 17 January 2017, https://www.hongkongfp.com/2016/08/27/the-complex-design-of-hong-kongs-legislative-elections-ensure-that-nothing-will-change/

Planning Department 2020, *Land Utilization in Hong Kong 2019*, https://www.pland.gov.hk/pland_en/info_serv/statistic/landu.html

Poon, A 2005, *Land and the Ruling Class in Hong Kong*, Alice Poon, Richmond.

Raworth, K 2012, *A Safe and Just Space for Humanity: Can We Live Within the Doughnut?*, Oxfam Discussion Paper, February 2012, https://www.oxfam.org/sites/www.oxfam.org/files/dp-a-safe-and-just-space-for-humanity-130212-en.pdf

Simpson, A 2020, "Hong Kong Named the Most Expensive Housing Market in the World," *Hong Kong Tatler*, 6 June, viewed 16 March 2021, https://hk.asiatatler.com/life/hong-kong-most-expensive-housing-market-in-the-world

Social Welfare Department 2021, *Statistics on Waiting List for Subsidised Residential Care Services for the Elderly*, https://www.swd.gov.hk/storage/asset/section/632/en/LTC_statistics_HP-Eng(202103).pdf

Task Force on Land Supply 2018, *How to Tackle Land Shortage? Land for Hong Kong: Our Home, Our Say!* viewed 17 March 2021, https://www.legco.gov.hk/yr17-18/english/panels/dev/papers/dev20180529-booklet201804-e.pdf

Time Out Hong Kong 2016, "Tycoons: The Men Who Rule Hong Kong," *Time Out*, 4 October, https://www.timeout.com/hong-kong/blog/tycoons-the-men-who-rule-hong-kong-100416

Trade and Industry Department 2020, *Hong Kong – The Facts (Trade and Industry)*, viewed 8 April 2021, https://www.gov.hk/en/about/abouthk/factsheets/docs/trade_industry.pdf

Transport and Housing Bureau 2014, *Railway Development Strategy 2014*, viewed 23 March 2021, https://www.thb.gov.hk/eng/psp/publications/transport/publications/rds2014.pdf

Transport and Housing Bureau 2020, *Long Term Housing Strategy Annual Progress Report 2020*, https://www.thb.gov.hk/eng/policy/housing/policy/lths/LTHS_Annual_Progress_Report_2020.pdf

Transport and Housing Bureau (THB) 2021, *Report of the Task Force for the Study on Tenancy Control of Subdivided Units*, https://www.thb.gov.hk/eng/contact/housing/studyOnTenancyControl_Report.pdf

United Nations 2014, *World Urbanization Prospects: The 2014 Revision Highlights*, United Nations, New York, https://population.un.org/wup/publications/files/wup2014-report.pdf

United Nations 2015, *Transforming Our World: The 2030 Agenda for Sustainable Development*, United Nations General Assembly, https://www.un.org/ga/search/view_doc.asp?symbol=A/RES/70/1&Lang=E

United Nations 2017, *New Urban Agenda*, UN-Habitat, New York, https://habitat3.org/wp-content/uploads/NUA-English.pdf

United Nations Development Programme 2009, *Charting a New Low-Carbon Route to Development*, United Nations Development Programme, New York.

UN-Habitat 2011, *Global Report on Human Settlements 2011: Cities and Climate Change*, UN-Habitat, United Nations, file:///G:/0000_files%20worked%20at%20home/RGC/2014-16/2_Shenzhen/LSE/Abstract&Paper/REVISION/2011_UN_Habitat_Cities_Climate_Change.pdf

Water Supplies Department 2019, *Total Water Management Strategy: Strategy for Sustainable Water Supply in Hong Kong*, viewed 21 March 2021.

Wilkinson, C 2012, "Social-Ecological Resilience: Insights and Issues for Planning Theory," *Planning Theory*, vol. 11, no. 2, pp. 148–169.

World Bank 2010, *Cities and Climate Change: An Urgent Agenda*, The World Bank, Washington, DC.

366   Urban Policy

Useful Websites

District Profiles: 2016 Population By-census
https://www.bycensus2016.gov.hk/en/bc-dp-new-town.html

Environment Bureau: Resources and Publications
https://www.enb.gov.hk/en/resources_publications/index.html

Exploring Doughnut Economics
https://www.kateraworth.com/doughnut/#

Hong Kong: Asia's World City
https://www.brandhk.gov.hk/html/en/

Hong Kong Fact Sheets
https://www.cedd.gov.hk/eng/publications/fact-sheets/hong-kong-fact-sheets/index.html

Land Utilization in Hong Kong 2019
https://www.pland.gov.hk/pland_en/info_serv/statistic/landu.html

Lantau Tomorrow Vision
https://www.lantau.gov.hk/en/lantau-tomorrow-vision/index.html

Long Term Housing Strategy Annual Progress Report 2020
https://www.legco.gov.hk/yr20-21/english/panels/hg/papers/hgcb1-387-1-e.pdf

Melhado Case
https://legalref.judiciary.hk/lrs/common/search/search_result_detail_frame.jsp?DIS=15259&QS=(%24Melhado)&TP=JU

New Development Area
https://www.landsd.gov.hk/en/land-acq-clearance/new-development-area.html

Oxfam International
https://www.oxfam.org/en

Protection of the Harbour Ordinance
https://www.elegislation.gov.hk/hk/cap531

Study on Existing Profile and Operations of Brownfield Sites in the New Territories –
Feasibility Study
https://www.pland.gov.hk/pland_en/p_study/comp_s/Brownfield/TheStudy_e.html

Sustainable Development Goals
https://sdgs.un.org/goals

The Intergovernmental Panel on Climate Change
https://www.ipcc.ch/

The Land Registry
https://www.landreg.gov.hk/en/home/index.htm

The New Urban Agenda
https://habitat3.org/the-new-urban-agenda/

Urban Glossary: Urban Studies, Faculty of Social Science, the Chinese University of Hong Kong
https://urban-glossary.cuhk.edu.hk/category/alphabetical/b/

Village Houses in the New Territories
https://www.landsd.gov.hk/en/land-disposal-transaction/village-houses-NT.html

Further Reading

Chen, HW, Ng, MK, Es, M, Lee, J, Mak, WWS & Tong, Y 2018, "Socio-Spatial Polarization and the (Re)-distribution of Deprived Groups in World Cities: A Case Study of Hong Kong, *Urban Geography*, vol. 39, no. 7, pp. 969–987, https://doi.org/10.1080/02723 638.2017.1421392. An article that highlights how government policies impact the geographical distribution of the disadvantaged.

Cheng, J (ed) 2020, *Evaluation of the C. Y. Leung Administration*, City University Press, Hong Kong. A good collection for learning how to evaluate urban policies from different angles.

Cheng, J (ed) 2013, *Evaluating the Tsang Years 2005–2012*, City University Press, Hong Kong. A comprehensive evaluation of the administration of Donald Tsang from different perspectives.

Cheng, J (ed) 2007, *HKSAR in Its First Decade*, City University Press, Hong Kong. A good collection for tracing the evolution of urban developments in Hong Kong.

Cheng, J and Lo, S (eds) 1997, *1997 Transition: Hong Kong's Challenges*, Hong Kong: The Chinese University Press of Hong Kong. This book offers insights to pre-1997 Hong Kong and issues related to its return to Chinese rule.

Leary-Owhin, ME & McCarthy, JP, *Routledge Handbook of Henri Lefebvre, The City and Urban Society*, Routledge. To learn how to understand urban development from the perspective of the production of space in different socioeconomic and cultural settings.

Mottershead, T (ed) 2004, *Sustainable Development in Hong Kong*, Hong Kong: Hong Kong University Press. So far the only book on sustainable development in Hong Kong.

Ng, MK 2014, "Intellectuals and the Production of Space in the Urban Renewal Process in Hong Kong and Taipei," *Planning Theory and Practice*, vol. 15, no. 1, pp. 77–92. If you want to know what intellectuals can do to transform urban development, read this article.

Ng, MK et al. 2021, *Sustainable Communities for People's Multifaceted Well-being*, CUHK: Knowledge Transfer Project, 51p. (bilingual), https://www.iofc.cuhk.edu.hk/post/ sustainable-communities-for-people-s-multifaceted-well-being. This booklet provides an overview of key concepts on sustainable urban development in the twenty-first century.

Ng, MK & Mak, WS 2020, "The Right to Spatial Development for Human Flourishing," *Transactions of the Association of European Schools of Planning*, vol. 4, no. 1, pp. 22–32, http://transactions-journal.aesop-planning.eu/volume-4/article-33/. If you want to know why you should have a right to the city, read this article.

Part IV: Political Environment

15

Changing Relations between Hong Kong and the Mainland since 2014

Peter T. Y. Cheung

A "high degree of autonomy" under the "one country, two systems" (OCTS) framework was promised by China's preeminent leader Deng Xiaoping and enshrined in the Basic Law (BL) of the Hong Kong Special Administrative Region (HKSAR) in order to ensure its smooth unification with the People's Republic of China (PRC). After the former Chief Executive (CE) Leung Chun-ying's appointment in 2012, tensions between the Hong Kong community and Mainland authorities had aggravated, as epitomized by the growing anti-Mainland sentiments responding to the challenges of increasing socioeconomic integration and the outbreak of the Occupy Central Movement (OCM), which ruined the trust between Hong Kong and the Mainland. Yet the most devastating blow to the precarious experiment of OCTS erupted in the 2019 Anti–Extradition Law Amendment Bill (Anti-ELAB) Movement, culminating in the promulgation of the draconian National Security Law (NSL) by Beijing in mid-2020, and the subsequent overhauling of the Hong Kong political system in March 2021.

This chapter analyzes the politics of the changing relations between the central authorities in Beijing and Hong Kong since 2014 and particularly in 2019–2022 (for an analysis of Mainland–Hong Kong relations 1997–2012, see, e.g., Cheng 2009, PTY Cheung 2012, and Lo 2008; and for the period 2012–2017, see PTY Cheung 2018, Fong 2017, and Loh 2018). For the sake of simplicity, central authorities, central government, Central People's Government (CPG), and Beijing will be used interchangeably. My focus will be on key central initiatives in governing Hong Kong, as space limitation forbids a more comprehensive analysis of their multifaceted relationship.

The Changing National and Global Contexts since 2014

Beijing's strategy in governing Hong Kong can only be understood by taking into account the drastically changing national and global environments since President Xi Jinping assumed power in 2012. First, a "hard authoritarian" mode of governance was consolidated in Mainland China through a popular anti-corruption campaign and a reshuffling of the political leadership, relying upon legal means to strengthen the party's governance capacity and establishing authority through institutional changes of the party-state (Shambaugh 2017). The promotion of Xi's thoughts on "socialism with Chinese characteristics in the new era," the assertion of party power under his centralized control over state institutions, and the amendments of the PRC constitution in 2018 (which highlighted Xi's thoughts), the leadership of the CCP and the abolition of term limits for Presidents and Vice-Presidents, among other things, marked the firm consolidation of Xi's rule.

Second, a security state has been established under Xi where stability and order are primary (TM Cheung 2020). National security now encompasses both internal and external security and traditional and nontraditional security. The National Security Law promulgated in 2015 covers both broad territorial, political, economic, and defense dimensions and specific sectors such as finance, resources and energy, food, culture, technology, the internet and information, minorities, religion, terrorism, social order, the environment, nuclear power, and outer space. Toward the end of President Hu Jintao's term, national security came second after national sovereignty and before "China's political system established by the Constitution and comprehensive social stability, and the basic safeguards for ensuring sustainable economic and social development" (Information Office of the State Council 2011) as China's core interests. These were later consolidated as "national sovereignty, national security, and development interests." The Chinese leadership increasingly perceives the external environment as highly volatile and hostile. While Sino-American relations began to deteriorate as the US pivoted to Asia in President Barack Obama's second term, the conflictual relationship worsened rapidly after Donald Trump assumed the presidency in 2016 and initiated the trade war against China in 2018. The intensifying strategic competition between the two great powers is rooted in structural competition between an incumbent superpower and a rising challenger over a range of issues, from regional security and military rivalry to economic and technological contests and domestic and global governance models (Medeiros 2019). Since assuming office in 2021, President Joe Biden has continued and broadened the stringent strategy in confronting China, as he sees China as "the only competitor with both the intent to reshape the international order and, increasingly, the economic, diplomatic, military, and technological power to advance that objective" (*South China Morning Post* 13 October 2022).

Last but not least, the once critical role of Hong Kong in China's economic development has changed over time, even though it remains China's most important international financial center and offshore RMB center. While Hong Kong has contributed significantly to China's economic reform and opening by serving as a model, financier, trading partner, and gateway to the capitalist global economy for some 30 years since 1978, other key cities such as Beijing, Shanghai, Guangzhou, and Shenzhen have emerged as new growth poles and drivers of innovation and technology, foreign investment, and international trade. In 1997, Hong Kong's GDP was approximately 18 percent of that of the Mainland, but it had dwindled to 2.5 percent by 2019 (World Bank 2021). Although no longer enjoying double-digit growth, China's economy has recorded robust annual growth of six to seven percent from 2012 to 2019. The central authorities under Xi increasingly expect Hong Kong to follow the national development strategy and closely integrate with the Mainland.

The Occupy Central Movement, the Umbrella Movement, and Their Profound Repercussions

Before examining Beijing's strategies in enforcing "comprehensive jurisdiction," it is first necessary to recount the impacts of the OCM and the Umbrella Movement (UM) because they constitute one of the most severe challenges to the central authorities and the Hong Kong government since 1997 (see e.g., Ma and Cheng 2020). The OCM was conceived initially by law academics Benny Tai and others as a civil disobedience campaign, but young activists like Joshua Wong spearheaded the massive protests that erupted on 29 September 2014. With unexpected popular support, these protests and the subsequent occupation of the main segments of Central and Admiralty in the central business district and the commercial areas in Causeway Bay and Mong Kok for 79 days were considered the "Umbrella Movement" (Mainland officials and analysts mainly use the term "illegal Occupy Central" movement). The OCM and UM occurred largely as a political reaction by different pan-democratic groups to the 8.31 Decision of 2014 by the Standing Committee of National People's Congress Standing Committee (SCNPC) on the method for electing the CE and the formation of the Legislative Council (LegCo) in 2016. While Beijing considered the 8.31 Decision as the feasible path for universal suffrage under OCTS, the pan-democratic and other groups criticized the decision for its high threshold over the nomination of candidates (Chen 2021, Chapter 2) and the requirement that the CE has to be "*a person who loves the country and loves Hong Kong (aiguoaigang)*." Drawing upon months of deliberation in the community, the OCM supporters wanted to use the movement to press for more democratic reforms, but central officials and the official media characterized the movement as a "color revolution" colluding with foreign countries to destabilize Hong Kong and the PRC (*South China Morning Post* 11 October 2014). This massive and extended contention not only widened the gulf between the CPG and the pan-democrats and the younger generation but also entrenched the polarization of Hong Kong society into the "yellow ribbon" camp supporting the protesters and the "blue ribbon" camp supporting the police, the government, and the CPG.

The impacts of the OCM and UM are transformational in many respects. First, the confrontation led to the political awakening of young people, who later became the major force in subsequent political movements. Reflecting frustration over the failure of the moderate pan-democrats in fighting for democracy, localist and even pro-independence or self-determination groups have appeared on the political landscape. In 2015–2016, several such groups emerged, such as Youngspiration, Demosistō (led by the former convener of Scholarism Joshua Wong and dissolved in 2020), the Hong Kong National Party (later banned in 2018), and Hong Kong Indigenous, which called to "Liberate Hong Kong, Revolution of Our Times"—a controversial slogan that later became the key motto of the 2019 Anti-ELAB Movement but was viewed as pro-independence and subversive by the CPG and the Hong Kong government. Candidates and political groups associated with the UM and displaying a localist and self-determination orientation appeared in the 2015 District Council (DC) elections and the 2016 LegCo elections, further leading to fragmentation of the opposition and polarization of the political spectrum. The election debut of candidates belonging to the "umbrella soldiers" even gained eight seats with five percent of the votes in the 2015 DC elections (JTM Lam 2017: 360–362). The fragmentation of the pro-democracy camp deepened in the 2016 LegCo elections because the localist parties and candidates associated with the UM made further gains, winning a total of eight seats with 19 percent of the votes, mainly at the expense of the traditional pan-democratic parties, which only won 21 seats with 36 percent of votes, as compared to 27 seats and 56 percent of votes in 2012 elections (Kaeding 2017: 160–161).

Second, the failure of the OCM and UM to get concessions from the central authorities widened the rift between those demanding democracy in Hong Kong and Beijing's stringent policy (CY Cheung 2017), fueling concerns for its local identity, civic community, and the boundaries of OCTS and contributing to low confidence in the government and the CPG. With the rising conflicts arising from the growing influx of Mainland visitors and their impact on communities, various brands of anti-Mainland discourses and localism defending Hong Kong's distinctive social and cultural identity and economic interests surfaced after 2010 (WM Lam 2018; Veg 2017). The tense political atmosphere after 2014 also provided the context for the first violent confrontation in Mong Kok between localist political groups and the police over the clearing of street food hawkers in February 2016. The violent clashes marked the radical localists' first use of force after the failure of peaceful protests like the OCM. With China's increasing authoritarian turn, the subsequent heavy sentencing of protesters who participated in the Mong Kok riots might also have fueled the soaring discontent against the police, the government, and the Mainland authorities (Ma 2020: 31–42). According to the Asian Barometer survey, public confidence in the CE and the HKSAR government had dropped respectively from 59.9 percent in 2012 to 37.3 percent in 2016 and from 63.6 percent to 44.4 percent, and confidence in the CPG had plummeted from 53.4 percent to 35.6 percent (Ma 2020: 13; see Chapter 10 in this volume). Given the domination of pro-establishment forces in the LegCo, filibustering and obstructive actions had also become the main tool for the pan-democratic opposition to express their discontent over unpopular government policies or issues involving the Mainland, such as the colocation controversy.

From the Experiment of "High Degree of Autonomy" to "Comprehensive Jurisdiction"

There is no shortage of analysis on Beijing's governance of Hong Kong in recent years (see e.g., Cheng 2020; WM Lam 2020; Lau 2017; Lo et al. 2019; Lo et al. 2021; Tian 2018 and 2020; Zhu 2020; Yan 2015). These works highlight, for instance, the united front strategy, the countermobilization efforts, the "legalization without democratization" strategy, and the adoption of patron-client tactics in co-optation. Drawing upon these works, this chapter argues that Beijing's strategies in governing Hong Kong under "comprehensive jurisdiction" can be conceptualized into the following interrelated components: (a) asserting constitutional and legislative authority; (b) securitization of Hong Kong's governance; (c) overhauling the electoral system; (d) emphasizing ideological authority and strengthening united front work; (f) responding actively to external influence over Hong Kong affairs; (f) incorporating Hong Kong into the national development framework; and (g) revamping the governing team and central organs in Hong Kong and Macao affairs. Other key initiatives concern rectifying, for instance, education, civil society, the mass media, and the legal sector, but these merit separate treatment beyond the scope of this chapter.

The central approach to governing Hong Kong under "comprehensive jurisdiction" involves asserting central authority under a unitary, socialist constitutional order and emphasizing its legitimacy to exercise such authority so that "OCTS" can "sail steadily and go the distance" (*xingwen zhiyuan*). The Chinese political lexicon emphasizes that the central initiatives are in line with the original dictates set by preeminent leader Deng Xiaoping (e.g., patriots administering Hong Kong) and the original intent of the OCTS policy, but the changing times call for Beijing's active fixing of loopholes of the Hong Kong political system to truly implement the OCTS experiment. Such narratives not only buttress the continuity, consistency, and hence legitimacy of its strategies but also fend off accusations that Beijing has disregarded the promise of the "high degree of autonomy" model that characterized the pre-2020 period.

Asserting constitutional and legislative authority

Since China is a unitary state led by the highly centralized CCP, the center's constitutional supremacy is the most powerful means to ensure its mandates are enforced in Hong Kong. The White Paper on the Practice of the "One Country, Two Systems" Policy in the HKSAR issued in June 2014 by the State Council constitutes an authoritative and systematic attempt to articulate the authority of the center (*zhongyang*) and to correct the "misunderstanding" of OCTS among the Hong Kong people. Reiterating that Hong Kong's high degree of autonomy was authorized by the CPG and both the Chinese constitution and the BL formed the constitutional foundation of the HKSAR, the document first used "comprehensive jurisdiction" to depict the power of the central authorities over Hong Kong, which encompassed not merely the interpretative power of the BL and other central powers as stipulated in the BL, but also the growing application of central authority emanating from the Chinese constitution (Chan 2021). In his speech on the twentieth anniversary of the implementation of the BL in May 2017, then-Chairman of the SCNPC, Zhang Dejiang, reiterated that the resumption of Chinese sovereignty over Hong Kong means it has the power of "comprehensive jurisdiction" (*People's Daily* 28 May 2017). Aside from national defense and foreign affairs, the central authorities should formulate measures, institutions, and mechanisms to exercise its powers in the following areas: recording and reviewing the laws of Hong Kong, appointing the CE and principal officials, interpreting and amending the BL, determining the development of the political system, directing both the CE and reporting by the CE, among others. In short, the repertoire of policy instruments for implementing "comprehensive jurisdiction" was already formulated well before major changes unfolded in 2020–2021 (see also Tian 2017). On 1 July 2017, Xi Jinping stressed the primacy of "one country" in his important speech on the 20th anniversary of Hong Kong's reunion with the PRC (*Xinhua Net* 1 July 2017). Aside from emphasizing that "Hong Kong needs to improve its systems to uphold national sovereignty, national security and development" and "the relevant institutions and mechanisms for implementing the Basic Law and raising public awareness of the Constitution and the Basic Law in Hong Kong, particularly among civil servants and the young people," he laid down the three bottom lines (*dixian*) that must not be crossed, including any activities endangering national sovereignty and national security, challenging the power of the central authorities and the authority of the BL, and using Hong Kong to infiltrate and sabotage the Mainland (*Xinhua Net* 1 July 2017).

As the mistrust between the Mainland and Hong Kong further heightened, and the localist political forces emerged, Beijing used its constitutional power decisively. For instance, the disrespectful behavior against China by newly elected legislators to express their dissent during their oath-taking for LegCo offices infuriated the national leadership and prompted the SCNPC to preemptively interpret Article 104 of the BL in November 2016, which led to the disqualification of two new legislators and later another four through a judicial review by the government. Most importantly, this interpretation officially made upholding the BL and bearing allegiance to the HKSAR a requirement and precondition for standing for elections and taking public office.

The SCNPC also exercised its constitutional prerogative to make critical decisions shaping Hong Kong's governance without going through the pathway of the BL (Chan 2021), in this case concerning a major cross-boundary infrastructure project which had aroused political opposition and divided the Hong Kong community. Two major projects facilitating further integration with the Mainland—the high-speed rail link and the 55 km Hong Kong-Macao-Zhuhai bridge—were completed in 2017 and 2018, respectively. The Hong Kong government and the business community believed the rail link would greatly benefit Hong Kong by connecting it with the national high-speed rail network, while the bridge would connect Hong Kong with the blooming Pearl River Delta and the rest of the Mainland. The high-speed rail project already aroused considerable protests when it was deliberated in the LegCo in 2009–2010. Unlike the previous colocation arrangement for the Shenzhen Bay bridge, which applied Hong Kong laws to the boundary control area located inside Shenzhen, this colocation arrangement for the high-speed rail allowed Mainland laws to be applied to passengers who had exited Hong Kong immigration checkpoints and passengers coming from the Mainland who had not passed through the Hong Kong immigration checkpoints in the Mainland port area in the West Kowloon terminus, and to passengers throughout the entire train. Seeing this as a violation of OCTS, as Mainland jurisdiction would penetrate inside Hong Kong, the pan-democratic legislators and other groups strongly opposed the legislation, though to no avail. The agreement on colocation was first signed between the Hong Kong government and Guangdong province in mid-November 2017. However, in view of the different legal and political challenges, the SCNPC simply made an authoritative decision in late December 2017 to declare that this agreement accorded with the BL and the Chinese constitution before implementation through local legislation.

Further, in the aftermath of the OCM and UM, some Hong Kong people expressed their political discontent by booing the national anthem at football matches in 2015, which further angered the central authorities. In response, the SCNPC passed a national anthem law that would apply to the entire nation and inserted it into the Annex III of the BL in November 2017. Afterward, the National Anthem Ordinance was passed in the LegCo in June 2020 after much confrontation and obstruction by pan-democrats (*South China Morning Post* 4 June 2020).

The exercise of central authority by drawing upon the Chinese constitution has become increasingly prevalent in governing Hong Kong (Chan 2021; CY Lam 2020). In mid-August 2020, using the request of the Hong Kong government in response to the COVID-19 pandemic as the justification to delay the LegCo elections for one year, the SCNPC made a decision to extend the term of the incumbent LegCo members for not less than one year (*South China Morning Post* 11 August 2020). In mid-November 2020, the SCNPC further decided to require legislators to uphold the BL and pledge allegiance to the HKSAR to vet election candidates or legislators who were deemed to support Hong Kong independence, deny PRC sovereignty over Hong Kong, solicit foreign intervention over Hong Kong affairs, or exhibit other behavior damaging national security, and empowered the Hong Kong government to immediately act on this decision, which disqualified four opposition legislators (who had lobbied the US government to sanction the PRC or the HKSAR officials) and prevented them from staying in the extended term of the LegCo, prompting all other opposition lawmakers to resign en masse (*South China Morning Post* 11 August 2020). The adoption of decisions (*jueding*) by the SCNPC has been increasingly used to exercise power directly over Hong Kong beyond the interpretation of the BL (Chan 2022). Other path-breaking exercises of central constitutional and legislative authority—such as the legislation on the NSL in 2020 and the revamping of the electoral system in 2021—will be analyzed in later sections.

Safeguarding national security and securitization of Hong Kong's governance

After 2014, national security became a prominent frame for the CPG to understand and tackle Hong Kong's governance challenges. There were periodic calls for legislation of Article 23 of the BL from the pro-establishment camp, but it was never put on the government's decision agenda. The eruption of the political crisis arising from the 2019 Anti-ELAB Movement became a critical juncture in securitizing Hong Kong's post-1997 governance (for analysis of the 2019 crisis, see e.g., Lee et al. 2019; Lo et al. 2021). Emboldened by the domination of pro-establishment forces in the LegCo, which allowed the passage of controversial bills such as the colocation arrangement for high-speed rail terminus, the CE Carrie Lam wanted to extradite a Hong Kong man accused of the murder of his girlfriend in Taiwan by amending the extradition bill to cover those jurisdictions with which Hong Kong has not established a rendition arrangement (including the Mainland, Taiwan, and Macao). Under this amendment, people became deeply concerned with the extension of the Mainland's extradition authority to Hong Kong because of their skepticism toward the Mainland legal system.

The failure of the Hong Kong government to tackle the mounting crisis by the summer of 2019 created the worst-case scenario in OCTS: the incapacity of the local agent to maintain order risked inviting the sovereign to restore order by any means at its disposal. As the protests became more extensive, violent, and confrontational since July, Beijing perceived these as attempts by the opposition camp and even Western governments to undermine the authority of the Hong Kong government and the CPG and to destabilize Hong Kong and the Mainland (Lau 2020; Tian 2020). Starting from early and mid-August, the spokesperson of the Hong Kong and Macao Affairs Office (HKMAO) mentioned the "emergence of terrorism" and in early September claimed that the protestors wanted to turn Hong Kong into "an independent or semi-independent political entity" and demanded "stop violence and terminate chaos" (Lo et al. 2021: 178–179). Then, HKMAO Director Zhang Xiaoming warned that the protests showed signs of a "color revolution," buttressing the hard-line approach used by the police in cracking down on the protests. When the Hong Kong government seemed to have failed in dealing with the situation, the People's Armed Police moved to Shenzhen in early August and conducted exercises dealing with rioters, seemingly sending a strong warning to the protesters (Lo et al. 2021: 168–170). By autumn, central leaders had come out openly to support Carrie Lam and her government in restoring order. Given the grave situation, Beijing found it hard to back down, especially when the protestors demanded not only the resignation of the CE but also universal suffrage for the LegCo and the CE. Although Carrie Lam suspended the legislative process indefinitely on 15 June, she only formally withdrew the bill on 4 September after large-scale riots broke out in late June.

Unlike the largely peaceful OCM and UM, growing violence against the government arising from pent-up political frustration erupted in every district amid aggressive police tactics, such as extensive use of tear gas and rubber bullets. The intensity and spread of street battles involving firebombs, stoppage of traffic (including at the airport and periodic interference with the subway and main roads), vandalism (such as damaging banks, restaurants, and shops with Mainland or pro-establishment investments), and expression of anti-Mainland sentiments did not end even after the government finally withdrew the bill in early September (for details, see Ibrahim and Lam 2020). From Beijing's perspective, the localist and pro-independence political ideas, plus the violent confrontations and chaos threatening social and economic activities, constituted blatant challenges to law and order, the authority of the CPG, and national security

(Hong Kong and Macao Affairs Office of the State Council 2019). The expression of pro-independence slogans, the destruction of symbols of national sovereignty such as the national flag and national emblem and vandalism against the Central Liaison Office (CLO), as well as efforts in engaging external support and demanding sanctions against the PRC, had clearly crossed Xi's bottom lines and enraged the central authorities.

Riding the extreme dissatisfaction against Carrie Lam and her government, the pro-democracy camp registered a landslide victory against the pro-establishment camp in the 2019 DC elections with a record 71.2 percent turnout rate (2.93 million voters). While the pro-establishment camp still received 41.27 percent of votes (1.2 million), the pro-democracy camp had increased by almost 1 million votes to 56.62 percent (1.67 million), hence taking over the majority in 17 of the 18 DCs, which used to be strongholds for Beijing's supporters (JTM Lam 2021: 12). In addition to such a sweeping victory for the opposition and the sudden collapse of the pro-establishment forces, the opposition's plan to get over half the seats in the LegCo in the planned 2020 elections—and later half the seats of the Election Committee (EC) for CE elections—became an imminent danger to the central authorities because these were regarded as outrageous efforts to "seize power," threaten the socialist system in the Mainland, and endanger the country (Xia 2021).

In the midst of the massive protests in 2019, the fourth plenum of the nineteenth Central Committee of the CCP held in October 2019 decided on a package of measures to implement "comprehensive jurisdiction," including: (a) perfecting the appointment system of the CE and principal officials; (b) using the authority in interpretation by the SCNPC and exercising the power of the central authorities under both the BL and the Chinese constitution; (c) establishing and improving the legal system and implementation mechanism for safeguarding national security; (d) improving the reporting system of the CE; (e) perfecting the integration of Hong Kong and Macao into the Guangdong-Hong Kong-Macao Greater Bay Area (GBA) (Box 15.1) to resolve the deep-seated contradictions and problems that affect social stability and long-term development; (f) strengthening the education of public officials and especially the younger generation to enhance their national awareness and patriotism, and (g) preventing and suppressing the intervention of foreign forces into Hong Kong and Macao affairs and their engagement in secessionist, usurping, penetrative, and disruptive activities (Pei 2020; *Xinhua Net* 5 November 2019). In early 2020, the reshuffling and upgrading of the ranks of central officials in Hong Kong and Macao affairs further heralded a major shift of central strategy with the appointment of Luo Huining, former Party Secretary in Shanxi province known for his anti-corruption efforts, as Director of CLO, and Xia Baolong, Vice Chairman of Chinese People's Political Consultative Conference (CPPCC), as Director of the

HKMAO under the State Council. Both officials, who did not have connections to Hong Kong affairs but were trusted by Xi and recognized for their hard-line approach, reflected Xi's determination to take decisive actions to rectify the unstable situation in Hong Kong (*South China Morning Post* 7 January 2020 and 13 February 2020), whereas their respective predecessors, Wang Zhimin and Zhang Xiaoming, were seemingly demoted for failing to handle the 2019 crisis.

The decision on safeguarding national security in Hong Kong by the NPC in late May and the enactment of the NSL—a national law—by the SCNPC in June 2020 constitute a milestone defining Hong Kong's practice of OCTS. A host of global and domestic factors created the policy window for this pathbreaking law to be introduced earlier than later. The global spread of the COVID-19 pandemic has seriously weakened the economies in Western democracies and their ability to respond to developments in Hong Kong. The pandemic provided not only a perfect justification for the Hong Kong government to impose restrictions over mass gatherings, which led to a de facto banning of all protests, but also a pretext for delaying the legislative elections scheduled in autumn 2020. Rather than waiting for Hong Kong to legislate on national security (i.e., Article 23 of the BL), this national law was enacted by the SCNPC, directly inserted into Annex III of the BL, and became part of the constitutional instruments on 30 June 2020.

The NSL legislation process suggests that the CPG will not be hesitant to exercise its constitutional prerogative to legislate or add national laws to the BL annex should Hong Kong fail to address its problems. As part of the BL framework, all the institutions, organizations, and citizens have the constitutional duty to uphold this law, hence accounting for its sweeping coverage and power, and it overrides all other local legislations (Article 62). Article 3 states that "[t]he executive authorities, legislature and judiciary" of the HKSAR "shall effectively prevent, suppress and impose punishment for any act or activity endangering national security in accordance with this Law and other relevant laws." More importantly, new institutional mechanisms ensure direct central supervision of the HKSAR in national security. A new central organ, Office for Safeguarding National Security in the HKSAR (OSNS), is established in Hong Kong. A Committee for Safeguarding National Security in the HKSAR (CSNS) comprising the CE and other senior officials is created and a central advisor (the CLO director) will be assigned to oversee the implementation of the NSL. Under certain circumstances beyond the handling capacity of the HKSAR (Article 55), the OSNS can directly exercise jurisdiction over these cases, which will then be directly handled by the Supreme People's Procuratorate and the Supreme People's Court in the Mainland. While Hong Kong still has to legislate on Article 23 of the BL, the central authorities can now exercise direct and wide-ranging power over all NSL-related matters.

The prioritization of security over all other matters has defined the main themes of Hong Kong's governance since mid-2020. As the implementer of NSL, the government had already introduced a host of measures, including rolling out NSL education, censoring guidelines for screening movies, oath-taking by civil servants, real-name registration for telephone SIM cards, and monitoring the media and others. In July 2021, a Deputy Director of the HKMAO stressed that these efforts should be further strengthened in the near future (*Ming Pao* 6 July 2021).

Overhauling the electoral system to ensure "patriots administering Hong Kong"

In the aftermath of the 2019 crisis, Hong Kong's electoral system was thoroughly revamped to achieve "patriots administering Hong Kong." As early as 1984, Deng Xiaoping had articulated the need to rely upon "patriots" as the mainstay in governing Hong Kong, and the criteria for a patriot are "to respect one's own nation, sincerely support the resumption of the exercise of sovereignty over Hong Kong by the motherland, and not to impair Hong Kong's prosperity and stability" (*HKSAR Government Press Releases* 5 March 2021). The full stipulation is "the administration of Hong Kong by Hong Kong people with patriots as the main body" (*aiguozhe weizhutide gangrenzhigang*), a principle that has been reiterated regularly by Beijing as tensions arose in the relations between the CPG and the Hong Kong community. In January 2021, Xi underscored that only through the implementation of "patriots administering Hong Kong" could "comprehensive jurisdiction over the HKSAR be effectively implemented, the constitutional order as set out in the Constitution and the Basic Law be effectively safeguarded, various deep-seated problems be effectively resolved, and the long-term stability and prosperity of Hong Kong be achieved" (Hong Kong and Macao Affairs Office of the State Council 2021; *HKSAR Government Press Release* 5 March 2021). In late February, Xia Baolong elaborated on this principle and insisted that all key appointments of executive, legislative, and judicial branches, as well as key statutory bodies, must be held by "patriots" and not be taken by anyone who "goes against China and disrupts Hong Kong" (*South China Morning Post* 22 February 2021). Patriots should exhibit three attributes: "sincerely safeguarding national sovereignty, security, and development interests"; "respecting the fundamental system of the country" (which means not opposing the socialist system led by the CCP) and "constitutional order" of the HKSAR; and "doing one's utmost to maintain its prosperity and stability" (*South China Morning Post* 22 February 2021). Further, in early January 2021, oath-taking was introduced to require the 180,000 civil servants to take an oath pledging to uphold the BL, bear allegiance to the HKSAR, be dedicated to their duties, and be responsible to the government (*South China Morning Post* 19 April 2021).

The decision on "improving the electoral system" by the NPC and the subsequent amendment of Annex I and II of the BL on 30 March 2021, followed by the local legislation by the Hong Kong government, has completely restructured the political system (*South China Morning Post* 30 March 2021). These efforts will put the central authorities in even greater control over the entire elite selection process, likely because it no longer trusted the Hong Kong electorate, or probably even the government or the pro-establishment camp, to meet its expectations, in view of the results of the DC elections in November 2019. First, the national legislature has asserted its constitutional authority over Hong Kong's political development, replacing the previous Annex I and II of the BL, which detail the methods for selecting the CE and forming the LegCo, with a new version through delegating its powers to the SCNPC, and sidestepped the previous "five-step procedure" of amendment of these annexes involving the CE's report, the determination by SCNPC, the proposal of a bill by the government, the two-thirds majority approval in the LegCo, and then the SCNPC's approval. Such a "five-step procedure" disappeared in the new Annexes, meaning that the initiative of future political reform rests entirely in the hands of Beijing. Through delegation from the NPC, the SCNPC has much more leeway to exercise its power to decide on Hong Kong's political development on the basis of the Chinese constitution rather than just relying on the interpretation of the BL (CY Lam 2021).

Second, both the executive branch and legislative branch of the Hong Kong government will be selected through a tightly controlled electoral system where pro-Beijing organizations and groups representing Mainland interests are highly privileged (see Chapter 3 in this volume). For instance, the membership of the EC for electing the CE will be expanded from 1,200 to 1,500, and a new fifth sector comprising Hong Kong deputies from the NPC, delegates from the CPPCC, and representatives from other Mainland bodies in Hong Kong will be created. A convener of the EC with the position of "state leader" will be appointed, highlighting its role as an agent of the center.

Third, the membership of the LegCo is expanded from 70 to 90, but 40 will be returned by the EC, whereas only 20 will be elected from directly elected geographic constituencies and 30 from the functional constituencies. The constituencies for directly elected geographical constituencies are expanded to 10, with each returning two members. Both the number and groups of functional constituencies are revamped to reduce the influence of the opposition in the professional sectors and from the business community and to augment those representing the Mainland. Fourth, the CSNS plays a key role in vetting the candidates for the LegCo elections, as it is tasked to issue an opinion to the Candidate Eligibility Review Committee, which will not be subject to judicial review. Last, the block voting for passing motions, bills, and amendments introduced by individual members in the LegCo are also changed to require approval from (a) the EC as well as (b) both the GCs and FCs.

These dramatic steps demonstrate not only the further interlocking of the Hong Kong and Mainland state organs but also Beijing's determination to exercise a maximum degree of control over the vetting, nomination, and election of LegCo members and the passage of future legislation to ensure "patriots administering Hong Kong" and "executive-led governance." According to John Burns, an expert on the Chinese party-state, the electoral changes have placed the CCP "at the core of Hong Kong's political system" (Burns 10 April 2021). First, he suggested that the CLO would go beyond its traditional united front work and play a key role in vetting at least 1,612 positions, such as the EC, the LegCo, the CE, and principal officials. The organizational management of the CCP will likely be extended to different sectors in Hong Kong, as an increasing number of officials and candidates for public offices will be under its purview. Second, coordinating and balancing the competing interests of local and Mainland organizations, which are given more representation in the EC, is another key task for the CCP. Third, the CCP will need to employ different strategies to discipline many officials and candidates for public office, mainly because the party cannot use its own party disciplinary mechanism as in the Mainland. Fourth, the party will continue to lead the united front and mobilize support for Beijing. Given the complex set of nomination, selection, and vetting involved for candidates for all key public offices, the challenges in political control and coordination mean that the CCP will play a pivotal role in Hong Kong's governance because it is unlikely that any CE or political parties can have the capacity to manage such a complex setup.

Emphasizing ideological authority and strengthening united front work

With the failure of the Hong Kong government to introduce the moral and national education proposal in Hong Kong in 2012, the contention over cultivating a stronger Chinese identity and patriotism has become an issue in Hong Kong's governance. In the autumn of 2019, official Mainland media criticized the Liberal Studies curriculum in Hong Kong and the involvement of teachers in student activism during the protests. By December 2020, 269 protest-related complaints had been made against teacher misconduct since June 2019, and 154 teachers were disciplined (*South China Morning Post* 24 May 2021). In April 2021, under growing criticism from both the pro-establishment camp and the government for covering controversial subjects and becoming politically biased (e.g., using materials from pro-democratic and anti-Mainland media sources by some teachers), the Liberal Studies subject in the secondary school curriculum, which was actually introduced by the government in the post-1997 education reform to cultivate independent thinking and social awareness among students, was officially succeeded by a Citizen and Social Development subject, which focuses more on cultivating national identity and a better appreciation of the Mainland's achievements starting from 2021–2022. To cultivate a stronger national identity and a correct understanding of the NSL and to prevent students from engaging in disobedience or protests, as happened in 2019, the Education Bureau has issued detailed guidelines for all primary and secondary schools to teach the NSL (*South China Morning Post* 4 February 2021), while universities will devise their own plans to teach the subject.

Strengthening united front work is another key central response to tackle the governance challenges in Hong Kong (Cheng 2020; Lo et al. 2019). To build connections with the grassroots and buttress the patriotic political forces, an elaborate system of united front work has been developed. These networks utilized both patronage of business elites as well as mass organizations, particularly (a) hometown associations; (b) three local federations in Hong Kong Island, Kowloon, and the New Territories through networks of women bodies, youth, and cultural societies and business chambers; and (c) service-oriented NGOs (Cheng 2020). These patronage networks managed by the CLO channeled lots of resources to the pro-establishment parties and politicians to help strengthen their political influence, gauge public sentiment, and build their grassroots base. Other strategies adopted included the outsourcing of counterprotest work, using existing state organs for tackling dissent, and employing extended stigmatization based on an elaborate network of agents, groups, and alliances. Scholars argued that the CLO "plays the role of organizer, facilitator, coordinator, and mobilizer in united front politics" (Lo et al. 2019: 366). Yet increasing dependence upon the CLO for political support and coordination by the CE and the Hong Kong government risks undercutting their legitimacy and effectiveness as they might have fewer incentives to respond to community demands. These developments suggest an increasing reliance on authoritarian instruments in governing Hong Kong, but the contrasting conceptions of citizenship and post-materialistic political values of many Hong Kong people, especially the younger generation, explain why there was strong resistance to the political compliance expected by the Mainland through these united front strategies (Lo et al. 2019: 137).

Responding actively to foreign influence and Hong Kong's precarious future as an international financial center

The 2019 political crisis brought the most serious international repercussions and hence the most severe impacts on OCTS and the city's future as an international financial and business center. Not only Taiwanese political parties, but more importantly, the Democratic Progressive Party government had used the crisis as a justification to denounce the OCTS framework for Taiwan, and Tsai Ing-wen had exploited the Hong Kong situation to help her bid for reelection in January 2020 (Lo et al. 2021: 298–303). The extradition bill itself had also aroused consternation among the business and professional sectors in Hong Kong, given its many legal ramifications. The months of protests in 2019, which turned violent in late summer, had disrupted traffic and deterred business as well as visitors, especially from the Mainland, and called into question the order and stability of the city. Moreover, protestors had extended their protest overseas and appealed to many foreign governments and communities, much to the wrath of Beijing. For instance, former Democratic Party leader Martin Lee led a delegation to the US Capitol and met Secretary of State Mike Pompeo and other officials, as well as members of Congress (*South China Morning Post* 16 May 2019), while *Apple Daily* founder Jimmy Lai later met US Vice President Mike Pence and Pompeo in Washington, DC, in mid-June 2019, all of which triggered strong admonition from Beijing (*South China Morning Post* 9 July 2019). From August until November, various protests were held to rally support from the US to pass the Hong Kong Human Rights and Democracy Bill and put pressure on China (Lo et al. 2021: 292–298), which was considered evidence of collusion with foreign forces (Lau 2020).

These efforts by the protesters and critics of the Hong Kong government were instrumental in persuading the US Congress to pass the Hong Kong Human Rights and Democracy Bill in November 2019, which was regarded by Beijing as a most flagrant foreign intervention into China's domestic affairs and evidence of collaboration with foreign powers by these opposition figures. In response to the imposition of the NSL, the Trump administration signed the Hong Kong Autonomy Act, which sanctioned officials in the Mainland and Hong Kong for violating Hong Kong's autonomy. It further announced in July 2020 that Hong Kong would no longer be treated differently from China in trade, and by late September 2020, goods imported from Hong Kong would be marked "Made in China" (*South China Morning Post* 11 August 2020). Other foreign governments also responded to the NSL by raising serious concerns over Hong Kong's fate under OCTS and suspending their extradition treaties with Hong Kong. Since different officials in Hong Kong and the Mainland were also under US sanctions in 2020–2021, such actions motivated China to respond with an unprecedented anti-sanction law in June 2021 (*South China Morning Post* 11 June 2021).

Hong Kong's openness and connections with the global capitalist economy are key factors contributing to its rise as an international financial center and a global city. In fact, its status as a global business, financial, and transportation hub has contributed enormously to China's rapid economic growth. OCTS almost by definition requires international acceptance of Hong Kong's special status; foreign countries will only treat Hong Kong differently if it is indeed distinguishable from other parts of the PRC, and if they consider the OCTS promises largely kept. With the promulgation of the NSL, reactions of the OECD countries—Hong Kong's key business and trading partners—toward the wavering of the promised OCTS and a "high degree of autonomy" are highly critical. It may be unrealistic to expect these liberal democracies not to respond to the prosecution of pro-democracy opposition politicians, the disciplining of the media such as the closure of *Apple Daily* (a leading anti-communist media group) in June 2021, and the likely rectification of other key sectors such as education, the mass media, and the legal sector as championed by pro-Beijing political forces in recent years. Hong Kong's future as a truly international financial center can only continue so long as the international community sees that OCTS is still in place (see Chapter 16 in this volume). As Hong Kong is considered part of the Mainland system after 2020–2021, whether foreign governments would allow its companies to sell high-tech products or invest in technology sectors in the city remains to be seen, and this may affect Hong Kong's role as a window for transferring Western technology to the Mainland. Since China is unlikely to open up its capital account any time soon, Hong Kong may still have a role to play as an offshore RMB center and China's international financial gateway for some time, but business is unlikely to remain usual as in the pre-2020 period.

Incorporation of Hong Kong into the national development framework

Another key central strategy is to incorporate Hong Kong into the national development framework. In the aftermath of the OCM and UM, Beijing has expedited the integration of Hong Kong into the Mainland economy by formulating the GBA planning. Xi Jinping aspired to achieve "national rejuvenation" and put forward his grand strategy of "One Belt, One Road," commonly called the Belt and Road Initiative (BRI), in 2015 to counter the US strategy of weakening China's expanding global influence (Zhao 2020). In addition to the BRI, which may open new opportunities for Hong Kong's finance and business services, the GBA planning is the first strategic development plan formulated by the central government that the Hong Kong government must fully implement because it is initiated by the central authorities. A framework agreement was first signed in Xi's presence during the twentieth anniversary of Hong Kong's reunification with the PRC in July 2017, and the full document was promulgated by the National Development and Reform Commission in early 2019. This initiative seeks to facilitate Hong Kong's integration with Macao and nine other cities in the Pearl River Delta to develop into a "world-class bay area" (Yu 2019). While sustaining its conventional positions as a global financial, trade, and transportation hub, Hong Kong was also tasked with developing into an international innovation and technology center. Instead of highlighting Hong Kong's role in China's development and in view of Hong Kong's continuing political turmoil since the OCM, the primary aim of this plan is to incorporate Hong Kong into the broad scheme of national development and to integrate it socially, economically, and culturally with the neighboring region. In fact, the central government has also been giving more support to other Chinese cities, as shown in the decentralization of more policy autonomy to boost Shenzhen's development into a technology and finance hub in 2020 (*South China Morning Post* 17 October 2020).

Unlike previous cross-boundary cooperation between Hong Kong and Guangdong, this GBA initiative was initiated by Xi. The CE formally became a member of the Mainland policy process by joining the Leading Group for the Development of the Guangdong-Hong Kong-Macao GBA under the State Council. Before 2014, Hong Kong's leaders could often directly access the central leadership, but it is now put into a group together with 10 other cities. Various policies were soon promulgated by Beijing in 2019 to lower taxes and relax other administrative restrictions to assist Hong Kong people working and residing in Guangdong. Guangdong and other cities also took advantage of this opportunity to articulate their developmental visions while also following the central dictate to help Hong Kong integrate with their region.

The Outline of the 14th Five-Year Plan (FYP) promulgated in 2020 prioritized the imperative to enforce "comprehensive jurisdiction" and the NSL, as well as to adopt measures to enable Hong Kong and Macao residents to work and live in the Mainland, and to strengthen their national awareness and patriotism while enhancing the city's status as an international financial, trade, and shipping center and international aviation hub, among others (*Xinhua Net* 12 March 2021b). Hong Kong is also obliged to follow the priorities set out in national development planning, and to play its part as designated in China's grand plan. In an unprecedented "briefing" for both lawmakers and top officials held in late August 2021, central officials demanded that with central support, both the governing elites and the Hong Kong community should actively take initiatives to align with the 14th FYP and expedite integration through converging not just their policies, industries, and markets but also their ideas and thinking with that of the Mainland (*South China Morning Post* 23 August 2021). However, whether Hong Kong's competitiveness and unique characteristics under OCTS (such as openness and the rule of law under the common law system) can be maintained under "comprehensive jurisdiction" and whether it will still be welcomed by foreign investors as the preferred destination for business in Asia remains to be seen. Furthermore, the neighboring Shenzhen has risen as China's leading innovation and technology hub. Shenzhen's average GDP growth was 21.6 percent per annum from 1979 to 2019, and its GDP surpassed that of Hong Kong in 2018 (*South China Morning Post* 3 September 2020). In Xi Jinping's speech commemorating the 40th anniversary of the establishment of the Shenzhen Special Economic Zone in mid-October 2020, he did not mention Hong Kong's crucial role in supporting Shenzhen's development, at least in the first two to three decades since its establishment. He also designated Shenzhen as the "key engine" of the future development of the GBA, signaling a shift in his view on Hong Kong as an important player in the area (*Xinhua Net* 14 October 2020). Whether Hong Kong will continue to thrive as an international business and financial center amid Shenzhen's rise into an innovation and service economy prioritized by Xi constitutes an existential challenge to this once thriving global city in Asia.

Revamping the governing team and central organs on Hong Kong and Macao affairs

In response to the growing geopolitical risks and international threats confronting China, the central authorities took swift steps to revamp the personnel and organs governing Hong Kong and Macao. No longer just offering support or hinting at Hong Kong's shortcomings, the central leadership had openly underscored the problems in Hong Kong and showed the policy directions for the HKSAR administration to follow. In his speech on the 25th anniversary of the HKSAR on 1 July 2022, Xi not only tried to reassure Hong Kong and the world that OCTS, being such a successful system, will continue in the long run, but he also detailed his priorities for Hong Kong's development and expectations for the governing team (*South China Morning Post* 1 July 2022). His "hopes" include (a) improving the quality of governance through better government performance and better managing the relations between the government and the market; (b) boosting the momentum of development, including the alignment with national development strategies such as the 14th FYP, the GBA planning, and the BRI initiative, as well as "breaking the impediments of vested interests"; (c) addressing the difficulties of the people's livelihood to meet their desires for "a better life, a bigger apartment, more business start-up opportunities, better education for kids and better elderly care"; and (d) upholding harmony and stability through focusing on development and particularly helping "young people overcome difficulties in education, employment, business start-up and home-buying" (*South China Morning Post* 1 July 2022). Such a list of unprecedented "demands" delivered by Xi on this highly symbolic occasion apparently suggests increasing central impatience with the performance of the HKSAR government, which cannot be dissociated from the accumulation of socioeconomic and political discontents since 1997.

The HKSAR government's legislative and executive branches are put in the hands of the patriots after the restructuring of the Hong Kong polity. The Seventh

LegCo elections were held on 19 December 2022 under the new electoral system and turned out 90 members, many of whom were new faces and none were from the former opposition camp (see Chapter 10 in this volume). With strong central backing and no contenders, John Lee Ka-chiu, a former senior police officer, Secretary for Security, and Chief Secretary for Administration (June 2021–April 2022) was elected the CE by the revamped EC with 99.2 percent of the vote in May 2022 (*South China Morning Post* 8 May 2022). Together with Eric Chan Kwok-ki, a former immigration director, the No. 1 and No. 2 officials of the HKSAR both came from the disciplinary force, signaling Beijing's preference for the more reliable disciplinary officers and abandonment of the once elitist Administrative Officers.

Personnel and institutional changes were also introduced in 2023. In January 2023, Zheng Yanxiong, the former head of the OSNS, replaced the retiring Luo Huining as the Director of the CLO (*South China Morning Post* 14 January 2023). Although not a Central Committee member, Zheng's background in national security seems to be what concerns Beijing most in governing Hong Kong in the post-2019 period. Furthermore, as part of the comprehensive restructuring of the State Council to establish tighter central party control over key policy portfolios, the Hong Kong and Macao Affairs Office was changed from an administrative agency under the State Council to become the Hong Kong and Macao Affairs Office directly under the party's Central Committee, although its nominal name under the State Council will be kept (*South China Morning Post* 19 March 2023). Executive Vice-Premier, Ding Xuexiang, a member of the Politburo Standing Committee and a close confidant of Xi, would serve as the leader of the party's Central Leading Group of Hong Kong and Macao Work (*South China Morning Post* 15 March 2023). The upgraded Hong Kong and Macao Office, which held its first meeting in mid July 2023, shows that Xiao Baolong continues to serve as its director and Zhou Jie, a former deputy party secretary and security chief from Henan Province, is appointed as its executive deputy director (*South China Morning Post* 11 July 2023). The other deputy directors include the two directors of the liaison office from Hong Kong and Macao, one veteran diplomat, and one Beijing expert in national security and international relations from the Chinese Academy of Social Sciences. Hence, future initiatives regarding Hong Kong and Macao will come directly from the party center to achieve better coherence in governing the SARs in an increasingly precarious global environment, whereas the other agencies, such as the CLO, will be mainly tasked with implementation.

Conclusion

Hong Kong's experience since 2014 shows how the previous "high degree of autonomy" model is being revamped to converge with the Mainland system of authoritarian governance under the "comprehensive jurisdiction" model. The central authorities have employed comprehensive measures in recasting the rationales, rules, and processes of Hong Kong's political system, which features several distinct characteristics: (a) the active use of the SCNPC as the institutional mechanism to steer Hong Kong's governance; (b) the penetration of central authority into the local government structure through the national security advisor in the CSNS and the role of the OSNS in vetting candidates in elections; (c) further interlocking of Hong Kong and Mainland political systems through the provision of formal roles for NPC delegates, CPPCC delegates, and Mainland mass organizations, and other bodies in the EC; (d) the formal integration of Hong Kong into the Chinese policy process through the CE's membership in the Leading Group on the GBA of the State Council; and (e) implementation of national policies and preferences, most notably educational changes (such as patriotic education and NSL education) and the GBA planning, among others. With the celebration of the centenary of the party in the HKSAR on 1 July 2021, the CLO Director made it plain that "advancing the cause of OCTS" means upholding the leadership of the CCP (*South China Morning Post* 12 June 2021). The White Paper on democracy in Hong Kong under OCTS issued by the State Council in December 2022 further offers an official narrative of Hong Kong's political development before and after 1997 to legitimize the various central initiatives in overhauling the governance of the HKSAR as democratic progress (*South China Morning Post* 18 December 2022).

While Hong Kong may have its own legal, administrative, and political structures distinguishable from the authoritarian Mainland system, the essence of the political order has undergone important transformations to implement "patriots administering Hong Kong." President Xi's report to the 20th National Congress of the CCP in October 2022 reiterated that the two SARs should enhance "their overall governance and management capacity" and improve "their judicial and legal systems" (Xi, 2022). Revamping other state organs, such as the judiciary and the civil service, and other social institutions—such as schools and universities, the media, the professional sectors, and NGOs—will follow suit to achieve the objective of "comprehensive jurisdiction." With the growing centralization of party control over state administration since March 2023, the central leadership has now kept Hong Kong and Macao affairs tightly under its purview. Although the structures of the "two systems" remain, the essence and logic of the emerging political order are experiencing a homogenization process (*tongzhihua*) to converge more closely with the evolving system of governance in the Mainland well before 2047, as China is rising as an authoritarian superpower.

The development of the Mainland–Hong Kong relationship since 2014 witnesses not merely the rising activism and preemption by the central authorities but also her extensive efforts in remaking state-society relations under the dictates of the party-state and recasting state-economy relations through cross-boundary socioeconomic and administrative integration. How will Hong Kong's previous characteristics, such as its openness, pluralistic way of life, global connections, cosmopolitanism, the common law, and socioeconomic and political freedoms fare under "comprehensive jurisdiction"? Some believe the Mainland's forceful imposition of legal, political, and administrative power over Hong Kong will fuel apathy, frustration, and even resistance against the gradual waning of civil liberties, partial democracy, and limited government. Beijing and the pro-establishment camp, however, believe that with the remolding of the current political system and the removal of the opposition and dissent, Hong Kong could experience a revival and focus its energy on livelihood and economic challenges confronting it, such as housing, poverty, and economic restructuring and benefit from the Mainland's economic development. Not unlike previous episodes of its recent past, this unique global city is again facing enormous social, economic, and political challenges and uncertainties, albeit in the even more tumultuous and unpredictable early twenty-first century.

Acknowledgments

The author is grateful for the grants for this study from the Department of Social Sciences and the Faculty of Social Sciences and Liberal Arts at the Education University of Hong Kong, and for the research assistance provided by Billy Tong and Siwei Huang. The valuable comments from Albert Chen, Cora Chan, Edmund Cheng, Cheung Kwok-wah, C. Y. Lam, and the editors on earlier drafts are much appreciated, but all errors are the author's responsibility. The views expressed do not represent those of the funding bodies.

Box 15.1: Greater Bay Area planning

The Outline Development Plan of the Guangdong-Hong Kong-Macao Greater Bay Area (GBA) is a strategic development plan promulgated by the National Development and Reform Commission in early 2019 to promote the development of the nine cities in the GBA (formerly called the Greater Pearl River Delta—Guangzhou, Shenzhen, Zhuhai, Foshan, Huizhou, Dongguan, Zhongshan, Jiangmen, and Zhaoqing), as well as Hong Kong and Macao SARs, encompassing a total area of 56,000 square kilometers with a combined population of roughly 70 million at the end of 2017 into a "world class bay area" by 2035 (Constitutional and Mainland Affairs Bureau 2019). This planning, which was under President Xi Jinping's direct steering, aims to facilitate and incorporate the development of these two SARs into national development so that they could achieve greater social, economic, cultural, and spatial cooperation and integration with the Mainland. It is considered a new endeavor of "one country, two systems." The planning document mainly sets out the strategic positioning and policy goals to be achieved: (a) a vibrant, world-class city cluster; (b) a globally influential international innovation and technology hub; (c) an important support pillar for the Belt and Road Initiative; (d) a showcase for in-depth cooperation between the Mainland and Hong Kong and Macao; and (e) a quality living circle for living, working, and traveling. A Leading Group on the Development of the Guangdong-Hong Kong-Macao GBA headed by the Executive Vice-Premier was established to plan and prioritize the specific implementation measures.

Questions

1. What will be the key features of the evolving framework of "one country, two systems" if Hong Kong is aligning administratively, politically, and legally with the essential elements of the Mainland system of governance?
2. Will Hong Kong continue to maintain a high degree of autonomy, a high level of competitiveness, and a vibrant civil society when it is increasingly integrated into the Greater Bay Area socially, economically, and administratively?
3. Will Hong Kong sustain its position as an international financial, trade, and transportation center in the next decade in view of the keen competition from other cities in Asia, the AI and technological transformation, and the growing tensions in global politics?
4. How can Hong Kong continue to contribute to the development of the Mainland so that it can still thrive as a cosmopolitan, vibrant, and prosperous global city for China in the coming decade?

Bibliography

Burns, J 2021, "Hong Kong's Electoral Changes: The Communist Party Is Taking Over," *Hong Kong Free Press*, viewed 30 June 2021, https://hongkongfp.com/2021/04/10/hong-kongs-electoral-changes-the-communist-party-is-taking-over/

Chan, C 2021, "Can Hong Kong Remain a Liberal Enclave within China? Analysis of the Hong Kong National Security Law," *Public Law*, pp. 271–292.

Chan, C 2022, "From Legal Pluralism to Dual State: Evolution of the Relationship between the Chinese and Hong Kong Legal Orders," *Law & Ethics of Human Rights*, vol. 16, no. 1, pp. 99–135.

Chen, AHY 2021, *The Changing Legal Orders in Hong Kong and Mainland China: Essays on "One Country, Two Systems,"* City University of Hong Kong Press, Hong Kong.

Cheng, EW 2020, "United Front Work and Mechanisms of Countermobilization in Hong Kong," *China Journal*, no. 83, pp. 1–33.

Cheng, J 2009, "The Story of a New Policy," *Hong Kong Journal*, no. 15.

Cheung, CY 2017, "'One Country, Two Systems' after the Umbrella Movement: Problems and Prospects," *Asian Education and Development Studies*, vol. 6, no. 4, pp. 385–400.

Cheung, PTY 2012, "The Changing Relations between Hong Kong and the Mainland since 2003," in WM Lam, PLT Lui and W Wong (eds), *Contemporary Hong Kong Government and Politics*, Expanded 2nd ed., Hong Kong University Press, Hong Kong.

Cheung, PTY 2018, "In Beijing's Tightening Grip: Changing Mainland-Hong Kong Relations amid Integration and Confrontation," In BCH Fong and TL Lui (eds), *Hong Kong 20 Years after the Handover: Emerging Social and Institutional Fractures After 1997*, Palgrave Macmillan, London.

Cheung, TM 2020, "The Chinese National Security State Emerges from the Shadows to Center Stage," *China Leadership Monitor*, 1 September.

Constitutional and Mainland Affairs Bureau 2019, "Outline Development Plan for the Guangdong-Hong Kong-Macao Greater Bay Area," viewed 2 July 2021, https://www.bayarea.gov.hk/filemanager/en/share/pdf/Outline_Development_Plan.pdf

Fong, BCH 2017, "One Country, Two Nationalisms: Center-Periphery Relations between Mainland China and Hong Kong, 1997–2016," *Modern China*, vol. 43, no. 5, pp. 523–556.

HKSAR Government Press Release 2021, "CE Statement on NPC's Deliberation on Improving HKSAR Electoral System to Implement 'Patriots Administering Hong Kong,'" viewed 30 June 2021, https://www.info.gov.hk/gia/general/202103/05/P2021030500393.htm

Hong Kong and Macao Affairs Office of the State Council 2019, "Guowuyuan Gangaoban xinwen fayanren jieshao dui dangqian Xianggang shitai de kanfa" [Views of spokesperson of Hong Kong and Macao Affairs Office of the State Council on current situation of Hong Kong], viewed 12 July 2021, https://www.hmo.gov.cn/xwzx/xwfb/xwfb_child/201908/t20190806_21095.html

Hong Kong and Macao Affairs Office of the State Council 2021, "Xi Jinping tingqu Linzheng Yuee shuzhi baogao" [Xi Jinping Hears Working Report by Carrie Lam], viewed 30 June 2021, https://www.hmo.gov.cn/xwzx/zwyw/202101/t20210127_22354.html

Ibrahim, Z & Lam, J (eds) 2020, *Rebel City: Hong Kong's Year of Water and Fire*, World Scientific Publishing Co Pte Ltd, Singapore; South China Morning Post Publishers Limited, Hong Kong.

Information Office of the State Council 2011, "China's Peaceful Development," viewed 29 June 2021, http://english.www.gov.cn/archive/white_paper/2014/09/09/content_281474986284646.htm

Information Office of the State Council 2014, "The Practice of the 'One Country, Two Systems' Policy in the Hong Kong Special Administrative Region," viewed 30 June 2021, http://english.www.gov.cn/archive/white_paper/2014/08/23/content_281474982986578.htm

Keading, MP 2017, "The Rise of 'Localism' in Hong Kong," *Journal of Democracy*, vol. 28, no. 1, pp. 157–171.

Lam, JTM 2017, "Hong Kong District Council Elections 2015: A Political Litmus Test for the Occupy Central Movement," *Asian Education and Development Studies*, vol. 6, no. 4, pp. 354–371.

Lam, JTM 2021, "The 2019 District Council Election in Hong Kong: A Localism Perspective," *Asian Affairs: An American Review*, vol. 48, no. 2, pp. 113–132.

Lam, CY 2020, "Cong lihui renqi zhengyi kan renda changweihui jueding de zhidu ji yingxiang" [The institution of SCNPC decision and its implication reflected in the dispute of LegCo terms], *Ming Pao*, 21 August, B13.

Lam, CY 2021, "You wubuqu bian yibuqu de qishi" [The implication behind "five-steps" replaced by "one-step"], *Ming Pao*, 17 March, B08.

Lam, WM 2018, "Changing Political Activism: Before and after the Umbrella Movement," in BCH Fong and TL Lui (eds), *Hong Kong 20 Years after the Handover: Emerging Social and Institutional Fractures After 1997*, Palgrave Macmillan, London.

Lam, WM 2020, "China's Changing Ruling Strategies on Hong Kong and Their Implications," *Contemporary Chinese Political Economy and Strategic Relations: An International Journal*, vol. 6, no. 3, pp. 953–992.

Lau, SK 2017, *Huigui hou Xianggang de dute zhengzhi xingtai: yige ziyou weiquan de teshu gean* [Political pattern of Hong Kong after its return: A special case of liberal authoritarian polity], The Commercial Press (Hong Kong) Limited, Hong Kong.

Lau, SK 2020, "Xianggang xiuli fengbo beihou de shencengci wenti" [Deep-seated problems exposed by Hong Kong's extradition law protest], *Hong Kong and Macao Journal*, no. 1, pp. 3–12.

Lee, FLF, Yuen, S, Tang, G & Cheng, EW 2019, "Hong Kong's Summer of Uprising: From Anti-Extradition to Anti-authoritarian Protests," *China Review*, vol. 19, no. 4, pp. 1–32.

Lo, SSH 2008, *The Dynamics of Beijing-Hong Kong Relations: A Model for Taiwan?* Hong Kong University Press, Hong Kong.

Lo, SSH, Hung, SCF & Loo, JHC 2019, *China's New United Front Work in Hong Kong: Penetrative Politics and Its Implications*, Palgrave Macmillan, Singapore.

Lo, SSH, Hung, SCF & Loo, JHC 2021, *The Dynamics of Peaceful and Violent Protests in Hong Kong: The Anti-extradition Movement*, Palgrave Macmillan, Singapore.

Loh, C 2018, *Underground Front: The Chinese Communist Party in Hong Kong*, 2nd ed., Hong Kong University Press, Hong Kong.

Ma, N 2020, *Fankang de gongtongti: 2019 Xianggang fansongzhong yundong* [Rebellion community: 2019 anti-extradition movement], Rive Gauche Publishing House, New Taipei.

Ma, N & Cheng, EW (eds) 2020, *The Umbrella Movement: Civil Resistance and Contentious Space in Hong Kong*, Amsterdam University Press, Amsterdam.

Medeiros, ES 2019, "The Changing Fundamentals of US-China Relations," *The Washington Quarterly*, vol. 42, no. 3, pp. 93–119.

Pei, M 2020, "Investigation of A Death Long Feared: How China Decided to Impose Its National Security Law in Hong Kong," *China Leadership Monitor*, 1 September.

Shambaugh, D 2016, *China's Future*, Polity, Malden, MA.

Tian, F 2017, "Tongzhan zhigang yu yifa zhigang de xietiao ji youhua" [Coordination and optimization between ruling Hong Kong by united front and ruling Hong Kong by law], *Journal of the Central Institute of Socialism*, no. 3, pp. 77–83.

Tian, F 2018, *Houzhanzhong zhigang: fali yu zhengzhi* [Hong Kong governance after Occupy Central: Jurisprudence and politics], City University of Hong Kong Press, Hong Kong.

Tian, F 2020, *Kangming qitu: Xianggang xiuli yu liangzhi jibian* [Disobedience the wrong path: The Anti–Extradition Law Amendment Bill movement in Hong Kong and dramatic change of the two systems], Sinminchu Publishing Company Limited, Hong Kong.

Veg, S 2017, "The Rise of 'Localism' and Civic Identity in Post-Handover Hong Kong: Questioning the Chinese Nation-State," *China Quarterly*, no. 230, pp. 323–347.

World Bank 2021, World Development Indicators, viewed 29 June 2021, https://databank. worldbank.org/source/world-development-indicators

Xi, Jinping 2022, "Hold High the Great Banner of Socialism with Chinese Characteristics and Strive in Unity to Build a Modern Socialist Country in all Respects," viewed 27 March 2023, https://www.fmprc.gov.cn/eng/zxxx_662805/202210/t20221025_10791908. html

Xia, B 2021, "Quanmian luoshi aiguozhe zhigang yuanze tuijin yiguoliangzhi shijian xingwen zhiyuan" [Fully implement principle of "patriots administering Hong Kong" promote sound and sustained practice of "one country, two systems"], *Bauhinia Magazine*, viewed 14 July 2021, https://bau.com.hk/2021/03/43249

Xinhua Net 2017, "Xi Jinping zai qingzhu Xianggang huigui 20 zhounian dahui ji Xianggang tebie xingzhengqu diwujie zhengfu jiuzhi dianli shangde jianghua" [Xi Jinping's speech at meeting marking Hong Kong's 20th return anniversary, inaugural ceremony of fifth term HKSAR government], viewed 30 June 2021, http://www.xin-huanet.com/politics/2017-07/01/c_1121247124.htm

Xinhua Net 2019, "Zhonggong zhongyang guanyu jianchi he wanshan zhongguo tese shehui zhuyi zhidu tuijin guojia zhili tixi he zhili nengli xiandaihua ruogan zhongda wenti de jueding" [Several important decisions by the Central Committee of the Chinese Communist Party on upholding and improving the system of socialism with Chinese characteristics and advancing the modernization of China's system and capacity for governance], viewed 30 June 2021, http://www.xinhuanet.com/ politics/2019-11/05/c_1125195786.htm

Xinhua Net 2020, "Xi Jinping: Zai Shenzhen jingji tequ jianli 40 zhounian qingzhu dahui shangde jianghua" [Xi Jinping: Speech at the celebration meeting for the 40th anniversary of the Shenzhen Special Economic Zone], viewed 29 June 2021, http://www. xinhuanet.com/politics/2020-10/14/c_1210840649.htm

Xinhua Net 2021a, "Guanyu quanguo renmin daibiao dahui guanyu wanshan Xianggang tebie xingzhengqu xuanju zhidu de jueding (caoan) de shuoming" [Explanation on the draft of the decision on improving the electoral system of the Hong Kong Special Administrative Region], viewed 9 July 2021, http://www.xinhuanet.com/ politics/2021-03/05/c_1127172464.htm

Xinhua Net 2021b, "Zhonghua Renmin Gongheguo guomin jingji he shehui fazhan di shisi ge wunian guihua he 2035 nian yuanjing mubiao gangyao" [Outline of the

14th Five-Year Plan for National Economic and Social Development of the People's Republic of China and the Long-Range Objectives through the Year 2035], viewed 30 June 2021, http://www.xinhuanet.com/fortune/2021-03/13/c_1127205564.htm

Yan, X 2015, *Xianggang zhi yu luan: 2047 de zhengzhi xiangxiang* [Rule and chaos in Hong Kong: Political imagination of 2047], Joint Publishing (Hong Kong) Company Limited, Hong Kong.

Yu, H 2019 "The Guangdong-Hong Kong-Macao Greater Bay Area in the Making: Development Plan and Challenges," *Cambridge Review of International Affairs*, pp. 1–29.

Zhao, S 2020, "China's Belt-Road Initiative as the Signature of President Xi Jinping Diplomacy: Easier Said than Done," *Journal of Contemporary China*, vol. 29, no. 123, pp. 319 335.

Zhu, H 2020, "Beijing's 'Rule of Law' Strategy for Governing Hong Kong," *China Perspectives*, 19 November.

Useful Websites

News website of the Communist Party of China
http://cpc.people.com.cn

National People's Congress of the PRC
http://www.npc.gov.cn

The State Council
www.gov.cn

Hong Kong and Macao Affairs Office of the State Council
http://www.hmo.gov.cn

Liaison Office of the Central People's Government in the HKSAR
Constitutional and Mainland Affairs Bureau, HKSAR Government
www.cmab.gov.hk

Greater Bay Area website, HKSAR Government
www.bayarea.gov.hk

Greater Bay Area website, China
http://www.cnbayarea.org.cn

Further Reading

Bush, RC 2016, *Hong Kong in the Shadow of China: Living with the Leviathan*, Brookings Institution Press, Washington, DC. This is a systematic analysis of Hong Kong's social, political, and economic conditions up to 2015, primarily from an American perspective.

Cheung, A 2021, *Erci guodu – Xianggang 2020 zhengju fansi: weiji yu qianlu* [The second transition: Reflections on the political situation of Hong Kong in 2020: Crisis and the way ahead], Chung Hwa Book Company (Hong Kong) Limited, Hong Kong. This is an exploration of Hong Kong's prospects in light of the 2019 political crisis and the National Security Law.

Ghai, Y 1999, *Hong Kong's New Constitutional Order: The Resumption of Chinese Sovereignty and the Basic Law*, 2nd ed., Hong Kong University Press, Hong Kong. This is an important work on Hong Kong's constitutional, legal, economic, social, and political systems as a special administrative region of China.

Lau, SK 2000, "The Hong Kong Policy of the People's Republic of China, 1949–1997," *Journal of Contemporary China*, vol. 9, no. 23, pp. 77–93. This is a useful article summarizing the evolution of Beijing's policy toward Hong Kong.

Lau, SK 2015, *Yiguoliangzhi zai Xianggang de shijian* [Practice of one country, two systems in Hong Kong], The Commercial Press (Hong Kong) Limited, Hong Kong. This provides an analysis of the tensions and challenges in implementing "one country, two systems," especially in light of Beijing's concerns.

Lui, TK, Chiu, SWK & Yep, R (eds) 2018, *Routledge Handbook of Contemporary Hong Kong*, Routledge, London. This is a comprehensive academic handbook analyzing the social, economic, political, and other trends and policy issues confronting Hong Kong.

16

Hong Kong's International Status at a Crossroads

Li Hak-yin and Ting Wai

Hong Kong was regarded as a free and international city with a unique non-sovereign entity status in the past. Given the rapid political and social changes in Hong Kong since the Umbrella Movement in 2014, the Anti–Extradition Law Amendment Bill (Anti-ELAB) Movement in 2019, and the legislation of the National Security Law (NSL) in 2020, Hong Kong's international status has been changed drastically in the post-2020 era. More devastatingly, Hong Kong has been caught into political disputes between China and Western countries, which arouses international concerns over whether Hong Kong can still maintain its high level of autonomy under "one country, two systems."

This chapter attempts to reexamine Hong Kong's international status and whether the city can still play any significant role independently, as well as the impacts posed by the NSL. First and foremost, it summarizes the key literature on Hong Kong's international status. Second, it offers a brief background on the major political developments in Hong Kong since 2014, which have led to the tug of war between China and the West over Hong Kong. Third, this chapter analyzes Hong Kong's changing international status from multiple perspectives, including the Western triad of the United States (US), Europe—particularly the United Kingdom (UK) and the European Union (EU)—and Japan, the general perception of Hong Kong as an international cosmopolitan society and financial center, and the views of international civil society. Some key questions are worth exploring in depth. For example, how does the Western triad view the rapid changes in Hong Kong? What policy instruments has the Western triad adopted to respond to the situation in Hong Kong? Has Hong Kong's status as a unique non-sovereign entity been affected? To what extent could international civil society support Hong Kong's efforts to maintain its institutional pillars and autonomy? Last but not least, this chapter evaluates the future of Hong Kong's international status by reviewing the possible challenges and their implications for the world. This chapter concludes with the paradoxical phenomenon that more Western pressure over Hong Kong will only drive China to more assertively curb Hong Kong's autonomy in international relations, because Beijing has long feared that Hong Kong can be manipulated by foreign powers to bargain with China or even threaten the security of the Chinese Communist Party (CCP) regime.

Hong Kong's international status has been widely discussed and examined since the 1950s. One reason is that Hong Kong historically served as a bridge between China and the West and had considerable geostrategic importance in East Asia during the Cold War. A second reason is that, during British colonial rule, Hong Kong earned a promising international profile through the signing of various international treaties and participation in numerous regional and international organizations. This made Hong Kong a unique non-sovereign entity even after its return to China as a Special Administrative Region (SAR) in 1997. Last but not least, Hong Kong has been observed and monitored by the international community since its handover to China, especially by the Western triad, all of which have political and economic interests in Hong Kong. However, Western attention to and rhetorical support for Hong Kong has aroused Chinese suspicion and criticism of foreign interference in its internal affairs. Beijing responded with increasing intervention in Hong Kong's politics after the Umbrella Movement in 2014, and China has further tightened its control over Hong Kong since the Anti-ELAB Movement in 2019; for example, the disqualification of pan-democratic Hong Kong legislators and the establishment of the NSL in 2020 stimulated international concern that Hong Kong could become just another Mainland city, and that Hong Kong's declining autonomy has caused considerable damage to its international status.

A Tug of War between China and the West

The literature on Hong Kong's international status can be divided into three periods with different focuses and approaches. The first phase can be traced back to the 1950s, when Hong Kong had become a middleman between China and the West. At the very beginning of the Cold War, China suffered international isolation for its participation in the Korean War. Beijing did not resume sovereignty over Hong Kong but adopted the "long-term consideration, full utilization" policy by turning Hong Kong into an international channel for importing various necessities and materials and for trading with other countries (Miners 1998: 5; Chen 2007: 9–11). From the Western perspective, Hong Kong was regarded as a foothold from which to observe and comprehend China. It was also an important outpost for American intelligence services and financial activities in Asia (Paau 2002: 10).

Second, around the time of Hong Kong's handover, a large body of studies pointed out the unique status of Hong Kong in the international community. As early as 1986, Sung Yun-wing regarded Hong Kong as a window to China, not only because it was an entrepôt for the reexport and transshipment of Chinese products around the globe, but also because it contributed to China's modernization via investments and technological transfer (Sung 1986: 83–101). Other studies focused on Hong Kong's status as a non-sovereign entity, which paradoxically allowed Hong Kong to be an international actor via its membership in international treaties and organizations while also drawing worldwide attention to Hong Kong's development (Tang 1993: 205–215; Ting 1997: 2–72; Davis 1997: 70–77). Some specific studies illustrated the potential impact Hong Kong could have on the regional order and on China-US relations. James C. Hsiung viewed Hong Kong as a "reversible window" between China and the West in the fields of investment and capital flow. Hong Kong's "one country, two systems" policy could affect China's unification with Taiwan, and Hong Kong's future interactions with China could also affect Washington's diplomatic calculations in the region (Hsiung 1998: 237–244). Kenneth Lieberthal believed that Hong Kong could shape Sino-US relations, but such a scenario would depend on whether the clash of perceptions between China and the US over Hong Kong can be solved, as China firmly regards Hong Kong as part of its internal affairs (Lieberthal 1997). James T. H. Tang further added that Hong Kong could be a source of conflict between China and the US because the two countries have different understandings of trade, human rights, and Hong Kong's political development (Tang 1997: 419–433). Last but not least, Lau Siu-kai pointed out that the fundamental constraint on Hong Kong's international profile indeed comes from Beijing. Not only is the Chinese government suspicious of foreign intervention, but Chinese leaders fear that Hong Kong could become a base for subversion against the central government, as well as a Western bargaining chip through which to threaten China in the future (Lau 2000: 77–93).

Third, the studies of Hong Kong's international status since the handover have become more diversified in terms of theoretical approaches. The middleman perspective is further conceptualized by Ting Wai and Ellen Lai. Economically, Hong Kong has become the Western triad's capitalist enclave to explore the Chinese market, while most of Hong Kong's outward investment has gone to China. Politically, the West still treats Hong Kong as a bridgehead for advocating freedom and the rule of law in Asia. Nevertheless, Hong Kong's international status can be jeopardized due to the "Mainlandization" of Hong Kong (Boxes 16.1 and 16.2), increasing intervention from Beijing, and the deterioration of judicial independence, freedom, and the rule of law (Ting and Lai 2012: 349–367). In a recent study, Li Hak-yin finds that Hong Kong was gradually inclined to side with Beijing from 2012 to 2017, during Leung Chun-ying's administration, by compromising its unique international status. There have been various deteriorations in fields such as human rights, the rule of law, press freedom, and the free flow of people. Beijing has begun to utilize Hong Kong for its diplomatic interests in improving relations with the Philippines, as well as to warn Singapore regarding its relations with the US and Taiwan (Li 2020: 219–246).

Simon Shen employed other approaches—such as identity, branding, public diplomacy, and paradiplomacy—to illustrate Hong Kong's international status. His study argued that Beijing's support of Margaret Chan, a former Hong Kong government official, to become the head of the World Health Organization (WHO) was a Chinese diplomatic mission to improve its international image by making use of Hong Kong's identity (Shen 2008: 361–382). In another study, Shen evaluated Hong Kong's government policy in its quest to be branded as "Asia's World City" (Shen 2010: 203–224). He also discovered in a later study that some influential Hong Kong tycoons helped to liaise with other countries and secure China's overseas interests through both public diplomacy and paradiplomacy (Shen 2016: 69–90; 277–291). In addition, Tim Summers found that the UK is becoming uneasy about speaking for the interests of Hong Kong people, fearing that such involvement could jeopardize its trading relations with China. Meanwhile, international opinion and support seem to be the remaining means for Hong Kong people to voice their concerns regarding democratization (Summers 2016: 1–25).

The above show that Hong Kong's international status is not static but can be changed and affected from time to time by domestic political developments in Hong Kong and interventions from Mainland China, as well as by foreign perceptions of the changes in Hong Kong. These three variables are interlocking, with one variable triggering the responses of the other two. Specifically, Hong Kong's democratic movements always lead to contrasting responses from China and the Western triad. On the one hand, China attempts to contain Hong Kong's democratization, which can pose a demonstrative effect on Chinese people in the Mainland. On the other hand, the Western triad delivers moral and rhetorical support for Hong Kong's democratization to maintain this capitalist enclave on China's doorstep. However, China regards Western support for Hong Kong as a foreign intervention in its internal affairs, even believing that the West plans to turn Hong Kong into a base for subversion. Hence, China is increasing and enhancing its political control and manipulation over Hong Kong. Finally, Hong Kong's autonomy and international status suffer because of the confrontations between China and the West. When Hong Kong people resist Chinese intervention with the West standing on their side, Beijing responds with even more overwhelming policies toward Hong Kong.

Since the Umbrella Movement: Challenges to the External Relations of Hong Kong

The Umbrella Movement in 2014 and the Anti-ELAB Movement in 2019 illustrate the above pattern. When the West has further expressed concerns over the situation of human rights and freedom in Hong Kong, China considers those Western concerns to be foreign interventions by further constricting Hong Kong's autonomy.

The yellow umbrella became a symbol of Hong Kong's democratic movement in 2014, when protestors used umbrellas to protect themselves against the police use of tear gas. The original movement was known as "Occupy Central with Love and Peace," which was a civil disobedience campaign proposed by two university professors, Benny Tai and Chan Kin-man, as well as a Baptist Minister, Chu Yiu-ming. By paralyzing the central business district area, pan-democratic forces hoped to persuade China to live up to its promise of a truly free and open election of both the Legislative Council (LegCo) and the Chief Executive (CE) of Hong Kong, by universal suffrage. The movement was later sparked in late September by student protests organized by Scholarism, an association of high school students. Meanwhile, the *People's Daily* questioned whether the Umbrella Movement was anything different from previous "color revolutions" allegedly instigated by the US to intervene in other countries' internal affairs under the cover of supporting democracy and human rights (Hua 2014). Nevertheless, the West spoke for the Umbrella Movement. The EU Commissioner for Foreign Affairs and Security Policy, Catherine Ashton, said in October 2014 that "We have conveyed our concerns and expressed our support for the introduction of universal suffrage on many occasions to our interlocutors from Hong Kong" (Ashton 2014). In November, during the Asia-Pacific Economic Cooperation (APEC) meeting, American president Barack Obama told Chinese president Xi Jinping that the US believed Hong Kong's election should be "transparent and fair and reflective of the opinions of people there," and Xi rebutted that the Hong Kong issue is a domestic affair in China and the US should not comment on it (Barber 2014). Next, British prime minister David Cameron clashed with China in December because Beijing rejected a visit of the British House of Commons Foreign Affairs Committee to Hong Kong, with China labeling the visit as "post-colonial interference" (Borger and Norton-Tylor 2014). The Japanese government did not comment much on Hong Kong, probably because Japan was experiencing a most difficult time with China after its nationalization of the Diaoyu Islands in 2012; thus Tokyo avoided further provocation of Beijing.

Since the Umbrella Movement, several political issues have demonstrated the increasing number of Chinese interventions in Hong Kong, which have caused international concern regarding the deterioration of "one country, two systems," the result being another round of confrontation between China and the West over Hong Kong. The first issue was the disappearance of five Hong Kong booksellers from the Causeway Bay Books store in late 2015, some of whom later appeared on Chinese television admitting to the crime of illegal book trading. The incident was regarded as a severe blow to Hong Kong's human rights and judicial independence due to the mysterious nature of China's cross-border arrests. Many wondered whether the real reason behind the abductions was that the books published were critical of the Chinese government. Second, pro-independence candidates such as Edward Leung and Andy Chan were disqualified from participating in the 2016 LegCo elections. Third, even after the elections in September 2016, more elected pro-independence legislators, such as Yau Wai-ching and Sixtus Leung as well as pan-democratic legislators such as Nathan Law, Lau Siu-lai, Edward Yiu, and Leung Kwok-hung, were disqualified due to doubts about their sincerity in the oath-taking process and their loyalty to the central government in Beijing.

Foreign perceptions of Hong Kong changed accordingly. For example, the US-China Economic and Security Review Commission issued an annual report to the US Congress. It said:

> The case of Hong Kong—particularly as it relates to the book-sellers incident and encroachment on press and academic freedoms, and the new loyalty "pledge" required for legislative candidates—reflects a broader pattern of behavior in which Beijing disregards norms, agreements, or laws (either in spirit or in letter) in pursuit of its objectives . . . Nonetheless, many in the Hong Kong business community, including US-based and global firms, are beginning to question Hong Kong's future as a global financial center due to the deterioration of the "one country, two systems" model. (US-China Economic and Security Review Commission 2016)

The British government shares a similar view:

> Nevertheless, during the reporting period, a number of developments caused concern in Hong Kong and internationally, affecting confidence in "one country, two systems." These developments included events surrounding the LegCo elections and the subsequent oath-taking by elected legislators, as well as continuing concerns about the exercise of rights and freedoms guaranteed by the Joint Declaration, including freedom of expression and the freedom of the press. (Foreign and Commonwealth Office 2017)

Thereafter, the Chinese government responded more bluntly to Western concerns about Hong Kong. In 2017, on the 20th anniversary of Hong Kong's handover, the Chinese Foreign Ministry declared that the Sino-British Joint Declaration was "now history and of no practical significance . . . The British side has no sovereignty, no power to rule and supervise Hong Kong after the handover" (Ministry of Foreign Affairs of the People's Republic of China 2017). Meanwhile, Chinese president Xi Jinping gave the following sharp warning during his visit to Hong Kong:

> Any attempt to endanger China's sovereignty and security, challenge the power of the Central Government and the authority of the Basic Law of the HKSAR or use Hong Kong to carry out infiltration and sabotage activities against the Mainland is an act that crosses the red line, and is absolutely impermissible. (*China Daily* 2017)

Thereafter, Hong Kong is no longer a free and open international city for exchanges. In October, Benedict Roger, Deputy Chair of the British Conservative Party's Human Rights Commission, was refused entry into Hong Kong. In August 2018, Councillor Kenichiro Wada of Shiroi City, Japan, faced the same situation because of his support for Taiwan's independence and the alleged possibility that Japan would intervene in Hong Kong's elections (Lam 2018). In the same month, the Chinese Ministry of Foreign Affairs requested that the Foreign Correspondents' Club (FCC), Hong Kong cancel a talk that was to be delivered by the pro-independence Hong Kong National Party's Andy Chan. The FCC declined to comply with the request but, very soon, the Hong Kong National Party was banned, and FCC Vice President Victor Mallet's application to renew his working visa was declined by the Hong Kong government.

The proposed extradition bill in early 2019 was another watershed, dragging China and the West into a new round of disagreement and conflict. The foreign business community, human rights groups, and many ordinary Hong Kong citizens feared that any person in Hong Kong could be sent back to China for trial, as they are not confident that the Chinese legal system could uphold justice. One million Hong Kong people took to the streets to protest the bill on 9 June, and a further 2 million filled the streets on 16 June after the police's suppression of a demonstration on 12 June and CE Carrie Lam's promise to delay the bill. Some events spiralled out of control; for example, protestors broke into the LegCo building on 1 July, while the gangs in white shirts attacked protestors in black shirts and other ordinary citizens in Yuen Long on 21 July, with the police failing to show up until half an hour later. On 12 August, protestors occupied the Hong Kong International Airport. Even though the Hong Kong government withdrew the bill in September, many demonstrations continued in different parts of Hong Kong, demanding an independent investigation of the police's excessive use of force (Lau 2019).

The West sympathizes with Hong Kong's Anti-ELAB Movement, especially the Western triad, which has put more pressure on China. First, both the US Congress and President showed their support for Hong Kong. Nancy Pelosi, the speaker of the House of Representatives, issued a statement on 6 August 2019 calling for a suspension of the transfer of American munitions to Hong Kong's police and working towards the enactment of the Hong Kong Human Rights and Democracy Act (Speaker of the House 2019). Meanwhile, there was speculation as to whether Beijing would suppress demonstrations in Hong Kong by military force. President Donald Trump brought Hong Kong into the consideration of the China-US trade deal, saying, "No, I think it would be very hard to deal if they do violence, if it's another Tiananmen Square" (Ng 2019). In September, the US Congress invited Hong Kong activists Joshua Wong and Denise Ho to testify to the latest situation in Hong Kong. Finally, the Hong Kong Human Rights and Democracy Act was approved by the US Congress and signed by President Trump in November. The act requires an annual review of Hong Kong's autonomy for the territory to maintain its special status with the US.

Second, British foreign secretary Jeremy Hunt warned of a potential Chinese crackdown on demonstrations in Hong Kong in July 2019, stating that the UK would not "gulp and move on" (BBC 2019). The UK also rebutted China's denial of the Sino-British Joint Declaration over worries about the chaos caused by the extradition bill and emphasized that "maintaining Hong Kong's high degree of autonomy and upholding its rights and freedoms in full, is the way to guarantee Hong Kong's future success and the prosperity of its people" (Foreign and Commonwealth Office 2019). The EU sent a démarche to Hong Kong to demand a reconsideration of the extradition bill as early as May (Cheung, Cheung, Sum and Lum 2019). Then, in July, the European Parliament passed a resolution demanding that Hong Kong withdraw the bill and implement direct elections for the CE and all seats in the LegCo. It further stated that it "condemns the constant and increasing interference by China in Hong Kong's internal affairs" (European Parliament 2019).

Third, when Japanese prime minister Shinzo Abe met with Chinese president Xi Jinping during the G20 Osaka Summit in late June, Abe reiterated to Xi "the importance of the continued prosperity of a free and open Hong Kong under 'one country, two systems'" (Ministry of Foreign Affairs of Japan 2019a). Abe emphasized the same point to Chinese premier Li Keqiang during the ASEAN Summit in November (Ministry of Foreign Affairs of Japan 2019b). The Japanese response to Hong Kong's Anti-ELAB Movement was mild in comparison with those from the US and Europe.

In contrast, China sees the numerous demonstrations in Hong Kong and the accompanying Western pressure as tremendous foreign interventions in Hong Kong that are behind the Anti-ELAB Movement. In August 2019, the former CE of Hong Kong, Tung Chee-hwa, also a vice-chairman of the Chinese People's Political Consultative Conference (CPPCC), suggested that there must be foreign manipulations due to the movement's organization and scale. He said, "Hong Kongers shall by no means be used by them." (*People's Daily* 2019). Meanwhile,

Yang Jiechi, a CCP Political Bureau member and Director of the Office of the Foreign Affairs Commission of the CCP's Central Committee, cautioned the US and other countries to stop intervening in Hong Kong, which is part of China's domestic affairs (Chen 2019). In addition, Director of the Hong Kong and Macao Affairs Office of the State Council, Zhang Xiaoming, questioned the movement for its "clear color revolution characteristics" since protestors were raising other demands, such as to "liberate Hong Kong" or even calling for Hong Kong's independence (Yang 2019). Later, in December, Chinese foreign minister Wang Yi sharpened similar criticism and Beijing's discontent (Ministry of Foreign Affairs of the People's Republic of China 2019). More significantly, Chinese leader Xi Jinping warned US president Donald Trump on a call regarding Hong Kong: "These actions have interfered in China's internal affairs, harmed China's interests and undermined mutual trust and cooperation between the two sides" (Holland and Liu 2019).

Nevertheless, Western support for Hong Kong's Anti-ELAB Movement has only driven China to squeeze Hong Kong comprehensively with the passing of the NSL. The NSL came into effect on 30 June 2020, targeting secession, subversion, terrorism, and collusion with foreign or external forces. Even though the law is very new to Hong Kong, many activists and pan-democratic affiliates have either fled Hong Kong or been arrested by police. First, Nathan Law and Ray Wong were accused of lobbying foreign forces for sanctions against government officials in Hong Kong and China. Second, pro-democratic media tycoon Jimmy Lai was sued for similar reasons. Third, 53 pan-democratic candidates were arrested in January 2021, ostensibly for organizing primaries to coordinate voters in the run-up to the LegCo elections held in September 2021. However, they were accused of having as their ultimate aim the overthrow of the Hong Kong government. These cases have not yet gone to final trial, but they show the power of the NSL, which can deter Hong Kong people from seeking help from the international community or challenging the Hong Kong administration or central government by whatever means in future. The US, UK, Canada, and Australia issued a joint statement expressing their "serious concern" about the mass arrest for breaching the Sino-British Joint Declaration, stating that it undermined "one country, two systems" and that they believe the NSL is "being used to eliminate dissent and opposing political views" (US Department of State 2021a).

Multiple Perspectives on the Changing International Status of Hong Kong

Perspectives of the Western triad

First and foremost, have the increasing Chinese interventions since the Umbrella Movement and the NSL legislation upset Hong Kong's unique non-sovereign entity status from the perspective of the Western triad? US Secretary of State Michael Pompeo responded to that question immediately and bluntly on 30 June 2020:

> The Chinese Communist Party's decision to impose draconian national security legislation on Hong Kong destroys the territory's autonomy and one of China's greatest achievements. Hong Kong demonstrated to the world what a free Chinese people could achieve – one of the most successful economies and vibrant societies in the world. But Beijing's paranoia and fear of its own people's aspirations have led it to eviscerate the very foundation of the territory's success, turning "one country, two systems" into "one country, one system." (Pompeo 2020a)

The British Secretary, Dominic Raab, also briefed the UK Parliament on 1 July that the NSL could infringe upon the rights of Hong Kong people, which have been protected under the United Nations (UN) International Covenant on Civil and Political Rights as guaranteed by the Sino-British Joint Declaration. He said that China "has failed to do so with respect to Hong Kong, by enacting legislation which violates its autonomy and threatens the strangulation of its freedoms" (Foreign and Commonwealth Office and The Rt Hon Dominic Raab MP 2020). Simultaneously, the EU's statement expressed "grave concerns" and included the following comment:

> The European Union is concerned that the law risks seriously undermining the high degree of autonomy of Hong Kong, and having a detrimental effect on the independence of the judiciary and the rule of law. Both of these principles remain essential for the continued stability and prosperity of Hong Kong, and are therefore of vital interest to the European Union and the international community. (Council of the European Union 2020a)

Also, Japanese chief cabinet secretary Yoshihide Suga regarded the situation in Hong Kong as "regrettable" and said that "the enactment of the national security law undermines the credibility of the "one country, two systems" principle (Johnson and Sugiyama 2020). Obviously, the Western triad believes that Hong Kong's autonomy, freedom, and rule of law could be greatly undermined by the NSL.

The Western triad has come up with various policy instruments to address Hong Kong's changing status, with the toughest policy coming from the US and milder responses from the UK and the EU, while Japan acts passively with a wait-and-see attitude.

The US has offered Hong Kong special status since the handover, enshrined in its Hong Kong is regarded as a "separate customs territory" in that its economic relations, trade, import quotas, certificates of origin, access to sensitive technologies, and cultural and educational exchanges such as the Fulbright Academic Exchange Program are not affected by the PRC (US Congress 1992a), and the existing US laws and treatment of Hong Kong remain the same unless "Hong Kong is not sufficiently autonomous to justify treatment under a particular law of the United States" (US Congress 1992b). However, the act also addresses American support for Hong Kong's democratization and human rights. The American President can review whether the act should be continued or not, according to political developments in Hong Kong (US Congress 1992c). In a nutshell, Hong Kong is an independent non-sovereign entity from the American point of view, and it is treated differently from the PRC.

The change in US policy came even before the implementation of the NSL. On 29 June 2020, the US stopped exporting its defense and dual-use technologies to Hong Kong because Washington "can no longer distinguish between the export of controlled items to Hong Kong or Mainland China" (Pompeo 2020b). Second, on 1 July, the American Congress passed the Hong Kong Autonomy Act, which was later signed by President Donald Trump. The act gives the US government the power to sanction "foreign individuals and entities that materially contribute to China's failure to preserve Hong Kong's autonomy" (US Congress 2020a). Third, on 14 July, President Trump issued an executive order on "Hong Kong normalization," invoking the powers in the Hong Kong Policy Act to modify existing American laws and treatment of Hong Kong. The affected areas cover various fields, such as immigration, Hong Kong passport holders' privilege, arms export control, license exceptions to Hong Kong, transfer of criminals, the Fulbright exchange program, and capital blockades on persons who assist and implement the NSL (The White House 2020). Fourth, the US launched economic sanctions against 11 officials in Hong Kong and China in August, including the CE of Hong Kong, Carrie Lam, the Commissioner of the Hong Kong Police Force, Chris Tang, and the Director of the Hong Kong and Macao Affairs Office of China's State Council, Xia Baolong (US Department of the Treasury 2020a). Four more Hong Kong and Chinese officials were sanctioned in November (Pamuk and Brunnstrom 2020). A month later, the US expanded the sanctions to 14 vice-chairpersons of China's National People's Congress (US Department of the Treasury 2020b). Prosecutors with the Hong Kong Department of Justice who are involved in the cases against the democrat activists in Hong Kong have also been sanctioned by Washington. Other American policies include the requirement that Hong Kong products exported to the US must be labelled as "made in China" and the proposed Hong Kong People's Freedom and Choice Act of 2020, which would have offered "temporary protected status" to Hong Kong citizens who have faced political persecution under the NSL (US Congress 2020b). While the bill failed to gain sufficient votes in the Senate in December, similar bills may be proposed in future.

Although the rhetoric in the statements by the UK and EU put Hong Kong in the world's spotlight, their policies are softer than those of the US. The British government first proposed an indirect path for 3 million Hong Kong people to obtain citizenship in the UK in July 2020. Only those with British National (Overseas) passports can join the scheme, and applicants must support themselves financially to live in the UK for five years before they can make a formal application for British citizenship (*BBC* 2020a). More importantly, the British government does not issue any guarantee that the future citizenship application will be approved. Second, London suspended its extradition treaty with Hong Kong and has extended its arms embargo from its original coverage of Mainland China to Hong Kong for fear that shackles and smoke grenades could be used by the Hong Kong government to suppress demonstrations. The British response is nothing special. Many countries, such as Canada, have adopted the same policy, while France, Germany and other EU members have also revoked their extradition treaties with Hong Kong. Nevertheless, the UK has not yet imposed any sanctions on officials in Hong Kong and China, which led to criticism of the British "hedging strategy" by Hong Kong activist Nathan Law (Wintour 2020), a strategy that was probably due in large part to concerns about damaging trading and investment relations with China, especially during the "Brexit" era since 31 December 2020.

Similarly, the EU's moral support for Hong Kong has not been transformed into concrete policies. On 28 July, the EU announced "a coordinated response package of measures" in various areas, such as asylum, visa policy, and residence policy; the limitation on exporting sensitive equipment and technology; and the member states' extradition agreement with Hong Kong (Council of the European Union 2020b). The EU's coordinated response allows each member state to decide the scope and implementation of their policy toward Hong Kong in those areas, but not many EU member states have carried out substantive measures. An exception is Germany's prohibition on exporting technologies that can be used for surveillance (The Hong Kong Trade Development Council 2020). While the EU continues to speak for Hong Kong's political freedom and democratization, the EU has not delivered any dedicated policy to Hong Kong people or any sanctions against China. Instead, the EU reached a common consensus with China in the form of the Comprehensive Agreement on Investment

(CAI) on 30 December 2020, after more than seven years of negotiations. The deal offers EU companies greater access to the Chinese market, tackles the Chinese internal subsidies of state enterprises and the forced transfer of technologies, and socializes China in complying with labor rights and sustainable development. Beijing promises only to make efforts to ratify the International Labour Organization Conventions on forced labor, but there is no deadline or enforcement mechanism. The EU faces a dilemma between upholding human rights and democracy for Hong Kong people on one hand and reaching a formal investment deal with China in the interests of European companies on the other. There is also a clash between the European Parliament and the European Commission. Former Belgian prime minister and European Parliament member Guy Verhofstadt suggests not ratifying the deal "without commitment and proof that the human rights of Hongkongers, Uygurs and Tibetans improve," while the EU Commission's spokesman Eric Mamer offers the contrasting stance that "We have separate lines of dialogue with China on the rule of law, democracy," and the EU needs to engage with China continuously to solve the climate change crisis (Lau 2021). The diverging interests among its member states and the internal complexities make the EU voice soft and weak. Nevertheless, the European Parliament froze the ratification of the treaty in May 2021 due to Chinese sanctions on EU personnel.

Japan has always been a quiet actor within the Western triad regarding Hong Kong's political development. Some members of the Diet (the Japanese parliament) have discussed various policy options, such as a fast tracking of Japanese permanent residency to talented Hong Kong people (Miki 2020), or sanctions against individuals and organizations who violate human rights in Hong Kong (Ota 2020). Nevertheless, nothing has been translated into policy yet. The Japanese administration is very cautious about speaking up for Hong Kong, probably because of its economic ties with Beijing and the fact that some Japanese citizens have been arrested and detained in Mainland China. Tokyo maintains a low profile in criticizing Beijing.

From the Western triad's perspective, Hong Kong's international status has changed after 2020. Hong Kong has gradually become another Chinese city. The Western triad can no longer treat Hong Kong as an independent entity with a high level of autonomy; they are cautious on sharing information, technologies, and munitions with Hong Kong, which could be retrieved and used by China. Besides, the Western triad is short of effective policy to maintain the status quo of Hong Kong with their diplomatic gestures and statements, while China is determined to resume its full sovereignty in Hong Kong. Last but not least, the Western triad lost its political enclave in East Asia when Hong Kong could no longer display the attractiveness of Western political values such as human rights, the rule of law, and democracy.

General perceptions of Hong Kong as an international financial center

Second, is Hong Kong still regarded as an international, cosmopolitan, and open society? Can Hong Kong maintain its position as an international financial center? There are various indicators that reflect the international perceptions of Hong Kong after 2020, such as responses from foreign business corporations and international organizations.

Foreign business corporations' views on Hong Kong have been upset by the NSL. The American Chamber of Commerce in Hong Kong conducted a survey in August 2020. Altogether, 55.85 percent of the American companies had adopted a "wait and see" attitude towards Hong Kong's post-NSL developments, and 51.3 percent said their companies had not been affected so far. However, 4.55 percent of the companies were still planning to reallocate their capital, assets, and other business operations in the short term, while 31.17 percent were leaving Hong Kong in the medium to long term. Also, 33.77 percent and 35.06 percent of them are "extremely concerned" and "somewhat concerned" about the NSL, respectively. In addition, 9.09 percent of respondents had decided to leave Hong Kong in the short term, and 44.16 percent would do so in the medium to long term (American Chamber of Commerce in Hong Kong 2020). The Chamber's 2023 survey showed that US-China relations, overseas public perceptions of Hong Kong, and a weakening global economy are the biggest challenges of the American companies in Hong Kong, while 38 percent of them have already been negatively impacted by the NSL (American Chamber of Commerce in Hong Kong 2023). Their European counterparts share a similar view. The Head of the EU Office to Hong Kong and Macao, Carmen Cano de Lasala, warned that "[w] e have 1,600 companies operating in Hong Kong, more than we have in Japan or the United States . . . the law has created a lot of fear and uncertainty on what the offences of subversion and collusion with foreign powers mean and how [the law] will be implemented" (Cheung 2020). Moreover, in the survey carried out by the Japan External Trade Organization, 15 percent and 52 percent of the Japanese companies were "very concerned" and "concerned," respectively, with the NSL, while 67 percent feared the limitation of information freedom, and 60 percent were concerned about the rule of law in Hong Kong (Kihara 2020).

In addition, Hong Kong's position as an international financial and commercial center is in doubt. The first evidence is that the number of regional headquarters of foreign corporations in Hong Kong decreased from 1,541 in 2019 to 1,411 in 2022—the first drop in the last decade. Although the number of Chinese companies using Hong Kong as their regional headquarters jumped significantly from 216 in 2019 to 251 in 2022, other countries such as the UK, Japan, and Australia have reduced the number of companies using Hong Kong as their regional headquarters (Census and Statistics Department 2022). The second piece of evidence is that foreign companies have increasingly viewed Hong Kong's business favorability negatively. The Hong Kong Census and Statistics Department's annual survey found that foreign companies' satisfaction with the "free flow of information" was 62 percent in 2018 but decreased to 45 percent in 2022. Meanwhile, the foreign companies' satisfaction with the "rule of law and independent judiciary" was 51 percent in 2018 but declined to 34 percent in 2022 (Census and Statistics Department 2018 and 2022). Besides, a hedge fund advisor commented that "Hong Kong as we know it is dead . . . It will become just another city in China. The hedge fund community will move on to Singapore and elsewhere" (Lockett and Shane 2020). For example, the US hedge fund Elliott Management closed its Hong Kong office and moved its staff to London and Tokyo in January 2021. Other funds indicated that they had the same plan for diversifying the risks in Hong Kong (*Nikkei Asia* 2021). Also, the *Financial Times* interviewed a dozen major law firms in Hong Kong, Tokyo, and Singapore. These firms received increasing questions from clients on "whether to write Hong Kong out of governing law and arbitration clauses" in their business contracts because of the NSL and the Mainlandization of Hong Kong (Kinder and Lewis 2021). The third piece of evidence is suggested by the International Monetary Fund (IMF). Hong Kong can no longer serve as China's funding and investment channel because of various American sanctions that have caused a US-China trade war. Around one-third of China's equity financing, two-thirds of Chinese offshore bond insurance, and more than half of China's inward and outward direct investment are managed in or pass through Hong Kong (International Monetary Fund 2021).

Worse still, the rapidly deteriorating commercial environment in parallel with the limitation on liberty (especially press freedom and freedom of association) are reflected by the descending world ranking of Hong Kong in terms of economic freedom. The Heritage Foundation has removed Hong Kong from the list of countries/regions in its latest ranking of the Index of Economic Freedom since Hong Kong is now regarded as part of Mainland China rather than a separate and autonomous economic entity. From 1995 to 2019, Hong Kong ranked No. 1 for 25 years as the freest economy in the world (Jim 2021).

Last but not least, the status of Hong Kong's international financial center is further challenged by the US. The American government issued the "Hong Kong Business Advisory" on 16 July 2021 to illustrate the potential threats caused by the NSL: "data privacy risks; risks regarding transparency and access to critical business information; and risks for business with exposure to sanctioned Hong Kong or PRC entities or individuals" (US Department of State 2021b).

The evidence above suggest that Hong Kong has lost the nimbus of an international financial center, and there are serious implications toward the global business world. In the post-2020 era, internally Hong Kong's freedom and rule of law have been questioned because of the NSL, while externally Hong Kong has been caught by a trade war and geopolitical rivalry between China and the US. Under this very intense atmosphere, the responses from foreign companies in Hong Kong is understandable. They are probably afraid that their operations will be affected due to the lack of free flow of information and the potential danger of being obliged by Hong Kong's monitoring institutions to reveal their internal data. Also, foreign companies have gradually lost their faith in Hong Kong while Chinese business activities in Hong Kong have been constrained by the American sanctions. As a consequence, more foreign businesses may leave Hong Kong in the future, due to its internal and external uncertainties.

International civil society perspective

Third, can the international civil society offer any help to Hong Kong in terms of maintaining its high degree of autonomy? Will the international nongovernmental organizations (NGOs) and mass media still regard Hong Kong as their fundamental base in Asia-Pacific?

With the legislation of the NSL, China aims to control Hong Kong's civil society as well as its connections with the international community. Article 9 of the NSL offers the Hong Kong government power to supervise "schools, universities, social organizations, the media, and the internet," while Article 54 deals with foreign nongovernmental organizations and news agencies. Human Rights Watch has forewarned that it would be possible for even peaceful speeches and activities to fall into the categories of secession, subversion, terrorism, and collusion with foreign forces, as the law keeps those definitions very vague and broad (Human Rights Watch 2020).

Already, many social activists and human rights groups have fled Hong Kong, as the city can no longer offer much space for political lobbies and discussions, needless to say other activities and campaigns. Nathan Law emphasizes the only available option to comment and expound Hong Kong's human rights and democratization is to "continue the advocacy work on the international level" (*BBC* 2020b). Similarly, in 2021, Amnesty International abandoned both the local "section" office and regional office of Asia-Pacific in Hong Kong. The chair of its organization board, Anjhula Mya Singh Bais, explained the devasting impacts brought by the NSL: "Hong Kong has long been an ideal regional base for international civil society organizations, but the recent targeting of local human rights and trade union groups signals an intensification of the authorities' campaign to rid the city of all dissenting voices" (Amnesty International 2021).

Meanwhile, the international mass media have been forced to reduce their risks from Hong Kong. The first alarm that warned of the changing understanding of Hong Kong as a free and vibrant city was raised by Reporters sans frontières (Reporters Without Borders). Its Secretary General and Director General, Christophe Deloire, said in 2017 that "Hong Kong was the place where we originally wanted to open an office in Asia, but the declining degree of freedom may make their work difficult without 'legal certainty'" (Horton 2017). The organization finally picked Taiwan for its Asian bureau. Besides, in July 2020, the *New York Times* announced that it was moving its digital news operation to South Korea's capital, Seoul. The paper explained the importance of Hong Kong as "an Asian headquarter(s) for English-language news outlets drawn to the city's openness to foreign companies, proximity to the Chinese Mainland and rich tradition of a freewheeling press . . . as a window on China," but went on to state that the NSL has brought more uncertainty. For instance, some of its reporters' applications for Hong Kong working visas were denied for no apparent reason (Grynbaum 2020). Other online social media also cast votes of no confidence in Hong Kong. For example, Facebook denied the Hong Kong government's request for access to user data, Naver migrated its data backup center from Hong Kong to Singapore, and even the Chinese company TikTok left Hong Kong because of the NSL (Somasundaram 2020). According to the World Press Freedom Index, Hong Kong's ranking dropped significantly—from No. 58 in 2013 to No. 80 in 2021 and then to No. 148 (worse than Rwanda) in 2022—because of the Hong Kong government's tougher policy on censorship, Beijing's threatening NSL, and increasing pro-Beijing factions in Hong Kong (Reporters Without Borders 2023).

Hong Kong's traditional status as a hub for international NGOs and mass media has inevitably been weakened. Not only can the international civil society not do much to preserve Hong Kong's autonomy, but it is also difficult for them to maintain their operations in the city. The international civil society's concerns could be the alleged "evidence" of foreign forces behind the Hong Kong pan-democratic camp and activists, enabling Beijing and the Hong Kong administration to use the NSL against them. More importantly, with fewer international NGOs and mass media in Hong Kong, the free flow of information, which almost all foreign companies and global businesses rely on, is further limited. Hence, it affects the business environment as well as Hong Kong's status as an international financial center.

Hong Kong's Future: Challenges and Implications for the World

Since the increasing Chinese interventions in Hong Kong after the Umbrella Movement in 2014, Hong Kong's international status has been challenged and upset, and the legislation of the NSL has set Hong Kong on an irreversible path toward what many regard as "one country, one system." From the Western triad's policy responses and the reactions of foreign companies as well as the helplessness of international civil society, all the evidence shows that Hong Kong is no longer a free and open society with a high level of autonomy, or a unique non-sovereign entity that can maintain a free flow of information, rule of law, and judicial independence—the necessary conditions for its role and status as an international financial center.

The rapid change of Hong Kong's international status carries several implications for the world. First, Hong Kong is no longer a "window" between China and the West. Not only have Hong Kong people lost their freedom to criticize both their own administration and the central government in Beijing, but Hong Kong can hardly act as a gateway for political communications with the outside world on human rights, freedom, and democracy, which may be targeted by the NSL. Beijing's grasp on Hong Kong reached a climax in 2023 by moving the Hong Kong and Macao Affairs Office from the State Council to the CCP's Central Committee. With the party's direct supervision on Hong Kong affairs, it can be expected that self-censorship will prevail in various sectors, such as the mass media, education, the legal profession, and civil society, to avoid being trapped by the law and the party.

Second, the trend of Hong Kong's Mainlandization is increasing. Apart from the NSL, Hong Kong's administration is attempting to synchronize itself with Beijing's interests. For example, former CE Carrie Lam suddenly postponed her policy address in October 2020. The central government had set out a blueprint for the Guangdong-Hong Kong-Macao Greater Bay Area, and the role of Hong Kong seemed to have already been decided. Carrie Lam wished to get acquainted with the relevant policies before delivering her annual policy address. However, the real reason was that the date originally planned for her policy address clashed with the 40th anniversary of the establishment of the Shenzhen Special Economic Zone. Carrie Lam postponed her speech because she had to attend the anniversary event chaired by Xi Jinping (Kawase 2020).

The current CE, John Lee, closely aligns his administration with Beijing. Hong Kong followed China's "Zero COVID" policy by neglecting many local experts' advice about "living with COVID," as many Western countries did. For instance, government pandemic adviser and microbiologist Yuen Kwok-yung repeatedly suggested that Hong Kong should not block the free flow of people as an international city and financial center, and that Hong Kong was not equipped with the necessary resources to follow China's "Zero COVID" policy. Hong Kong's pandemic restrictions were among the strictest in the world, presumably to prevent COVID-19 transmission to Mainland China. The measures aimed to secure a safer environment in Hong Kong, with the hope that, once the situation improved, Mainland China would agree to reopen the border and restore people flow with Hong Kong. However, Hong Kong's rigid anti-COVID-19 policy led to serious complaints from foreign companies, while international exhibition businesses and tourism turned to competitors like Singapore and other Western countries. Besides, John Lee's new policy narratives—"to tell Hong Kong's story," "Hong Kong as a gateway connecting China and the world," and "Wealth for Good in Hong Kong" (to attract family office business)—serve to tackle the negative impacts brought by the NSL and the "Zero COVID" policy. But these policies only add weight to Hong Kong's Mainlandization, as the government puts political correctness above all to follow China's policy rather than following scientific advice, at the cost of Hong Kong's economy and business environment. The debate on COVID-19 policies also shows the changing Hong Kong government's mentality; "internal" exchanges with Mainland China now look more important than international. When Hong Kong leaders think more from the "one country" perspective, they position Hong Kong as a city of China. Thus, Hong Kong's international status would be limited and restricted from within by Hong Kong leaders themselves.

Third, Hong Kong cannot serve as a model for Taiwan anymore. Tsai Ing-wen made the criticism that the NSL proves that "one country, two systems" is not feasible for Taiwan because "[w]e are very disappointed that China is not able to carry out its promises" (Hernández and Myers 2020).

Fourth, some financial centers in the region may explore opportunities to share if not to replace Hong Kong's status as an international financial center. For example, Seiji Kihara, a Japanese lawmaker, has suggested that Tokyo should seize the moment (Miyasaka 2020), and even President Xi announced in 2020 that Shenzhen would be a "core engine" of the Greater Bay Area for better integrating Hong Kong and Macao (Zhang and Rui 2020). Obviously, Hong Kong would face external challenges from other regional financial centers, while Beijing doubts Hong Kong's political loyalty and hence is preparing Shenzhen as a potential replacement.

Last but not least, Hong Kong may be caught in the deglobalization or decoupling process between China and the US. Washington's perception of the rise of China began to change during Barack Obama's administration; its "pivot to Asia" policy and the Trans-Pacific Partnership share the same goal as Donald Trump's trade war and Indo-Pacific strategy, though the means are different. The American grievances regarding the rapid economic rise of China, which is partly a result of some "misbehaviors" of China, such as hacking foreign companies to acquire their high technologies, set out a confrontational agenda by lowering dependency on Chinese raw materials, its supply chains, and even its market. If the role of Hong Kong is no longer regarded by the US as the same as before, then less participation by the US in Hong Kong's economy may be detrimental to Hong Kong's interests as an international and cosmopolitan city. However, given the continuous Chinese suspicions of foreign forces behind Hong Kong and the surging Chinese nationalism under Xi's "Chinese Dream" to rejuvenate Chinese civilization, Hong Kong's status as a free international city can be compromised, even at the expense of "one country, two systems."

In the foreseeable future, more mass media, foreign business corporations, and both local and foreign professional talents will leave Hong Kong. The resulting brain drain and the new wave of emigration may pose significant challenges to Hong Kong's future development. There are already 105,000 Hong Kong people who have migrated to the UK since 2021 (Laura 2023), some of whom, needless to say, are middle class and have talents in various industries and business sectors. By contrast, the increasing number of Mainland companies, both state and civilian, in Hong Kong will play a dominating role in its economic and financial sectors. Marxists believe that controlling the "infrastructure"—that is, the economy—is essential, as it determines the "superstructure"—that is, the cultural, political, and legal institutions of society. Will the Beijing government become more proactive in interfering in Hong Kong's financial and monetary policy? This unanswered question remains an indicator of the further marginalization of Hong Kong as an international city.

In a nutshell, the "international character" (or internationalness) of Hong Kong is deemed to be in decline, while its "Chinese character" (or Chineseness) will tend to increase. These two characters are not necessarily mutually exclusive. Since becoming a Chinese city in 1997, Hong Kong has remained an international city, buttressed by its robust institutions. Now, however, overwhelming control of all the institutions and sectors of Hong Kong by the CCP is turning Hong Kong into a city that is not unique anymore, thus losing its competitiveness. Its increasing "Chineseness," not only in terms of national and cultural identification but also in terms of the "direct rule" under Beijing, challenges the robustness of Hong Kong's institutions, thus repugning the *raison d'être* of Hong Kong as an open and liberal international city.

To conclude, the implementation of the NSL reflects Beijing's resolute determination to control Hong Kong's politics and society. While the Beijing and Hong Kong administrations have repeatedly denied that the NSL could upset Hong Kong's prosperity or its status as an international financial center, this chapter argues that the negative impacts caused by Chinese interventions affect the external relations and international status of Hong Kong. In the post-2020 era, could the Chinese leaders ignore those figures such as the declining rankings, deteriorating reputation of Hong Kong, as well as foreign companies and people leaving the city? When Hong Kong's uniqueness, competitive edge, and its status as a free international city are in decline, is it really in the interest of China's future development?

Acknowledgments

This work was supported with research funding from Tokyo International University.

Box 16.1: Internationalization

Internationalization is the process of turning Hong Kong into an international city with Western attention and presence. China appreciates the status of Hong Kong as an international city, as it benefits Chinese national interests. But China only welcomes economic internationalization, not political internationalization of Hong Kong. While China recognizes that participation of the Western triad in Hong Kong's economy is crucial in maintaining economic internationalization, it emphasizes that political interference by the West in Hong Kong's domestic political development should be forbidden.

Box 16.2: Mainlandization

Mainlandization is the process of turning Hong Kong from a relatively international city into a "Chinese" city, with an increase in "Chinese" characteristics, though this might not necessarily result in the decrease of Hong Kong's "international" character. The character of a modern international city is shaped by a competent, efficient, and non-corrupt civil service, the rule of law, very clear "rules of the game" for market mechanisms, and liberty of expression and association. People in Hong Kong are worried that these characteristics are in the process of erosion, thus rendering Hong Kong an image that is similar to other Chinese cities. Some people say that this would result in the "provincialization" of Hong Kong, which means downgrading Hong Kong into a city of no special international status.

Questions

1. How does the Western triad view the rapid changes in Hong Kong?
2. What policy instruments has the Western triad adopted to respond to the situation in Hong Kong?
3. Has Hong Kong's status as a unique non-sovereign entity been affected if not undermined?
4. To what extent could the international civil society support Hong Kong's efforts to maintain its institutional pillars and autonomy?
5. Will Hong Kong lose its uniqueness and competitive edge, becoming just like any other Mainland Chinese city?

Bibliography

American Chamber of Commerce in Hong Kong 2020, "AmCham Temperature Survey Findings: OFAC's Sanction on Hong Kong and National Security Law," 13 August, https://www.amcham.org.hk/news/amcham-temperature-survey-findings-ofacs-sanction-hong-kong-national-security-law

American Chamber of Commerce in Hong Kong 2023, "AmCham HK's Latest Members Business Sentiment Survey Shows Cautious Optimism in 2023," 30 March, https://www.amcham.org.hk/news/amcham-hks-latest-members-business-sentiment-survey-shows-cautious-optimism-2023

Amnesty International 2021, "Amnesty International to Close Its Hong Kong Offices," 25 October, https://www.amnesty.org/en/latest/news/2021/10/amnesty-international-to-close-its-hong-kong-offices/#:~:text=Amnesty%20International%20will%20close%20its,by%20the%20end%20of%202021

Ashton, C 2014, "Situations in Hong Kong," European Commission, 22 October, https://ec.europa.eu/commission/presscorner/detail/en/SPEECH_14_718

Barber, E 2014, "Obama Issues a Warning over Xi Jinping's Growing Power," *Time*, 4 December, https://time.com/3617581/obama-xi-jinping-china-hong-kong/

BBC 2019, "Hong Kong Protests: Jeremy Hunt 'Keeping Options Open' over China," 4 July, https://www.bbc.com/news/uk-politics-48865907

BBC 2020a, "UK Unveils New Special Visa for Hong Kong's BNO Holders," 22 July, https://www.bbc.com/news/world-asia-china-53503338

BBC 2020b, "Nathan Law: Leading Young Democracy Activist Flees Hong Kong," 3 July, https://www.bbc.com/news/world-asia-china-53271740

Borger, J & Norton-Taylor, R 2014, "David Cameron Steps into Row over UK Delegation's Hong Kong Visit," *Guardian*, 1 December, https://www.theguardian.com/world/2014/dec/01/david-cameron-uk-foreign-affairs-committee-hong-kong-house-of-commons-china

Census and Statistics Department 2022, "Companies in Hong Kong with Parent Companies Located Outside HK," https://www.censtatd.gov.hk/hkstat/sub/sp360.jsp?tableID=133andID=0andproductType=8

Census and Statistics Department 2018 and 2022, "Report on Annual Survey of Companies in Hong Kong with Parent Companies Located Outside Hong Kong," https://www.censtatd.gov.hk/hkstat/sub/sp360.jsp?productCode=B1110004

Chen, J 2007, "1949: Xianggang weihe meiyou huigui" [1949: Why Hong Kong did not return to China], *Wenshi Bolan* [*Vision*], vol. 7, pp. 9–11.

Chen, Z 2019, "Yang: Foreign Interference in HK Affairs Intolerable," *China Daily*, 2 August, https://www.chinadailyhk.com/articles/0/206/9/1564713122138.html

Cheung, G 2020, "National Security Law Tarnishes Hong Kong's Image and Leaves European Union Firms Revisiting Plans, Bloc's Envoy Says," *South China Morning Post*, 19 August, https://www.scmp.com/news/hong-kong/politics/article/3097877/national-security-law-tarnishes-hong-kongs-image-and-leaves

Cheung, T, Cheung, G, Sum, LK & Lum, A 2019, "11 EU Representatives Meet Hong Kong Leader Carrie Lam to Protest Against Controversial Extradition Bill as Government Gathers 100 Officials to Build United Front," *South China Morning*

Post, 24 May, https://www.scmp.com/news/hong-kong/politics/article/3011627/hong-kong-government-gathers-100-officials-meeting-build

China Daily 2017, "Full Text: Xi's Speech at Meeting Marking HK's 20th Return Anniversary, Inaugural Ceremony of 5th-Term HKSAR Gov't," *China Daily*, 1 July, https://www.chinadaily.com.cn/china/hk20threturn/2017-07/01/content_29959860.htm

Council of the European Union 2020a, "Declaration of the High Representative on Behalf of the European Union on the Adoption by China's National People's Congress of a National Security Legislation on Hong Kong," 1 July, https://www.consilium.europa.eu/en/press/press-releases/2020/07/01/declaration-of-the-high-representative-on-behalf-of-the-european-union-on-the-adoption-by-china-s-national-people-s-congress-of-a-national-security-legislation-on-hong-kong/#

Council of the European Union 2020b, "Hong Kong: Council Expresses Grave Concern over National Security Law," 18 July, https://www.consilium.europa.eu/en/press/press-releases/2020/07/28/hong-kong-council-expresses-grave-concern-over-national-security-law/

Davis, MC 1997, "International Commitments to Keep: Hong Kong Beyond 1997," *World Affairs*, vol. 160, no. 2, pp. 70–77.

European Parliament 2019, "European Parliament Resolution of 18 July 2019 on the Situation in Hong Kong (2019/2732(RSP))," 18 July, https://www.europarl.europa.eu/doceo/document/TA-9-2019-0004_EN.html

Foreign and Commonwealth Office 2017, "Six-Monthly Report on Hong Kong: July to December 2016," 24 February, https://assets.publishing.service.gov.uk/government/uploads/system/uploads/attachment_data/file/594542/1Six_-monthly_report_on_Hong_Kong_-_January_to_June_2016.pdf

Foreign and Commonwealth Office 2019, "Six-Monthly Report on Hong Kong: January to June 2019," 31 October, https://assets.publishing.service.gov.uk/government/uploads/system/uploads/attachment_data/file/856991/Hong_Kong_Six-monthly_Report_Jan-Jun19.pdf

Foreign and Commonwealth Office and The Rt Hon Dominic Raab MP 2020, "National Security Legislation in Hong Kong: Foreign Secretary's Statement in Parliament," 1 July, https://www.gov.uk/government/speeches/foreign-secretary-statement-on-national-security-legislation-in-hong-kong

Grynbaum, MM 2020, "New York Times Will Move Part of Hong Kong Office to Seoul," *New York Times*, 14 July, https://www.nytimes.com/2020/07/14/business/media/new-york-times-hong-kong.html

Hernández, JC & Myers, SL 2020, "As China Strengthens Grip on Hong Kong, Taiwan Sees a Threat," *New York Times*, 18 September, https://www.nytimes.com/2020/07/01/world/asia/taiwan-china-hong-kong.html

Holland, S & Liu, R 2019, "In Phone Call with Trump, China's Xi Says US Interfering in Internal Affairs," *Reuters*, 21 December, https://www.reuters.com/article/us-usa-china-idUSKBN1YO1UN

Horton, C 2017, "Reporters Without Borders Picks Taiwan for Asian Bureau," *New York Times*, 6 April, https://www.nytimes.com/2017/04/06/world/asia/reporters-without-borders-asia-hong-kong.html?_r=0

Hua, Y 2014, "Why Is the US So Keen on 'Color Revolutions,'" *People's Daily*, 11 October, http://en.people.cn/n/2014/1011/c98649-8793283.html

Human Rights Watch 2020, "China: New Hong Kong Law a Roadmap for Repression," 29 July, https://www.hrw.org/news/2020/07/29/china-new-hong-kong-law-roadmap-repression

Hsiung, JC 1998, "Hong Kong as a Nonsovereign International Actor," *Asian Affairs: An American Review*, vol. 24, no. 4, pp. 237–244.

International Monetary Fund 2021, "People's Republic of China: 2020 Article IV Consultation-Press Release; Staff Report; and Statement by the Executive Director for the People's Republic of China," 8 January, https://www.imf.org/en/Publications/CR/Issues/2021/01/06/Peoples-Republic-of-China-2020-Article-IV-Consultation-Press-Release-Staff-Report-and-49992

Jim, C 2021, "Hong Kong Dropped from Economic Freedom Index as Policies 'Controlled from Beijing,'" *Reuters*, 4 March, https://www.reuters.com/article/us-hongkong-economy/hong-kong-dropped-from-economic-freedom-index-as-policies-controlled-from-beijing-idUSKBN2AW0OI

Johnson, J & Sugiyama, S 2020, "Tokyo Toughens Tone after Beijing Passes Hong Kong Security Law," *Japan Times*, 30 June, https://www.japantimes.co.jp/news/2020/06/30/national/politics-diplomacy/japan-delivers-toughest-words-yet-china-hong-kong-security-law/

Kawase, K 2020, "Hong Kong Leader Postpones Policy Address to Attend Xi's Speech," *Nikkei Asia*, 12 October, https://asia.nikkei.com/Politics/Hong-Kong-leader-postpones-policy-address-to-attend-Xi-s-speech

Kihara, T 2020, "Hong Kong Downsizing Considered by One-Third of Japanese Companies," *Nikkei Asia*, 20 October, https://asia.nikkei.com/Business/Business-trends/Hong-Kong-downsizing-considered-by-one-third-of-Japanese-companies

Kinder, T & Lewis, L 2021, "Companies Consider Writing Hong Kong out of Legal Contracts," *Financial Times*, 31 January, https://www.ft.com/content/1070440a-0993-4c19-9797-2c0e781fd7db

Lam, J 2018, "Immigration Officers Detain Japanese Politician Kenichiro Wada at Hong Kong Airport for Two Hours before Denying Him Entry to City after Pro-Democracy Stance Upsets Beijing," *South China Morning Post*, 10 August, https://www.scmp.com/news/hong-kong/politics/article/2159149/immigration-officers-detain-japanese-politician-hong-kong

Lau, S 2019, "United Nations Human Rights Body Takes Aim at Hong Kong Police over Use of Weapons," *South China Morning Post*, 13 August, https://www.scmp.com/news/china/diplomacy/article/3022623/united-nations-human-rights-body-takes-aim-hong-kong-police

Lau, S 2021, "Hong Kong Arrests Threaten Passage of EU-China Investment Deal, European Parliament Members Say," *South China Morning Post*, 7 January, https://www.scmp.com/news/china/diplomacy/article/3116713/european-parliament-members-say-hong-kong-arrests-threaten

Lau, SK 2000, "The Hong Kong Policy of the People's Republic of China, 1949–1997," *Journal of Contemporary China*, vol. 9, no. 23, pp. 77–93.

Laura, W 2023, "105,000 Hongkongers Start New Lives in UK since BN(O) Visa Scheme Began 2 Years Ago," *South China Morning Post*, 23 February, https://www.scmp.com/news/hong-kong/society/article/3211282/more-105000-hongkongers-start-new-lives-uk-bno-scheme-began-2-years-ago

Li, HY 2020, "Hong Kong's Role as a Mediator between China and the West: Changes under C. Y. Leung Administration," in JYS Cheng (ed), *Evaluation of the C. Y. Leung Administration*, City University of Hong Kong Press, Hong Kong, pp. 219–246.

Lieberthal, K 1997, "Hong Kong between the US and China," *Journal of the International Institute*, vol. 5, no. 1, http://quod.lib.umich.edu/j/jii/4750978.0005.101?rgn=main;view=fulltext

Lockett, H & Shane, D 2020, "Hong Kong Hedge Funds Explore Exit as National Security Law Looms," *Financial Times*, 9 June, https://www.ft.com/content/2acb077f-9f81-4457-9932-5223334facee

Miki, R 2020, "Japan Weighs Shortcut to Green Cards for Hong Kong Financial Talent," *Nikkei Asia*, 2 July, https://asia.nikkei.com/Spotlight/Japan-immigration/Japan-weighs-shortcut-to-green-cards-for-Hong-Kong-financial-talent

Miners, N 1998, *The Government and Politics of Hong Kong*, 5th ed., Oxford University Press, Hong Kong.

Ministry of Foreign Affairs of Japan 2019a, "Japan-China Summit Meeting and Dinner," 27 June, https://www.mofa.go.jp/a_o/c_m1/cn/page3e_001046.html

Ministry of Foreign Affairs of Japan 2019b, "Japan-China Summit Meeting (Premier Li Keqiang of the State Council of the People's Republic of China)," 4 November, https://www.mofa.go.jp/a_o/c_m1/cn/page3e_001126.html

Ministry of Foreign Affairs of the People's Republic of China 2017, "Foreign Ministry Spokesperson Lu Kang's Regular Press Conference on 30 June 2017," 30 June, https://www.fmprc.gov.cn/mfa_eng/xwfw_665399/s2510_665401/t1474637.shtml

Ministry of Foreign Affairs of the People's Republic of China 2019, "Wang Yi Talks about 2019 China's Diplomacy: Firmly Defend Our Core National Interests, Provide a Strong Support for Achieving the Two Centenary Goals," 13 December, https://www.fmprc.gov.cn/mfa_eng/zxxx_662805/t1724312.shtml

Miyasaka S 2020, "Japan Fires up Plans to Scout Hong Kong Talent for Financial Hub," *Nikkei Asia*, 13 June, https://asia.nikkei.com/Spotlight/Japan-immigration/Japan-fires-up-plans-to-scout-Hong-Kong-talent-for-financial-hub

Nikkei Asia 2021, "Hedge Fund Elliott Pulls out of Hong Kong," January 20, https://asia.nikkei.com/Business/Finance/Hedge-fund-Elliott-pulls-out-of-Hong-Kong

Ng, T 2019, "Donald Trump Says Tiananmen Square-Style Crackdown in Hong Kong Would Harm Trade Talks," *South China Morning Post*, 19 August, https://www.scmp.com/news/hong-kong/politics/article/3023340/us-president-donald-trump-says-tiananmen-square-style

Ota, N 2020, "Japan Eyes Bill to Sanction Human Rights Abuses in Hong Kong," *Asahi Shimbun*, 30 July, http://www.asahi.com/ajw/articles/13591720

Paau, DSL 2002, "Xianggang: Zhong Mei guangxi zhong de xin yinsu" [Hong Kong: New factor in Sino-US relations], *Meiguo Yanjiu* [American Studies Quarterly], vol. 16, no. 3, pp. 7–35.

Pamuk, H and Brunnstrom, D 2020, "US Imposes Sanctions on Four Chinese Officials over Hong Kong Crackdown," *Reuters*, 10 November, https://www.reuters.com/article/us-usa-china-hongkong/u-s-imposes-sanctions-on-four-chinese-officials-over-hong-kong-crackdown-idUSKBN27P2F2

People's Daily 2019, "No Compromise with 'Black Sheep' Attempting to Disrupt Hong Kong's Social Order: Tung Chee-hwa," *People's Daily*, 1 August, http://en.people.cn/n3/2019/0801/c90000-9602296.html

Pompeo, MR 2020a, "On Beijing's Imposition of National Security Legislation on Hong Kong," US Department of State, 30 June, https://www.state.gov/on-beijings-imposition-of-national-security-legislation-on-hong-kong/

Pompeo, MR 2020b, "US Government Ending Controlled Defense Exports to Hong Kong," US Department of State, 29 June, https://www.state.gov/u-s-government-ending-controlled-defense-exports-to-hong-kong/

Reporters Without Borders 2023, "Hong Kong," https://rsf.org/en/hong-kong

Shen, S 2008, "Borrowing the Hong Kong Identity for Chinese Diplomacy: Implications of Margaret Chan's World Health Organization Campaign," *Pacific Affairs*, vol. 81. no. 3, pp. 361–382.

Shen, S 2010, "Re-branding without Re-developing: Constraints of Hong Kong's 'Asia's World City' Brand (1997–2007)," *Pacific Review*, vol. 23, no. 2, pp. 203–224.

Shen, S 2016, *Hong Kong in the World: Implications to Geopolitics and Competitiveness*, Imperial College Press, London, pp. 69–90; 277–291.

Somasundaram, N 2020, "Hong Kong Security Law Sparks Race for Asia's Next Financial Capital," *Nikkei Asia*, 19 August, https://asia.nikkei.com/Spotlight/The-Big-Story/Hong-Kong-security-law-sparks-race-for-Asia-s-next-financial-capital

Speaker of the House 2019, "Pelosi Statement in Support of Hong Kong Protestors," 6 August, https://www.speaker.gov/newsroom/8519-3

Summers, T 2016, "British Policy toward Hong Kong and Its Political Reform," *Issues and Studies*, vol. 52, no. 4, pp. 1–25.

Sung, YW 1986, "The Role of Hong Kong in China's Export Drive," *Australian Journal of Chinese Affairs*, no. 15, pp. 83–101.

Tang, JTH 1993, "Hong Kong's International Status," *Pacific Review*, vol. 6, no. 3, pp. 205–215.

Tang, JTH 1997, "Hong Kong in United States-China Relations: The International Politics of Hong Kong's Reversion to Chinese Sovereignty," *Journal of Contemporary China*, vol. 6, no. 16, pp. 419–433.

The Hong Kong Trade Development Council 2020, "EU Imposes Export Controls on 'Sensitive' Equipment and Technologies Headed to Hong Kong," 29 July, https://hkmb.hktdc.com/en/NDk3MTM2ODQ2/hktdc-research/EU-Imposes-Export-Controls-on-%E2%80%9CSensitive%E2%80%9D-Equipment-and-Technologies-Headed-to-Hong-Kong

The White House 2020, "The President's Executive Order on Hong Kong Normalization," 14 July, https://www.whitehouse.gov/presidential-actions/presidents-executive-order-hong-kong-normalization/

Ting, W 1997, "The External Relations and International Status of Hong Kong," *Occasional Papers in Contemporary Asian Studies*, University of Maryland School of Law, no. 2, pp. 2–72.

Ting, W & Lai, E 2012, "Hong Kong and the World," in WM Lam, PLT Lui and W Wong (eds), *Contemporary Hong Kong Government and Politics*, Hong Kong University Press, Hong Kong, pp. 349–367.

US-China Economic and Security Review Commission 2016, "2016 Annual Report to Congress," November, https://www.uscc.gov/sites/default/files/2019-11/Chapter%20 3,%20Section%203%20-%20China%20and%20Hong%20Kong.pdf

US Congress 1992a, "S.1731 – United States-Hong Kong Policy Act of 1992," sections 102 (3), 103 (1), 103 (8), 105 (3), https://www.congress.gov/bill/102nd-congress/ senate-bill/1731/text

US Congress 1992b, "S.1731 – United States-Hong Kong Policy Act of 1992," sections 201 (a) and 202 (a), https://www.congress.gov/bill/102nd-congress/senate-bill/1731/text

US Congress 1992c, "S.1731 – United States-Hong Kong Policy Act of 1992," sections 2 (5) and (6) and 203, https://www.congress.gov/bill/102nd-congress/senate-bill/1731/ text

US Congress 2020a, "H.R. 7440 – Hong Kong Autonomy Act," https://www.congress.gov/ bill/116th-congress/house-bill/7440

US Congress 2020b, "H.R. 8228 – Hong Kong People's Freedom and Choice Act of 2020," https://www.congress.gov/bill/116th-congress/house-bill/8228

US Department of the Treasury 2020a, "Treasury Sanctions Individuals for Undermining Hong Kong's Autonomy," 7 August, https://home.treasury.gov/news/press-releases/ sm1088

US Department of the Treasury 2020b, "Hong Kong-Related Designations," 7 December, https://home.treasury.gov/policy-issues/financial-sanctions/recent-actions/ 20201207

US Department of State 2021a, "Joint Statement on Hong Kong," 20 January, https://www. state.gov/joint-statement-on-hong-kong/

US Department of State 2021b, "Risks and Considerations for Businesses Operating in Hong Kong," 16 July, https://www.state.gov/risks-and-considerations-for-businesses-operating-in-hong-kong/

Wintour, P 2020, "Chinese Officials Linked to Hong Kong Arrests Escape UK Sanctions," *Guardian*, 10 December, https://www.theguardian.com/politics/2020/dec/10/ chinese-officials-linked-to-hong-kong-activist-arrests-escape-uks-new-sanctions

Yang, S 2019, "Central Govt Official Identifies HK Turmoil as 'Color Revolution' for First Time," *Global Times*, 7 August, https://www.globaltimes.cn/content/1160700.shtml

Zhang, P & Rui, G 2020, "China Unveils Plan to Turn Shenzhen into 'Core Engine' of Reform," *South China Morning Post*, 13 October, https://www.scmp.com/news/china/ politics/article/3105215/china-unveils-plan-turn-shenzhen-core-engine-reform

426 Hong Kong's International Status at a Crossroads

Useful Websites

American Chamber of Commerce in Hong Kong
https://www.amcham.org.hk/news/amcham-temperature-survey-findings-ofacs-sanction-hong-kong-national-security-law

Full text: Xi's speech at meeting marking 20th anniversary of HK's return, inaugural ceremony of 5th-term HKSAR gov't, *China Daily*, 1 July 2017
https://www.chinadaily.com.cn/china/hk20threturn/2017-07/01/content_29959860.htm

H.R. 7440 – Hong Kong Autonomy Act, United States Congress
https://www.congress.gov/bill/116th-congress/house-bill/7440

HKSAR Census and Statistics Department
https://www.censtatd.gov.hk/hkstat/sub/sp360.jsp?tableID=133andID=0andproduct Type=8

HKSAR Constitutional and Mainland Affairs Bureau
https://www.cmab.gov.hk/en/home/index.htm

HKSAR Department of Justice, International Law Division
https://www.doj.gov.hk/en/about/orgchart_ild.html

HKSAR Trade and Industry Department
https://www.tid.gov.hk/english/aboutus/publications/pub_maincontent.html

Human Rights Watch
https://www.hrw.org/news/2020/07/29/china-new-hong-kong-law-roadmap-repression

Reporters Without Borders
https://rsf.org/en/hong-kong

The President's Executive Order on Hong Kong Normalization, The White House
https://www.whitehouse.gov/presidential-actions/presidents-executive-order-hong-kong-normalization/

Further Reading

Congress of the Unites States, "S.1731 – United States-Hong Kong Policy Act of 1992," https://www.congress.gov/bill/102nd-congress/senate-bill/1731/text. A fundamental and official American policy toward Hong Kong that has helped to shape Hong Kong's unique international status as a non-sovereign entity.

Foreign and Commonwealth Office and Foreign, Commonwealth and Development Office, The United Kingdom, "Six-Monthly Reports on Hong Kong," https://www. gov.uk/government/collections/six-monthly-reports-on-hong-kong. A collection of the British government's regular evaluation of the implementation of the Sino-British Joint Declaration in Hong Kong.

Li, HY 2020, "Hong Kong's Role as a Mediator between China and the West: Changes under C. Y. Leung's Administration," in Cheng, JYS (ed), *Evaluation of the C. Y. Leung Administration*, City University of Hong Kong Press, Hong Kong, pp. 219–246. A review of Hong Kong's international status from 2012 to 2017 under Leung

Chun-ying's administration, while Beijing has begun to play a greater role in Hong Kong's external relations.

Shen, S 2016, *Hong Kong in the World: Implications to Geopolitics and Competitiveness*, Imperial College Press, London. An overview of Hong Kong's external relations with both theoretical and empirical discussions, such as paradiplomacy, public diplomacy, branding, and the role of Hong Kong's non-state actors.

Ting, W 1997, "China, the United States, and the Future of Hong Kong," in B Leung and J Cheng (eds), *Hong Kong SAR: In Pursuit of Domestic and International Order*, the Chinese University Press of Hong Kong, Hong Kong, pp. 241–257. An investigation of how US policy was shaped to maintain the status quo in Hong Kong after 1997.

Ting, W 2000, "Europe, China and the Future of Hong Kong," in Neves, MS and Bridges, B (eds), *Europe, China and the Two SARs: Towards a New Era*, Macmillan, London, pp. 226–244. An examination of how Europe affected the transformation of Hong Kong before 1997.

Ting, W 2004, "An East-West Conundrum: Hong Kong in between China and the United States after the Chinese Resumption of Sovereignty," in YC Wong (ed), *One Country, Two Systems in Crisis: Hong Kong's Transformation since the Handover*, Lexington Books, Lanham, MD, pp. 187–208. This is an in-depth analysis of how Hong Kong situates itself between China and the United States, and how the relationship between the two powers will influence the future of Hong Kong.

Ting, W & Bridges, B 2002, "Thinking in Triangles: France, Germany and Hong Kong," *East-West Dialogue*, vol. VI, no. 2 and vol. VII, no. 1, June, pp. 320–340. A detailed analysis of the part played by two European states, France and Germany, in Hong Kong's economic, social, and political development.

17

Conclusion

Looking to the Future

Lam Wai-man, Percy Luen-tim Lui, and Wilson Wong

As of 2023, Hong Kong has entered the third decade as a special administrative region under the sovereignty of China. Like its previous editions, this volume attempts to provide an updated, comprehensive, and critical analysis of the development of Hong Kong's governing institutions, major policy areas, and relationship with China and the world in the context of governance and the experiment of "one country, two systems" (OCTS). Along with this attempt, topics related to political parties and the electoral systems, the mass media and public opinion, political culture and identity, and civil society in Hong Kong are also examined with regard to how successful they have been in promoting a more effective, accountable, and legitimate governance.

Political Institutions

This part of the volume covers major political institutions of the HKSAR, which include the executive, the legislature, the judiciary, the civil service, and the local administrative bodies. All these political institutions have, to a different degree, been affected by the Anti-ELAB Movement in 2019, the enactment of the NSL in 2020, and the implementation of the electoral system reform in 2021.

In Chapter 2, Li Pang-kwong examines the composition of the HKSAR executive, the powers that it enjoys, how it functions, its relationship with the legislature, and factors that affect its performance. Li also studies the notion of executive-led government and concludes that the executive-led government has been replaced by the executive-driven government (which means that, though the executive does not possess the power to constitute the legislature, the pro-government political figures are in the majority of the legislature). Under the executive-driven government, the HKSAR government has to build its majority coalition in the LegCo by persuasion and performance, not by institutional default. Li also examines the political dynamics developed since the Anti-ELAB Movement. He asserts that the new electoral arrangements put in place since 2021 have made room for the CE and the executive to judge and confirm the eligibility of LegCo candidates, through which it is easy to exclude anti-government candidates for the LegCo elections. Subsequently, one sees the return of an overwhelming majority of pro-government legislators in the LegCo. Moreover, one also sees the suppression of the influence of the opposition camp to the bare minimal level. As a result, though not equipped with the power to constitute the legislature, the CE, with the support from the Central People's Government (CPG), can dictate the decision of the legislature as he/she sees fit. Under such institutional arrangements, a variant form of the executive-led government is being brought back in. Though, with the growing support of the CPG, the CE could be released from the pressure of losing the majority in the ExCo and the LegCo, but the question of how to return a credible and capable CE with an effective governing team remains the pressing issue to be addressed.

In Chapter 3, by comparing the performance of the sixth term HKSAR LegCo with the 1995–1997 LegCo, Percy Lui finds that the greater the number of pro-democracy legislators the LegCo has, the greater its assertiveness to discharge its duties, and vice versa. Lui also examines other factors (such as the constitutional constraints imposed by the Basic Law) that would affect the capacity and performance of the HKSAR LegCo. After discussing why the sixth-term HKSAR LegCo had performed unsatisfactorily, Lui moves on to examine plausible impacts of major political developments, including (1) disqualifying legislators: rounds 1 and 2 (November 2016 and July 2017, and November 2020); (2) the Anti-ELAB Movement (June 2019–early 2020), the enactment of the NSL (July 2020), and the COVID-19 pandemic (December 2019–mid 2023); and (3) reforming the LegCo electoral methods (March 2021) on the performance of the future terms of the HKSAR LegCo. Under the new electoral methods, the seventh-term HKSAR LegCo is composed by an overwhelming majority of pro-government legislators. Though whether the future LegCo would act like the earlier Provisional Legislative Council (which acted more like an arm of the administration than as a watchdog of the government) remains to be seen, it is fair to predict that it would not be as assertive and aggressive as the previous terms HKSAR LegCo in checking the behavior and performance of the Hong Kong government.

In Chapter 4, Lai Yan-ho studies the HKSAR Judiciary. Lai observes that though Hong Kong enjoys a separate judicial system from the Mainland, when the central authorities become more aggressive in exercising direct or indirect control over Hong Kong, the latter lacks ability to resist exercise of power by the sovereign. Consequently, whether the courts can still uphold impartiality and act as guardians of human rights when adjudicating judicial reviews or criminal trials related to anti-government protests became questionable. By examining the trials of the activists in the Umbrella Movement (UM), Lai asserts that public order laws and the courts have been weaponized by the government to silence the political opposition. These practices became more prominent in the Anti-ELAB Movement in 2019. As there are many pending trials related to the movement, it is important to see how the verdicts and sentences of these Anti-ELAB cases will affect the criminal justice system, judicial independence, and the rule of law in Hong Kong. Moreover, given the introduction of the NSL in Hong Kong by the CPG, the whole judicial system as well as the enjoyment of judicial autonomy in Hong Kong is now undergoing a drastic change. Above all, Lai notes that various surveys conducted after the enactment of the NSL show that citizens have become much less confident in the rule of law and judicial independence in Hong Kong. As Lai argues, it would be a challenging task for the judiciary and the governments of both HKSAR and PRC to rebuild public trust in the judiciary.

In Chapter 5, Wilson Wong studies the features of and roles that the Hong Kong civil service played in the governance of Hong Kong before and after the 1997 handover, including the post-2020 era. When Hong Kong was a British colony, the political system was a bureaucrat-dominated system with only bureaucrats but no professional politicians. Major public policies were formulated by senior civil servants (belonging to the administrative officer grade) and implemented by the civil service. As Wong points out, the civil service is taken as the "institutional conscience" of Hong Kong, and the civil service system is designed to ensure that civil servants can make the best policies based on their own expertise and judgment, without being threatened or biased by both internal and external pressures. Wong also analyzes the details of reforms to the civil service system after the handover. These reforms include the ASPO, politicization of the civil service (especially under the Leung and Lam administrations), public sector reform and civil service reform. Despite all these reforms and the changing role, Wong notes that the Hong Kong civil service remains an influential actor in the governance of the HKSAR. With reference to the need to make use of emerging technologies to continuously improve public services, Wong asserts that the civil service should invest much more aggressively in areas like collaborative governance and digital governance to strengthen its capacities to cope with the new circumstances and challenges in the post Anti-ELAB Movement era.

In Chapter 6, Rami Chan studies the HKSAR's local government system and its complex web of advisory and statutory bodies. Chan first details the development, functions, and the empowerment of the DCs in 2001 and 2006. He examines in detail the political role of the DCs (elections of the DCs have been political battlegrounds for various political parties to gain influence in district administration and in Hong Kong politics). He argues that the passage of the government's constitutional reform package in June 2010 has transformed a DC from a simple advisory body into a dynamic arena for power struggle. Though the Anti-ELAB Movement helped the pan-democrats achieve a landslide victory in the 2019 DC elections (which gave birth to the first ever pan-democrat-dominated DCs: 17 out of 18), the subsequent political developments such as the enactment of the NSL and the electoral reform in March 2021 have removed almost all the political influence of the DCs in the name of reinforcing DCs to align their status as not an "organ of political power," according to the Basic Law. The narrowing political environment after the enactment of the NSL would also significantly affect the role and function of advisory and statutory bodies. When political loyalty becomes a priority on the selection and appointment of membership, it will further affect the creditability of these consultative bodies.

Mediating Institutions and Political Actors

With the limitations of institutional politics in Hong Kong discussed above, mediating institutions have played some important functions to compensate for the participation gap. In the last edition of this volume, we cast doubt as to how political stability and effective governance could be maintained without substantial and genuine reforms to the political system, given the inevitable changes in the political landscape and constraints on the political development of Hong Kong. The past decade witnessed blatant politicization and divisions in society and open conflicts between the authorities and the people, as well as among the people until 2021.

Chapter 7 analyzes the democratic reforms in Hong Kong by Lai Yan-ho and Sing Ming. The chapter provides an overview of the path of democratization in Hong Kong since the colonial era. The blockade of a fair and open process for nominating candidates in future CE elections in 2014 contributed to the outbreak of the UM. Demands for universal suffrage continued and were heightened during the Anti-ELAB Movement in 2019. Nevertheless, the NSL introduced in 2020—and the subsequent arrests, disqualifications of democratic lawmakers, and so forth—brought about gigantic changes to the political landscape in Hong Kong. Popular confidence in democracy, the rule of law, and freedom in Hong Kong also witnessed sharp falls until recently. The question is whether the support for freedom and democracy in Hong Kong in the last few decades would go further. The future democratic development in post-2020 Hong Kong will hinge upon the interplay among the CPG, domestic pro-establishment and pro-democracy forces, and the global environment.

432   Conclusion

In Chapter 8, on political parties and elections, Kwong Ying-ho and Mathew Y. H. Wong provide a historical review of party politics and elections in Hong Kong and highlight the dynamics among the Chinese government, the Hong Kong government, and pro-Beijing, pro-democracy, and localist parties in Hong Kong. Hong Kong had a multiparty system with polarized ideological spectrums. In the past decade, the traditional classification of pro-democracy and pro-Beijing political parties was challenged through the rise of localist organizations, leading to a new spectrum between "pro-establishment" and "non-establishment." Regarding elections, the chapter provides a review of the results of various LegCo elections and seat allocations among the political parties. Owing to the executive-dominant system of Hong Kong—in which the power of the executive branch is guaranteed, whereas the legislature is fragmented and given relatively limited power—popular support for political parties has been low. Additionally, Hong Kong people are generally skeptical of party politics because of various factors, notably including the Chinese government's strategies in Hong Kong. As such, party politics has remained weak and the development of political parties stagnant regardless of their political orientations. In the legislative elections in 2021, the pro-establishment camp gained a sweeping victory and consolidated its political influence. The development of political parties and elections in Hong Kong will depend on whether the authorities take further steps to transform the political party system in Hong Kong, as well as the development of the pro-establishment camp amid the changes.

Chapter 9, by Stephan Ortmann on civil society, traces the emergence of civil society in colonial times and its development into a liberal civil society in the 1990s. The chapter then takes stock of the situation after the handover regarding the development of the vast united front network of political parties, trade unions, business elites, newly created counterprotest organizations, hometown associations, neighborhood organizations, and so forth, which attempted to provide an alternative to the liberal civil society and curb its expansion. Social conflicts culminated in the UM and were then heightened by the Anti-ELAB Movement, which saw unprecedented mobilizations in Hong Kong. However, the NSL, promulgated in 2020, would weaken the civil society, allowing only depoliticized nongovernmental organizations endorsed by the state. Also, businesses that side with pro-democracy activists have also encountered more political pressure. Ortmann argues that Hong Kong has changed to an illiberal authoritarian regime, which would seriously impact the growth of the civil society.

Chapter 10, by Lam Wai-man on political identity, culture, and participation, reviews the conflicting readings by scholars before and after the handover of Hong Kong's political culture as politically passive and analyzes the developments of the subject matter after 2012. In the 2010s, the Hong Kong identity had shed much of its Chineseness and instead developed into a new Hong Konger identity, with consolidated cultural and value contents capable of generating and sustaining political actions. The development of localism—namely, community-oriented localism, civic localism, and nativist localism—signified another landmark turn in the Hong Kong identity. Another climax happened in the Anti-ELAB Movement, during which localism in Hong Kong took an ideological and strategic turn into Hong Kong nationalism or "civic nationalism," which further led to a brand of Hong Konger identity geared toward greater political autonomy for Hong Kong. These existed alongside the activist character of the local political culture, marked by people's growing fundamental social and political demands and increased endorsement of radicalized and confrontational strategies. Despite these, civility and the rule of law had long been ascribed as indispensable elements of the colonial order, and the political culture in Hong Kong still embodied elements of political passivity, such as low interest in politics and low sense of political efficacy. Meanwhile, political trust had dwindled over the years and especially after the Anti-ELAB Movement, until recently. The changing political culture had enhanced institutional and noninstitutional participation, collective actions, and social movements in Hong Kong, such as the formation of community, professional, and political organizations by locals driven by social and political consciousness. After the promulgation of the NSL, the above organizational activism has been restrained, and it is likely that institutional participation would become the more popular form of expression.

Chapter 11, by Joseph M. Chan and Francis L. F. Lee on mass media and public opinion, discusses the definitions of public opinion, the roles of the mass media, and their effects in the process of public opinion formation. Structural factors shape the operation of media organizations and constrain journalists' capabilities in adhering to their professional ideals. In Hong Kong, since most local media organizations are business enterprises, they are subject to ownership influence, advertisers, and market-driven journalism. Since the early 2010s, the trends of ownership of Hong Kong media by Mainland Chinese capital and the co-optation of media owners have allowed more Chinese control or influence over the Hong Kong press. Particularly, the passage of the NSL has imposed immense pressure on Hong Kong media to self-censor and further eroded the resilience of journalistic professionalism. Alongside the importance of the media is public opinion, which has become a key factor of governance in Hong Kong. Regarding this, government officials are in general identified as the "primary definers," whereas journalists are the "secondary definers." Meanwhile, citizens and various social forces may shape the representation of public opinion in the media, especially through collective actions. However, Chan and Lee assert that the NSL would also result in a chilling effect marked by self-censorship in all social sectors.

434　Conclusion

Policy Environment

The chapters on policy environment focus on "governance in action." It serves the purpose of illustrating how political forces and policy actors compete to determine "who gets what, when and how" in each policy area, as structured by the political institutions in Hong Kong. Although the three chapters are written independently by different authors, similar conclusions are made. They conclude that public policy should be approached as conscious and rational choices by policymakers with consideration of the public interest, a long-term perspective, and fairness to all citizens. On the other hand, they are also shaped by the macro-political systems and the overall power dynamics in Hong Kong, which explain the similar patterns and observations identified across chapters. Many policies in Hong Kong are dominated by those who enjoy more power in the governing institutions at the expense of the less represented and organized groups, which led to questions and reflections on the necessity and desirability of reforms on both the policy level and the level of macro-political institutions.

In Chapter 12, by Wilson Wong and Raymond Yuen on economic policy, a central theme is that economic policy is shaped by more than economic forces. The image of a "market economy" is more a myth than a reality, as political considerations often override economic logic in shaping economic policy. One of the examples is Hong Kong's fiscal system, under which the politically powerful are often taxed less but benefit more. Owing to the new and major developments in Hong Kong's politics and governance, there have been corresponding changes to expedite the shift from an approach of a relatively invisible hand in economic policy toward an increasingly visible hand marked with budgetary punctuations. The old doctrines of economic policy, such as positive nonintervention and fiscal prudence with a balanced budget, are given less adherence, as Hong Kong's economic policy is becoming more similar to the Mainland, which prefers a more interfering government and a planned economy. These changes are translated into a more aggressive model of industrial policy and budgetary punctuations, including higher public expenditure and a budget deficit. There are doubts about how a balance can be struck between a more visible role of government and sustainable fiscal health, especially during a period of economic decline in both Hong Kong and the Mainland. Given the inseparable linkage between economic policy and governance, another challenge for the HKSAR government is how to coordinate economic transformation with structural reforms in its governance system.

Chapter 13, by Wong Hung on social policy, describes the social policy in the post-1997 era as no more than "old wine in new bottles." Social policy of the HKSAR government still has the same economic pragmatism origin as its colonial past. In practice, Hong Kong has never claimed or committed to be a welfare state and has limited welfare provision. The practical and piecemeal responses produced are inadequate for addressing the fundamental needs and problems, leading to sharp deteriorations of the social conditions in Hong Kong, which include deepening of poverty and a widening wealth gap. According to the principle of "one country, two systems," the Hong Kong government should have the will to govern. A more comprehensive, long-term, and people-oriented planning for social policy should be adopted, with greater participation of the civil society to make Hong Kong people enjoy life with better health care, housing, and social security. However, the HKSAR government seems to lose its will to govern and tends to wait for the CPG to take political leadership in handling the social problems and rising class conflicts. In this connection, the latest strategy of the Hong Kong government to further integrate Hong Kong into the development of the Greater Bay Area and Mainland China can only offer a vague framework. It remains unable to provide solid grounding for formulating a people-oriented social policy.

Chapter 14, by Ng Mee Kam on urban policy, points out the need for Hong Kong, as a world city, to adopt the New Urban Agenda of the United Nations to call for a paradigm shift in urban planning, development, and management to achieve the Sustainable Development Goals (SDGs). Hong Kong has been facing challenging urban issues related to its legacies as a British colony and a specific brand of "state-led liberal capitalism" that focuses on economic growth. There is a need for concerted tripartite efforts by the now multilevel governments, the private sector, and the civil society to integrate ecological and social justice considerations during economic and spatial development. Shifting away from an urban biased mode of development bequeathed by the colonizers and the government's reliance on land and property-related revenues, the pathway toward the future should "leave no one, no place, and no ecology behind." Instead of developing the Lantau Tomorrow Vision, an alternative New Territories Tomorrow Vision is preferred to strategically reimagine and replan the rural New Territories, where most of the land resources lie. This would require a reorientation of the government from reclaiming land from the sea to restoring and "reclaiming" land, practicing integrated planning that respects nature and promotes conservation of tangible and intangible heritages. While the government should have enough resources to undertake this challenge, the question is if they would have such a vision and mission.

Political Environment

As a global city and part of China, Hong Kong's politics are undoubtedly shaped by the external environment beyond domestic forces. We have devoted the last two chapters of this book to the political environment of Hong Kong, including its relations with the Mainland and the wider world.

Chapter 15, by Peter T. Y. Cheung on the changing relations between Hong Kong and the Mainland, analyzes the changing strategy of Beijing in governing Hong Kong since President Xi Jinping assumed power in 2012. Against the background of the consolidation of the hard authoritarian mode of governance and the establishment of a security state in Mainland China, the once indispensable role of Hong Kong in China's economic development has changed. These along with the profound repercussions of the OCM and UM have transformed the relations between Hong Kong and the Mainland ever since. Overall, Beijing's "comprehensive jurisdiction" over Hong Kong can be conceptualized into several components, including asserting constitutional and legislative authority, the securitization of Hong Kong's governance, overhauling the electoral system, emphasizing ideological authority and strengthening united front work, responding actively to external influence over Hong Kong affairs, incorporating Hong Kong into the national development framework, and revamping the governing team and central organs in Hong Kong and Macao affairs. While Hong Kong may maintain its own systems as different from the Mainland, with "patriots administering Hong Kong," the revamping of other state and social institutions, and the reeducation of values and ideologies in Hong Kong, the emerging political order in Hong Kong will inevitably undergo a homogenization process.

Chapter 16, by Li Hak-yin and Ting Wai on Hong Kong's international status, reexamines Hong Kong's international status. The chapter summarizes the key literature around Hong Kong's international status, offers a backgrounder on Hong Kong's major political developments since the UM, analyzes Hong Kong's changing international status from multiple perspectives, and evaluates Hong Kong's future international status by reviewing possible challenges and their implications. The UM and the Anti-ELAB Movement served as the source of conflict between China and the West over Hong Kong. While China saw numerous demonstrations in Hong Kong and Western pressures as tremendous foreign interventions in Hong Kong, the West and foreign business corporations have also been upset because of the increasing Chinese interventions toward Hong Kong and the NSL. The rapid change in Hong Kong's international status carries several implications for the world: Hong Kong is no longer a "window" between China and the West; the trend of Hong Kong's Mainlandization is increasing; Hong Kong is no longer a model for Taiwan; and Hong Kong is caught in the deglobalization or decoupling process between China and the US. The increasing direct control of Hong Kong by Beijing challenges the robustness of Hong Kong's institutions. In the future, the international character of Hong Kong will decline while its Chinese character increases, although these two characters are not necessarily mutually exclusive to each other.

Discussion

Based on the critical analysis of the chapters in this volume, we would like to highlight several major changes to the governance and politics in Hong Kong in recent years.

Evolution of the "one country, two systems" principle

The "one country, two systems" (OCTS) principle has steadily evolved in the past two decades. Simply put, the evolution of the principle is reflected in a shift of emphasis from "two systems" to "one country," and a corresponding development in the understanding of the notion of a "high degree of autonomy." One can examine the evolution of the OCTS principle from four different periods: (1) from 1997 to 2003, (2) from 2003 to 2014, (3) from 2014 to 2019, and (4) from 2019 onward.

In the first period, the emphasis is on the differences between the two systems, which granted the HKSAR a high degree of autonomy to manage its own affairs, except national defense and foreign affairs. During this period, the CPG was conscious not to give the impression that it was exercising undue intervention in the HKSAR's governance. To paraphrase a comment from the former President of China, Jiang Zemin, "the river water would not mix with the well water." Such a comment vividly characterized the spirit of the OCTS principle until July 2003.

July 2003 marks the beginning of the second period of the implementation of the OCTS principle. On 1 July 2003, more than 500,000 people took to the streets to protest the perceived poor performance of the HKSAR government, especially its proposals to enact a national security law to give effect to Article 23 of the Basic Law. Both the HKSAR government and the CPG were shocked by the "1 July march," as it was the first time in the history of Hong Kong that so many people had publicly demonstrated against the government. Alarmed by the growing discontent of the Hong Kong people toward the government's performance, the CPG began to take a more proactive approach in the governance of the HKSAR. A case in point is its greater involvement in negotiating a political reform package with the Democratic Party in May 2010. Though the CPG has taken a more proactive approach in its dealing with the HKSAR, there was no evidence that it has significantly restricted the degree of autonomy that the HKSAR government enjoyed during this period.

In June 2014, when Hong Kong society was debating the next move in reforming its political system (including the planning of the Occupy Central Movement by the pan-democratic camp), the State Council of China issued the *White Paper on The Practice of the "One Country, Two Systems" Policy in the Hong*

Kong Special Administrative Region. The main theme of the White Paper is the CPG's reassertion of its "comprehensive jurisdiction" over the HKSAR. Later, on 31 August 2014, the SCNPC announced its Decision (31 August Decision), which set the parameters for the further development in the HKSAR's political reform. In the eyes of the CPG, the emphasis of the OCTS principle then was clearly on "one country," and subsequently, a narrower interpretation of the notion of a "high degree of autonomy" that the HKSAR enjoys in governing itself. Moreover, the Occupy Central Movement (which took place on 28 September 2014) and the subsequent development in the HKSAR politics (like the 2016 LegCo elections) gave a big boost to localism, which emphasized "two systems" more than "one country."

Lastly, in response to the Anti-ELAB Movement, the CPG enacted the NSL for the HKSAR on 30 June 2020. Furthermore, to ensure that patriots would govern the HKSAR, the SCNPC issued a decision on 11 March 2021 to improve the electoral systems of Hong Kong (including the electoral systems of the EC and the LegCo). Today, as some critics assert, the emphasis on the OCTS principle is primarily on "one country," not on "two systems." Such an emphasis naturally would result in a much more restrictive understanding of the notion of a "high degree of autonomy" that the HKSAR government would possess in governing Hong Kong. The developments in Hong Kong politics are closely tied with the further integration of Hong Kong with the Mainland.

Securitizing Hong Kong

The securitization of Hong Kong has remained a top agenda for the government. The Anti-ELAB Movement in 2019 eventually led to thousands of arrests and prosecutions. In June 2020, the National Anthem Ordinance, which criminalizes insults to the national anthem of China, came into effect. Additionally, the NSL—which criminalizes separatism, subversion, terrorism, and foreign interference—was promulgated on 30 June 2020. With the implementation of the NSL, an Office for Safeguarding National Security of the CPG and a Committee for Safeguarding National Security of the HKSAR were set up in the territory. The wide-ranging provisions of the NSL are perceived by some as having unfathomable, chilling effects in society.

Since 2020, all civil servants have been required to swear allegiance and sign a pledge declaring that they would uphold the Basic Law, bear allegiance to the HKSAR, and be accountable to the HKSAR government. With the passing of the oath-taking requirement bill in the LegCo in March 2021, the mandatory oath of allegiance has been extended to cover DC members and all personnel hired on non-civil service terms. This has led to massive resignations of District Councilors. Along with this was the launch of a further electoral system reform for Hong Kong on 11 March 2021, which drastically altered the election methods of the Election Committee (EC) subsector elections and the LegCo elections in 2021, the CE election in 2022, and the status of the DCs.

Since the promulgation of the NSL, there have been a series of arrests and prosecutions, with many trials pending and suspects long detained in custody; of democrats and localists for joining or organizing the 4 June commemoration and the 1 October protest in 2020 not approved by the police; participation in the pan-democrats organized primaries for the 2020 LegCo elections (postponed to December 2021 due to the COVID-19 pandemic); and the publication of seditious materials. Furthermore, the police raided the offices of *Apple Daily* and *Stand News*. *Apple Daily* and *Stand News* closed after the police raids and arrests, and *Hong Kong Citizen News* also disbanded in January 2022.

Reconstituting the identity of younger generations has been one of the foremost tasks of the government. For example, the former CE, Carrie Lam, stressed that students should be trained to become law-abiding, respect different opinions, and adopt a responsible attitude as members of society. She had reiterated the importance of cultivating students' understanding of the country's development, the Basic Law, the implementation of "one country, two systems," and the importance of national security. She further urged teaching young people to respect and preserve the dignity of the national flag and the national anthem, as well as to develop in them a sense of identity, belonging, and responsibility toward the country, the Chinese race, and society. Since the subject of Liberal Studies was blamed by pro-establishment figures for encouraging students to participate in protests, it was replaced by "Citizenship and Social Development" in the 2021–2022 school year onward. The term of CE John Lee started in 2022. In a similar vein, his government has also sought to boost Hong Kong's economic and social development through active promotion of the city's integration into the national development alongside ensuring its social stability, patriotism, and national security.

Refocusing on economic development and greater integration with the Mainland

The focus of the HKSAR government after the enactment of the NSL and the reform to the electoral systems has been on economic development, which is understandable since the Hong Kong economy, like other economies in the world, was hit hard by the COVID-19 pandemic. A major strategy that the government relies on is to further integrate the Hong Kong economy with the Mainland. The rationale behind the further economic integration between the two sides is simple—the further development of the Hong Kong economy would enhance the well-being of the Hong Kong people, which, in turn, would restore and enhance the legitimacy of both the CPG and the HKSAR government.

Indeed, such an integration began as early as 2002, when Hong Kong negotiated a closer economic partnership with China. The two sides signed the Closer Economic Partnership Agreement (CEPA) on 29 June 2003. The signing of CEPA and the opening up of "individual visits" by Mainland residents to the HKSAR in August 2003 signaled the beginning of Hong Kong's greater economic integration with the Mainland. Later, there was an initiative to bring together nine provinces of southern China (Guangdong, Fujian, Hunan, Guangxi, Hainan, Sichuan, Guizhou, Jiangxi, and Yunnan) along with Hong Kong and Macao to form a common market, which has been described as the "Pan-Pearl River Delta" (PRD, or simply 9+2).

Like the development in the political front, there is a steady increase in the economic integration between the HKSAR and the Mainland. This is especially so after the Occupy Central Movement and the Anti-ELAB Movement. The CPG and the HKSAR government believe that the future development of the Hong Kong economy lies in the Mainland in general (Hong Kong has been covered in China's National Five-Year Plans, including the 12th, 13th, and 14th, since its return to China) and the Greater Bay Area (GBA) initiative (which was launched in 2017) in particular. The GBA comprises the two special administrative regions of Hong Kong and Macao, and the nine municipalities of Guangzhou, Shenzhen, Zhuhai, Foshan, Huizhou, Dongguan, Zhongshan, Jiangmen, and Zhaoqing in Guangdong Province. The HKSAR government asserts that the GBA would generate new impetus for the growth of the Hong Kong economy and bring new development opportunities to different sectors of the HKSAR. As such, one can expect the CPG and the HKSAR government to adopt more measures in the future to facilitate further integration of the Hong Kong economy with the Mainland. Overall, it is fair to say that the shifting of emphasis from "two systems" to "one country" as well as the greater integration of the Hong Kong economy with the Mainland would have far-reaching impact on governing style and the degree of autonomy that the HKSAR government possesses in governing the HKSAR.

Readjustment of civil society

With the promulgation of the NSL and the 2021 electoral system reform, pro-autonomy and pro-independence political parties were disbanded, while traditional pro-democracy political parties were marginalized. The pro-establishment camp, on the contrary, has grown in number, influence, and political power. As seen with the 2021 Legislative Council elections, of the 90 legislators returned, there was only one non-establishment figure.

The civil society in Hong Kong became very polarized between the pro- and anti-establishment political identities and political participation after the Occupy Movement in 2014. This rift was heightened during and after the Anti-ELAB Movement in 2019. Nevertheless, the many "red lines" that emerged with the NSL have utterly paralyzed if not wiped out the anti-establishment camps. As of 2023, prominent civil society organizations had either ceased operation or disbanded, including the Civil Human Rights Front, the Hong Kong Professional Teachers' Union, the Hong Kong Confederation of Trade Unions, and the Hong Kong Alliance in Support of Patriotic Democratic Movements of China. Other relatively moderate social and professional organizations and unions have also gone silent or dissolved. Various universities cut ties with their student organizations, which had been the backbone of pro-democracy movements in Hong Kong in the past decade. Campus statues and symbols associated with local resistance were removed, including the Pillar of Shame at the University of Hong Kong and the Goddess of Democracy at the Chinese University of Hong Kong.

With the authorities' directive that "patriots rule Hong Kong," civil society organizations have to be depoliticized and politically correct in order to survive. The growing stringent patriotic atmosphere has prompted many people to leave Hong Kong. It was reported that the net outflow of people from June 2020 to mid-2021 in the "Hong Kong exodus" was 89,200 (Bao 2021). Remaining oppositionists, largely frustrated or alienated, would choose "lying flat" (*tǎng píng*), which literally means being knocked out of a fight or out of action. Others looking for alternatives would resort to supporting pro-democracy businesses in the Yellow Economic Circle and becoming involved in informal social and literal activities, and so on. Nevertheless, these businesses and activities may also be seen as a concerted effort against the government. In short, the civil society, which had fueled not only the political but also social and economic developments in Hong Kong over the past decades, has been shocked and hammered. In 2023 and the years onward, the challenge for the civil society will be in finding its path to recovery and repositioning itself.

Bibliography

Bao, J 2021, "Hong Kong Exodus Set to Accelerate in 2022," *Asia Times*, 27 August, viewed 3 January 2022, https://asiatimes.com/2021/08/hong-kong-exodus-set-to-accelerate-in-2022

Index

35-plus strategy, 42, 69
831 decision, 5, 66, 87, 168, 195, 223, 373, 438

Accountability System for Principal Officials (ASPO), 3–4, 14–15, 35–36, 38, 46, 111, 121–123, 205, 430
activism, 4–5, 20, 78, 170, 214, 217, 224, 233, 241–243, 248–249, 254–245
administrative absorption of politics, 116, 134
administrative officers, 114–116, 136, 360
administrative state, 112–114, 118
advisory bodies, 124, 149–150
ageing, 352. *See also* health policy
agencification, 126
agenda-setting, 274. *See also* public opinion
Anti-ELAB movement, 3, 6–7, 20, 62, 68, 176–177, 206, 225–228, 282, 371, 378–379, 403, 405–407, 440–441
anti-rich sentiment, 325–326
Apple Daily, 7, 18–19, 97, 231, 271, 386–387, 439
Area Committees, 16, 19, 33, 147, 155
Asian Financial Crisis, 3, 120, 201, 304, 324, 330
authoritarianism, 76; electoral, 14; hard, 372, 426; soft, 3, 19, 112
autocratization, 162–163
autonomy, high degree of, 8, 10, 83, 163, 192, 331, 376, 414, 437–438; judicial, 84–85, 93, 98, 430, 438

bargaining model, 162–166
Basic Law: 1–2, 22, 82–83, 113, 137, 161, 193, 217; interpretations, 2, 4, 6, 18, 67, 84–87, 144, 165, 170–171, 377–378; decisions, 87–89, 146, 377
Annex I, 4
Annex II, 4, 17, 59, 62, 199
Annex III, 87
Article 1, 170
Article 2, 170
Article 5, 88
Article 18, 8, 18, 87
Article 23, 3, 9–10, 93, 217, 437
Article 45, 167, 181, 195
Article 48, 14
Article 49, 14
Article 50, 14
Article 52, 14
Article 54, 36
Article 56, 36
Article 64, 58
Article 73, 14
Article 74, 17, 41, 57, 59, 62, 65, 72
Article 79, 65
Article 98, 137
Article 104, 6, 18, 66, 70, 85–86, 144, 171
Article 107, 296
Article 158, 18, 84–85
Article 159, 170
basic rights and freedoms, 78, 82, 94–95, 229, 404

Index

Belt and Road Initiative (BRI), 6, 8, 387, 393

big market, small government, 293, 304, 319, 324, 332, 334, 348, 350

bills, 57–58; government's, 59; private members', 16–17, 59, 62–63, 72–73

block voting, 145, 156, 384

blue ribbons. *See* polarization, political

British colonial legacy, 32, 42–44, 111–116, 174, 250, 304–306, 331, 345–347, 400

British National (Overseas), 7, 232, 410

brownfield sites, 345, 347–348, 356–357, 360

budgets, 38–39, 58, 173, 295–296, 302, 321, 348

bureaucracy, 44, 113–114, 119–121, 123–124, 129, 305, 312

bureaucrat-dominated model, 111–113, 120, 430

bureaus, 35–38, 61, 114, 119–121

business politicians, 113

business sectors, 40, 47, 54, 176, 200, 204, 205, 306, 311, 418

Candidate Eligibility Review Committee, 17–18, 34, 43, 54, 71, 96, 178, 349, 383

capitalism in Hong Kong, 293; crony capitalism, 306, 355; productivist welfare capitalism, 320; state-led liberal capitalism, 342, 435

Care Teams. *See* District Services and Community Care Teams

censorship, 78, 174, 215, 382, 415; self-censorship, 19, 174, 271–273, 284

Central People's Government (CPG), 32, 95, 111, 163, 229, 270, 299, 319, 429

Chan, Kin-man, 5, 90–91, 175, 222, 403

Chan, Ho-tin, 5, 207

Chan Ho-wun, Figo, 172

Chan, Yuen-han, 333

Chief Executive, 8, 163, 204–205; powers of, 14, 34, 41,122; Policy Unit, 37,

276; Council of Advisors, 37; governing coalition, 34, 45

Chief Executive election, 5, 15–16, 33–34, 53, 71, 96, 145–147, 167–168, 178, 181, 192, 195, 199

Chinese identity, 195–196, 244, 247, 257–258, 384

Chiu, Andrew Ka-yin, 68

Chow, Alex Yong-kang, 90, 175

Chow, Ting, Agnes, 5–6, 69, 90, 171, 220

Chu, Hoi-dick, Eddie, 172

Chu, Yiu-ming, 5, 91, 175, 222, 403

Citizen and Social Development (subject), 385, 439

city of protests, 281

civic nomination, 167–168, 181

Civic Party, 166, 194, 271

Civic Passion, 167

civil disobedience, 91, 169, 222, 250, 282, 373, 403

Civil Human Rights Front, 176, 227, 230, 282

civil servants, 4, 8, 35, 44, 111–114, 122–124, 129, 331, 382–383, 438; as guardian of public interests, 115–116; recruitment, 9, 117, 120

civil service, 3, 14–15, 46, 111; depoliticization, 117–118; disciplinary system, 118–119; managerial discretion, 118–119; politicization, 123–124, 127, 142–143; reform, 124, 127

civil society, 20, 165–166, 176, 180, 214–217, 230–235, 251, 280–283, 414–415, 441

climate change, 342

Closer Economic Partnership Arrangement (CEPA), 10, 307, 440

colocation arrangement, 8, 18, 87–88, 377

color revolutions, 373, 379, 403, 407

collusion, government-business, 304, 306, 325

commercial environment, 412–414

Committee for Safeguarding National Security, 34, 43, 94, 98, 229, 381

common goods, 215

Index 445

common law, 69, 77–78, 82–83, 90, 94, 101, 175, 388, 392
comprehensive jurisdiction, 2–3, 19, 83, 168, 375–390, 436–438
Comprehensive Social Security Assistance, 329, 356
Constitution, of PRC, 83, 88–89, 376
consultative system, 134–135, 220, 276, 284, 431
contentious politics, 89, 221–229, 248–249
co-optation: business sectors, 220, 306; media sectors, 270, 278–279
core values, Hong Kong, 76, 111, 245–247
Court of Final Appeal, 18, 56, 84, 88
COVID-19 pandemic, 70, 143, 228, 302, 381, 416–417, 439
criminal justice, 78, 89–93; bails, 18, 95, 97
critical minority, 57

decolonization, 163
democracy, 1, 77, 82, 112–113, 127–128, 136, 162–166, 215, 242, 284, 306, 431–432; media as surrogate democracy, 277
Democratic Alliance for the Betterment and Progress of Hong Kong (formerly Democratic Alliance for the Betterment of Hong Kong), 55, 194, 197, 203, 206
Democratic Party, 4, 15, 40, 55, 146, 166, 193, 230, 281, 437
democratization, 1, 3, 16, 20, 76, 79, 91, 112–113, 161, 198, 201, 401; backsliding, 162–163
Demosistō, 6, 69, 171–172, 196, 220, 256, 374
digital divide, 303
digital governance, 127
Ding, Xuexiang, 390
diplomacy, 402; internal, 6
disqualification, 5–7, 18, 170–173, 404, 431; elected legislators and councillors, 66–67, 70, 85–88, 145, 196,

377–378; candidates, 143, 178, 197, 207–208
disruptive technologies, 127
District Council, 8, 18–19,135–136, 145, 276; dual councillors, 140; functions and composition, 137–143, 154–155
District Council election, 2, 68, 136, 139–145, 154, 179, 380
District Council (Second) Functional Constituency, 4, 135, 140, 142, 147, 155, 166, 178, 199, 241, 251
District Fight Crime Committee, 16, 19, 33, 147, 155
District Fire Safety Committees, 16, 19, 33, 155
District Health Centre, 327–328
District Services and Community Care Teams, 155, 349

economic pragmatism, 320, 326, 334, 435
editorial independence, 20, 277–280
Elderly Health Care Voucher, 327
Electoral Affairs Commission, 5, 170, 248–249
electoral frauds, 148
electoral reforms, 3, 8, 19, 145–147, 154, 163, 178, 198, 208, 223, 230, 349, 373, 439
emergency powers: Public Order Ordinance, 2, 78, 89–91, 175, 430; Seditious Publication Ordinance, 78; Emergency Regulation Ordinance, 7, 78, 92–93
equity-efficiency trade-off, 298, 312
ethnic identity, 243–244
European Union (EU), 399, 408, 410
executive, 14–16, 31–32, 163, 179, 391
Executive Council, 5, 15, 35–37, 46, 112, 306
executive-driven government, 41–42
executive-led government, 1, 11, 14–16, 41–42, 47, 111–113, 135, 192, 205, 348
executive-legislature relation, 17, 39–41, 56, 123, 173, 192, 198, 383–384

externalities, 297–298, 312

filibustering, 17, 173, 375
final adjudication, 18, 79, 84–85
Finance Committee, LegCo, 39, 58, 60–61
fiscal policy, 295–297, 310, 318; inequality, 300–303, 311
Fishball Revolution. *See* Mong Kok riots
Five-Year Plan (FYP), 6, 102, 388, 440
foreign interventions, 232, 386, 401–402, 406–407, 436
freedoms. *See* basic rights and freedoms
Fugitive Offenders and Mutual Legal Assistance in Criminal Matters Legislation (Amendment) Bill, 7, 31, 40, 176
functional constituency (FC), 17, 39, 53, 71, 145–147, 178, 199, 204, 209, 349; first past the post, 55; preferential elimination, 55; corporate voting, 16, 33, 200

Gazette, 58
generalists, 116, 122, 129, 305
geographical constituency (GC), 17, 39, 53, 71, 145, 148, 178, 199, 206; list system, 55, 200; binominal voting system, 200, 203
gerrymandering, 147–148
Gini Index, 303, 350
governance, 284, 343–344, 384, 389–390
governing ideologies, 3, 14, 310
governor, 14, 32, 36, 41, 52, 56, 112, 136, 198, 200
Greater Bay Area (GBA), 8, 12, 14, 313, 387–389, 392–393, 416–417, 435, 440
Guangzhou-Shenzhen-Hong Kong Express Rail Link (XRL), 4, 8, 87, 221, 325–356, 377

Hare quota, 200
health policy, 327–329
Heung Yee Kuk, 181, 346, 348
high land price policy, 301, 350–351, 355, 357

Hong Kong Alliance in Support of Patriotic Democratic Movements of China, 441
Hong Kong and Macao Affairs Office (HKMAO), 10, 93, 380, 390, 409, 416
Hong Kong Confederation of Trade Unions, 3, 333, 441
Hong Kong Federation of Trade Unions, 333
Hong Kong identity, 195–196, 216, 223, 228, 240, 244–246, 257, 402
Hong Kong Indigenous, 6, 207, 220, 256, 374
Hong Kong-Macao-Zhuhai bridge, 377
Hong Kong National Front, 69, 256
Hong Kong Professional Teachers' Union, 225, 230, 233, 271, 441
housing, 3, 9, 323–326, 351–352; cubicle flats, 325, 351; Home Ownership Scheme (HOS), 296, 324; Long Term Housing Strategy (LTHS), 324, 352; My Home Purchase Plan, 326, 329; public housing, 216, 296, 311, 347, 351; Tenants Purchase Scheme (TPS), 324; tong lau, 325
hybrid regime, 13, 76, 163, 192, 215

identity politics, 246–247, 259–260
income inequalities, 303, 380–381
Independent Commission Against Corruption (ICAC), 78, 118, 216
Individual Visit Scheme, 307
industrial policy, 304–307; economic restructuring, 308–311
informational freedom, 412–413
institutional conscience, of civil service, 117, 127
integration: economic, 9, 11–13, 308, 313, 331–332, 439–440; national, 5–6, 9, 11–13, 242, 373, 375, 387–389, 436, 439–440
interest groups, 193, 209, 281
internationalization, 419
international status: as international financial center, 373, 385–388,

412–418; extradition treaties, 410; foreign perceptions of Hong Kong, 404–405, 408–412; non-sovereign entity, 399–400, 408–409

Japan, 405–406, 408, 411–412, 417
job-residence imbalance, 354–356
journalism, 268; citizen, 20, 243, 254–355; market-driven, 269
journalistic professionalism, 267–268, 273, 285
journalists, 255, 267–268, 273, 285
judges, 14, 18, 56, 79, 83–84, 94–97, 168
judicial authority, 79, 81, 98
judicial-executive relation, 77, 88, 96
judicial independence, 18, 76, 81–84, 87, 93–96, 98–101, 169, 174, 178, 404, 416, 430
judicial reviews, 6, 18, 66, 79, 81, 84–87, 94, 96, 229, 377, 383, 430
judiciary, 18, 76–79, 177, 391; functions, 92; politicization of, 81; structure and institutions, 79–81
July 1 demonstration, 3, 10, 40, 140, 221, 224, 227, 230, 281–282, 437
June Fourth incident, commemoration vigil, 98, 145, 154, 195, 228. See also Tiananmen incident

Kwok, Ka-ki, 70
Kwok, Wing-hang, Dennis, 70, 207

laissez-faire, 1, 293, 304, 318–321, 332, 348
Lam, Cheng Yuet-ngor, 6, 34, 150, 225–226, 294, 305, 321, 325, 379, 405, 409, 416, 439
land sales, 301, 348
Lantau Tomorrow Vision, 219, 310, 325, 352, 435
Lau, Siu-lai, 6, 66, 170, 172, 240, 404
law and order, 6, 69, 89–91, 250, 379
Law, Kwun-chung, Nathan, 66, 69, 86, 90, 170, 175, 232, 404, 407
law, weaponization of, 89–93, 163, 430

League of Social Democrats, 166, 172, 194
Lee, Cheuk-yan, 333
Lee, Ka-chiu, 9, 31, 34, 37, 294, 319, 390, 416
legal system: colonial, 78–99. See also common law
Legislative Council (LegCo), 52–53, 112, 173, 276; committees and panels, 60–61, 73; composition, 16–17, 53, 198, 202–203, 383; debates, 59–60; dual councillors, 140; functions and power, 56–61, 65; motions, 59–60, 65; provisional, 2, 53, 56, 429; separate vote count system, 16–17, 62, 65, 72–73
Legislative Council (LegCo) election, 2, 4, 42–43, 70–71, 88, 165–165, 170–173, 178–179, 202–203, 207–208, 241, 251, 380. See also 35-plus strategies; disqualification; primaries
legislature, 16–17, 34, 52, 62, 161, 173, 178, 192, 266, 391
legislature-executive relation. See executive-legislature relation
Leung, Chun-yin, 4, 61, 153, 222, 305, 319–324, 402
Leung, Kai-cheong, Kenneth, 70
Leung, Kwok-hung (Long-hair), 65–66, 86, 170, 172, 404
Leung, Sixtus Chung-hang, 6, 66, 85, 88, 170–171, 220, 404
Leung, Tin-kei, Edward, 6, 207, 404
Liaison Office of the Central People's Government (CLO), 206, 220, 380, 390
Liberal Party, 40, 194
Liberal Studies (subject), 9, 12, 280, 384, 439
localism, 4, 178, 192, 195–196, 202–203, 245–247, 257, 374, 433, 438
Low-income Working Family Allowance, 330, 351
Luo, Huining, 10, 380, 390

MacLehose, Murray, 1, 216

Mainlandization, 401–402, 413, 416–417, 419. *See also* integration
Mandatory Provident Fund (MPF), 40, 299, 355
market economy, 163, 293, 300, 310, 434
media, 20, 267–268; international mass media, 414–415; National Security Law, 270–272; performance and constraints, 269–270; political forces, 270–272; social, 20, 127, 225, 254–255, 264, 286, 415
Member Self-recommendation Scheme for Youth (MSSY), 151–152, 156
middle class, 301, 303, 311, 326, 418
minimum wage, 330, 332–334, 355
mixed economy, 293, 300
mobilization, 20, 116, 140, 169, 241, 280–283, 432; countermobilization, 282; demobilization, 283; self-mobilization, 286
monetary policy, 295–297; pegging between Hong Kong dollars and US dollars, 297, 311
Mong Kok riots, 5, 170, 196, 224, 374–375
Moral and National Education curriculum, 4, 12, 166, 222, 242–243, 384

nationalism: 5, 12; Chinese, 12, 215–216, 221, 246, 417; civic, 246; ethnic, 24
national flag and national emblem, 7, 9, 380, 439
National People's Congress, 22, 33, 42, 53, 71, 102, 135, 145–146, 270, 349, 409
national security, 7, 9, 11, 19, 94–95, 97, 164, 179, 229, 372, 376–382, 438–439
National Security Department, 178, 208
National Security Law (NSL), 3, 7, 11, 69–70, 93–97, 146–147, 177–179, 198, 206, 229–233. 270–272, 280, 283, 371, 381, 407, 414–415, 417, 437–439
national sovereignty, 10, 372, 376, 380, 382
New Territories, rural, 345–348, 356–359

New Urban Agenda, 340–344, 359
nonpartisan, 118, 192, 197, 204–205. *See also* partisan

Occupy Central Movement (OCM), 5, 90, 167–169, 174–175, 222–224, 250, 371, 373, 403, 437–438, 440
Office for Safeguarding National Security of the CPG (OSNS), 95–96, 381, 438
Old Age Allowance, 57, 329–330
One Belt, One Road. *See* Belt and Road Initiative (BRI)
One Country, Two Systems (OCTS), 2, 6–12, 22, 69, 82–83, 163, 192, 217, 221, 308, 331, 371, 375–376, 385–387, 404, 437–439
opinion polling, 265–267
organizations: civil society, 94, 180, 218–219, 344, 441; community, 139, 142, 221, 255–256; international nongovernmental, 414–415; political, 195, 217–218, 245, 255–256; professional, 245, 256, 258, 441; social, 215, 217, 232
overall jurisdiction. *See* comprehensive jurisdiction

partisan, 34, 45, 203. *See also* nonpartisan
patriots administering Hong Kong, 11, 16, 42, 71, 83, 146, 165, 178, 199, 242, 271, 349, 373, 375, 382–384, 389–390, 430, 438, 441
Patten, Christopher, 2, 53, 112, 136, 164, 193, 241–242, 320
People's Power, 194
polarization, political, 6, 198, 224–225, 282, 374, 441
policy addresses, 56, 59
policy formulation, 32, 36–38, 284
political apathy, 217, 240, 250
political appointment system, 43–44, 113, 121–123. *See also* Accountability System for Principal Officials (ASPO)

political culture, 19, 247–248, 250, 257–259, 280, 284, 432–433
political identity, 228, 240, 242, 247, 259, 432–433
political neutrality, 2–3, 118
political participation, 20, 86, 251–253, 259, 441; discursive, 243, 253–254, 258, 266–267
political parties, 20, 44–45, 139–140, 148, 191, 197–198, 204–206, 432
political public relations, 279–280
positive nonintervention, 294, 296, 304, 311, 318–321
post-80s generation, 325
poverty, 303, 325, 329–331, 342–343, 350–351: relative, 330; Commission on Poverty, 330–331
press freedom, 174, 231, 270–272, 284
primaries, 7, 68–69, 98, 144, 178, 197, 206, 230, 407, 439. *See also* 35-plus strategy; Legislative Council (LegCo) election
principal officials, 32–37
privatization, 125. *See also* reform under public sector
pro-Beijing, 10, 113, 147, 168, 179, 192, 194–208, 223–224, 230, 242, 247, 251, 383
pro-democracy, 17, 20, 56, 67–69, 148, 162–172, 174–179, 192, 194–208, 217, 233, 247, 282, 374, 380, 440–441
pro-establishment, 11, 17, 20, 67–68, 140–146, 150–151, 166–167, 219, 224, 243, 255–256, 375, 384–385, 439–440
proportional representation system, 39, 55, 146, 165, 200, 209
public expenditure, 302–303, 311, 313
public goods, 297, 312
public nuisance, 90–91, 175, 282
public opinion, 116, 265–267, 271–272, 280–284; bottom-up, 281; government's influence, 278–279; institutions and channels, 276–277; media effects, 274–275

public sector: economic functions, 295; reform, 124–127; size and scope, 297–299

Radio Television Hong Kong (RTHK), 19–20, 269, 271, 277–278, 286
referendum: civic, 167–168, 223; *de facto*, 4
rent seeking, 306, 313
riots, 89, 92, 176, 216, 226, 378
rule-based governance, 82
rule of law, 18, 76–77, 82–84, 98–100, 163, 169, 220, 229, 250, 388
Rural Representative Election, 172

Scholarism, 5, 167, 181, 222, 374, 403
securitization, 378–382, 438–439
security state, 372
self-determination, 5, 7, 66, 163, 170–172, 178–179, 196, 244, 374
Sino-American relations, 372, 401; Hong Kong's roles, 401, 417
Sino-British Joint Declaration, 1, 20, 163, 193, 406, 408
social movements, 234, 402. *See also* Anti-ELAB movement, Occupy Central Movement, Umbrella Movement
social policy, 318, 320–321, 335–336; CCP influence, 331–332; colonial heritage, 331; policy areas, 322–323
Societies Ordinance, 2, 7, 89
speech freedom, 98, 124, 174, 229
stability: economic, 297; political, 116, 134, 164, 251, 431; social, 240, 251, 329, 380, 439
Standing Committee of the National People's Congress (SCNPC), 2, 5, 18, 66, 70, 82, 84, 87–89, 93, 102, 144, 165, 195, 377–378
Stand News, 7, 97, 272, 439
statuary bodies, 149–150, 153
Studentlocalism, 69, 256
Super District Council. *See* District Council (Second) Functional Constituency

450   Index

Sustainable Development Goals (SDGs), 340–344, 359

Tai, Yiu-ting, Benny, 5, 68, 90–91, 175, 222, 373, 403
Tang, Ping-keung, Chris, 143, 231, 409
taxes, 301, 311–313
Tenants Purchase Scheme (TPS), 324
Tiananmen Incident, 79, 164, 193, 201, 217
Tsang, Donald Yam-kuen, 4, 15, 34–36, 45, 121, 305, 319–326, 330–333
Tung, Chee-hwa, 3, 34–35, 55, 121, 221, 281, 304, 306, 319–320, 323, 406
tycoons, 113, 200, 220, 299, 348, 355, 402, 407

Umbrella Movement, 20, 66, 89–91, 169, 174–175, 195–196, 222–224, 250, 282, 373, 403
unemployment, 330
united front, 11, 219–220, 282, 375, 384–385, 432, 436
universal suffrage, 4–5, 87, 91, 135, 165–166, 220, 226, 373, 379, 403, 431
urban policy, 340; economic structure, 354–356; growth-at-all-cost mentality, 348–350, 358–359; new development areas, 345, 353, 356; new towns, 345–346, 350; small house policy, 347; urban biased, 345–348
Urban Renewal Authority, 126, 153, 325
urban-rural divide, 354–356
United States' Policy in Hong Kong: Hong Kong Autonomy Act, 7, 386, 406; Hong Kong Human Rights and Democracy Act, 7, 386, 406; sanctions, 409
utilitarian familism, 240

veto, 36, 63, 67, 172, 208; power of the Chief Executive, 14, 34, 43
Voluntary Health Insurance Scheme (VHIS), 328–329

Wage Protection Movement (WPM), 333
waste management, 358
water management, 347, 357–358
White Paper on the Practice of the 'One Country, Two Systems' Policy, 2, 82, 168, 376, 437
Wong, Toi-yeung, Ray, 220, 407

Xi, Jinping, 11, 82, 215, 372, 376, 387, 403–407, 436
Xia, Baolong, 10, 271, 380, 382, 409

Yau, Wai-ching, 6, 66, 86, 170, 404
yellow ribbons. See polarization, political
Yeung, Ngok-kiu, Alvin, 70
Youngspiration, 85, 172, 196, 220, 256, 374
Yiu, Chung-yim, 66

Zhang, Dejiang, 10, 376
Zhang, Xiaoming, 10, 15, 71, 379, 381, 407